SAP PRESS e-books

Print or e-book, Kindle or iPad, workplace or airplane: Choose where and how to read your SAP PRESS books! You can now get all our titles as e-books, too:

- ▸ By download and online access
- ▸ For all popular devices
- ▸ And, of course, DRM-free

Convinced? Then go to **www.sap-press.com** and get your e-book today.

SAP® BW: Administration and Performance Optimization

 PRESS

SAP PRESS is a joint initiative of SAP and Galileo Press. The know-how offered by SAP specialists combined with the expertise of the Galileo Press publishing house offers the reader expert books in the field. SAP PRESS features first-hand information and expert advice, and provides useful skills for professional decision-making.

SAP PRESS offers a variety of books on technical and business-related topics for the SAP user. For further information, please visit our website: *www.sap-press.com*.

Amol Palekar, Bharat Patel, and Shreekant Shiralkar
SAP NetWeaver BW 7.3—Practical Guide
2013, 789 pp., hardcover
ISBN 978-1-59229-444-2

Buntic Georgian and Andrew Joo
100 Things You Should Know About SAP NetWeaver BW
2013, 367 pp., paperback
ISBN 978-1-59229-447-3

Bjarne Berg and Penny Silvia
SAP HANA: An Introduction (3rd edition)
2014, app. 615 pp., hardcover
ISBN 978-1-4932-1164-7

Xavier Hacking and Jeroen van der A
Getting Started with SAP BusinessObjects Design Studio
2013, 468 pp., hardcover
ISBN 978-1-59229-895-2

Joe Darlak and Jesper Christensen

SAP® BW: Administration and Performance Optimization

Galileo Press

Bonn • Boston

Galileo Press is named after the Italian physicist, mathematician, and philosopher Galileo Galilei (1564 – 1642). He is known as one of the founders of modern science and an advocate of our contemporary, heliocentric worldview. His words *Eppur si muove* (And yet it moves) have become legendary. The Galileo Press logo depicts Jupiter orbited by the four Galilean moons, which were discovered by Galileo in 1610.

Editor Emily Nicholls
Acquisitions Editor Kelly Grace Weaver
Copyeditor Miranda Martin
Cover Design Graham Geary
Photo Credit iStockphoto: 5787447/©THEPALMER
Layout Design Vera Brauner
Production Kelly O'Callaghan
Typesetting III-satz
Printed and bound in the United States of America, on paper from sustainable sources

ISBN 978-1-59229-853-2
© 2014 by Galileo Press Inc., Boston (MA)
1st edition 2014

Library of Congress Cataloging-in-Publication Data
Library of Congress Cataloging-in-Publication Data Christensen, Jesper.
SAP BW : administration and performance optimization / Jesper Christensen and Joe Darlak. -- 1st edition.
pages cm
ISBN 978-1-59229-853-2 (print) -- ISBN 1-59229-853-2 (print) -- ISBN 978-1-59229-854-9 (e-book) --
ISBN 978-1-59229-855-6 (print and e-book) 1. SAP NetWeaver BW. 2. Database management. 3. Data warehousing.
4. Business intelligence--Data processing. 5. Management information systems. I. Darlak, Joe. II. Title.
TK5105.8885.S24C47 2014
005.75'85--dc23
2014009936

Contents at a Glance

PART I Initial System Setup

1   Configuring Your System Environment 21

2   Data Architecture and Loading 109

3   Data Management 157

4   Roles and Authorizations 217

PART II Performance Tuning

5   Data Modeling and Loading for Performance 253

6   Reporting Performance Tuning 357

PART III Administration Tasks in Your SAP BW System

7   Daily Tasks 425

8   Weekly Tasks 455

9   Monthly Tasks 481

10 Quarterly Tasks 509

11 Yearly Tasks 547

PART IV Support for Your BI Initiatives

12 BI Competency Center 575

Dear Reader,

As the hallmark of a successfully operated system, efficiency is the ideal to which all administrators aspire: how to set it up *better*; how to maintain it *better*; how to get *more* out of it—*faster*.

So if a thoughtfully architected and strategically managed SAP BW system is the key to your business' success, then a comprehensive guide to system administration and performance tuning will be the resource that never leaves your desk. After all, with guidance for efficiently executing daily, weekly, monthly, quarterly, and yearly tasks, how can it? From system configuration to data architecture to data modeling to data reporting, Joe Darlak and Jesper Christensen's guide to optimizing your SAP BW 7.x system will help you achieve the highest efficiency standard.

We at SAP PRESS would be interested to hear your opinion of this book. What did you think about *SAP BW: Administration and Performance Optimization*? How could it be improved? As your comments and suggestions are the most useful tools to help us make our books the best they can be, we encourage you to visit our website at *www.sap-press.com* and share your feedback.

Thank you for purchasing a book from SAP PRESS!

Emily Nicholls
Editor, SAP PRESS

Galileo Press
Boston, MA

emily.nicholls@galileo-press.com
www.sap-press.com

Contents

Foreword 13
Preface 15

PART I Initial System Setup

1 Configuring Your System Environment 21

1.1   Infrastructure Architecture 22
       1.1.1   SAP NetWeaver 7.40 Components 23
       1.1.2   SAP BW 28
       1.1.3   SAP BW Data Model 30
       1.1.4   BI Content 35
       1.1.5   New Versions, New Features 37
1.2   System Landscape 42
       1.2.1   Promote to Production Strategy 44
       1.2.2   Source System Interface 44
       1.2.3   Post-Copy Automation 46
       1.2.4   Change Management 51
       1.2.5   Transport Organizer 58
1.3   System Sizing 78
       1.3.1   SAP Benchmarks 82
       1.3.2   Quick Sizer 86
       1.3.3   Productive Sizing 90
       1.3.4   BWA Sizing 95
1.4   System Settings 98
       1.4.1   Profile Parameters 99
       1.4.2   Implementation Guide 101
       1.4.3   BI Basis Customizing 103
       1.4.4   Global Settings and Exchange Rates 106

2 Data Architecture and Loading 109

2.1   Data Flow in SAP BW 110
       2.1.1   The Data Flow Diagram 110
       2.1.2   Data Flow Components 111
       2.1.3   New Features for SAP BW 7.40 115
2.2   Layer Architectures of a Data Warehouse 117

2.2.1 Layered Scalable Architecture 117
2.2.2 Layered Scalable Architecture with SAP HANA 123
2.3 Graphical Modeling 125
2.3.1 Data Flow Templates 127
2.3.2 SAP-Delivered Data Flow Templates 128
2.4 Data Load Automation 134
2.4.1 Process Chains 135
2.4.2 Process Variants in Detail 140

3   Data Management 157

3.1 Master Data 158
3.1.1 Master Data Design 159
3.1.2 Master Data Loading 170
3.1.3 Master Data Maintenance 176
3.2 Transaction Data 184
3.2.1 InfoProvider Partitioning 184
3.2.2 Repartitioning 187
3.2.3 InfoProvider Maintenance 191
3.2.4 Aggregates 194
3.2.5 BW Accelerator 195
3.3 Temporary Data 196
3.3.1 SAP BW Archiving Objects 201
3.3.2 Archiving Request Administration Data 202
3.3.3 Statistics and Technical Content 204
3.4 Data Retention Strategy 205
3.5 Near-Line Storage 212

4   Roles and Authorizations 217

4.1 Authorization Concept in AS ABAP 217
4.1.1 Authorization Fields 220
4.1.2 Activity Fields 220
4.2 Standard Authorization Objects 221
4.2.1 Developer and Administrator Authorizations 222
4.2.2 Reporting Authorizations 224
4.3 Analysis Authorizations 225
4.3.1 Creating an InfoObject for Analysis Authorizations 225
4.3.2 Defining Analysis Authorizations 228
4.3.3 Automatically Generating Analysis Authorization 229

4.4	Roles	231
	4.4.1 Administrator Roles	232
	4.4.2 End-User Roles	232
	4.4.3 Role Templates	233
4.5	User Administration	236
	4.5.1 Defining Users	236
	4.5.2 Assigning Analysis Authorizations to Users	238
	4.5.3 User Administration Tools	241
4.6	Troubleshooting Authorization Problems	242
	4.6.1 Standard Authorization Errors	242
	4.6.2 SAP BW Analysis Authorization Errors	246

PART II Performance Tuning

5 Data Modeling and Loading for Performance 253

5.1	Data Modeling for Performance	253
	5.1.1 Enhanced Data Modeling with SAP BW 7.40	257
	5.1.2 Semantic Partitioning	262
	5.1.3 InfoCube Modeling	267
	5.1.4 DSO Modeling	279
	5.1.5 Virtual InfoProviders	291
	5.1.6 HybridProvider	314
5.2	Data Loading for Performance	317
	5.2.1 Extraction Processing	317
	5.2.2 Transfer Processing	332
	5.2.3 Load Processing	346
	5.2.4 ABAP Guidelines	352

6 Reporting Performance Tuning 357

6.1	Identifying Performance Problems	357
	6.1.1 Using SAP BW-Specific Tools	357
	6.1.2 Using Workload Monitors	368
	6.1.3 Performance Testing	384
	6.1.4 Analyzing Query-Specific Performance Issues	385
6.2	Reporting Performance Tuning	405
	6.2.1 Database Optimizations	405
	6.2.2 Query Optimization	411
	6.2.3 Frontend Tool Optimization	414

PART III Administration Tasks in Your SAP BW System

7   Daily Tasks **425**

7.1   Daily Administration Tasks 425
    7.1.1   Checking Database Storage 426
    7.1.2   Checking Workload 430
    7.1.3   Checking BWA 437
    7.1.4   Performing System Checks 439
    7.1.5   Automating Daily Tasks 445
7.2   Daily Data Load Monitoring Tasks 446
    7.2.1   Monitoring SAP BW CCMS Alerts 446
    7.2.2   Monitoring Process Chains 448
    7.2.3   Monitoring InfoPackages and RDA Daemons 449
    7.2.4   Monitoring DSO Activations 451
    7.2.5   Checking Aggregates 451

8   Weekly Tasks **455**

8.1   Weekly Administration Tasks 455
    8.1.1   Reviewing SAP EarlyWatch Alert 456
    8.1.2   Rebuilding BWA Indexes 461
    8.1.3   Cleaning PSA and Change Logs 464
    8.1.4   Cleaning Application Logs 467
    8.1.5   Executing BW Housekeeping Task List 469
    8.1.6   Executing Other Housekeeping Tasks 470
    8.1.7   Executing RSRV Consistency Checks 472
8.2   Weekly Performance Tuning 473
    8.2.1   Monitoring BI Statistics 474
    8.2.2   Compressing InfoCubes 477
    8.2.3   Rebuilding DB Indexes and Statistics 477
    8.2.4   Monitoring Cache Usage 478

9   Monthly Tasks **481**

9.1   Monthly Administration Tasks 482
    9.1.1   Scheduling System Restart 482
    9.1.2   Changing Portal Settings 489
    9.1.3   Checking SAP Notes 490
    9.1.4   Taking Action on the EarlyWatch Alert 493
    9.1.5   Executing RSRV Cleanup Tasks 493
    9.1.6   Collecting BWA Usage 495
    9.1.7   Forecasting Storage Capacity 497

9.2   Monthly Performance Tuning 499
         9.2.1   Conducting File System Housekeeping 500
         9.2.2   Archiving/Near-Lining Data 503
         9.2.3   Monitoring Data Load Statistics 505

10   Quarterly Tasks 509

10.1   Quarterly Administration Tasks 509
         10.1.1   Managing Users and Licenses 510
         10.1.2   Testing System Refresh 515
         10.1.3   Maintaining Hardware 523
         10.1.4   Updating SAP Kernels 524
         10.1.5   Applying Database Updates and Parameters 525
         10.1.6   Patching Operating System 528
         10.1.7   Validating System Parameters 528
         10.1.8   Reviewing Open Transport Requests 530
10.2   Quarterly Performance Tuning Tasks 530
         10.2.1   Reorganizing the Database 531
         10.2.2   Deleting Obsolete Queries and Reports 532
         10.2.3   Deleting Obsolete Data Flows 536
         10.2.4   Reviewing Configuration Settings 536

11   Yearly Tasks 547

11.1   Yearly Administration Tasks 548
         11.1.1   Upgrading SAP BW 548
         11.1.2   Applying SAP BW Support Packs 553
         11.1.3   Performing SAPgui Maintenance 558
         11.1.4   Testing High Availability and Disaster Recovery ... 563
         11.1.5   Assessing System Risks 564
11.2   Yearly Performance Tuning Tasks 564
         11.2.1   Reviewing Data Flow 564
         11.2.2   Reviewing External Performance and Optimization 565
         11.2.3   Re-Partitioning InfoProviders 566

PART IV Support for Your BI Initiatives

12   BI Competency Center 575

12.1   Centralized Support Organization 577
         12.1.1   BICC Governance 579
         12.1.2   Project Delivery 581

	12.1.3	Service Delivery	584
12.2	Roles and Skill Sets		585
	12.2.1	Business Roles	586
	12.2.2	IT Roles	589
12.3	Team Structure		596
	12.3.1	BICC Governance	596
	12.3.2	Project Delivery	597
	12.3.3	Service Delivery	598
12.4	Best Practices		599
	12.4.1	Vision and Strategy	599
	12.4.2	Governance	601
	12.4.3	Guidelines	602
	12.4.4	Compliance	603

Appendices 605

A	Checklists	607
A.1	Development Checklists	607
A.2	Housekeeping Checklists	614
B	Transaction Codes	619
C	Reports and Utilities	629
D	The Authors	639
Index		641

Foreword

Data warehousing has changed dramatically over the last 20 years. From custom-developed data models and programs, the industry has moved into standardized data warehouses with pre-delivered content. SAP BW has been in the forefront of this revolution since the 1990s. Now, with the 7.40 version taking full advantage of SAP HANA in-memory platform, SAP BW is experiencing a rebirth as the enterprise data warehouse for most Fortune-500 organizations.

With its new business content, new developer interfaces, and simplified data architecture, the latest release of SAP BW leverages the inherent speed of third-generation hyper-fast databases. It removes the need for use of complex multi-layered systems, objects such as persistent staging areas, and write-optimized DataStore objects or aggregates in order to get the desired performance.

The current release of SAP BW is a much simpler system than it was even a few months ago. All these changes have resulted in a platform that is more agile and can be modified quickly based on business needs in days or weeks, instead of months and years. It also provides a new platform that takes advantage of SAP's best-of-breed tool for reporting and analytics that was acquired with the Business-Objects merger a few years ago.

SAP BW: Administration and Performance Optimization is the first book to explore the many new features of SAP BW 7.40 in a practical manner. To answer questions on how to implement the fourth-generation data warehouses, the book provides developers, managers, and administrators with in-depth advice and step-by-step examples in all areas of the enhanced tool. This book starts with the basic of system setup, data modelling principles, and system sizing that are useful for beginners. However, these basic concepts are followed by in-depth expert advice on technical aspects of high-performance data loading and SAP BW security best practices. As is expected of a book of this nature, it follows these chapters with detailed, actionable advice on performance optimization for SAP HANA and non-HANA–based SAP BW systems from both a database and a reporting perspective. The last chapter of the book completes the picture with guidelines on building a BI Competency Center and the appendices offer helpful checklists.

If you, like me, have bought most of the dozens of BW books published in the last decades, you will find this book to be the most comprehensive of its kind. For any SAP BW developers and managers looking to simplify their landscape with more agile and higher performing data models, this is the book that should be on your desk. Even if you are not planning to move to SAP HANA in the near future, you will find many practical examples on how to performance tune and clean up your SAP BW 7.x system with the new tools provided by SAP.

Overall, this is the most important and comprehensive SAP BW resource to arrive on the market in many years!

Dr. Bjarne Berg, Ph.D.
CIO of COMERIT, Inc.
Professor of SAP University Alliance at Lenoir Rhyne University

Preface

The idea for this book has been germinating in our minds for the past decade during which we have been consulting on the topics covered in these pages with our clients, many of whom are the largest Fortune 100 corporations. We noticed some time ago that there were no publications devoted to maintaining a healthy SAP BW system, and concluded that a guideline describing not only what to do but when to do it would be extremely beneficial to the architects and managers with whom we had previously worked, and, more importantly, those we have not yet had the opportunity to advise.

When we finally decided to document our combined knowledge, SAP NetWeaver 7.31 had been recently released and our clients were starting to benefit from its new features and functionality. During the course of writing the book, SAP NetWeaver BW 7.40 was also released with significant new functionality for SAP HANA; therefore, we have included advice on usage of the new features and functionality of both these software versions.

Considering the disruptive nature of in-memory technology, this is an exciting time in the world of data warehousing. Organizations can now start to leverage business intelligence and predictive analytics on a scale never before possible. SAP BW remains a critical component in SAP's in-memory data fabric architecture, so it's never been more important to understand your BW technology and know how to keep your system healthy on the verge of exploding demand from your business.

However, this book is not intended to provide guidance for SAP BW powered by SAP HANA only, but rather is intended to provide guidance for SAP BW with specific recommendations for each database. Of course, no guideline on maintaining a healthy data warehouse would be complete without architecture and design guidelines to instruct the reader how to build it right in the first place. Therefore, we have written this book with four main areas in mind: system design, performance tuning, administration, and support.

In Part I, which spans the first four chapters, you will learn how to architect an SAP BW system and its landscape and which tasks are needed to set up the system during your first implementation project. We start by covering system landscape design, system connections, change management, and system parameters. Next, you will learn the principles of data architecture and master the process of defining and setting up a fully automated data load schedule. Subsequently, you will learn techniques for managing data in the warehouse to keep performance high and storage requirements low. Finally, you will learn how to secure your data with user roles and authorizations.

In Part II of this book, which includes Chapter 5 and Chapter 6, you will learn how to design and optimize performance in your SAP BW system. First we will explore data model design guidelines for optimal performance and review detailed tips and performance tuning techniques to improve overall warehouse performance. We will then cover how data loads can be tuned to minimize the time taken to refresh data in SAP BW. Subsequently, we will walk through the best practices that improve query and report performance.

Part III of this book includes Chapters 7 through 11; it will cover the administrative tasks you should execute in a live SAP BW system. Explore the tasks that should be performed on a daily basis in the system to ensure a well-tuned and high-performing system. Walk through the weekly tasks you should perform to proactively monitor the system. Master the monthly tasks that help management trust in the system's stability and ensure that you get credit for your hard work. Understand the tasks that should be performed quarterly to avoid long-term system health issues, and then explore the yearly system maintenance tasks that will ensure your system can continue to deliver value to the organization at a lower cost.

The final part of the book includes Chapter 12 and the appendices; it will cover how to support your SAP BW system. We will review the skill profiles required to support an SAP BW system and learn how to build a BI Competency Center for long-term success of your BI initiatives.

We feel the level of detail provided in each part of this book is appropriate, and we hope you agree, considering that an attempt to catalog everything we have ever learned about SAP BW could easily exceed many of the longest tomes ever written (and by the time we would have finished writing it, much of its content would probably be obsolete).

As we wrote this book, we truly gained respect for the authors of previous SAP books because we realized just how challenging it is to write something of this scope in one's spare time while working full time, traveling, and raising families. Fortunately, we had strong support from our wives and children, our friends, and our peers, who all encouraged us to persevere. While the writing process has taken significantly longer than either of us expected, we are now looking forward to sharing the results with you, our readers.

Joe Darlak and Jesper Christensen

To my wife, Laurie, my son, Jake, and my daughter, Ella: You are my greatest sources of strength and inspiration. I am deeply indebted to each of you for your boundless support and encouragement. I owe everything to you. Thank you.

Joe Darlak

To my two sons, Matthias and Lukas, and my wife, Susan: Thank you for your support and encouragement in writing this book. I love you.

Jesper Christensen

Part I
Initial System Setup

Implementing a world-class data warehouse requires three basic things: the right technology, tools, and components to satisfy user consumption; correctly sized infrastructure to support user demands; and the right system landscape to mitigate risk. Assembling these requirements is akin to laying the right foundation—choose wisely or risk the consequences.

1   Configuring Your System Environment

SAP introduced Business Information Warehouse (BIW) back in 1998 with the generally available (GA) release of version 1.0E. Back in those early days, BIW was designed and built based on the data warehousing principles espoused by data pioneer Ralph Kimball. In fact, training classes for version 1.2A at the SAP Partner Academy in the United States listed Kimball's book *The Data Warehouse Toolkit* as prerequisite reading.

Almost immediately, SAP dropped the word *Information* from the solution's name, and it became simply Business Warehouse, which it kept until the 2004 release of the NetWeaver platform. Over time, through the advent of many functional and technical improvements, the solution has grown and developed in the direction of Bill Inmon's corporate information factory, yet the founding principles of Kimball's data model remain.

Most recently, *NetWeaver* has been dropped from the title, so the solution is now known as SAP Business Warehouse (BW). The latest version is 7.40, which is optimized for SAP HANA, SAP HANA Cloud, and SAP Mobile. The SAP HANA database and its in-memory technology are innovative technologies that enable considerable flexibility in data modeling and architecture never available before. Although this book is not written specifically for SAP BW powered by SAP HANA, much of the advice and instruction provided here will prepare any BW system on a traditional database platform for an efficient migration to SAP HANA.

Regardless of the version implemented, choosing the right components, correctly sized infrastructure, and the right system landscape lays the foundation for delivering a well-designed and administered data warehouse. The end results provide the characteristics of a robust reporting solution:

- Data integrity
- Risk mitigation
- Efficient automation
- Performance optimization
- Ease of maintenance

We will cover data warehouse design and administration in subsequent chapters of this book. In this chapter, we cover new SAP BW features and functionalities in Section 1.1, how to design a system landscape in Section 1.2, how to size those systems in Section 1.3, and system settings in Section 1.4. Let's begin by exploring the infrastructure architecture of SAP BW.

1.1 Infrastructure Architecture

Two distinct types of architecture are involved in a data warehouse. The first is the *data architecture*, which deals with the data flow from the source systems into the data warehouse, through the transformation layers, and into the reporting environment. Data architects are responsible for ensuring that design guidelines are followed in the development and implementation of reporting and analysis solutions that ultimately meet business reporting requirements. Data architecture will be covered extensively in Chapters 2, 3, and 5.

The second type of architecture is *infrastructure architecture*, which deals with the technical decisions regarding which applications and interfaces are required to satisfy user consumption and support user growth in demand. This area is usually the responsibility of business intelligence (BI) architects, who ensure that all applications work seamlessly together within your system landscape.

For most companies that employ SAP R/3 or SAP ERP as their enterprise resource planning software, SAP BW is the default choice for business intelligence because the components are so well integrated with other SAP modules. Let's review the components delivered with SAP BW 7.40.

1.1.1   SAP NetWeaver 7.40 Components

We can divide SAP NetWeaver into nine major functional areas of innovation, as described in Table 1.1. Notice that SAP BW is one of them.

SAP NetWeaver Function Area	Purpose
SAP NetWeaver Application Server	Provides development and runtime environments for development in ABAP and Java. The application server is included in all SAP NetWeaver systems.
SAP BW	Manages information as a proven platform for online analytical processing (OLAP) solutions.
SAP Gateway	Enables developers to create applications that link business users to SAP software from any environment and through any device.
SAP Portal	Connects people and increases user productivity as the central point of information and collaboration in and across enterprises.
SAP Process Orchestration	Orchestrates processes by providing tools and methodologies to integrate business processes across system boundaries.
SAP Identity Management	Secures access, manages users and identities, and provides authorizations that empower users to access the systems for their daily work in a governed fashion. SAP NetWeaver single sign-on provides secure login procedures based on security standards such as certificates or SAML.
SAP Information Lifecycle Management	Manages systems with tools and procedures to install, upgrade, update, and patch SAP solutions in close coordination with SAP Solution Manager. Customers can manage complete solution landscapes from a single console fulfilling SLAs in a reliable way with minimal downtimes.
SAP Auto-ID Infrastructure	Delivers capabilities to integrate all automated sensing devices, including RFID readers and printers, Bluetooth devices, embedded systems, and barcode devices.
SAP NetWeaver Master Data Management (MDM)	Ensures cross-system data consistency and helps integrate business processes across the extended value chain.

Table 1.1 SAP NetWeaver Functional Areas and Their Purposes

Of all these function areas, only the SAP NetWeaver Application Server is included in all SAP NetWeaver implementations. The purpose of the SAP NetWeaver Application Server is to provide programmers with an efficient means of expressing business logic and to insulate them from the need for technical coding specific to the database, operating system, or hardware on which the application server is installed.

SAP NetWeaver Application Servers are commonly referred to as *instances*, and in some cases incorrectly referred to as *systems*. To prevent confusion, it is important to understand the difference between instances and systems as they relate to ABAP, Java, and dual-stack systems.

► An SAP *system* is a set of installed software components that provides a defined set of functionalities. Each one is installed and configured as a unit and consists of a logical database, one or more application server instances (ABAP and/or Java), central services (such as a message server and enqueue server), and optional components (such as TREX and LiveCache). The system is identified by its unique SAP system ID, or SID, which consists of three letters or digits (e.g., DV1, QA1, or PD1).

There are three different types of systems: the ABAP system, the Java system, and the dual-stack system, which offers both technologies in one system. These system types consist of the corresponding instance types in a homogeneous way, meaning only one type is permitted in the system: ABAP instance *or* Java instance *or* dual-stack instance.

> **Recommendation**
>
> Java stack separation is recommended prior to upgrading to SAP NetWeaver 7.40 and required to migrate to SAP HANA. Dual-stack systems are not supported in SAP HANA.

► An application server *instance* is an administrative unit that integrates SAP system components running on one physical host. Application server instances provide data processing functions and offer corresponding services. Instances are started, stopped, and monitored as one unit. There can be multiple instances on one host belonging to the same system or different systems. An instance can be uniquely identified by the host name and a two-digit instance number.

Each instance type consists of different processes. The main instance types are the following:

- *ABAP server instances* consist of common components such as Internet Communication Manager (ICM), Internet Graphics Server (IGS), and different types of ABAP work processes: dialog (for mostly interactive use), batch (for background processing), update (for update processing), and spool (for printing).

- *Java server instances* consist of common components such as ICM, IGS, and Java server processes, each running on one Java Virtual Machine (JVM).

- *Dual-stack instances* are a combination of ABAP and Java parts in one instance.

- *Central services instances* (SCS) consist of a message server for communication between instances and an enqueue server for lock management. Each ABAP or Java system has one SCS; dual-stack systems can have either one shared or two separate SCS instances.

- *Web Dispatcher server instances* are application-level gateways for HTTP requests to an SAP Web Application Server. They act as a software web switch controlling access to and from the Internet, thus contributing to security while balancing the SAP system load. Each SAP system has one web dispatcher.

- *SAP NetWeaver Search and Classification (TREX) instances* are search engines for SAP NetWeaver applications and can find information in both structured and unstructured data. Each SAP system has one TREX instance.

- *Enqueue replication server instances* are used only in high availability (HA) solutions to ensure that the lock table in the enqueue server is not flushed if the SCS fails.

Combinations of the different server types form the basis of a complete SAP system. The BI architect is responsible for ensuring that these combinations are configured correctly and work efficiently, regardless of the function area of the of the SAP NetWeaver system. In this book, we cover only the SAP BW functional area.

A complete SAP BW system has multiple software components installed. You can see which components are installed in the SAP system on any screen from the SAP GUI by going to menu item System • Status and selecting the Detail button under the Component version field. Figure 1.1 gives an example of installed software components.

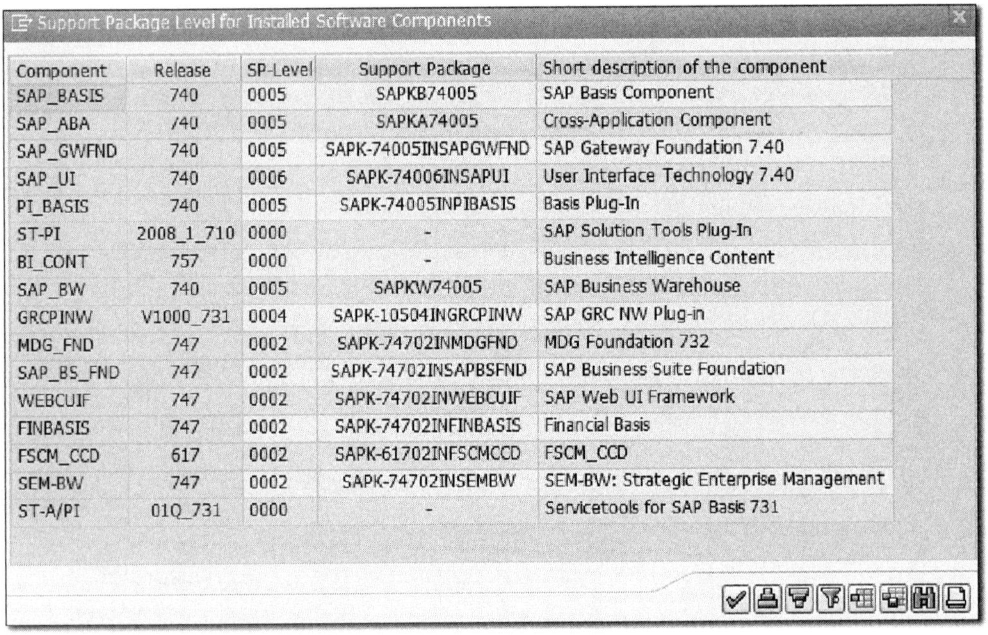

Support Package Level for Installed Software Components

Component	Release	SP-Level	Support Package	Short description of the component
SAP_BASIS	740	0005	SAPKB74005	SAP Basis Component
SAP_ABA	740	0005	SAPKA74005	Cross-Application Component
SAP_GWFND	740	0005	SAPK-74005INSAPGWFND	SAP Gateway Foundation 7.40
SAP_UI	740	0006	SAPK-74006INSAPUI	User Interface Technology 7.40
PI_BASIS	740	0005	SAPK-74005INPIBASIS	Basis Plug-In
ST-PI	2008_1_710	0000	-	SAP Solution Tools Plug-In
BI_CONT	757	0000	-	Business Intelligence Content
SAP_BW	740	0005	SAPKW74005	SAP Business Warehouse
GRCPINW	V1000_731	0004	SAPK-10504INGRCPINW	SAP GRC NW Plug-in
MDG_FND	747	0002	SAPK-74702INMDGFND	MDG Foundation 732
SAP_BS_FND	747	0002	SAPK-74702INSAPBSFND	SAP Business Suite Foundation
WEBCUIF	747	0002	SAPK-74702INWEBCUIF	SAP Web UI Framework
FINBASIS	747	0002	SAPK-74702INFINBASIS	Financial Basis
FSCM_CCD	617	0002	SAPK-61702INFSCMCCD	FSCM_CCD
SEM-BW	747	0002	SAPK-74702INSEMBW	SEM-BW: Strategic Enterprise Management
ST-A/PI	01Q_731	0000	-	Servicetools for SAP Basis 731

Figure 1.1 The Installed Components for an SAP BW System

Table 1.2 offers a description of the components in Figure 1.1 plus a few others. Most SAP BW systems have at least seven of these components, and some have additional, optional components.

Component	Mandatory	Optional	Description
BI_CONT	X		BI Content provides all delivered business content.
PI_BASIS	X		Basis Plug-In includes all interface connectivity and functionality.
SAP_ABA	X		Cross-Application Component provides all ABAP functionality.
SAP_BASIS	X		SAP Basis Component contains all SAP base functionality.
SAP_BW	X		SAP BW includes all BW-specific items and functionality.

Table 1.2 SAP BW Components (Required and Optional)

Component	Mandatory	Optional	Description
SAP_UI	X		SAP User Interface (UI) contains old and new NetWeaver 7.40 UI technologies, such as Web Dynpro ABAP and SAPUI5.
ST-A/PI	X		Service Tools for Applications Plug-In provides analysis tools for service delivery.
ST-PI	X		SAP Solution Tools Plug-In provides Basis and trace tools service delivery and system monitoring.
BI_CONT_XT		X	BI Content for BOBJ I provides delivered content for use with BusinessObjects.
FINBASIS		X	Financial Basis is a technical prerequisite for SEM-BW.
GRCPINW		X	SAP Governance, Risk and Compliance (GRC) Plug-In for NetWeaver systems provides access control via automated user management from a connected SAP GRC system.
MDG_FND		X	SAP Master Data Governance (MDG) tracks changes to master data and helps keep it consistent.
PCAI_ENT		X	Landscape Virtual Management Enterprise enables execution of post-copy automation (PCA) task lists.
SAP_BS_FND		X	SAP Business Suite Foundation contains common search and analytics models and is required for SEM-BW and MDG_FND.
SAP_GWFND		X	SAP NetWeaver Gateway Foundation offers development and generation tools to create OData services to a variety of client development tools.
SEM-BW		X	Strategic Enterprise Management (SEM) includes balanced scorecard functionality.
WEBCUIF		X	SAP Web UI Framework is required for SEM-BW.

Table 1.2 SAP BW Components (Required and Optional) (Cont.)

As with any system, maintenance is required with every installed component. The maintenance required for each component includes applying resolutions to known issues. SAP releases periodic *support packages* containing defect resolutions that can be applied to the SAP system. In most cases, the support packages for each component are grouped in a *support package stack* (SPS) to simplify their application and ensure consistency among them.

Once a component is installed, it cannot be uninstalled. Therefore, we recommend due diligence when identifying which components are truly needed in every system. The optional components described are recommended for specific use cases only. Even without them, SAP BW is a complete data warehouse.

1.1.2   SAP BW

SAP BW is a fully functional data warehousing application that enables the integration, transformation, and consolidation of relevant business information from productive SAP applications and external data sources. The data warehousing process includes data modeling; data extraction, transformation, and load (ETL); and the administration of the data warehouse management processes. The central tool for data warehousing tasks in SAP BW is the Data Warehousing Workbench.

By using in-memory technologies, SAP BW can deliver high performance with large quantities of data. In particular, in-memory technologies efficiently process demanding scenarios with high data volumes, high query frequency, and complicated calculations.

Reporting performance alone can be improved by storing data as indexes in SAP Business Warehouse Accelerator (BWA). Replacing a traditional relational database with an SAP HANA database improves both data load performance and reporting performance.

Regardless of whether in-memory technology or traditional relational databases are used, SAP BW is delivered with different tools and services to support development of SAP BW objects and processes, the supply of data into the system landscape, the execution of tests and traces, and the monitoring of the systems landscape.

SAP BW is also a fully functional business intelligence application that provides reporting and analysis tools and functions that enable companies to make well-formed tactical and strategic decisions. Its online analytic processor provides OLAP functions and services, as well as services for BW-integrated planning and analysis process design.

SAP Business Explorer (SAP BEx), previously known as the SAP Business Intelligence Suite, provides flexible reporting and analysis tools for strategic analysis, operational reporting, and decision-making support within a business. SAP BEx tools can also be used to create planning applications and for data entry in BW Integrated Planning. SAP BEx tools include the following:

- *SAP BEx Query Designer* is used to define queries with filter, navigation, and calculation functionality. Queries designed by this tool are used by all other tools in the SAP BEx Suite to access data within BW InfoProviders.

- *SAP BEx Analyzer* is an analytical reporting and design tool embedded in Microsoft Excel. BEx Analyzer provides easy-to-use context menus and drag-and-drop functionality to navigate in queries created in SAP BEx Query Designer.

- *SAP BEx Web Application Designer* (WAD) is the central desktop application used to create web applications and generate HTML pages containing BW-specific content, such as tables, charts, or maps. It enables OLAP navigation of SAP BEx Query data in all web applications and business intelligence cockpits that can be integrated into the portal. It also is used to create web-based planning applications.

- *SAP BEx Report Designer* is used to create enterprise reports on SAP BEx Queries with optimal settings for generating, displaying, and printing PDFs.

- *SAP BEx Broadcaster* is used to distribute any SAP BEx object to a wide range of users and includes functions for performance optimization and exception reporting. SAP BEx Broadcaster can pre-calculate SAP BEx Queries, SAP BEx web applications, SAP BEx Analyzer workbooks, and SAP BEx Enterprise Reports and broadcast them by email to the portal in various formats (HTML, MHTML, ZIP, etc.) or as hyperlinks. The tool can also generate alerts and broadcast based on master data (known as *bursting*).

You can also evaluate SAP BW data by using the SAP BusinessObjects products, which have been enabled by efficient and effective use of interfaces in the SAP BW Analytic Engine. This integration with SAP BusinessObjects broadens the scope for reporting tools with SAP BEx and offers a premium experience for end users. SAP BusinessObjects does not replace SAP BEx since SAP BEx Queries are still required for integration, but instead complements the reporting capabilities and allows other modes of access to BW data.

SAP BusinessObjects Integration includes the following tools:

- *SAP BusinessObjects Business Intelligence (BI)* allows access to the SAP BEx web application in the BI launch pad.

- *SAP BusinessObjects Dashboards* can be used to visualize BW data in the form of dynamic and interactive dashboards.

- *SAP Crystal Reports* can be used to generate form-based reports on BW data.

- *SAP BusinessObjects Web Intelligence (WebI)* can be used to create display-only or ad-hoc reports.

- *SAP BusinessObjects Analysis* enables analysis of BW data in either the OLAP edition or the edition for Microsoft Office, which is based on Microsoft Excel.

> **Recommendation**
>
> Using SAP BusinessObjects products may require separate licensing, so be sure to check the licensing conditions of your contract.

Recall that the BEx Query is the foundation for all types of reports from the SAP BEx Suite to SAP BusinessObjects. However, before queries can be built, the underlying data models must already exist. There are many different types of data models available within SAP BW, and choosing the right one depends on the sources of data and the business reporting requirements.

1.1.3   SAP BW Data Model

InfoProvider is the generic term for any data model in SAP BW that provides information from the data warehouse for reporting and analysis. There are many different types of InfoProviders: some store data physically, while others are only views on data stored elsewhere. All InfoProviders, however, are seen as uniform objects in BEx Query Designer.

InfoProviders are built of *InfoObjects*, which are the smallest information units in BW and the structural building blocks of all BW InfoProviders. There are five types of InfoObjects:

- *Characteristics* represent business information, such as company code, customer, or product, which describes transactions or master data in the BW source systems. Characteristics can have master data attributes, texts, or hierarchies.

- *Key figures* represent numeric information, such as quantity, amount, or number of items, which are the facts in a transaction.

- *Units* provide unit of measurement or currency information for key figures.

▶ *Time characteristics* represent temporal information, such as date, fiscal period, and calendar month.

▶ *Technical characteristics* represent administrative information, such as request number, which is used solely for data load or OLAP processing within BW and has no other value to the business.

Although all InfoProviders are built using IntoObjects, characteristic InfoObjects with attributes can be InfoProviders themselves. This type of InfoProvider can be used for master data reporting.

The most common type of InfoProvider—and the one that BW was originally designed to deliver—is the InfoCube. A standard *InfoCube* is a multi-dimensional object; it is a set of relational tables structured as an extended star schema, which includes a fact table in the middle surrounded by up to 16 dimension tables (see Figure 1.2). The fact table consists of key figures, and the dimension tables consist of characteristics and/or units.

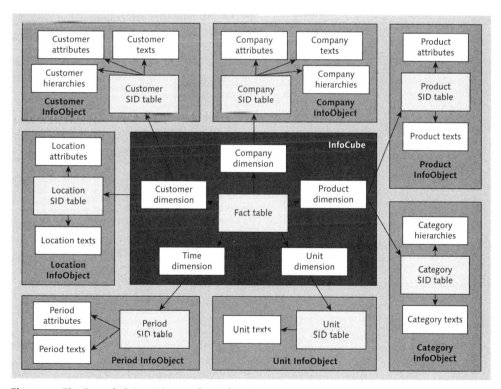

Figure 1.2 The Extended Star Schema of an InfoCube

The extended star schema is an architectural concept that improves performance when reporting on large datasets and supports analytical processing by facilitating filtering, navigation, and aggregation of facts. The dimensions of the fact table are linked to the fact table using dimension IDs (DIMIDs), which are four-byte fields of sequential numbers contained in the key part of both tables. The key figures in the fact table are thus related to the characteristics in the dimension tables—or, in other words, the dimensional characteristics determine the granularity at which the key figures are stored in the InfoCube.

The second most common InfoProvider is the standard *DataStore object* (DSO), which is a data staging object consisting of three transparent flat table structures: an activation queue, an active data table, and a change log. While InfoCubes are good for reporting on summarized and/or aggregated data, DSOs are good for loading and storing detailed data and propagating delta records through to InfoCubes. Because DSOs are used for data staging and business transformations, there are usually more of them than InfoCubes in any given system, but they are less likely to be used for reporting and analysis because their structure is not optimized for it.

Figure 1.3 shows how the three DSO tables work together during the data load.

1. The *activation queue* is filled with new records when they are loaded by request to the DSO. These records are stored here until they are activated. After the activation of all requests, this data is deleted.

2. The *active data table* contains the active data and is called the "A table." Active data tables are built according to the DSO definition, which contains a key field section and a data field section—each consisting of InfoObjects of all types.

3. The *change log* contains the change history for the delta update from the DSO into other data targets, such as other DSOs or InfoCubes.

The activation queue and change log are almost identical in structure: the activation queue has an SID, the package ID, and the record number as its key, whereas the change log has the request ID, the package ID, and the record number as its key.

Data can be loaded into the activation queues of DSOs by several sources simultaneously because a queuing mechanism enables a parallel insert. The key fields allow records to be labeled consistently in the activation queue.

During activation, the data in the activation queue is compared to the data in the active data table, meaning that new records are inserted and changed records are updated. These changes are recorded in the change log and are then available for loading to subsequent data targets, such as other DSOs or InfoCubes.

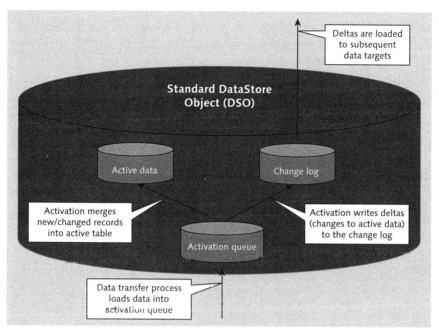

Figure 1.3 The DataStore Object Activation Process

In many cases, it is necessary to report on data that is *not* stored in a single Info-Object, InfoCube, or DSO. In these cases, a view of data from multiple InfoProviders is necessary. SAP BW lets you model or derive many types of virtual InfoProviders that do not store data physically but instead join or union data from others. Table 1.3 lists these InfoProviders, but we'll cover them in more detail in Chapter 5.

InfoProvider	Description
Aggregation Level	Redefines the granularity of single InfoProviders used for planning purposes
BEx Query	Reads data from a query using the data federator interface, thus allowing for pre-aggregation of results
CompositeProvider	Combines data from analytic indexes in BWA or SAP HANA and Info-Providers by using a union, left outer join, or inner join
HybridProvider	Combines historic data with real-time data from InfoProviders designed to separate data already loaded into BW from a small set of new data not yet loaded

Table 1.3 Virtual InfoProviders That Can Be Modeled in BW

InfoProvider	Description
InfoSet	Combines data in master data-bearing characteristics, InfoCubes, and DataStore objects by using a *join* on tables of the relevant InfoProviders
MultiProvider	Combines data from other InfoProviders by using a *union* on tables of the relevant InfoProviders
TransientProvider	Reads data from derived InfoProviders based on a classic InfoSet or an SAP HANA analytic index
VirtualProvider	Reads a small set of data in real time from the source system or another InfoProvider based on a data transfer process, BAPI, function module, or SAP HANA model

Table 1.3 Virtual InfoProviders That Can Be Modeled in BW (Cont.)

With the exception of MultiProviders, the use cases for many of the virtual Info-Providers listed in Table 1.3 are usually limited to specific applications and smaller sets of data because providing reporting performance equivalent to standard InfoCubes can be a significant challenge. In most cases, relying on traditional modeling techniques is the better alternative. Please refer to Chapter 5 for more information on data modeling for performance.

Before moving on to the next section on SAP's delivered content, it may be helpful to review the primary functional areas of the SAP BW solution:

▶ Data transfer processes leverage extraction, transformation, and load (ETL) functionality to extract data from a specific source, apply transformation rules, and load it into the data warehouse.

▶ The data warehouse stores data in various InfoProviders with multi-dimensional or transparent flat table structures.

▶ BEx queries access the information in InfoProviders and deliver it to end users for reporting and analysis via a selection of tools in either the BEx Suite or SAP BusinessObjects Suite.

This SAP BW solution provides substantial functionality to address any business reporting requirement, but there is no need to start development from scratch. SAP contains a large number of pre-defined *business content* in the form of DataSources, InfoObjects, DSOs, InfoCubes, authorization roles, queries, etc., enabling everyone to leverage SAP's experience and reduce implementation cycles. The business content can be modified to meet an organization's specific requirements; however, custom development will take longer to implement.

1.1.4 BI Content

With BI Content, SAP delivers pre-configured role- and task-based information models and reporting and analysis scenarios based on industry standards. BI Content models and scenarios cover all business areas and integrate content from almost all SAP applications and even some selected external applications.

BI Content information models are designed with three purposes in mind:

- For use in specific industries without modification (out of the box)
- To be adapted to any degree of detail
- To serve as a template or as an example for customer-defined models

As a result, BI Content for SAP BW enables quick and cost-effective implementation by providing models that can be used as guidelines during implementation. These information models include the following:

- DataSources (delivered as a plug-in for the OLTP Source System)
- InfoObjects (key figures and characteristics)
- InfoSources
- Transformations
- InfoProviders (InfoCubes and DSOs)
- Process chains
- Variables
- Data mining models
- Queries
- Workbooks
- Web templates
- Roles
- Aggregation levels
- Planning functions
- Planning function types

For BusinessObjects customers, BI Content Extensions contain dashboards and Crystal Reports to extend the data models for consumption in that suite of tools. In addition, SAP BW provides demo content, which includes sample data.

Recall from Figure 1.1 that both BI Content and BI Content Extensions are delivered as add-ons to SAP BW. Different versions of business content are relevant for each SAP NetWeaver release (see Table 1.4 for valid BI Content versions by release).

SAP NetWeaver Release	BI Content Version
SAP NetWeaver 7.40	BI Content 7.47
	BI Content Extensions 7.47
SAP NetWeaver 7.31	BI Content 7.47
	BI Content Extensions 7.47
	BI Content 7.46
	BI Content Extensions 7.46
SAP NetWeaver 7.30	BI Content 7.37
	BI Content Extensions 7.37
	BI Content 7.36
	BI Content Extensions 7.36
	BI Content 7.35
	BI Content Extensions 7.35
SAP NetWeaver 7.03	BI Content 7.47
	BI Content Extensions 7.47
	BI Content 7.46
	BI Content Extensions 7.46

Table 1.4 Cross-Reference of BI Content Version by SAP NetWeaver Release

BI Content should always be installed in every environment and leveraged to the greatest possible extent. The sheer complexity of some business content extractors provide reason enough for many existing SAP customers to invest in SAP BW as a data warehousing solution. The integration with other SAP applications (which is driven by business content) adds such significant value that it cannot be ignored. For systems on SAP HANA, there is now specific Business Content optimized specifically for that database included in BI Content release 7.47. This new content utilizes SAP HANA-optimized transformations, consolidated InfoObjects, and more line item details and, in some cases, leverages BW models and SAP HANA models in combined scenarios.

1.1.5 New Versions, New Features

SAP BW on SAP HANA continues to be the cornerstone of SAP's strategic vision for enterprise data warehousing providing organizations a solid data foundation to capture, store, transform, and manage data in a scalable, enterprise-ready data warehouse. SAP BW on SAP HANA will continue to evolve to meet the growing challenges imposed on IT such as the need to manage exploding data volumes, new data sources, and real-time information access.

New Features for SAP BW 7.40

The latest release of SAP BW running on SAP HANA, SAP BW 7.40, is a great example of how SAP BW has evolved to meet these new challenges. SAP has continued to move more of the process-intensive functions from the SAP BW application into the database to take advantage of the inherent in-memory performance improvements and reduce the need for data transfers between the primary application server and the database server. Figure 1.4 compares SAP BW on SAP HANA with a traditional BW setup.

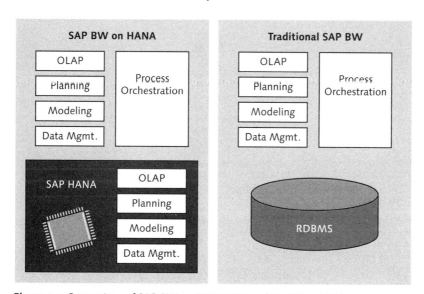

Figure 1.4 Comparison of SAP BW on SAP HANA and Traditional BW

The key system-related features available with SAP BW 7.40 include converged planning solutions like BPC unification, enhanced mobile enablement, and BW content optimized for SAP HANA.

However, these are just a few of the new features available with SP5. Table 1.5 offers a full list of features by category. Note that since SAP NetWeaver 7.40 is optimized for SAP HANA, many of these new features are available for only that database platform. But even without SAP HANA, there are still many application-level features available for traditional relational databases.

Category	BW 7.40 Feature	Availability
Analytic Manager	Inventory Key Figures for DSOs, VirtualProviders, CompositeProviders	SAP HANA only
	OLAP: Calculation Push-down	SAP HANA only
	OLAP: Current Member	
	OLAP: FIX Operator	
	OLAP: Multidimensional FAGGR	
	OLAP: Stock Coverage Key Figure	SAP HANA only
	PAK Enhancements	SAP HANA only
	Planning Function Push-down	SAP HANA only
	Planning on Local Providers in BW Workspace	SAP HANA only
	Planning: ODATA & Easy Query Extensions	
	Planning: Support on SAP HANA views for facts and master data	SAP HANA only
EDW	Bulk Load Capabilities (only for field-based DSOs)	SAP HANA only
	Data Request Housekeeping	
	DTP for Hierarchies: Extract Multiple Hierarchies Request by Request from PSA into Data Target	
	Field-based DataStore Objects	SAP HANA only
	SAP HANA Analysis Process	SAP HANA only
	Open Hub: Push data into a Connected Database	
	Open ODS Layer—Open ODS View	SAP HANA only
	Operational Data Provisioning—Data Services Integration	

Table 1.5 New SAP BW 7.40 Features

Category	BW 7.40 Feature	Availability
EDW	Operational Data Provisioning—ODQ for SLT	
	Operational Data Provisioning—Optional PSA and Renewed Integration with SAP Extractors and BW Data Mart Scenario	
	Support of Smart Data Access	SAP HANA only
	Transformation based on HAPs (In-Memory Transformations)	SAP HANA only
Enhancement	Extension of Max Characteristic Value	
	Extra-Long Text	
	High-Cardinality InfoObject (SID-less)	
	XXL Attributes	
Metadata and modeling	BW Modeling Tools in Eclipse	SAP HANA only
	BW Workspace Enhancements: Data Cleansing	SAP HANA only
	CompositeProvider	SAP HANA only
	SAP HANA Model Generation for BW InfoProvider	SAP HANA only
	InfoObjects based on Calculation View	SAP HANA only
	New Web Dynpro-based Master Data Value Maintenance	
	Re-Modeling Toolbox Enhancements	SAP HANA only
Miscellaneous	SAP HANA-Optimized BW Business Content	SAP HANA only
NLS	Monitoring for Sybase IQ integrated in DBA cockpit	
	Optimized Query Access to NLS Data in Sybase IQ leveraging SDA	
	Support to Archive InfoProviders containing Non-Cumulative Key Figures	

Table 1.5 New SAP BW 7.40 Features (Cont.)

Most of the new features listed in Table 1.5 will be covered in more detail in the following chapters when specific BW object and functionality are reviewed.

But before progressing into system landscapes, let's take a look at what's new from a Basis perspective in SAP NetWeaver versions 7.31 and 7.40.

New Functionality in SAP NetWeaver 7.31

The new capabilities available with SAP NetWeaver 7.31 follow the "innovation without disruption" philosophy. A good example is the introduction of ABAP Development Tools for SAP NetWeaver, also known as *ABAP in Eclipse* for short. Eclipse is an open development platform comprised of extensible frameworks, tools, and runtimes for building, deploying, and managing software across the lifecycle.

ABAP in Eclipse provides developers a more intuitive style of user interaction, including wizards, auto-arrangement of panes, and elaborated task lists so they can manage different programming perspectives in parallel. The perspective approach enables work in multiple systems and on multiple development objects at the same time in one Eclipse session—each object is shown in its own tab.

> **Recommendation**
>
> Not all ABAP objects are natively supported in Eclipse. However, these objects can still be edited in Eclipse via an embedded SAP GUI session.

In addition to ABAP in Eclipse, many plug-ins are available that serve the need for innovative program models, such as SAP HANA database access and user interface handling based on SAPUI5, which is SAP's native implementation of the HTML5 protocol. As a result, the SAP HANA Studio, SAP HANA Cloud tools, and design time tools for SAPUI5 are based on Eclipse.

With all plug-ins based on Eclipse, developer productivity is dramatically increased since the learning curve is less steep in a homogeneous tool environment.

SAP NetWeaver 7.31 also delivered many innovations for the Java stack, most notably in the area of Process Integration (PI) and Business Process Management (BPM). Both PI and BPM can now be deployed on a single Java stack, reducing complexity compared to previous dual stack deployments.

The PI and BPM modeling and configuration tools have been moved to Eclipse, as well. Business process patterns are available to model application-to-application (A2A) and business-to-business (B2B) processes in a consistent and governed fashion.

Aside from the ABAP developer tools, there is no compelling reason to upgrade BW implementations to SAP NetWeaver 7.31. In contrast, there are many new capabilities for BW in SAP NetWeaver 7.40, especially when powered by an SAP HANA database.

New Functionality in SAP NetWeaver 7.40

SAP NetWeaver 7.40 is a follow-up release to SAP NetWeaver 7.30, which was designed as an enhancement package to ensure compatibility with previous SAP NetWeaver releases. It runs on all established database platforms but was heavily optimized for SAP HANA; objects such as SAP HANA views and stored procedures can now be defined directly in the ABAP dictionary and consumed in ABAP programs.

In addition, SAPUI5 and SAP Gateway are now integral parts of the SAP NetWeaver 7.40 platform, making it easy to build innovative applications, such as predictive analytics, on top of the SAP NetWeaver 7.40 platform (including Suite on HANA). In previous releases on a traditional database environment, all of the code (user interface code such as Web Dynpro, application logic, and database operations) was executed on the ABAP application server level. With SP5 of NetWeaver 7.40 in an SAP HANA environment utilizing innovative user interface technologies, code previously written in ABAP moves to the appropriate layer. Not surprisingly, there are two main use cases for this latest release:

1. SAP BW powered by SAP HANA

2. ABAP custom development on top of SAP HANA (either optimizing and accelerating existing ABAP applications or developing new applications)

SAP delivers step-by-step guidelines and best practices for optimizing existing programs for SAP HANA, an approach that empowers ABAP programmers to delegate database-intensive operations and calculations to the database layer.

In a traditional SAP environment, the data is always brought to the ABAP application layer for processing. In an SAP HANA environment, code can be executed in the database directly on the data, so many I/O operations can be avoided. For example, stored procedures can be executed purely on the database layer, providing significant performance benefits when compared to a traditional database environment.

In addition to the delegation of code to the database layer, user interface code can be promoted to the browser layer (SAPUI5). But that does not mean that the application server layer has no purpose. The application server layer is still integral to providing application logic and orchestration, connectivity, and system management.

SAP offers innovative user interface technologies to address the needs of both power users and occasional users. The transaction-oriented application UIs are typically powered by Web Dynpro and Floorplan Manager; these are very robust and come with rather sophisticated development tools. This allows developers and power users to develop, extend, and configure the user interface of solutions, such as the SAP Business Suite. To better support innovative technologies such as cloud and modern mobile and desktop applications, SAP has delivered the SAPUI5 development toolkit. This is ideally suited to serve occasional users with a high degree of interaction.

SAPUI5 is SAP's implementation of the standard HTML5 protocol, which is supported by modern browser technology. SAP leverages the HTML5 standard to the greatest extent possible to cover requirements such as browser and device independence. SAPUI5 makes it easy to embed domain-specific UI technology, such as charting libraries. SAPUI5 is rather platform-independent and available for all major SAP runtime platforms, such as AS ABAP, AS Java, SAP HANA Cloud, and SAP HANA XS.

SAPUI5 was developed in a release-independent fashion but is integrated into SAP NetWeaver 7.40 for easy deployment. SAP UI5 offers a rich control library and access to business data with Gateway services. The user interface logic is based on JavaScript.

On the Java side, SAP NetWeaver 7.31 Java and SAP NetWeaver 7.40 Java are based on the same internal code line, meaning they are identical. Therefore, SAP NetWeaver functional areas such as SAP Enterprise Portal, SAP Business Process Management, and SAP PI are enabled to run directly on SAP HANA, thus enabling consolidation of the number of systems employed in any given system landscape.

1.2 System Landscape

A *system landscape* contains all of the SAP systems in a logical group, which can be either horizontal or vertical.

Horizontal landscapes consist of all the systems that are linked by transport routes to support a *promote to production* (PtP) strategy, which is the process by which system changes are developed, tested, and migrated to the productive environment. A typical horizontal landscape includes three systems: development, quality assurance (QA), and production. The BW landscape in Figure 1.5 is an example of a horizontal landscape.

In contrast, vertical landscapes consist of all the systems that serve the same function in the PtP strategy. For example, all the systems that run productive services are the *production landscape*, as shown in Figure 1.5.

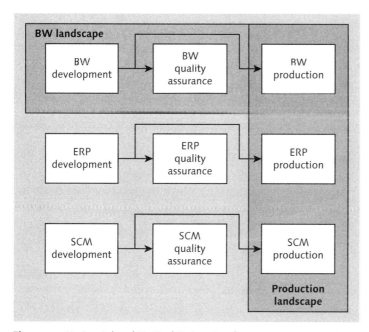

Figure 1.5 Horizontal and Vertical System Landscapes

In the following sections, we will cover both the horizontal and vertical landscapes in more detail, starting with a recommended PtP strategy (Section 1.2.1) and then moving on to vertical landscape integration in terms of source system interfaces (Section 1.2.2). Then, we will discuss how to copy systems within a horizontal landscape (Section 1.2.3), followed by an introduction to change management and client configuration as they relate to the PtP strategy (Section 1.2.4). This section concludes with a deep dive into the configuration of the transport organizer, including specific tasks for SAP BW systems (Section 1.2.5).

1.2.1 Promote to Production Strategy

SAP recommends a three-system horizontal landscape for all SAP applications, and most companies implement it with a three-system PtP landscape, complete with a development system, a QA system, and a production system. The QA system serves many purposes, including providing an environment for the following:

- *Consolidation* of development to ensure that nothing is missing from transports before import into production
- *Integration* testing of solutions insulated from ongoing development
- *User acceptance* of solutions, using production-quality data because QA systems can be routinely refreshed from production
- *Cutover* preparation of solutions, including identification of access needs, specific procedures, and data load estimates
- *Regression* testing of solutions to ensure that they do not break anything else currently operating in production

The three-system PtP strategy can be extended to include a second or third QA system, isolating the environments used for the previously outlined testing purposes from one another. Additional systems for sandbox development and training are common, but because they are not part of the transport route, they are not considered part of the PtP strategy.

The most important consideration in defining a PtP strategy is that it should closely align with the PtP strategy of the data warehouse source systems, such as ERP. In other words, the BW system PtP landscape should have no fewer systems than the PtP landscape of its source systems.

1.2.2 Source System Interface

SAP BW provides an open architecture in many areas: data can be extracted from various sources, including productive SAP applications, external databases, and flat file sources. Integrated planning enables end users to enter data directly into the data warehouse. Data can also be made available for consumption by downstream applications using the open hub interface.

All source systems for each BW system should be aligned within the same vertical landscape. Therefore, the BW development system should be fed from the development source systems, the BW quality assurance system should be fed from the quality assurance source systems, and the BW production system should be fed from the production source systems, as shown in Figure 1.6.

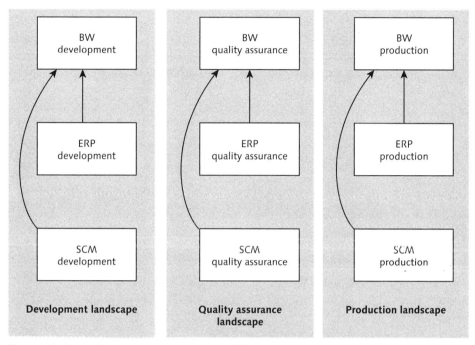

Figure 1.6 Source System Interfaces Aligned within Vertical Landscapes

> **Warning!**
>
> It is not recommended to connect source systems from a different vertical landscape to BW (i.e., production data should not be fed directly into a development system). Many objects used to load data into SAP BW from source systems such as DataSources, transfer rules, and DTPs are source system-dependent. These inter-landscape connections result in duplicate objects in the development environment (i.e., one transfer rule for development ERP and a duplicate transfer rule for production ERP).
>
> Only the development transfer rules should be transported through to production, but the risk of transporting the wrong rules is quite high. The two sets of rules will quickly fall out of sync, and it will be extremely difficult to keep them both functioning. This will eventually wreak havoc on the integrity of the BW landscape change and transport system.

Even though it is not recommended to connect one source system to SAP BW systems in different vertical landscapes, it is possible to connect one source system to multiple BW systems within the same vertical landscape. This is possible because delta queues can be cloned to feed multiple SAP BW systems from a single SAP source system; the caveat, however, is that delta queues should be cloned only for BW systems within the same vertical landscape in the PtP landscape. For example, if an SAP BW training system were created as a copy of a QA system, the source system connections could be cloned so that they feed both SAP BW QA and SAP BW Training with minimal risk. However, if the SAP BW training system is not in the transport path, it needs to be regularly refreshed from SAP BW QA to keep in sync with development changes, and each time, the delta queues need to be cloned anew.

Cloning delta queues involves a multi-step process, which can be automated with the Post Copy Automation tool from SAP Landscape Virtualization Management. Let's turn our attention there now.

1.2.3 Post-Copy Automation

With the Enterprise edition of SAP Landscape Virtualization Management (LVM), customers can install the Post-Copy Automation (PCA) add-on on systems to be copied. In most landscapes, the QA system is refreshed (copied) from production on a routine basis. A valid license is required to download the add-on PCAI_ENT_10 from SAP Service Marketplace. To install the add-on in any SAP system, component SAP_BASIS must meet or exceed the following release level:

SAP NetWeaver Version	Support Pack
SAP NetWeaver 7.00	Support Package 14
SAP NetWeaver 7.01	Support Package 00
SAP NetWeaver 7.02	Support Package 00
SAP NetWeaver 7.10	Support Package 14
SAP NetWeaver 7.11	Support Package 09
SAP NetWeaver 7.30	Support Package 01
SAP NetWeaver 7.31	Support Package 01
SAP NetWeaver 7.40	Support Package 01

Table 1.6 Minimum Support Pack Levels Required for PCA

Because its implementation may require substantial effort, the PCA add-on should be installed only in those systems that will be copied. While PCA can be used in all SAP systems, if there are no plans to use PCA in landscapes other than SAP BW, the add-on needs to be installed only in the SAP BW landscape. However, prerequisite SAP Notes need to be applied in all source systems so that delta queues and RFC destinations can be recreated after system copies of SAP BW.

In most cases, the SAP Notes for PCA require manual steps, so this effort should not be taken lightly. Figure 1.7 gives an example of the effort to apply PCA prerequisite SAP Notes in an SAP BW 7.30 system and all its source systems—note that 60% of the notes require manual steps.

SAP System	BW	ERP	SCM	CRM	SRM	
Release	730	731	702	702	702	
Component SAP_BASIS SP Level	7	2	10	10	10	Total
SAP Notes (automated corrections)	15	2	2	2	2	23
SAP Notes (manual corrections)	23	3	4	4	4	38
SAP Notes - Total	38	5	6	6	6	61

Figure 1.7 Substantial Effort of Patching PCA for Systems Below SAP BW 7.40

So why go through with this effort? The answer is that PCA standardizes and automates system copy tasks. Even though SAP has published a how-to on performing database copies for BW systems, very few companies follow these instructions verbatim. In fact, in our experience, no two companies perform database copies the same way, and, even more concerning, no single company performs database copies consistently and correctly. The end result is sometimes many weeks of root-cause analysis and troubleshooting to identify steps that were omitted or performed incorrectly during the last system copy procedure.

Using PCA for system copies offers five main benefits:

▶ PCA enforces SAP standard best practices for system copies. The task lists are maintained and delivered by SAP, so any issues with the tool are fully supported.

▶ PCA mitigates the risk of human error and eliminates the risk of omitting steps in the tasks it covers. Some tasks require input parameters, which can be prepopulated in the source system and saved as variants for execution later in the copied system. Using variants ensures identical execution time after time. The task lists also ensure that all tasks are executed successfully in the correct sequence—no steps can be skipped.

▸ PCA executes tasks faster by stringing task lists together. This level of automation facilitates seamless execution. Using variants enables anyone to execute post-copy tasks, so there is no need to wait for specific skillsets to execute any post-copy tasks—anyone can pull the trigger.

▸ PCA provides an audit trail of who did what and when. The logs can be evaluated in case of subsequent issues. Logs like the one in Figure 1.8 can be used to confirm that the correct parameters were entered and the steps executed in the correct sequence.

▸ PCA is customizable, so client-specific tasks can be added to task lists. Any transactions or programs that can be executed in the SAP application are candidates for automation in a PCA task list.

▸ SAP continues to deliver new task lists to facilitate other areas of need in BW, such as pre- and post-upgrade, pre- and post-migration, and housekeeping task lists.

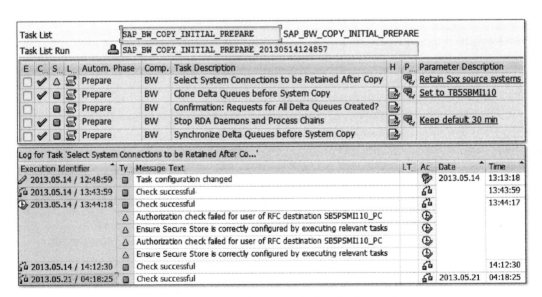

Figure 1.8 PCA Task List to Clone Delta Queues before the System Copy

In some special use cases, such as an OS/DB migration to SAP HANA, PCA can be used to clone delta queues in the source systems before a system copy is performed (see Figure 1.8). The copied system can then be upgraded and migrated to SAP HANA with minimized downtime of the existing production system on its traditional database. The cloned delta queues can feed the newly migrated copy, and as soon as data loads are caught up, the users can be transitioned from the old system to the new system. This migration approach reduces the migration risks for large databases.

PCA task lists can be maintained and executed via Transaction STC01 in client 000 only. Previously executed task lists can be reviewed, resumed, and maintained in Transaction STC02. Figure 1.9 highlights different status symbols for each task list execution.

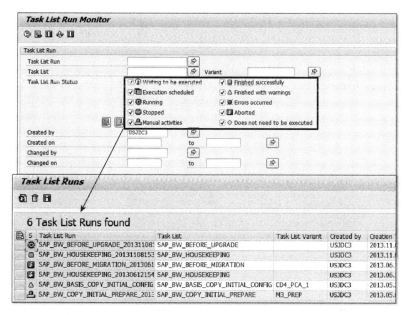

Figure 1.9 The Task List Run Monitor (Transaction STC02)

After the database copy is executed and the SAP system is restarted, the post-copy task list cleans up unneeded system tables from the original system (see Figure 1.10).

After cleaning and initial setup, the task list re-configures the new system based on parameters input, including executing the logical system name conversion (Transaction BDLS) and configuring RFC connections to source systems, licenses, and system profiles (see Figure 1.11).

49

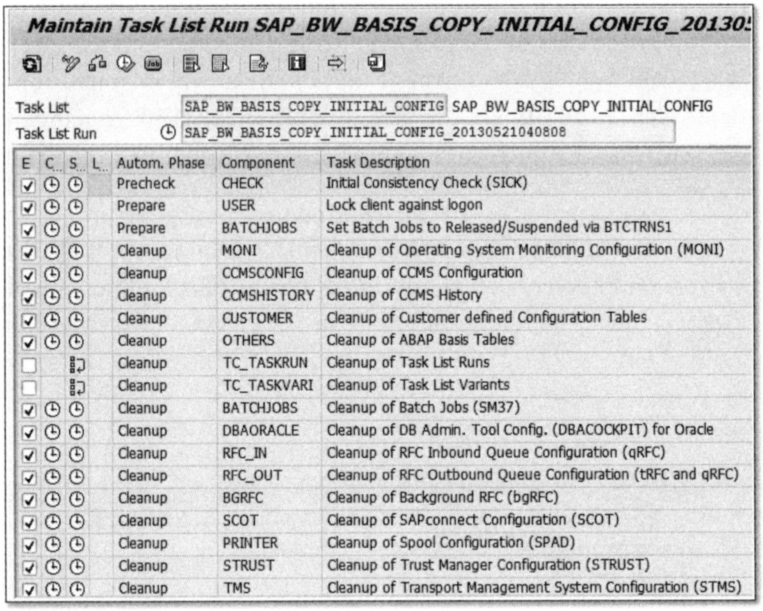

Maintain Task List Run SAP_BW_BASIS_COPY_INITIAL_CONFIG_20130!

E	C	S	L	Autom. Phase	Component	Task Description
✓	⊕	⊕		Precheck	CHECK	Initial Consistency Check (SICK)
✓	⊕	⊕		Prepare	USER	Lock client against logon
✓	⊕	⊕		Prepare	BATCHJOBS	Set Batch Jobs to Released/Suspended via BTCTRNS1
✓	⊕	⊕		Cleanup	MONI	Cleanup of Operating System Monitoring Configuration (MONI)
✓	⊕	⊕		Cleanup	CCMSCONFIG	Cleanup of CCMS Configuration
✓	⊕	⊕		Cleanup	CCMSHISTORY	Cleanup of CCMS History
✓	⊕	⊕		Cleanup	CUSTOMER	Cleanup of Customer defined Configuration Tables
✓	⊕	⊕		Cleanup	OTHERS	Cleanup of ABAP Basis Tables
☐		🔁		Cleanup	TC_TASKRUN	Cleanup of Task List Runs
☐		🔁		Cleanup	TC_TASKVARI	Cleanup of Task List Variants
✓	⊕	⊕		Cleanup	BATCHJOBS	Cleanup of Batch Jobs (SM37)
✓	⊕	⊕		Cleanup	DBAORACLE	Cleanup of DB Admin. Tool Config. (DBACOCKPIT) for Oracle
✓	⊕	⊕		Cleanup	RFC_IN	Cleanup of RFC Inbound Queue Configuration (qRFC)
✓	⊕	⊕		Cleanup	RFC_OUT	Cleanup of RFC Outbound Queue Configuration (tRFC and qRFC)
✓	⊕	⊕		Cleanup	BGRFC	Cleanup of Background RFC (bgRFC)
✓	⊕	⊕		Cleanup	SCOT	Cleanup of SAPconnect Configuration (SCOT)
✓	⊕	⊕		Cleanup	PRINTER	Cleanup of Spool Configuration (SPAD)
✓	⊕	⊕		Cleanup	STRUST	Cleanup of Trust Manager Configuration (STRUST)
✓	⊕	⊕		Cleanup	TMS	Cleanup of Transport Management System Configuration (STMS)

Task List: SAP_BW_BASIS_COPY_INITIAL_CONFIG SAP_BW_BASIS_COPY_INITIAL_CONFIG
Task List Run: SAP_BW_BASIS_COPY_INITIAL_CONFIG_20130521040808

Figure 1.10 PCA Task List-Cleaned System Table After the Database Copy

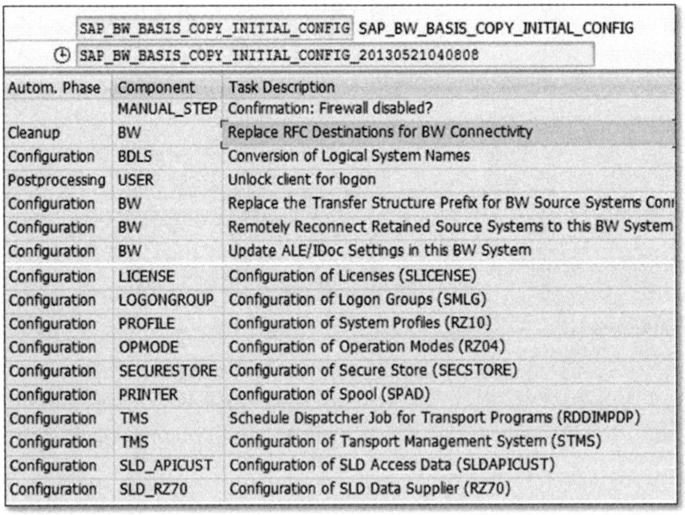

SAP_BW_BASIS_COPY_INITIAL_CONFIG SAP_BW_BASIS_COPY_INITIAL_CONFIG
⊕ SAP_BW_BASIS_COPY_INITIAL_CONFIG_20130521040808

Autom. Phase	Component	Task Description
	MANUAL_STEP	Confirmation: Firewall disabled?
Cleanup	BW	Replace RFC Destinations for BW Connectivity
Configuration	BDLS	Conversion of Logical System Names
Postprocessing	USER	Unlock client for logon
Configuration	BW	Replace the Transfer Structure Prefix for BW Source Systems Coni
Configuration	BW	Remotely Reconnect Retained Source Systems to this BW System
Configuration	BW	Update ALE/IDoc Settings in this BW System
Configuration	LICENSE	Configuration of Licenses (SLICENSE)
Configuration	LOGONGROUP	Configuration of Logon Groups (SMLG)
Configuration	PROFILE	Configuration of System Profiles (RZ10)
Configuration	OPMODE	Configuration of Operation Modes (RZ04)
Configuration	SECURESTORE	Configuration of Secure Store (SECSTORE)
Configuration	PRINTER	Configuration of Spool (SPAD)
Configuration	TMS	Schedule Dispatcher Job for Transport Programs (RDDIMPDP)
Configuration	TMS	Configuration of Tansport Management System (STMS)
Configuration	SLD_APICUST	Configuration of SLD Access Data (SLDAPICUST)
Configuration	SLD_RZ70	Configuration of SLD Data Supplier (RZ70)

Figure 1.11 PCA Task List-Reconfigured System after the Database Copy

Now that you have a general idea of the system landscape and source system connections, the next step is to plan development and customization in the system and their role in client configuration.

1.2.4 Change Management

Before the SAP BW system can be used to load data and report on company-specific business processes, it must be adapted to the business requirements. This is usually done in an SAP implementation project, but adapting and configuring are also ongoing processes. Even after the system is used productively, changes to the SAP configuration will still need to be made, due either to business or organizational changes in your company or to the implementation of new SAP functions, often linked to an upgrade to a new SAP release.

SAP provides various tools for modifying the SAP software. The tools used depend on the type and extent of the business requirements. Any modifications made with these tools are stored in tables in the SAP database:

▶ **Customizing tools**
The most important configuration tool is the Implementation Guide (IMG), which is accessed via Transaction SPRO. The IMG can be used to make almost all configurations possible in the SAP standard. Any modifications made to the SAP software in the IMG are known as Customizing settings, or *Customizing* for short. This includes setting up default system behavior referenced during data loads and reporting.

The IMG splits the various Customizing settings into IMG activities and displays them in a hierarchical overview. This overview shows the recommended process flow and assignment to the different applications of the SAP system. The IMG lets you filter out the relevant IMG activities for a particular section of the SAP applications. IMG activities can also be grouped logically into IMG projects, which are then worked on as an implementation project by a particular team. The requirements of a project and its progress can be documented in the IMG project.

Changes made in the IMG are placed in the Customizing tables of the SAP database. The contents of these tables are known as Customizing data. When the SAP applications are used productively, the SAP runtime system analyzes this Customizing data and uses it to control the business processes.

Most Customizing data is client-specific, meaning that different Customizing settings can be chosen for each client in the SAP system that do not affect each other. Changes to the Customizing settings in one client have no effect on system actions in another client.

However, there is also a significant amount of cross-client data that is relevant for all clients (such as the factory calendar). Note that changes to these types of Customizing settings affect all clients in the SAP system.

▶ **ABAP Workbench**

SAP provides the ABAP Workbench as a complete programming environment. The ABAP Workbench includes tools for defining data structures (ABAP Dictionary), developing ABAP programs (ABAP Editor), and designing interfaces (Screen Painter and Menu Painter), as well as many other functions. These tools can be used to develop custom report programs or transactions, or to modify or make enhancements to existing SAP programs. These enhancements are known as *customer exits*.

The changes made in the ABAP Workbench are placed in the Repository tables of the SAP database. The contents of these tables are known as Repository data or Repository objects. Apart from a few exceptions, the Repository data is cross-client. As with cross-client Customizing, changes to Repository objects affect all clients of an SAP system.

▶ **Data Warehousing Workbench**

SAP provides the Data Warehousing Workbench to activate and develop all backend SAP BW objects. There are no SAP BW objects active by default, even though, as previously discussed, there are thousands of business content objects delivered by SAP. All activation, modification, and new development, as well as most production-level support, such as process chain and data load monitoring, can be done within the Data Warehousing Workbench.

The changes made in the Data Warehousing Workbench are also placed in the Repository tables of the SAP database. Even though the Repository data is cross-client, in SAP BW systems, the Data Warehousing Workbench can be accessed in only a single client; thus, access to it is prevented from all other clients.

▶ **Change and Transport System (CTS)**

The CTS is the central tool for managing changes to Customizing and Repository data made in the IMG, ABAP Workbench, or Data Warehousing Workbench. The CTS records all changes in change requests. The changes in change requests can be linked together logically or be completely independent of each other. Developers in a team can use a common request or individual requests, and they can create documentation for each task in a change request to describe their changes in more detail. This makes it easier to understand the purpose of each change.

When the developer has completed his or her work, the transport can be released. Upon release, two files that can be imported into other clients or SAP systems are created in the file system: a data file and a co-file. The definitions of the objects locked in the request are written to the data file, and the logs of the request are written to the co-file. The logs of the co-file are updated every time the transport is imported into another client or SAP system. This automatic procedure is known as a *transport*.

> **Recommendation**
>
> Before a change request is released, only the object name is locked in the request. The changes—not the request—are stored in the Repository tables. Upon release, the Repository tables are read for the objects locked in the request, and the table entries are written to the request data file, preserving the version of the objects at that specific point in time.

Transports of changes by the CTS allow development in one environment, testing in the QA environment, and then productive use in the production environment. This mitigates the risks faulty settings and program errors place on productive operations.

Transports of changes between clients and systems are subject to rules set in the CTS configuration in the system landscape. One rule may be that changes are transported into a test environment before they can be copied to the production environment. All transports are logged, so you can see when a change request was imported into a client or system and whether there were any errors.

- ▸ **Application data**
  In contrast to Customizing and Repository data, application data is not part of the configuration of the SAP software. Application data is the business data that the SAP applications process when they are used productively. It is split up into master data (such as material masters, customer masters, and vendor masters)

and transaction data (such as sales orders and financial documents). Application data is always client-specific.

The CTS does not manage changes to application data, and it is impossible to transport application data into other clients or systems.

When a user logs on to an SAP system, he or she logs on to a specific client of that system. Any activities carried out in the system using these tools are always carried out in one client. When planning the SAP system landscape, it is necessary to consider which clients are needed for which activities. In addition to any customer-specific clients, each SAP system may have been installed with the default clients listed in Table 1.7.

Client	Description	Purpose
000	SAP reference client	▸ Used to set up new "neutral" clients by client copy ▸ Contains sample customizing table entries but no application data ▸ Not a working client ▸ Do not change or delete this client
001	Production preparation client	▸ Created as a copy of client 000 ▸ Used sometimes as a working/productive client ▸ Do not delete if used as a working client
066	EarlyWatch client	▸ Created during installation years ago ▸ Used only as a service client that enabled SAP to access the system remotely and perform EarlyWatch functions with regard to analyzing errors and performance ▸ Not used anymore and can be safely deleted (its function has been replaced by SAP Solution Manager)

Table 1.7 Default SAP Clients and Purposes

A comprehensive change management strategy limits developer tool access to the appropriate system in the landscape. Multiple clients can exist within each SAP system; each should have a specific role, but only one client in each system can be used to access the Data Warehousing Workbench. Therefore, most SAP BW systems are limited to a single client in addition to the default clients above. The role of the working client in each SAP BW system should correspond with the intended role of each system.

Let's take a look at the central client roles:

- **Customizing and development client (Customizing)**
  Since there is always a need to adapt the SAP software for company-specific business needs, each SAP system landscape requires a client where Customizing settings—and possibly ABAP Workbench developments—can be made.

- **Quality assurance client (Test)**
  Before the Customizing settings and Workbench developments can be used productively, they need to be tested extensively for errors. Any faulty settings can seriously disrupt productive operations, and at worst, lead to the loss of productive data. The integrated nature of the various SAP applications means there are many dependencies among the different Customizing settings. Even an experienced Customizing developer may not discover these dependencies immediately. The correctness of the settings can be guaranteed only with extensive testing.

- **Production client (Production)**
  A separate client is required for productive use of the SAP system. It is essential that no Customizing settings or Workbench developments are made directly in production (and also that no tests are carried out) in order to mitigate the risk of disruption.

These three clients—Customizing, Test, and Production—are the central clients that exist in every system landscape. Standard system landscapes have precisely one client for each of these client roles. Figure 1.12 gives a sample configuration of client roles by SAP system as seen from Transaction SCC4.

Recommendation

We recommend that you make all Customizing settings in the Customizing client of the development system and then use the CTS to transport them to the other clients and systems.

We also recommend that no Customizing settings or Workbench developments be made in the quality assurance or production clients. This can be controlled by the appropriate client settings.

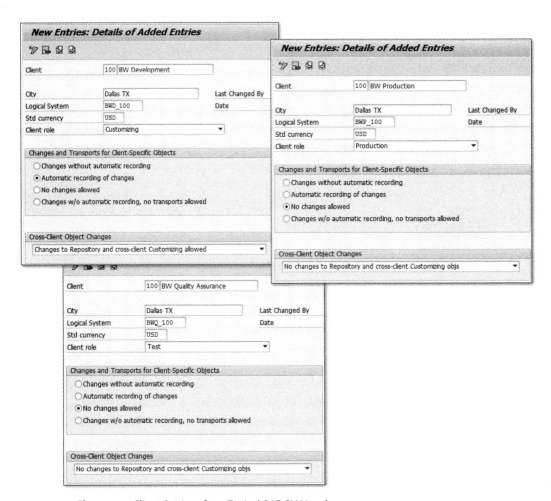

Figure 1.12 Client Settings for a Typical SAP BW Landscape

Note the change settings in the systems shown in Figure 1.12. The development system is set to automatically record client-specific changes and allows changes to cross-client objects. However, the QA and production systems do not allow either type of change; this corresponds with the client roles and their respective SAP systems in the landscape. In the development client, one other setting is needed to enable development: the system change option, which is highlighted in Figure 1.13. This can be set in Transaction SE03.

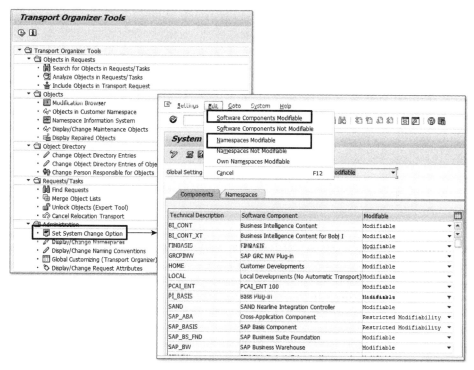

Figure 1.13 Setting the System Change Option (Transaction SE03)

To enable system changes, first set the global setting to MODIFIABLE. Then, set all software components and namespaces to MODIFIABLE using the commands under the EDIT menu.

In SAP BW systems, these central roles are suitable for all environments, including sandbox and training systems, which are usually created by copying another environment defined as one of the central roles. There are additional client roles available, such as DEMO and TRAINING/EDUCATION, but they are not as relevant for SAP BW systems because they are intended for use in multi-client SAP systems. Since SAP BW systems are limited to a single working client, there is no need to consider these client roles.

In multi-client systems, it is important to note that each extra client takes up additional system resources (main memory and database space). They also need to be administrated. For example, user access authorizations need to be maintained, and changes need to be distributed to/from these clients using CTS. The advantages and disadvantages should be carefully weighed before setting up other clients. The other client roles are as follows:

- **Prototype or sandbox client (Demo)**
  A sandbox client can be configured to test any client-specific Customizing settings. Any settings that should be retained need to be re-created in the customizing client. To prevent conflicts between the prototype client settings and real settings in the Customizing client, changes to cross-client Customizing data and Repository objects are restricted in the prototype client. The CTS does not record changes made to client-specific Customizing data and does not transport them from the prototype client.

- **Training client (Training/Education)**
  A training client can be configured to prepare end users for new functionality or new reporting areas to be transported into the production client. The users can use the new functions in this client, which has special application data for training. This client also restricts changes to Customizing data and Repository objects.

This section has provided an overview of the roles of clients and systems in a system landscape and contained essential information on where to perform development and customizing activities. It also introduced and explained important terms and concepts regarding the Change and Transport System (CTS), which helps organize development projects in the Data Warehousing Workbench, the ABAP Workbench, and Customizing, and then transport the changes between the SAP Systems in your system landscape. Now, let's discuss in more detail how the CTS can be used to organize changes.

1.2.5 Transport Organizer

The transport organizer is fully integrated into the Data Warehousing Workbench, the ABAP Workbench, and Customizing tools. Navigation among them is possible in both directions, enabling developers to do two important things:

- Switch to the transport organizer from all transactions of the Data Warehousing Workbench, the ABAP Workbench, and Customizing

- Switch to the appropriate Workbench editor by double-clicking individual objects in an object list

The transport organizer records and documents all changes to Repository and Customizing objects, as listed in Table 1.8.

Object Type	Object Description
Repository	SAP BW objects
	ABAP Dictionary objects
	ABAP programs
	Screens
	User interface definitions
	Documentation
Customizing	Settings for control tables

Table 1.8 Transportable SAP Objects by Type

The transport organizer helps organize development projects by allowing the distribution of project work across individual developers or teams by using different change requests. These change requests record all changes made to development objects and Customizing settings. Objects from the areas of Customizing, the ABAP Workbench, and the Data Warehousing Workbench are managed and recorded in separate requests. Special checks have been implemented for each of these applications.

The transport organizer can be accessed from a request overview (Transaction SE09) that clearly shows all change requests and can display several levels of detail, right down to the object list itself.

Developments, corrections, and repairs are recorded in tasks and transported using change requests. The target system and type of transport are assigned automatically and do not need to be maintained by the user. Several users can work together on a project by organizing their development work in tasks. These tasks belong to a common change request. Access to the transport organizer functions can be controlled for different user groups by assigning appropriate authorizations.

Once Repository objects have been included in a change request, they can be edited only in that request. This means that until the change request has been released, the objects are locked against development work or maintenance by other developers not working on this change request. These developers are only allowed to display the objects.

This is how the transport organizer prevents uncoordinated, parallel changes to objects. Only make changes to the original objects. A warning appears if you try to change a non-original object.

The transport organizer is activated automatically every time a Repository object is edited. An object has to be in a change request before a user can create or change it. Entering objects in requests ensures that all changes made in the Data Warehousing Workbench or in the ABAP Workbench are registered. Changes to Customizing data are also registered by the transport organizer.

A package (formerly known as a development class) and responsible developer are assigned to each Repository object. This package indicates which area the object belongs to. This enables the ability to quickly contact a person in connection with any object. The structure of the entire Repository is based on packages, which can assist developers starting their work.

The transport organizer provides version management for all ABAP Workbench objects, enabling you to compare or retrieve previous versions of these objects. This lets developers document or restore versions released before or after a particular change request or development project.

Recommendation

There is no version management for Data Warehousing Workbench objects. These objects have only three versions:

- 'D' for SAP-delivered business content versions
- 'M' for modified versions
- 'A' for active versions

After an object is edited and subsequently activated, the modified and active versions are the same.

All developers working on a change request should be required to write structured documentation when releasing their tasks. This documentation should state the objectives of the development and clarify the contents of the request. Even though all changed objects are automatically recorded in the object list of the change request, some SAP BW objects record only a unique ID, which is difficult to interpret, so the documentation can help here. All the information in a change request—the object list together with the documentation and version management—provides complete control over all revisions.

Development projects should not be worked on in a production system, but only in the development system. Later in this chapter, we will discuss some exceptions for specific types of SAP BW objects to ensure that production support can be managed efficiently. To ensure that objects remain consistent, each Repository object has a defined original location. Changes are generally made at the original location to prevent unintentional, parallel work on the same object. The original location of Repository objects can be changed with relocation transports.

If several development systems are being used, it may be necessary to transport objects specifically to SAP systems that are not supplied with regular change transports. If necessary, the transport attributes of the object (original system, development class, and transport layer) can be changed. The transport types required for this are managed by the extended view of the transport organizer (Transaction SE01).

To transport Repository and Customizing objects from the development system to other SAP systems in the system group, transport routes are used. These are defined when the system group is configured in the transport management system (TMS). The transport involves exporting objects from the source system in which the objects were changed and importing them into one or more target systems.

When a change request is imported into a system, it processes the contents in a specific sequence. Table 1.9 walks through the import sequence. Some steps may be omitted if there are no relevant objects in the request.

Sequence	Import Step	Description
0	Selection for import	Adds the request to the import buffer
1	Import ABAP Dictionary objects	Imports domains, data elements, structures, and tables
2	ABAP Dictionary activation	Activates domains, data elements, structures, and tables

Table 1.9 Change Request Import Steps in Sequence

Sequence	Import Step	Description
3	Import	Imports all other objects
4	Check versions	Updates versions of all ABAP objects
5	Method execution	Activates all non-ABAP objects
6	Generation of programs and screens	Activates all remaining ABAP objects

Table 1.9 Change Request Import Steps in Sequence (Cont.)

Note

Mass imports of change requests can be imported synchronously or asynchronously. The most important difference is that a synchronous import executes each step in Table 1.9 in sequence for each request, whereas an asynchronous import executes each step for all requests before executing the next step for all requests. If the same object is contained in multiple requests, the asynchronous method activates only the last version because the previous versions are overwritten before the activation steps are executed.

A transport log is created automatically for each change request. If errors occur in the production system after an import has taken place from a quality assurance system, the log provides answers to the following questions:

▶ Which objects were transported?

▶ Who requested the transport?

▶ Why was the transport performed?

There are transport organizer tools available for searching for, displaying, editing, and analyzing change requests and transports. For more information on these tools, please refer to the SAP documentation.

Transport Management Configuration

System changes are migrated to the productive environment according to the PtP strategy covered in Section 1.2.1. All changes, whether new development, corrections to existing development, repairs to SAP-delivered objects, or customizing table entries are migrated using transports requests. Transports contain all necessary and relevant information about the included objects so that the latest object versions can be moved from one system to another.

Transports can be organized, moved, and monitored between SAP systems in a horizontal landscape using the TMS. No user actions at the operating system level are necessary because all transport-related information and functions are mapped in the SAP system.

The TMS provides the following functions:

- Configure transport layers and routes using a graphical editor
- Display import queues for all SAP systems in the transport domain
- Import all requests in an import queue
- Import all requests in a project
- Import individual requests
- Configure and conduct TMS Quality Assurance
- Configure transport workflow

In order to begin transporting, TMS must first be configured in all SAP systems in the landscape. The initial TMS configuration includes the following tasks:

- **Configure the transport domain.**
  That is, define which SAP systems in the system landscape form a transport domain, define which transport groups are needed, and decide which SAP system is to be the transport domain controller.

  A *transport domain* is formed by all the SAP systems within a horizontal landscape that share the same TMS settings. In the domain, one system has the reference configuration, which is distributed to all other systems in the domain. The TMS automatically generates RFC connections among the systems in a domain so that they can communicate.

  A *transport group* is formed by all systems in a domain that share a file system directory where the data files and co-files are written when a change request is released. These files can be imported into any system that shares the same group, as illustrated by BW TRANSPORT DOMAIN A in Figure 1.14. The files can also be copied to the file directories of other transport groups within the same domain, as illustrated by the dotted line between BW TRANSPORT GROUP 2 and BW TRANSPORT GROUP 3 in BW TRANSPORT DOMAIN B. Normally, all systems in a domain form a single group; however, this may not be possible if one or more systems have different hardware platforms, there are high security levels preventing access to file systems from other systems, or a system has a slow network connection.

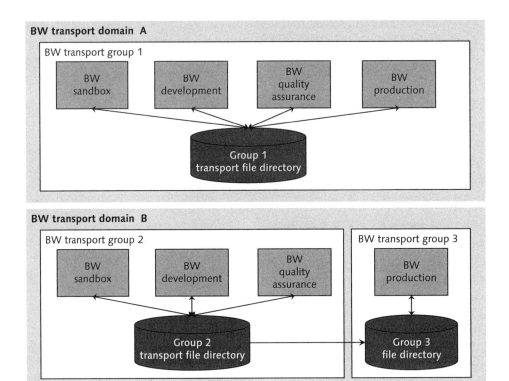

Figure 1.14 Transport Domains and Groups Sharing File System Directories

Changes to the domain are restricted to the system with the reference configuration, which is called the *transport domain controller*. The transport domain controller can be any system that has high availability, high security precautions, and the highest possible release. The production system meets these requirements and is normally configured as the domain controller.

Make sure to have a *backup domain controller* available in case the domain controller fails. Depending on the frequency of database refreshes from production to QA, the development system may have higher availability than the QA system and be a better candidate for the backup controller.

▶ **Configure the transport layers.**
A *transport layer* groups all development projects from the same SAP system that will be transported on the same transport routes.

Each development system in the landscape must be assigned a default transport layer before development can begin. Objects delivered by SAP belong to the transport layer SAP. Other transport layers are generally needed only when new development systems are included in the system landscape.

▶ **Configure the transport routes.**

Transport routes are used to define in which target system change requests are consolidated and which SAP systems are forwarded requests automatically. Recall from Figure 1.5 that the PtP strategy forms the basis for the transport routes in the landscape. Figure 1.15 shows the two types of transport routes in a three-system landscape: consolidation routes and delivery routes.

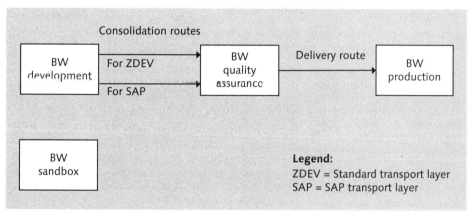

Figure 1.15 Transport Routes for a Sample SAP BW Landscape

Consolidation routes are used to transport objects of each transport layer from a starting point, or source, to a transport target. In a three-system landscape, the source is the development system, and the target is the QA system. Any new or modified objects assigned to a transport layer with a consolidation route are included in transportable change requests. After the request has been released, the objects can be imported into the consolidation system. Objects assigned to transport layers without consolidation routes will be included in local change requests (or in customizing requests without a transport target), which cannot be transported to other SAP systems.

Delivery routes transport objects from a consolidation system to production or other systems. A delivery route ensures that all change requests imported into the route's source system are automatically flagged for import into the route's target system. Delivery routes can be configured with the same source system and different target systems (parallel forwarding), and multiple delivery routes can also be configured in sequence (multilevel forwarding).

Configuring sequential delivery routes to virtual systems and then to production can help mitigate the risk that untested changes are imported into production.

▶ **Choose the transport schedule and strategy.**

The transport strategy is set by default to queue-controlled mass transports but can be re-configured to work with single transports or workflow-controlled transports instead.

The mass transport strategy imports the entire content of the queue asynchronously. By default, the import option to leave the transport request in the queue for later import is activated. Mass imports can be scheduled periodically; this approach is useful for consolidation routes so that changes are imported quickly into the QA system, allowing developers to test their work almost immediately, correct any errors, and consolidate all changes before moving to production. These automatic imports are usually scheduled every 15, 30, or 60 minutes.

Note

Imports that are scheduled asynchronously perform the import steps for all selected requests at one time. For example, if 100 requests are selected for asynchronous import, the data dictionary activation step executes for all 100 requests before the main import is executed for any of them. This is especially useful if dependent objects are contained in subsequent transports—it can prevent many import errors and eliminate the need to re-import requests again.

Note

The import option to leave the transport request in the queue for later import keeps requests in the correct chronological location in the queue. This is useful in cases of preliminary single imports for individual requests that will be followed by a mass import because it prevents older objects from being imported at the next regular import of all the requests. It is also useful in case errors are raised during import: the requests can be re-imported without adding them all back to the queue in the correct sequence.

The single transport strategy is useful only if the number of transports is extremely low. By default, the import option to leave transport requests in the queue for later import is deactivated.

The workflow-controlled transport strategy generates transport proposals to link all related requests when they are exported. The import options correspond to those for single transports, but imports process transport proposals in the TMS work list instead of transport requests.

▶ **Configure the QA approval procedure.**
In a three-system landscape, the consolidation route target system can be configured as a QA system. All requests imported into the QA system are included in the QA work list, and only those completely approved can be imported into the delivery systems.

There are three delivered approval steps: by request owner, by user department, and by system administrator. By default, only the system administrator check is active.

▶ **Configure the transport workflow.**
The *transport workflow* facilitates automatic imports of transport proposals into specific target systems while requiring explicit approvals to guarantee the quality of those systems.

Once the transport proposal is approved, the requests contained in the proposal are automatically imported into the specified target systems. If rejected, the proposal can be modified and resubmitted.

▶ **Configure development packages.**
Formerly known as development classes, *packages* are assigned to Repository objects created at the start of a development project. Packages are also assigned to transport layers (the SAP system proposes the standard transport layer). All Repository objects created in the same package belong to the same transport layer and are transported according to the associated transport routes.

Customizing settings (i.e., table entries) do not usually belong to a package because they are generally not Repository objects listed in the object directory. Therefore, they are always assigned to the standard transport layer.

SAP-delivered Repository objects always belong to the pre-installed SAP transport layer and cannot be assigned to custom transport layers. Modifications to SAP standard objects by SAP Notes should be transported along the same routes as customer developments. To do this, configure the same consolidation route for the SAP layer as for the standard transport layer of the development system; this means that the source and destination of the two consolidation routes must be the same. When a two- or three-system group is configured, this consolidation route is created automatically for the SAP layer.

Once TMS is configured in all SAP systems in the landscape, it is important that development and customizing be performed only in the development system and not in the QA or production systems; this will ensure the integrity of the change control system. The settings to control which systems developers make changes in was covered earlier.

In SAP BW systems, there are additional SAP BW-specific configuration tasks that must be completed in the TRANSPORT CONNECTION pane of the Data Warehousing Workbench. Let's take a look at them now.

SAP BW-Specific Transport Configuration

SAP BW systems use many source system-dependent objects, such as Data-Sources, transfer rules, and DTPs. For these types of objects, the source system is part of the definition and is captured in change requests in the development system. When a change request containing these objects is imported into a target system, the definition must be converted to reflect the source systems of that target system; otherwise, activation will fail because the source systems of the development system do not exist (nor should they).

The conversion rules should be configured in each target system independently because they will differ for each. To maintain the conversion rules, go to the TRANSPORT CONNECTION screen in the Data Warehousing Workbench and select the CONVERSION button, as shown in Figure 1.16. Note that several clients in the development ERP system are converted to a single client in the production ERP system.

> **Note**
>
> Conversion rules should be configured for all source systems connected to the development SAP BW system. If no conversion rule is configured for a source system and a related object is imported, it is imported as-is. This results in activation errors because the development source system should not be connected to the target systems (i.e., non-development systems).

Within the transport connection screen, object changeability settings should also be configured independently in each target system in the landscape. The object changeability settings override the system change settings and client settings with regard to cross-client object changes; in effect, the object changeability settings enable the editing of specific object types directly in production.

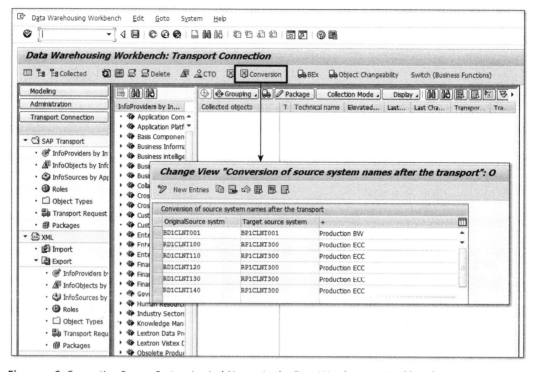

Figure 1.16 Converting Source System Logical Names in the Data Warehousing Workbench

The object changeability configuration can be reached via the TRANSPORT CONNECTION screen of the Data Warehousing Workbench shown in Figure 1.17. Every type of SAP BW object can be configured with one of three values:

▸ *Not changeable* is the default value.

▸ *Changeable original* only allows editing of objects originally created in this system.

▸ *Everything changeable* allows editing of objects imported into this system.

Although all development should be done in the development system and then transported into production, there are legitimate reasons some object types should be changeable directly in production. Allowing these changes in production does present a risk to the integrity of the change and transport organizer, but it also enables end-user development of ad-hoc queries and real-time support for data load issues. Table 1.10 shows recommended settings for object types that should be changeable in a production environment.

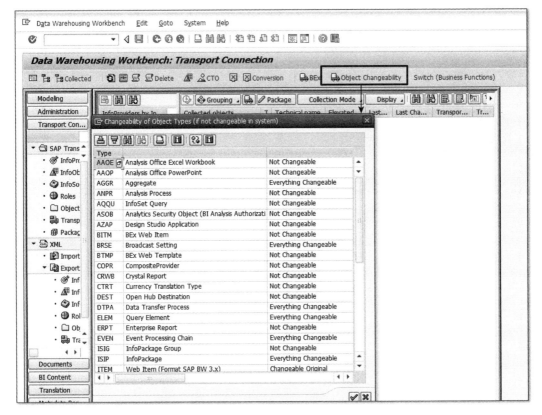

Figure 1.17 Object Changeability Configuration

Recommendation

All changes made directly in production to data load objects should be tracked and either reverted immediately upon resolution or implemented in the development environment and transported through the landscape.

Changeability Requirement	Object Types	Recommended Setting
Data load support team needs to adjust process chains and/or schedules to resolve ad-hoc production data load issues.	▸ InfoPackage ▸ Data transfer process ▸ Process chain ▸ Process chain starter	Everything changeable

Table 1.10 Object Changeability Recommendations

Changeability Requirement	Object Types	Recommended Setting
End users need to create ad-hoc queries and/or reports directly in production to analyze business data	▸ Query element ▸ Query view ▸ Workbook ▸ BEx web item ▸ BEx web template	Changeable original

Table 1.10 Object Changeability Recommendations (Cont.)

Note

Enabling development of queries and reports directly in production may result in a proliferation of queries and reports that need to be managed. A process to replace end-user reports in production with validated reports from development should be agreed with the business. In addition, a routine process to delete unused or obsolete reports from production should be implemented to control the proliferation of reports and limit the impact on system tables.

Best Practice

Authorizations should be implemented to prevent the creation of global query elements, such as variables, structures, and restricted or calculated key figures. These objects can be reused in other queries, which may make it difficult to replace them but, most importantly, if the same technical names are later used by an object imported from development, the definition could be overwritten and neither object may work properly.

In the development system, the standard transport system can be turned off to enable the SAP BW transport connection. In the standard transport system, developers are prompted to assign a package every time they create a new BW object. If the developer chooses a transportable package, he or she is prompted to include the object in a transportable change request.

During large SAP BW implementations, when development on many subject areas is occurring in parallel, the standard transport system can result in import errors if transports are not expertly coordinated. These errors can occur anytime dependent objects are not included in the same request—and coordinating an n:m level of dependencies can prove futile and frustrating.

For example, imagine a simple scenario in which one developer activates business content InfoObjects and saves them into a change request under his user name.

These business content InfoObjects may then be used by other teams of developers who are building unrelated InfoProviders for their own subject areas. If the teams release their change requests first, they will fail on import in the target system because the dependent InfoObjects do not yet exist there. While this scenario can also happen with ABAP and Data Dictionary development, it is far more common with SAP BW InfoObjects and global query elements because of the encouraged reusability of such object types.

If the standard transport system is turned off, developers are not prompted to assign packages to newly created BW objects (only BW objects are affected; all other ABAP and Data Dictionary objects still trigger a dialog box) because they are created as local objects with package $TMP by default. When using the BW transport connection, all objects that should be transported must be collected and assigned to transportable packages and then to change requests in the TRANSPORT CONNECTION screen of the Data Warehousing Workbench. The transport connection wizard identifies all dependent objects and illustrates whether they are local objects and need to be transported. The benefit of the SAP BW transport connection is that all objects can be collected at one time into segregated requests and released in the proper sequence to assure successful import in the target systems.

To deactivate the standard transport system, go to the TRANSPORT CONNECTION screen of the Data Warehousing Workbench and choose the menu item EDIT • TRANSPORT • SWITCH-OFF STANDARD. To activate the standard transport system, select EDIT • TRANSPORT • SWITCH-ON STANDARD.

> **Note**
>
> If changes are made to the BEx object types after they have already been transported once, they are automatically recorded in a change request by prompting the developer with a dialog box. This can slow development in the BEx tools if many different objects are being changed; sometimes the dialog box can "hide" behind other open windows on your desktop, which makes you search for it—if you expect it—or wait for it if you don't (and at this point it will never appear by itself).

BEx objects such as query elements, query views, web templates, web items, enterprise reports, and workbooks can also be given special treatment in the BW transport connection. This special treatment enables change requests to be assigned to BEx objects in advance rather than during maintenance of those objects.

If the standard transport system has been deactivated, a single BEx transport request can be declared for all BEx development, or different BEx transport requests can be declared for specific packages. In this case, it is best to assign a different package to each subject area to retain flexibility when releasing BEx transport requests.

In addition to these BEx objects, objects from the planning and broadcasting settings also use the BEx transport requests. Even if the standard transport system has been activated, these objects continue to be written to the BEx transport request(s).

When using BEx transport requests, we recommend that you declare new requests immediately after releasing the old ones. For more information, you can reach the BEx transport request declaration screen via the BEx button in the TRANSPORT CONNECTION screen of the Data Warehousing Workbench, as shown in Figure 1.18.

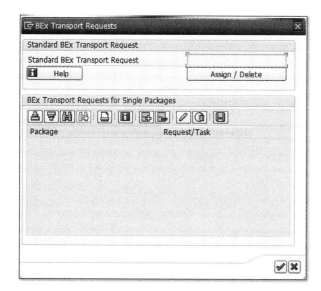

Figure 1.18 BEx Transport Request Assignment Window

Recommendation

Deactivate the standard transport system for initial development. As soon as the production system is deployed and stabilized, reactivate the standard transport system.

If the standard transport system is not active, all objects need to be collected using the transport connection wizard when they are ready to be transported for the first time. Initially, new objects are created automatically as local objects in the package $TMP. The developer must take the following steps manually in the TRANSPORT CONNECTION screen of the Data Warehousing Workbench:

1. Collect objects together with all dependent objects.

2. Specify a transportable package and a transportable request.

The collected new objects (package = $TMP or empty) are then written to the specified request. The collected objects are now subject to the automatic transport connection, and the system automatically records changes to them from this point on in the development system. The object collector needs to be used again to transport new objects created until the standard transport system is activated.

Collecting objects into transports via the transport connection wizard is a powerful capability and should be approached with caution. Ideally this task should be managed by a seasoned veteran on large projects; because not everything in the development system should be migrated to production, a gate keeper is needed to prevent those unwanted changes from being collected.

Before collecting any object, it is a good idea to configure the wizard. The following settings are recommended for most needs:

▶ SPECIFY THE SOURCE SYSTEM: Choose which source system to collect objects from by selecting the SOURCE SYSTEM button.

▶ Set GROUPING to ONLY NECESSARY OBJECTS: Prevent the wizard from collecting all objects in the data flow before and/or after the object chosen.

▶ Set COLLECTION MODE to START MANUAL CONNECTION: This setting ensures that the wizard will start collecting dependent objects only when executed; otherwise, it starts collecting them as soon as an object is dragged into the collection window (see Figure 1.19). If multiple objects are being collected, the automatic setting is inefficient because it collects dependencies for the first object, then for the first and second object, and then for the first, second, and third objects, and so on.

▸ Set DISPLAY to LIST to segregate objects of different types or set DISPLAY to HIERARCHY to see the dependencies between objects.

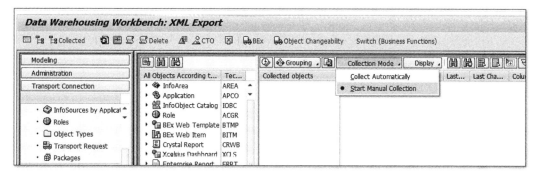

Figure 1.19 The Transport Connection Screen in the Data Warehouse Workbench

When collecting objects for an initial transport, there is a specific sequence in which objects of different types should be released. Before releasing any objects collected using the wizard, you should migrate all OLTP source system objects. This includes any Data Dictionary objects and ABAP programs in the source systems, followed by the application component hierarchy and then the DataSources in those same systems.

> **Note**
>
> All DataSources, including those from the SAP BW system itself, must be replicated in the SOURCE SYSTEM screen of the Data Warehousing Workbench of the target system before transfer rules, transformations, DTPs, or InfoPackages dependent on them can be imported and activated successfully.

In the SAP BW system, before collecting any objects using the wizard, ensure that the following objects are released and imported successfully in the target system(s):

▸ Development packages (formerly known as development classes)

▸ Analysis authorizations

▸ Security roles (developer, support, testing, and end user)

▸ Custom data classes for SAP BW InfoProvider tables

- Data Dictionary objects used by DataSources
- ABAP programs and customer exits used by DataSources
- DataSources—remember to replicate these before importing SAP BW objects

> **Note**
>
> Before migrating custom data class table entries, the database administrator should create the custom tablespaces in the database of the target systems. If BW objects are transported and their custom data class refers to a tablespace that does not exist, the InfoProvider may not activate successfully.

The first transport released from the SAP BW development system containing objects collected using the transport connection wizard should contain only InfoObjects and InfoObject Catalogs—sometimes InfoObjects should be migrated in two transports, one for attributes and the next for the master data InfoObjects that use the attributes of the first transport and/or any reference InfoObjects that refer to the InfoObjects of the first transport. If one transport is used and not every InfoObject activates successfully, simply re-import the same transport a second time before importing any subsequent transports—all remaining objects should activate successfully the second time.

> **Recommendation**
>
> Do not use InfoObject catalogs! They serve no functional purpose and only result in import errors if not transported with all InfoObjects assigned to them. The catalogs offer no added value, and any discrepancy between the objects in the development system and the target system results in an error, which can be time consuming to resolve.

Each subsequent transport collected should contain only the objects of each type in sequence. Transporting a large number of objects this way keeps the transports small and minimizes import errors while simplifying resolution to any errors which are received.

- InfoAreas—if the InfoAreas do not exist in the target system, the InfoProviders are activated under the node NOT ASSIGNED
- InfoSources for master data—attributes, text, and hierarchies
- InfoProviders—including DataStore Objects, InfoCubes, InfoSets, etc.

- InfoSources for transaction data—including transfer structures, communication structures, transfer rules, update rules, InfoPackages, DTPs, transformations, and ABAP code containing ETL logic used in any of these objects
- MultiProviders
- Queries and query elements—including variable customer exit code
- Query views
- BEx analyzer workbooks and workbook folders (if used)
- BEx web templates
- Portal objects
- Jump targets
- Process chain variants and local process chains
- Meta process chains

For smaller projects, the CTO import process imports and activates object types in the correct sequence, so objects do not need to be separated in as many transports as the initial migration. Please note that objects of the same type are imported and activated alphabetically, so any dependencies between them may be resolved only by importing the same transport a second time.

> **Best Practices**
>
> The following best practices are based on lessons learned from many past global implementations. Following these recommendations will minimize the difficulties associated with transporting BW objects and facilitate a successful project delivery.
>
> - Do not collect objects into transports until the development is complete and stable.
> - Leave all objects assigned to package $TMP (local objects) until it is absolutely ready to transport.
> - Delete all obsolete objects in the development system so that they will not be inadvertently transported to the QA and production systems.
> - Collect and release objects in the recommended sequence to minimize the risk of errors and facilitate resolution if any occur.
> - Ensure that each transport imports successfully before proceeding with the next transport.
> - Import dependent transports into production in the same sequence as they were imported into QA, including all transports that ended with errors.

- Keep track of both the transport errors in QA and the action steps taken to resolve them. These action steps will come in handy when importing those same transports into production.

- Avoid making any changes directly in QA or production—all changes should be made in development and transported.

- Do not delete any objects from transports in development to preserve the integrity of the change management system. If an object is deleted in development, that deletion is captured in one and only one transport. If the object is then deleted from the transport, the object deletion is never transported to the target systems. The deletion of objects from transports is the primary cause of inconsistencies between the production and development systems.

- Verify that all source system transports required for ETL objects in SAP BW are successfully imported, tested in Transaction RSA3, and replicated in SAP BW prior to initiating the SAP BW transports.

- Document changes contained in each transport—this will help in root cause analysis if unexpected issues result after the import and will also help when transporting SAP BW objects, such as query elements, DTPs, and InfoPackages, which are listed in the object list as unique IDs and are difficult to interpret without mapping to the technical name.

For more information on the SAP BW transport connection, transport management system, or transport organizer, see the information posted in SDN on these topics. It is important to define the system landscape and understand the infrastructure requirements before procuring hardware, but there is one more topic that is essential to the procurement process: calculating what size hardware is the right size for a specific data warehousing need.

1.3 System Sizing

System sizing is the process of translating data warehousing and business reporting requirements into hardware requirements. The hardware and database sizes are influenced by business aspects such as the number of users and how often they execute reports, as well as technological aspects such as the network load and computing capacity required to meet performance expectations.

Sizing calculations determine the hardware requirements of an SAP system, such as network bandwidth, physical memory, CPU power, and I/O capacity. SAP provides a wide range of tools that help estimate these hardware requirements. The simplest sizing approach is to leverage the SAP sizing benchmarks and guidelines offered for the SAP Business Suite, SAP BusinessObjects solutions, SAP Industry Solutions, and SAP NetWeaver solutions. These sizing benchmarks are available in the SAP Service Marketplace and will be reviewed in more detail in Section 1.3.1.

SAP's most prominent tool is the Quick Sizer, a self-service tool available for free on SAP Service Marketplace. This tool was developed in close cooperation with SAP's hardware partners to help customers determine the parameters of their hardware needs and is used more than 40,000 times a year by SAP customers. The SAP Service Marketplace also offers a wide range of documentation on how the Quick Sizer can be used; we take a closer look in Section 1.3.2.

The Quick Sizer and other sizing guidelines can be used only for the *initial sizing* of SAP standard solutions. An initial sizing is helpful for budgeting but cannot be guaranteed to deliver the right capacity for every requirement and must be confirmed by proper testing. This sizing approach requires many assumptions about the usage and setup of a productive system.

The alternative to initial sizing is *productive sizing*. Productive sizing is the process of estimating supplemental hardware requirements to roll out either new or existing functionality to new users. Depending on the stage of a solution's lifecycle, the productive sizing approach may differ. For example, when rolling out new functionality, the approach may contain more conceptual estimates than factual measurements, and when rolling out existing functionality to new users, the approach may contain more factual measurements than conceptual estimates.

Independent of the approach, measuring and analyzing current resource consumption such as table growth, CPU utilization, and memory usage in order to predict future resources is a key to success. This approach applies equally to SAP BW applications and ancillary systems such as BW Accelerator. The extra load on the system caused by additional users or new applications can then be extrapolated from the analysis of existing consumption.

Ask any SAP Basis expert how big a system is needed, and they may just respond, "the bigger, the better." While it may be sage advice in some cases, this statement can be true only if budget is of no concern. Indeed, more powerful hardware not only costs more, but also accrues higher energy and maintenance costs than smaller systems.

When considering all costs involved, the more economical approach is to calculate the correct sizing requirements to ensure that any hardware purchase meets all business and performance requirements. Sizing your SAP solution correctly has been proven cost effective and worth the effort, often providing a reduction in total cost of ownership.

An initial sizing estimate can determine whether a high-end, intermediate, or even low-end enterprise server architecture is needed. A more advanced sizing estimate can be calculated as soon as more information about the activity of expected users, anticipated data volumes, and processing requirements is available.

> **Note**
>
> Sizing should never be considered a one-time event; instead, it should be recognized as an iterative process that will be repeated using different methodologies and/or tools over the lifecycle of a system's implementation and through its service operation until it is decommissioned.

There are three basic sizing models, which are usually employed independently — each has its own advantages and disadvantages:

- **User-based sizing**
  There are three different types of active users (low, medium, and high) who use the system to different extents, and the categorization is based on the number of navigations executed. Merely counting the users does not provide an adequate requirement. The disadvantage of this sizing model is that this estimation says very little about the actual throughput these users produce.

- **Throughput-based sizing**
  Compared to the more straightforward user-based approach, the throughput-based approach allows more input parameters. This sizing model accepts additional parameters, such as data targets loaded, and accounts for peak and average usage. This model is quite thorough because it relies on expected throughput. However, it also relies on a number of assumptions (e.g., records loaded, queries executed, etc.) that need to be cross-checked against the individual installation.

- **Customer performance test**
  Performance and stress testing is conducted in a production system with customer data. This approach may require an iterative testing approach, and the effort can result in considerable impact to the project, in terms of both schedule and cost.

The results of these sizing models provide estimates for hardware components such as CPU, disk space, and memory. The more information that can be detailed in the model, the more accurate the sizing estimate will be. There are important key performance indicators that help determine sizing, listed by their related hardware component:

- CPU
  - Data load volumes/hour
  - Query navigation steps/hour
  - Number of cores and processing power of servers
- Disk space and disk I/O
  - Data volume residing in the database
  - Database read and write activity
- Memory
  - Allocation requirements per user or process
  - Buffer and cache sizes
  - Overhead requirements
- Network bandwidth
  - Transferred records/volumes of data
  - Network times and roundtrips

SAP provides estimating and monitoring tools that can help determine these key performance indicators. In cooperation with its technology partners, SAP ensures that there is a proper sizing procedure for all applications.

Initial sizing results can serve to provide budgetary estimates for the hardware needed for any SAP BW implementation for all systems in a horizontal landscape. Each system in the landscape may have a single server with a combined database instance and primary application server (PAS) instance, or separate servers for database and PAS instances—as is usually the case with SAP BW on SAP HANA. Additional application server (AAS) instance needs will also be evident in the sizing estimate.

As a general rule of thumb, most sizing activities focus on the production system and then discount storage and computing capacity for the other systems in the landscape, working backwards from production.

The quality assurance system is normally copied from the production system, so the storage capacity must be the same as production, but the CPU capacity can be anywhere from 10–50% of production. In many cases, the sandbox, development, and quality assurance instances can be installed on the same hardware, with the production being the only separately hosted instance.

Normally the development system is about 5–10% of the storage size of the production system, and the sandbox is copied routinely from the development instance. Both of these systems need less CPU capacity than the QA system, so probably 5–20% of production.

With the help of SAP Standard Application Benchmarks, estimates for CPU and memory consumption can be converted into hardware specifications for particular SAP software components.

1.3.1 SAP Benchmarks

SAP Standard Application Benchmarks help customers and partners find the appropriate hardware configuration for their IT solutions. Working together, SAP and hardware partners developed the SAP Standard Application Benchmarks to test the hardware and database performance of SAP applications and components. The SAP benchmarking procedure is standardized and well defined. It is monitored by the SAP Benchmark Council, which is made up of representatives of SAP and technology partners involved in benchmarking. Originally introduced to strengthen quality assurance, the SAP Standard Application Benchmarks can also be used to test and verify scalability, concurrency, power efficiency, and multi-user behavior of system software components, RDBMS, and business applications.

While the majority of benchmarks are run online, the SAP BW Benchmarks are run in the background. Previous versions of the SAP BW Benchmarks for SAP NetWeaver 7.0 include the *Data Mart Benchmark* (BI-D), which includes query activity only, and the *Mixed Load Benchmark* (BI-MXL), in which query activity and data load/update activity are executed in parallel. The BI-XML benchmark can be run with or without BWA.

The only valid benchmark for SAP BW 7.30 and later is the *Enhanced Mixed Load Benchmark* (BW-EML), which meets the current demands of typical business warehouse customers. These demands are covered by the following three major requirements:

▶ **Near real-time reporting**

Instant results from analytical applications on last-minute data is crucial for timely decision making.

▶ **Ad-hoc reporting capabilities**

Data volumes in data warehouses continue to grow dramatically as a result of increased complexity and a need for more detailed granularity, which in turn requires more sophisticated and complex analysis methods. Analytical applications must facilitate navigation through huge amounts of data by providing extensive slicing and dicing functionality. Ad-hoc query capabilities are required to satisfy these demands because it is inherently difficult to predetermine frequent navigation patterns and pre-calculate intermediate results to speed up reporting performance.

▶ **Reduction of TCO**

Typical data warehouse sizes can reach tens or hundreds of terabytes; in many cases, the same data is stored redundantly throughout the warehouse. Significant savings can result from keeping data redundancy at a low level while still maintaining layered data models. SAP BW 7.30 on SAP HANA helps reduce the total cost of ownership by allowing reports to run directly on DataStore objects (the core building elements of a layered warehousing architecture), often eliminating the need to maintain data redundantly in multi-dimensional InfoCube data structures.

As the latest addition to the family of SAP BW Application Benchmarks, the BW-EML Benchmark has been developed with these three customer requirements in mind.

Like its predecessor, the BW-MXL Benchmark, the BW-EML Benchmark focuses on a mix of multi-user reporting activity and data load activity in parallel. The data model includes three InfoCubes and seven DSOs, which all share the same set of fields. Each object holds one year of data—there are seven years of data in the DSOs, with the last three years of data in the InfoCubes. The InfoCube data model includes a full set of 16 dimensions consisting of 63 characteristics with cardinalities up to one million different values and one complex hierarchy. This model also consists of 30 different key figures, including some requiring exception aggregation. In the DSO data model, the high cardinality characteristics have been defined as key members, while all other characteristics have been defined as data members.

The SAP BW-EML Benchmark can be executed with various different initial data load volumes loaded from ASCII flat files:

▸ 500 million records initial load (e.g., 50 million records per InfoProvider)

   ▸ 500 thousand records delta load

▸ One billion records (e.g., 100 million records per InfoProvider)

   ▸ 1 million records delta load

▸ Two billion records (e.g., 200 million records per InfoProvider)

   ▸ 2 million records delta load

Even larger data volumes can be defined for distributed server landscapes. The total record length in the ASCII files is 873 bytes. After the initial load, delta loads equal to one thousandth of the initial records are loaded. A single benchmark run is supposed to last at least one hour, while the delta data has to be loaded in small chunks every five minutes. Each InfoCube and DSO has to be loaded with the same number of records.

During that same hour, reporting activity is executed in parallel with the delta loads. Two sets of the same four reports are defined on two MultiProviders—one based on the three InfoCubes, and the other based on the seven DSOs.

Reports are executed with a random selection on a specific year, thus picking the InfoCube or DSO containing the data randomly. These random values for filter parameters ensure that different partitions of data are accessed. Subsequent navigation steps are then executed within each report with the cache disabled. Although the reports follow similar navigation patterns, the drill-down and slice-and-dice characteristics have been grouped by cardinality, and respective objects are selected randomly. This randomization ensures that a huge number of different characteristics combinations are covered in a multi-user reporting scenario and guarantees a high degree of reproducibility of the reporting results since only characteristics of the same cardinality are considered for each randomized operation.

Traditionally, the key measurement for benchmarks has been the *SAP Application Performance Standard* (SAPS), which is a hardware-independent unit of measurement that describes the performance of a system configuration in the SAP environment. It is derived from the Sales and Distribution (SD) Benchmark, where 100 SAPS is defined as 2,000 fully business-processed order line items per hour.

In technical terms, this throughput is achieved by processing either 6,000 dialog steps (screen changes), 2,000 postings per hour in the SD Benchmark, or 2,400 SAP transactions. In the SD Benchmark, fully business processed means the full business process of an order line item: creating the order, creating a delivery note for the order, displaying the order, changing the delivery, posting a goods issue, listing orders, and creating an invoice.

If a sizing calculation suggests a configuration of 10,000 SAPS for a particular solution, the benchmark table can be consulted for a comparable sample configuration. The benchmark tables can be sorted by the SAPS column to provide a view of configurations that are likely to fulfill the requirements.

However, the benchmark key figure for all SAP BW-related benchmarks is not SAPS; instead, it is the number of ad-hoc navigation steps per hour. Given the differences of the queries and data models, results of the BW-EML Benchmark can not be compared to those of the BW-MXL benchmark. See Figure 1.20 for examples of BW-EML Benchmarks results for IBM and HP hardware based on 500 million and one billion records and between 65,000 and 129,000 ad-hoc navigation steps per hour.

SAP BW Enhanced Mixed Load (BW EML) Standard Application Benchmark Results

500,000,000 records

Date of Certification (mm/dd/yyyy)	Technology Partner	Number of Records	Ad-Hoc Navigation Steps per Hour	Operating System-Release Database Server	RDBMS Release	SAP NetWeaver Release	Number & Type of Database/Application Servers	Certification Number
8/8/2013	IBM	500,000,000	66,900	i 7.1	DB2 for i 7.1	SAP NetWeaver 7.30	IBM Power System 750 Express Server, 4 processor / 32 cores / 128 threads, POWER7+, 4.06 GHz, 32 KB(D) + 32 KB(I) L1 cache and 256 KB L2 cache per core, 10 MB L3 cache per core, 512 GB main memory	2013020

1,000,000,000 records

Date of Certification (mm/dd/yyyy)	Technology Partner	Number of Records	Ad-Hoc Navigation Steps per Hour	Operating System-Release Database Server	RDBMS Release	SAP NetWeaver Release	Number & Type of Database/Application Servers	Certification Number
09/25/2013	HP	1,000,000,000	129,930	SuSE Linux Enterprise Server 11	SAP HANA 1.0	SAP NetWeaver 7.30	1 database server: HP DL580 G7, 4 processor / 40 cores / 80 threads, Intel Xeon Processor E7-4870, 2.40 GHz, 64 KB L1 cache and 256 KB L2 cache per core, 30 MB L3 cache per processor, 512 Gb main memory 1 application server: HP BL680 G7, 4 processor / 40 cores / 80 threads, Intel Xeon Processor E7-4870, 2.40 GHz, 64 KB L1 cache and 256 KB L2 cache per core, 30 MB L3 cache per processor, 512 Gb main memory	2013027
05/16/2013	HP	1,000,000,000	65,990	SuSE Linux Enterprise Server 11	SAP HANA 1.0	SAP NetWeaver 7.30	1 database server: HP DL580 G7, 4 processor / 40 cores / 80 threads, Intel Xeon Processor E7-4870, 2.40 GHz, 64 KB L1 cache and 256 KB L2 cache per core, 30 MB L3 cache per processor, 512 Gb main memory 1 application server: HP BL680 G7, 4 processor / 40 cores / 80 threads, Intel Xeon Processor E7-4870, 2.40 GHz, 64 KB L1 cache and 256 KB L2 cache per core, 30 MB L3 cache per processor, 512 Gb main memory	2012023

Figure 1.20 SAP BW EML Benchmark Results

> **Note**
>
> The benchmarks are updated frequently and can be accessed via *http://www.sap.com/solutions/benchmark/bweml-results.htm*.

These results can be used to determine an appropriate hardware configuration for any given sizing requirement, assuming that there are sample benchmark configurations for a given requirement available. If there are not enough sample configurations, however, it may be necessary to consult more traditional benchmarks using SAPS or extrapolate a configuration from the existing certified benchmarks. The Quick Sizer is a good way to determine sizing requirements. We will cover this in the next section.

1.3.2 Quick Sizer

The Quick Sizer is a free, web-based application that uses a proven sizing methodology developed in close cooperation with SAP technology partners. By measuring the hardware resource consumption of realistic business processes in both SAP internal and actual customer systems against SAP Standard Application Benchmarks, SAP has derived different sizing guidelines for each SAP application. Quick Sizer leverages these up-to-date sizing guidelines to calculate CPU, disk, memory, and I/O resource requirements in a hardware- and database-independent format as it guides users through a structured questionnaire.

To reiterate, Quick Sizer provides the following benefits free of charge:

▸ Simplified online sizing based on input of business-oriented figures

▸ Proven sizing methodology developed in close cooperation with SAP technology partners

▸ Up-to-date sizing algorithms based on SAP Standard Application Benchmarks

Business requirement inputs to the Quick Sizer are simple figures such as the number of users running reports or the expected number of records loaded for each reporting area. These figures are translated by Quick Sizer into hardware-independent requirements that enable initial budget planning. Based on the results, SAP technology partners can propose a complete system configuration for any system landscape or component.

The Quick Sizer uses two independent sizing approaches: user-based and through-put-based. In the first approach, users are grouped per business task according to their estimated usage activity. A rough sizing recommendation is provided based on this information.

As shown in Figure 1.21, developing the Quick Sizer is an iterative process that continuously brings together technology partners, customers, and SAP. The algorithms used in the Quick Sizer are updated based on customer and partner feedback and experience. The end result is a tool that calculates the right combination of processing performance (in SAPS), disk space (in MB), disk I/O, and main memory (in MB).

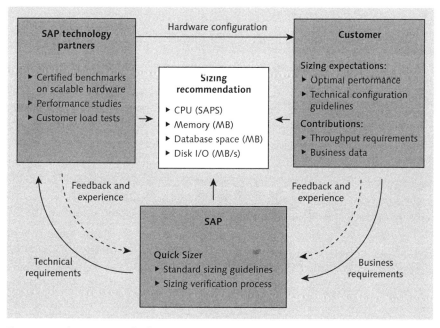

Figure 1.21 The Sizing Method Using the Quick Sizer

Let's walk through the simple, seven-step process for using the Quick Sizer for an SAP BW implementation, as illustrated in Figure 1.22. The first few steps are quite straightforward. First, launch the Quick Sizer web application from within the SAP Service Marketplace.

> **Note**
>
> An SAP UserID is required to access the Quick Sizer. It can be found in the SAP Service Marketplace via *http://service.sap.com/quicksizing*.

Second, choose a customer number (if more than one are available) and provide a project name. Third, select the SAP application to be sized from the TREE OF ELE-MENTS pane. For sizing SAP BW, choose the Business Warehouse application.

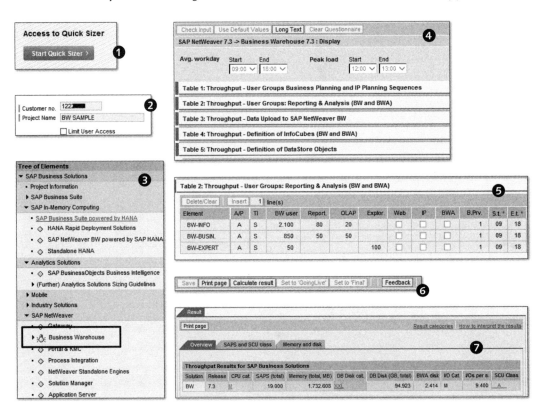

Figure 1.22 Using Quick Sizer for SAP BW

As soon as an application is chosen, an input screen is generated in the main window of the Quick Sizer. At this time (step four), it is necessary to start entering information about how the application will be used. Enter the start and end times of the average workday, as well as the start and end times of the peak loads on the system using a 24-hour format. For systems used globally or 24/7, enter start and end times of '00' and '24,' respectively.

Step five is to enter the business-oriented figures into the generated input screen. For SAP BW, there are five different tables requiring input:

1. User Groups Business Planning and IP Planning Sequences: Accepts input for user groups that are defined by the planning functions they execute and the data volumes they use.

2. User Groups, Reporting & Analysis: Accepts input for user groups based on the types of reports executed and the number of navigation steps per hour. Table 1.11 defines each user group.

3. Data Upload to SAP BW: Accepts input on how many records will be loaded into SAP BW during the peak time interval.

4. Definition of InfoCubes (BW and BWA): Accepts input on the data model definition and data volume loaded to each InfoCube and whether the InfoCube is loaded into the BW Accelerator.

5. Definition of DataStore Objects: Accepts input on the data model definition and data volume loaded to each DSO.

User Group	Navigation Steps/Hour	Report Types	Typical Distribution Ratio
Information consumer	1	Static reports	71%
Business user	11	Analytical reports with navigation	26%
BW expert	33+	Ad-hoc reports	3%

Table 1.11 User Groups for SAP BW Sizing

Recommendation

If there are any questions about the population of this data into the Quick Sizer, we recommend that you access the help documentation available from a link in the upper-right corner labeled How to fill in the questionnaire.

When all input information has been entered into the Quick Sizer, the sixth step is to save and then calculate results.

The seventh and final step is to review and analyze the results, consult the SAP BW-EML Benchmark results, and contact hardware vendors.

Even if you have already calculated a sizing estimate or have received one made by partners, use the Quick Sizer to verify it. SAP's comprehensive sizing methodology helps ensure that all hardware components needed to build a balanced system infrastructure, such as database and application servers, are adequately equipped to fulfill business requirements. But remember, the Quick Sizer is designed only for initial sizing of requirements, not to validate the size of productive systems.

1.3.3 Productive Sizing

Let's quickly look at how to validate current capacity and project growth in a productive SAP BW system.

Data Sizing

Most SAP BW systems retain data longer than source systems such as ERP; the data remains available for business logic and reporting for many years after it has been archived from the system of record. In addition, there is redundancy in the data flow; as data is staged throughout the data warehouse, the same data may be stored in more than one DSO and/or InfoCube. For SAP BW systems with high adoption rates by the businesses they support, it is common for them to experience organic growth consistently over time. Of course, not all ERP tables are loaded into SAP BW, but a good rule of thumb is to expect a larger database in the SAP BW system than the source systems.

When sizing the disk space for a new content or functional implementation in an operational BW system, use the same disk size calculation used by the throughput sizing method. This method takes into consideration the number of objects per year, their size, and the length of time they will remain in the system before they are archived. The following data types are assumed to have little influence on the disk size and are therefore not considered in the sizing calculation:

- System tables as defined by the minimum system requirements
- Objects that reside in the system for only a very short time. Typically, this includes "intermediate" or temporary data, such as IDocs, spool jobs, batch input jobs, job logs, application logs, and temporary tables.

▶ Master data usually does not contribute greatly to the overall disk sizing. In general, preference should be given to document type transaction data; however, if very large master data tables do exist, they should also be considered in the sizing activity.

In the throughput sizing method, the sizing calculation can ignore tables that are either small or rarely used, hardware-dependent table compression, and custom tables and indexes.

For disk growth analysis in operational systems, monitor the database statistics in Transaction DB02 and/or the DB monitor of the hardware vendor. Historical statistics will indicate monthly organic growth, which is simply the storage growth resulting from loading one month of data into existing data models. To confirm the monthly organic growth rate, focus on the growth rates of the 20 largest tables. If this is excessive, consider data archiving possibilities by agreeing on a data retention period with the business and estimating growth only until that period. See Chapter 3, Section 3.3 for more information on archiving.

Armed with the monthly growth rate, check the total available disk size and the amount of free space remaining to determine the time period when existing storage will be exhausted. When the throughput sizing of new data models is taken into account, the amount of storage needed to meet future loading requirements should be straightforward to determine.

The more difficult sizing calculations are often related to processing power, or CPU capacity, which has a significant impact on the performance of SAP BW and must take into account both throughput and user sizing approaches.

Processing Sizing

Processing power is important in OLAP systems because processing massive amounts of records for reporting is quite intensive. In addition, loading and activating large data sets also contributes significantly to the CPU requirements. To calculate processing power correctly, the Quick Sizer needs to know the number of sizing-relevant objects, their size, and the time frame in which they are being processed.

The Quick Sizer results for CPU sizing are divided into requirements for the application and the database layer and are specified in SAPS, rather than GHz. For SAP BW performance, it is also important to leverage high-speed network connections between the PAS and DB servers (if separate), as well as from the DB to the storage network—a minimum 10 Gbps connection is recommended and is, in fact, required for SAP HANA appliances.

When sizing new CPU requirements for existing systems, several transactions are available to analyze existing processing capacity in an operational system, such as ST03 and ST06. Table 1.12 offers a list of recommended transactions and the available analytical functions and metrics.

Transaction Code	Description	Available Metrics/Functions
ST03G	Global Workload Statistics	▸ Detailed workload analysis ▸ Distributed statistical records ▸ Application log
ST03N	Workload and Performance Statistics	▸ Response time analysis ▸ Load history and distribution ▸ BI Workload
ST06	Operating Systems Monitor	▸ Number of CPUs ▸ CPU utilization ▸ CPU bottlenecks ▸ Top 40 CPU processes
STAD	Statistics Display for All Systems	▸ Stats records by time ▸ Stats records by transaction ▸ Transaction totals

Table 1.12 Useful Transactions for Monitoring CPU Utilization and Capacity

In an operational system, go to Transaction ST06 to monitor current capacity and analyze average and peak CPU utilization; if it routinely exceeds 70-80%, additional capacity is likely needed before going live with additional functionality or content. As a rule, 20% of the processes cause 80% of the load, so monitoring the top 40 processes (also in Transaction ST06) will identify the areas needing the most focus. If the sizing calculation indicates a need for more CPU capacity, you can extend existing hardware in the following ways:

▸ Adding more application servers

▸ Adding more CPUs

▸ Replacing existing CPUs with faster CPUs

The number of SAPS defined for a specific configuration may change between releases. If the resource consumption of Release B differs from that of Release A, the number of navigation steps processed by the configuration per hour will change, and the number of SAPS will be different, too.

For example, a configuration that delivered 10,000 SAPS in Release A will deliver 9500 SAPS in Release B, if Release B has a resource consumption that is 5% higher than that of Release A.

In most cases, adding application servers is the easiest route. We recommend that you use a few larger application servers instead of many smaller ones. This will reduce complexity of the landscape and should benefit support and procurement costs, assuming economies of scale. In addition, it should reduce network traffic, providing a potential performance boost.

Memory Sizing

In general, the highest contributor to memory consumption in an SAP BW system is reporting users. System settings such as buffers and caches also influence the memory requirements of the application server. During initial sizing, the Quick Sizer accounts for this by adding one application server as a memory offset to the user-specific memory requirements.

In Java applications, the memory required by Garbage Collection also plays an important role and, therefore, is also included in the Quick Sizer's memory sizing.

Let's take a look at a few helpful transactions for monitoring memory usage.

Transaction Code	Description	Available Metrics/Functions
SM04	User list	▸ List of users logged on
ST02	Setups/tune buffers	▸ Buffer sizes ▸ Swap usage ▸ Extended heap memory

Table 1.13 Useful Transactions for Monitoring Memory Usage

Transaction Code	Description	Available Metrics/Functions
ST06	Operating systems monitor	► Physical memory ► Swap size ► Free memory ► Virtual memory
ST07	Application monitor	► Active users by application ► Buffer size by application ► Response time by application

Table 1.13 Useful Transactions for Monitoring Memory Usage (Cont.)

In an operational system, check the number of active users in Transaction ST07. Go to Transaction ST06 to monitor current capacity and analyze average peak memory utilization. Also, check Transaction ST02 to detect whether swap space is being used; this indicates whether existing buffer sizes are too small already. If the sizing calculation indicates a need for more memory capacity, you can extend existing hardware in the following ways:

► Add more application servers

► Add more memory

► Replace existing memory with faster memory

When migrating an existing BW system on a traditional relational database to SAP BW on SAP HANA, the most accurate sizing can be estimated by running sizing program /SDF/HANA_BW_SIZING within the SAP BW before migration.

> **Note**
>
> Program /SDF/HANA_BW_SIZING is available only with ST-PI support pack SP06—there are no advance corrections that can be applied to earlier versions. See SAP Note 1736976 for more information. This note is frequently updated, so check it routinely.
>
> If the prerequisite is not available, you can execute the database-dependent sizing scripts provided in SAP Note 1637145 directly in the database.

If the sizing program is not available, a rough estimate can be calculated using the results of database-dependent sizing scripts (SAP Note 1637145) and the following formula:

RAM Total = ((colstore_tables_footprint * free_memory_factor /
colstore_compression_factor) + (rowstore_tables_footprint /
rowstore_compression_factor)) * source_db_compression_factor +
(50GB * number_of_hosts)

where `colstore_tables_footprint` and `rowstore_tables_footprint` are provided by the database scripts; the `free_memory_factor` is 2 (this represents that
only 50% of memory should be filled with data, and the remaining 50% should be
available for calculations and processing); the average `colstore_compression_`
`factor` is approximately 4, based on the authors' results from previous migrations; the average `rowstore_compression_factor` is 1.5; and the `source_db_`
`compression_factor` should be based on the type of compression active in the
existing database.

This calculation is remarkably similar to the one used to size the SAP BW Accelerator, with two exceptions. First, there are no row store tables in BWA, and, second, there is no overhead for each BWA host.

1.3.4 BWA Sizing

The SAP BW Accelerator (BWA) is ideal for many customer scenarios. It will
remarkably improve response times of any queries with either high data selection
or high data manager times, or large aggregation (that is, a high ratio between the
number of records selected and the number of records transferred).

BWA also provides significant improvement to the end-user experience, especially in scenarios when unpredictable user behavior and ad-hoc reporting lead to
low OLAP cache hit ratios and low usage of aggregates and offer no possibility to
pre-calculate reports.

As of SAP BW 7.30 and BWA 7.20, scenarios based on MultiProviders, queries
with exception aggregation, and real-time reporting based on HybridProviders
scenarios can be accelerated with BWA. Before this release combination, only
InfoCubes could be loaded into memory, which limited the data footprint in
BWA. Now that DSOs can be loaded into BWA, the demand for memory space in
the BWA appliance is higher than ever.

To ensure good performance, keep 50% of the memory in the BWA hardware
available for query execution joins and aggregation activities. Because the memory consumption of any BWA index is far smaller than the memory consumption

of the InfoProvider on the database, a sizing calculation is needed. SAP has delivered program RSDDTREX_MEMORY_ESTIMATE, which analyzes InfoCubes and/or DSOs and estimates the memory consumption of their BWA indexes. See SAP Note 917803 for instructions on how to execute this sizing program.

> **Note**
>
> The results of program RSDDTREX_MEMORY_ESTIMATE reflect the current data size, so future growth must be considered and then multiplied by two to calculate BWA memory and three for BWA disk.

Sizing for the BWA is also integrated in Quick Sizer; there is a BWA checkbox for each InfoCube and DSO input. Checking this box on one or more InfoCube and DSO delivers hardware results for BWA. The Quick Sizer delivers a good first pass at sizing, but this should be confirmed by adequate testing in live use-case scenarios.

> **Note**
>
> Use the Quick Sizer for initial sizing only; do not use Quick Sizer for retro calculations. In a production environment, statistical BWA data is the best basis for sizing.

> **Recommendation**
>
> Resize BWA at regular intervals and, when necessary, add additional blades or increase the amount of memory per existing blade.

BWA is delivered as an appliance, so minimum hardware requirements are in place to guarantee that it performs well. The appliance's performance is influenced by the following components:

- Number of blades
- Amount of memory per blade
- Speed and number of CPUs (or CPU cores) per blade
- Speed of storage system
- Speed of network connection between BW system and BW Accelerator

In order to size the BWA appliance, three factors need to be determined:

- Total amount of memory
- Total amount of disk space
- Number of SAPS for query processing

Once these factors are known, the number of blades and amount of storage space required can be derived. Backup blades are not taken into account for sizing. For high-availability setups, one or more extra blades are required as backup for automatic failover. All other components are determined by the hardware vendor.

> **Note**
>
> The total amount of memory determines the SAP pricing of the BWA appliance.

The following steps describe the BWA sizing process:

1. Select which InfoCubes and DSOs should be indexed with BWA.
2. Determine the initial data volume requirement for each InfoCube, DSO, and related master data.
3. Provide periodic organic data growth rates per InfoProvider.
4. Enter data volume and growth rates into Quick Sizer to calculate SAPS, total main memory, and storage space requirements.
5. Alternatively, use the sizing program to determine the memory requirement for the current data volume and calculate total memory and storage requirements based on the sizing formula.

For post-implementation sizing check, the BWA statistical information is the best source of data. This information can be found in tab USAGE • ACCESS STATISTICS of the TREX Admin tool. The only relevant measure for re-sizing is the disk size (KB) of all InfoCubes, DSOs, and master data objects loaded into BWA indexes. To be within sizing limits, the following statement needs to be true:

SUM (Disk Size in KB) is less or equal to 0.5 * <SUM of main memory of all blades>

> **Note**
>
> Other measures (e.g., memory size) are not reliable for sizing because they fluctuate during different times of data loads and do not cover worst-case scenarios.

If the statement is not true and the disk size ratio is higher than 50% of total available memory, you should compare the index sizes against the disk sizes for the largest indexes and re-index (either drop and re-create or reorganize) any indexes that are 20% larger than the disk size. If this does not reduce the ratio to below 50%, check SAP Knowledge Base Article (KBA) 1872296 on high-memory consumption. If no solution is found, please consider the following two available options:

▶ Carrying out a new sizing for the BWA hardware

▶ Deleting cubes from BWA

With all topics on sizing now reviewed, it is time to complete our coverage of the system environment. The next section covers the remaining configuration items that need to be addressed before an SAP BW system is fully ready for use. This configuration includes performance tuning in terms of profile parameters, basic system settings, and other parameters.

1.4   System Settings

After the initial installation of an SAP BW 7.40 system or after any hardware changes, functional implementations, or technical upgrades, many settings and parameters should be configured and/or reviewed before the system is considered ready for use.

The first step is to configure the *profile parameters*, which define how the system uses the available hardware in terms of CPU, memory, and database. There are parameters that also cover end-user interaction with the system, such as password requirements and idle timeout durations. In fact, many of the profile parameters should be reviewed and adjusted every time the hardware configuration is changed or the application is patched or upgraded.

Once the profile parameters are defined for an initial installation, the SAP Implementation Guide should be configured. The IMG structures the SAP application to the requirements of the company; specific SAP BW configuration should be reviewed after initial implementation and after every upgrade.

For SAP BW, there are also basic system settings that can be configured in the Data Warehousing Workbench that tailor the way the system is used by the support team. These settings should not be overlooked.

Lastly, there are specific parameters that should be configured within additional hardware appliances such as BWA and SAP HANA to improve the performance and functionality of those technologies when used with SAP BW.

In this section, we'll explore all four of these system setting categories further, beginning with profile parameters.

1.4.1 Profile Parameters

One of the first steps when installing any SAP system is to configure the profile parameters, which manage memory use, database, and user interaction. Profile parameters can be reviewed in Transaction RZ10 and changed individually in Transaction RZ11.

Profile parameters must be set optimally for the SAP BW system to perform efficiently. The recommendations for SAP BW systems are not always the same as those for ERP systems. Table 1.14 lists important SAP Notes related to initial parameter configuration of an SAP BW system.

SAP Note	Description
1044441	Basis parameterization for NW 7.0 BI systems
0192658	Setting basis parameters for BW Systems
0830576	Parameter recommendations for Oracle 10g
1171650	Automated Oracle DB parameter check
0702728	Profile parameter for export/import buffer instances
0656060	OLAP: Cache main memory displacement not functioning
0480710	Profile parameters for table buffers
0879941	Configuration parameters for SQL Server 2005
0814704	MaxDB Version 7.6 parameter settings for OLTP/BW
0390016	DB2/390: BW: Database settings and performance
0541508	iSeries: Checking the system parameters for BW
0374502	DB6: BW performance: Note overview

Table 1.14 Important SAP Notes for SAP BW Configuration

Performance problems can occur if the parameter values for the memory areas (buffers, program memory, and extended memory) are too small. On the other hand, if the values are set too large, errors may occur when starting SAP, or runtime errors may occur. Short dumps indicating that memory sizes are too small are usually the result of poor programming rather than real memory issues, so unwarranted increases in memory parameters can encourage bad coding practices. Most often, the optimal settings depend on the hardware (i.e., CPU and RAM), database release, application release, and operating system release. It can be a tricky balance to strike.

In SAP BW systems, the size of the global cache is dependent on the shared memory buffer, which is defined by the profile parameter `rsdb/esm/buffersize_kb`. The global cache setting can be maintained in Transaction RSRCACHE and should not exceed 90% of the shared memory buffer.

After going live, the parameters should be reviewed and adapted as required to support the specific requirements of each implementation. An easy way to ensure that parameter values remain optimally configured in a productive system is to monitor the EarlyWatch Alert for recommendations tailored to each system. Profile parameters are specific to each application server, so be sure to check and review all profiles for consistency.

Recommendations

Consider the following best practices related to profile parameters:

▸ Save the old profile before you make any changes. If the instance does not start with the new parameters, start it with the old profile.

▸ Use program `sappfpar` to check the validity of parameters values.

▸ Test all parameter settings in the QA environment before making them in production.

In general, changes to profile parameters become active only the next time the relevant instance is restarted. To reduce downtime, some well-known parameters are *dynamically switchable*; many of these have only recently become dynamic since the release of SAP NetWeaver 7.30. Dynamically switchable parameters take effect immediately without the need for a system shutdown. To determine which profile parameters can be switched dynamically, call Transaction RZ10 and choose menu item PROFILE • DYN. SWITCHING • DISPLAY PARAMETERS.

As soon as all the profile parameters are tuned and SAP is restarted (if necessary), the configuration task can continue with the SAP Implementation Guide.

1.4.2 Implementation Guide

The SAP Implementation Guide (IMG) is the tool that adjusts the SAP system to the installer's requirements. In other words, the IMG facilitates the implementation and configuration of an SAP system in a given company.

The implementation guide is a hierarchical structure of application areas in the component hierarchy. It contains all the work steps required for a complete implementation with documentation for each step.

There are three implementation guide variants:

▸ The *SAP Reference IMG* contains IMG activities for the full set of work steps for all applications in the SAP System. It also contains the full functionality of all possible Customizing settings across all countries and application components. All Customizing activities are assigned to one or more components. Not all functions in the hierarchy need to be implemented; only those functions chosen from the application components are implemented. This results in individual Customizing projects for implementing the SAP system in a given company.

▸ A *project IMG* is a separate implementation project created to reduce the complexity of the configuration process in the SAP Reference IMG. An implementation project will contain only those functions needed for the processes covered by the project. Separate project IMGs can be generated for each implementation project and for release updates. The scope of the project IMG can be determined by countries, components, or Customizing activities.

▸ A *project view IMG* can be generated to structure project activities by selecting attributes by specified criteria. For example, the mandatory activities view contains only required activities and excludes any optional activities.

Regardless of the variant chosen, the IMG leads the implementation project team through all required Customizing settings while providing documentation for all required configuration steps. To access the IMG, call Transaction SPRO in the SAP system. In general, the guide can be used to do the following:

▸ Configure SAP functions in a quick, safe, and cost-effective manner

▸ Adapt standard functions to meet company requirements

- Manage, edit, and analyze implementation or upgrade projects
- Document and monitor implementation phases with a project management tool
- Transfer configuration data automatically from the quality assurance system to the production system to ensure consistency

In an SAP BW implementation, you can use the IMG to configure SAP BW-specific settings by following the menu path SAP CUSTOMIZING IMPLEMENTATION GUIDE • SAP NETWEAVER • BUSINESS WAREHOUSE, as shown in Figure 1.23.

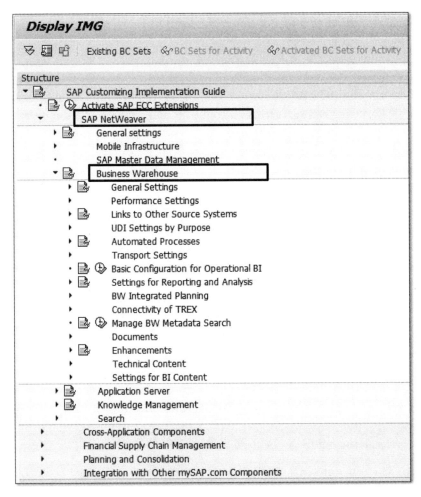

Figure 1.23 SAP Reference IMG for Business Warehouse (Transaction SPRO)

More specifically, the IMG can be used as a one-stop shop to configure general printer settings, fiscal year settings, default DSO object settings, authorization settings, settings for displaying SAP documents, links to other systems (such as flat files, ERP and other data sources, Microsoft Analysis services, and Crystal Enterprise, etc.), UD Connect Settings (such as Java Connectors, the RFC Destination for the J2EE engine, availability monitoring, etc.), automated processes (such as batch processes), transport settings, reporting-relevant settings (such as BEx settings and default reporting settings), and Business Content settings.

In the next section, we will cover some of these SAP BW basic system settings, which deserve more attention.

1.4.3 BI Basis Customizing

Many of the customizing settings in the IMG can also be accessed directly via a transaction code. Many of the transaction codes for BI Basis customizing tasks follow the naming convention RSCUSTVxx, where xx ranges from 01 to 30. Each of these transactions should be checked and configured as necessary. Recall that the benefit of using the IMG is the availability of documentation explaining the impact of each activity. Table 1.15 offers a list of important IMG activities and related transactions.

IMG Activity	Description	Transaction
Maintain number range objects	Buffer number ranges for high cardinality SID values and DIMIDs	SNRO
Maintain permitted extra characters	Specify additional characters that can be loaded into key fields	RSKC
Printer setup	Define the local printer LOCL (and any others)	SPAD
Update mode for master data	Choose to create master data even if not available	RSCUSTV9
Set material number display	Define the length of material number the same as in ERP	OMSL
Set up technical content	Activate all technical content objects	RSTCT_INST_BIAC

Table 1.15 Common Customizing Settings in the IMG

IMG Activity	Description	Transaction
Activate update of statistics from DWB	Activate updating of statistics	RSA1
Maintain runtime parameters of DSOs	Improve performance when processing data in DSOs	RSODSO_SETTINGS
Global cache settings	Specify maximum memory sizes for cache	RSRCACHE
Maintain control parameters for the data transfer	Specify limits for the size and number of records per data package	RSCUSTV6
Define logical system	Create a unique logical system for the BW client	BD54
Assign logical system to client	Assign the logical system to the SAP BW client	SCC4
Set options for uploading flat files	Specify flat file defaults	RSCUSTV1
Change source system name after transport	Transport setting for mapping source system, done in target (QA and production)	RSLGMP
Create destination for import post-processing	Specify connection information for post-import processing	RSTPRFC
Activate personalization in BEx	Reporting-relevant setting that enables end users to save report variants and pre-fill popular variables	RS_PERS_ACTIVATE
Activate conversion of InfoObjects	Activate the DataStore for converting InfoObjects in BI Content	RS_CONV_ACTIVATE
Set standard web templates	Specify default web templates	RSCUSTV27
Determine settings for web templates	Specify web template properties	RSCUSTV28
BW enhancement	Create a project and activate customer exit programs for use with DataSources, BEx variables, and virtual characteristics/key figures.	CMOD

Table 1.15 Common Customizing Settings in the IMG (Cont.)

One of the customizing activities that deserves special mention is the Maintain Permitted Characters item, which can be accessed via the IMG via program RSKC_ ALLOWED_CHAR_MAINTAIN or directly in Transaction RSKC. This setting determines which ASCII characters are permitted to be used in key fields of tables, or in SAP BW terms, as those generating SID values in SAP BW InfoObjects. SAP provides the following list of permitted characters by default:

' !"%&''()*+,-./:;<=>?_0123456789ABCDEFGHIJKLMNOPQRSTUVWXYZ'

When data is loaded to key fields (those generating SID values), the system checks whether each character in each data value is permitted against this list, with two exceptions:

▶ If these characters are capitalized in any of the other installed languages in your system, then they are also accepted in characteristic values, assuming the languages were installed before any additional characters were added to the list.

▶ If lower-case values are enabled in the InfoObject, then lower-case values of characters in the list are also accepted.

Before adding characters to the permitted characters list, install all the languages that will be used later. All languages installed subsequently will not be checked, and the additional capitalized characters of those languages will not be permitted, thus requiring the use of this transaction.

> **Note**
>
> Only a limited number of characters can be added to this list, so be prudent in adding them. More importantly, once a character has been added, it cannot be removed because there is no way the system can know whether a value with that character has already been loaded or not. To override the restrictions and allow all special characters, enter the string 'ALL_CAPITAL' and nothing else in this transaction.

One other important customizing activity deserves special attention: maintaining the configuration table RSADMIN. This activity is not included in the IMG. This configuration table allows additional performance settings to be activated or enabled in the system. By default, no parameters are included in this table, but they can be added manually using program SAP_RSADMIN_MAINTAIN. For a complete list of valid parameters, see SAP Note 912367.

1.4.4 Global Settings and Exchange Rates

Global settings in an SAP BW system refer to the currencies, units of measure, fiscal year variants, and factory calendars. These settings should not be maintained directly in SAP BW; rather, they should be extracted or transferred from one or more ERP source systems. There are many tables behind these settings that are identical in structure between ERP and BW, and failure to keep them in sync could affect the integrity of BW reports on ERP transaction data. Table 1.16 gives a list of tables related to each global setting.

Global Setting	Tables Updated
Currencies	TCURC, TCURF, TCURN, TCURS, TCURT, TCURV, TCURW, TCURX
Units of Measurement	T006, T006A, T006B, T006C, T006D, T006I, T006J, T006T
Fiscal Year Variants	T009, T009B, T009C, T009T, T009Y
Factory Calendars	TCALS, TFACD, TFACS, TFACT, TFAIN, TFAIT, THOC, THOCD, THOCI, THOCS, THOCT, THOL, THOLT, THOLU

Table 1.16 Tables Updated for Each Global Setting

You can transfer these settings in the SOURCE SYSTEMS screen of the Data Warehousing Workbench (Transaction RSA13) by right-clicking the selected source system and choosing TRANSFER GLOBAL SETTINGS.

There are three modes available for transferring global settings:

▸ **Simulation**
  Use this mode to simulate the updates that will occur without committing any changes. The output will show a list of related tables and the number of records that will be updated.

▸ **Update tables**
  Use this mode to update records to the related tables. When you select this mode, any new or existing records in the source system are reflected in SAP BW by overwriting previously transferred values.

> **Note**
> The update mode does not work for factory calendars. The factory calendar tables can only be rebuilt.

▶ **Rebuild tables**
Use this mode to reconstruct the related tables by first deleting the old entries and then writing the new entries. Rebuilding is useful when configuration has been deleted from the source system and those entries also need to be deleted from the SAP BW system.

Recommendation

Schedule a job to update these tables periodically using program RSIMPCUST. This will keep this information synchronized with the source ERP system.

Exchange rate settings are similar to global setting, except they must be transferred to SAP BW separately by specifying exchange rate types. Failure to keep exchange rates in sync with the SAP ERP source systems will affect the accuracy of currency conversions executed during reporting.

The three modes available for transferring exchange rates are similar to those available for global settings, except only table TCURR is updated:

▶ **Simulation**
Use this mode to simulate the updates that will occur without committing any changes. The output will show the number of records that will be updated.

▶ **Update exchange rates**
Use this mode to update records to SAP BW. By selecting this mode, any new or existing records in the source system will be reflected in SAP BW by overwriting previously transferred values.

▶ **Transfer exchange rates again**
Use this mode to reconstruct the table by first deleting the old entries and then writing the new entries. Rebuilding is useful when rates have been deleted from the source system and those entries also need to be deleted from the SAP BW system.

Recommendation

Schedule a job to update exchange rates periodically using program RSIMPCURR. This program could be added as a second step in the same job used to transfer global settings—in any case the currencies must exist before the exchange rates can be successfully transferred.

At this point, the BW system is optimally configured and ready for productive use. The next chapter will cover data architecture strategies and data loading principles.

Practicing good data warehousing is as much an art as it is a science. It takes a systematic yet creative approach. The role of a data architect is part passionate dictator, part principled realist, and part gifted artisan.

2 Data Architecture and Loading

An *enterprise data warehouse* (EDW) is a unified database for all business information in an organization. Although there are many interpretations of what makes an enterprise-class data warehouse, the following features are often included:

- Standard approach for organizing and representing data
- Normalized design to provide data integrity (a single version of the truth)
- Robust infrastructure with a high level of stability and security
- Scalable solution to enable growth

The primary attraction of an EDW is that it delivers a "single version of the truth" across all business departments in a consistent and efficient manner. An EDW imposes a standard treatment of data and can grow with the needs of the business without compromising the security or integrity of that data.

While it may be impossible to define a single methodology or best practice that handles all requirements without some snag, hitch, or exception, the first step when implementing an enterprise data warehouse is to define the data architecture standards, including data loading guidelines.

Unfortunately, defining and implementing an enterprise-ready and scalable data architecture is sometimes seen as a lower priority than building the data models and reports requested by the business. In many poorly implemented data warehouses, too narrow a focus is placed on the ability to load specific data at the granularity and frequency needed to satisfy current requirements, instead of on implementing a well-designed standard architecture and process for loading all data. And usually data is managed just enough that it does not adversely impact performance and/or support costs (direct or indirect); any other considerations are deferred until later.

The truth is that data architecture should never be an afterthought and should always be considered as part of the original design. A good data architect anticipates future reporting needs and data growth and proactively incorporates such needs into a scalable design that can be easily enhanced and maintained.

In this chapter, we'll cover the basics of data architecture, including how to model data flows in SAP BW 7.40 (Section 2.1), including use of recommended layer architectures (Section 2.2) and the delivered tools for graphical modeling (Section 2.3). Then, we'll dive into data load automation (Section 2.4). In the next chapter, we'll cover data management principles in detail.

2.1   Data Flow in SAP BW

The data flow in a data warehouse describes the path by which data flows from its source through the architected layers of a warehouse until it is available in its final form and then consumed by the end user or downstream application. Within SAP BW, the data flow defines which objects and/or InfoProviders are loaded with data, from which data sources, and by which processes. These objects and processes are used to extract, transform, and load (ETL) data into the warehouse so that it can be used for analysis, reporting, and planning.

Understanding the data flow in an existing SAP BW system is a crucial prerequisite to being able to support that system. The single most important deliverable for achieving this aim is the data flow diagram. Let's take a closer look.

2.1.1   The Data Flow Diagram

The data flow diagram should be "evergreen"—it should be updated as part of the project delivery process. In this way, it is always current when needed. If there is no data flow diagram, the first step of any data warehousing effort should be to develop one. And even though this document may be difficult to keep up to date, its value exceeds the costs of maintaining it. In our experience, it is always enlightening to those who see it for the first time: "Wow. I didn't know we loaded data from there!"

The data flow diagram should be available outside the SAP system (for example, accessible via Excel, PowerPoint, or Visio). While the system can provide data flow documentation (see Section 2.3 on graphical modeling) on a single flow, there is additional information that cannot be captured in the system-generated data flow, such as DataStore or master data lookups and other dependencies. Figure 2.1 shows the sample data flow diagram; it uses dotted lines to illustrate lookups from master data and other DataStores.

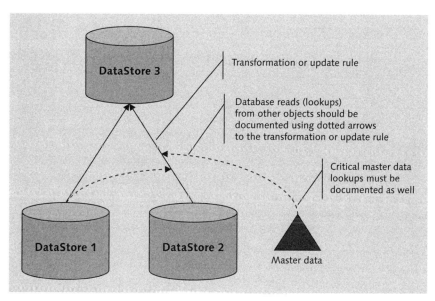

Figure 2.1 Sample Data Flow Diagram

In SAP BW, a wide array of data flow design options is available to support customer-specific process requirements. Data can be transferred to SAP BW from any source and, in some cases, the source data can be accessed directly. Simple or complex transformations, cleansing, or consolidation rules can be applied to data once transferred into SAP BW, and then the data can be stored in many different types of InfoProviders based on the customer-specific layer architecture. Let's review the definitions of the most common data flow components.

2.1.2 Data Flow Components

SAP BW 7.40 introduced significant conceptual and technological changes to objects used in the data flow. Figure 2.2 illustrates the most important components of the new data flow.

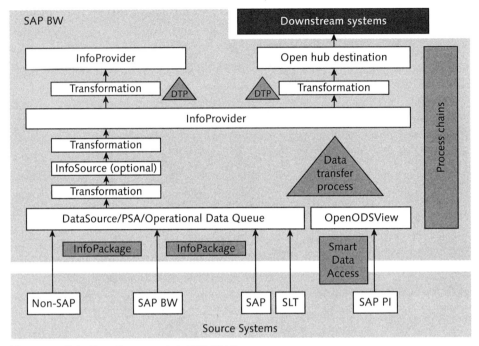

Figure 2.2 Data Flow Components in SAP BW 7.x

In SAP BW, a *DataSource* is a set of fields used to extract data from a source system and transfer it to the BW system. DataSources can also provide data for direct access. DataSources include metadata about the extraction mechanism (such as delta or full load) and the source of the data (such as a domain, table, view, or function module) and can be defined for the extraction of text, attribute, or transaction data.

Since SAP NetWeaver 7.0, the new DataSource object can be edited or created independently of 3.x objects via Transaction RSDS. This new DataSource (also object type RSDS) enables real-time data acquisition, as well as direct access to File and DB Connect source systems. When the DataSource is activated in BW, the system creates a *persistent staging area* (PSA) table in the PSA. The PSA is the entry layer of SAP BW, and each active DataSource is a persistent object in the data flow.

Before data can be processed in BW, it has to be loaded into the PSA using an *Info-Package*. Selection parameters can be specified for transferring data into the PSA in the InfoPackage. In the 3.x data flow, InfoPackages can be used to load data into the PSA only, into the PSA and subsequent data target in parallel or sequentially, or directly into the data target. However, in the new data flow, InfoPackages load data only into the PSA.

In BW 7.x, the two sets of rules—transfer rules and update rules—are replaced by *transformation rules*. Transformation rules offer an intuitive graphic user interface; simplified rule maintenance; and additional functionality, such as quantity conversion, performance-optimized lookups of master data and DataStore objects, and the option to create an end routine or expert routine.

Transformations convert data from the source format to the target format in SAP BW by mapping the DataSource fields to the InfoObjects of the data target. Rule groups can be used to execute different mappings based on source field values. They enable data consolidation and cleansing from multiple sources, as well as semantic synchronization of data. As a result, InfoSources are no longer mandatory with transformations; they are optional but can still be used to connect multiple sequential transformations (i.e., complex multistep processes) or consolidate redundant transformations from multiple sources or to multiple targets.

InfoObjects are the building blocks of data structures in SAP BW. They contain all the metadata about the field from which they are sourced, including data type and length, texts, hierarchies, attributes, and compound keys. There are four basic types of InfoObjects: characteristics, key figures, units/currencies, and time characteristics.

InfoProviders are persistent data repositories built out of InfoObjects that provide data for analysis, reporting, and planning. InfoProviders are used in the layer architecture of the Data Warehouse to receive data from DataSources and send data to other InfoProviders. There are several different types of InfoProviders; each will be discussed in more detail in Chapter 4:

- InfoCubes store transactional data in a multidimensional model and are designed to facilitate complex data analysis in real time. Grouping characteristics into the dimensions of an InfoCube serves two primary functions: enforcing simplicity when modeling business transactions and improving query performance.

- DataStore objects (DSOs) store transaction data at an atomic or granular level, which can be consolidated from multiple sources or cleansed prior to loading. The major benefit of using DSOs is the delta mechanism they provide; when data is activated, only deltas are sent to subsequent data targets.

- ▶ OpenODSViews are available only in SAP BW powered by SAP HANA systems; they allow the combination of external data sources, such as SAP HANA tables and artifacts, with BW data models by defining associations between single fields of the external sources with InfoObjects or other OpenODSViews. Subsequently, the external data can be consumed in reporting scenarios without the need to replicate that data in an SAP BW-managed persistence. If the external data is in a separate SAP HANA system, it can still be read using Smart Data Access.

After migrating to SAP BW powered by SAP HANA, existing InfoCubes can be optimized for SAP HANA to leverage the in-memory computing power of HANA.

> **Note**
>
> Update rules cannot load to or read from SAP HANA-optimized InfoCube objects due to their architecture. Therefore, any InfoCubes either loaded from or read into update rules in a 3.x data flow cannot be converted to SAP HANA-optimized InfoCubes until the 3.x data flows have been migrated to 7.x data flows. Only then can the conversion to an SAP HANA-optimized InfoCube be performed.

Data transfer processes (DTPs) distribute data within *SAP* BW from one persistent object to another using transformations and filters. Sources for the data transfer include DataSources and InfoProviders; targets include InfoProviders and other downstream systems via open hub destinations. DTPs replace export DataSources InfoSpokes. DTPs make the data load processes more transparent and facilitate performance optimization by allowing configuration of parallelization specifically for each DTP. They are more flexible during load processes because delta processes to different data targets can be scheduled independently. DTPs also simplify error handling by sorting out incorrect records in an error stack and writing the data to a buffer after the processing steps are complete.

In SAP BW, *process chains* are used to schedule the processes associated with the data flow, including InfoPackages and data transfer processes.

The complexity of data flows can vary widely depending on the requirement. At an absolute minimum, a data flow must have at least one of each the following objects: a DataSource, a transformation, an InfoProvider, an InfoPackage, and a data transfer process.

Data flows and their components can be modeled in the modeling functional area of the Data Warehousing Workbench. A graphical user interface helps create top-down models and facilitates adherence to best practices by allowing modeling based on data flow templates provided by SAP. With top-down modeling, a model blueprint can be created and saved on the SAP BW system and, later, used to create a persistent data flow.

2.1.3 New Features for SAP BW 7.40

Recall from Chapter 1 that SAP BW remains the cornerstone of SAP's enterprise data warehouse strategy. This means SAP BW will not be replaced by SAP HANA; on the contrary, SAP BW is enhanced by SAP HANA. SAP does not advise any customer to try to replicate SAP BW application functionality in a standalone SAP HANA environment.

In line with this message, SP5 of SAP BW 7.40 represents a significant investment by SAP to further improve SAP BW as a world-class enterprise data warehousing solution. It brings significant advancements to the platform and delivers new functionality to meet the evolving needs of businesses for a structured, yet flexible, analytics database with the ability to quickly deliver changing reporting requirements while reducing development time and costs.

Most of the new functionality in SP5 is applicable to only SAP BW systems powered by SAP HANA. Here are some of the key data provisioning features now available:

▶ SAP HANA *Smart Data Access* (SDA) provides enhanced data provisioning flexibility. SDA enables direct read access to relational and non-relational sources via ODBC as if they are persistent tables in SAP BW. This means SAP BW analytic services can be performed on external data that is not replicated in SAP BW—the external data read via SDA can be joined with data stored in SAP BW using OpenODSViews.

▶ *Operational Data Provisioning* (ODP) offers a unified technology for data provisioning and consumption in SAP BW. ODP acts as the hub for all data flowing into BW from external sources, both SAP and non-SAP, and encompasses the *Operational Delta Queue* (ODQ), which supports an "extract once, deploy many" approach for sources and a unified configuration and monitoring service for all source and target types. A time stamp-based recovery mechanism and configurable data retention periods enable greater and more flexible data management. An intelligent parallelization option for loading data targets in high volume scenarios offers reduced loading time.

▶ *Direct Update* to SAP BW InfoProviders from SAP ERP extractors delivers simplified data provisioning from SAP source systems, allowing for multiple targets without the need for the PSA. The concept also works for transferring data between BW systems.

▶ Simplified trigger-based table replication to SAP BW is available with SAP Landscape Transformation (SLT) via new source system type ODP-SLT. The ability to load SLT data directly into SAP BW provides a more robust mechanism for real-time reporting compared to existing capabilities. The PSA is not required, thus enabling a simplified data flow model.

▶ Extended capabilities of the Open Hub Service allow exporting data from SAP BW directly to tables residing in any relational database (RDBMS) supported by SAP, including Sybase ASE and IQ. This complements the existing capability to feed BW Open Hub data into SAP HANA for native HANA modeling.

▶ The *HANA Analytical Process* (HAP) enables HANA-native statistical functions and algorithms to be applied directly on BW InfoProvider data in a more accessible, powerful, and flexible way than with the existing Analysis Process Design tool. The new functions and algorithms available are those within the *Predictive Analytics Libraries* (e.g., clustering, association, regression analysis, anomaly detection, weighted scoring, and exponential smoothing).

▶ The *Planning Application Kit* (PAK) improves integrated planning performance by pushing down planning functions into SAP HANA. The PAK also paves the way for unified planning, which combines the best of three SAP planning technologies (SAP HANA, SAP BPC, and SAP BW-IP) into a unique planning solution. It combines the EPM Excel add-in, flexible BPC administrative user interface, and powerful BW-IP/PAK planning manager within a super-fast HANA planning engine.

At this time, only the combination of SAP BW and SAP HANA enables customers to take advantage of all the new functionality and features currently available as of SP5 for SAP BW 7.40. Nevertheless, it is important to recognize that SAP is continuing to invest in SAP NetWeaver in order to simplify the data modeling process, reduce the complexity of the landscape, and increase the agility of development by combining the strengths of an SQL-oriented approach in SAP HANA with its integrated EDW application SAP BW.

2.2 Layer Architectures of a Data Warehouse

As data is loaded into the data warehouse, it is staged at various points and granularities along the data flow until it is ready for consumption. Each staging point is considered a *layer* of the data warehouse architecture. Architecting data in SAP BW principally involves designing the layers—the data staging and data models— of a data warehouse.

2.2.1 Layered Scalable Architecture

The concept of *layered scalable architecture* (LSA) provides a framework for designing and implementing best practice data flows. The LSA framework divides the data flow into two distinct layers: the enterprise data warehouse layer, which includes data acquisition and corporate memory, and the architected data mart layer, which includes data distribution and analysis.

Figure 2.3 illustrates the structure of the different layers in LSA, which SAP highly recommends implementing for its performance and structural benefits.

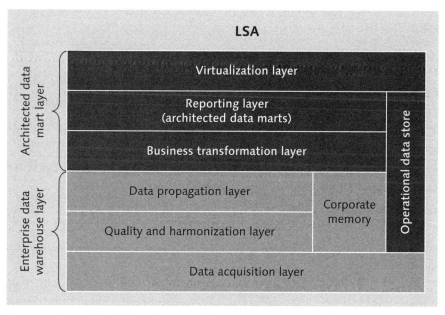

Figure 2.3 Layered Scalable Architecture of an Enterprise Data Warehouse

Depending on specific requirements, a data warehouse may also contain either additional or fewer layers; the data in each layer does not necessarily have to be saved in persistent format.

The LSA introduces three main rules regarding the location of business transformation logic in the data flow:

▸ No business logic transformations should be performed in the enterprise data warehouse layer. This ensures that data models in the data warehouse layer can be reused for different data marts. Only quality checks, cleansing, and data harmonization transformations should be included in this layer.

▸ All transformations, including data lookups from master data or other transaction data, should be performed between DSOs to insulate the logic from reloading requirements.

▸ All business logic transformations should be performed in the architected data mart layer.

Let's dissect the primary horizontal layers shown in Figure 2.3.

The *enterprise data warehouse* layer (EDW) at the base consists of four different sub-layers:

▸ **Data acquisition**
The data acquisition layer is the entry point for data in the BW system and is usually the PSA table, although it can be designed as a *pass-through* DSO, which does not retain history; all content is deleted after it is distributed to subsequent data targets, much like a PSA table. The benefit of using a pass-through DSO is the ability to write validation reports and/or lookups against the pass-through DSO. The data in the data acquisition layer is identical in format to the data extracted from the source.

▸ **Quality and harmonization**
Data is cleansed and homogenized in the quality and harmonization layer and stored in standard DSOs, which provide beneficial delta mechanisms. This layer is particularly important if data is merged from multiple sources and, therefore, is sometimes also called the consolidation layer. There should be no business logic in the transformations of this layer so that the data can be reused for multiple data marts.

▶ **Data propagation**

The *data propagation* layer is used to distribute data to one or more architected data marts. To accelerate performance, semantically partitioned DSOs should be used for this layer.

▶ **Corporate memory**

The corporate memory contains a complete history of all loaded data and is stored in write-optimized DSOs. The corporate memory should be loaded independently of the update to the other layers and is therefore not in the critical path of the data flow. It is intended to serve as a complete source for reconstructions, which can prove especially useful if the source system data is routinely archived.

The *architected data mart* layer consists of three sub-layers:

▶ **Business transformation**

In the business transformation layer, all business logic and lookups from other data targets should happen in this layer so that history can be restated by full repair loads from the data propagation layer instead of full loads from the source. This layer should also use semantically partitioned DSOs.

▶ **Reporting**

The reporting layer contains data in its final format as it is needed for consumption in reporting, analysis, or planning. This layer is modeled mainly using InfoCubes, which should also be semantically partitioned to improve data load performance, but also could contain VirtualProviders, HybridProviders, or InfoSets.

▶ **Virtualization**

The virtualization layer contains only MultiProviders and CompositeProviders. Queries should always be built on a virtual InfoProvider to insulate them from changes to the underlying data models. This way, if a field is removed from or changed in an underlying data model, the impact to the end user is minimized.

The *operational DataStore* is a bit unique because it spans both the enterprise data warehouse layer and the architected data mart layer but belongs to neither. By definition, the operational DataStore supports operative data analysis and, therefore, needs to be loaded at a much higher frequency (typically near real-time) and may also be stored at a lower granularity than the other data warehouse layers.

Semantic Partitioning

Semantic partitioning is an architectural design to enable parallel data loading and query execution. The performance benefits are so significant that semantic partitioning should be deployed on virtually every data model. In SAP NetWeaver 7.30, SAP introduced the semantically partitioned object (SPO) to facilitate development and reduce the maintenance burden of these objects.

Sample partitioning criteria could be region, company, controlling area, actual/plan, or calendar year. Semantic partitions that are created in this way are called *domains* in the LSA. Figure 2.4 illustrates the use of geographic domains (Europe, Asia, and America) as the basis for semantically partitioning a data model. This figure can be read from the bottom up or the top down. During data loading, data is split into the partitions by domain (from the bottom up); during query reads, data access is also split by domain (from the top down).

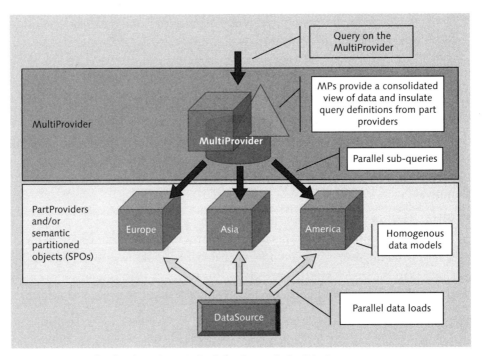

Figure 2.4 Example of a Three-Domain Basis for Semantic Partitioning

Depending on the structure of the source systems, the data flow can either merge or split data into domains. Figure 2.5 and Figure 2.6 turn Figure 2.3 on its side for sample data flows. Recall that the corporate memory is not split into domains.

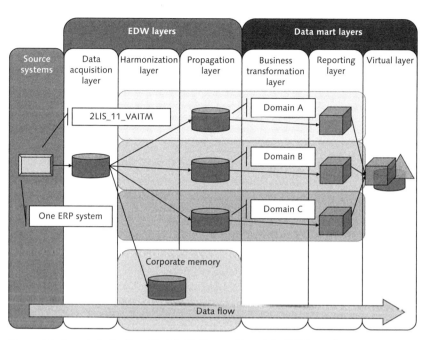

Figure 2.5 Sample Data Flow That Splits Transactions into LSA Domains

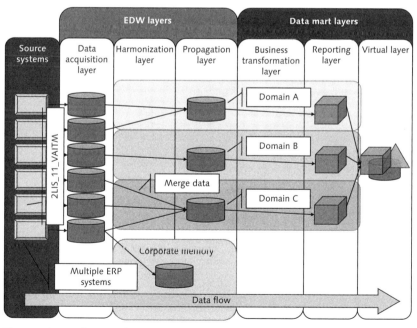

Figure 2.6 Sample Data Flow Merging Transactions into LSA Domains

The concept of merging or splitting data flows into domains requires special consideration for how to minimize the additional maintenance burden posed by multiple redundant transformations. Rest assured: the solution to this problem is covered in the LSA and is reviewed in the section below.

InfoSources in the LSA

InfoSources are not obsolete! Even though they are not required for use with transformations, they still offer significant benefits in complex data flows. By placing an InfoSource before and after transformations, as seen in Figure 2.7, it is possible to bundle the transformation logic so that it has to be maintained only once. In fact, SAP even recommends that InfoSources be used before and after all InfoProviders to insulate all transformation logic from changes to InfoProviders.

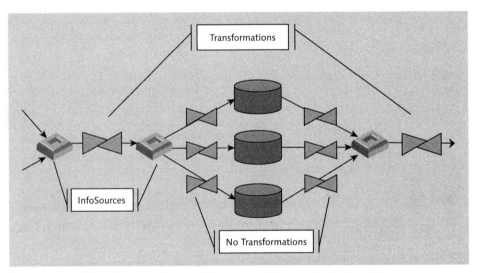

Figure 2.7 Insulating Transformation Logic between InfoSources in the Data Flow

---

Best Practice

Write transformation routine code in program includes and call them from the start, end, or expert routines. The use of program includes provides the following benefits, which are not available to code written directly in the transformation routines themselves:

► Version management: A program include is like any other ABAP program and has full version control functionality.

> ▶ Portability: Using forms in the includes to read master data into internal tables, for example, can be reused in other transformations.
>
> ▶ Ease of maintenance: Most changes to the include logic can be handled directly through the program editor and do not require editing and/or activation of the transformation.

Notice that there are no transformations between the inbound InfoSource and the InfoProviders or between the InfoProviders and the outbound InfoSource. This data flow logic is automatically implemented in this way for SPOs.

To recap, the recommended LSA provides performance and structural benefits for both simple and complex data flows by leveraging the functionality BW offers. Adopting LSA is highly recommended as a best practice for BW implementations running on traditional relational databases. However, when running SAP BW on in-memory databases like SAP HANA, LSA needs to be optimized to take advantage of new in-memory computing capabilities.

2.2.2 Layered Scalable Architecture with SAP HANA

SAP BW powered by SAP HANA provides greater flexibility in data modeling and better performance during data loading. Indeed, the performance benefits of SAP HANA require a different approach to layer architecture than LSA. This new and improved layer architecture is called LSA++.

In LSA++, the data acquisition layer is replaced by the *Open Operational DataStore Layer*, which allows consumption of externally managed data sources using field-based modeling. This layer no longer requires persistence of the data in the SAP BW application. External data, typically located in a non-BW–managed schema of the SAP HANA database, can be consumed virtually and combined with EDW core InfoProviders without the need to create InfoObjects first.

The core EDW layer remains the same in LSA++ (see Figure 2.8), with additional services added for operational and flexible reporting. Let's consider the main differences between LSA++ and LSA:

▶ Queries run just as fast on DSOs as they do on InfoCubes. Therefore, an explicit reporting layer is not required because queries can be defined directly on the data propagation or business transformation layers.

▶ Virtual data marts using CompositeProviders can be built to combine Info-Providers.

▶ VirtualProviders and TransientProviders can be built to access data directly in the SAP HANA database.

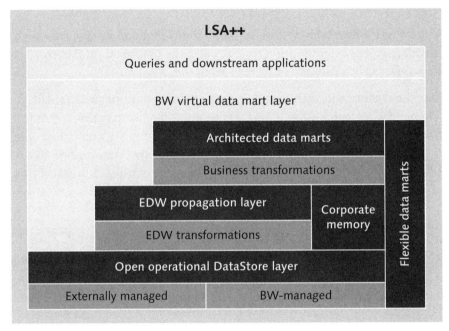

Figure 2.8 Layered Scalable Architecture with SAP HANA (LSA++)

The *EDW propagation layer* in the LSA++ consists primarily of standard DSOs. These offer the following advantages:

▶ Faster activation times and loading times

▶ Greater flexibility: queries report directly on the data propagation layer

The architected data mart layer in the LSA++ consists of SAP HANA-optimized InfoCubes and/or standard DSOs (in the business transformation layer).

SAP HANA-optimized InfoCubes offer the following advantages:

▶ Data can be loaded faster because no dimension tables are populated.

▶ Data modeling is simpler.

   ▶ Multidimensional modeling is not necessary because the dimensions are used only as structuring criteria and do not have any effect on system performance.

   ▶ Aggregates and database indexes are not required.

▶ Remodeling is quicker because the dimensions do not contain any data.

The *virtual data mart layer* of the LSA++ replaces the virtualization layer. The virtual data mart layer contains all InfoProviders that do the following two things:

▶ Combine data using joins or unions, such as MultiProviders and CompositeProviders

▶ Access data such as TransientProviders and VirtualProviders directly in the SAP HANA database

Overall, the layers of LSA and LSA++ are more alike than different. Each architecture is tailored to a specific type of database (relational or in-memory); both provide substantial benefits over the use of other architectures that are not layered and/or not scalable. To facilitate adoption of LSA or LSA++, SAP has introduced the ability to model data flows directly in the Data Warehousing Workbench and delivered business content templates depicting several different flows at various levels of complexity.

2.3   Graphical Modeling

LSA scenarios can be modeled as data flows (and data flow templates) in the Data Warehousing Workbench in the MODELING screen, which is structured like other object trees using InfoAreas. In the object tree, the symbol displayed in the object information column indicates whether a data flow has been created as a template. The data flow maintenance screen can be opened for a data flow by choosing the context menu command DISPLAY or CHANGE.

The graphical user interface of the maintenance screen facilitates the creation and documentation of data flows and data flow templates and has many advantages, listed in Table 2.1.

Application Scenario	Advantages
Top-down modeling of new data flows	▸ Top-down modeling enables quick and structured modeling directly in SAP BW. ▸ Data flow templates enable blueprint modeling without creating persistent objects in the database. ▸ Creation of persistent objects can be handled subsequently by adding the required technical properties to the template objects.
Either structuring an implementation using data flows *or* organizing existing models in data flows after upgrading to 7.30	▸ Modeling objects can be grouped and stored as a persistent view for an enterprise model. ▸ Data flows can be organized according to application areas or Data Warehouse layers. ▸ Data flows and their elements can be easily documented. ▸ All dependent objects belonging to a data flow can be collected and transported. ▸ Naming conventions can be applied to models so that they can be reused.
Defining modeling standard using data flow templates	▸ You can model templates quickly and simply by copying and adapting them to a data flow. ▸ Predefined data flow templates for LSA have been delivered as SAP Business Content. ▸ Templates can facilitate creation and adoption of company-wide standards. ▸ Use of templates can help to reduce development costs.

Table 2.1 Advantages of Graphic Data Flow Modeling in Different Scenarios

A data flow can contain persistent and non-persistent objects. SAP defines *persistent objects* as objects that already exist and are saved in the metadata tables in the database and that can also be displayed in the object trees of the Data Warehousing Workbench (e.g., in the InfoProvider tree). A persistent object can be used in multiple data flows.

SAP defines *non-persistent objects* as objects that have been created in the data flow maintenance by specifying an object type and a name. These objects do not exist in the database tables and cannot be displayed in any other object tree of the Data Warehousing Workbench. Non-persistent objects can be displayed and used only in the data flow in which they were created.

Data flow templates represent data flow scenarios with all required and dependent objects. They can be used to provide scenario documentation and are ideal for storing and documenting best practice modeling architecture. Data flow templates can support the complex modeling of the LSA layers, as well as fast modeling of simple, standard data flows.

2.3.1 Data Flow Templates

SAP provides documented data flow templates that can be used when implementing LSA scenarios. The data flow or data flow template is a standalone TLOGO object type (DMOD). Data flows and data flow templates can be transported and have a Repository connection, document connection, and connection to version management.

A data flow can be saved and used as a data flow template if it contains only non-persistent objects. These objects are placeholders with a technical name and description.

> **Note**
>
> Delivered SAP data flow templates are displayed in the InfoArea object tree only if they exist in an active version. However, you do not need to install the SAP data flow templates from Business Content to use them in customer-specific data flows. Simply display the content version of the SAP data flow templates in the Data Flow Maintenance by clicking the APPLY DATA FLOW TEMPLATE button and integrate them into your data flow.

> **Note**
>
> Since queries and reporting objects do not belong to the data flow, they will not be displayed in the data flow.

Creating Data Flows or Data Flow Templates

Data flows and data flow templates can be created in the data flow tree in the Data Warehousing Workbench MODELING screen. The procedure is basically the same for both objects.

> **Note**
>
> The technical name of a data flow is limited to 30 characters. The last four characters are filled with TMPL if you are creating a data flow template.

A data flow is consistent and can be activated if all persistent objects contained in the data flow exist and have the object status *Active*. If the data flow contains non-persistent objects, warnings appear during the consistency check. However, the data flow can still be saved and activated.

A data flow template can contain only non-persistent objects, but an existing data flow can also be saved as a template.

> **Recommendation**
>
> If you use persistent objects in your data flow and then save the flow as a template later on, the system uses the persistent objects to create non-persistent objects for the template. The technical names and descriptions of the persistent objects are applied to the non-persistent objects.

2.3.2 SAP-Delivered Data Flow Templates

SAP has delivered several data flow templates to address requirements for most data flow scenarios in an LSA environment, so let's examine a few. For further information on each, see the documentation in the BW system that is displayed automatically when you view the SAP data flow template.

SAP data flow template LSA100, shown in Figure 2.9, provides a simple and basic structure for the levels and data flow logic. Use this template to model simple flows with small data volumes and without complex transformations. This template does not split data or merge data into domains, nor does it include a corporate memory.

In this scenario, all business transformations should occur between the two DSOs (the first in the data propagation layer and the second in the business transformation layer). If there is no business logic, the second DSO is unnecessary, and data can be loaded directly to the InfoCube in the reporting layer. Most implementations using delta-enabled DataSources have surely implemented this scenario without attempting to adhere to LSA guidelines.

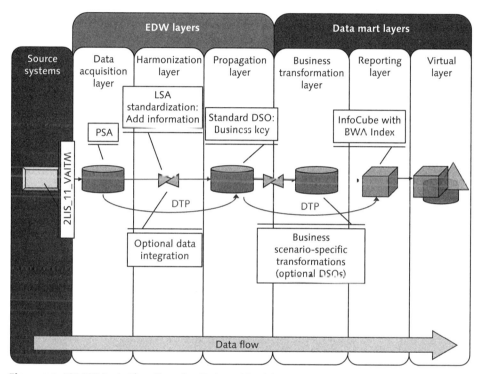

Figure 2.9 LSA100 Basic Flow (Layering Data and Logic)

SAP data flow template LSA110, shown in Figure 2.10, introduces the corporate memory layer, which is intended to store the load history. The corporate memory should be modeled using a single write-optimized DSO (no domains or semantic partitioning). Since the corporate memory is independent of the data loads to the other layers, it is not part of the data load critical path.

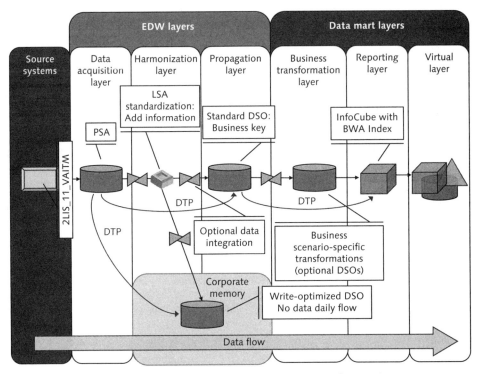

Figure 2.10 LSA110 Basic Flow Extensions (CM and Harmonization InfoSource)

To obtain greater transparency and flexibility, the LSA recommends using Info-Sources in front of all InfoProviders that store data. SAP data flow template LSA315, shown in Figure 2.11, is a simplification of SAP data flow template LSA310, which introduces the InfoSource concept.

InfoSources bundle transformation logic in a single transformation to simplify development effort when implementing domains or semantic partitioning. They also insulate transformation logic from changes in DataSources or InfoProviders, and vice versa.

SAP data flow template LSA320, shown in Figure 2.12., offers a solution for cases in which performance problems occur while loading large data volumes in a simple data flow. In this template, the data flow is split into domains immediately after the PSA. The domains are modeled using a semantically partitioned DSO, which requires the use of InfoSources in the inbound data flow.

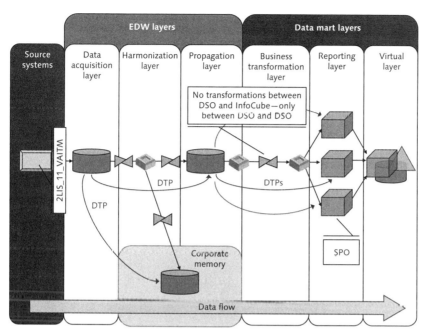

Figure 2.11 LSA315 Scalability (InfoSources and Single ERP Source)

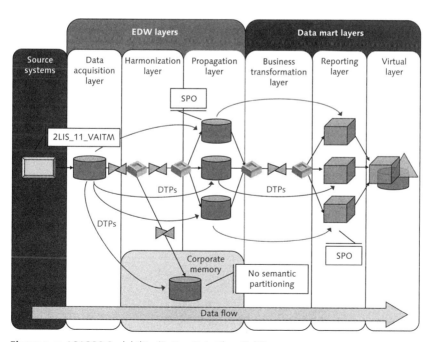

Figure 2.12 LSA320 Scalability (Entire Data Flow Split)

SAP data flow template LSA330, shown in Figure 2.13, is very similar to template LSA320. The difference is the addition of a pass-through DSO in the data acquisition layer. This makes it possible to handle errors at a very early stage and also simplifies data splitting and validation. The pass-through DSO should be modeled as a write-optimized DSO for performance reasons, and its contents should be deleted routinely after data is distributed to the data propagation layer and corporate memory.

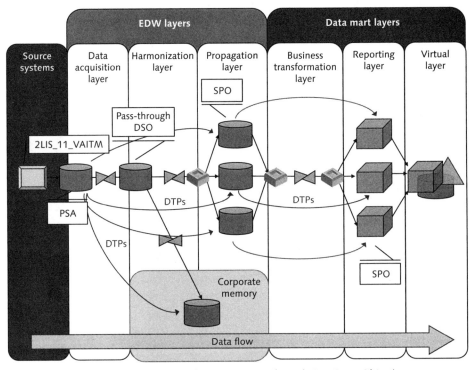

Figure 2.13 LSA330 Scalability (Flow Split Using a Pass-Through DataStore Object)

SAP data flow template LSA410, shown in Figure 2.14, can be used to model scenarios in which more than one source system is connected to an SAP BW system for the same business processes. In this scenario, the data loaded from multiple sources has to be consolidated, or merged, into domains.

In this scenario, the data harmonization layer is the most complex because data from multiple sources must be homogenized and synchronized.

SAP data flow template LSA420, shown in Figure 2.15, is based on SAP data flow template LSA400. LSA420 illustrates the role of the business transformation layer in a scenario in which data from two business areas is combined for reporting.

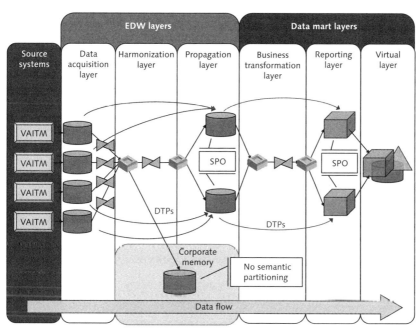

Figure 2.14 LSA410 Scalability and Domains (Strategic Flow Collect)

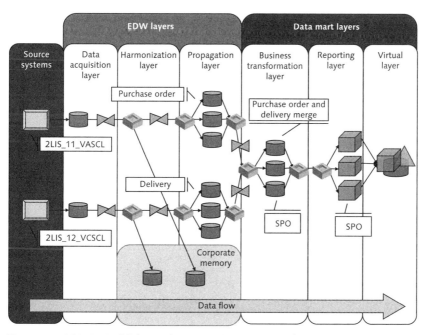

Figure 2.15 LSA420 Scalability and Domains (Business Transformation Layer)

The `LSA4xx` templates are the most complex of the SAP-delivered data flow templates and are ideally the ones that all standard data architectures should be based on, considering that they are scalable and enterprise class.

Now that you understand the data flow and ETL process, let's move on to data load automation, and we'll cover process chains in detail.

2.4 Data Load Automation

Many steps and processes must be performed to move data along its data flow path through the Data Warehouse. These data flow processes can be controlled with *process chains*, which are used to schedule data loads and execute processes in the Data Warehouse in a structured way. During runtime, they enable the greatest possible parallelization while preventing lock situations when processes execute simultaneously.

Process chains operate under event control. If a process completes with a certain result (for example, "successfully finished"), then one or more follow-on processes can be triggered. By definition, process chains allow central control, automation, and monitoring of the SAP BW processes and efficient operation of the enterprise data warehouse. Because the process chains are integrated in the Alert Monitor in the Computer Center Management System (CCMS), processing of SAP BW processes is embedded in the central SAP monitoring architecture of the CCMS.

Since the introduction of process chains with SAP BW 3.0B, automating data loads in SAP BW has become easier and more robust. In SAP NetWeaver 7.0, more process variants were released; these have increased the flexibility and automation capabilities of process chains. Two new process variants that have increased the ability to model complex processes more than any others are the *Decision between multiple alternatives* variant and the *Interrupt process* variant.

With the release of SAP NetWeaver 7.30, even more process variants have been released, such as the *Is the previous run in the chain still active?* variant. This particular variant was intended to be released earlier but was redacted from SAP NetWeaver 7.0.

It is not uncommon for process chains to receive minimal consideration during the design phase of a project; in fact, they are often the last piece of the development cycle and are therefore a lower priority. However, you should not underestimate the complexity of designing and implementing efficient process chains.

Let's examine process chains more closely.

2.4.1 Process Chains

In an operational data warehouse, data needs to be extracted from source systems, loaded through the data flow, and made available to end users or downstream applications according to agreed-upon schedules. Dependencies among data flows complicate the scheduling of these data loads. In SAP BW, process chains are used to schedule and execute all the activities related to the flow of data through the system.

Technically, a process chain is simply a sequence of scheduled processes connected using events triggered by a predecessor process. Conceptually, however, process chains are efficient and flexible tools that can be used to do the following:

▶ Automate complex process flows using event-controlled processing

▶ Visualize those processes using network graphics

▶ Centrally control and monitor processes

Let's hone in on the process chain structure even further.

Process Chain Structure

All process chains consist of a start process and individual application processes. Some also contain *collection processes*, which allow multiple chain strings to be merged into one individual string. The *start process* starts the chain based on standard background job control options. All other processes in the chain are scheduled to wait for an event signaling success or failure of the previous process.

See Figure 2.16 for an example of a delivered technical content process chain to load statistics data to InfoCubes 0TCT_C22 and 0TCT_C23 and their aggregates. Notice that the start process on the right triggers two chain strings; each chain string loads one InfoCube and its aggregate. Each step in the data load needs to be explicitly specified in the process chain, so no automated roll-ups occur even if configured in the MANAGE INFOCUBE screen.

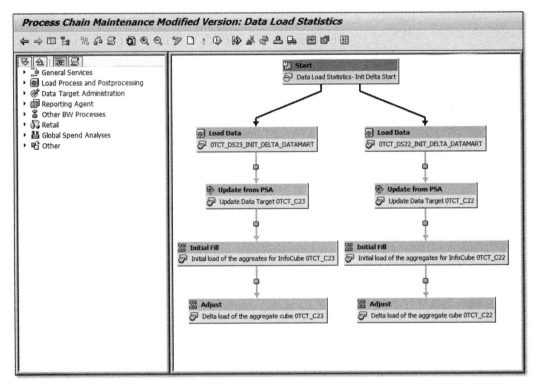

Figure 2.16 Sample Technical Content Process Chain (Transaction RSPC)

The application processes are the actual activities to be executed. SAP BW 7.40 supports process types assigned to the following categories, as seen on the left in Figure 2.16:

► GENERAL SERVICES

► LOADING PROCESS AND POST-PROCESSING

► DATA TARGET ADMINISTRATION

► REPORTING AGENT

► OTHER BW PROCESSES

► RETAIL

► GLOBAL SPEND ANALYSIS

► OTHER

Other SAP applications, such as SAP Business Planning and Consolidation (BPC) for NetWeaver, SAP Supply Chain Management (SCM), and SAP Master Data Management (MDM) have their own processes. In addition, custom processes can also be implemented.

Critical Path

When you are designing process chains, the main objective is to reduce the overall load duration by executing the optimal number of processes in parallel, which you do by efficiently using the available background processes without sacrificing performance. Take care to respect dependencies between processes and to ensure that the parallel processes are sufficiently organized to avoid database conflicts.

The *critical path* is the longest running sequence of dependent steps in a chain. It represents the shortest possible duration of the chain and must be completed before reporting is available to end users.

If data is looked up from another data target during ETL, such as a DSO or an InfoObject, then loading data to that data target is also in the critical path (e.g., data looked up must be active prior to the ETL logic; therefore, the ETL logic is *dependent* on the load to the data target).

Once the critical path has been identified, all other steps should be organized on parallel near-critical paths.

The following considerations should be taken when loading master data:

▸ Split attributes by criticality and dependence into local chains to improve scheduling flexibility and runtime.

  ▹ Critical and dependent (C&D) master data and/or DSOs must be active prior to subsequent lookups/ETL; if master data is not active, the lookup will not return the correct value, resulting in the need for reloads.

  ▹ Critical and non-dependent (C&ND) master data is not needed for lookups but is needed for reporting, so it must be loaded with every transaction data chain. Master data cannot be loaded in parallel with transaction data because this can result in database contention (table locks), which cause loads to fail.

  ▹ Though non-critical (NC) master data rarely changes, don't overlook it. Load NC master data once daily, weekly, or monthly.

- Load texts of critical master data with the attributes so they are available in reports, but don't include them in the same local chain.

  - Split C&D texts from C&D attributes and C&ND texts from C&ND attributes to provide the greatest flexibility.

  - Texts load quickly, generate the SID values, and, therefore, can improve attribute load performance if loaded prior to attributes, but they can reduce critical path runtime if scheduled after attributes in parallel with transaction data.

- You can load hierarchies in parallel with transaction data and activate them at the end of the critical path.

- Bundle attribute change runs (ACRs) and PSA deletions at the end of each relevant local chain to reduce overhead and simplify the local chains.

The C&D master data is in the critical path because it must be active before transaction data can be loaded. As soon as all C&D master data is loaded and activated, both transaction data and non-dependent master data and texts can be loaded. These subsequent master data loads should not be in the critical path, so it is best to recommend times to load them without extending the critical path.

Now that all master data needed for lookups is loaded and activated, transaction data can be loaded. The critical path for transactions still has the same definition: it is the longest running sequence of dependent steps in the load process. Until the critical path is complete, all data is not available for reporting. The process chains should be designed around the critical path; there should be no unnecessary or non-critical processes or loads impeding the processes in the critical path.

Figure 2.17 shows how to identify the critical path. All durations are in minutes. The critical path is the longest path in the diagram. The data load paths vary in duration, but Path 7 is the critical path because it takes 50 more minutes to load than any other process, as shown in Table 2.2.

All optimization efforts should focus on reducing the critical path. The performance of each step in the critical path should be evaluated for potential savings in terms of extraction, transformation, load processing, or activation time. If a chain is optimized to the extent that it is no longer the longest-running process, it stops being the critical path, and the focus should shift to the next-longest process—

these are called *near-critical paths*. The near-critical path in Figure 2.17 is Path 4 because it is the second-longest process in the illustration.

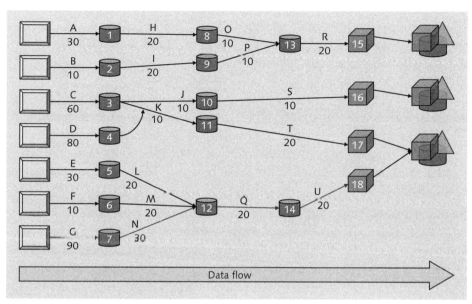

Figure 2.17 Transaction Data Critical Path

Path	Sequence	Duration	Path Type
Path 1	A-H-O-R	80 minutes	
Path 2	B-I-P-R	60 minutes	
Path 3	C-J-S	80 minutes	
Path 4	(C&D)-K-T	110 minutes	Near-critical
Path 5	E-L-Q-U	90 minutes	
Path 6	F-M-Q-U	70 minutes	
Path 7	G-N-Q-U	160 minutes	Critical

Table 2.2 Process Chain Sequence and Duration

Now that we understand process chains and the critical path sequence of steps, let's dive into the specific steps that make up process chains.

2.4.2 Process Variants in Detail

In the context of process chains, a process is any procedure with a defined beginning and end, so it can be either internal or external to an SAP system. When a process chain is activated and scheduled, the individual processes are scheduled in the background. Upon completion of each process, it can trigger one or more events, which then start other processes.

A process is characterized by the following terms:

- The *process type* is the kind of process, such as the load process type *Execute InfoPackage*; all process types are available in the process chain maintenance screen. The process type defines which tasks the process executes and which properties can be configured during maintenance. The process type is set in the RSPROCESSTYPES view.

- The *process variant* is the name of a specific process type saved in a process chain. For example, a process variant of type *Execute InfoPackage* can be defined to use a specific InfoPackage that extracts data from DataSource 0PLANT_ATTR. In this way, each process can have multiple variants; for example, a system with 1,000 InfoPackages may have 1,000 Execute InfoPackage process variants. The user generally defines the process variant at the time when the process is created or scheduled. However, the user does not always define the process variant; for some process types, the variants are determined internally and stored as GUIDs.

- The *process instance* is the runtime value of the process variant. In the Execute InfoPackage process variant for 0PLANT_ATTR, the process instance would be the name of the request. Once the process ends, the instance is transferred to the process chain management and saved. The logs for the process are stored under the process instance.

A distinction should be made between the three main types of processes (start, application, and collection processes) because each is handled in a different way by the process scheduler. Let's look at each now.

Start Processes

The start condition of every process chain is defined in its start process. Each process chain has a unique start process, and each start process has all the background control options available to directly schedule it. Start processes can be scheduled to start immediately (when activating the process chain), at a specified time, or after a particular event. Upon activation of the process chain, the start process is scheduled in the background based on the selections.

If more extensive scheduling options are required, use the SAP Scheduling Framework to start the chain using the API function module RSPC_API_CHAIN_START.

Alternatively, the start of a process chain can be triggered using a metachain. A *metachain* is a process chain that calls other process chains. If the start process is defined to start using a metachain, it is not scheduled after activation. The process is scheduled only when the metachain that calls it is running.

The start process is the only process that can be scheduled independently. All other processes are scheduled to wait for an event.

The start process has the following special features:

▸ Only the start process can be scheduled without a predecessor process.

▸ The start process cannot be a successor of another process.

▸ Only one start process is allowed for each process chain.

▸ A start process can be used only in a single process chain.

If you want to define more than one start condition to execute a process chain or part of a process chain, use the interrupt process, as well as the start process

Interrupt Process

An interrupt process can be used to simulate a second start process in a process chain. An *interrupt process* stops a chain from executing until it is triggered to restart. This functionality is useful when two independent process chains must be executed before a third can be triggered. To configure this type of logic, the third chain should be scheduled based on the conclusion of the first process chain, but it should include an interrupt process waiting for the conclusion of the second chain. When the second chain completes, the interrupt is tripped, and the third chain continues to be processed.

Previous Run Active?

The newest process variant was originally developed for NetWeaver 7.x but not fully released until NetWeaver 7.30. The *Previous run active?* variant can be used after the start process to prevent regularly scheduled chains from running more than one instance concurrently. It works by checking whether any previous executions of the same chain are still running. For example, if a chain is scheduled to run every two hours, and the first execution takes three hours to complete, the second chain (scheduled to start at the second hour) would start as planned but end right away because the previous run is still active. The third chain (scheduled to start at the fourth hour) would also start as planned and execute to completion.

But what if it were important to start the next chain as soon as the first chain ended at the third hour and not wait another hour until the third chain's scheduled start time? A good solution to this scenario is to use an interrupt process to trigger the next execution when the previous chain completes. This avoids a two-hour delay when the previous chain runs only a few minutes late (see Figure 2.18).

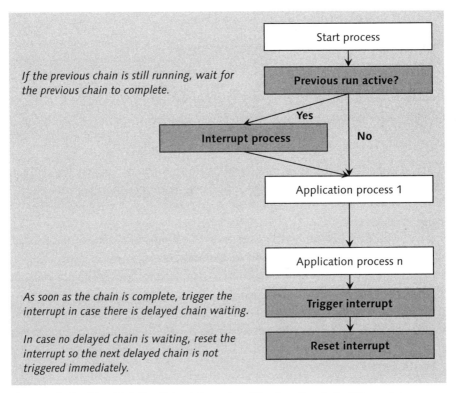

Figure 2.18 Combined Solution Using Interrupt and Previous Run Active? Processes

Interrupt process variants wait for a second event to trigger before their condition is satisfied. This second event is triggered at the end of the previous chain (use program BP_RAISE_EVENT). Since the interrupt process can be satisfied before a chain is interrupted, it is necessary to develop a program to reset the interrupt process.

Create program `ZBW_RESET_INTERRUPT` to force the reset of the interrupt process (see Listing 2.1). At the end of each chain, trigger the interrupt to start any chain that has been interrupted, then immediately reset the interrupt in case there were no chains waiting for the interrupt. In this way, the next chain that should be interrupted is not immediately satisfied and has to wait until the previous chain does indeed complete successfully.

```
report  zbw_reset_interrupt.
parameters: p_chain type rspc_chain.
parameters: p_var   type rspc_variant.

delete from rspcinterruptlog
 where variante = p_var
   and chain    = p_chain
   and log_id   = ''.

if sy-subrc = 0.
  message s143(rspc).
else.
  message s144(rspc).
endif.
```

Listing 2.1 Program Code to Reset Interrupts

Utilizing the interrupt variant in this way offers flexibility with minimal risk of overlap or contention errors in scheduling data loads. Designing process chains in this way will significantly reduce the level of effort required to monitor and resolve daily loading issues. You should always look for additional opportunities to build data loading processes that are error preventive or self-correcting in nature. Using such designs liberally and often ensures robust, flexible, and efficient data loads into any BW system.

Application Processes

Application processes include all the data flow processes that should be automated in process chain maintenance. They represent activities typically performed in the operational use of BI. Table 2.3 gives a list of all available application process types in SAP BW 7.30.

Note

In process chains, the automatisms of the integrated processes are ignored and have to be implemented using process chain types.

For example, if a DSO is set to activate automatically when loaded, this setting is ignored in the process chain. A separate process type variant to activate the DSO must be explicitly included in the process chain.

Process Category	Application Process Type
General services	▸ Interrupt Process
	▸ Start Process
	▸ AND (Last)
	▸ OR (Each)
	▸ EXOR (First)
	▸ ABAP Program
	▸ OS Command
	▸ Local Process Chain
	▸ Remote Process Chain
	▸ Workflow (Remote Also)
	▸ Decision Between Multiple Alternatives
	▸ Is the previous run in the chain still active?
	▸ Start Job in SAP BusinessObjects Data Services
Load process and post-processing	▸ Execute InfoPackage
	▸ Read PSA and Update Data Target
	▸ Save Hierarchy (3.X)
	▸ Update DataStore Object Data (Further Update)
	▸ Delete Overlapping Requests from InfoCube
	▸ Data Transfer Process
	▸ Close Request for an InfoPackage (RDA/Push)
	▸ Quality Status/Set Data Release
	▸ Trigger Delta Merge
	▸ Start Load Process for Real-Time Data Acquisition (RDA)
	▸ Stop Real-Time Data Acquisition (RDA) Load Process
	▸ Trigger Event Data Change (for Broadcaster)

Table 2.3 NetWeaver 7.30 Application Processes Supported by Process Chain Maintenance

Process Category	Application Process Type
Data target administration	▸ Delete Index
	▸ Generate Index
	▸ Construct Database Statistics
	▸ Initial Fill of New Aggregates
	▸ Initial Activation and Filling of SAP HANA/BWA Indexes
	▸ Roll Up of Filled Aggregates/BWA Indexes
	▸ Compression of the InfoCube
	▸ Activate DataStore Object Data
	▸ Complete Deletion of Data Target Contents
	▸ Delete Entire Content of Linked Transactional ODS
	▸ Archive Data from an InfoProvider
Reporting agent	▸ Exception Reporting
	▸ Print in the Background
	▸ Precalculation of Web Templates
	▸ Precalculation of Value Sets
Other BW processes	▸ Replicate BW user authorizations to HANA database
	▸ Attribute Change Run
	▸ Adjustment of Time-Dependent Aggregates
	▸ Deletion of Requests from PSA
	▸ Deletion of Requests from the Change Log
	▸ Delete Requests from Write-Optimized DSO
	▸ Execute Planning Sequence
	▸ Switch Realtime InfoCube to Plan Mode
	▸ Switch Realtime InfoCube to Load Mode
	▸ Reorganize Attributes and Texts for Master Data
	▸ Execute SAP HANA Analysis Process
	▸ Execute Analysis Process
	▸ Update Explorer Properties of BW Objects
Retail	▸ Send POS Sales Data to XI System

Table 2.3 NetWeaver 7.30 Application Processes Supported by Process Chain Maintenance (Cont.)

Process Category	Application Process Type
Global spend analysis	▸ Automatic Classification ▸ DataStore Object-Replication ▸ Master Data Update with Global Keys
Other	▸ Event in SAP CPS ▸ Job in SAP CPS ▸ Last Customer Contact Update (Retraction) ▸ Sybase IQ Partition Monitor

Table 2.3 NetWeaver 7.30 Application Processes Supported by Process Chain Maintenance (Cont.)

In the process chain maintenance screen, you can access documentation for a process type by selecting the process type in the overview tree and choosing [F1]. You can also call the same documentation by choosing Further Help from the dialog box when adding a process to the process chain.

Though we can't cover each of the almost 100 process types listed in the table in detail, several are particularly noteworthy.

Loading Processes
With a process chain start and interrupt structure in place, it is now possible to extract and load data into the BW system from its source systems. The most important process variants are *Execute InfoPackage* and *Data Transfer Process*, which load data from DataSources. These process variants are nothing more than the InfoPackages and DTPs themselves, but these objects deserve special attention in this section because each of them can spawn parallel processes.

As a general rule of thumb, all data should be loaded through the PSA and not directly into the data target. See Figure 2.19 for the InfoPackage Processing option to load only to the PSA ❶. While this may seem redundant compared to loading the data target directly because each record is written to the database twice (once to the PSA and then again to the data target), it significantly accelerates data load error resolution because all the data is stored in the PSA, where it can either be analyzed for inconsistencies and duplicates or validated for completeness before and even after it is loaded to the data target. In addition, if there is a non-data–related error writing to the data target (a bug in the business logic of a transformation, etc.), the data does not need to be re-extracted from the source system, which could take substantially longer than simply reloading from the PSA.

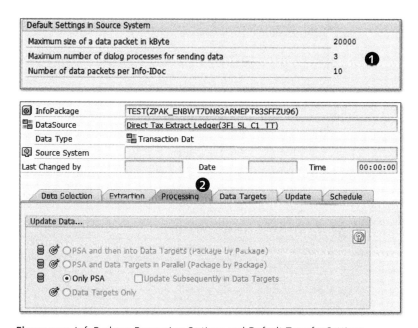

Figure 2.19 InfoPackage Processing Options and Default Transfer Settings

Data is split into data packets when it is loaded into the PSA, and the default size of each data packet can be controlled via customizing Transaction RSCUSTV6 in the source system but overwritten in the InfoPackage ❷. The optimum settings for each DataSource depend on the record size and extraction logic, but the default settings should be suitable for most extracts.

Subsequent updates from the PSA to InfoProviders are handled by DTPs, which can also be executed in parallel (see Figure 2.20). In this example, data is both extracted in parallel ❶ and subsequently procesed in parallel ❷. The number of parallel processes used by DTPs can be specified in the DTP itself, but the default values for all DTPs are set in Transaction RSBATCH, which can be used to specify the number of parallel processes ❶ and the job class (priority A, B, or C) ❷ of each process type variant, which is relevant for parallel processing in the SAP BW system (see Figure 2.21).

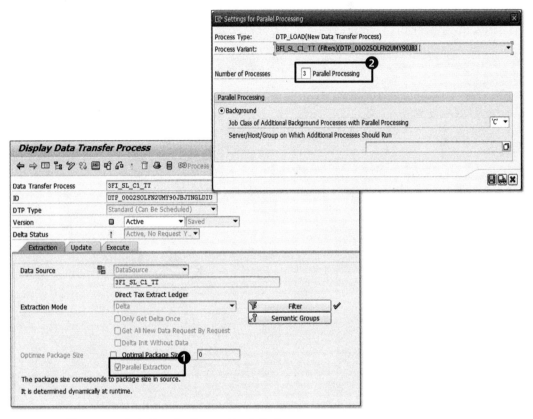

Figure 2.20 Data Transfer Process Parallelization

As illustrated in Figure 2.21, many SAP BW process types allow parallel processing. It is important to understand the default settings and how they impact the performance of the system when designing process chains to extract, transform, and load data.

> **Note**
>
> There must be enough background work processes (type BTC) available in the system for executing parallel BW processes. More background work processes (at least 50% more) are needed with parallelization than without.

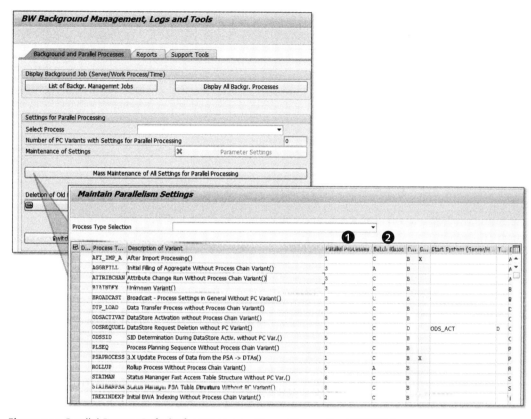

Figure 2.21 Parallel Process Defaults for BW Process Types (Transaction RSBATCH)

You can improve individual load performance by maintaining all the settings related to ETL (both parallelism and data package size). If the extract or transformation logic executed in each data package performs lookups of large amounts of data, smaller packages with a higher degree of parallelism may improve data package performance, as well as the end-to-end duration of the load process. However, if more batch work processes are consumed by this higher degree of parallelism, fewer jobs in other chains can be scheduled concurrently, or there could be deadlocks while waiting for work processes to free up.

To help manage these scheduling priorities and enable a high-level view of all loads scheduled within the system, you should group loading processes with chains, and then group these chains within other chains. This tactic helps segre-

149

gate loading processes from one another and simplifies the view of all existing processes (so administrators do not have to scroll up and down and side to side to understand complex load scenarios).

Local Process Chains

Process chains can be scheduled as processes within *metachains*. A *local process chain* is called by a metachain—both must exist in the same system. In addition to local process chains, metachains can also call *remote process chains*, which are process chains in other systems.

Using local process chains to group logical units of work can simplify the metachains and facilitate troubleshooting. For example, local chains can be built to load specific InfoProviders and include all the explicit automatisms required, such as index deletion, index generation, database statistics construction, compression, aggregation, or BWA rollups. In this way, the metachain would contain a local process chain to load an InfoCube, but all the detail steps would not clutter the graphical view of the process chain.

Local process chains also facilitate data load optimization efforts by enabling reorganization of processes. For example, if a metachain executes several local chains sequentially and one is determined to be outside of the critical path, then it can easily be moved into a parallel path.

ABAP Programs

The ABAP program process type can be used to execute programs in the background with or without variants. Programs can be scheduled via the following options:

▶ **Synchronous, local**
Specify the program name and variant under PROGRAM TO CALL = PROGRAM (as shown in Figure 2.22). The program is started after the event for the predecessor process is triggered and executed in the background on the same server on which the process chain is scheduled. The process chain waits until the program has finished before it continues with any possible successors.

▶ **Asynchronous**
Choose this option if your program is asynchronous—meaning it is a *distributed process*. Distributed processes utilize different work processes for specific tasks; the ending task is not always the same as the starting task.

In an asynchronous process, the process chain management does not equate the end of the process with the end of the background process. The process status remains active, and successor events are not automatically triggered.

To signal the end of the process, the program must call the remote-enabled `RSPC_ABAP_FINISH` function module. The process is then indicated as completed, and the successor events are triggered. Pass the process variant as input to the function module by adding the following data declaration to the program `PARAMETERS variant TYPE rspc_variant`.

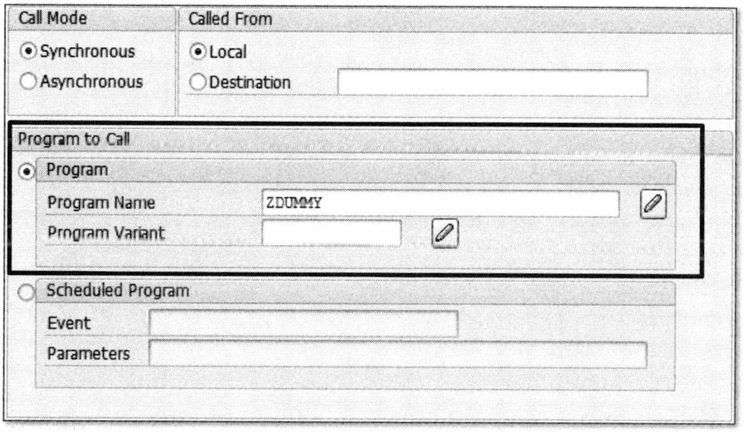

Call Mode	Called From
⦿ Synchronous	⦿ Local
○ Asynchronous	○ Destination

Program to Call
- ⦿ Program
  - Program Name: ZDUMMY
  - Program Variant:
- ○ Scheduled Program
  - Event:
  - Parameters:

Figure 2.22 ABAP Process Variant Configuration Settings

Recommendation

The process chain management does not recognize the program termination.

Therefore, the chain itself terminates when restarted because the old run is not finished. To avoid this, manually set the process to TERMINATED in the chain log view in the process monitor (PROCESS TAB page). Do this prior to restarting.

▶ **Asynchronous, local**
Choose this option if the program is asynchronous (it requires a user decision or makes an asynchronous RFC) or the program is already scheduled in the background. In this case, the program must be scheduled to wait for a batch event. Enter the event and, if necessary, the parameter under SCHEDULED PROGRAM.

▶ **Asynchronous, destination**

Choose this option to schedule a program on the target server waiting for an event. Specify the destination for the target system and enter the event and parameter, if any, by choosing SCHEDULED PROGRAM. This option is only available for target systems as of Service API 3.0A.

Note

SAP recommends using the synchronous, local option by writing a local program that synchronously calls a remote-enabled function module in the target system. The enables the following benefits:

▶ The process can be monitored using process chain management.

▶ Logs can be written and issued by the program and displayed in the process chain maintenance log view.

▶ Error messages can be raised to terminate the job, process, and process chain. Therefore, write your logs as success messages.

▶ It is not possible to evaluate the error messages to trigger subsequent processes. Instead, use decision variants.

Decisions between Multiple Alternatives

Decision variants enable conditional logic within the process chains, such as if-then-else statements. The decision variant uses functions in the formula builder to evaluate the conditional statement; the last "else" statement does not require a function because it is accepted if no other conditions are satisfied (see Figure 2.23).

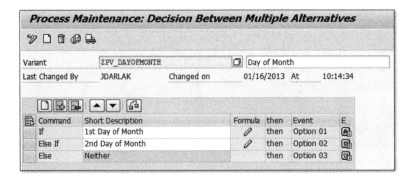

Figure 2.23 Example Conditional Statement in a Decision Variant

The function library of the formula builder contains all the standard Boolean, mathematical, string, and date functions available in transformation rules. In addition, the function library contains enhanced date and time functions and new process chain category functions (see Figure 2.24 for a screenshot of available date and time functions).

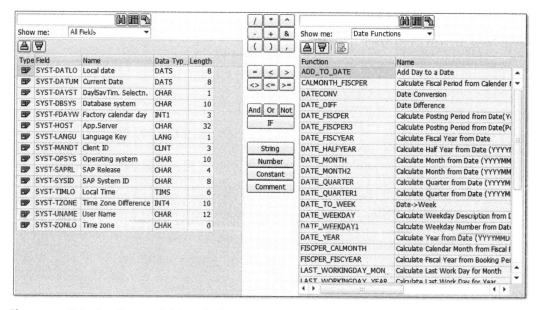

Figure 2.24 Date Functions Available in the Function Builder

In the date functions category, the new function DATE_WEEKDAY1 calculates the day of the week based on the current date as a technical specification (1-7) from the date. This allows a process chain to execute a different chain string during the weekend than during the week.

In the new process chain category, there are three new functions that allow access to additional information about the process chain execution:

▶ PREDECESSOR_PARAMETER: Runtime parameter of direct predecessor

▶ PROCESS_PARAMETER: Runtime parameter of a process in the current chain

▶ PROCESS_VALUE_EXISTS: Process in chain has parameter value

While there are many functions available, it is also possible to create user-defined functions in the function library by using an enhancement implementation of BAdI RSAR_CONNECTOR to create function classes and methods.

Obsolete Process Types for SAP HANA Database
The following process types are no longer needed when using SAP HANA database because indexes are obsolete:

▶ Initial Filling of New Aggregates

▶ Update Explorer Properties of BW Objects

▶ Rolling Up Filled Aggregates/BWA Indexes

▶ Adjust Time-Dependent Aggregates

▶ Construct Database Statistics

▶ Generate Index

▶ Delete Index

When using the SAP HANA database, it is no longer possible to select these process types in process chain maintenance.

> **Recommendation**
>
> Existing process chains that use the obsolete process do not have to be modified before migration to SAP HANA. The relevant process variants are not executed in the chains and do not terminate with errors.

Collection Process

A collection process merges several parallel paths, or chain strings, to form a single string in the process chain. Collection processes are handled as multiple occurrences of the same process, and the system guarantees that all processes of the same name trigger the same event. The following collection processes are available in the process chain maintenance:

▶ **AND process (last)**
The AND process does not start until all the events of the predecessor processes, including the last process, have been successfully triggered.

Use this collection process to combine processes when subsequent processing is dependent on successful completion of all predecessor processes.

▶ **OR process (every)**
The OR process starts every time a predecessor process event has been successfully triggered.

Use this collection process to avoid multi-scheduling the actual application process. Include a subsequent process only once and have it executed every time a predecessor completes successfully.

▶ **XOR process (first)**
The XOR process starts only when the first event in one of the predecessor processes has been successfully triggered.

Use this collection process to schedule processes in parallel and trigger subsequent processes after any predecessor process completes.

With the power to automate data loads comes the responsibility to manage that data. As we will discover in the next chapter, it is important to recognize that the data loaded into the data warehouse must be actively and effectively managed to keep costs low and system performance high.

Effectively managing data growth in your data warehouse can be an intensive and massive task. Fortunately, planning for growth and performance up front during design can simplify and facilitate the data management effort.

3   Data Management

As data is loaded into a data warehouse, it is propagated through the data flow and replicated throughout the LSA architecture. For example, data extracted from a table in SAP ERP could be loaded into the PSA, one or more DSO layers, change logs, the corporate memory, and InfoCubes. The result of this data propagation is data replication and an increased storage requirement over and above the original source system. In some cases, data may be denormalized to improve data load performance and/or reporting performance (i.e., including sales order header information in the sales order item data flow). *Denormalization* is the intentional duplication of columns in multiple tables, and it increases data redundancy.

Failure to proactively manage data loaded into SAP NetWeaver can seriously jeopardize system performance and directly affect the total cost of ownership. Housekeeping activities must be an integral part of the operational concept of a complex enterprise data warehouse. Planning and executing housekeeping activities regularly in the system ensures optimum utilization of system resources and thereby optimizes the overall system performance.

This chapter introduces many concepts regarding monitoring and managing data loads for master data (Section 3.1) and transaction data (Section 3.2), as well as monitoring temporary data resident in the system (Section 3.3). An integral part of any data monitoring and housekeeping effort is a data retention strategy (Section 3.4), which may include a hybrid approach using all tools at one's disposal, such as aggregation, near-line storage, archival, and data deletion (Section 3.5).

3.1   Master Data

Before one can understand how best to maintain master data, one must understand not only what master data is, but also what it is not. Master data defines what is important to a business; it is unique information of reference owned and maintained by the business and reused many times in transactions. Master data management is the collection and execution of practices to ensure uniform, governed, and high-quality master data.

High-quality master data has a few important characteristics:

- Relevant to the business
- Free of duplicates
- Complete
- Accurate
- Consistent across systems and entities

Master data that will not be used or is irrelevant is not master data, and should be removed or flagged for deletion from the source system. Master data that does not exist in the source system is not used in transactions and so should be removed from the data warehouse. Master data that is used but is inaccurate, incomplete, or inconsistent can adversely impact operational performance, analytical capabilities, legal compliance, and segregation of duties and lead to loss of business opportunities. It needs to be corrected, completed, or made consistent.

In SAP BW, master data is handled differently from transaction data: it is loaded differently, stored differently, activated differently, and maintained differently, so managing master data effectively in SAP BW requires a three-pronged approach:

1. Design master data well, taking into consideration the requirements and source of the data.
2. Plan an effective data loading strategy by identifying master data dependencies, as discussed in Chapter 2, Section 2.4.1; optimizing loading parameters; and configuring system settings.
3. Routinely maintain master data objects using available system utilities to monitor for and repair common issues.

Let's focus on this three-pronged approach, but only relevant items that have not already been covered earlier in this chapter.

3.1.1 Master Data Design

Master data is designed as *InfoObjects*, the building blocks of all other data structures in BW. The InfoObject definition contains all the metadata about the data, such as the field type and length, whether it has a conversion routine, and how it should be displayed. *Metadata* is data about data—it is the information that distinguishes one field from another and it is comprised of the InfoObject definition that contains all the specifications for the three types of master data, in addition to information used by the BW application to interpret those specifications.

Three basic types of master data can be loaded into SAP BW:

▶ Attributes

▶ Hierarchies

▶ Texts

InfoObjects can handle very complex data models themselves. A single InfoObject may consist of up to 11 tables and views in the database (in the list below, x represents either C for the customer name space or 0 for the SAP name space):

▶ SID table (/BIx/S)

▶ Attribute tables

  ▷ Attribute view (/BIx/M)

  ▷ Time-independent attributes (/BIx/P)

  ▷ Time-independent attribute SID table (/BIx/X)

  ▷ Time-dependent attributes (/BIx/Q)

  ▷ Time-dependent attribute SID table (/BIx/Y)

▶ Hierarchy tables

  ▷ Hierarchy table (/BIx/H)

  ▷ Hierarchy SID structure (/BIx/I)

  ▷ Hierarchy interval table (/BIx/J)

  ▷ Hierarchy SID table (/BIx/K)

▶ Text table (/BIx/T)

The SAP BW architecture encourages master data portability between data models. For example, a customer in sales data models is always consistent with a customer in delivery data models, and a material in production data models is consistent with materials in shipment data models. When you are designing InfoObjects needed in a reporting or data modeling scenario, you should take care to identify all master data that shares the same values and reuse existing InfoObjects.

To ensure that the master data is always consistent, validate the values from different sources and confirm that they are also consistent. If they are not, take steps to ensure consistency or use different master data objects instead. If the existing InfoObject only needs a different description to be suitable for this use case, create a *Reference InfoObject*, which is an InfoObject that shares the same master data tables as an existing InfoObject. Reference InfoObjects ensure consistency in InfoObject values and improve overall system performance by reducing the number of master data loads.

Recall from Chapter 1, Section 1.1.3 the five different types of InfoObjects; all of them have definitions, although not all are considered master data:

1. Characteristics
2. Key figures
3. Units
4. Time characteristics
5. Technical characteristics

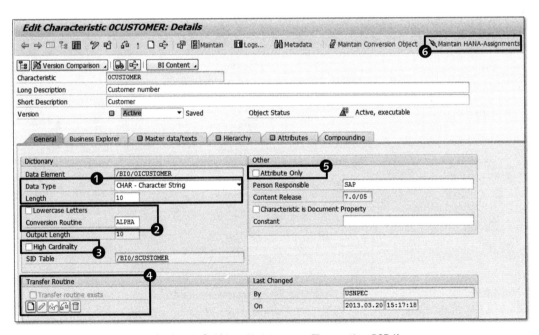

Figure 3.1 General Tab in InfoObject Maintenance (Transaction RSD1)

To keep master data relevant and correct, fields must be mapped carefully from source systems to SAP BW, especially from flat files or non-SAP data sources. The first step when defining a new characteristic InfoObject is to specify the data type and length—which is done on the GENERAL tab of InfoObject maintenance (Transaction RSD1). See Figure 3.1 for the GENERAL tab definition of InfoObject 0CUSTOMER, where ❶ defines its data type and length as a CHAR 10.

Table 3.1 lists the four data types available for characteristic InfoObjects. In most cases, characteristic InfoObjects are either be alphabetic (CHAR) or numeric (NUMC) because all date and time characteristics should be created as reference objects of 0DATE or 0TIME, and not as custom characteristics.

Data Type	Content	Character Length
CHAR	Numbers and letters	1-250
NUMC	Numbers only	1-250
DATS	Date	8
TIMS	Time	6

Table 3.1 Data Types Available for Characteristic InfoObjects

> **Note**
>
> As of SAP BW 7.40 SP2, InfoObject values can be now be up to 250 characters in length. Previously, they were limited to 60 characteristics. See SAP Note 1823174 for more information.

One of the most common mistakes is not assigning the proper conversion routines to fields. Conversion routines such as the ALPHA routine cannot be added after master data has been loaded, so the ALPHA-converted InfoObjects must be defined correctly up front.

> **Note**
>
> As a general rule of thumb, if the field in the source system is ALPHA converted, the corresponding InfoObject in BW should be, as well. Because most non-SAP source systems do not have conversion routines, these fields may need to be converted during loading.

ALPHA conversion routines are valid only for character fields. When values are inserted into an ALPHA-converted field, they are left padded with zeroes if the value is numeric or right-padded with spaces if it is alphabetic. This ensures that data is mapped correctly, regardless of source. Table 3.2 shows how values are loaded differently for ALPHA-converted fields versus non-converted fields. Notice that 1, 01, and 0001 are all treated as the same value in an ALPHA-converted field but stored as three unique values in a non-converted field.

Value in Source	CHAR 5 InfoObject; No Conversion Routine	CHAR 5 InfoObject; ALPHA-Converted
1	1	00001
01	01	00001
0001	0001	00001
'ABC'	'ABC'	'ABC '
'ABC '	'ABC '	'ABC '
'ABC '	'ABC '	'ABC '

Table 3.2 Comparison of ALPHA-Converted and Non-Converted Fields

In this way, the ALPHA conversion routine can help preserve the integrity of data in the data warehouse, especially if the data is loaded from multiple sources. Otherwise, there could be multiple values used in transaction data, but only one would correctly map to the master data. If the mapping of transaction data to master data is not corrected, this could not only lead to a loss of business due to data integrity issues in reporting, but also propagate throughout the warehouse and cost more to fix the longer the root cause remains.

In many cases, it is common for data loaded from non-SAP sources into ALPHA-compliant fields to fail. The solution is to call CONVERSION_EXIT_ALPHA_INPUT in the InfoObject field routine. This ensures that data is in the proper format no matter where it is used. Please note that you must activate all existing transfer rules, update rules, and transformations after coding the routine for it to take effect in existing ETL. New ETL will automatically pick up the routine without any additional action required.

> **Note**
>
> ALPHA-converted fields cannot be extended (e.g., from CHAR 10 to CHAR 12). If the length of the field were extended, the existing values would not have the correct number of left-padded zeroes.

> Be wary of online resources that suggest that ALPHA-converted fields can be easily extended by removing the ALPHA conversion routine assignment. This is extremely bad advice because once it is removed you cannot easily add it back!

If there is a need to ALPHA-convert an InfoObject that has already been loaded and used, the solution is to complete the following steps:

1. In the transformation rules for the InfoObject, call the function module CONVERSION_EXIT_ALPHA_INPUT to explicitly perform the conversion.

2. Activate all transformations where the InfoObject is used so that the new rule takes effect.

3. Reload all master data to ensure that all attribute values are assigned to the ALPHA-compliant value.

4. Reload all transaction history from all sources to eliminate non-ALPHA–compliant values.

5. Once all transaction data has been reloaded, use the RSRV function to delete master data that is no longer used. This function checks all usages of the InfoObject before deleting any master data. This step should eliminate all non-ALPHA–compliant values from the master data.

6. Execute program RSMDEXITON.

> **Note**
>
> Program RSMDEXITON is not fully supported by SAP in SAP BW 7.x, so it should be fully tested.

After the data type, conversion routine, and length have been defined, the next things to consider are the LOWERCASE LETTERS flag ❷ and the HIGH CARDINALITY flag ❸ in Figure 3.1. If the master data values contain lower case values, the lowercase checkbox should be checked; otherwise, only capitalized values are accepted.

The HIGH CARDINALITY flag is new with SAP BW 7.40 SP5. High cardinality InfoObjects enable business scenarios that require extremely high volumes of master data (e.g., sales invoice analysis). InfoObjects flagged as high cardinality do not generate SIDs to overcome the limitation on standard InfoObjects of two billion records, meaning they have no SID table. High-cardinality InfoObjects can be used only in InfoProviders that store the key values, and not the SID values of characteristics.

> **Note**
>
> The HIGH CARDINALITY flag can be set only on InfoObjects with a data type of CHAR or NUMC and a length greater than or equal to 10.
>
> ▸ High-cardinality InfoObjects cannot be used in the following ways:
>
>   ▸ In InfoCubes
>
>   ▸ As a compounding parent
>
>   ▸ As a navigational attribute
>
>   ▸ In hierarchies
>
>   ▸ In SAP HANA analytic processes
>
> ▸ Response times may be impacted during reporting on high-cardinality InfoObjects because SID values need to be generated as local SIDs.

It is also possible to define custom coding for this InfoObject that is executed every time 0CUSTOMER is loaded from any source to any data target. This custom code is maintained in the TRANSFER ROUTINE ❹ grouping.

The last important option to consider is the ATTRIBUTE ONLY? flag ❺, which is remarkably similar to the HIGH CARDINALITY flag. If the InfoObject will be used only as a display attribute and not as navigation attribute and will never be used in an InfoCube, it can be set as attribute only and no SIDs are generated for its values. Attribute-only InfoObjects can still be used in other InfoObjects, DSOs, or InfoSets.

Free text fields should never be loaded to an InfoCube but can be loaded to DSOs without SID activation. Free text fields should generally not be ALPHA-converted because 1 and 01 may be deliberately different. Free text fields, by default, have no edits/validations on them and, therefore, may never have duplicate values. Thus, these fields should be modeled as non-navigational fields in SAP BW, meaning they shouldn't have SIDs generated. To model these fields, choose ATTRIBUTE ONLY to make them display-only. Load them into DSOs with or without BEx reporting flags, but not to InfoCubes. Most free text also needs lowercase characters enabled.

For SAP BW installations on SAP HANA, there is one more point of interest on the GENERAL tab: InfoObject assignments to field-based providers such as OpenODS-Views can be maintained using the button MAINTAIN HANA ASSIGNMENTS ❻, as seen in Figure 3.1.

The next tab in the InfoObject definition is the BUSINESS EXPLORER tab, which defines how the InfoObject interacts with BEx queries and reports. To reduce development effort and improve consistency in BEx queries and reports, define the default DISPLAY and BEX DESCRIPTION in this tab before starting with front-end development, as illustrated by ❶ in Figure 3.2. Spending a little time up front here will save hours of rework later.

However, the most important settings on this tab from a performance and master data perspective are the AUTHORIZATION RELEVANT checkbox ❷ and the QUERY FILTER VALUE SETTINGS for QUERY EXECUTION field ❸.

InfoObjects defined as *authorization relevant* can have access restrictions on specific values assigned to users. Even if full authorizations are provided for all values, the authorization check still executes, possibly impairing query performance. Therefore, define InfoObjects as authorization relevant only if they indeed will be restricted. This topic will be covered in more depth in Chapter 4.

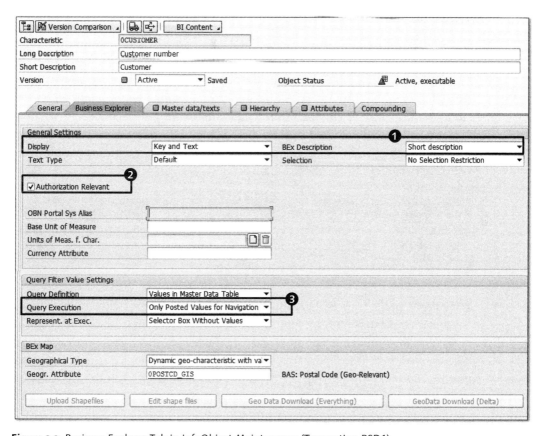

Figure 3.2 Business Explorer Tab in InfoObject Maintenance (Transaction RSD1)

The query filter value selection for query execution defines which values the end users see when filtering on a dimensional or navigational attribute in a BEx query. Choose source as ALL MASTER DATA VALUES if the number of values is relatively small—but ensure that the values are correct. Incorrect or unused values will confuse the end users and result in slower adoption of reporting out of SAP BW. If the number of master data values is large, use ONLY POSTED VALUES FOR NAVIGATION for performance reasons and to ensure that only relevant values are shown in the report, which increases usability and speeds up adoption. Please note that all general settings on this tab can be edited and overwritten at the query level.

The MASTER DATA/TEXTS tab (see Figure 3.3) is relevant only for characteristics for which attributes or texts will be loaded from a source system of record. If the characteristic has neither attributes nor texts, the appropriate checkboxes on this tab should be explicitly unchecked (they are checked by default when a characteristic is created).

If attributes and/or texts will be loaded, the appropriate checkboxes must remain checked, as indicated by ❶ and ❷, respectively. Before any data can be loaded, the APPLICATION COMPONENT field ❸ must be populated, or no transformations can be created to load the InfoObject. All information regarding texts is defined on this tab as well, including whether short, medium, or long texts exist and whether they are language-dependent or time-dependent. Only select checkboxes that are relevant for the source of master data being loaded; the simplest possible table structure provides the best performance.

> **Note**
>
> As of SAP BW 7.40 SP2, InfoObjects support extra-long texts, which can be up to 1,333 characters in length. The previous limit was 60 characters. See SAP Note 1823174 for more information.

To improve performance of lookups to master data during data loads, specify the MASTER DATA READ ACCESS method ❹. By defining a read class, the same code can be used to look up data from the master data tables of this InfoObject every time it is accessed, providing a level of control over access methods during transformation routines and minimizing the need for start and/or end routines in transformation logic to read master data tables into memory.

For installations on SAP HANA, the InfoObject master data tables can be exposed to HANA using the checkboxes in the grouping labeled EXTERNAL SAP HANA VIEW ❺.

External SAP HANA views are not used by SAP BW but can be used as an SAP HANA-native access interface to BW models and data.

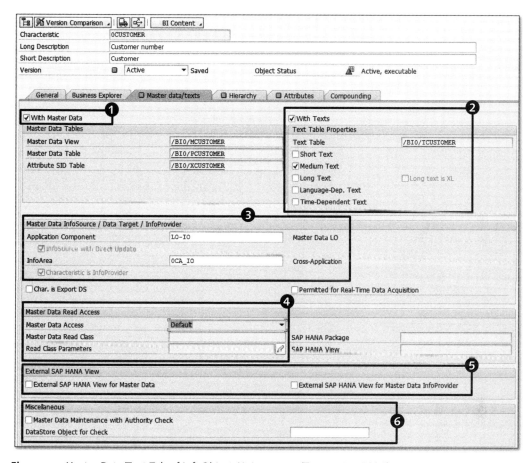

Figure 3.3 Master Data/Text Tab of InfoObject Maintenance (Transaction RSD1)

Note

There are many limitations on characteristics when exposing master data to SAP HANA:

- The MASTER DATA READ ACCESS field must be set to DEFAULT.
- Authorization-relevant navigational attributes are not supported.
- Compounding is not supported.
- Conversion routines (such as date and ALPHA) are not supported.
- Hierarchies are not supported.

> ▸ ATTRIBUTE ONLY? characteristics are not supported.
>
> ▸ High-cardinality InfoObjects must have master data.

Lastly, it is possible to control maintenance of specific values of the master data of an InfoObject by specifying MASTER DATA MAINTENANCE WITH AUTHORITY CHECK ❻. If this indicator is not set, it is possible only to permit or forbid master data maintenance for all characteristic values of an InfoObject. If the indicator is set, use authorization object S_TABU_LIN to specify key values for which users have authorization to maintain.

Hierarchies for an InfoObject are defined on the HIERARCHY tab (see Figure 3.4). Select the checkbox WITH HIERARCHIES to enable hierarchies and configure whether they are time dependent or version dependent or contain intervals.

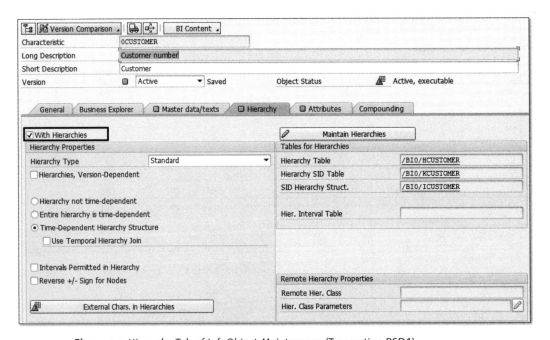

Figure 3.4 Hierarchy Tab of InfoObject Maintenance (Transaction RSD1)

The master data tables are defined on the ATTRIBUTE tab (see Figure 3.5), which lists all display and navigational attributes of OCUSTOMER. Time dependency should be used only where it is needed to mirror settings in the source systems (such as employee data). Limit the use of time-dependent master data for cases in which reporting requirements dictate the need to report different values over time because it impacts performance and data-loading flexibility.

We recommend that you use navigational attributes instead of posting repeated values directly in the InfoProvider in order to reduce data duplication (3NF) and increase reporting flexibility. Of course, most fields posted in the original transactions should remain as dimensional characteristics to preserve transactional integrity, but any groupings or other information about those fields should come from attributes.

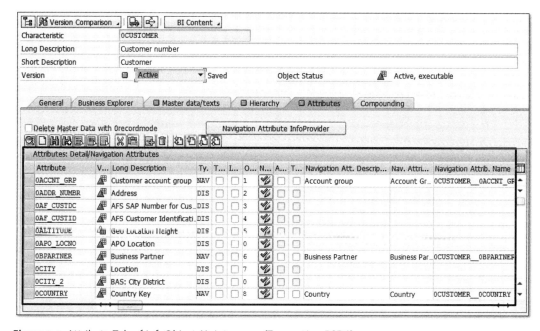

Figure 3.5 Attribute Tab of InfoObject Maintenance (Transaction RSD1)

Recommendation

Always add 0LOGSYS as a navigational attribute of master data bearing InfoObjects and populate it with the logical system of the source system from which it is loaded. This helps identify any records generated or created via transactional loads and allow them to be segregated from true master data loaded from the system of record.

Using flags as navigational attributes can help performance of lookups during transactional data loads and reporting when used as query filters. All flags with the same values, such as YES/NO, should be referenced from a single InfoObject that has texts loaded once; there is no reason to load Yes/No texts to more than one object. The same logic applies to all other objects that share the same master data: load it once and create reference objects everywhere a different description is needed.

> **Recommendation**
>
> When defining flags for use in reporting, follow the standard SAP convention of using only two values: *X* and *blank*. The conventional method of using *Y* for *Yes* and *N* for *No* always includes a third unexpected value: *blank*. This third value either is easily overlooked, resulting in poor data integrity, or adds unnecessary complexity to business logic or reporting logic.

There are performance limits to the number of navigational attributes and total attributes an InfoObject should have — respectively, there should be no more than 80 of the former and 100 of the latter. Failure to adhere to these limits can significantly affect master data activation performance with larger data sets. While there are no published benchmarks, most data sets with more than two million values suffer performance impacts when the number of attributes exceeds the prescribed limits. When this happens, performance of activation can be improved by creating secondary indexes on master data /BIx/P and /BIx/X tables with the following fields in sequence:

1. CHANGED

2. OBJVERS

These indexes cannot be transported because the tables themselves are generated locally during InfoObject activation, so they need to be created in each system individually. It is possible to develop an ABAP program to enable this activity without opening the client or data dictionary change authorization checks.

Secondary indexes can also be used to improve system performance, especially in modeling situations in which the number of values is excessively large and the InfoObject's attributes are used as either lookup values during master data loading or join conditions in InfoSets or CompositeProviders.

3.1.2   Master Data Loading

This is the second piece of the three-pronged approach. When new master data is loaded, records are inserted directly into the master data tables, and no activation is required. However, when changes to master data are loaded, existing texts are overwritten immediately, but existing attributes and hierarchies cannot be activated immediately because any aggregates that contain these objects must be adjusted. In InfoCubes, data referring to hierarchies or navigational attributes is not stored in the cube, but joined during query execution. To improve query performance, this data is stored in aggregates. To ensure that queries accessing data from InfoCubes or aggregates return consistent results, the master data and aggregates must be adjusted at the same time. Therefore, the following tasks must be coordinated:

▶ Activating master data changes to attributed and hierarchies

▶ Realigning aggregates containing navigational attributes

▶ Realigning aggregates defined on hierarchy levels

Regardless of whether aggregates exist, the system does not automatically activate master data changes. Instead, changes to existing attributes or hierarchies are loaded into the master data tables as modified versions. There are then two records in the master data tables: the first is the active record marked for deletion with field OBJVERS = 'A' for active and field CHANGED = 'D' for deletion, and the second is the changed record marked for insertion with field OBJVERS = 'M' for modified and field CHANGED = 'I' for insertion.

These changes can only be activated subsequently by a process called a *hierarchy/ attribute change run* (CR). There are two phases in the change run:

1. The *startup phase* checks which attributes and hierarchies have changed since the last CR and then identifies which aggregates must be adjusted before these changes can be activated and which InfoCubes the aggregates are built on.

2. The *work phase* adjusts the aggregates determined in the first phase in a cube-by-cube manner. This phase can be executed in parallel if the RSADMIN parameter CR_MAXWPC is set to a value greater than one. After the aggregates are adjusted, the attribute and hierarchy changes are activated, followed by the official release of the adjusted aggregates.

During the attribute and hierarchy activation step of the second phase, the records marked for deletion are physically deleted, and the records marked for insertion are activated. After the activation, it is not possible to determine the previous values because there is no change history recorded for master data.

> **Note**
>
> See SAP Note 825927 for more information on controlling change run behavior via RSADMIN parameters.

To monitor the status of running CRs or those needing to be executed, use program RSDDS_CHANGERUN_MONITOR. Figure 3.6 displays the program screens. First, if no CR is running, there is a list of InfoObjects that need to be activated. In this case, 0CUSTOMER master data needs to be activated. Choose the InfoObject icon ❶ to select which InfoObjects to process. Then, click the Execute button ❷. Use the Refresh button to monitor the activation process ❸. When the activation is complete, the screen is blank, as indicated by ❹; just re-execute the program check if any more master data needs to be activated.

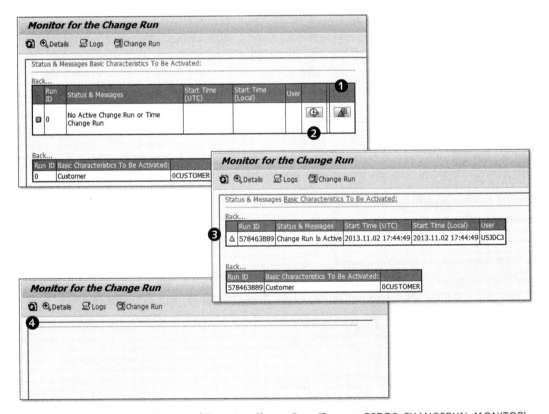

Figure 3.6 Monitoring and Executing Change Runs (Program RSDDS_CHANGERUN_MONITOR)

If a characteristic is loaded via multiple sources with the possibility of a subsequent load overwriting values from a previous load, or if it contains time-dependent attributes or texts, you should consider using the process type REORGANIZE ATTRIBUTES AND TEXTS FOR MASTER DATA in a process chain before executing a change run. This process type first compares data in the active and modified versions of the time-dependent and non-time-dependent attributes with each other. If there are no differences between the active and modified versions, the modified version is deleted, minimizing or eliminating the need to execute a change run. In a second step, the process type checks time-dependent texts and attributes to determine whether time intervals exist with identical attribute values or text entries. If this is the case, the relevant time intervals are combined into larger intervals.

> **Recommendation**
>
> When loading master data in process chains, it is most efficient to load all non-dependent data first and then execute a single mass change run, rather than an individual CR for each InfoObject loaded.

During the insertion of new master data, new SID values need to be generated for each value. It is advisable to buffer the number ranges that generate the SID values for master data loads that result in the generation of a large number of new SIDs during extraction. The same statement is true for InfoObjects without master data that are loaded as transaction data, and for dimension IDs (DIMIDs) that are generated when new values are loaded into InfoCube dimension tables.

One way to identify the SID tables and dimension tables with the largest number of values is to use the SAP EarlyWatch Alert (EWA) or program SAP_INFOCUBE_ DESIGNS. Another way is to search the number range table NRIV for objects (field OBJECT) that start with 'BIM*' for InfoObject SIDs or 'BID*' for dimension table DIMIDs. Sort the results descending by field NRLEVEL to identify the largest number-range object values; these are good candidates for buffering. In addition to buffering SIDs and DIMIDs based on monitoring historical volumes or high rates of organic table growth, it is also good practice to proactively buffer number ranges whenever you know in advance that a large data load of new records will be taking place.

With the high volume and high growth rate tables identified, the next step is to determine the correlated number-range objects to be buffered. For SIDs, use Transaction SE16 to view the InfoObject entry in table RSDCHABASLOC. Field

NUMBRANR contains the last seven digits of the number-range object; prefix these digits with 'BIM' to get the number-range object. For DIMIDs, view the dimension table entry in table RSDDIMELOC to find the corresponding number-range object when prefixed with 'BID'.

Next, go to Transaction SNRO and enter the number-range object to configure the number of values that should be buffered (see Figure 3.7). Choose MAIN MEMORY BUFFERING and enter the number of values to be buffered. If 100 new SID values are generated every data load, the buffer value should be set to something greater than or equal to 100. In past experience, buffering 100-500 values has proven very efficient.

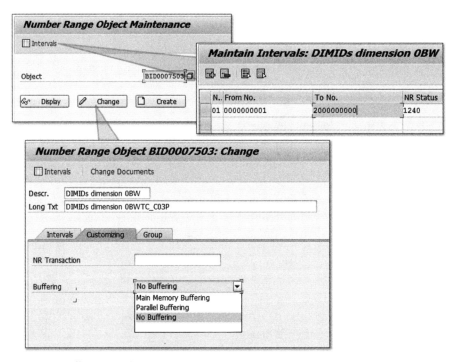

Figure 3.7 Buffering Number Ranges (Transaction SNRO)

> **Note**
>
> Loading performance can be improved by buffering the number ranges of master data SIDs using Transaction SNRO. We recommend that you buffer the number ranges of the InfoObjects that have—or will have—high volumes or high growth rates.

Although master data can be maintained directly (i.e., attribute values can be created and changed) via Transaction RSDMD, you should reserve this transaction for correcting master data issues that cannot be resolved through a full repair load. In a data warehouse, all data should have a system of record. This means master data that does not currently exist but is needed for reporting, such as YES/No flag texts, still need to be loaded from somewhere.

Try to avoid using flat files for loading data that do not have a source system of record, such as SAP ERP. Instead, create a fixed value domain in Transaction SE11 and enter all the values there. Fixed-value domains are transportable data dictionary objects, so all value changes are not only recorded, but also more likely to be tested in the QA system to ensure that the new values are correct before SIDs are generated in production for them. Domains can be created directly in the SAP BW system or in the SAP ERP system; the decision should depend on where responsibility lies for maintaining the values. If it is the SAP BW support team, create them in SAP BW; if the business owns the data and should maintain the values, then create them in SAP ERP. A DataSource can be created on a fixed-value domain to load texts from any SAP source.

If data must be loaded from a flat file, it should be loaded via an automated and repeatable process. Flat files can be loaded in batch processing only when the files exist on the application server. To enable batch loading, transfer all flat files to the SAP system's application server file directory (via FTP or other means) and load them from there. Never load flat files from a user's desktop unless the user is testing in a sandbox environment. When loading from the file system, use dedicated file paths and file names to identify each file and what data it contains. In the SAP BW system, logical file names and paths should be configured in Transaction FILE to match the file names and paths in the file systems. These logical file names can then be specified in the DTPs or InfoPackages for loading. It is a good idea to leverage operating system scripting to archive flat files by date so that data errors can be isolated and corrections can be made when necessary.

> **Note**
>
> When data is loaded from flat files, non-SAP sources, or even non-standard Data-Sources, be especially careful when mapping transformation routines for compound InfoObjects. Always ensure that the fields being mapped to the compounded Info-Objects are populated before updating the base InfoObject. This requires the use of ABAP code in the routine, but will preserve the data integrity of the values being loaded.

When loading master data, there are several other performance considerations that should be taken into account, including InfoPackage and DTP settings. These considerations are the same for transaction data and will be covered in Section 3.2.

3.1.3 Master Data Maintenance

Finally, master data maintenance is the third prong. To check the health of master data objects and repair inconsistencies, perform consistency checks on the data and metadata stored in a BI system. Pre-defined consistency checks are available in the analysis and repair environment, which can be accessed using Transaction RSRV. The analysis and repair environment contains a collection of utilities for all areas within SAP BW. Figure 3.8 shows the utilities available for master data ❶ and hierarchies ❷.

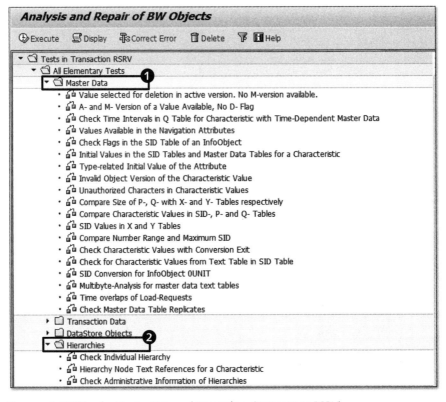

Figure 3.8 Utilities for Master Data and Hierarchies (Transaction RSRV)

Nineteen utilities are available for master data, and many of these will check for errors and repair any that are found. Each utility accepts parameters and can be executed manually or in process chains using the program RSRV_JOB_RUNNER. These utilities should be executed when unexpected behavior is noted in the system. The following list documents the check conducted by each utility and specifies whether an inconsistency, if found, can be repaired:

▶ VALUE SELECTED FOR DELETION IN ACTIVE VERSION. NO M-VERSION AVAILABLE.
This elementary test checks whether there are characteristic values in the active (A) version that have been flagged for deletion (D flag is set) that have no modified (M) version. These characteristic values are lost during activation.

This inconsistency can be repaired.

▶ A- AND M- VERSION OF A VALUE AVAILABLE, NO D-FLAG.
This test checks whether there are characteristic values in both the active (A) and modified (M) versions, where the active version is not flagged for deletion (D flag is not set). This would lead to a short dump during activation.

This inconsistency can be repaired.

▶ CHECK TIME INTERVALS IN Q TABLE FOR CHARACTERISTIC WITH TIME-DEPENDENT MASTER DATA.
The Q table for a characteristic includes the values for the time-dependent attributes. For characteristics without time-dependent master data, there is no Q table. In this case, this test does not execute any checks. With this test, you can check the Q table for a characteristic to see if the time intervals included for a specification also include the time frame from 01.01.1000 to 31.12.9999 without any gaps or overlaps. The test is executed for both the active version and the most recently changed version.

If the test is executed in Repair mode, all detected inconsistencies are removed, if possible. For example, if the deletion flag (CHANGED column) is incorrectly set ('D' instead of being blank, or vice versa) with an active data record (OBJVERS = 'A'), this type of inconsistency can be removed in most cases.

> **Note**
>
> In the case of characteristics with navigation attributes, the respective Y table has to be rebuilt after repairing the Q table. Note that changes to the X or Y tables for a characteristic require reconstruction of all aggregates that use a navigation attribute for the characteristic or one of the characteristics that refer to the characteristic. To rebuild the Y table, perform the steps specified in SAP Note 323140.

If inconsistencies still remain after a repair run, it can take up to three repair runs to remove all inconsistencies.

▶ VALUES AVAILABLE IN THE NAVIGATION ATTRIBUTES.
This quick test checks whether a characteristic's navigational attribute values also exist in the SID table of the navigation attribute. It compares the number of entries in the attribute table (P or Q table) with the number of entries in the X or Y table. If the numbers are not the same, the first 50 attributes that fail the test are written to the application log.

Inconsistencies between the P and X or between the Q and Y tables are revealed with this test. In contrast to the test COMPARE THE SIZE OF THE P AND X TABLES WITH THE Q AND Y TABLES, this test gives information about which navigation attribute is the source of inconsistency between the tables. An inconsistency leads to incorrect numbers in reporting: missing entries operate like (invisible) filters; the case of having more entries in the X than in the P table or having more entries in the Y than in the Q table should not happen and points to severe inconsistencies, which could be the result of system errors when deleting master data.

This inconsistency can be repaired.

▶ CHECK FLAGS IN THE SID TABLE OF AN INFOOBJECT.
This elementary test checks three things:

▹ Whether the specified InfoObject has master data (see InfoObject maintenance, MASTER DATA tab, WITH MASTER DATA checkbox)

▹ Whether the master data tables are available

▹ Whether there are records in the SID table for which the data flag (DATAFL) is set, but not the check flag (CHCKFL)

These types of records lead to errors in the systems and must be corrected.

This inconsistency can be repaired.

▶ INITIAL VALUES IN THE SID TABLES AND MASTER DATA TABLES FOR A CHARACTERISTIC.
After the tables are created on the database, an *initial record* (also called an initial entry) is written in the SID tables and master data tables of a characteristic. This test checks whether there are valid initial records in the SID tables and master data tables. Depending on the master data table, an initial record has different forms:

▹ In an SID table, the initial record has the following structure: the values of the characteristic and (if the characteristic is compounded) higher-level characteristic are blank. The SID field is also blank (= 0). The three indicators CHCKFL, DATAFL, and INCFL have the value 'X'.

- ▶ In a P table, all the fields of the initial record are blank, with the exception of the OBJVERS field, which has the value 'A'.

- ▶ In a Q table, all the fields of the initial record are blank, with the exception of OBJVERS = 'A', DATEFROM = '01.01.1000' and DATETO = '31.12.9999'.

- ▶ In an X table, all the fields are blank, with the exception of the OBJVERS field, which has the value 'A'.

- ▶ In a Y table, all the fields are blank, with the exceptions of the OBJVERS field, which has the value 'A', DATEFROM = '01.01.1000', and DATETO = '31.12.9999'.

This inconsistency can be repaired—the missing initial records are generated.

- ▶ TYPE-RELATED INITIAL VALUE OF THE ATTRIBUTE.
  This test checks the P table and Q table of characteristics with data types NUMC, DATS, or TIMS for initial entry values using SPACE instead of 0. This inconsistency can be repaired.

- ▶ INVALID OBJECT VERSION OF THE CHARACTERISTIC VALUE.
  This test checks that only the following valid combinations of values for OBJVERS and CHANGED fields exist in master data tables, respectively:

  - ▶ 'A' + 'D'
  - ▶ 'A' + ' '
  - ▶ 'M' + 'I'
  - ▶ Other combinations are recognized as errors.

No repair options are available.

- ▶ UNAUTHORIZED CHARACTERS IN CHARACTERISTIC VALUES.
  This test checks the characteristic values existing in the SID table against the following criteria (using the same function module used when data is loaded, RRSV_VALUE_CHECK_PLAUSIBILITY):

  - ▶ Only permitted characters occur in the characteristic values.
  - ▶ The characteristic values match the data type of the characteristic.
  - ▶ The values are available in internal format for characteristics with specific conversion routines.
  - ▶ The values have "meaningful" times for time characteristics.

- The values of the superior characteristics are made up of the above checks for compounded characteristics.

If errors are found, the SID for the characteristic value is also specified. Analyze whether this SID still occurs in the (dimension tables of) InfoCubes. If so, the requests that include invalid characteristic values have to be deleted and reloaded.

If the characteristic values are not used in the InfoCubes, the transaction data is correct. Invalid values could be used in hierarchies or as attribute values for other characteristics.

▶ COMPARE SIZE OF P-, Q- WITH X- AND Y- TABLES RESPECTIVELY.
This simple test compares the number of entries in P, X, Q, and Y tables of the characteristic; they need the same amount of entries at all times. Please note that it is possible, although unlikely, that this test finds no errors, even though P and X, or Q and Y tables are inconsistent to each other.

The X or Y tables are rebuilt in the repair mode. If errors still exist after the repair, there might be missing entries in the SID tables for the navigation attributes of the characteristic. To check this, use the (elementary) tests:

- TYPE-BASED INITIAL VALUES FOR THE ATTRIBUTE.
- INITIAL VALUES IN THE SID- AND MASTER DATA • TABLES FOR A CHARACTERISTIC.

▶ COMPARE CHARACTERISTIC VALUES IN SID-, P- AND Q- TABLES.
This test checks whether the same characteristic values exist in the S, P, and Q master data tables, and if so, it checks the values against the following criteria:

- Characteristic values in the SID table that have been loaded in data records (DATAFL = 'X') also have the check flag (field CHCKFL) = 'X'.
- Characteristic values in the P table that have been loaded in data records have the object version (field OBJVERS) = 'A'.
- Characteristic values in the Q table that have been loaded in data records have the object version (field OBJVERS) = 'A'.

There is no repair option for these inconsistencies.

▶ SID VALUES IN X AND Y TABLES.
This test checks for inconsistencies between the values in the P and X and/or the Q and Y tables.

This inconsistency can be repaired.

- COMPARE NUMBER RANGE AND MAXIMUM SID.
  This elementary test checks whether a number-range object exists for the SIDs of the characteristic. If so, it checks whether the largest SID used is smaller than or has the same status as the number-range object.

  This inconsistency can be repaired.

- CHECK CHARACTERISTIC VALUES WITH CONVERSION EXIT.
  This test checks whether all the values in the SID table of a characteristic with a conversion routine are valid internal values. In this test, the values are first converted from the internal to external format and then back from the external into the internal format. If the result value does not agree with the original, it is not valid.

  There is no repair option for these inconsistencies.

> **Note**
>
> Use Transaction RSMDCNVEXIT to perform conversion for the entire SAP BW system. See SAP Note 447341 for more information about this transaction.

- CHECK FOR CHARACTERISTIC VALUES FROM TEXT TABLE IN SID TABLE.
  The test checks that all key field values in the text table of a characteristic also exist in the SID table for the characteristic.

  This inconsistency can be repaired.

- SID CONVERSION FOR INFOOBJECT 0UNIT.
  This test checks whether the entries in the SID table for 0UNIT lie within valid interval limits as determined by the number-range object `BIM9999996`.

  This inconsistency can be repaired in some cases. In others, there is no repair option. Please read the documentation for this utility in RSRV carefully before proceeding.

- MULTIBYTE-ANALYSIS FOR MASTER DATA TEXT TABLES.
  This test checks text table entries against multibyte code pages for corrupt character values.

  There is no repair option for these inconsistencies.

- TIME OVERLAPS OF LOAD-REQUESTS.
  This test checks whether concurrently running requests have updated the same

master data records during processing (in case of duplicate data records in different data packages).

There is no repair option for these inconsistencies.

Three utilities are available for hierarchies:

▶ CHECK INDIVIDUAL HIERARCHY.
This test checks the parent-child relationships in the hierarchy tables for consistency. This includes checking whether certain artificial (invisible) hierarchy nodes exist and are sorted correctly in the hierarchy.

There is no repair option for these inconsistencies.

▶ HIERARCHY NODE TEXT REFERENCES FOR A CHARACTERISTIC.
This test checks the consistency of hierarchy nodes that are characteristic values by validating the SID entries and the existence of text entries in the hierarchy K-table.

This inconsistency can be repaired.

▶ CHECK ADMINISTRATIVE INFORMATION OF HIERARCHIES.
This check tests the existence and consistency of administration information for the specified hierarchy.

This inconsistency can be repaired.

Use the Transaction RSRV consistency checks to investigate when master data-related issues are encountered, or periodically to confirm the health of the system. Be cautious when using customized ABAP programs to manipulate master data tables and/or entries because this may lead to inconsistencies that cannot be repaired by the discussed checks.

In many cases, invalid or incorrect master data values are loaded and used in transaction data. If there are values that should not exist and have no system of record, there may be a mapping inconsistency somewhere in the data flow. Once the mapping is corrected, the erroneous values should be deleted. However, even if the transaction data is cleaned up, the erroneous master data remains.

Master data values can be deleted only if they are no longer used in any transactions. The first time transaction data is loaded for a master data value, the master data record is flagged in the SID table. These flags preserve the referential integrity of the system by preventing the deletion of any master data that has been used in transactions. However, these flags are not cleared when transaction data is deleted.

It is still possible to delete master data that is no longer used in transactions, but first the system must update the flags by re-determining whether master data values are still being used. Three different algorithms are available for this purpose; each one is optimized for various datasets (small, medium, or large). The algorithm can be chosen explicitly for the delete operation by the user, or the system automatically selects the appropriate one.

To delete master data, right-click the InfoObject in the Data Warehousing Workbench and choose entry DELETE MASTER DATA from the context menu. The pop-up shown in Figure 3.9 allows you to confirm whether master data is used in the system, and if not, whether master data can be deleted. As illustrated, it is possible to choose whether entries in the SID tables and the text tables of a characteristic are to be retained or deleted.

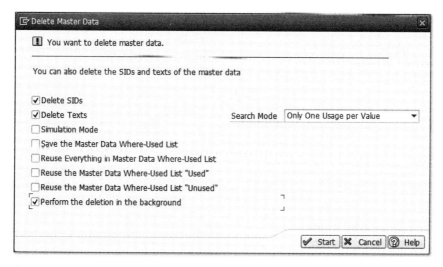

Figure 3.9 Master Data Deletion Screen

Note

If SID table entries for any characteristic values are deleted, the SID values assigned to those characteristic values are lost. If master data for those characteristic values are ever reloaded, new SID values have to be created for the characteristic values. This has a negative effect on the runtime required for loading. In some cases, deleting entries from the SID table can also lead to serious data inconsistencies if the list of used SID values generated from the where-used list is incomplete.

Deleting entries from the SID table is only necessary, or useful, in exceptional cases. The option of deleting master data but retaining the entries from the SID table is usually sufficient.

It is important that the master data in the SAP BW system reconcile with the source systems. Remember that master data management is the collection and execution of practices to ensure uniform and governed master data of high quality, which is both relevant to the business and free of duplicates. Master data that does not exist in the source system is not used in transactions, so it should be removed from the data warehouse. The maintenance and deletion of master data in SAP BW is critical to high quality in reporting.

3.2 Transaction Data

Managing transaction data is conceptually different from managing master data, and the data volumes and organic growth require more constant attention. While master data is usually loaded into a single InfoObject with little redundancy (unless poorly designed), transaction data is staged throughout the warehouse, as described earlier in this chapter, resulting in deliberate redundancy throughout the layers of the architecture.

The advent of SAP HANA and new features like Smart Data Access (SDA) and Operational Data Provisioning (ODP) provide enhanced data provisioning flexibility. This new functionality can help reduce the need to replicate data throughout the data warehouse but does not eliminate it. Most transaction data is still persisted in the data warehouse layer architecture.

To combat the reporting performance impact resulting from the consistent and inevitable growth of data volumes in InfoProviders, it is necessary to resort to an age-old tactic—divide and conquer. This is not only a relational database problem, since even in-memory appliances such as SAP HANA are not immune, considering that the record-count limit for tables in SAP HANA is two billion rows. In SAP BW, the divide-and-conquer tactic is employed on multiple levels in multiple ways.

3.2.1 InfoProvider Partitioning

Earlier in Chapter 2, Section 2.2.1, the concept of semantic (or logical) partitioning was introduced. The introduction of semantically partitioning objects (SPO) accompanied the release of SAP BW 7.30 and can be used for both DSO staging layers and InfoCube layers. Design and use cases for SPOs will be covered in Chapter 5.

For now, let's turn our attention to physical or database partitioning, where the database partitions tables based on specific values defined within the BW application. The OLAP processor then knows where to look for data requested by either of those characteristics, or it will query each partition in parallel if data is requested by any other characteristic. The results are then joined together and presented to the user.

> **Note**
>
> Partitioning is supported by SAP HANA, IBM DB2 (for z/OS and i), Oracle, and Microsoft SQL Server but limited to a specific subset of time characteristics: InfoCubes and DSOs can be partitioned only by calendar month or fiscal year period. For IBM DB2 for Linux, UNIX, and Windows, multidimensional clustering is available instead. Clustering is more flexible than partitioning because it can be configured on more than one characteristic and is not limited to time characteristics.

Though both InfoCubes and DSOs can be partitioned, they handle physical partitioning differently. In DSOs, only the active table is partitioned, and data loaded to the activation queue by request is written to the correct partition during activation. The change log is not partitioned because it is not queried by end-user reporting.

Since InfoCubes are multi-dimensional models with only DIMIDs in the fact tables, they need a different structure to enable efficient partitioning. To optimize read performance, a partitioning column is added to the fact table and used in query joins. The master data IDs (SIDs) of the partitioning characteristics are then filled in the partitioning column according to the entries in the time dimension when new data requests are loaded.

Standard InfoCubes have two fact tables—the F-fact table and the E-fact table. The *F-fact table* is always partitioned by data package to improve data load performance. This means that all records loaded from one source at one time are written to the same partition. Records are aggregated during the transformation or update rules so that only inserts need to be performed, substantially improving database write performance.

Only the *E-fact table* partitioning can be changed, and by default it is not partitioned at all. Because partitioning is available only by calendar year or fiscal period, the only reason not to partition the E-fact table would be that neither time characteristic exists in the InfoCube. Regardless of the partitioning strategy, data is only written to the E-fact table during compression. During compression, all records with the same key values across the data package partitions in the F-fact table are aggregated into a single record in the E-fact table. In this way, the data volume of the InfoCube can be managed when a high number of delta records results in substantial growth.

> **Note**
>
> If E-fact table partitioning is based on fiscal year period (OFISCPER), the fiscal year variant (OFISCVARNT) must be set to a constant in the InfoProvider. If data has already been loaded to the InfoCube and all data records in the cube are assigned to just one fiscal variant, you can use program RSDU_SET_FV_TO_FIX_VALUE to set the fiscal variant to a fixed value.

Consider a single sales order, which may endure four or five changes over its lifetime. Each change, when loaded through a DSO, generates two delta records; the first is a reversal of the previous values loaded (before image), and the second is the new value (after image). If left uncompressed, the F-fact table would store from nine to 11 records for this one sales order, which would need to be aggregated during query execution. Compression reduces these records to a single record in the E-fact table, reducing data volume to an average 10% of the F-fact table and, therefore, significantly improves both data loading and query performance. Use program SAP_INFOCUBE_DESIGNS to check the size of the E-fact and F-fact tables to identify InfoCubes with large F-fact tables that are candidates for compression.

> **Note**
>
> SAP recommends that the number of partitions not exceed specific thresholds to maintain optimal performance:
>
> ▸ F-fact table should not exceed 30-50 partitions
> ▸ E-fact table should not exceed 100-120 partitions

> **Recommendation**
>
> Always compress with elimination of zeroes turned on unless there is a specific need to report zero-value records, as opposed to records that do not exist (null values).

Over time in an operational data warehouse, data may need to be reloaded to correct business logic bugs or erroneous mappings between stage layers. If data is selectively deleted from InfoCubes, specific values are deleted from both the E-fact and the F-fact tables. In this case, there may be empty partitions in the F-fact table if all the records are selectively deleted. Empty partitions add no value and claim space on the database even though they are empty, so they should be dropped from the database. Use report SAP_DROP_EMPTY_FPARTITIONS to drop empty partitions in the InfoCube fact table.

> **Note**
>
> See SAP Note 590370, Too Many Uncompressed Requests (F-table Partitions), for more information on report SAP_DROP_EMPTY_FPARTITIONS.

3.2.2   Repartitioning

After data is loaded to an InfoCube, the partitioning properties cannot be changed using the maintenance interface or by transport request. However, it may be necessary to repartition the E-fact table for various reasons. SAP has provided a repartitioning tool that provides three different types of repartitioning:

▶ ATTACHING PARTITIONS

Use this option to add partitions to an E-fact table or DSO-active table that is already partitioned, but only before the initial number of partitions has been exhausted. For example, if the initial partitioning covered the time period up to December 2014, new partitions need to be added to ensure that data for 2015 and beyond does not get written to the overflow partition. If data for 2015 has already been written to the overflow partition, use the complete partitioning option.

▶ MERGING PARTITIONS

Use this option to merge empty or almost-empty partitions of an E-fact or DSO-active table that is already partitioned. If older partitions contain few or no data records, due to either fewer business transactions during a particular time period or data management activities such as archiving, these partitions should be merged into the underflow partition in order to reduce the number of partitions in the database catalog.

▶ COMPLETE REPARTITIONING

Use this option to partition an E-fact table or DSO-active table that has data but has never been partitioned, or to repartition these tables based on new requirements. This option is useful if the original partitioning schema needs to be adjusted because some partitions are too large, or data has been loaded to the overflow partition before new partitions could be added. Complete repartitioning is suitable for general use and can be used for creating partitions for the first time, as well as adding and merging partitions.

> **Note**
>
> Complete repartitioning always requires additional disk space as the data in the fact tables are copied to shadow tables. Depending on the size of the DSO or InfoCube, complete repartitioning could take several hours because the original data is physically copied, new indexes are created, and table statistics are calculated.

Unlike complete repartitioning, in which the data from partitioned tables must be completely copied and converted, the options to attach and merge partitions involve only a sequence of database catalog operations if there is not yet data in the overflow partition or the partitions to be merged are empty. Therefore, the runtime for these database catalog operations is usually just a few minutes.

> **Note**
>
> Read the corresponding documentation in SAP Note 1008833 before executing repartitioning using program RSDU_REPART_UI.

See Figure 3.10 for a screenshot of the repartitioning interface that can be accessed by executing program RSDU_REPART_UI. After selecting the InfoProvider to be repartitioned, select a processing option ❶ based on the use cases described earlier. To execute the repartitioning option, choose INITIALIZE ❷. To monitor a current or previous repartitioning job, choose MONITOR ❸. In this example, new partitions have been successfully added to a COPA InfoCube.

A complete list of the processing steps for repartitioning an InfoCube is compiled in Table 3.3. A repartitioning request can be canceled and reset with minimal side effects in any processing step before SWITCH_EFACT. Up to this point, the repartitioning request is working on only shadow tables and aggregates, but it may be necessary to reactivate inactive aggregates and E-fact and F-fact table views.

> **Note**
>
> The processing steps SWITCH_EFACT and SWITCH_FFACT are critical, and if any errors occur, they must be corrected manually by SAP Support.

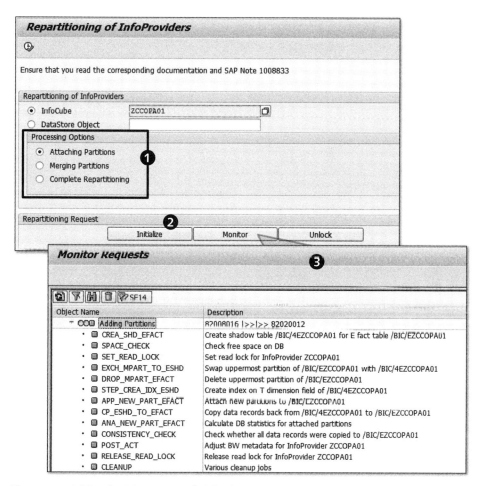

Figure 3.10 Adding Partitions to an InfoCube (Program RSDU_REPART_UI)

Processing Step	Description
CREA_SHD_EFACT	Create an empty shadow table for the F-fact table with a partitioning column. The shadow table uses the naming convention /BI<x>/4E<InfoCube>.
CREA_SHD_FFACT	Create an empty shadow table for the F-fact table with a partitioning column. The shadow table uses the naming convention /BI<x>/4F<InfoCube>.

Table 3.3 Repartitioning Tasks in Sequence of Execution

Processing Step	Description
SPACE_CHECK	Check whether there is sufficient free disk space to execute the repartitioning.
COPY_TO_SHD_EFACT	Copy the data records from the E-fact table to the shadow table /BI<x>/4E<InfoCube> using parallel processing.
COPY_TO_SHD_FFACT	Copy the data records from the F-fact table to the shadow table /BI<x>/4F<InfoCube> using parallel processing.
CREA_IDX	Create an index on both shadow tables.
SET_READ_LOCK	Set a read lock for the InfoCube because correct results cannot be guaranteed during repartitioning.
INA_AGGR	Deactivate all aggregates for the InfoCube.
DELETE_FACTVIEW	Delete the E-fact and F-fact table views.
CHECK_EFACT	Check if data records have been completely copied from the E-fact table to the corresponding shadow table /BI<x>/4E<InfoCube>.
CHECK_FFACT	Check whether data records have been completely copied from the F-fact table to the corresponding shadow table /BI<x>/4F<InfoCube>.
SWITCH_EFACT	Replace the E-fact table with the corresponding shadow table /BI<x>/4E<InfoCube> and rename the indexes.
SWITCH_FFACT	Replace the F-fact table with the corresponding shadow table /BI<x>/4F<InfoCube> and rename the indexes.
CREA_FACTVIEW	Create the views of the E-fact and F-fact tables.
POST_ACT	Adjust the SAP BW metadata, activate the update rules, and generate and activate the load program.
REPA_IDX	Check whether all indexes were created correctly and recreate or repair missing or incorrect indexes.
ANALYZE	Calculate database statistics for E-fact and F-fact tables.
RELEASE_READ_LOCK	Release the read lock (the InfoCube is now available for reporting again).
CLEANUP	Execute various cleanup operations.

Table 3.3 Repartitioning Tasks in Sequence of Execution (Cont.)

After you process step `SWITCH_FFACT`, the fact tables have the target structure and the shadow tables have the original structure, so it does not make sense to reset the repartitioning request after this step is reached. Because the SAP BW metadata has not yet been adjusted, errors occurring on or after processing step `CREA_FACT-VIEW` should only be recovered forward.

After processing step `POST_ACT`, the SAP BW metadata is consistent with the new structure of the fact tables. The subsequent processing steps are not critical and can be executed manually, if necessary. While it is possible to reset or delete the repartitioning request after this point, it still does not make sense to do so because the repartitioning is almost complete.

> **Note**
>
> After repartitioning, the shadow tables /BI<x>/4F<InfoCube> and /BI<x>/4E<Info-Cube> contain the original data in the original structure, which can be valuable for recovery or analysis if errors occur. Therefore, these tables are not deleted as part of the CLEANUP step and must be deleted manually.

3.2.3   InfoProvider Maintenance

Recall that Transaction RSRV provides consistency checks for SAP BW-specific objects. It includes several utilities for transaction data, which may need to be used far more routinely than those for master data. Figure 3.11 shows transaction data, DataStore, and PSA utilities available in Transaction RSRV.

The following utilities are relevant for InfoCubes:

▶ CONSISTENCY OF THE TIME DIMENSION FOR AN INFOCUBE
This test checks whether the time characteristics of the InfoCube used in the time dimension are consistent. For example, if an InfoCube has both `OCALDAY` and `OCALMONTH`, the date mapped to calendar day should be in the same month as what is mapped to calendar month. Time-characteristic consistency is extremely important for non-cumulative InfoCubes and partitioned InfoCubes. Inconsistencies result in performance impacts and the return of incorrect data to queries.

There is no automatic repair option available for inconsistent transactions—data needs to be reloaded with consistent values. However, inconsistent time-dimension table entries can be deleted if they are no longer used.

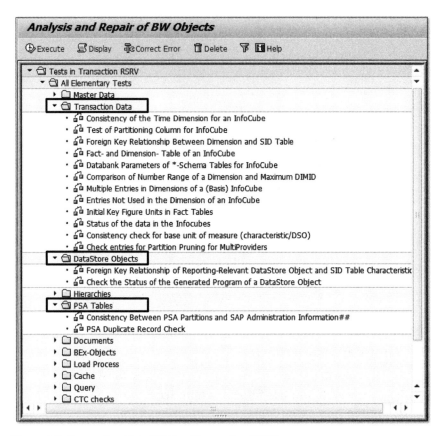

Figure 3.11 Transaction Data Utilities (Transaction RSRV)

▶ TEST OF PARTITIONING COLUMN FOR INFOCUBE
This test checks whether the partitioning column is populated for all records in the F-fact table.

This inconsistency can be repaired.

▶ FOREIGN KEY RELATIONSHIP BETWEEN DIMENSION AND SID TABLE
This test checks whether each SID value in the dimension table entry exists in the appropriate SID table.

There are no automatic repair options. Try deleting unused dimension table entries and test again. If the issue is not solved, the InfoCube needs to be dropped and reloaded to ensure referential integrity.

- FACT AND DIMENSION TABLE OF AN INFOCUBE
  This elementary test checks the foreign-key relationship between a fact table and a dimensions table. It checks whether the DIMIDs in the fact table exist in the appropriate dimension tablets.

  There are no automatic repair options. Try deleting unused dimension table entries and test again. If the issue is not solved, the InfoCube needs to be dropped and reloaded to ensure referential integrity,

- DATABANK PARAMETERS OF *-SCHEMA TABLES FOR INFOCUBE
  This test checks whether the database parameters are set correctly for all the tables that belong to the star schema of an InfoCube. This test is database-dependent, so it may not be relevant to all databases. Read the log for more information.

- COMPARISON OF NUMBER RANGE OF A DIMENSION AND MAXIMUM DIMID
  This elementary test checks whether a number-range object exists for the dimension of an InfoCube, and, if so, whether the largest DIMID is less than or equal to the current value of the number range object.

  This inconsistency can be repaired.

- MULTIPLE ENTRIES IN DIMENSIONS OF A (BASIS) INFOCUBE
  This elementary test checks whether there are any redundant entries in a dimension table — that is, more than one DIMID with the same SIDs, which can occur when using parallel loading jobs.

  An inconsistency can be repaired.

- ENTRIES NOT USED IN THE DIMENSION OF AN INFOCUBE
  This test checks whether all DIMIDs are used in a fact table. This inconsistency can occur if records are deleted from the fact table or compressed with elimination of zeroes.

  Deletion of unused dimension entries can help control the growth of dimension tables and improve performance.

  Inconsistencies can be repaired.

> **Note**
>
> Unused dimension entries can also be detected and deleted by scheduling report RSDDCVER_DIM_UNUSED on a regular basis.

▶ INITIAL KEY FIGURE UNITS IN FACT TABLES
This check tests whether any records exist in the E-fact and F-fact tables with zero key figure values and blank unit values.

There is no automatic repair option. Data must be reloaded to resolve this inconsistency.

▶ STATUS OF THE DATA IN THE INFOCUBES
This test checks whether InfoCube entries exist in table RSMDATASTATE and, if so, whether the field values are consistent.

There is no automatic repair option—inconsistent InfoCubes should be reactivated.

The following checks are relevant only for DSOs:

▶ FOREIGN KEY RELATIONSHIP OF REPORTING-RELEVANT DATASTORE OBJECT AND SID TABLE CHARACTERISTICS
This test checks whether each characteristic value in the active table exists in the appropriate SID table.

There are no automatic repair options. Data must be reloaded to either the InfoObject or DSO to resolve this inconsistency.

▶ CHECK THE STATUS OF THE GENERATED PROGRAM OF A DATASTORE OBJECT
This test checks whether the generated program for a DSO exists in the active version.

There are no automatic repair options. Reactivate the DSO to resolve this inconsistency.

In most cases, the utilities available in Transaction RSRV can help identify and resolve data inconsistencies within InfoProviders. However, there are many other checks that should be performed routinely to assess the overall design of each InfoProvider and ensure that it is delivering optimal performance.

If the number of entries in a dimension table exceeds 10-20% of the number of entries in the fact tables of an InfoCube, the dimension may need to be remodeled. See Chapter 5 for more information on modeling InfoProviders for optimal performance.

3.2.4 Aggregates

The usage of aggregates needs to be monitored on a regular basis. Over time, end-user behavior and data models can change, rendering some aggregates obsolete while fostering a need for new aggregates. Since aggregates are redundant copies of data in InfoCubes at a summarized level, proliferation of such objects can significantly impact a system's storage-capacity needs. In addition, rolling up aggregates during transaction data loads and the re-alignment during master data activation can adversely impact the data loading schedule. Therefore, it is prudent to control aggregate proliferation and monitor aggregate usage to ensure that existing ones are providing a performance benefit. This section covers aggregate management; aggregate design will be covered in Chapter 5.

Table RSDDAGGRDIR provides the information on the number of times an aggregate is used by queries. Check the table periodically and deactivate those aggregates for which the field CALLS = 0 and object version OBJVERS = 'A'. Aggregates can be deactivated programmatically using function module RSDDK_AGGREGATES_DEACTIVATE.

In systems in which BWA has replaced the need for aggregates, you should deactivate aggregates rather than deleting them. Inactive aggregates are not filled, are never used when executing queries, and do not have an impact on master data change runs. However, if there is ever an issue with the BWA appliance or indexes, the inactive aggregates can be quickly activated and filled to ameliorate the situation.

3.2.5   BW Accelerator

The use of BWA can dramatically improve query performance on InfoCubes and DSOs, but the technology requires a specific hardware appliance with separate licensing arrangements with SAP. In most cases, licensing is based on the amount of productive memory used, so it is economically beneficial to limit the data stored in BWA indexes. In addition, the creation or roll-up of indexes is executed during the data load process and, therefore, can increase data load durations, although index roll-ups are generally much faster than aggregate roll-ups.

Routine monitoring and maintenance of BWA indexes can help ensure that the investment provides the most value to the end users. First, it is important to choose the right queries to optimize. Up-to-date statistics are critical to identifying queries that are candidates for BWA. Review statistical data from table RSDDSTAT_OLAP for queries with high Data Manager times, as opposed to OLAP processing times. These queries spend more time hitting the database than the OLAP processor, where calculations and conversions are performed.

Even when the right indexes are in place, they still need to be monitored to ensure that they are using the appropriate amount of BWA memory. Over time, BWA indexes can grow and become larger than fact tables in the BI system. To identify these indexes, periodically execute the BI and BWA table comparison check in Transaction RSRV, and rebuild indexes for which there is a significant deviation. In addition to index growth, it is also necessary to adjust or rebuild indexes after changes are made to the relevant InfoProvider. If delta indexes are used, they must be routinely merged with the main index. However, it is also prudent to routinely rebuild the entire index to ensure that memory is being released from the delta indexes.

There are additional Transaction RSRV checks available for BWA that should be used in conjunction with BWA alerts. BWA alerts can be configured via the TREX Admin tool on the BWA itself. Use Transaction RSDDBIAMON to access BWA and monitor the indexes on it.

> **Recommendation**
>
> Execute all the Transaction RSRV checks for BWA whenever a new BWA revision is applied.

As indexes grow in size, it may be necessary to also reorganize or redistribute indexes across the blades in the appliance. This capability can be launched from the BI Accelerator Monitor RSDDBIAMON2.

3.3 Temporary Data

During the load processing of large volumes of master and transaction data into BW, there is usually a significant amount of storage consumed by temporary transaction data and system-related metadata. Routine housekeeping activities should remove unused, unwanted, and unneeded data; these activities are the focus of Part III of this book, which covers administration activities for a live SAP BW system. Performing these activities regularly ensures optimal utilization of system resources and increased system performance.

According to SAP's Data Volume Management (DVM) service, data deletion is one of the four recommended methodologies to check potential database growth. (The other methodologies are avoidance, summarization, and archiving.) As shown in Figure 3.12, one-third of the storage space in the average SAP BW database is occupied by temporary data (PSA and DSO change logs). This should not be a surprise. In fact, in our experience, we have observed PSA and change-log data consuming up to two-thirds of the storage space in some SAP BW systems!

The size of the PSA and change logs can be explained by the fact that entries in these tables are never updated or overwritten. The only operations on these tables are inserts or deletions. For example, full loads on a periodic basis increase the size of the PSA table much faster than the actual data target, which is either overwritten, in the case of a DSO or an InfoObject, or dropped and reloaded, in the case of an InfoCube or InfoObject. For delta loads, changes to previously extracted records are overwritten in DSOs and InfoObjects or compressed into a single record in InfoCubes (assuming compression occurs routinely).

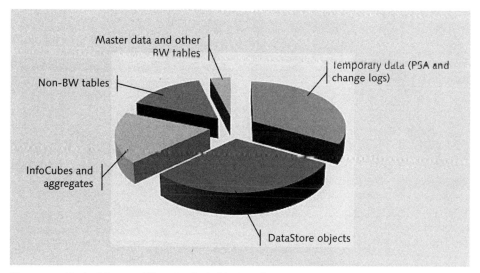

Figure 3.12 Typical Storage Allocation by Table Type for an SAP BW System

From a strategic perspective, the only reasons to retain entries in the PSA tables are to facilitate error resolution and mitigate the need to re-extract data from sources that are either poor-performing or delta-capable. In the case of full loads, only the latest PSA entry should be retained; all other entries can be deleted once the latest entry is successfully loaded into the PSA. For delta loads, a retention period for PSA data should be set based on the risk of data loss (i.e., data should not be deleted from the PSA before it is loaded to all subsequent data targets). In most cases, 15 days is more than sufficient to mitigate this risk. In many cases, a full repair load can be executed to recover any lost deltas without a significant performance impact, so this risk is usually applicable for delta DataSources that require the population of setup tables in the source system before full repairs can be carried out, such as LIS DataSources in the logistics cockpit.

The deletion strategy for PSA tables should differentiate between master data and transaction data, full loads and delta loads, and DataSources and setup tables. Change logs should be treated like delta loads for transaction data. An additional consideration should be the periodicity of the data load from the source. For example, if a full InfoPackage is loaded monthly, the previous month's load should be retained in the PSA, meaning the retention period should be 31 days. Table 3.4 illustrates a sample deletion strategy for daily loads in a typical SAP BW system.

Table Type	DataSource	Extraction Mode	Delete Entries Older Than
PSA	Master data	Full	1 day
PSA	Master data	Delta	3 days
PSA	Transaction data	Full	1 day
PSA	Transaction data	Delta	8 days
PSA	Transaction data with setup table	Delta	15 days
Change log	Transaction data	Delta	8 days

Table 3.4 Sample Deletion Strategy for Daily Load PSA and Change Log Tables

The best way to delete data from the PSA and change log tables is by scheduling the relevant process variants in the process chains after data has been loaded successfully. These process variants enable flexible deletion using selection criteria, and the parameter screens accept parameters with patterns on DataSource (for PSA tables) and DSOs (for change logs). Even though the acceptance of patterns in the selection criteria simplifies maintenance of the deletion jobs, PSA and change log tables are still too easily omitted from cleansing. To combat this, there are custom programs published on SCN that can help identify those tables with entries that are "unmanaged" or otherwise excluded from existing deletion variants.

For one time use, PSA tables can be deleted using either program RSPSADEL1 or function module RSATREE_PSA_DELETE_BATCH. We don't recommend that you use these programs routinely because PSA deletions should not be scheduled while data is being loaded; it is best to schedule the relevant process variants directly in the process chains after data has been loaded. This helps mitigate the risk of database contention by ensuring that these conflicting jobs do not overlap.

In SAP BW, database objects such as tables or views are created dynamically during query execution or other processes and read data from InfoProviders. These tables have the '/BIO/0' name prefix and are always created within the ABAP Dictionary, so they are visible with Transaction SE11 and other SAP DDIC transactions. All these temporary tables are released and dropped during normal system operation and so do not need to be deleted unless a large number of temporary tables have been created due to some exceptional circumstance. If the situation warrants cleansing, use program SAP_DROP_TMPTABLES to delete these temporary tables.

> **Note**
>
> For further details on program SAP_DROP_TMPTABLES, please refer to SAP Note 1139396 and make sure the latest version of the program is available (Note 1106393). Similar information on temporary indexes used during BWA processing can be found in SAP Note 1168412.

The next group of tables that should be cleansed routinely — in order of impact on storage capacity in a typical SAP BW system — is the metadata tables, such as request administration and application logs. Many of the request administration tables can be archived using SAP-delivered archiving objects in Transaction SARA, which will be covered in the next section. Many of the remaining tables and logs can be cleansed using standard programs; Table 3.5 offers a list of recommended activities and programs.

Executable	Type	Description
SM58	TCODE	Delete tRFC queues
RSWR_BOOKMARK_REORG	PGM	Reorganize BEx web application bookmarks
RSRD_BOOKMARK_REORGANISATION	PGM	Reorganize BEx broadcaster bookmarks

Table 3.5 Routine Housekeeping Activities for SAP BW

Executable	Type	Description
RSWB_ROLES_REORG	PGM	Reorganize roles and favorites workbooks
SLG2	TCODE	Delete expired application logs
RSRLDREL	PGM	Delete links between ALE and Idocs
RSBATCH_DEL_MSG_PARM_DTPTEMP Use parameters DEL_MSG = 3, DEL_PAR = 3 and DEL_DTP = X	PGM	Delete BI background management messages and parameters
RSAR_PSA_PARTITION_CHECK, SAP_PSA_PARTNO_CORRECT, RSAR_PSA_CLEANUP_DIRECTORY and RSAR_PSA_CLEANUP_DEFINITION	PGM	Check and clean PSA tables
RSSM_ERRORLOG_CLEANUP	PGM	Reorganize PSA error log
RSB_ANALYZE_ERRORLOG	PGM	Analyze the error log
RSBM_ERRORLOG_DELETE	PGM	Delete old or inconsistent error DTPs
RSPC_INSTANCE_CLEANUP and RSPC_LOG_DELETE	PGM	Delete old process chain logs
RS_FIND_JOBS_WITHOUT_VARIANT	PGM	Delete jobs without variant
RSBTCDEL2	PGM	Delete old job logs
RSSODFRE	PGM	Reorganize hidden folder Office Documents
RSBCS_REORG	PGM	Reorganize SAP Office/Business Workplace documents
SCU3	TCODE	Check table change logs (DBTABLOG)
RSTBPDEL	PGM	Delete old table change logs (DBTABLOG)

Table 3.5 Routine Housekeeping Activities for SAP BW (Cont.)

Executable	Type	Description
SP12 TEMSE DATA STORAGE • CONSISTENCY CHECK	TCODE	Reorganize TemSe and spool (printing)
SP00041	PGM	Delete old spool requests
RSTS0024	PGM	Delete orphaned job logs
RSTT_TRACE_DELETE	PGM	Delete BW RSTT traces
ANALYZE_RSZ_TABLES	PGM	Check entries of RSZ tables (BI query elements)

Table 3.5 Routine Housekeeping Activities for SAP BW (Cont.)

Note
SAP strongly recommends, and we agree, that you perform these housekeeping activities for log and metadata tables larger than 100 MB or 100,000 lines.

3.3.1 SAP BW Archiving Objects

It is not uncommon for systems that have been in operation for extended periods of time to have large system tables. However, this is unnecessary because much of this information can be archived using standard archiving objects; Table 3.6 shows the SAP BW information that can be archived with minimal configuration. The properties of each archiving object can be seen and maintained in Transaction AOBJ.

Archiving Object	Description
BWREQARCH	Request administration and log information
IDOC	IDoc types RSINFO, RSSEND, and RSREQUEST
RSECPROT	BI authorization logs
RSEC_CHLOG	BI authorization change logs

Table 3.6 SAP BW Archiving Objects

Archiving is configured and executed using Transaction SARA (archive administration). Before archiving can be executed, the archive file path must be defined. For each archiving object listed in Table 3.6, choose CUSTOMIZING and then select CROSS CLIENT FILE NAMES/PATHS under BASIS CUSTOMIZING. Define the file name and path, which can also be accessed directly in Transaction FILE. Return to the Customizing menu and confirm or change the default technical settings for the archiving object.

Once the configuration is complete, you can execute archiving in two steps: write data to the archive file and then delete the data from the tables. Both steps must be executed before the archiving run is considered complete. You can monitor the status of current and previous archiving runs using the MANAGEMENT button.

> **Note**
>
> In the technical settings for the archiving object, you can configure deletion to happen automatically after the archive files are successfully written.

In some cases, there are alternatives to using Transaction SARA to archive data. For example, each archiving object, such as BWREQARCH, has programs that can be used to produce the same result:

▶ RSREQARCH_WRITE

▶ RSREQARCH_DELETE

▶ RSREQARCH_RELOAD

In other cases, records can be deleted directly without archiving. For example, it may not make much sense to archive authorization logs (archiving object RSECPROT) if they are used only to trace and resolve authorization issues. Once the issues have been resolved, the traces do not need to be kept and can be deleted.

3.3.2 Archiving Request Administration Data

Every time a request is displayed in the extraction monitor, the data transfer process (DTP) monitor, or the administration of an InfoProvider, the system checks whether the administration tables and log tables of the DTP/InfoPackage are complete. If the entries for each request are incomplete or missing in the table, the technical and QM status is reset in all the targets filled by those requests. As these tables grow, performance is naturally affected, but records cannot be deleted from these tables, or else the administration/display of requests fails.

When archiving request administration data, administration and log information about requests is stored in archive files and deleted from system tables. However, totals records are retained in relevant tables to prevent the status of archived requests from being changed because the detail information is missing. In this way, the reduction in request administration tables improves performance of all the request-related activities just described without affecting the status set by the system.

> **Note**
>
> The header table of the requests, table RSREQDONE, is not archived. It contains one record for each request that contains information about the status of the archiving.

Request data is archived from the tables shown in Table 3.7.

Table	Changes upon Archiving
RSSELDONE	One record remains in the table for each archived request; further records for the same request are deleted after archiving.
RSLDTDONE	Entries for the selected request are deleted after archiving.
RSDELDONE	
RSHIEDONE	
RSRULEDONE	
RSMONMESS	
RSMONRQTAB	
RSMONFACT	
RSUICDONE	
RSTCPDONE	
RSCRTDONE	
RSMONICTAB	
RSMONIPTAB	

Table 3.7 Request Administration Tables Affected by BWREQARCH

Table	Changes upon Archiving
RSBMONMESS	
RSBMNODES	Entries for the selected request are compressed after archiving.
RSBMLOGPAR	

Table 3.7 Request Administration Tables Affected by BWREQARCH (Cont.)

The archiving concept for request administration data is based on the SAP NetWeaver data archiving concept. The archiving object BWREQARCH contains information about which database tables are used for archiving and which programs are executed (the write, delete, and reload programs). These programs are executed in the archive administration transaction. In addition, archiving runs for requests can be managed in the Administration functional area of the Data Warehousing Workbench.

Note

For certain functions and processes that access requests, request administration data is reloaded to the administration and log tables.

Recommendation

To avoid reloading data from the archive unnecessarily, you should archive administration data only from requests that are more than three months old and will probably not be edited again.

3.3.3 Statistics and Technical Content

In prior BW versions, statistics tables also had a tendency to grow quite large. These tables start with Transaction RSDDSTAT* and record statistics on everything from data loading to end-user reporting. As soon as data is loaded in the technical content data targets, it can be purged from the redundant database tables. These tables can be deleted manually using Transaction RSDDSTAT or program RSDDSTAT_DATA_ DELETE, but the recommended approach is to set the RSADMIN parameter TCT_KEEP_ OLAP_DM_DATA_N_DAYS. As of SAP BW 7.30, the default value for this parameter is 14 days, so unless there is a need to keep the data for shorter or longer periods, nothing else needs to be done. The older data is deleted automatically when deltas are loaded successfully into the technical content data targets.

A new technical content introduced with SAP BW 7.30 is Database Volume Statistics (InfoCube `0TCT_C25`), which provides information on data volumes of various BW objects. With this content, database volumes can be analyzed according to InfoArea, application component, SAP BW object types, and SAP BW-specific table classifications. The purpose of this data model is to analyze database growth and size from an SAP BW perspective, using typical SAP BW taxonomy and dependencies:

- Hierarchical display of InfoArea (for InfoProviders) and application component (for DataSources).
- Database table size (before and after DB compression)
- Logical database size (number of rows × record size)
- Derivation of BW object metadata information from the underlying database table name

This technical content can be leveraged to support the following use cases, among others:

- Providing support for housekeeping activities like archiving and periodic PSA and change log deletion.
- Service-level agreement (SLA) monitoring of implemented reporting scenarios for cross-charging costs to business departments.

Examining all available statistical information, including reporting statistics, data loading statistics, and database growth can also be very useful in helping define a data retention strategy for the data models in the warehouse, which is the subject of the next section.

3.4 Data Retention Strategy

In an operational data warehouse, it is natural for the volume of data to perpetually increase, which is known as *organic growth*. Constant changes to business and legal requirements mean that this data must be available for longer than ever before. The impact of keeping a large volume of data in the system is generally a decrease in performance and an increase in administration effort. To combat and manage these impacts, you should implement a data aging strategy early in the lifecycle of the data warehouse; such a strategy can have a profound influence on design and architecture.

Efficient storage of historical data for comprehensive enterprise data warehousing is essential to maintaining a healthy and high-performing system. Consider the following advantages of a carefully planned data retention strategy:

- Reduced infrastructure costs
  - Storage capacity costs
  - Processing capacity costs
- Improved performance of the SAP BW system
  - Query performance
  - Data-loading performance
  - System administration performance
- Reduced administration and maintenance effort
  - Reloading and re-partitioning effort
  - Data management effort

When considering a data retention strategy, there are always trade-offs: benefits and costs, as well as advantages and risks. The decision on what data should remain available and accessible to end users is fraught with consequences.

However, the good news is that there is solid advice available since this dilemma has been wrestled with many times before. To start, it may be helpful to consider some of the following questions:

- At what point does a lack of processing capability incurred by the data volume become unacceptable? In other words, what is the data volume threshold above which response times are intolerable?
- Are there any catastrophic consequences associated with loss of processing for this system?
- What other systems or processes does the data retention strategy affect or feed? How many downstream systems rely on data availability in this data warehouse?
- What is the cost and elapsed time of restoring or recreating the data that is no longer retained?
- Is there a legal requirement (such as a litigation hold, court order, or law) to retain the data or keep the system operational?

▶ What are the exposures related to residual risks of keeping old data available for reporting? What liabilities are inherent in lieu of adopting a strictly enforced data retention strategy?

The greatest complexity related to defining a data retention strategy is that answering these questions requires candid discussion and agreement among infrastructure, technical support, and business representatives. To add a bit more complexity is to recognize that the data retention requirements for each subject area or line of business may be completely different. The good news is that a data retention strategy need not be "one size fits all." In fact, multiple options are available, and the success of the whole strategy may depend on defining unique data-aging tactics for each area based on specific data content and the business value of accessing that data.

The specific options or tactics available range from doing nothing (i.e., keeping all data available online forever) to deleting data directly from the database, with no option for recovery. Thankfully, there are also several options in between! Again, because these options may influence design and architecture, defining the data aging or retention strategy should not be deferred, or a significant effort to re-design or re-architect may result.

The key point is that as data ages, details lose relevance. Keeping irrelevant data online not only adversely impacts performance (in read and write operations), but also increases administration and maintenance efforts and costs. The following list ranks different data retention tactics in order of data availability online, and, indirectly, data relevance:

1. Detail InfoProviders

2. History InfoProviders

3. Summary InfoProviders

4. Near-line storage (NLS)

5. Traditional archiving

6. Data deletion

Note

Traditional archiving is not available for customer data loaded to SAP BW InfoProviders; however, it is available for system administration data, such as IDocs and application logs. Please refer to the previous section for more details on archiving.

From a purely technical perspective, the first step to defining which tactic is suitable for each data set is to determine the usage of the relevant data sets. The technical content statistics are a great place to start—check the number of navigations and number of users who are executing queries on each InfoProvider for that data set (i.e., subject area). Ranking each InfoProvider by usage and performance is a good way to initiate discussions with the business on the need for a data retention strategy. The flaw in this approach is the inability to decipher the age of the data being queried from the statistical information available, so engaging the business on end-user behavior is critical to fully understanding how the data is being consumed. A general guideline to follow is illustrated by Table 3.8 data used more frequently should be kept online, and data used less frequently is a candidate for being kept offline.

	Detail Info-Providers	Historical Info-Providers	Summary Info Providers	Near-line Storage	Data Archiving	Data Deletion
Frequently queried data	X	X	X			
Rarely used data	~	X	X	X		
Very rarely used data		~	X	X	X	
Expired or obsolete data			~	X	X	X

Table 3.8 Data Retention Tactics versus Data Access Frequency

While no single tactic should be employed for all data sets, Table 3.8 illustrates some general guidelines that can be employed fairly consistently. Before proceeding, it would be a valuable exercise to review the tactics above in a little more detail and evaluate the advantages and disadvantages of each approach.

The first three tactics (detail, historical, and summary InfoProviders) influence the design of the data models in the warehouse, the fourth one (NLS) influences the system architecture, and the final two (data archiving and data deletion) influence only the warehouse administration.

First and foremost, any and all data that is frequently accessed should remain available in full detail. In fact, all available details of each transaction should be available in order to minimize the need to enhance the data structure to add data fields later. This is the default tactic and is represented by the first column in Table 3.8, labeled DETAIL INFOPROVIDERS. The other columns represent alternative tactics to the default.

The use of history InfoProviders involves the creation of a new InfoProvider where old data is loaded at the original granularity, or level of detail. Current data remains in the original InfoProvider. After data is moved to the history cube, it must be deleted from the original InfoProvider so that queries do not return duplicate data.

The historical InfoProvider tactic provides the following benefits:

► Storing historical data in a semantic partition improves performance of read/write access to the original InfoProvider because most loading and querying is done against current data in the original cube, which has less data.

► All data, current and historical, remains available online and can be accessed in the same query when both the historical and current InfoProviders are part-providers of the same MultiProvider.

► There is no custom programming required to implement historical InfoProviders, so development is simple. Mapping transformation rules from the original InfoProvider to the historical InfoProvider are 1:1.

However, the historical InfoProvider is associated with a few disadvantages:

► The cost/benefit value associated with maintaining historical data is low. As the older data loses relevance and is accessed less frequently but remains on-line, the cost per storage unit equals the cost of more relevant data.

► Unless an automated mechanism is developed, data moved from the original InfoProvider to the historical InfoProvider must be selectively deleted from the original InfoProvider, which requires planning and execution effort, as well as data-loading downtime.

► There is not a reduction in infrastructure costs (storage capacity) or in administration effort. In fact, the existence of historical data may result in increased administration effort because changes made to the original InfoProvider may need to be applied to the historical InfoProvider to keep results consistent.

Rather than keeping historical data at the same granularity as relevant or current data, another option is to simplify the data model and summarize the data. As the details lose relevance, this approach can be very practical to keep the relevant information available. The following are advantages of a summary InfoProvider:

▶ Storing summarized data in a specific InfoProvider improves performance of read/write access to the original InfoProvider because most loading and querying is done against current data in the original cube, which has less data.

▶ Summarized data, current and historical, remains available online and can be accessed in the same query when both the summarized and current InfoProviders are part-providers of the same MultiProvider.

▶ There is minimal custom programming required to implement summary Info-Providers, so development is simple. Mapping transformation rules from the original InfoProvider to the summary InfoProvider are usually 1:1.

▶ Data in the summary InfoProvider can be aggregated by more than one characteristic, thus compounding the value of the summary InfoProvider.

▶ Query response times against the summary InfoProvider are faster.

▶ The reduction in storage capacity is directly correlated to the reduction in granularity, as long as the data in the original InfoProvider is deleted.

▶ A reduction occurs in infrastructure, maintenance, and administration costs, including backups, because the database holds less data.

The summary InfoProvider tactic is prone to the following disadvantages:

▶ An analysis effort needs to be conducted to determine whether each InfoProvider is a candidate for summarization based on the business use cases for queries on the data contained within the InfoProviders.

▶ If data is not deleted from the original InfoProvider, there is neither a reduction of cost and effort nor an improvement of performance regarding the original InfoProvider.

▶ In many cases, queries may need to be adapted if historical data is summarized, or new queries may need be to be created.

Beyond summarized data, there is no other online data storage option. The next alternative is to move data out of the database and onto a near-line storage (NLS) database. As of SAP BW 7.30, there are three primary options: PBS, SAND, and SAP-NLS. The PBS and SAP-NLS options are based on Sybase IQ technology, and all three employ a columnar architecture to compress data. The next section will dive deeper into the NLS options, but for now, the advantages of implementing NLS include the following:

▶ Data stored in NLS can reach compression ratios of up to 95%, significantly reducing storage capacity requirements and costs in the original database.

▶ Less expensive media can be used for the NLS solution, further reducing the cost of the reduced storage capacity.

▶ Data in NLS can be accessed by the original queries with little or no maintenance and only a nominal performance impact.

▶ Data that is near-lined can be restored to the original database, if necessary.

The disadvantages of NLS as a data retention tactic include the following:

▶ Data stored in the NLS solution does not meet the same performance benchmarks as data that remains online—there is a performance impact, which is usually acceptable for older data.

▶ Only static data can be near-lined. Once near-lined, no deltas can be loaded unless the near-lined data is restored to the original database. It then needs to be moved again to the NLS database.

▶ When data is moved from the original database to the NLS database, no new data can be loaded to the original InfoProvider until the NLS process is completed.

▶ Each NLS solution has a license and maintenance cost that, in some cases, depends on the volume of data stored in the NLS solution.

▶ In order to look up data from NLS in transformation rules, a specific ABAP coding needs to be added to ensure that the NLS data is queried.

When data is truly no longer relevant for any end-use scenario, or liability policies dictate that data should be purged from all production systems, selective deletion of data from BW InfoProviders is the best and sometimes only option. The following are advantages of deleting data:

▶ Cheapest cost option from an infrastructure perspective—once the data is deleted, there are pure cost savings

▶ Minimal maintenance required—especially if a custom programming solution is developed to selectively delete irrelevant data from InfoProviders

- Better performance reading and writing to the InfoProviders that have less data volume

- Less storage capacity needed for all InfoProviders being cleansed in this way

- A healthier system as redundant and irrelevant data is deleted

The disadvantages of data deletion, on the other hand, are quite stark:

- Very risky if no archiving was done previously, and important or legally needed data is no longer available

- Recovery of deleted data can come only from the source system and if the data is archived from the source, recovery can be extremely costly and difficult; if data has been deleted from the source system, no recovery is possible

- Additional administration is required to detect candidate data for deletion and confirm whether it can be deleted

It is important to note that these tactics are not mutually exclusive, and every tactic could be employed in a single scenario. The keys to defining a successful data-aging strategy include the following:

- Forecasting the impact of future data growth on capacity and performance

- Developing a cost model for data storage and maintenance

- Profiling data activity and access for all data sets

- Defining data retention tactics for all data sets

- Choosing and implementing technology to minimize impact to the business

In the next section, we'll discuss the NLS solutions for SAP BW 7.40 in more detail.

3.5 Near-Line Storage

The SAP BW NLS interface was previously introduced in release BW 7.0 but could only be used with software developed by SAP development partners. The most promising solution was developed in Germany by software company PBS, a long-time SAP development partner whose main focus is on archiving. In its SAP BW NLS implementation, PBS opted for the analytic database platform Sybase IQ as the storage location for its NLS data and leveraged the column-based architecture of the database to achieve compression rates of 90-95%. SAP subsequently acquired Sybase and developed its own NLS solution for Sybase IQ, which was delivered with SAP BW release 7.30 SP09 and can be used with all supported database versions.

The SAP-NLS integration with BW enables the archiving of rarely accessed data from the online database to a near-line database, where it is dramatically compressed. The near-line data can still be accessed by BW processes, such as queries and data loads, while reducing the storage capacity requirements of the online database. SAP-NLS thus provides a balance between cost and performance. Additional benefits can include data-loading performance improvements and a reduction in the BWA footprint.

The objective is to achieve a steady state for storage capacity by near-lining historical data and keeping current data online. Figure 3.13 gives a real-life projection for a 25 TB database. In this example, all but two years of data would remain online—anything older would be near-lined. Over time, the online database size would remain relatively constant while the compressed near-line data would grow at a nominal pace, avoiding the future costs of additional storage capacity.

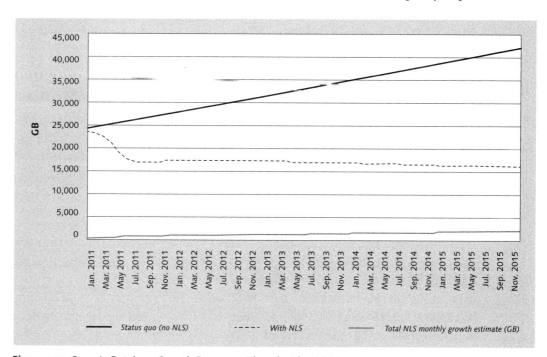

Figure 3.13 Organic Database Growth Forecast with and without NLS

The near-line process removes data in time slices to the Sybase IQ DB. All near-lined time intervals of an InfoProvider are then locked for load processes in SAP BW, so only static data is a candidate for NLS. Any data that could change—either by full load or delta—should remain online or, if already near-lined, will need to be restored from NLS before it can be loaded successfully. The archiving process is highly complex but can be easily managed in both directions using SAP BW Data Archiving Processes (DAP), which can also be scheduled in process chains.

Apart from this restriction, the near-lined data remains available at any time for all other processes in SAP BW, such as query-read accesses and ETL-process lookups. Queries that analyze data over longer periods of time are split and procure data from the online database and Sybase IQ.

> **Note**
>
> Consult SAP Notes 1737415 and 1796393 to install and configure NLS using Sybase IQ.

The overall recommended SAP data management strategy is to use SAP HANA DB with SAP-NLS to deliver a multi-temperate, color-coded persistence management concept. There are three temperatures—hot data, warm data, and cold data—as illustrated in Figure 3.14:

▶ *Hot data* is active data that needs to be accessed frequently by read and write processes. This data is stored online in the main memory of the SAP HANA database.

▶ *Warm data* is less frequently accessed data that is stored in the SAP HANA database file system. This data is loaded into the main memory for processing, but then displaced with higher-priority hot data once processing is finished.

▶ *Cold data* is rarely used data that is stored in the Sybase IQ database of NLS. This data can be accessed from NLS for read-only operations.

The non-active data concept was originally developed to optimize the displacement strategy for BW tables in SAP HANA, where tables with warm data are flagged and prioritized for displacement from the main memory whenever they are used. If the warm data tables are partitioned, only the partitions affected by the transaction are loaded to the main memory. The non-active concept enables a more efficient use of the main memory.

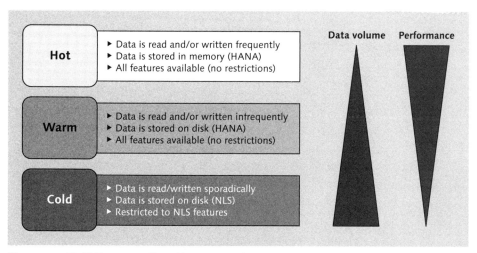

Figure 3.14 Multi-Temperate Data Management Strategy

Next, Chapter 4 will introduce you to authorizations and roles.

*Securing access to functionality and business information is of high
importance in most SAP BW systems, so understanding the security roles
and authorizations used in SAP BW is an important first step.*

4 Roles and Authorizations

Because SAP BW is based on the SAP NetWeaver platform, it uses the SAP
NetWeaver role-based security framework. The standard SAP NetWeaver security functions have been enhanced with customizable SAP BW analysis authorizations to enable flexible security that matches the organization structure in each
company.

This chapter discusses the most important concepts to understand within the topic
of roles and authorizations. We will start by providing an overview of the authorization concept in SAP BW (Section 4.1). We will then go through the standard authorization objects provided by SAP (Section 4.2), followed by a section on how to
define and set up analysis authorizations (Section 4.3). Roles, which tie the authorizations together and are used to assign functionality and data access to end users,
will be covered in Section 4.4. The process of assigning roles and other user administration activities will be covered in Section 4.5. Finally, we'll conclude the chapter
with a brief discussion of troubleshooting authorization problems (Section 4.6).

4.1 Authorization Concept in AS ABAP

The SAP NetWeaver general authorization concept is mainly built on the AS ABAP
authorization objects. An *authorization object* contains one or more authorizations
fields; these authorizations are assigned to users via roles and profiles.

> **Recommendation**
>
> The SAP BW web-based reporting requires users to be set up in the AS Java system to
> allow them to execute reports. However, unless other AS Java functionality is used, it
> requires limited setup.

The AS Java authorization concept uses Access Control Lists (ACLs) to control access to individual objects in the Java system and roles to assign activities to users. We recommend that you use the standard Portal role `Business Explorer` to define the initial set of authorizations needed in AS Java for end users.

A more detailed discussion of Java is outside the scope of this chapter, which focuses on AS ABAP authorizations only.

AS ABAP authorizations can be used to protect most functions, objects, or values in the system. When you perform an action, the authorization check compares the values for the individual fields of an authorization object or an authorization assigned to the user with the values set for executing an action in the program. A user is authorized to perform an action only if the authorization check is successful for *every field* in an authorization object or authorization. For example, if someone has access to execute a query based on the query name but does not have access to the InfoArea where the InfoProvider is located, he cannot execute the query. This enables complex user authorization checks. It is possible to grant access, but denying access by entering values that a user does not have access to is not possible.

The SAP NetWeaver authorizations are structured into authorization object classes. A class can have one or more authorization objects, and each authorization object can have one or more authorizations. This is depicted in Figure 4.1.

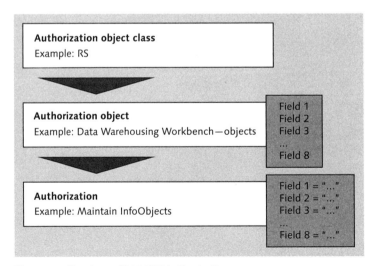

Figure 4.1 Structure of SAP BW Authorizations

All SAP BW authorizations are included in authorization object class RS. The authorization objects like the one in Figure 4.2 can be displayed in Transaction SU21, which also includes all other standard authorizations available in the system.

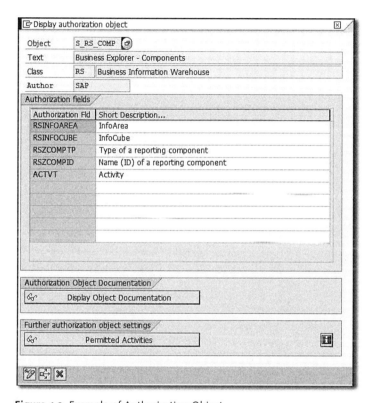

Figure 4.2 Example of Authorization Object

It is not enough to grant access to the authorization objects in class RS because SAP BW also makes use of a lot of standard SAP NetWeaver functionality for system communication, system settings, and maintenance. (This will be covered more in Section 4.4, where we will look at the content of the standard roles provided by SAP.)

An authorization object contains one or more authorization fields and activity fields. These will be covered in the following sections.

4.1.1   Authorization Fields

Authorization field values control the values for which a user has access. Each authorization object can have one or more authorization fields.

Authorization fields can be maintained with the following:

1. Specific values

2. Patterns where the character * is a wildcard

3. Ranges that can be ranges of specific values or patterns

4. Full access using * only in the value

We recommend that you use patterns based on naming conventions for technical SAP BW objects because it minimizes the maintenance effort for the authorizations when new objects are created.

For example, consider an InfoArea where all objects for sales could be in a SALES InfoArea, as shown in Figure 4.3. Secured InfoProviders could have a specific prefix (SAL_C*) for unsecured full access sales InfoProviders and another (SAL_SC*) for sales InfoProviders with information that requires specific access, as shown in Figure 4.3.

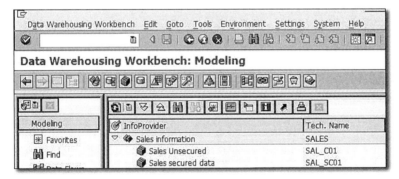

Figure 4.3 Naming Conventions for Authorizations

4.1.2   Activity Fields

The activity field controls the types of activities that the user has access to perform for the authorization object. The predefined set of activities defined in SAP BW can be found in table TACT. Table 4.1 lists the most commonly used activity fields in SAP BW.

Activity	Description
01	Create or generate
02	Change
03	Display
06	Delete
07	Activate, generate
16	Execute
22	Enter, include, assign

Table 4.1 Common Activities in Authorization Objects in SAP BW

Developers and administrators should have access to all activities in the development system. The following activites should be limited in the test and production systems for objects that are transported through the system landscape:

▶ 01: Create or generate

▶ 02: Change

▶ 06: Delete

We recommend that you maintain a separate namespace for objects like queries, web templates, and reports that are created directly in production.

Now that we have covered the authorization concept, we will move to describing the standard authorization objects provided by SAP. These are required to grant access to use the SAP BW functionality.

4.2   Standard Authorization Objects

SAP BW comes delivered with a set of standard authorization objects that control access to general SAP NetWeaver functionality, SAP BW administration, and SAP BW reporting objects. These objects can be divided into two types: developer and administrator authorizations and reporting authorizations. We'll discuss each in more detail next.

4.2.1 Developer and Administrator Authorizations

Standard SAP BW developer and administrator authorizations are available to limit access to creating and maintaining the non-reporting objects in the system.

The SAP BW standard authorization objects that control access to the administrator workbench and other administrator functionality are listed in Table 4.2.

Authorization Object	Description
BO_CA_CES	Content Administration: BOE System Definition
BO_CA_JOB	Content Administration: Operations on Content-Related Jobs
BO_CA_RPT	Content Administration: Operations on Reports
RSANPR	Authorization for Analysis Process
RSCRMRTUPD	Real-Time Update from CRM
S_RSEC	Infrastructure of the Analysis Authorizations
S_RS_ADMWB	Data Warehousing Workbench—Objects
S_RS_AINX	Analytical Index
S_RS_ALVL	Planning: Aggregation Level
S_RS_DMOD	Data Warehousing Workbench—Data Flow
S_RS_DS	Data Warehousing Workbench—DataSource (Release > BW 3.x)
S_RS_DTP	Data Warehousing Workbench—Data Transfer Process
S_RS_HIER	Data Warehousing Workbench—Hierarchy
S_RS_HIST	Authorizations for TLOGO Object History
S_RS_HYBR	Data Warehousing Workbench—HybridProvider
S_RS_ICUBE	Data Warehousing Workbench—InfoCube
S_RS_IOBC	Data Warehousing Workbench—InfoObject Catalog
S_RS_IOBJ	Data Warehousing Workbench—InfoObject
S_RS_IOMAD	Data Warehousing Workbench—Maintain Master Data
S_RS_ISET	Data Warehousing Workbench—InfoSet

Table 4.2 Administration Authorization Objects

Authorization Object	Description
S_RS_ISNEW	Data Warehousing Workbench—InfoSource (Release > BW 3.x)
S_RS_ISOUR	Data Warehousing Workbench—InfoSource (Flexible Update)
S_RS_ISRCM	Data Warehousing Workbench—InfoSource (Direct Update)
S_RS_KPCAT	KPI Monitoring: Authorization for KPI Catalog
S_RS_KPI	KPI Monitoring: Authorization for KPI Definition
S_RS_LOPDO	LOPD: Customizing Authorizations
S_RS_LPOA	Data Warehousing Workbench—Semantically Partitioned Object
S_RS_MPRO	Data Warehousing Workbench—MultiProvider
S_RS_ODSO	Data Warehousing Workbench—DataStore Object
S_RS_OHDST	Data Warehousing Workbench—Open Hub Destination
S_RS_PC	Data Warehousing Workbench—Process Chains
S_RS_PLENQ	Lock Settings
S_RS_PLSE	Planning Function
S_RS_PLSQ	Planning Sequence
S_RS_PLST	Planning Function Type
S_RS_PPM	Authorization Object for BI Planning Process Management
S_RS_RSFC	Authorization Object for Transaction RSFC
S_RS_RSTT	Authorization Object for RS Trace Tool
S_RS_THJT	Data Warehousing Workbench—Key Date Derivation Type
S_RS_TR	Data Warehousing Workbench—Transformation
S_RS_UOM	Data Warehousing Workbench—Quantity Conversion Type
S_RS_WSPAC	BW Workspace

Table 4.2 Administration Authorization Objects (Cont.)

These authorization objects must be maintained for developers and administrators to grant access to enable development and system administration.

Reporting end users require access to a lot of the administrator authorization objects with activities 03 (Display) and 16 (Execute) to be able to access the data in the system when executing queries.

4.2.2 Reporting Authorizations

Standard SAP BW authorization objects are available to limit access to reporting components such as queries, reports, and dashboards.

Table 4.3 lists reporting-related authorization objects.

Authorization Object	Description
S_RS_AO	Analysis Office: Authority Object
S_RS_AUTH	BI Analysis Authorizations in Role
S_RS_BCS	BEx Broadcasting Authorization to Schedule
S_RS_BEXTX	Business Explorer—BEx Texts (Maintenance)
S_RS_BITM	Business Explorer—BEx Reusable web items (NW 7.0+)
S_RS_BTMP	Business Explorer—BEx Web Templates (NW 7.0+)
S_RS_COMP	Business Explorer—Components
S_RS_COMP1	Business Explorer—Components: Enhancements to the Owner
S_RS_CPRO	Authorization Object for BW Composite Provider
S_RS_CTT	Data Warehousing Workbench—Currency Translation Type
S_RS_DAS	Business Explorer—Data Access Services
S_RS_EREL	Business Explorer—Enterprise Report Reusable Elements
S_RS_ERPT	Business Explorer—Enterprise Reports
S_RS_FOLD	Business Explorer—Folder View On/Off
S_RS_PARAM	Business Explorer—Variants in Variable Screen
S_RS_TOOLS	Business Explorer—Individual Tools
S_RS_XCLS	Front-End Integration—Xcelsius Visualization

Table 4.3 Reporting Authorization Objects

Developers and administrators require access to these authorization objects to be able to execute queries and reports in the system, as well as troubleshoot problems reported by end users.

4.3 Analysis Authorizations

You use SAP BW analysis authorizations to control access to business information. In this section, we'll walk you through the basics: creating an InfoObject for analysis authorizations, defining analysis authorizations, and generating analysis authorizations.

4.3.1 Creating an InfoObject for Analysis Authorizations

Analysis authorizations are created based on the InfoObjects in SAP BW for which your organization requires separate information access. Usually, these are organizational or geographical InfoObjects with more or less static values, such as company code; profit center; country or region; or groupings such as accounts groups, customer groups, or material groups.

To avoid having complex authorizations, you should use specific InfoObjects for analysis authorizations. It is possible to define analysis authorizations on all types of InfoObjects, but you shouldn't use InfoObjects that have fast changing values, such as order numbers, customer numbers, and material numbers. This would require massive maintenance effort in ensuring that authorizations are updated frequently.

Note that analysis authorizations are not delivered by SAP as standard objects. You must define which InfoObjects have to be checked for authorizations before analysis authorizations can be defined for them. In order to do this, you have to create a specific security-relevant InfoObject and assign it as an attribute updated with the same values as the original InfoObject.

Consider, for example, a company code for which the standard object `OCOMP_CODE` is used in several InfoProviders. Creating a new InfoObject `ZSECCOMP` that is authorization-relevant as an attribute of `OCOMP_CODE` (such as the one shown in Figure 4.4 and Figure 4.5) allows for only specific InfoProviders requiring authorization to be maintained with analysis authorizations.

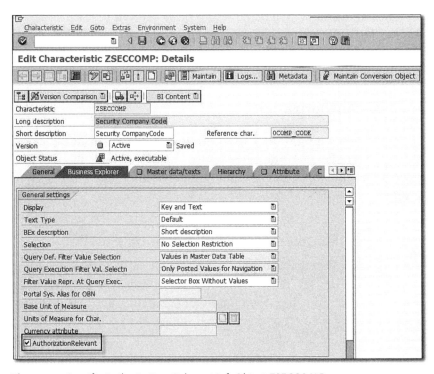

Figure 4.4 Specific Authorization-Relevant InfoObject ZSECCOMP

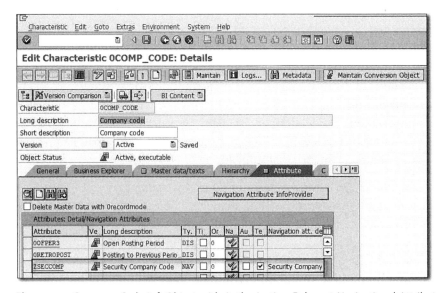

Figure 4.5 Company Code InfoObject with Authorization-Relevant Navigational Attribute

Analysis authorization can then be defined based on the navigational attribute, and the navigational attribute can be selectively switched on in the InfoProviders, as shown in Figure 4.6.

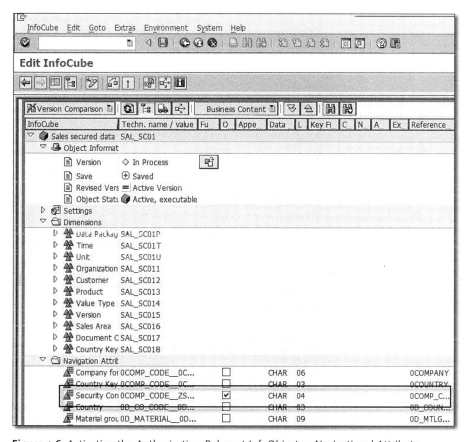

Figure 4.6 Activating the Authorization-Relevant InfoObject as Navigational Attribute

Analysis authorizations are created and maintained in Transaction RSECADMIN. This transaction also provides additional functionality to generate analysis authorizations and assign them to end users. We recommend that you limit access to this transaction and related authorization object S_RSEC to security and system administrators only.

> **Recommendation**
>
> Some business content InfoObjects are delivered with the authorization flag set. These can be switched off if you do not need authorization checks on these objects. Switching this flag off keeps you from having to define analysis authorizations for these objects.

4.3.2 Defining Analysis Authorizations

Go to Transaction RSECADMIN • INDIVIDUAL MAINTENANCE to define a new analysis authorization. In the example, we will create an analysis authorization for company code 1000.

The following three special characteristics must always be included in the analysis authorization:

- 0TCAACTVT (Activity in Analysis Authorizations)
- 0TCAIPROV (Authorizations for InfoProvider)
- 0TCAVALID (Validity of an Authorization)

These are required in order to provide access to InfoProviders, so the system gives an authorization error if they are absent. They are, by default, assigned access to display all data without a validity date.

Once you've added these three InfoObjects, you can add the additional InfoObjects you have configured as authorization relevant, as displayed in Figure 4.7.

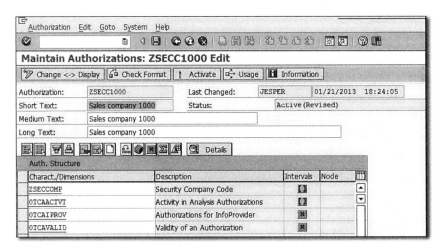

Figure 4.7 Analysis Authorization Example

You can click the icon in the INTERVALS column to maintain the authorized values for your characteristic. In our example in Figure 4.8, we assign access to company code 1000.

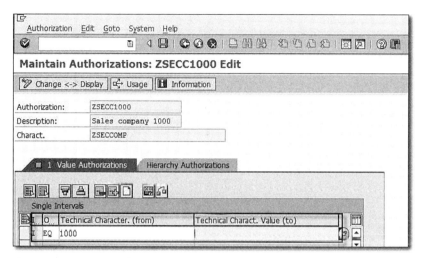

Figure 4.8 Assigning Values in the Analysis Authorization

You can use user exit variables to provide authorization based on dynamic authorizations determined at runtime in ABAP.

Another option is to assign access based on hierarchy nodes. This is especially useful when hierarchies are already defined on the InfoObject and the definition of the hierarchy can be used for access to business information.

Restricting access to specific key figures can be done via InfoObject OTCAKYFNM. Don't set this InfoObject as authorization relevant unless it is required to restrict access to key figures. The key figure InfoObject name should be maintained as authorized values, so you should set specific naming conventions for these key figures to allow for easy maintenance.

4.3.3 Automatically Generating Analysis Authorization

A standard analysis authorization 0BIALL is generated automatically in the system for all authorization-relevant InfoObjects. This is assigned to the SAP_ALL profile by default to ensure that SAP_ALL has full access in the system. This analysis authorization should not be maintained manually.

It is also possible to automatically generate analysis authorizations in Transaction RSECADMIN based on uploaded data (Figure 4.9).

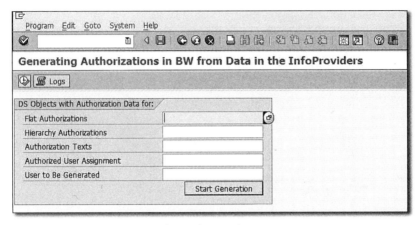

Figure 4.9 Generation Program for Analysis Authorizations

The DataStore objects (DSOs) for generating authorizations have the same structure as the authorizations. SAP provides the following five template DSOs that can be used:

- Authorization data (values) (0TCA_DS01)
- Authorization data (hierarchies) (0TCA_DS02)
- Description texts for authorizations (0TCA_DS03)
- Assignment of authorizations to users (0TCA_DS04)
- Generation of users for authorizations (0TCA_DS05)

The actual data used in the generated authorizations is in the template DSOs 0TCA_DS01 and 0TCA_DS02.

> **Recommendation**
>
> The program deletes all generated analysis authorizations as a first step and then re-generates them. Consequently, schedule the generation for a time when users are not logged on to the system; otherwise, they would experience authorization errors.

4.4   Roles

SAP BW uses the SAP NetWeaver role-based authorizations concept. Users are defined with one or more roles assigned.

It's possible to combine roles into *composite roles*—a combination of one or more roles—for easier maintenance of users and roles. But you should define a role-based security model with as few composite roles as possible to minimize support costs and make it easier for users to request access. You can create both basic and composite roles via Transaction PFCG, which is used for role maintenance, as shown in Figure 4.10.

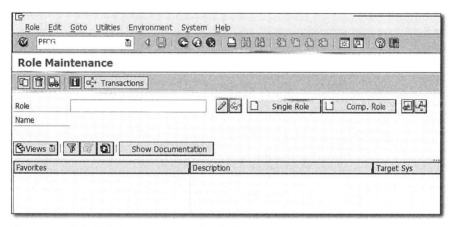

Figure 4.10 Role Maintenance (Transaction PFCG)

Analysis authorizations are assigned to roles using authorization object S_RS_AUTH with the assigned value of the defined analysis authorization.

Recommendation

The combined authorizations for the roles assigned to a user are evaluated when authorization checks are executed.

In this section, we'll cover the different role types in SAP BW for administrators and end users. We'll conclude with a discussion of the most useful role templates provided by SAP.

4.4.1 Administrator Roles

Administrator roles are required to support the SAP BW system. These roles are normally granted to members of the support organization and vary by system in the landscape.

Table 4.4 shows the roles that are regarded as best practices in an SAP BW system landscape.

Development System	Test System	Production System
Developer	Production Developer	Production Developer
Development Support	Production Support	Production Support
Change and Transport Manager	Change and Transport Manager	Change and Transport Manager
Basis Support Development	Basis Support—Production	Basis Support—Production

Table 4.4 Recommended Administrator Roles by System in Landscape

SAP does provide some template roles that can be used as a starting point for defining the support roles, but these roles have extensive access to Basis administration tasks. Therefore, you should modify them to reduce the risk of giving too many people access to change system settings.

4.4.2 End-User Roles

There are three general types of end users in an SAP BW system, as follows:

- Authors and analysis: Authors and analysts require advanced analysis functionality and the ability to perform special data analysis. To accomplish their tasks, they need useful, manageable reporting and analysis tools.

- Executives and knowledge workers: Executives and knowledge workers require personalized, context-related information provided in an intuitive user interface. They generally work with pre-defined navigation paths but sometimes need to perform deeper data analysis.

- Information consumers: Information consumers require specific information (snapshot of a specific data set) to be able to perform their operative tasks.

End users' roles should be defined to give access to reporting functionality and reports. We recommend that you limit the number of roles that are created in the system as much as possible to make maintenance easier and avoid confusion when end users request access to reports.

You should decide on end-user roles based on three dimensions, as follows:

1. Business process
2. Business function
3. Business role

Each of these could lead to a different number of technical roles to be defined in the system. Try to choose the method that best suits your organizational setup.

An additional dimension to the end-user roles is access to business information. This access is controlled via analysis authorizations.

We recommend that you assign analysis authorizations via roles if there are fewer than 100 roles to be maintained. If there are more than 100 roles, you should maintain the access via user assignment in Transaction RSECADMIN by generating the analysis authorizations, as described in Section 4.3.3.

In addition to the end-user roles that allow for executing the reports, you can also have a role for super users that allows them to create ad hoc queries and reports directly in production. This role should allow the users to create the objects with a specific name prefix and be limited to that exact prefix. It should also not have access to create global, calculated, and restricted key figures and structures.

4.4.3 Role Templates

SAP delivers a set of standard role templates. The templates for SAP BW user roles start with S_RS_R (with the exception of the roles for Business Planning, which start with S_RS_PL). The templates for SAP BW workspace user roles start with S_RS_T.

Use the template roles when creating new roles to quickly add all the authorizations from the template into the profile for the new role.

Table 4.5 describes the most useful role templates and the tasks that they facilitate.

Technical Name of Template	Description	Tasks
S_RS_RDEAD	BW Role: BW Administrator (development system)	▸ Maintaining the source system and uploading metadata ▸ Executing queries for the statistics InfoCubes ▸ Maintaining aggregates ▸ Maintaining analysis authorizations ▸ Scheduling broadcast settings ▸ Maintaining currency and quantity conversion types, as well as key date derivation types
S_RS_ROPAD	BW Role: BW Administrator (productive system)	▸ Maintaining the connection to the source system and executing queries for the statistics InfoCubes.
S_RS_RDEMO	BW Role: Modeler (development system)	▸ Defining the InfoObjects, InfoProvider, transformation rules, data transfer process, and process chains ▸ Scheduling broadcast settings ▸ Maintaining currency and quantity conversion types, as well as key date derivation types
S_RS_ROPOP	BW Role: Operator (productive system)	▸ Uploading data from the source system ▸ Executing the data transfer processes ▸ Monitoring processes
S_RS_RREDE	BW Role: Reporting Developer (development system)	▸ Designing queries, reports, and web applications ▸ Maintaining analysis authorizations and their assignments to roles ▸ Scheduling broadcast settings ▸ Maintaining currency and quantity conversion types, as well as key date derivation types

Table 4.5 Role Templates Delivered in SAP BW

Technical Name of Template	Description	Tasks
S_RS_RREPU	BW Role: Reporting User	► Executing queries in BEx Analyzer or on the web
S_RS_PL_PLANMOD_D	BW Role: Planning Modeler (development system)	► Defining aggregation levels ► Defining data slices and characteristic relationships ► Defining planning functions, planning sequences, and planning function types ► Defining queries and web applications
S_RS_PL_ADMIN	BW Role: Planning Administrator	► Defining data slices ► Executing planning functions and planning sequences
S_RS_PL_PLANNER	BW Role: Planner	► Displaying plan data in queries and web applications ► Manually entering data in queries that are ready for input ► Executing planning functions and planning sequences
S_RS_TWSPA	BW Workspace Administrator	► Creating BW Workspaces, defining their properties, making central data available in them, and managing the BW Workspaces
S_RS_TWSPD	BW Workspace Designer	► Loading personal data into the Workspace and then creating CompositeProviders
S_RS_TWSPQ	BW Workspace Query User	► Executing queries on CompositeProviders

Table 4.5 Role Templates Delivered in SAP BW (Cont.)

A full list of role templates can be accessed in Transaction PFCG • UTILITIES • TEMPLATES, as shown in Figure 4.12. It is also possible to define new templates from this same screen.

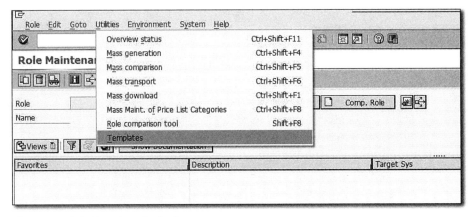

Figure 4.11 Role Templates in the System

Using template roles provides a quick start to defining the roles required in the SAP BW system. Of course, you can expect some modification to authorizations from the standard templates when defining the roles that will be assigned to the users in the system via user administration.

4.5 User Administration

User administration includes tasks such as defining users and assigning analysis authorizations to users. We'll cover these tasks next, and then conclude the section with a brief discussion of some additional tools that can help with user administration.

4.5.1 Defining Users

Users are defined and maintained in AS ABAP in Transaction SU01. This transaction should be assigned to security administrators; other administrators and developers should have access to the display-only transaction, Transaction SU01D.

Transaction SU01, which is shown in Figure 4.12, provides access to the following main tasks:

▶ Create users

▶ Maintain users

▶ Display users

- ▶ Delete users
- ▶ Copy users
- ▶ Lock and unlock users
- ▶ Change password for users

Recommendation

Users are maintained with basic information, such as name and address. We recommend that you always maintain email addresses because they are used for information broadcasting functionality.

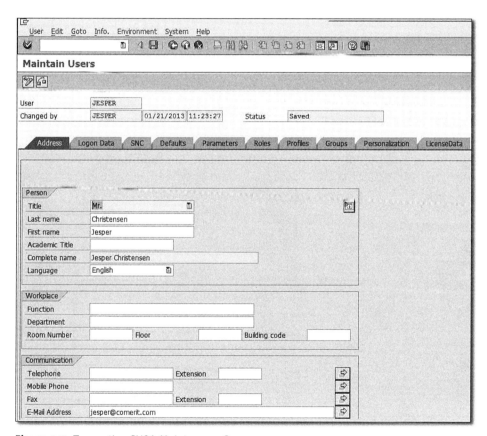

Figure 4.12 Transaction SU01 Maintenance Screen

Logon information that is also maintained includes the user group, which can be used to limit maintenance access to specific users.

When roles are assigned in the ROLE tab, corresponding profiles are automatically added to the PROFILE tab.

> **Recommendation**
>
> Users in AS Java can be read from the AS ABAP user store. This is the recommended approach for SAP BW because the users must be present in AS ABAP to enable query executions.

4.5.2 Assigning Analysis Authorizations to Users

You can assign analysis authorizations to users via roles or directly in Transaction RSECADMIN. Recall from earlier in this chapter that you should choose the method based on the number of roles that the authorization requires and the company's general authorization strategy. Most companies prefer using the role-based assignment because it is aligned with the rest of the SAP systems in the landscape. Let's explore both.

Assigning Analysis Authorizations to Roles

Analysis authorizations are assigned to roles using the authorization object S_RS_ AUTH. You can see the analysis authorization created earlier assigned in a role in Figure 4.13.

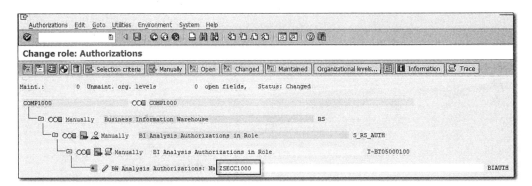

Figure 4.13 Analysis Authorization Assigned in a Role

Make sure to have a clear naming convention in place for the analysis authorizations to enable maintenance via ranges or patterns. Once the analysis authorization is assigned to the role, it is applied to all users that the role is assigned to in user administration.

Assigning Analysis Authorizations to Users in Transaction RSECADMIN

Assigning analysis authorizations directly to users is an SAP BW-specific functionality; it does not provide the same reporting capabilities as when roles are used.
You can make assignments individually or en masse via the USER tab in Transaction RSECADMIN, as shown in Figure 4.14.

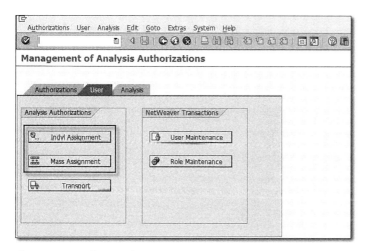

Figure 4.14 Analysis Authorization Assignment Options (Transaction RSECADMIN)

When selecting the individual maintenance options, you can select a specific user
and maintain the assigned analysis authorizations. It is also possible to see which
analysis authorizations are assigned via the sub-tab ROLE-BASED under the ROLES
tab in Figure 4.15.

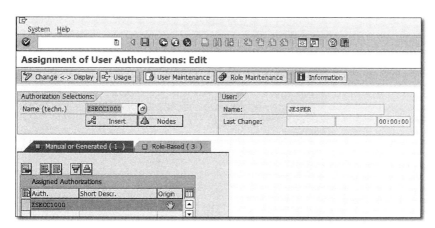

Figure 4.15 Analysis Authorization Assigned via Individual Maintenance

The mass maintenance option in Figure 4.16 provides two radio-button options to assign the analysis authorizations to users: AUTHORIZATIONS and USER.

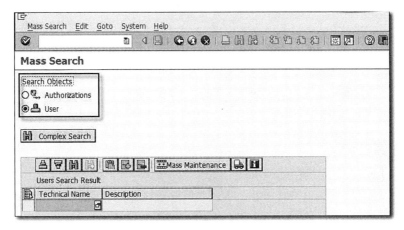

Figure 4.16 Mass Maintenance Search Options

The COMPLEX SEARCH button provides various options to select the users for mass maintenance.

Once the users or authorizations have been selected, it is possible to maintain them all in one action and add additional users with the same authorization. You can see in in Figure 4.17 that an additional user, TESTAUTH, is assigned with the same authorization values.

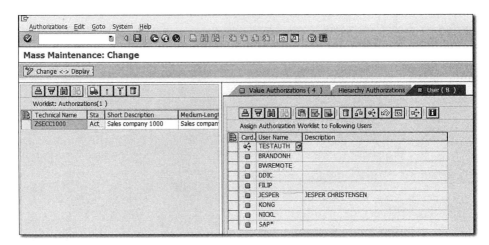

Figure 4.17 Mass Maintenance Screen Example

You can also change the authorized values, which then update the analysis authorization when it is saved and activated.

4.5.3 User Administration Tools

There are some tools to assist you in user administration. Next, we'll briefly introduce the User Information System and SAP GRC Access Control.

User Information System

The User Information System shown in Figure 4.18 provides detailed analysis capabilities of all aspects of the AS ABAP user roles and authorizations.

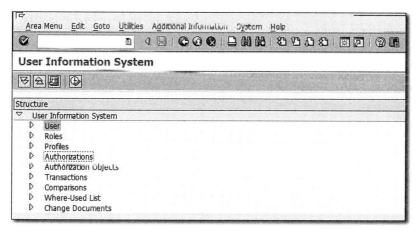

Figure 4.18 Transaction SUIM Provides Detailed Analysis of Users and Authorizations

In addition to the standard User Information System, additional reporting capability provided in Transaction RSECADMIN displays users assigned to specific analysis authorizations. This is possible via the MASS ASSIGNMENT button of the USER tab.

SAP GRC Access Control

SAP Governance Risk and Compliance (GRC) Access Control is a recommended tool to manage access and maintenance for many SAP and non-SAP systems in a landscape. SAP GRC Access Control provides an enterprise-wide role and user management platform that streamlines user audits and analysis of segregation of duties.

In addition, SAP GRC contains capabilities to manage super administrator activities via privileged user IDs and subsequently report on the usage and tasks performed.

User administration is a never-ending task in an SAP BW system and also causes the most incidents with end users when they are missing access or have other types of authorization problems. We will cover how to troubleshoot authorizations problems in the next section.

4.6   Troubleshooting Authorization Problems

The most common authorization problems identified when administrating an SAP BW system relate to missing authorizations.

There are three types of problems:

1. Missing authorization for standard authorization objects

2. Missing authorization for analysis authorization

3. Missing Java portal authorizations

The last of these, SAP NetWeaver AS Java authorization errors, are not common for SAP BW, so we won't discuss them at length in this section. If they do occur, the result is normally a clear message stating which object the user does not have access to. It is then possible to assign the access to the object via the user management engine (UME).

Let's look more closely at the other two types of errors.

4.6.1   Standard Authorization Errors

When executing tasks via SAP GUI, you can always get details for authorization errors by executing Transaction SU53, which is shown in Figure 4.19.

Several items are displayed here: the check authorization and the roles and authorizations assigned to the user. This makes it easy to analyze whether the error is caused by a missing role or missing authorization in an existing role.

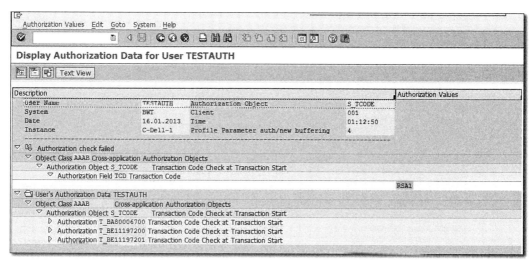

Figure 4.19 Transaction SU53 Error

You can also use the standard authorization trace (Transaction ST01) to analyze errors related to standard authorization objects, as shown in Figure 4.20. This is especially helpful when errors occur in reporting and the error is not obvious based on the error message.

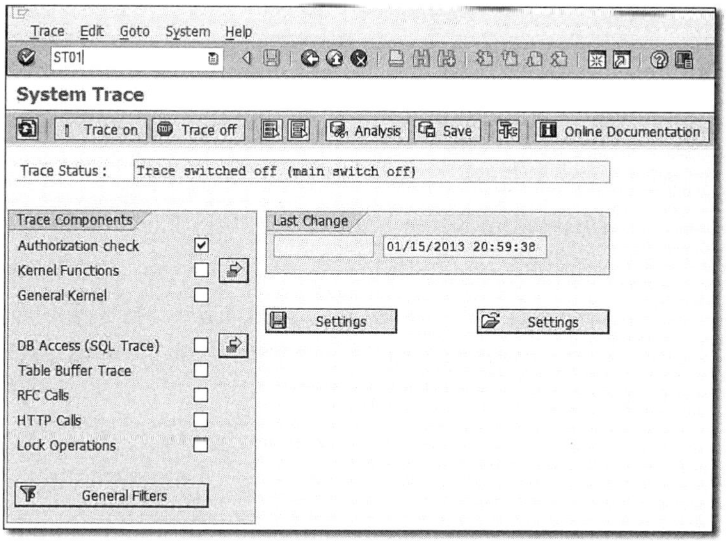

Figure 4.20 Standard Authorization Trace (Transaction ST01)

Make sure that you set a general filter before activating the trace to avoid tracing for all users that are active in the system. To do this, click the GENERAL FILTERS button and then set the user that should be traced, as shown in Figure 4.21.

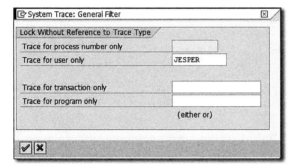

Figure 4.21 Setting a Filter for a Specific User before Activating the Trace

Once this is set, click the TRACE ON button and execute the tasks that caused the authorization errors. Once the tasks are completed, remember to switch off the trace; otherwise, it continues to trace the user activity.

Once the trace has been recorded, it can be analyzed via the ANALYSIS button. To find the trace, limit the selection by the user that was traced and the date and time that the trace was recorded. Figure 4.22 shows an example of limiting the trace time parameters from 1/15/2013 to 1/17/2013.

The trace report should be read as follows:

▶ RC=0: Authorization check was successful

▶ RC <> 0: Authorization check failed

The error lines are also highlighted in red to indicate that they failed. A sample trace report (with no errors) is shown in Figure 4.23.

Based on the result from either Transaction SU53 or Transaction ST01, you can assign the missing authorizations or roles related to the authorization error message.

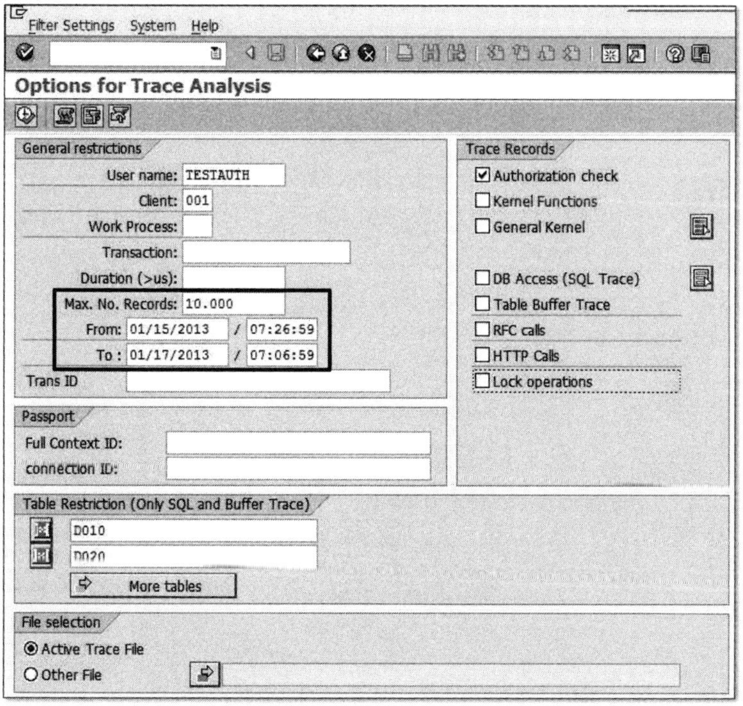

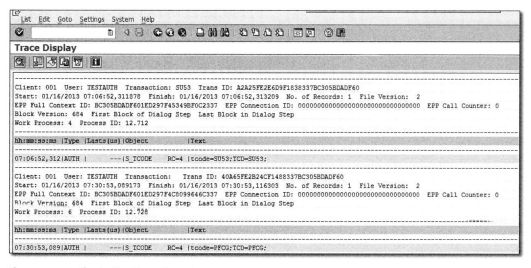

Figure 4.22 Selection Options for Analysis of Authorization Trace

Figure 4.23 Authorization Trace Report

4.6.2 SAP BW Analysis Authorization Errors

SAP BW analysis authorization errors can be analyzed using the analysis log in Transaction RSECADMIN. The log provides a detailed breakdown of the analysis authorizations checked during the query execution, including the checked values.

As shown in Figure 4.24, there are two ways to analyze authorization errors: either executing a query as another user or configuring the log recording for a user and then asking the user to execute the query while the recording is on.

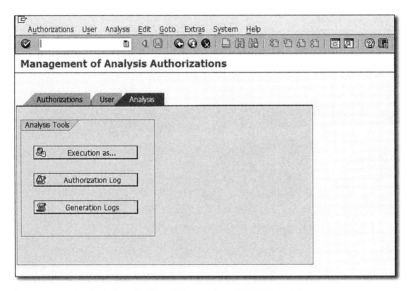

Figure 4.24 Analysis Log Options (Transaction RSECADMIN)

Both of these options result in a detailed authorization log, which can become quite hard to read if you perform too many authorizations or navigations. We recommend that you use bookmarks in either Transaction RSRT or the BEx tools to create the shortest possible log.

As shown in the Authorization Check Log in Figure 4.25, the log has three sections:

▶ Header: Contains basic information for the execution.

▶ InfoProvider check: Contains the access check for the InfoProvider.

▶ Authorization checks: Contains the main checks for the analysis authorizations. These are separated into sub-numbers (SUBNR) based on the checks required by the structures in the query definition. The number of SUBNRs depends on the complexity of the query executed; many are possible.

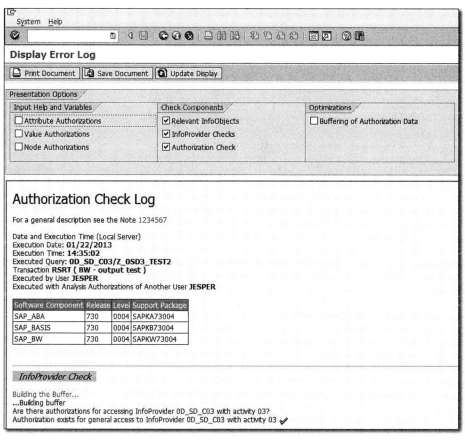

Figure 4.25 Authorization Log Header and InfoProvider Check

Recommendation

You can see that the log may display an unsuccessful partial check in the first iteration steps but that the check as a whole is successful. The important result is the one that is delivered after the last step.

However, if a sub-selection is not authorized, the system displays the following lines:

ALL AUTHORIZATIONS TESTED
MESSAGE EYE 007: YOU DO NOT HAVE SUFFICIENT AUTHORIZATION (in yellow)
NO SUFFICIENT AUTHORIZATION FOR THIS SUB SELECTION (SUBNR) (in yellow).

Let's consider the two options for analyzing authorization errors.

Execute as Other User

Executing as a different user allows a security or system administrator to execute a query with the authorizations of another user. Figure 4.26 shows the execution as another user, Filip, and the WITH LOG option selected.

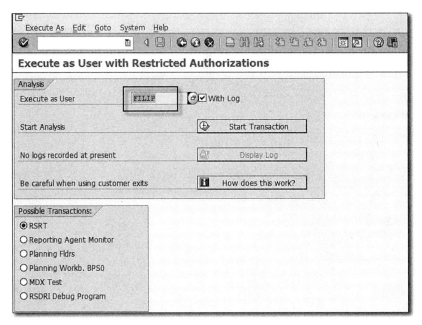

Figure 4.26 Executing the Query as Another User

If you execute as another user with a log recording activated, you can analyze it for errors.

The default option for executing the query is via the Query Monitor (Transaction RSRT). This allows for selecting a query and a bookmark, as shown in Figure 4.27.

Recommendation

The function module RSEC_GET_USERNAME should be used to avoid problems with authorization-user exit variables when executing them as another user from RSECAD-MIN.

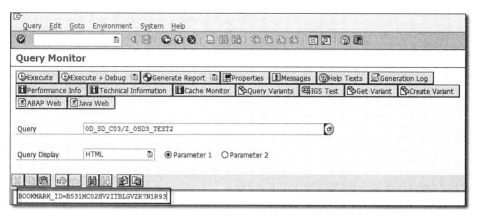

Figure 4.27 Executing a Query in Transaction RSRT with BOOKMARK_ID

The functionality for executing the authorization check as other users can be secured via authorization object S_RSEC and values for TCODE and Transaction RSECADMOBJ set as RSUDO; we recommend that you assign this functionality only to security administrators.

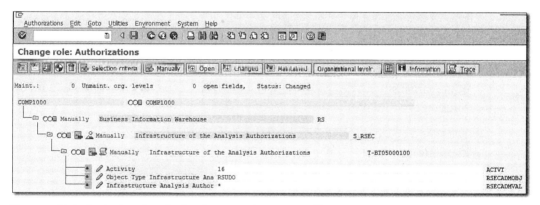

Figure 4.28 Authorizations Required to Execute a Query as a Different User

Configure Authorization Log

The other primary option for troubleshooting authorization errors is to activate an authorization log recording for a specific user to enable troubleshooting of authorization errors. This is done from Transaction RSECADMIN • ANALYSIS tab • AUTHORIZATION LOG.

Once the user has been activated, recording logs are generated for all actions done by that user, as shown in Figure 4.29. Therefore, remember to deactivate the recording immediately once the required log has been generated.

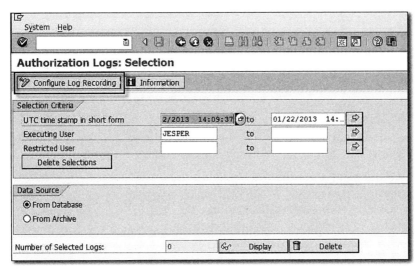

Figure 4.29 Activating Authorization Log Recording for a User

SAP BW provides advanced functionality to define and manage users and access to functionality and business information. The security definition must be a part of the initial system design to ensure that it is designed and incorporated into the solution to avoid costly reworking down the road.

The following chapters in Part II offer detailed tips and performance tuning techniques to improve overall system performance.

Part II
Performance Tuning

No other areas require more administration and performance-tuning effort than data modeling and data loading. Before commencing development work, you should define and document design guidelines, best practices, and a development methodology. Consider supportability and performance up front during design, especially when it comes to data staging in the data flow.

5 Data Modeling and Loading for Performance

Practicing good data modeling is as much an art as it is a science. It takes a systematic, yet creative approach. The role of a data architect is part passionate dictator, part principled realist, and part gifted artisan. While it is impossible to define a methodology or best practice that will handle all requirements without some snag, hitch, or exception, a good data architect employs well-defined principles systematically across all development in the data warehouse. Maintaining consistent development practices and continuity across subject areas serves to improve the supportability of the warehouse content over a longer period of time.

You may recall from Chapter 2 that data architecture has a real influence on supportability and performance, but the keys to an efficient and maintainable data warehouse are well-designed data models supported by a pragmatic approach to extraction, transformation, and load (ETL) processes.

In this chapter, we'll cover data modeling for optimal performance, including a review of all InfoProvider options available in SAP BW 7.40 (Section 5.1). Then, we'll provide an in-depth review of all ETL processes, including specific performance-tuning advice (Section 5.2).

5.1 Data Modeling for Performance

The objective of efficient data modeling is to deliver data integrity and reporting accuracy in a design that loads quickly, is easy to maintain, and delivers fast reports. For each report that needs to be delivered, you need to gather the complete set of business requirements from the end user before a solution can be designed. In some cases, a single data model can deliver many reports; in others, a single data model may deliver only one report. Without considering all the requirements, you may not be able to design a solution that meets the expectations of the users.

To gather the business requirements, you can use a standard set of questions to lay the framework for a data model:

- ▶ What data is needed to satisfy the report, and where is it stored?
- ▶ Which dimensions and/or characteristics are needed?
- ▶ What granularity is needed along each dimension?
- ▶ What filters and variables are needed to limit the result set?
- ▶ What key figures and calculations are needed?
- ▶ Do any calculations require non-cumulative key figures?
- ▶ Do any calculations require exception aggregation?
- ▶ How often is the source data updated?
- ▶ How often does the data in the report need to be updated?
- ▶ How many records are aggregated into a typical result set?
- ▶ How many users execute this report, and how often do they use it?

These questions are just a sample set—there are certainly more—but the answers are necessary for you to envision the solution at a functional level (from the top down). As soon as the functional design is documented, it can be reviewed with the business to identify any outstanding questions, inconsistencies, or omissions. The functional design should include a data flow and all architectural considerations. In most cases, data is extracted to the data warehouse following the principles of an enterprise data warehouse (EDW) and staged per the principles of LSA or LSA++ (see Section 2.2 on layered architectures in Chapter 2).

Once a functional design has been approved, it is time to proceed to a detailed design. The detailed design is more or less managed from the bottom up. At this point, each field in the report should be linked to a source field in the source database. The detailed design includes the details of all InfoObjects that are building blocks of all data models and are critical to the delivery of correct information in the right format (see Section 3.1.1 on master data design in Chapter 3).

The detailed design should also define the correct granularity to ensure accurate and consistent results. And last but not least, a good data model design considers performance optimizations for loading data into the warehouse and through the layers as quickly as possible and delivering the data to the report(s) quickly.

Proper InfoObject modeling begins with normalizing master data in *third normal form* (3NF), which maintains that every non-key attribute of an InfoObject should provide a fact about the full key and only the full key. Normalization is implemented with one purpose: to maintain data integrity. During the normalization process, InfoObjects with attributes are decomposed into more InfoObjects with attributes. However, the more InfoObjects with attributes there are, the more tables need to be joined to deliver a full dataset. In some cases, it may be necessary to subsequently add attributes for performance or history reasons. *Denormalization* is the process of optimizing the read performance or scalability of a database by adding redundant data or grouping data.

Normalization and denormalization techniques can also be applied to transaction data InfoProviders. Consider a few examples of denormalization techniques:

▶ Materialized views are database objects that contain the results of a query. They can be created by using the SAP BEx Broadcaster to pre-calculate result sets or denormalizing attributes from one InfoObject or InfoProvider to another Info-Provider in order to limit the number of joins and improve response time of queries with complex analytic processing.

▶ Star schemas are multidimensional models, also known as fact-dimension models. All InfoCubes are extended star schemas that are inherently redundant to the DSOs that stage data before them. In SAP HANA, InfoCubes are no longer necessary to deliver optimal read performance.

▶ Prebuilt summarized data sets such as aggregates are, by definition, redundant. With BWA, aggregates are less valuable, assuming that ample memory is available to replace them with BWA indexes; with SAP HANA, aggregates are completely obsolete.

> **Recommendation**
>
> If a denormalization approach is followed, it is the designer's responsibility to keep the redundant data in sync across the relevant database tables in a timely manner. It is this increase in logical complexity that makes this approach hazardous. Failure to keep data in sync results in data inconsistencies between reports and subjects the support team to end-user questions or complaints. In the worst case, a lack of data integrity and consistency could significantly affect adoption rates.

Many of the principles employed by SAP BW to improve performance, such as multidimensional modeling and aggregates, have been developed for use with traditional relational databases to circumvent limitations or constraints of that technology. With the advent of the in-memory database SAP HANA, significant changes to the way data models should be developed have arisen as more and more logic is pushed down to the database layer. This requires adapting to new ways of thinking and a departure from the best practices of the past.

Most of the new features available with SAP BW 7.40 are designed specifically for use with SAP HANA. The combination of SAP BW 7.40 and SAP HANA provides the following benefits:

▶ Simplification of the data modeling processes by providing one common modeling environment

▶ Increase in the agility of the EDW by enabling the seamless consumption of data from HANA into BW and BW into HANA

▶ Reduction in the complexity of the EDW landscape by processing large amounts of data faster

▶ Combination of the strengths of both an SQL-oriented approach with an integrated EDW application, enabling reuse of SAP BW services to manage and analyze data

Some of the features SAP BW 7.40 has to offer are applicable to all databases, so migration to SAP HANA is not necessarily required. However, it is not possible to take advantage of all the new features without SAP HANA.

In this section, we will first cover the enhanced data modeling capabilities delivered with SAP BW 7.40 (Section 5.1.1) before reviewing semantic partitioning in detail (Section 5.1.2). We'll then cover modeling in detail for InfoCubes (Section

5.1.3), DataStore objects (Section 5.1.4), VirtualProviders (Section 5.1.5), and HybridProviders (Section 5.1.6).

5.1.1 Enhanced Data Modeling with SAP BW 7.40

Recall from Chapter 2 that SAP BW 7.40 delivers new data architecture features that harness the flexibility and performance of SAP HANA and/or enable access to data from new external systems:

- SAP HANA Smart Data Access as the logical EDW
- Operational Data Provisioning to further reduce data layers in BW

These new architecture capabilities of SAP HANA are driving innovations in data modeling. Here are some of the key enhanced data modeling features available with SP5 of SAP BW 7.40:

- Common Eclipse-based modeling tools
- Open ODS Views to easily integrate external data models (field based modeling)
- New CompositeProvider
- Inventory Key Figures for DSOs, VirtualProviders, and CompositeProviders

> **Recommendation**
>
> With the exception of Operational Data Provisioning, all of these new features are available only for SAP BW on SAP HANA systems.

Even in traditional database installations, there are enough new features to justify an upgrade or installation of SAP BW 7.40 in addition to enhancements and bug fixes to existing functionality. Each of these new features deserves more attention. We'll cover some, such as Open ODS Views and the new CompositeProvider, later in this chapter. The rest will be covered now before moving on to data modeling.

Eclipse-Based Modeling Tools

SAP has spent significant effort simplifying the modeling tools used in SAP BW 7.40 on SAP HANA. The new Eclipse-based tools are flexible, intuitive, and easy to use and include SAP HANA Studio, BW Modeling, and ABAP Development Tools. See Figure 5.1 for an example of an Eclipse-based maintenance screen for InfoObjects that can be accessed from SAP HANA Studio; it has all the same functionality as Transaction RSDIOBJ.

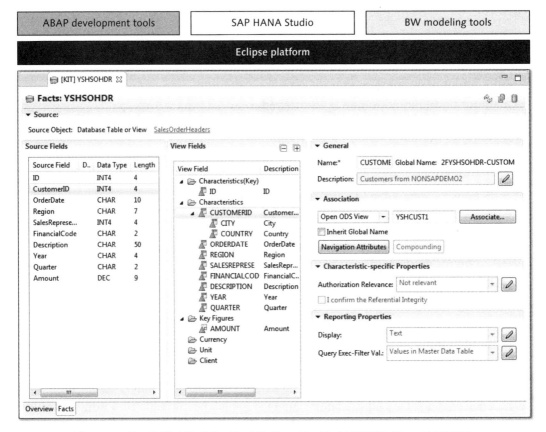

Figure 5.1 The Unified Modeling Tool Platform Used in SAP BW 7.40 on SAP HANA

For BW Modeling, the newly developed modeling tools include Open ODS Views and the new CompositeProvider, which can be accessed from both SAPgui ❶ and SAP HANA Studio ❷, as shown in Figure 5.2. These tools facilitate harmonization between the SAP BW and SAP HANA modeling environments by enabling integration and cross-consumption of models between them.

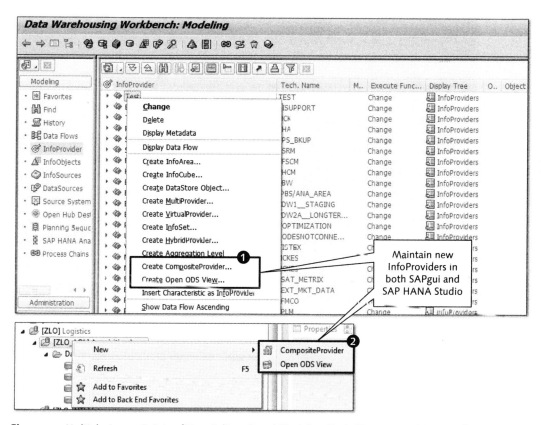

Figure 5.2 Multiple Access Points of New Eclipse-Based Modeling Tools (Transaction RSA11 and SAP HANA Studio)

Smart Data Access

Recall from Chapter 2 that SAP HANA Smart Data Access (SDA) uses ODBC connections to enable direct read access to relational and non-relational sources as if they were persistent tables in BW. SDA is available only in SAP HANA systems and can be used to read data from sources that were never before accessible by SAP BW, such as Sybase IQ, Sybase ASE, SAP HANA, Hadoop, and Teradata (see Figure 5.3). When a query is executed on the Open ODS View in the BW virtualization layer, the data is read directly from the source system, and the result is returned to the query. Therefore, no data is stored persistently in the SAP HANA database.

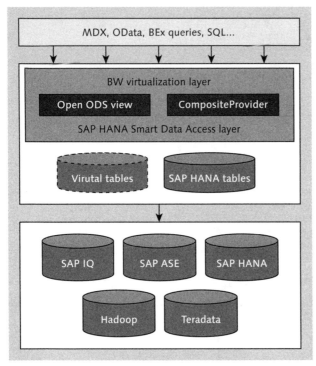

Figure 5.3 BW Virtualization Layer and Smart Data Access
(Transaction RSA11 and SAP HANA Studio)

On SAP HANA, there is no longer a need to physically move data into SAP BW—
as long as network performance is fast enough and the data volumes are not excessive, the virtual models reduce the data volume in SAP BW and data loading
latency to report on external data. By using the new objects, such as Open ODS
View and CompositeProviders, in the BW Virtualization Layer for LSA++, you can
now create a federated EDW.

Operational Data Provisioning

Operational Data Povisioning (ODP) enables the use of SLT and other BW systems
as sources for an SAP BW 7.40 system. As depicted in Figure 5.4, ODP creates a
shared technology platform for data extraction and allows for one-time extraction
to multiple data targets, without needing a PSA. The data persisted in the ODP is
highly compressed—up to 90%—so it consumes even less space than a PSA
would.

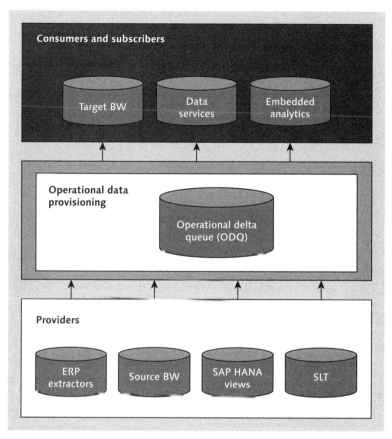

Figure 5.4 Operational Data Provisioning and the Operation Delta Queue

ODP offers the following benefits:

▸ Unified configuration and monitoring for all provider and subscriber types

▸ Timestamp-based recovery mechanism for all provider types with configurable data-retention periods

▸ Highly efficient compression that enables data compression rates up to 90% in operational delta queue (ODQ)

▸ Intelligent parallelization options for subscribers in high-volume scenarios

Regardless of the database installed and specific features available, the first step to building a data warehouse for optimized performance is to adhere to a layered scalable architecture, as covered in Chapter 2. Before you proceed into optimized data modeling, it is important to fully understand the semantic partitioning principles of LSA and LSA++.

5.1.2 Semantic Partitioning

Recall from Chapter 2 that semantic partitioning is an architectural design to enable parallel data loading and query execution. The performance benefits are so significant that semantic partitioning should be deployed on virtually every data model. Compared to standard InfoCubes or DSOs, a semantically partitioned object offers the following advantages:

▸ **Better performance**
The larger the data volumes, the longer the runtimes required for standard DSOs and standard InfoCubes. Semantic partitioning distributes the data across several different DSOs or InfoCubes with the same data model. The result is shorter runtimes when loading, activating, or querying data across different domains when data is partitioned by anything other than calendar year, like region, company, or controlling area.

▸ **Smaller BWA footprint**
If the partition is by calendar or fiscal year, more current partitions can be indexed, and older partitions can remain in traditional storage, resulting in lower cost for BWA memory. In an SAP BW on SAP HANA system, older partitions can be set to "cold" so that they are either near-lined or unloaded from memory before other tables.

▸ **Better scheduling flexibility**
For an EDW scenario involving several time zones, regional partitions defined by time zone can be loaded independently of each other.

▸ **Better error handling**
If a request for one region ends with an error, for example, the entire InfoProvider is unavailable for analysis and reporting. With a semantically partitioned object, the separation of regions into different partitions means that only the region that caused the error is unavailable for data analysis.

Prior to SAP BW 7.30, semantic partitions had to be implemented and managed manually, as shown in the Figure 5.5. For each partition, a separate and distinct data provider had to be built with transformations to and from it. Business transformations to look up data had to be coded to read dynamically from the correct partition. And changes to one model or transformation had to be manually replicated for each partition.

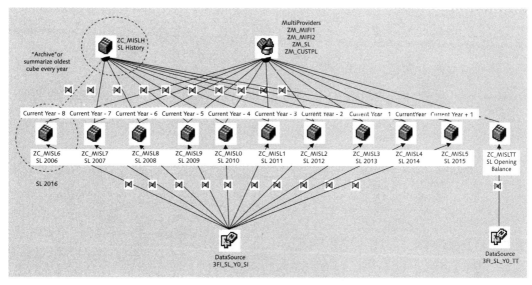

Figure 5.5 An Example of Semantic Partitions for Special Ledger Data

The model depicted in Figure 5.5 is designed for the special ledger, which has two DataSources. The data flow model for the totals table (TT) is not partitioned, but the data flow model for the detail ledger entries (SI) is partitioned by fiscal year. This model has ten partitions, each for one fiscal year from "current year - 8" (CY-8) to "current year + 1" (CY+1). For the current year, 2014, the data in Info-Cube ZC_MISL6 is from 2006 (CY-8), and the data in InfoCube ZC_MISL5 will be from 2015 (CY+1). Data loads to each InfoCube are managed by a filter in each transformation from the SI DataSource. At the end of the current year, CY-8 will be manually loaded to summary cube ZC_MISLH, which has a coarser level of granularity along more than one dimension, so the data volume will be reduced significantly. Once the summary data is validated, the detailed data in InfoCube for CY-8 will be dropped. Then, the transformation filter control mechanism will be updated manually to load "current year + 2," or 2016, into the empty cube ZC_MISL6.

These annual activities must be performed with some level of manual maintenance and control at the end of every year. In addition, any change to the model must be manually replicated to each model. If the SI model were loaded from DSOs that were also partitioned, the level of effort to add a single field would be 20 times the effort to update the non-partitioned TT InfoCube. Figure 5.6 shows a semantically partitioned data flow with both DSOs and InfoCubes prior to SAP BW 7.30.

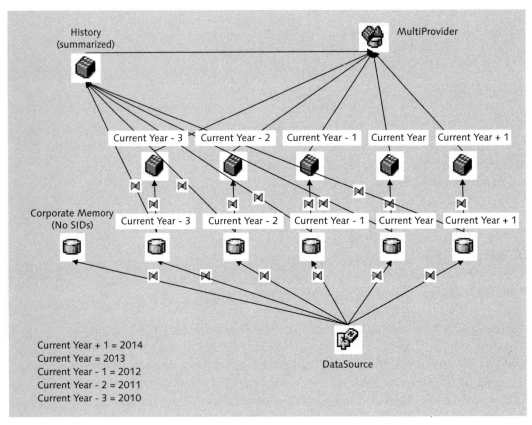

Figure 5.6 Semantically Partitioned Data Flow with DSOs and InfoCubes

The semantically partitioned object (SPO) InfoProvider type was introduced with SAP BW 7.30; the SPO is designed to automate the implementation of semantic partitioning, so it creates several objects with the same structure. These partitions are technically referred to as PartProviders. The introduction of the SPO has radically simplified the effort to design, build, and maintain semantically partitioned models in six easy steps (keep in mind that it is necessary to design and build only a single reference object):

1. Create a new InfoCube or DSO and check the box designating it a semantically partitioned object.

> **Note**
>
> The technical names of SPOs are limited to six characters.

2. Add all required InfoObjects to the InfoProvider. If the SPO is based on a DSO, all partitioning characteristics have to be included in the key.

3. Define the partitions in the appropriate maintenance screen and activate the SPO. Up to five InfoObjects can be used to define each partition, and up to 99 partitions are supported (multiple partitions can be created at one time). Partitions are characterized by distinct partitioning criteria—there can be no overlap between dimensions. No overflow partition is created automatically, so one must be modeled in the partitioning criteria. Exclusions are not supported for partitioning criteria, and only one interval or list of single values is allowed per InfoObject per partition.

4. Create a single transformation to map fields from the DataSource to the SPO. It is only necessary to design and build transformation logic to map the reference object—all filtering is automatically managed by the SPO partitioning criteria.

5. Create DTPs to load data via the transformation to the SPO.

6. Add the DTPs to a process chain and schedule the load.

Figure 5.7 shows an example of an SPO created to replicate the special ledger scenario with 10 partitions by year.

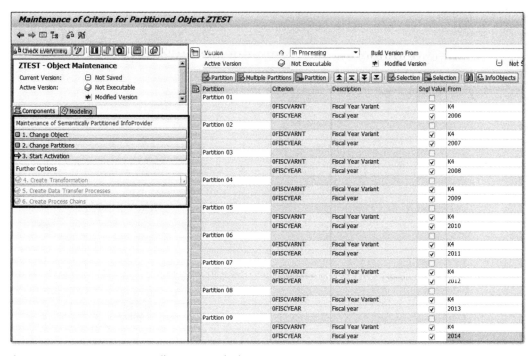

Figure 5.7 Creating a Semantically Partitioned Object

Recommendation

If the SPO is an InfoCube, deltas can be updated to the target InfoProvider using DTPs without any restrictions. If the source is an SPO based on a reference DSO, only full DTPs can be created. To perform delta updates, select the partitions of the SPO, rather than the SPO itself, as the source.

If the target is an SPO, perform the DTPs using the target SPO's wizard. The source of the DTPs must then be the outbound InfoSource of the source SPO, rather than the semantically partitioned object itself.

For analysis and reporting, data from semantically partitioned objects can be joined in a MultiProvider or CompositeProvider to enable seamless reporting to end users. For reporting needs requiring more flexibility, selected partitions can either be further updated to another InfoCube or included in a MultiProvider for specific analysis, as shown in Figure 5.8.

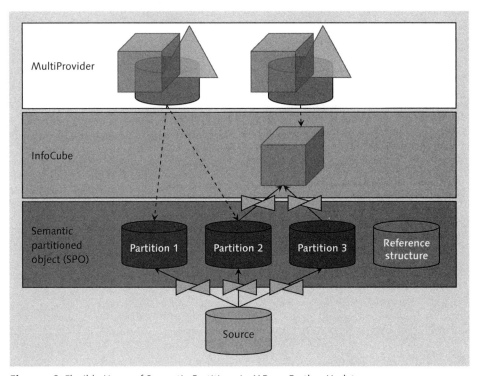

Figure 5.8 Flexible Usage of Semantic Partitions in MPs or Further Updates

> **Recommendation**
>
> If an entire SPO is further updated to another InfoProvider, navigation attributes cannot be used in the analysis. This is because the InfoSource that compiles the individual partitions for the update does not support navigation attributes. If you update only some of the partitions, this restriction does not apply.

When you are joining SPOs in a MultiProvider, each partition is explicitly represented in the MP. However, this increase in the number of joins in the MP should not impact query performance due to *partition pruning*, which forces the online analytic processor to read only the partitions that contain data requested from the query. In this way, the data is processed quickly, even without the use of a BW accelerator.

5.1.3 InfoCube Modeling

Recall from Chapter 1 that the standard InfoCube is a set of relational tables structured as an extended star schema, which includes a fact table joined to dimension tables (see Figure 1.2). The extended star schema is an architectural concept that improves performance in a relational database when reporting on large datasets and supports analytical processing by facilitating filtering, navigation, and aggregation of facts.

The dimension tables and fact table are linked to one another using dimension IDs (DIMIDs), which are four-byte fields of sequential numbers contained in the key part of both tables. The key figures in the fact table are thus related to the characteristics in the dimension tables; in other words, the dimensional characteristics determine the granularity at which the key figures are stored in the InfoCube.

> **Recommendation**
>
> The dimension IDs form a concatenated key, which enables the InfoCube to circumvent the limit of 16 key fields in traditional database tables.

While InfoCubes can hold up to 250 characteristics and 233 key figures, it is not recommended to build cubes with this many fields in them. First, an InfoCube with that many key figures would likely be sparsely populated, which means most key figures would be blank for each transaction. Because these blank key-figure values consume as much database storage space as populated ones, the result is high storage costs for lower performance. Any cube with 250 characteristics likely has so many combinations of characteristic values in each dimension that DIMID generation results in extremely slow data loads (even if the DIMIDs are buffered), and the dimensions themselves likely result in poor-performing queries.

InfoCubes can have a maximum of 16 dimensions. Three of these dimensions are used by SAP: time, unit, and package. The other 13 dimensions are available for customization. Correlated characteristics should be combined in dimensions to facilitate query building in the BEx Query Designer; this provides both functional and technical benefits. Functionally, it is easier to choose fields to add to a query from dimensional groups of related fields than one long list of all InfoObjects in the cube. Technically, the grouping of characteristics in dimensions can have a significant impact on both data loading and reporting performance.

> **Recommendation**
>
> For optimal performance, the number of rows in dimension tables should not exceed 10% of the number of rows in the fact table. Smaller dimension tables always provide better performance.

Too many characteristics and/or characteristic values can lead to dimensions that exceed the previously noted threshold. This has an impact on the performance of [F4] filter value selections on posted values and query navigation performance. In most cases, it makes sense to use all the dimensions available and set as many line-item dimensions as possible. In practice, though, most data modelers prefer to leave one or two dimensions available so that they are in a better position to handle future business requirements that are still currently unknown. Remodeling dimensions is not an easy task once the InfoCubes are productive and have data loaded into them—especially if the data cannot be simply and/or quickly reloaded. So, having a spare dimension or two to add unrelated characteristics to the cube to support future requirements can be immensely beneficial.

Characteristics that logically belong together (for example, sales district and sales area are both details of a sales region) should be grouped together in the same dimension. One method for visualizing characteristics that belong together is to create a granularity map, as shown in Figure 5.9. Detail characteristics representing a finer level of granularity should be placed closer to the center of the map, and coarser-granularity characteristics should be further out. For example, along the cost-center dimensional line, *cost center* is closer to the center, and *controlling area* is farther away from the center. Any characteristics that do not fit on a dimensional line may need their own dimension. If characteristics farther out on the line can be or are already navigational attributes of another dimensional characteristic, they should be used as navigational attributes unless there is a requirement to store a transactional value for that field in the cube.

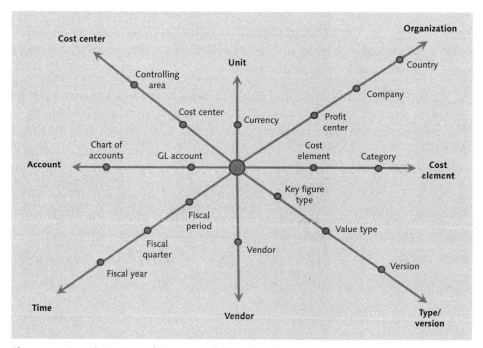

Figure 5.9 Granularity Map of Dimensional Characteristics

Recommendation

To reduce the potential need for future maintenance, facilitate MultiProvider and CompositeProvider assignments, and simplify query development, add all relevant time characteristics to the InfoCube up front. For example, if calendar day (0CALDAY) is the finest granularity in the transaction, then all coarser granularity time characteristics should also be added, such as calendar week (0CALWEEK), calendar month (0CALMONTH2), calendar month/year (0CALMONTH), calendar quarter (0CALQUART1), calendar quarter/year (0CALQUARTER), and calendar year (0CALYEAR). Failure to do this up front limits the flexibility and functionality of reporting down the road.

When you adhere to these design criteria, dimensions remain independent of each other, and dimension tables remain small when it comes to data volume.

Smaller dimension sizes are extremely beneficial to performance—InfoCubes with dimensions that adhere to the threshold percentage are optimized for data analysis.

To satisfy many reporting requirements, it may be necessary to group unrelated characteristics into the same dimension. The best way to perform a sanity check on the expected performance of these dimensions is to calculate both the maximum and expected number of dimension records and compare them against the expected number of records in the fact table.

For example, the characteristics in the type/version dimension are not always related, so a sanity check could prove instrumental in determining whether these characteristics should indeed occupy the same dimension, as shown in Table 5.1. In fact, there are a few more characteristics that could be evaluated for this dimension at the same time.

Dimensional Characteristic	Distinct Values
Key figure type	27
Currency type	13
Value type	10
Version	9
Valuation	3
Sender/receiver indicator	2

Table 5.1 Potential Unrelated Candidates for a Type/Version Dimension

To calculate the maximum possible number of dimension records, simply multiply the distinct values of all characteristics together:

Max values = 27 × 13 × 10 × 9 × 3 × 2 = 189,540

This result indicates that this could be a large dimension depending on the size of the fact table—if the fact table has only one million rows, this dimension table will exceed the optimal threshold at 19%. However, not all of these characteristics are mutually exclusive. For example, just because there are 10 distinct value types and nine distinct versions does not mean there are 90 valid combinations of the two. In fact, there may be a relationship between these two fields that predicates only

23 distinct combinations. Furthermore, perhaps the transactions to be loaded into this cube use only three of the 13 available currency types. If these statements are true, to calculate the expected number of values would require replacing 13 × 10 × 9 from the original formula with 3 × 23, as follows:

*Expected values = 27 × **3** × **23** × 3 × 2 = 11,178*

This new result shows that a dimension with six characteristics would satisfy the threshold in a cube with one million rows because the rows in the dimension would be less than 2% of the fact table. Such a dimension should perform well in almost any cube. What is interesting is the significant difference in the results of the calculations — all these characteristics have less than 30 distinct values, and yet in a completely mutually exclusive environment, the number of expected combinations could easily skyrocket and significantly impact performance.

> **Recommendation**
>
> Be careful storing multiple dates in dimensions other than the time dimension. The number of records in a dimension table with three mutually exclusive dates could easily exceed 48 million records in a single year.

Up to this point, the discussion has centered on the optimal design of a multidimensional InfoCube. This advice holds true for the standard InfoCube most of all, but there are several different types of InfoCubes, and each has a specific structure and use case. Table 5.2 gives a description of each available InfoCube type.

InfoCube Type	Description
Standard	▸ Standard InfoCubes have a multi-dimensional structure.
	▸ Standard InfoCubes are technically optimized for reporting, to the detriment of data loading.
	▸ Data is loaded to a standard InfoCube by a data-transfer process and stored physically in the database.
BWA-only	▸ BWA-only InfoCubes have a multi-dimensional structure.
	▸ Data is loaded to a BWA-only InfoCube by a data transfer process (DTP) and stored directly in the BW Accelerator.
	▸ BWA-only InfoCubes cannot be built in SAP HANA databases.

Table 5.2 InfoCube Types

InfoCube Type	Description
In-memory	▸ In-memory InfoCubes do not have physical dimension tables (except for the package dimension). ▸ Characteristics can still be added to dimensions for logical grouping purposes (helps locating characteristics when building queries). ▸ Data is loaded to an in-memory InfoCube by a data-transfer process and stored in the HANA database. ▸ In-memory InfoCubes are available as InfoProviders for analysis and reporting purposes. ▸ All new InfoCubes built in SAP HANA are in-memory by default; existing InfoCubes have to be manually converted.
Real-time	▸ Real-time InfoCubes have a multi-dimensional structure. ▸ Data is loaded to real-time InfoCubes when data is entered into BW Integrated Planning reports.
Semantically partitioned	▸ Semantically partitioned InfoCubes have a multi-dimensional structure. ▸ Semantically partitioned InfoCubes consist of multiple standard InfoCubes (partitions) with the same structure but different data. ▸ Data is loaded to a standard InfoCube by a data-transfer process and stored physically in the database. ▸ Semantically partitioned InfoCubes are available as InfoProviders for analysis and reporting purposes.

Table 5.2 InfoCube Types (Cont.)

Each different type of InfoCube has specific technical settings. We'll review each independently in the following sections, with the exception of the semantically partitioned InfoCube, which has already been covered in Section 5.1.2.

Standard InfoCube

The most often overlooked performance optimization available for standard Info-Cubes is fact table compression. Compression offers many benefits to both reporting and data loading.

For example, if the transactions in the InfoCube have an average of two deltas for each transaction posted, the number of records in an uncompressed InfoCube is five times more than the number of records in a compressed InfoCube. As an example, consider this: the initial transaction would be loaded to the InfoCube as an after-image. The first change to the transaction would result in two more records: a negation of the before-image and the new after-image. The second change would result in an additional two more records, for a total of five records in the InfoCube.

Upon compression with elimination of zeroes, the first four records would be compressed to two records and then deleted from the E-fact table, leaving only the final after-image available. This benefits reporting: less data is selected from the database, and less data is processed in the OLAP engine. The data is also physically partitioned by time period, meaning faster queries filtered by time. It also has a substantial benefit to data loading; less data in the F-fact table correlates with faster database indexing. Having fewer data packages in the F-fact table leads to more efficient management of the InfoCube. Having less data in the InfoCube reduces the cost of storage and the footprint in BWA. (Keep in mind that the BWA index must be fully dropped and re-built to reclaim the space taken by the records eliminated during compression.)

It is important to understand that physical partitioning and compression go hand in hand. Without compression, there is little reason to physically partition Info-Cubes, although the addition of the indexed partitioning column in the F-fact table provides a performance benefit when reporting on the partitioned time characteristic. Because the E-fact table is partitioned by the time characteristic and not filled unless you compress, partitioning without compression offers little benefit. On the other hand, compression alone, without physical partitioning, offers more from a data-loading perspective but delivers fewer benefits from a reporting perspective.

To further optimize performance, dimensions of standard InfoCubes can be flagged as line-item and/or as high cardinality. A *line-item dimension* can have only one characteristic in it. In this case, there is no dimension table created, and the SID of the characteristic InfoObject replaces the DIMID in the fact table. The line-item table improves data load performance by eliminating the need to generate a DIMID and write it to the dimension table, and improves query performance by eliminating a join in the analytic processor.

If the InfoCube has fewer than 13 characteristics, place each in its own dimension and flag them as line-item, especially if each characteristic has many navigational attributes. This provides the best performance.

> **Recommendation**
>
> Line-item dimensions can be reset only by dropping all data in the InfoCube. Therefore, if future requirements dictate a need to add a characteristic to an existing line-item dimension, the data must generally be dropped before the remodel can be executed.

For systems on an Oracle database, there is also a HIGH CARDINALITY flag, which is independent of the line-item dimension setting, available for dimensions. High cardinality simply means that a high number of records are expected in the dimension, usually in the tens or hundreds of millions. In normal usage, all dimension indexes are built using bitmap indexes in Oracle and are extremely efficient during lookups and when used to combine selection criteria. However, they do not handle large numbers of distinct values when compared to the total number of rows in the base table. Therefore, if there are a high number of distinct DIMIDs for a given dimension when compared to the rows in the fact table, the DB index for that dimension may perform poorly as a bitmap index. Such a dimension is naturally a candidate for the HIGH CARDINALITY flag.

When the HIGH CARDINALITY flag is set, a B*tree index is created for the index instead of the default bitmap index. B*tree indexes are not as efficient for reporting as bitmap indexes because only bitmap indexes can be used for star-join access, which is the most effective way of selecting data. In rare cases, building b*tree indexes is quicker than building bitmap indexes, but you should always test them for adverse impacts before proceeding.

> **Recommendation**
>
> Do not set the HIGH CARDINALITY flag unless you encounter severe performance issues when rebuilding database (DB) indexes on the affected InfoCube. Always test this setting for impacts on data loading and reporting before using it productively.

> **Recommendation**
>
> Never use HIGH CARDINALITY flags with characteristics in non-cumulative validity tables, or the result will be a significant impact to reporting performance.

If a dimension has a high number of rows and you encounter a severe performance issue with bitmap indexes, such as that building indexes takes hours, you should look for opportunities to remodel the dimensions so that they are more balanced and each has fewer rows before setting the HIGH CARDINALITY flag. This approach allows the preservation of reporting performance while also resolving the index performance issue.

Dropping and rebuilding DB indexes on the F-fact table is often faster than updating the same indexes during loading, assuming that the InfoCube is compressed regularly. Therefore, when loading data to InfoCubes, always delete the DB indexes prior to loading and rebuild them after loading (before rolling up). These processes should be handled in the process chains and should be a part of a standard PC template.

When loading data into standard InfoCubes, multiple DTPs can be executed in parallel only if the DB indexes are dropped before the loads. The data in each request is only visible after the last request has been successfully loaded. If data is subsequently loaded into an aggregate or BWA index, the data is not available until the requests are rolled up.

BWA-Only InfoCube

For systems with BWA, you can load data directly into a BWA index without staging it persistently in the BW database. This means that only the definition and structure of the InfoCube are known to the database. Storing InfoCube data directly in BWA and not on the database offers many benefits, as follows:

- Avoids data redundancy in the SAP BW system by storing cube data only once
- Improves database performance by preserving memory space and reducing load on the system
- Eliminates the need to create aggregates
- Improves data analysis performance by relocating it from SAP BW to BWA

For BWA-only InfoCubes, there is no E-fact table and only one dimension table—the package dimension, which is required to manage requests in the BW system. This is the only InfoCube table populated in the database.

The F-fact table is still created in the database because it is needed to drive the definition of the BWA index, but it remains empty. There are no dimensions because the F-fact table indexes are flattened, which means that the characteristic SIDs are written directly to the F-fact table in BWA. This improves data loading performance and simplifies cube design and development; dimensions do not need to be optimized for performance. Rather, InfoObjects can be logically placed in dimensions to facilitate query development.

Data is loaded to the BWA-only InfoCube using DTPs from the EDW layer in the warehouse, which remains a stable basis layer. When needed, the BWA index can be dropped and reloaded from the EDW layer. For technical reasons, multiple DTPs cannot load a BWA-only InfoCube in parallel, so multiple DTPs must be scheduled sequentially. However, parallelization within each DTP is possible.

> **Recommendation**
>
> There is no backup and restore process for BWA-only InfoCubes—the cubes have to be completely reloaded in case of error. There is also no selective deletion or request deletion capability for BWA-only InfoCubes.

Obviously, there are other administration functions that are not available for BWA-only InfoCubes, such as partitioning, compression, and reconstruction of the BWA index—data needs to be loaded to the BWA index; it cannot be reconstructed.

In-Memory InfoCube

In an SAP HANA environment, the principles of the LSA++ architecture should be implemented (see Chapter 2). InfoCubes (whether or not optimized for SAP HANA) are no longer necessary, except in the following use cases:

- Non-cumulative key figures (as of SAP BW 7.40 SP5) can be modeled in DSOs.
- Integrated planning can only be done on real-time InfoCubes.
- The external write-interface (RSDRI) works only for InfoCubes.

The in-memory InfoCube is a standard InfoCube optimized for use with SAP HANA. In SAP HANA, all InfoCubes are stored as columnar tables, where each field in the table is itself an index. Because of the way columnar databases work, multidimensional models like star schemas are no longer necessary to improve query performance, especially when the columnar tables are stored directly in memory. However, there is still a benefit to grouping characteristics into relevant dimensions—these dimensions facilitate query development by making it easier to locate characteristics in the cube.

In an in-memory InfoCube, characteristics can still be assigned to dimensions. However, the system does not create any dimension tables in the database, except the package dimension. Instead, the SID of each characteristic value is written directly to the fact table. This improves system performance during data loading because DIMIDs do not have to be generated and written to the dimension tables. The dimensions are simply used as a logical grouping of objects to facilitate query development in the BEx Query Designer.

In SAP HANA, changes to columnar tables are recorded in delta tables, which need to be subsequently merged with the main table. This activity is handled directly by the database, so partitioning and compression can no longer be used in the traditional sense. To manage this from the application level, four partitions are automatically created for InfoCubes, as shown in Figure 5.10:

- Partition 1: Non-compressed requests
- Partition 2: Compressed requests
- Partition 3: Reference points for inventory data
- Partition 4: Historic movements of inventory data

> **Recommendation**
>
> Partitions 3 and 4 are always created, even if there are no inventory/non-cumulative key figures present in the InfoCube

In an SAP HANA environment, in-memory InfoCubes are the default standard. It is no longer possible to build any InfoCubes with a physical DataStore except in-memory InfoCubes. In Figure 5.10, ❶ and ❷ illustrate that all standard InfoCubes are in-memory, which can be deselected only in the case of a VirtualProvider. Further, ❸ and ❹ illustrate the checkboxes to specify whether the InfoCube is also real-time or semantically partitioned, respectively. After a migration to HANA from any other database, InfoCubes are not automatically converted to in-memory InfoCubes—they have to be converted manually, one by one.

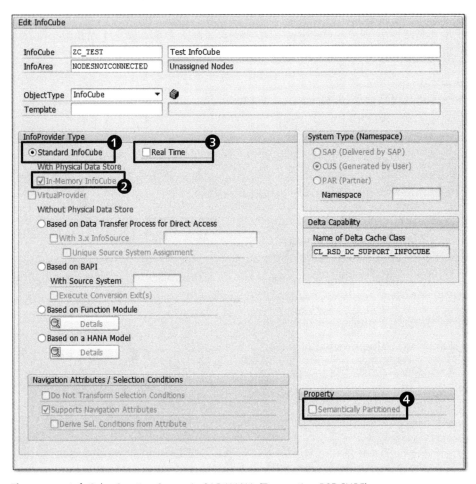

Figure 5.10 InfoCube Creation Screen in SAP HANA (Transaction RSDCUBE)

Real-Time InfoCube

Standard InfoCubes technically allow parallel write processes, but they are optimized for read access. You must drop all DB indexes from the InfoCube in order to load more than one DTP to it, and any data loaded in parallel is available only when all requests are successfully completed, DB indexes are re-created, and BWA indexes or aggregates have been rolled up. Real-time cubes differ from standard InfoCubes in their ability to support parallel write access, which makes them the perfect choice for Integrated Planning where multiple users enter data simultaneously during their planning sessions.

Real-time InfoCubes can be populated with data using the following two different methods:

- The transaction for entering planning data
- BW staging

Real-time InfoCubes can be converted from plan mode to load mode and back again. In plan mode, data cannot be loaded by BW staging. In load mode, data cannot be entered via planning. To convert the real-time InfoCube, right-click the cube in the InfoProvider tree and choose PLANNING-SPECIFIC PROPERTIES • CHANGE REAL-TIME INFOCUBE. By default, REAL-TIME DATA TARGET CAN BE PLANNED, DATA LOADING NOT PERMITTED is selected. Switch this setting to REAL-TIME DATA TARGET CAN BE LOADED WITH DATA; PLANNING NOT PERMITTED to load the cube using BW Staging.

> **Recommendation**
>
> The conversion can also be executed in the background using ABAP report SAP_CONVERT_NORMAL_TRANS. Alternatively, use the process chain variants *Switch Realtime InfoCube to Plan Mode* and *Switch Realtime InfoCube to Load Mode*.

In plan mode, data is written to a real-time InfoCube data request. When the number of records in the data request exceeds a threshold value, the request is closed and rolled up asynchronously into any defined aggregates.

Depending on the database on which they are based, real-time InfoCubes differ from standard InfoCubes in the way they are indexed and partitioned. In Oracle, there are no bitmap indexes on the fact table. The resulting reduction in read-only performance is acceptable in favor of parallel (transactional) writing and improved write performance.

5.1.4 DSO Modeling

While InfoCubes are good for reporting on summarized and/or aggregated data, DSOs are good for loading and storing detailed or atomic-level data and propagating delta records through to InfoCubes. DSOs store data in flat, transparent tables and can contain up to 16 key fields and a maximum of 749 total fields (key + data), or 1962 bytes, whichever comes first.

Because DSOs are used for data staging and business transformations, they are more widely used than InfoCubes and can account for up to 80% of the disk storage space used on the database. In a traditional DBMS, they are less likely to be used for reporting and analysis because their structure is not optimized for it. In SAP HANA, however, DSOs are used for both data staging and reporting; all columnar tables are optimized for read access because every field is indexed.

Table 5.3 lists different types of DSOs. Each DSO has a specific use case, functionality, structure, and/or loading mechanism.

DataStore Type	Description
Standard	▶ Standard DSOs have a three-table structure (New, Active, and Change Log). ▶ Standard InfoCubes are technically optimized for data loading, to the detriment of reporting. ▶ Data is loaded to a standard DSO by a DTP and stored physically in the database.
In-memory	▶ In-memory DSOs are the same as standard, but they reside in SAP HANA.
Write-optimized	▶ Write-optimized DSOs have a single-table structure (Active). ▶ No SIDs are generated in write-optimized DSOs. ▶ Data does not need to be activated in direct update DSOs. ▶ Data is loaded to write-optimized DSOs by a data-transfer process and stored physically in the database.
Direct update	▶ Direct update DSOs have a single-table structure (Active). ▶ No SIDs are generated in direct update DSOs. ▶ Data does not need to be activated in direct update DSOs. ▶ Data is loaded to direct update DSOs by APIs or Integrated Planning.
Semantically partitioned	▶ Semantically partitioned DSOs consist of multiple standard DSOs (partitions) with the same structure but different data. ▶ Data is loaded to a standard DSO by a DTP and stored physically in the database. ▶ Semantically partitioned DSOs are available as InfoProviders for analysis and reporting purposes.

Table 5.3 Description of DSO Types and Usages

Let's review each DSO described in Table 4.3 for best practices and performance tips to ensure a satisfactory level of performance.

Standard DSO

Recall from Chapter 1 that a standard DSO is a data-staging object that consists of three transparent, flat table structures: an activation queue, an active data table, and a change log (see Figure 1.3).

> **Note**
>
> Let's quickly review how the three DSO tables work together during the data load:
>
> ► The *activation queue* is filled with new records when they are loaded by request to the DSO. These records are stored here until they are activated. After all requests are activated, this data is deleted.
>
> ► The *active data* table contains the active data and is called the A table. Active data tables are built according to the DSO definition, which contains a key fields section and a data field section—each consisting of InfoObjects of all types.
>
> ► The *change log* contains the change history for the delta update from the DSO into other data targets, such as other DSOs or InfoCubes.

The activation queue and change log are almost identical in structure: the activation queue has an SID, the package ID, and the record number as its key, whereas the change log has the request ID, package ID, and record number as its key.

Data can be loaded into the activation queues of DSOs by several sources simultaneously because a queuing mechanism enables a parallel insert. The key fields allow records to be labeled consistently in the activation queue and keep them segregated by package.

During activation, the data in the activation queue is compared against the data in the active data table: new records are inserted, and changed records are updated (key figures can be set to overwrite or summation). The results of the changes (the deltas) are recorded in the change log and are then available for loading to subsequent data targets, such as other DSOs or InfoCubes.

It is the activation step that can usually be found at the center of most DSO performance issues. It can take a long time to generate SID values, and the more fields in the DSO and the larger the data volume, the poorer the activation performance. To ensure satisfactory performance for DSO activation, consider the following best practices:

► Set the runtime parameters in the implementation guide to improve performance when processing data in DSOs (go to Transaction SPRO and choose the

SAP CUSTOMIZING IMPLEMENTATION GUIDE, then navigate to SAP NETWEAVER • BUSINESS INTELLIGENCE • PERFORMANCE SETTINGS • MAINTAIN RUNTIME PARAMETERS OF DATASTORE OBJECTS, or, from the ADMINISTRATION area of the Data Warehousing Workbench, choose CURRENT SETTINGS • DATASTORE OBJECTS). The values for these settings depend on the processing power of the system and are valid for all DSOs.

Parameters for activation:

▸ Define the default data-package size for data activation by setting the minimum number of data records for each data package.

▸ Define how long the main activation process waits for a split process before determining that it has failed by setting the maximum wait time, in seconds.

Parameters for SID generation:

▸ Define the default package size for SID generation by setting the minimum number of data records for each data package.

▸ Define how long the SID generation runs before acknowledging failure by setting the maximum wait time, in seconds.

Parameters for rollback:

▸ Set the maximum wait time, in seconds, for rollback in the DSO.

Process parameters:

▸ Define the type of processing by selecting serial, parallel (batch), or parallel (dialog).

▸ Limit how many work processes are used at one time for data processing by setting the maximum number of parallel processes.

▸ Identify the server group to be used for parallel processing of data in DSOs. If no server group is defined, processing runs on the same server where the activation process was started.

▸ Order the key fields in the DSO from coarse to fine granularity, with coarse-grained fields at the top/left and fine-grained fields at the bottom/right. This ensures that the primary index is defined in the most practical manner—so that it is traversed in a coarse-to-fine direction, which should align with end-user usage in most reports and transformation logic in most data lookups. Alternatively, order the keys from most frequently accessed to least frequently accessed, if coarse-to-fine is not appropriate.

For example, if the compound InfoObject `0MAT_PLANT` is in the key, then `0PLANT` should come first in the key order (top-left), ahead of `0MAT_PLANT` (bottom-right). This helps ensure that filters or drill-downs on plant use the primary index. In most cases, the primary index is used if all fields in the selection conditions contain key fields from the top-left, with no gaps. In other terms, consider a DSO with eight key fields, numbered K1-K8, where K1 is the top-left key field and K8 is the bottom-right key field. All eight key fields are in the primary index. A selection condition that includes key fields K1-K4 in the where clause uses the index, whereas a selection condition with fields K5-K8 does not. Likewise, a selection condition with fields K1-K3 and K6 also does not use the primary index because K4-K5 are missing from the where clause.

▶ Do not generate SID values unless required. There is little reason to generate SIDs for staged data unless it will also be used for reporting. In the EDW layer of the warehouse, there may be many fields extracted from the DataSource that will never be propagated up to a reportable layer. Set the SID creation to Never Create SIDs or During Reporting for these DSOs (see the setting labeled Create SIDs in Figure 5.11).

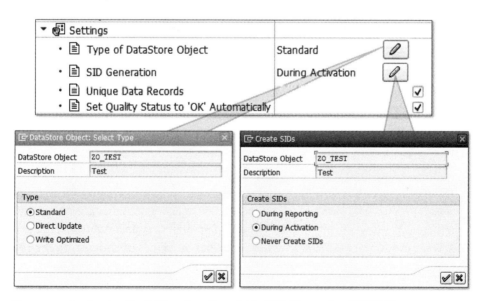

Figure 5.11 Configuring the Settings for a Reportable DSO (Transaction RSDODS)

▶ If there is no chance data loaded to the DSO will contain duplicate records (based on the key fields), set the Unique Data Records flag. Check this flag only if new unique records will be posted. During activation, the system does not need to compare the activation queue against the active table for existing records with the same keys. As a result, the activation runtime is reduced, especially in cases in which the active table contains a large number of records.

Recommendation

The UNIQUE DATA RECORDS property is valid only if SID generation is activated. If SID generation is not needed and data loads always deliver unique records, use a write-optimized DSO instead.

Table 5.4 shows the time saved in runtime activation for various configuration settings. The saving in runtime is influenced primarily by SID generation, and the specific percentages experienced differ depending on system configuration.

Runtime Savings by Technical Settings	Unique Data Records = ''	Unique Data Records = 'X'
Generation of SIDs During Activation = 'X'	0% (baseline)	~ 25%
Generation of SIDs During Activation = ''	~ 35%	~ 45%

Table 5.4 Relative Activation Times for DSO Configuration Options

- Limit the number of fields in the DSO to 300 fields or fewer. This is a subjective limit, but in our experience, DSOs with more than 300 fields suffer very poor performance during loading and activation, regardless of steps taken to optimize performance.

- Avoid loading free text fields to DSOs. If they must be loaded, set the InfoObjects as ATTRIBUTE ONLY to ensure that SIDs are never created for free text fields. Because free text fields are likely to have characters that are not permitted as key values (see more information on maintaining permitted characters in Section 1.4.3), they routinely result in activation errors in addition to the performance impact of generating SIDs for unique values that are probably not useful for filtering and/or drill-down usage.

- In systems using IBM DB2 databases, configure multidimensional clustering (MDC) on the active data tables by going to menu path EXTRAS • DB PERFORMANCE • CLUSTERING. At the database level, MDC enables quicker read access by reorganizing data into extents by cluster with block indexes, which are smaller and faster than traditional, secondary indexes. Simply choose one or more characteristics by which to group the data into clusters before loading data into the DSO.

▶ In a traditional DBMS other than DB2, configure partitioning for a similar benefit to clustering, with the limitation that partitioning is enabled only for time characteristics such as OFISCPER (fiscal period) and OCALMONTH (calendar year/month), just as it is for InfoCubes. To configure partitioning, go to menu path EXTRAS • DB PERFORMANCE • DB PARTITIONING.

▶ Create additional secondary indexes to satisfy selection criteria that do not access the primary index (check the query SQL trace, as discussed in Chapter 4). Secondary indexes can be created in DSO maintenance and can have a substantial positive impact on the performance of queries and transformation data lookups against the DSO.

Recommendation

Secondary indexes are updated during activation, so too many of them result in slower activation performance and could lead to activation errors, especially if the maximum wait time configured in the runtime parameters is too low.

In-Memory DSO

The in-memory DSO has the same structure and functionality as the standard DSO, with the exception that it exists in an SAP HANA database. In an SAP HANA environment, much of the activation logic has been pushed down into the database, so there is no time lost transferring data to and from the SAP BW application, thereby providing a substantial performance gain to data loads and activation times.

Recall from Chapter 2 that in SAP HANA, the layer architecture is adapted to LSA++, which replaces InfoCubes in the reporting layer with DSOs. As a result, DSO data models need to be updated to deliver the same reporting functionality as InfoCubes used to provide. In other words, all the characteristics and navigational attributes available in the InfoCube also need to be available in the DSO. From a modeling perspective, the biggest impact here is related to date fields. At least one date field needs to be mapped to a standard delivered business content time characteristic, such as calendar day (OCALDAY), which is specifically required in the following scenarios:

▶ Key date specifications for time-dependent master data

▶ Currency translation types with variable time references

▶ Data-archiving process configuration for NLS with Sybase IQ

Recommendation

To reduce the potential need for future maintenance, facilitate MultiProvider and CompositeProvider assignments, and simplify query development, add all relevant time characteristics to the in-memory DSO up front. For example, if calendar day (0CALDAY) is the finest granularity in the transaction, all coarser granularity time characteristics, such as calendar week (0CALWEEK), calendar month (0CALMONTH2), calendar month/year (0CALMONTH), calendar quarter (0CALQUART1), calendar quarter/year (0CALQUARTER), and calendar year (0CALYEAR) should also be added. Failure to do this up front will limit the flexibility and functionality of reporting down the road.

In SAP HANA, DSOs are stored as columnar tables, so by definition, each field is an index; this structure reduces the need for secondary indexes to improve selection condition performance. However, secondary indexes with multiple fields are still effective if these columns are used in a SELECT FOR ALL ENTRIES (SFAE) statement. In SFAE statements, the SAP HANA database essentially treats each condition as a select single, potentially negating the performance gain of a columnar table. Table 5.5 compares different SQL use cases.

Use Case	Pseudo SQL	Interpretation
Select for all entries (SFAE)	SELECT .. FROM <TABLE> WHERE (A,B,C,D,E) IN ((?,?,?,?,?) … (?,?,?,?,?)).	Acts like a series of select singles; an index will improve performance
Filter DTP or BEx query	SELECT .. FROM <TABLE> WHERE (A = ? OR A = ?) AND (B = ? OR B = ?).	Acts like a select * which performs well; no secondary index needed

Table 5.5 SQL Use Case Interpretation Regarding Benefits of Secondary Indexes

Where SFAE statements are used, a secondary index based on the entire where clause may still offer an improvement, although there have been marked improvements in this area since SAP HANA SP5 was released in 2013.

To recap, a standard DSO acts as a filter to prevent unchanged or duplicate data from updating InfoCubes. This filter mechanism is managed by the activation process, where only changes to the A table are written to the change log for further updating. There are many ways to optimize the DSO design to minimize the performance impact. However, the activation takes time, and in some scenarios, time may be too critical, or the delta functionality may not be necessary; in these scenarios, a write-optimized DSO may be the better choice.

Write-Optimized DSO

Write-optimized DSOs have a different structure and use case than standard DSOs. To start, they consist of a single active table, and when data is loaded using the DTP, it is immediately available for further processing. There is no activation step because data is not summarized or overwritten in the active table. Instead, the system generates a unique technical key for every record loaded to a write-optimized DSO. The technical, or primary, key consists of the following three fields:

1. `0REQUEST`: Request GUID
2. `0DATAPAKID`: Data package
3. `0RECORD`: Data record number

In addition to this technical key, a semantic key can be created based on the key fields in the DSO. Because data is not aggregated across the primary key, this DSO retains a history of all loaded data. If two data records with the same semantic key are extracted from the source, both records are saved in the DSO. However, the record mode responsible for aggregation remains, so data aggregation can take place in standard DSOs further on in the data flow.

The system does not generate SIDs for write-optimized DSOs, and there is no need to activate them. This enables data to be saved and further processed quickly. Reporting is possible on write-optimized DSOs if SIDs are set to generate during reporting; however, SID generation impacts query response time. See the setting labeled ❶ in Figure 5.12 for SID generation settings.

Recommendation

To improve query response time on write-optimized DSOs, include the semantic key in the query definition.

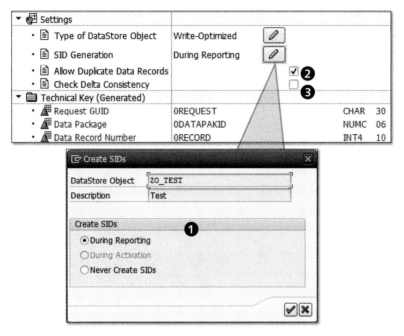

Figure 5.12 Write-Optimized DSO Configuration Settings (Transaction RSDODS)

A write-optimized DSO can be used in the following scenarios:

▸ As a consolidation, or harmonization, layer before you update the data to standard DSOs in the propagation layer. This accelerates the data through this layer and makes it available to the next layer twice as fast as with a standard DSO.

▸ As pass-through DSOs in the data acquisition layer; you need to report off this layer to validate data for Sarbanes Oxley or other compliance reasons. The data can then be dropped from the pass-through DSO as soon as the data has been sufficiently validated and successfully updated to the next layer.

▸ As a temporary storage area for large data sets needing complex transformations on the entire data set before it can be split into semantically partitioned objects. The complex transformations then need to be executed only once without activation before the data is split up.

▸ As the corporate memory layer for storing history. Business rules are only applied if and when the data is posted to other InfoProviders.

Write-optimized DSOs can be configured to allow duplicate values according to the semantic key (by design, the system-generated technical key never has duplicates). In this case, the system does not check whether the data is unique, and the active table may have several records with the same semantic key. See setting ❷ in Figure 5.12.

If the ALLOW DUPLICATE DATA RECORDS flag is left unchecked, as it is by default, the system generates a unique index on the semantic key of the InfoObject. This index has the technical name KEY.

> **Recommendation**
>
> If non-unique records are loaded to a write-optimized DSO that does not allow duplicates, the insert into the unique index will fail, causing the entire load to fail.

Since write-optimized DSOs do not have a change log, the system does not generate deltas in the sense of before- and after-images. It only sends requests with an initial data mart status as further updates. The before- and after-image must be passed through by mapping 0RECORDMODE to the DataSource field ROCANCEL on the inbound layers, or 0RECORDMODE of other DSOs on the outbound data flow.

When used like a PSA as a pass-through DSO in the acquisition layer, the write-optimized DSO should have its data deleted after a reasonable period of time. Normally, to maintain referential integrity, requests cannot be deleted from a DSO after they have already been further updated—the delta consistency check in DTP delta management prevents requests that have been retrieved with a delta from being deleted. In write-optimized DSOs, the delta consistency check is deactivated by default (see setting ❸ in Figure 5.12), so requests can be deleted regardless of their data-mart status.

However, if the write-optimized DSO is used anywhere else in the data flow, we recommend that you activate the delta consistency check to prevent requests from being inadvertently deleted.

Direct Update DSO

The direct update DSO differs from the standard DSO in terms of both its structure and how data is loaded. In a standard DSO, data is loaded in one table and activated in another, and the deltas are written to a third. In a direct update DSO, data is stored in a single table in precisely the same form in which it was written.

Similar to the write-optimized DSO, the direct update DSO has a single active table. Unlike the write-optimized DSO, data is not loaded via the data-transfer process to a direct update DSO; rather, data is usually received from BW Integrated Planning (IP), analysis processes, or external systems through application programming interfaces (APIs). An API is a set of rules and specifications that applications can follow to communicate with each other. APIs usually define routines, structures, object classes, and communication protocols. Table 5.6 offers a list of existing APIs available for use.

API	Description
RSDRI_ODSO_INSERT	Inserts new data with new keys
RSDRI_ODSO_INSERT_RFC	Same as RSDRI_ODSO_INSERT, but can be called remotely
RSDRI_ODSO_MODIFY	Inserts data with new keys to replace data with keys already in the system; the data is changed.
RSDRI_ODSO_MODIFY_RFC	Same as RSDRI_ODSO_MODIFY, but can be called remotely
RSDRI_ODSO_UPDATE	Changes data with keys in the system
RSDRI_ODSO_UPDATE_RFC	Same as RSDRI_ODSO_UPDATE, but can be called remotely
RSDRI_ODSO_DELETE_RFC	Deletes data

Table 5.6 APIs for Filling or Deleting Data from Direct Update DSOs

Direct update DSOs can receive data from IP if the planning-mode indicator is set. In this case, data can be written to the DSO only using IP or the Analysis Process Designer (APD). The APIs listed in the table above cannot be used when the planning mode is set because only IP can ensure all SID values exist for the characteristic values being stored in the DSO. IP also ensures consistency with the planning model with respect to characteristic relationships and data slices.

Because loading data by DTP is not supported, direct update DSOs are neither displayed in the administration tools nor in the monitor. However, data can still be further updated from a direct update DSO to additional InfoProviders. Since no change log is generated, however, you cannot perform a delta update to the Info-Providers at the end of this process.

> **Note**
>
> It is possible to switch between standard and direct update DSO types or change the Planning Mode indicator only if the DSO does not contain any data.
>
> If a standard DSO with update rules is switched to a direct update DSO, the update rules are set to inactive and can no longer be processed.

5.1.5 Virtual InfoProviders

Virtual InfoProviders do not store any data persistently; instead, all data is stored in other InfoProviders or database structures and is read by the virtual InfoProvider on demand. In this section, we will cover the following virtual InfoProviders:

- Aggregation level
- Analytical index
- CompositeProvider
- InfoSet
- MultiProvider
- Open ODS view
- TransientProvider
- VirtualProvider
- Query as InfoProvider

Let's look at each in more detail.

Aggregation Level

An *aggregation level* is a virtual InfoProvider specifically designed for Integrated Planning. An aggregation level represents a selection of characteristics and key figures from the underlying planning InfoProvider, which is either a real-time InfoCube (simple) or a MultiProvider (complex). The selection of characteristics in the aggregation level determines the planning granularity—the key figures are aggregated for the omitted characteristics.

Aggregation levels facilitate both manual planning and the use of planning functions at different granularities by pre-aggregating the results. More than one aggregation level can be created for an InfoProvider, enabling modeling at various levels of planning and hierarchical structures.

> **Note**
>
> Aggregation levels cannot be nested, so they cannot be included in MultiProviders.

Analytical Index

An *analytical index* is a new type of in-memory InfoProvider introduced in SAP BW 7.30, and it can be created only directly in BWA or an SAP HANA database. Analytical indexes are defined in the Analysis Process Designer (APD) or Workspace Designer and can be used immediately for reporting. All analytical indexes can be displayed and managed in the Analytic Index Overview (Transaction RSDD_LTIP).

Analytical indexes can be used in TransientProviders and CompositeProviders to address ad-hoc reporting needs, such as combining flat file data with BW InfoProvider data. Figure 5.13 gives an example of an analytical index definition in APD based on a query, although they can be easily sourced by a flat file. In APD, BEx queries can be used as an analytical index source if the property flag QUERY IS USED AS A INFOPROVIDER is set, enabling the pre-calculation and storage of query results.

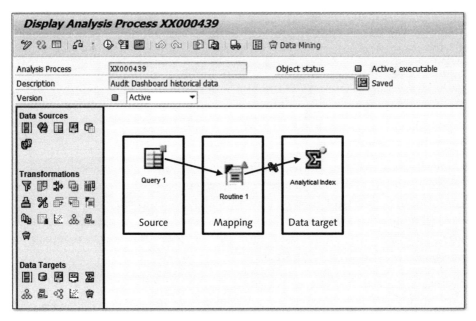

Figure 5.13 Analytical Index Mapping (Transaction RSANWB)

Analytic indexes store data in a star schema containing facts, dimensions (characteristics with attributes), and authorization data. During runtime, InfoObjects are automatically derived, so there is no need for modeling. As a result, they are great for quick and easy prototyping and can be created in a productive environment with no impact on live scenarios, assuming ample computing capacity and BWA or SAP HANA memory to support the analysis.

CompositeProvider

CompositeProviders were also introduced in SAP BW 7.30 but updated in BW 7.40 SP5. CompositeProviders are virtual InfoProviders designed to easily combine SAP BW InfoProvider data to non-BW data by union, inner join, or left outer join (LOJ). CompositeProviders leverage the full power of SAP HANA and cannot be used in systems on other databases unless BWA is installed. The non-BW data can be the following:

▶ An analytic index created with the APD

▶ An Excel file uploaded with the Workspace Designer

▶ A TransientProvider based on an SAP HANA model

There are three modeling areas for the CompositeProvider, which now has an Eclipse based maintenance screen, as illustrated in Figure 5.14. Each modeling area is configured for different user groups and application areas:

▶ **In BW Workspace Designer**
Business users can easily combine their own data from files with data from BW (DataSources, InfoProviders, or queries).

▶ **In the APD**
Administrators can combine data from multiple analytic indexes in a graphical environment to quickly create a prototype via Transaction RSLIMO. The data for the analytic indexes can come from APD data sources or SAP HANA models via TransientProviders.

▶ **In the Data Warehousing Workbench**
Developers and administrators can combine data from multiple InfoProviders and/or analytic indexes in a graphical environment via Transaction RSLIMOBW. The CompositeProvider offers more options than InfoSets or MultiProviders, but with that flexibility, comes risk. Always validate results carefully to ensure accuracy and data integrity.

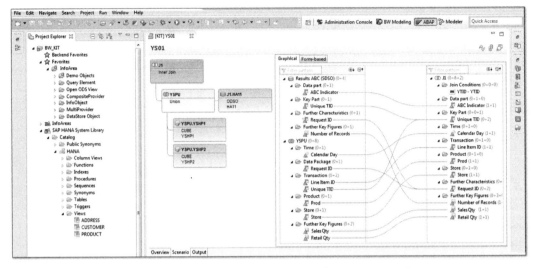

Figure 5.14 The "New" SAP BW 7.40 CompositeProvider Maintenance Screen

---

Recommendation

CompositeProviders can be transported only if they contain nothing but standard transportable BW InfoProviders.

The following constraints should be considered before designing and building CompositeProviders:

▸ CompositeProviders cannot be used in MultiProviders.

▸ Every CompositeProvider requires at least one InfoProvider with a union connection as its basis.

▸ Temporal joins are not possible in CompositeProviders (use InfoSets instead).

▸ Non-cumulative key figures cannot be used in a CompositeProvider.

▸ In SAP BW systems on HANA, queries with exception aggregation can be executed against only those CompositeProviders that contain standard, transportable SAP BW InfoProviders exclusively. In addition, exception aggregation is possible only against InfoObjects with SIDs.

▸ CompositeProviders cannot distinguish between unmapped key figures and booked zero values (MultiProviders can make this distinction).

▸ As with InfoSets, inner joins result in duplicated key figures in n:m relationships—divide key figures by number of records to calculate an average.

▶ For joins with a 1:n relationship, no division in the BEx query is necessary: simply uncheck the UNIQUE JOIN COLUMNS property of the joined InfoProvider. This is the default setting if the CompositeProvider is created via Transactions RSLIMO or RSLIMOBW. This setting results in accurate data but also transfers more data from the database.

For optimal performance, consider the following design principles:

▶ Inner joins are always faster than left outer joins. If the performance impact due to an LOJ is too great, consider modeling referential integrity into the Part-Providers during staging.

▶ If the model contains only unions, always use a MultiProvider. The analytic processor ensures the best execution plan is used.

▶ If no antijoins, temporal joins, or other InfoSet-only functionality is required, use CompositeProviders instead of InfoSets for their performance benefit.

CompositeProviders are widely expected to replace MultiProviders as the most commonly used virtual InfoProvider in SAP BW systems powered by SAP HANA.

InfoSet

InfoSets are virtual InfoProviders that do not physically store any data; rather, they join data from other InfoProviders, such as characteristic InfoObjects, InfoCubes, and DSOs. InfoSets have historically received a bad rap as poor-performing Info-Providers to be avoided, but this is an unfair assessment of their value! Until the introduction of the CompositeProvider, the InfoSet had the unique status as the only virtual InfoProvider that presents the intersection of data as a single record—as opposed to a MultiProvider, which presents the union of data as multiple records.

For example, consider the header and detail tables of a normalized model for sales orders. In this scenario, there is a sales order DSO and a sales item DSO. If these two DSOs are included in a MultiProvider, a report filtered on a single sales order with three items presents four rows in the result set: one row with the header fields populated and the item fields blank, and three rows with the item fields populated and the header fields blank (all rows would have the sales order populated).

However, in an InfoSet, the report displays only three rows, each with both the item fields and header fields populated. The data from the header table, the sales order DSO, is combined with each row from the sales item DSO when the data is joined. This particular view of presenting information may be a requirement for certain reports, and it is especially valuable for master data reporting.

This behavior can be explained by the following three different types of joins used in InfoSets, as Figure 5.15 shows:

- ▶ **Inner joins**
  An inner join, commonly referred to simply as a join, for tables A and B contains matching record pairs of both tables that satisfy the join predicate, or join condition. The join query compares each row of A with each row of B to find all matching pairs. Each matched pair is then combined into a result row.

- ▶ **Left outer joins**
  A left outer join (LOJ) for tables A and B contain all the records of the "left" table (A), even if the join condition does not find any matching record in the "right" table (B). A left outer join returns all the values from an inner join plus all values in the left table that do not match the right table.

- ▶ **Antijoins**
  An antijoin returns the diametric opposite of the inner join: the records that do not exist in both tables. This is extremely useful in both business scenarios, such as identifying which products are not selling, and technical scenarios, such as identifying referential integrity issues.

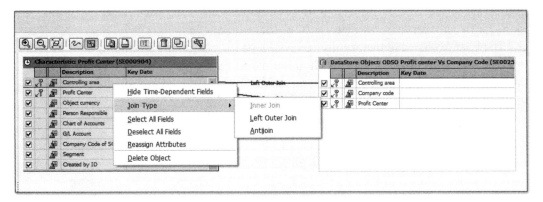

Figure 5.15 Join Types Available in the InfoSet (Transaction RSISET)

Inner joins provide the best performance and should be used by default. To improve performance on all joins, create secondary indexes on all table fields in the join conditions. If joining InfoObjects, always include OBJVERS as the first field of the secondary index—this field is included by default in the InfoSet join-predicate. To further improve performance, limit the number of joins in the InfoSet; fewer joins mean better performance.

> **Note**
>
> InfoSets are limited to a single "left" table for left outer joins. This limitation preserves the integrity of the results and minimizes the performance impact.

When rows are combined during the joins, there is one consideration that must be addressed in the Query Designer: all key figures from the header table must be divided by the number of records to present the correct results. Because each header table row is also combined with the detail table rows, it is doubled for each detail row in the result.

Returning to our example, all key figures in the sales order record are tripled when joined with the three sales item rows—the same value is displayed on each combined row in the result set. The solution is to use the number of records key figure, which is automatically available in each InfoSet, as a dividend for each key figure in the query. The steps are simple, as indicated in Figure 5.16: create a formula with the same name as the key figure ❷, and hide the original key figure. In the formula definition ❸, divide the original hidden key figure by the number of records ❶.

InfoSets can have multiple inner joins in either a hub and spoke or daisy chain design (see Figure 5.17). There is not a significant performance impact or benefit attributable to either option, although performance tests should be conducted on specific designs.

Each InfoSet can also be configured to use temporal joins to map periods of time. Without temporal joins, query result sets are determined by the query key date, but with them, it is possible to specify a particular point in time to evaluate the data. With temporal joins, the query key date is ignored in the InfoSet.

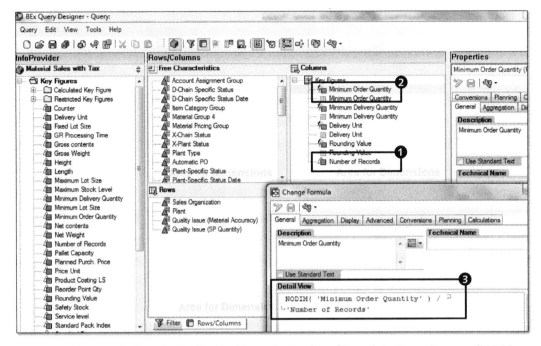

Figure 5.16 Steps for Dividing Key Figures by Number of Records to Ensure Accuracy (SAP BEx Query Designer)

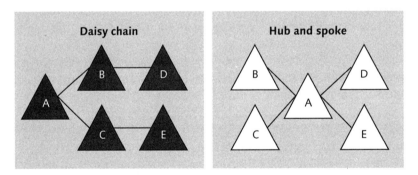

Figure 5.17 InfoSet Design Options

Each join can contain objects of the same or different object types. The individual objects can occur in a join more than once. Join conditions connect the objects in a join to one another (equal join condition). A join condition defines the combination of individual object records included in the result set.

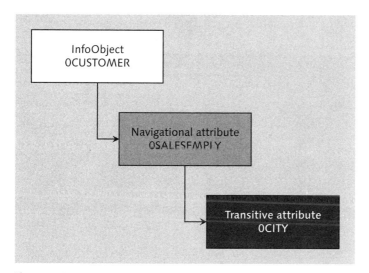

Figure 5.18 OCITY as a Transitive Attribute of OCUSTOMER

Every object added to an InfoSet is assigned a table number, such as T00001, and each field in that table is assigned a field number, such as F23 or F197. While this renaming enables the same object to be added to an InfoSet multiple times, it makes it extremely difficult to build queries based on a description and technical field name.

For example, consider an InfoSet that includes OMATERIAL, OMAT_PLANT, and OMAT_SALES. Each of these InfoObjects has the navigational attribute ODEL_FLAG (deletion flag). In the BEx Query Designer, there are three fields with the description DELETION FLAG (T00001_F23, T00002_F37, and T00003_11). So which one belongs to OMAT_PLANT? It is not easy to determine without looking at the InfoSet definition.

To simplify query building on InfoSets, always insulate the query development from the InfoSet with a MultiProvider. In the MultiProvider, add the same InfoObjects included in the InfoSet as PartProviders in the MultiProvider. Use these real InfoObjects as dimensional characteristics in the MultiProvider, but assign their values to the InfoSet technical fields.

Each superior InfoObject of a compound InfoObject must be distinct in the Multi-Provider. If more than one InfoObject in the InfoSet have the same compound InfoObject(s), create a reference object for them. For example, in Figure 5.19, ZPLANT ❶ has been created as a reference of OPLANT ❷ because OPLANT is compounded to both OMAT_PLANT and ZMAT_PQ2. Both ZPLANT and OPLANT have been added as PartProviders in the MultiProvider. They represent different compound InfoObjects — and should be mapped to one and only one of them, as indicated by ❸.

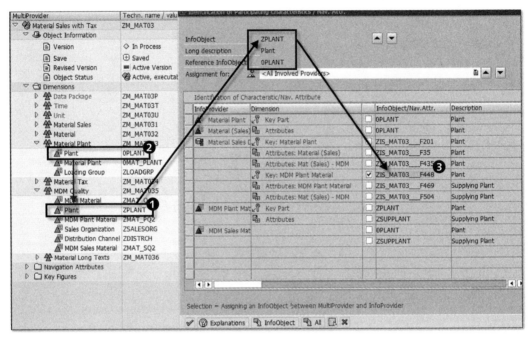

Figure 5.19 Ability of MultiProviders to Map InfoSet Technical Names to InfoObject Names (Transaction RSDCUBE)

If the InfoSet includes InfoObjects, the only dimensional characteristics in the MultiProvider should be key fields; use navigation attributes to map all other fields from the InfoSet. This further facilitates query development because it is then extremely easy to distinguish the source of each field. In the previous example, the following three easily distinguishable DELETION FLAG fields would then be available in the Query Designer: OMATERIAL__ODEL_FLAG, OMAT_PLANT__ODEL_FLAG, and OMAT_SALES__ODEL_FLAG.

Now that we've covered the InfoSet in detail, let's take a quick look at the Multi-Provider.

MultiProvider

A MultiProvider combines data from other InfoProviders, called PartProviders, for reporting and analysis purposes. The MultiProvider itself does not contain any data. Its data comes entirely from a union of the data in the PartProviders on which it is based. The following InfoProviders are eligible PartProviders for use in a MultiProvider:

▶ Aggregation levels

▶ DSOs

▶ HybridProviders

▶ InfoCubes

▶ InfoObjects

▶ InfoSets

▶ Semantically partitioned objects

▶ VirtualProviders

As shown in Figure 5.20, some, but not all, PartProviders contain data.

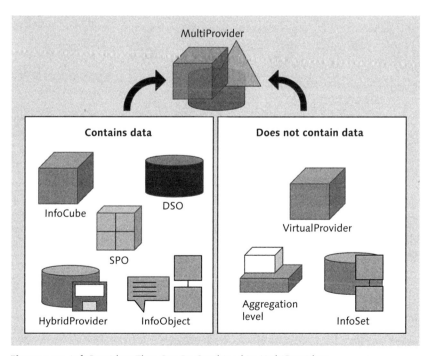

Figure 5.20 InfoProviders That Can Be Combined in MultiProviders

Like in-memory InfoCubes, MultiProviders have a multidimensional structure without physical dimension tables. This structure facilitates query development by organizing characteristics and their navigational attributes into dimensions for easy consumption. Dimensional characteristics, key figures, and navigational attributes can be assigned from the PartProviders to the MultiProvider.

> **Recommendation**
>
> To further facilitate query development, use hierarchy nodes on key figures to group them by PartProvider.

> **Recommendation**
>
> If an InfoObject does not exist in any PartProvider, it cannot be included in the Multi-Provider. In other words, the pool of candidate characteristics, key figures, and navigational attributes for a MultiProvider data model is limited to those existing in the Part-Providers.

A union operation is used to combine data from the PartProviders in a MultiProvider. Here, the system executes subqueries and then constructs a union set of the results from all subqueries. All values in these data sets are combined, and the complete result is returned to the query.

MultiProviders offer the following advantages:

▸ **Data model simplicity**
InfoProviders designed for individual subject areas are much simpler than those designed for multiple subject areas. Using MultiProviders allows InfoProvider designs to remain simple and small.

▸ **Architectural flexibility**
Smaller InfoProviders can be used in various combinations with other InfoProviders, enabling a flexible, object-oriented approach to data modeling. Multi-Providers are useful to combine the following:

  ▸ InfoProviders from different subject areas, such as sales and finance

  ▸ InfoProviders at different granularities, such as header and detail data

  ▸ InfoProviders with different values, such as actual and plan data

  ▸ SPOs across different data domains

  ▸ Virtual InfoProviders with physical InfoProviders

▶ **Better performance**
Combining data models in MultiProviders enables parallel processing during query execution. Parallel processing facilitates load balancing and better resource utilization. When a query is executed against a MultiProvider, parallel subqueries execute against each PartProvider. When the subqueries complete, the analytic processor unites the results and delivers them to the query.

▶ **Reduced query maintenance**
MultiProviders insulate queries from back-end changes to the PartProviders. In fact, one PartProvider could be completely replaced by a new PartProvider, without requiring any front-end changes to the query. This insulation is so valuable, MultiProviders should be used on every data model, even if there is no need to combine InfoProviders.

Recommendation

Never develop queries directly against an InfoProvider; always insulate the query from changes to the InfoProvider by including it in a MultiProvider. Then, develop all queries against the MultiProvider.

While most MultiProviders provide better performance without additional considerations, there are several design principles you should follow to ensure optimal performance during query execution on all MultiProviders.

First, limit the number of PartProviders in each MultiProvider. Modeling Multi-Providers with more than ten InfoProviders is also highly complex. Too many joins or parallel subqueries can adversely impact performance: splitting the queries and reconstructing the results takes a substantial amount of time and is generally counterproductive. Any MultiProvider with more than ten PartProviders other than SPOs should be subject to scrutiny; semantically partitioned objects count as a single PartProvider because query pruning is automatically handled for them as long as the SPO itself is included instead of its individual PartProviders.

Second, be cautious when combining InfoProviders in a MultiProvider if their data models are very different. A multitude of uncommon characteristics adds complexity to the data model and increases difficulty for query development, requiring detailed knowledge of the underlying data models. As an alternative in these modeling scenarios, use the report-report interface to link queries based on one InfoProvider to one or more queries on another.

Third, include query pruning design tactics in all PartProviders to prevent subqueries from executing against them if they do not contain data requested by the main query. The following query pruning approaches prohibit unnecessary subqueries from being executed in this sequence:

▶ **Query pruning based on characteristic constants**
Applying constants in the PartProviders where possible is the most effective query pruning tactic. If the PartProviders have been semantically partitioned but are not SPOs, the InfoProvider should have the requisite InfoObject values set as a constant. In InfoCubes and DSOs, you can specify constant values for InfoObjects by right-clicking them and selecting INFOOBJECT-SPECIFIC PROPERTIES from the context menu.

> **Note**
>
> Any number of InfoObjects can have a constant value, but each constant is limited to a single value and cannot be applied if data is already loaded to the InfoProvider.

▶ **Query pruning based on metadata restrictions**
If the PartProviders already have data in them, or constants aren't applicable because of restrictions of multiple single values or a range of values, or based on a compound InfoObject, you can manage required query pruning by maintaining partitioning criteria for all the PartProviders in a MultiProvider.

To implement metadata restrictions, enter partition criteria for a specific Multi-Provider using ABAP program RSPP_PART_MAINTAIN. The metadata restrictions are stored in table RSIPRORANGE. In Figure 5.21, the PartProviders in MultiProvider ZPRUNEMP1, which you can see in Transaction RSA1 ❶, are available for restrictions in program RSPP_PART_MAINTAIN ❷. The MultiProvider fields are mapped to the PartProvider fields ❸ and can be restricted based on existing values ❹.

> **Note**
>
> In program RSPP_PART_MAINTAIN, characteristics can be restricted only on values that exist in the MultiProvider using the equal ('EQ') and between ('BT') operator.

In the figure, DSO ZINVDSO1 contains data for only source system D1 and sales organization D005 to D015. Upon query execution, the system checks the requested values against this table to determine which PartProviders should be sub-queried.

Sales Forecasting	ZPRUNEMP1	=	Change
▸ ● Plan - CO Area 01	ZINV_IC1	=	Manage
· ● Plan - CO Area 02	ZINV_IC2	=	Manage
▸ ▣ Actuals - CO Area 02	ZINVDSO1	=	Manage
▸ ▣ Actuals - CO Area 01	ZINVDSO2 ❶	=	Manage
▸ ▣ Corrections - CO Area 02	ZINVDSO3	=	Manage

MultiProvider ZPRUNEMP1 Version M

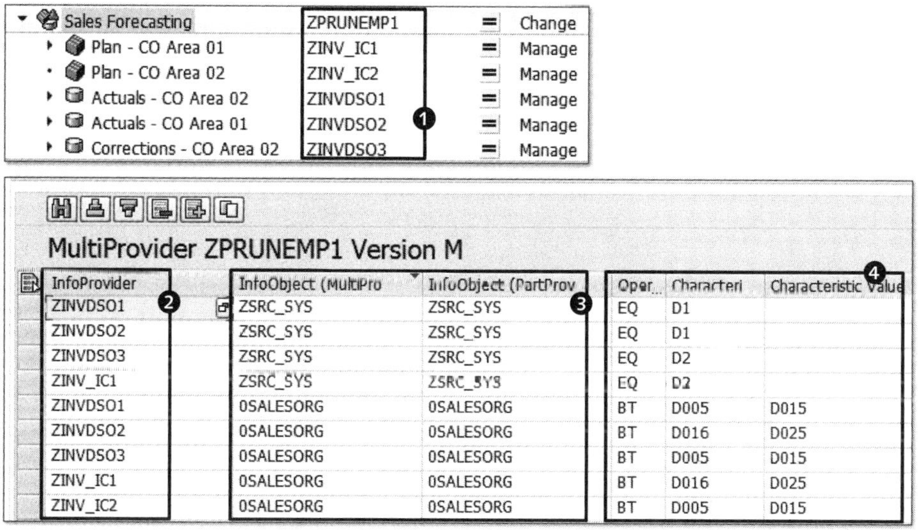

InfoProvider	InfoObject (MultiPro	InfoObject (PartProv	Oper...	Characteri	Characteristic Value ❹
ZINVDSO1 ❷	ZSRC_SYS	ZSRC_SYS ❸	EQ	D1	
ZINVDSO2	ZSRC_SYS	ZSRC_SYS	EQ	D1	
ZINVDSO3	ZSRC_SYS	ZSRC_SYS	EQ	D2	
ZINV_IC1	ZSRC_SYS	ZSRC_SYS	EQ	D2	
ZINVDSO1	0SALESORG	0SALESORG	BT	D005	D015
ZINVDSO2	0SALESORG	0SALESORG	BT	D016	D025
ZINVDSO3	0SALESORG	0SALESORG	BT	D005	D015
ZINV_IC1	0SALESORG	0SALESORG	BT	D016	D025
ZINV_IC2	0SALESORG	0SALESORG	BT	D005	D015

Figure 5.21 Query Pruning (Transaction RSA11 and Report RSPP_PART_MAINTAIN)

▸ **Query pruning based on MultiProvider hints**

If the MultiProvider contains only InfoCubes, subquery hints can be specified for each PartProvider InfoCube in table RRKMULTIPROVHINT. In this table, each characteristic for which a partitioning filter is valid should be added for each InfoCube in the MultiProvider that contains that characteristic. If a query has restrictions on this characteristic, the analytic processor checks which Info-Cubes can return data for the query by performing a quick read of their dimension tables. If the selected values are found in one InfoCube, the data manager can then completely ignore the remaining InfoCubes.

▶ **Query pruning based on PartProvider filters**
If none of these pruning techniques are applicable, the MultiProvider query can be restricted on virtual InfoObject `0INFOPROV`, which is included by default in all MultiProviders. You can implement this by either creating a hard filter on `0INFOPROV` in the query or using a customer exit variable if it is both necessary and possible to dynamically determine which InfoProviders should be queried.

Table 5.7 defines which pruning tactic is available for each PartProvider types. Any mixed MultiProvider models should consider the pruning tactics possible for each individual PartProvider type. However, these pruning tactics are important only if the MultiProvider is defined consistently.

PartProvider	Characteristic Constant	Metadata Restriction	MultiProvider Hint
InfoCube	Possible	Possible	Possible
DSO	Possible	Possible	Not possible
VirtualProvider	Possible	Possible	Not possible
SPO (InfoCube)	Possible	Automatic	Not possible
SPO (DSO)	Possible	Automatic	Not possible

Table 5.7 PartProvider Eligibility for Query Pruning Tactics

In the MultiProvider definition, each characteristic, navigation attribute, and key figure must correspond to at least one PartProvider characteristic, navigation attribute, or key figure. In other words, each MultiProvider field must be assigned to one or more PartProviders that contain the same field.

Special consideration must be given to the assignments of compound InfoObjects; compound characteristics and navigation attributes have to be identified consistently from PartProviders within a MultiProvider. Otherwise, the query results may be inconsistent. Data records that do not physically exist in any of the PartProviders may appear in the MultiProvider.

During activation of the MultiProvider, the system executes a consistency check for compound InfoObjects. If the consistency check fails, the MultiProvider cannot be activated.

Open ODS View

The *Open ODS View* is a new virtual object introduced with SAP BW 7.40 that integrates external data models into SAP BW, enabling a single BEx query to access data from both SAP BW and non-SAP BW data using SDA. In tandem with the new CompositeProvider, these two new objects form a new LSA++ Virtualization Layer in SAP BW on SAP HANA.

Open ODS Views are maintained from the SAPgui in Transaction RSODSVIEW, as shown in Figure 5.22. The field metadata, including data type, length, decimal places, lower-case values, and conversion routine are replicated from the source table and displayed on the FACTS tab ❶. The conversion routine column is populated only if a field is associated with an InfoObject (either via Transaction RSD1 or the ASSOCIATIONS tab).The tab titled PREVIEW FOR QUERY illustrates how the fields are made available for query development in the SAP BEx Query Designer ❷.

Many SAP customers have begun developing models in standalone SAP HANA systems and plan to migrate development later into the same database as their BW system as soon as it has been migrated to SAP HANA. Systems like this, with data models (SAP HANA tables and views) in the same database as SAP BW, are called *multiple components in one database* (MCOD). With managed persistence, the data in those SAP HANA tables can be consumed in SAP BW and further updated in subsequent data targets using field-based DSOs and SAP HANA-optimized transformations.

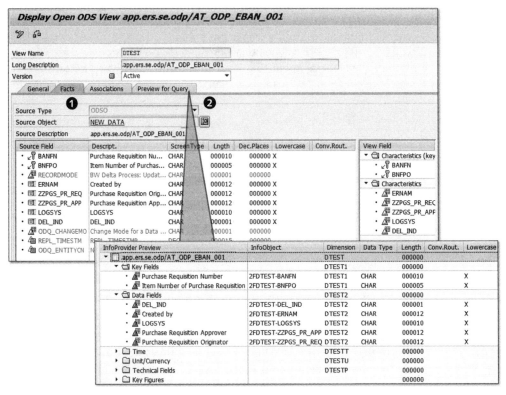

Figure 5.22 Open ODS View Maintenance (Transaction RSODSVIEW)

TransientProvider

TransientProviders were introduced as new virtual InfoProviders in SAP BW 7.30. They allow analysis and reporting of application data via BI tools without the need to model an InfoProvider in SAP BW or replicate data. They were originally designed to provide the benefits of SAP BW reporting to operational users in ECC by using the embedded BW system without the need for SAP BW skills. Transient-Providers eliminate the redundancy of storing data in both SAP BW and SAP ERP, reduce the overhead generated by replicating data between the systems, and deliver results with no data latency to the end user.

Instead of being modeled in the traditional sense, TransientProviders are generated as BW InfoProviders from the metadata of their source. TransientProviders are defined using InfoObjects, but these InfoObjects are also transient; that is, they are also generated from the metadata of the source fields.

The greatest advantages of a TransientProvider are that its metadata in SAP BW is not persisted (there is no InfoObject creation) and it is always generated at runtime. This means that, if the source metadata has changed, the TransientProvider is adapted automatically.

There are several types of TransientProviders available in SAP BW:

▶ DERIVED FROM A CLASSIC INFOSET
  The TransientProvider derived from a classic InfoSet is a generated InfoProvider used to access data from a classic InfoSet. There is no need to model the InfoProvider in the BW system or for the data to be replicated in the SAP BW system; the generated InfoProvider passes data through the SAP BW application to the BEx query for reporting and analysis.

The system automatically and dynamically creates the InfoProvider and corresponding InfoObjects using the classic InfoSet definition, provided that this has been released in the classic InfoSet maintenance transaction. Data can be called directly into BEx queries from the classic InfoSet.

Classic InfoSets offer the following functionalities:

▶ Classic InfoSets prepare texts automatically without the need to load master data.

▶ Selections made in the classic InfoSet maintenance transaction are available in the variables editor in the BEx query.

TransientProviders derived from classic InfoSets can easily be recognized in the Query Designer by their naming convention: the technical name of the TransientProvider consists of the prefix @1, concatenated with the technical name of the classic InfoSet. For example, if the technical name of the classic InfoSet is INFOSET_A, the name of the TransientProvider is @1INFOSET_A.

This type of TransientProvider offers the following functionality: for certain fields, such as those of type DATS, business content InfoObjects are used when creating the TransientProvider. The use of business content time characteristics, for example, enables the display of calendars and standard hierarchies for date fields in the BEx Query Designer and BI tools. On the contrary, any generated InfoObjects do not have master data and so do not support hierarchies or any display and navigation attributes.

▶ DERIVED FROM AN ANALYTIC INDEX
Analytic indexes can be created in the Analysis Process Designer and in BW Workspace Designer. During activation of each analytical index, a Transient-Provider is automatically generated by the system. There is no need to model the TransientProvider in the Data Warehousing Workbench or replicate data from the analytical index before the TransientProvider can be used in the BEx Query Designer.

Because the model is generated at runtime and the metadata of a TransientProvider is not saved, it is automatically adjusted when the source is changed. This makes TransientProviders suitable for ad hoc analysis. BEx queries created on TransientProviders are also automatically adjusted when the TransientProvider is changed. Only queries with complex formulas and restrictions might have to be manually adjusted.

> **Note**
>
> TransientProviders derived from analytical indexes cannot be transported; they must be created and/or generated in each system in the landscape.

▶ DERIVED FROM HANA MODEL
You can generate TransientProviders by publishing SAP HANA models in the BW system. The SAP HANA models published in the BW system are saved as an analytic index, and a TransientProvider is generated on this index. Transient-Providers based on SAP HANA models are suitable for ad hoc data or scenarios that change frequently.

These TransientProviders can then be linked to other SAP BW InfoProviders in a CompositeProvider. This enables the combination of ad hoc data with consolidated data from the SAP BW system and, also, the use of OLAP functions for analysis. If the SAP HANA model is changed, the analytic index is adjusted automatically at runtime.

> **Note**
>
> A TransientProvider derived from an SAP HANA model cannot be used as a data target in Analysis Process Designer.

To publish an SAP HANA model in the SAP BW system, the system reads the structure of the SAP HANA model from the SAP HANA database. The SAP BW system applies the structure to an analytic index. Models from any schema can be used here. The system automatically maps the authorizations from SAP HANA to the SAP BW analysis authorizations.

In the SAP HANA database, analytic privileges are used to define which users are allowed to view which data records for analysis purposes. Analytic privileges are handled as filters for database queries. Users see only the data for which they have an analytic privilege. In SAP BW, however, authorizations do not work as filters. Here, users can execute a query only if their analysis authorizations completely cover the relevant selection. If the query filter is not aligned with the user's analysis authorizations, an error message is displayed.

To resolve this discrepancy, analytic privileges are persisted both on the SAP BW system and in the SAP HANA database. At runtime, virtual analysis authorizations are created using an analytic-privileges mapping and then tailored to the authorizations that the database user (sap<SID>) has for the schema in the SAP HANA database. Only those analytic privileges are used for which the relevant InfoObjects are flagged as authorization relevant in SAP BW. An exception to this are users with analysis authorization object 0BI_ALL. Only the authorizations of the database user (SID) are included for these users.

> **Recommendation**
>
> The SAP BW database user is always used every time the SAP HANA database is accessed. The SAP BW database user and SAP BW user must be identical (1:1 user mapping), so the analytic privileges of the SAP BW database user can be mapped to the virtual analysis authorizations of the SAP BW system user.

VirtualProvider

Like the MultiProvider, VirtualProviders do not physically store any data and have a multidimensional definition. However, VirtualProviders are conceptually different from other virtual InfoProviders because they access data in real time directly from the source system, not from other data targets in the SAP BW system.

There are several options for accessing data in real time from the source system, and the access type is defined when the VirtualProvider is created—a radio button for choosing the VirtualProvider access type is available in the same transaction for creating standard InfoCubes (see Figure 5.23). The following access types are available:

▶ BASED ON DATA TRANSFER PROCESS FOR DIRECT ACCESS
Use this option for real-time access to data in an SAP source system. This type of VirtualProvider uses inverse transformations to pass query filters and variable values to the DataSource as selection criteria. Data is read from the source system, and the result set is passed back to queries using transformations and DTPs for direct access. Only the data requested is returned; subsequent navigation steps require the real-time ETL process to be repeated for a different data set.

> **Recommendation**
>
> Only use this type to access a small amount of data by a few users on an infrequent basis. Do not use this type if a large amount of data is required in the first navigation step by a large number of concurrent users on a frequent basis.

▶ BASED ON BAPI
Use this option to read data from external non-SAP systems without storing it in SAP BW. Each query triggers a data request with a dynamic structure determined by the characteristic selections. The non-SAP system transfers the requested data to the analytic processor using a BAPI. This access type is particularly suitable for reading data from non-relational structures in hierarchical databases.

Any read tool that supports the non-SAP system interface can be used. Because the transaction data is not managed in the SAP BW system, there is very little administrative effort on the SAP BW side with this VirtualProvider.

When a query is executed on this VirtualProvider, the data manager calls the VirtualProvider BAPI and transfers selection, characteristics, and key figure parameters. The external system then transfers the requested data to the analytic processor.

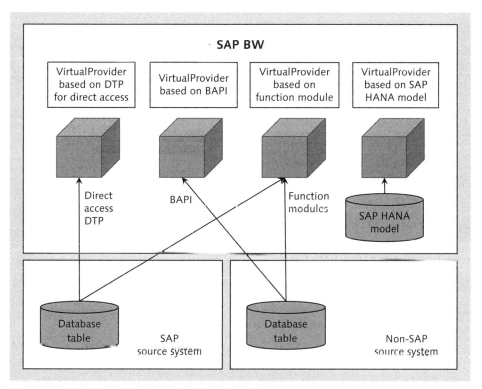

Figure 5.23 Real-Time Data Access for VirtualProviders

▶ BASED ON FUNCTION MODULE

This option reads data from non-SAP BW data sources, either local or remote, using a user-defined function module. Data can be changed in the function module before it is passed to the analytic processor. This VirtualProvider is more flexible but requires more implementation effort than other types. It is used primarily in the SAP Strategic Enterprise Management (SEM) application.

▶ BASED ON HANA MODEL

Use this option for stable scenarios to read SAP HANA analysis views or authorization views. This type of VirtualProvider can be used in a MultiProvider and can also use navigation attributes by selecting InfoObjects with master data access, either standard or SAP HANA attribute view.

Query as InfoProvider

The property QUERY IS USED AS A INFOPROVIDER can be set in the Query Designer. This enables the data federator interface in the SAP BW system to read data from the query. The main advantage to using queries as InfoProviders is the ability to calculate query functions in the Analytic Server before reading the data. This pre-calculation improves performance, especially with simple queries that return very large result sets. Supported query functions include the following:

▶ Standard aggregations (SUM, MIN, MAX)

▶ Formulas that are totaled before aggregation (+, −, constant factor)

▶ Unit conversions and currency translations

▶ Constant selections

▶ Formulas with quotients such as prices

▶ Formulas with exception aggregation

The following query scenarios cannot be activated as InfoProviders:

▶ Queries with two structures

▶ Queries with mandatory input variables

▶ Queries with non-cumulative key figures

▶ Queries with temporal hierarchy joins enabled

▶ Queries with technical names longer than 20 characters

▶ Queries based on TransientProviders or Aggregation Levels

When a query is activated as an InfoProvider, the following naming convention is applied: the data federator table is named by concatenating Q to the query name, and the InfoProvider is named by concatenating @ to the data federator table. For example, if a query has the technical name ZQUERY, the Data Federator table is given the technical name QZQUERY, and the InfoProvider is given the name @QZQUERY.

5.1.6 HybridProvider

Like analytic indexes, CompositeProviders, and TransientProviders, HybridProviders were also introduced with SAP BW 7.30. HybridProviders are designed to address the need for high performance in the following scenarios:

- ▶ Near real-time reporting on large data volumes (historic and current)
- ▶ Reporting across data from different sources, where at least one source is near-real time

For larger data volumes in a traditional DBMS, BW Accelerator is the preferred solution for improved query performance. For near real-time data, the solution could involve real-time data acquisition to a DSO and/or VirtualProvider. Combining these components into one solution addresses both needs. Hence, the HybridProvider is a combination of two InfoProviders (an InfoCube with a BWA index for historical data plus a DSO or VirtualProvider for near real-time data) presented as one single InfoProvider for transformations and reporting. This combination allows data to be analyzed in near-real time along with the historical data in BWA, ensuring good performance.

There are two types of HybridProvider, as follows, which are shown in Figure 5.24:

- ▶ BASED ON A DATASTORE OBJECT

  The HybridProvider based on a DSO is the combination of a DSO and an Info-Cube. The newest data is loaded to the DSO via Real-Time Data Acquisition (RDA). The InfoCube serves as an aggregate for historical data. If BW Accelerator is installed, the InfoCube can be indexed in BWA or configured as a BWA-only InfoCube. As of BWA 7.20 and SAP BW 7.30, the DSO can be indexed in BWA, too.

  A DTP for real-time data acquisition fills the DSO in the HybridProvider with current data in real time from any type of source. The daemon for real-time data acquisition activates this data, ensuring that the data is immediately available for analysis purposes. However, it can also be used independently of real-time data acquisition.

- ▶ BASED ON DIRECT ACCESS

  The HybridProvider based on direct access is a combination of a VirtualProvider and an InfoCube, both having the same structure. The newest data is not replicated into SAP BW, but instead is read directly in the source system using the VitualProvider.

  The VirtualProvider provides real-time data without the need to set up real-time data acquisition. There is no latency compared to real-time data acquisition, where the data is available in near-real time but not immediately. Data is loaded from only one DataSource to both the VirtualProvider and the InfoCube.

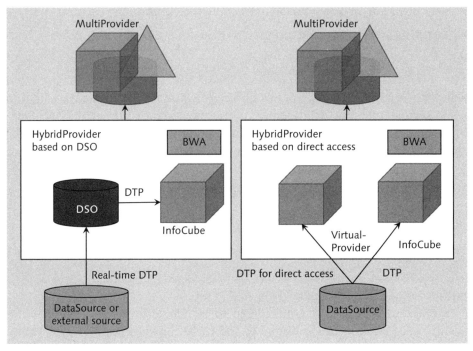

Figure 5.24 HybridProvider Types

HybridProviders are treated as a single object in the system, even though they are always a combination of two objects. During creation of a HybridProvider, the system generates all dependent metadata, including the InfoCube, transformations, DTPs, and process chains. Since only one object needs to be maintained, HybridProviders, like SPOs, provide a lower total cost of ownership.

The overall performance of the data warehouse processes depends on multiple factors. Good system performance begins with the design of the data model, but a complete layered architecture (LSA or LSA++) is the foundation of a performance-optimized data warehouse. Therefore, a robust strategy should be adopted to ensure that data models are designed according to concrete business requirements and implemented according to LSA guidelines. This approach mitigates the risk of architecture-related bottlenecks as usage and data volumes increase.

5.2   Data Loading for Performance

In addition to a clearly defined layer and data architecture, data provisioning and logistics can contribute substantially to the performance of the data warehouse. Decisions regarding data persistency and data provisioning should be made first. For data persisted in BW, the capabilities of SAP BW 7.40 have expanded with the ability to seamlessly provision data from tools such as SAP SLT and SAP Data Services.

Regardless of how the persisted data is provisioned, you should follow logical loading sequences to prevent errors and delays. There are also tactical configurations and technical settings to improve extraction, transformation, and load (ETL) performance. Data load schedules must be automated, yet flexible enough to handle multiple sources across the IT landscape while facilitating error detection, analysis, and correction.

In most new implementations, performance becomes an issue only after the system has been operational for a period of time and both data volume and usage have grown significantly. By the time performance becomes a concern, it usually requires substantially more time and effort to redesign the data flow logistics than to have adopted a proper design from the beginning. Adhering to best practice optimizes ETL performance and mitigates the risk of performance issues during data loading.

The following subsections cover best practices and recommended technical settings for each step in the data load process. These sections will concentrate on data ETL optimization, including load distribution and data retention for data persisted or staged through the layer architecture of the warehouse.

5.2.1   Extraction Processing

Data extraction from SAP source systems such as SAP ERP can be a performance bottleneck if there is extensive logic in the DataSource or if data volumes are high. In many companies, optimization efforts in SAP ERP can be obstructed if there is any risk to transaction processing performance. For example, creating secondary indexes on non-key fields to accelerate selection logic may not be acceptable to system architects if the index update adversely impacts transaction response times.

From an extraction-optimization perspective, it is important to use an efficient DataSource from the beginning. The focus of this section is to optimize the extraction of data from the source.

DataSources

In SAP source systems, SAP Business Content DataSources can be activated via Transaction SBIW, or custom DataSources can be defined in Transaction RSO2 to extract data to SAP BW. In most cases, SAP Business Content DataSources provide innumerable benefits, such as accurately denormalizing the data models in SAP ERP, looking up all relevant fields, applying standard business logic, and enabling delta queue extraction. However, sometimes enhancements to content DataSources negate the inherent efficiency in the original design. In these cases, custom-developed DataSources can provide better performance.

Custom DataSources can be based on data dictionary tables, views, domains, ABAP function modules, or SAP Queries (classic InfoSets). By default, customer DataSources extract the full data set delivered by the source, but they can also be configured to allow selection criteria to be entered in the SAP BW system.

> **Recommendation**
>
> When extracting from a data dictionary table, always build a view on top of it to insulate the DataSource from future changes to either the table or extensions to the DataSource.

For performance reasons, design and use delta-capable DataSources whenever practical. Delta extraction can be designed for DataSources in multiple ways, depending on the complexity of the source. If the source has a delta-capable field, such as a date field, timestamp, or a unique numeric key, define the DataSource as a GENERIC DELTA (see ❶ in Figure 5.25). Generic delta extractors capture the last value of the delta-relevant field upon extraction and then use this value to determine the delta dataset during the subsequent extraction.

You can extract two different types of delta records using a generic delta DataSource. When you are loading directly to InfoCubes, only additive deltas are possible (see ❸ in Figure 5.25). However, when you load to DSOs or master data, all records should have a *New* status. Regardless of type, it is important to set safety interval limits to ensure that no data is missed.

For example, if the delta-relevant field is specified as a calendar-day field, the initial extraction date, $D0$, is saved during initialization (see ❷ in Figure 5.25). All data available in the source until the time of extraction on date $D0$ is extracted. The next extraction only selects data from the *day after* the previous extraction date, *(D0 +*

1), to the current day, *D1*. In other words, the *lower limit* of the extraction range is the value *(D0 + 1)*, and the *upper limit* of the extraction range is the value *D1*.

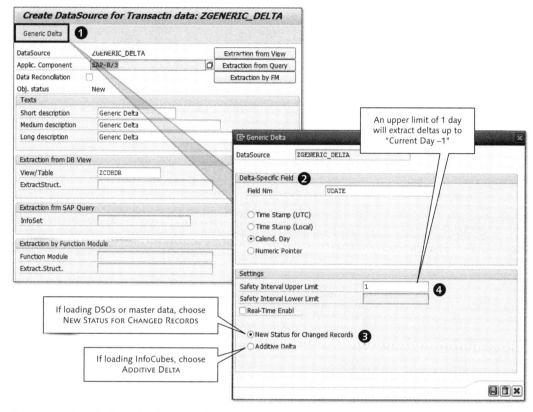

Figure 5.25 Generic Delta Configuration for Custom DataSources (Transaction RSO2)

Recommendation

To prevent the same data from being extracted twice, the previous extraction value is not included in subsequent extractions by default.

For example, if calendar-day data is extracted weekly, and the last extraction was January 10th, then the next extraction selects data from January 11th through January 17th; otherwise, data from the 10th would be included in both extractions and would be duplicated in the target BW system. However, if the previous extraction occurred mid-day on the 10th, then the rest of that day's data is missed during the subsequent extraction.

If delta data is extracted by timestamp, some recently posted transactions may not be updated in all base tables by the time the extraction executes. For example, if an initial extraction occurs at 12:00:00, a recently posted transaction stamped at 11:59:59 may not be saved in the base table if there are transactional system performance problems or update failures. If this transaction is updated to the base table at 12:00:30, it still has an 11:59:59 timestamp, so it is also missed in subsequent extractions.

To mitigate the risk of missing data as described in these examples, use safety intervals.

Generic deltas always need a safety interval to ensure that no records are missed during extraction. *Safety intervals* override the default behaviour of generic delta extractors by adjusting the upper and/or lower limits of the extraction range during each delta extraction. The lower-limit safety interval shifts the starting point of the extraction range, and the upper-limit safety interval shifts the end point. The safety intervals shift the upper and lower limits in one direction only: earlier in time. The units of the safety intervals are dependent on the delta-relevant field: calendar-day units are days, and timestamp units are seconds (numeric pointers have no units).

Recommendation

Lower limits cannot be set for additive deltas, so no duplicate records can be extracted to InfoCubes (see ❷ in Figure 5.26).

If the delta-relevant field is a calendar date, a lower-limit safety interval of one calendar day re-extracts the previous extraction date (January 10th, in this example). An upper-limit safety interval of one calendar day ends the extraction range at current day minus one (January 16th instead of January 17th).

Recommendation

For calendar-day delta-relevant fields, it is necessary to use only one limit. Setting an upper limit of one day excludes the current day from extraction, providing only a full day's worth of transactions to SAP BW.

If the delta-relevant field is a timestamp, a lower-limit safety interval of 3,600 seconds shifts the lower-limit back one hour before the previous extraction point, picking up any transactions that were not updated to the base tables in time. An upper-limit

safety interval of 3,600 seconds shifts the end point back one hour, so recent transaction remain unread until the subsequent extraction (see ❸ in Figure 5.26).

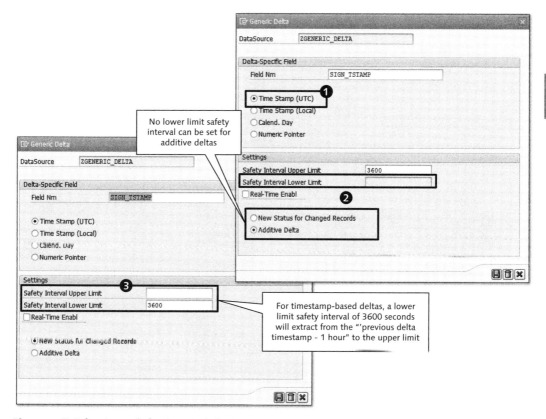

Figure 5.26 Safety Intervals for Generic Delta Extractors

For more complex scenarios—in which deltas should be triggered by changes to
table fields but there is no delta-relevant calendar day, timestamp, or numeric
pointer field—a DataSource can be configured as an ALE DELTA (see ❶ in Figure
5.27). An ALE delta DataSource uses change document, or change pointer, objects
to capture changes to specified table fields. When a change is captured, a pointer
to the changed record is written to the delta queue in Transaction RSA7.

There are dozens of standard SAP-delivered change document objects, such as
ADRESSE, which captures changes to table ADRC (see ❷ in Figure 5.27). Check table
TCDOB for a list of all available change document objects by table. If no standard

delivered objects meet the business requirements, you can create custom change document objects using Transaction SCDO, as you can see in Figure 5.28. Data-Sources using ALE deltas can be identified in tables `ROMDDELTA` and `RSMDDELTA`, which map DataSources or characteristics to change pointer object tables.

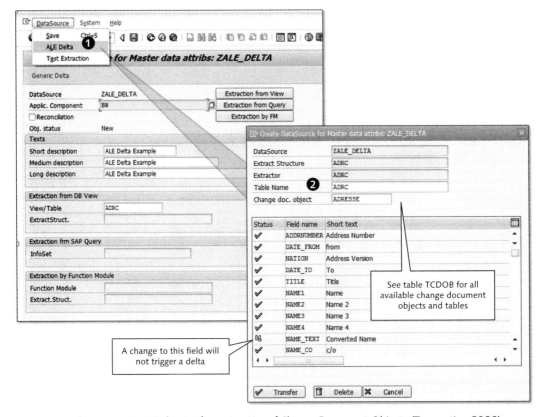

Figure 5.27 ALE Delta Configuration Use of Change Document Objects (Transaction RSO2)

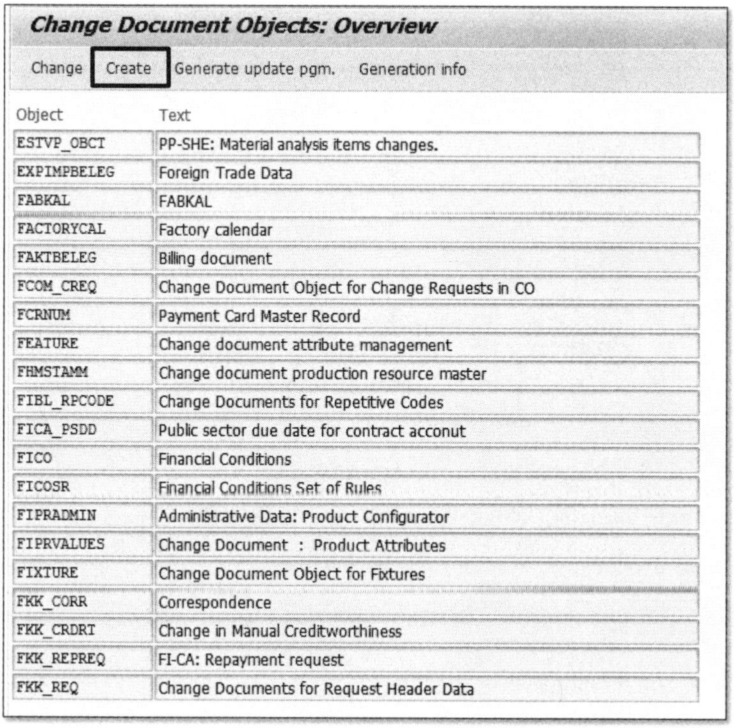

Figure 5.28 Creating Custom Change Document Objects (Transaction SCDO)

If a DataSource is not suitable for either the generic delta or the ALE delta configuration, extractions can be managed by selection criteria. To enhance the DataSource, select it from the application component hierarchy in Transaction RSA6. In the next maintenance screen, specify which fields should be available for selection from the InfoPackage in the SAP BW system (see Figure 5.29). All fields available in the DataSource are listed in this table unless they were explicitly hidden when delivered by SAP.

Recommendation

Some fields of SAP Business Content DataSources are hidden by definition. These fields can only be enabled for extraction by core modification of entries in table ROOSFIELD.

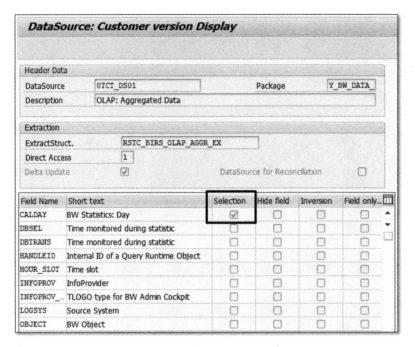

Figure 5.29 DataSource Maintenance (Transaction RSA6)

Any fields used for selection should be indexed in the database. If the fields are not key fields, create secondary indexes on them using Transaction SE11. When creating indexes with more than one field, order the fields in sequence of granularity—from the coarsest to the finest. Revisit the section on modeling DSO key fields in Section 5.1.4 for more information.

In Transaction RSA6, fields can be added to the DataSource extract structure. By default, these fields are hidden and not available for extraction until they are configured in the maintenance view, as seen in the HIDE FIELD column in Figure 5.29.

While business content DataSources can be enhanced by adding fields, enhancements should be limited because they can impact performance. In many cases, you can achieve better performance by creating a new DataSource based on a view joining the table where the additional fields exist to the original table. Otherwise, if an enhancement is implemented, the new fields are appended to the extract structure but must be filled by customer exit. See Section 5.2.4 for best practices and optimization tips for customer exit programming performance.

InfoPackages

When you use the traditional DataSource extraction method, InfoPackages trigger the data transfer from the DataSource in the source system to the PSA in SAP BW. They control package-related parameters for the data transfer and define the selection criteria.

InfoPackages can be scheduled independently but should always be included in process chains, even for initial history loads. This arrangement helps ensure a repeatable reload process.

InfoPackages support three modes of data extraction, as you can see in Figure 5.30:

▶ FULL UPDATE
This mode extracts all data from the DataSource based on the selection criteria specified in the DATA SELECTION tab. This mode is typically used for initial loads but also routinely for non-delta–capable DataSources.

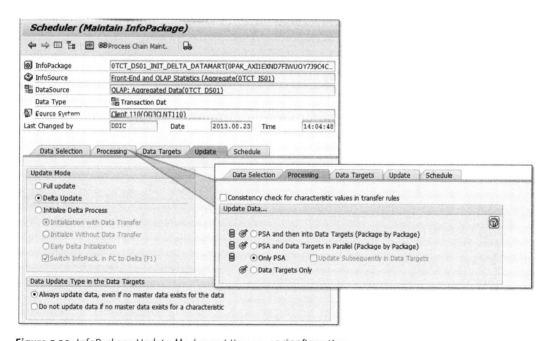

Figure 5.30 InfoPackage Update Modes and Processing Configuration

> **Recommendation**
>
> When extracting time-dependent data, pay explicit attention to the validity time interval settings on the UPDATE tab. The time interval determines the validity period of the time-dependent records that will be extracted. By default, the FIXED TIME INTERVAL START DATE is filled with the system date and END DATE with 31.12.9999, as shown in Figure 5.31. If retroactive updates are possible, set the interval to include older records. Coding a routine or variable for the time interval can ensure that the validity period adjusts over time.

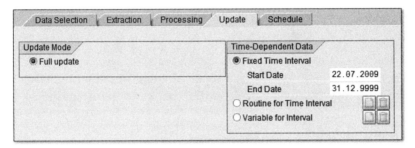

Figure 5.31 Time-Dependent Master Data Time Interval

▶ INITIALIZE DELTA PROCESS

Delta DataSources must be initialized, so the delta queue must be activated to capture deltas in the source system. This can be done with or without data transfer. If INITIALIZATION WITH DATA TRANSFER is chosen, all historical data is extracted, similar to a full load.

> **Recommendation**
>
> During initialization of transaction DataSources, data updates should be stopped in the source system; otherwise, records posted before the initialization is finished could be missed from extraction to SAP BW. If transactions cannot be stopped, initialization should be scheduled during periods of low system activity (i.e., Sunday morning).

For DataSources for which initialization extraction performance is a concern, choose option INITIALIZATION WITHOUT DATA TRANSFER to activate the delta mechanism and then use full repair loads to extract historical data. If the DataSource supports it, use the option EARLY DELTA INITIALIZATION, which starts the delta capture. Field ZDD_ABLE in the SAP BW table RSOLTPSOURCE or the source system table ROOSOURCE indicates whether a DataSource supports early delta initialization.

Recommendation

The option SWITCH INFOPACKAGE IN PC TO DELTA (F1) enables a single InfoPackage to be used for initializations and subsequent deltas. This way, only one InfoPackage needs to be created, and if the delta initialization is deleted, the next execution re-initializes. Once initialized, the InfoPackage is switched to extract deltas. This flexibility reduces the risk of a data-load error if used in process chains. However, there are benefits to controlling the initialization process with a separate InfoPackage, such as the ability to review the initialization settings later.

▶ DELTA UPDATE

Once the delta has been initialized, only new, changed and deleted records are extracted. This option is available for only delta-initialized DataSources. Table 5.8 lists the four delta types supported by DataSources in the source system.

Delta Type	Description
F	Flat file provides the delta
E	Extractor determines the delta (i.e., LIS, COPA)
D	Application determines the delta (i.e., LO, FI-AR/AP)
A	ALE change log pointer determines the delta

Table 5.8 Delta Types in Source System Table ROOSOURCE

As of SAP BW 7.x, InfoPackages must load to the PSA because further processing is handled by DTPs. In SAP BW 3.x, InfoPackages could load directly to the data target, as shown in Figure 5.30).

Parallelization techniques can optimize performance while loading data volumes, and there are multiple options, as follows:

▶ Leverage semantic partitioning capabilities in data modeling.

▶ Use multiple InfoPackages with non-overlapping selection conditions to split up large data volumes. Flat files can also be split up into smaller files and loaded in parallel.

Never use selection criteria in InfoPackages for initialization of delta DataSources because the same settings remain effective for subsequent deltas. Instead, initialize without data transfer and use multiple full loads with selection criteria for parallel loading of large data volumes.

▶ Define the degree of internal parallelization by setting the maximum number of dialog processes for parallel processing. It is possible to specify particular application servers for background job extraction, or use load balancing and let the system choose the most appropriate application server. Return to Section 2.4.2 on loading processes in Chapter 2 for more information on parallelization settings for data load processing.

The PROCESSING tab, shown in Figure 5.30, also includes a checkbox to enable consistency checks on master data. This setting ensures that no InfoObject values are inserted into SID tables during data loads, preventing corruption of master data values from sources without edit/validations. The validation logic behind this consistency check impacts data load performance and should be used only when you load data from flat files or other unsubstantiated sources. All SAP DataSources should be considered substantiated sources.

In tandem with parallelization, the data package size can also have an impact on extraction and load processing performance. Data is extracted from all DataSources using package fetch functionality, which enables the flexibility to optimize performance by minimizing processing and memory requirements.

The main memory requirement for extraction depends mainly on the size of the data package and can become very large. An optimally configured data package size can reduce the memory consumption. For more information and examples about specifying the parameters that influence the data package size, see SAP Notes 417307 and 409641.

You can configure the default size of each package for source systems by setting the maximum number of records in a data package in BI CUSTOMIZING, under CONNECTIONS TO OTHER SYSTEMS • MAINTAIN CONTROL PARAMETERS FOR DATA TRANSFER (Transaction RSCUSTV6).

In cases in which performance is poor because extraction logic requires a large memory requirement, you can adjust the default settings to reduce the number of records or the size of the data package. To override the default parameters, define the Info-Package-specific data transfer settings on the PROCESSING tab (see Figure 5.32).

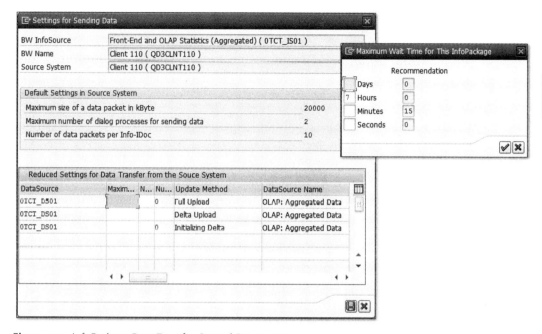

Figure 5.32 InfoPackage Data Transfer Control Parameters

There are different settings for the extraction and data transfer, depending on whether the data is loaded as PSA requests, in either the 7.x data flow (with DTPs) or 3.x DataSources, as long as they do not write to the data targets (InfoPackage processing option ONLY PSA) or the data is loaded directly to the data target in a 3.x data flow.

Recommendation

The information documented here is relevant for source systems with Service API release 7.0 or higher (Plug-In Basis 2005.1) or for 4.6C source systems (Plug-In 2004.1 SP10).

Requests that end in the PSA use qRFC with outbound queues by default. Therefore, these requests use the QOUT scheduler for data transfer from the source system to SAP BW (Transaction SMQS).

In the QOUT scheduler, specify the maximum number of dialog work processes used for the data transfer and the maximum processing time of the scheduler for the queue.

Requests that do not end in the PSA use the Service API (SAPI) to control the data transfer. These are PSA requests for 3.x DataSources that also write to data targets (for example, requests for 3.x DataSources with the InfoPackage processing option PSA AND THEN INTO DATA TARGETS) and requests in a data mart scenario (for example, updating a DSO in an InfoCube using an Export DataSource).

For these requests, set the default control parameters for data transfer for all Data-Sources under GENERAL SETTINGS • MAINTAIN CONTROL PARAMETERS FOR DATA TRANSFER in Transaction SBIW in the source system. The parameters are saved in the table ROIDOCPRMS. It is possible to override the default settings for specific DataSources in the InfoPackage under menu item SCHEDULER • DEFAULT DATA-SOURCE SETTINGS FOR DATA TRANSFER, as seen in Figure 5.32. These parameters are saved in the table ROOSPRMS.

> **Recommendation**
>
> For more information on requests that do not end in the PSA (SAPI-controlled data transfer), see SAP Note 1163359.

When loading data from flat files, always transfer the files to the application server (as described in Section 3.1.2 in Chapter 3) instead of loading from the client work station. Loading from the application server ensures not only an automated and repeatable process, but also optimal performance because it reduces network load. Files on the application server can be loaded in the background, thereby releasing the dialog work process for users.

If the volumes are excessively large, split the file into smaller parts. For optimal performance, create as many equally sized files as the number of CPUs available. The files can then be simultaneously loaded with multiple requests into the BI system. If possible, use fixed data-record lengths (ASCII files) for all flat files to save processing time because CSV files are converted to fixed data-record lengths during the loading process.

Persistent Staging Area

The persistent staging area (PSA) is the inbound storage area in SAP BW for data from the source systems. The extracted data is saved in transparent, relational database tables of the SAP BW system in the transfer structure format as defined in the Data-Source. Conceptually, the transfer structure in SAP BW is identical to the extract structure of the source system. In reality, there may be hidden fields in the extract structure that are not extracted to SAP BW. For fields that are extracted, the data format remains unchanged, so no summarization or transformations take place.

Each PSA-table is tightly coupled with its DataSource and generated by the SAP BW system upon activation of the DataSource. Data class and size category are the only technical PSA settings providing the possibility to assign separate tablespaces with different settings, like block size, extent size, and so on. When using SAP HANA as the database, these settings are not relevant.

For traditional 7.x DataSources, the PSA remains the entry point of all Data-Sources if data is loaded into SAP BW. Neither TransientProviders nor VirtualProviders with direct access use the PSA. The PSA is also not required for use of the Open ODS View.

Recommendation

The technical settings of the PSA can be found in the Transaction RSDS (even for 3.x DataSources, as seen in Figure 5.33).

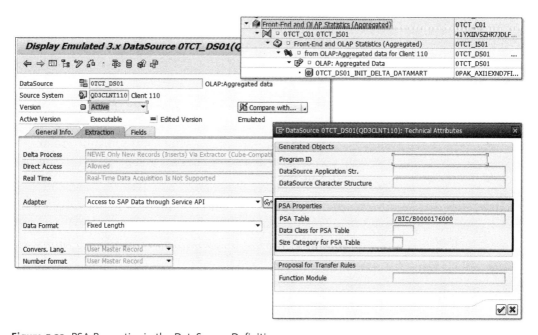

Figure 5.33 PSA Properties in the DataSource Definition

Using partitioning, you can split the dataset of a PSA table into several smaller, physically independent, and redundancy-free units. This separation can improve performance when reading and deleting from the PSA. In BI CUSTOMIZING, under CONNECTIONS TO OTHER SYSTEMS • MAINTAINING CONTROL PARAMETERS FOR DATA TRANSFER (Transaction RSCUSTV6), define the threshold number of data records after which a new partition is created. Multiple requests can be stored in each partition, but no request is split into more than one partition. In other words, all data records of each request are stored in a single partition, even if its size exceeds the defined partition size.

> **Note**
>
> Requests are not physically deleted from the PSA table until all requests in the PSA partition have been deleted. Then, the partition is dropped from the database.

5.2.2 Transfer Processing

After data is extracted to the PSA, it needs to be transferred to the data target. In a layered scalable architecture, data may be staged in several DSOs before it is available in the reporting layer. As discussed in Chapter 2, most transformations should be insulated between DSOs, although some simple data changes can be performed when you load the initial EDW layer.

Data Transfer Process

Recall that a data transfer process (DTP) is an object that triggers the data transfer between two persistent objects within SAP BW, such as from the PSA to a DSO or from a DSO to an InfoCube (see the boxed data target in Figure 5.34 for an example loading InfoCube 0TCT_VC06). A DTP can apply filters or semantic groups and control error handling. DTPs are used for standard data transfer, for real-time data acquisition, and for accessing data directly from the source system.

From a design perspective, DTPs can be used to separate delta processes for different data targets and filter data among the InfoProviders in different layers. You can realize peak performance of the transfer process by configuring technical settings according to best practices and optimizing parallel processing.

We recommend the following technical settings as best practices:

► Always set the DTP extraction mode from the PSA as Delta and never as Full. This setting controls how many requests are loaded from the PSA to the data target. When it is set to Delta, only new requests in the PSA are processed, but when it is set to Full, all existing requests in the PSA are processed, even those that have been processed previously. If the PSA is not cleansed routinely, especially for DataSources that support only the full update mode, performance can deteriorate significantly over time as the volume of processed data increases.

The default extraction mode for DTPs loading from one InfoProvider to another should also be Delta, but there could be initialization requirements that justify a Full mode. Avoid these scenarios as much as possible.

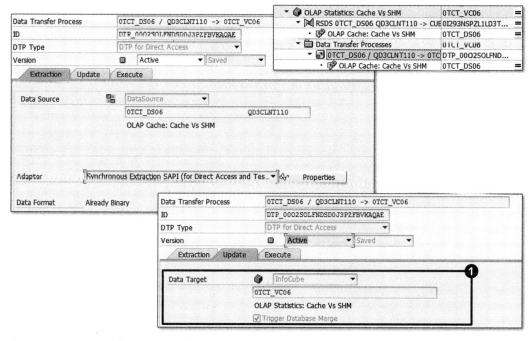

Figure 5.34 Data Transfer Process Definition

► As a general rule, do not edit the DTP description, especially when it is loading from a DataSource, because the source system is included in the description. The default descriptions are generated and will be automatically adjusted when importing into each system in the landscape. However, if the description is edited, it is fixed and transported as such.

In some special cases, such as when you apply filters in delta DTPs or use the full extraction mode, it may be prudent to edit the description to alert support staff of these specific use cases.

▸ When applying filters in the DTP, remove InfoObjects from the selection criteria for which no filtering is applied. The resulting clarity facilitates development and support.

▸ When loading from a DSO to a master data InfoObject, set the flag to HANDLE DUPLICATE RECORDS. This setting prevents a runtime error from occurring if there are multiple data records for the characteristic key in the data package. However, if the flag is set, the updating process is slower. To improve performance, deactivate the check, but only if the following requirements are fulfilled:

  ▹ The key of the DataSource provides unique data records.

Recommendation

For BI Content DataSources from SAP source systems, the field DELIVERY OF DUPLICATE DATA RECORDS on the GENERAL tab page in the BI DATASOURCE maintenance screen displays the behavior of the DataSource—this field is for informational purposes only and is not checked during extraction. Therefore, check the field manually (for value NONE) before deactivating the check in the DTP.

  ▹ Only a single request is transferred from the PSA when GET ALL NEW DATA IN SOURCE BY REQUEST on the EXTRACTION tab in the DTP maintenance transaction. More information is available later in this section.

  ▹ The key of the DataSource corresponds to the characteristic key of the target InfoObject or represents a subset of the characteristic key.

  ▹ The number of records for each characteristic key is not changed in the start or end routines of the transformation.

▸ Do not use error handling unless a specific use case is identified. Instead, use the default value NO UPDATE, NO REPORTING. With this setting, the system terminates the update of the entire data package if errors occur. The incorrect records are not written to the error stack because the request is terminated and has to be updated again in its entirety.

If error handling is required, define the key of the error stack using SEMANTIC GROUPING in the DTP. If any record has an error, all subsequent records with the same key are written to the error stack and not updated in the target, regardless of whether they have errors. This prevents records from being updated out of sequence when you use the error stack. However, subsequent lookups for these records from other data flows are not prevented, presenting a risk if the data flow is allowed to continue without failure.

> **Note**
>
> The use of the SEMANTIC GROUPING setting triggers a warning about potential performance degradation. However, with an SAP HANA database, there is no performance impact.

Request processing using a DTP can employ various methods of parallelization during its extraction and processing (transformation and update) steps. During DTP creation, the system selects the most appropriate and efficient processing mode in accordance with the global configuration settings and the specific source of the DTP.

Parallel extraction is enabled for a DTP when the following four conditions are met:

1. The source of the DTP must support parallel extraction, as the following do:
   - PSA of a DataSource
   - Write-optimized DSO
   - Change log of a standard DSO
2. Error handling must be deactivated.
3. The list for creating semantic groups in DTPs and transformations is empty.
4. The PARALLEL EXTRACTION field is selected (this is the default selection if the DTP source supports parallel extraction).

Parallel extraction requires more database resources, which could have a negative impact on the total time to process requests. The PARALLEL EXTRACTION field shown in Figure 2.20 in Chapter 2 offers two different processing mode options to influence the performance of data transfer. The two available options are PARALLEL EXTRACTION AND PROCESSING and SERIAL EXTRACTION, IMMEDIATE PARALLEL PROCESSING.

You can modify the system-defined processing mode of a standard DTP by changing the settings for error handling and semantic grouping. Table 5.9 gives tips on how to optimize performance of system-selected DTP processing modes.

Original State of DTP (Processing Mode)	Optimal Processing Mode	Optimal Settings for Better Performance
Serial extraction and processing of the source packages (processing mode 3)	Serial extraction, immediate parallel processing (processing mode 2)	Select a semantic grouping field
Serial extraction and processing of the source packages (processing mode 3)	Parallel extraction and processing (processing mode 1)	Deactivate error handling
Serial extraction, immediate parallel processing (processing mode 2)	Parallel extraction and processing (processing mode 1)	Deactivate error handling

Table 5.9 Optimizing DTPs Using Processing Modes

The following additional performance tips for DTPs optimize data loading:

▸ Set the number of permitted background processes globally for process type DTP_LOAD in Transaction RSBATCH (see Section 2.4.2 in Chapter 2 for more about loading processes).

▸ Adjust the number of parallel processes to optimize specific DTPs by overriding the global setting. This is particularly useful with massive data volumes or initial loads. In the DTP maintenance transaction, choose GOTO • BATCH MANAGER SETTING. Under NUMBER OF PROCESSES, specify how many background processes should be used to process the DTP (see Figure 5.35).

Recommendation

Always ensure that there are enough background work processes available for parallel processing. When multiple DTPs are executed at the same time, each one uses the number of background processes set in either global settings or the DTP-specific settings.

▸ By default, data is aggregated in the database using a GROUP BY statement during extraction from a DSO. When extracting data at the finest granularity (i.e., all key fields are extracted—which is almost always), aggregation has no effect. In these cases, select Suppress Database Aggregation on the Extraction tab to reduce the runtime of database extraction.

▶ Set an optimized size for each data package. The default setting for all DTPs for the size of a data package is set to 50,000 data records, which is based on the assumption that a data record has a width of 1,000 bytes. To improve performance, specify an optimal value for the data package size calculated from the size of the main memory. Enter this value under Package Size on the Extraction tab in the DTP maintenance transaction.

▶ Avoid processing large volumes of data by choosing Get All New Data Request by Request. This setting processes each request in the source one at a time, rather than bundling together all transfer-relevant requests from the source. Once processing is completed, the DTP request checks for further new requests in the source. If it finds any, it automatically creates an additional DTP request.

▶ Avoid processing small volumes of data when using non-overlapping filters in multiple DTPs during DataSource extraction. If a large amount of data is excluded by the filter criteria, this can result in very small data packages, possibly leading to poor extraction throughput if the overhead for each DTP exceeds the value of filter. Instead, replace the filter with semantic groups by activating error handling. This ensures that all data records belonging to each grouping key are extracted and processed within distinct data packages in the request.

▶ Extract full and initial loads from the active data table of DSOs instead of the change log. The change log can be larger than the active data table because it stores before- and after-images. Or, if it is cleansed during routine housekeeping, it may not contain all the data. To choose this setting, select Active Table (with Archive) or Active Table (without Archive) on the Extraction tab in Extraction from… or Delta Extraction from… in the DTP maintenance screen.

▶ Extract data from aggregates when InfoCubes are the source. During InfoCube extraction, the data is read from both the F-fact table and the E-fact table. To improve performance, use aggregates for the extraction, if they exist. Select Use Aggregates on the Extraction tab in the DTP maintenance screen. The system then compares the field structure from the transformation with the aggregates. If all InfoObjects needed in the transformation structure are used in an aggregate, the data is read from the aggregate during extraction instead of from the InfoCube tables.

> **Recommendation**
>
> When loading from one InfoProvider to another, if any of the key fields of the source InfoProvider are not assigned to target fields in the transformation, the key figures of the source are aggregated during extraction. You can prevent this automatic aggregation by implementing a start routine or using an intermediate InfoSource, however, please note that preventing aggregation can adversely affect the performance of the data transfer process. For more information, see SAP Note 1147419.

InfoSource

An InfoSource is a structure consisting of InfoObjects without persistence for connecting two transformations. InfoSources bundle transformation logic in a single transformation to simplify development effort when implementing data domains or semantic partitioning. They also insulate transformation logic from changes in DataSources or InfoProviders, and vice versa.

The InfoObjects that form the key of the records passing through an InfoSource can be specified in the definition. Because InfoSources are often used between DSOs for which `ORECORDMODE` is an important object, the best practice is to *not* specify any key fields so that each incoming record is passed through the Info-Source.

Adding an intermediate InfoSource in the ETL incurs additional processing and should be avoided as much as possible. However, in the following cases, it makes sense to use an intermediate InfoSource:

▸ When the same business logic should be applied to data loaded from different sources to the same data target (or from a single source to multiple targets). An intermediate InfoSource allows for central maintenance of common business logic. In Figure 5.35, source-specific transformations convert data into the Info-Source format. The common target transformation contains the common business rules across both sources. Alternatively, you can handle this scenario by maintaining the business logic in a single ABAP method, include, or function module and calling it from both source-specific transformations.

▸ When data should be flattened from multiple source records into a single target record. In Figure 5.36, two records for the same document item ❶ are flattened into one record by using different InfoSources that apply filters on each currency type, document currency ❷, and local currency ❸. The result is a single record with multiple key figures for each currency type ❹. Alternatively, you can handle this scenario by using rule groups in a single transformation.

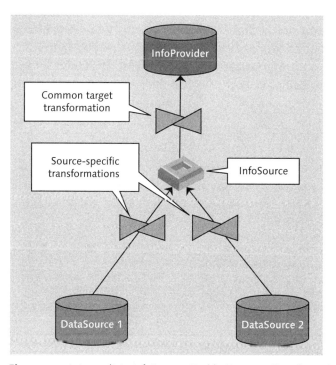

Figure 5.35 Intermediate InfoSources Enable Common Transformations

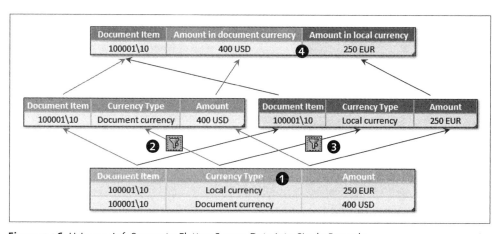

Figure 5.36 Using an InfoSource to Flatten Source Data into Single Records

Transformations

Transformations convert data from the source format to the target format in SAP BW by mapping the DataSource fields to the InfoObjects of the data target. The transformation process also enables consolidation, cleansing, and integration of data. Rule groups can be used to execute different mappings based on source field values, as shown in Figure 5.37. The DataSource fields are displayed in the box on the left, and the data target fields are in the box on the right, with the mapping arrows identifying links between the source fields and the target fields.

Transformations enable data consolidation and cleansing from multiple sources, as well as semantic synchronization of data. As a result, InfoSources are no longer mandatory with transformations; they are optional but can still be used to connect multiple sequential transformations (i.e., complex multistep processes) or consolidate redundant transformations from multiple sources to a single target or from a single source to multiple targets.

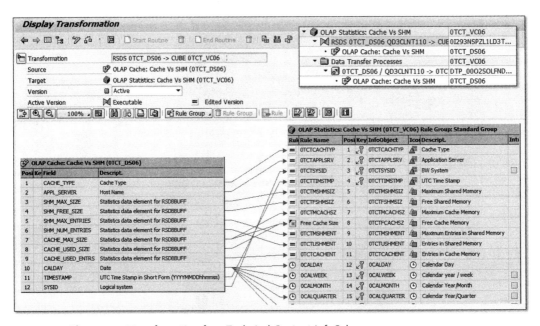

Figure 5.37 Transformation for a Technical Content InfoCube

Transformations should happen as early as possible in the data flow so that the transformed data is available to all further processes, but no complex transformations should happen between the PSA and the EDW layer. Because the PSA is not permanent, data may need to be reloaded from the source to correct data integrity issues that arise from poorly defined logic.

Individual transformation rules can have one of the following rule types (as seen in the dropdown menus in Figure 5.38):

▸ CONSTANT ❶: The target field is filled directly with the value entered.

▸ DIRECT ASSIGNMENT ❷: The target field is populated with the value of the assigned source field.

▸ FORMULA: The target field is calculated using the transformation library, together with the formula builder, without the need for ABAP coding.

▸ INITIAL: The target field is not populated. This rule type is available only if the target field is a characteristic.

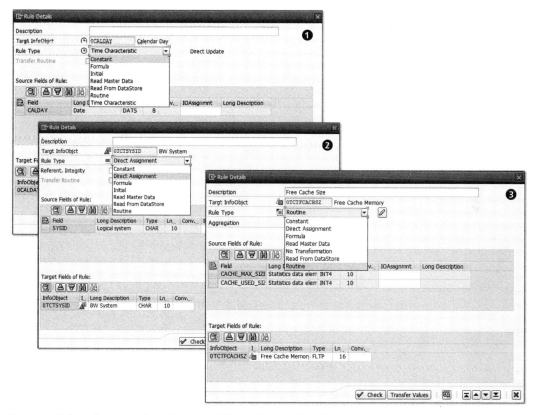

Figure 5.38 Transformation Rule Types for Different Types of InfoObjects

- No Transformation: The target field is not populated. This rule type is available only if the target field is a key figure.

- Read Master Data: The target field is populated from the attribute of the source field that is a characteristic with master data. This transformation type has been optimized and now buffers data in memory, removing the need to create custom coding for efficient reads.

- Read from DataStore: The target field is populated from a DSO data field when all key fields are provided by the source structure. This transformation type has been optimized and buffers data in memory, removing the need to create custom coding for efficient reads.

- Routine ❸: The target field is calculated using ABAP coding based on selected input fields.

- Time Characteristic: The target field is derived from the source field (i.e., calendar month from calendar day). This rule type is available only if the target field is a time characteristic.

> **Recommendation**
>
> Reading master data should be used with caution. From a modeling perspective, looking up and storing attributes persistently results in reporting historical values at that specific point in time. If the requirement is to report the current value of an attribute, use navigational attributes instead. If the requirements is to report historical truth (the value as of the time of the transaction), the lookup will not provide this accuracy if the attribute changes over time and the data is subsequently reloaded. To deliver historical truth, the value should be captured at the time of the transaction and loaded from the source.

When loading data to DSOs, the transformation rules support two types of aggregation behavior for key figures:

- **Summation**
  If the usual aggregation of the key figure is set to SUM in the InfoObject definition, records can be aggregated during data loading and added to any previous loaded values sharing the same record key. However, if the usual aggregation of the key figure is Minimum or Maximum, the transformation routine allows only the relevant option for each key figure. Use this behavior in the EDW layer if the source does not have the same key field structure as the target or if the DataSource is delta-capable. This behavior is used by default in all subsequent layers.

▶ **Overwrite**

This aggregation behavior overwrites any previously loaded values for the same record key. Use this behavior if full loads are written to the DSO or if a delta-capable DataSource sends the after-image (such as LIS or generic delta extractors).

InfoObject 0RECORDMODE in a DSO is used to identify the delta-image and how the record should be handled during the update to the DSO. If the DataSource extracts a suitable field, such as ROCANCEL, it should be mapped to 0RECORDMODE. Pay attention to how deletions (values D and R) are handled — by default, entries are physically deleted from the DSO. To retain records deleted from the source, set a deletion flag in the DSO and do not map 0RECORDMODE. Alternatively, deletions can be used in this way to cleanse records from non-delta-capable sources.

> **Recommendation**
>
> The referential integrity check for master data-bearing characteristics should always be switched on in the EDW layer transformation (source is PSA) if the source system is non-SAP.

Transformations support different points during which business logic can be coded in ABAP, as follows:

▶ **Start routine**

The start routine is executed once for each data package at the start of the transformation before any other routines are processed. The start routine has an internal table in the format of the source structure as input and output parameters called the source package. Code business logic in the start routine if the following scenarios are applicable:

- ▶ The logic depends on fields existing only in the source and not in the target.

- ▶ The logic must be applied before any aggregation takes place, or must be applied to the entire inbound data package, such as the modification or deletion of data in the source package.

- ▶ The logic applies to more than one mapping in the transformation, such as preliminary calculations that can be stored globally and re-used in other routines.

- ▶ Data required in the subsequent transformation mappings needs to be looked up from other data providers, such as master data characteristics or

DSOs. These tables can be read into memory once and accessed in subsequent routines.

> **Recommendation**
>
> In SAP HANA databases, the standard transformation routine functionality to read master data and DSO tables has been optimized and now buffers data in memory, removing the need to create custom coding for efficient reads.

- **Transformation routines**

  Transformation routines are executed for each record in the data package after the start routine and before the end routine. Code business logic in the individual transformation routines if the following scenarios are applicable:

  - The logic depends on fields existing in both the source and the target.
  - The logic is specific to a single field mapping.

- **End routine**

  The end routine is executed once for each data package after all other routines have processed. The end routine has an internal table in the format of the target structure as input and output parameters called the result package. Code business logic in the end routine if the following scenarios are applicable:

  - The logic depends on fields existing only in the target and not in the source.
  - The logic derives additional fields based on the contents of the result package.
  - The logic must be applied after aggregation takes place, or must be applied to the entire outbound data package, such as the derivation of fields based on other fields in the result package, the execution of data checks, or the deletion of records that should not be updated.
  - The logic applies to more than one mapping in the transformation, such as the creation of additional records.

> **Recommendation**
>
> Target fields that are populated in the end routine should be mapped with an *initial value* constant in the individual transformation routine with a rule description `Filled in end routine` so that it is immediately clear where the logic takes place.

▶ **Expert routine**

The expert routine allows the entire transformation to be programmed as one piece of code. In the expert routine, the other routines are irrelevant because all mappings must be coded from scratch—even the message transfer to the monitor must be coded by the developer. Expert routines should be used only in exceptional cases if there are no other options available.

Recommendation

In the expert routine, all fields are updated by default with overwrite mode (MOVE).

If the transformation logic requires access to all records with a particular key grouped together (typically in the start or end routine), the transformation can be configured to provide data packages by semantic groups (EDIT • DEFINE SEMANTIC GROUPS FOR PACKAGES), as shown in Figure 5.39. This was not possible before SAP BW 7.30; then, the semantic groups could be defined only in DTPs.

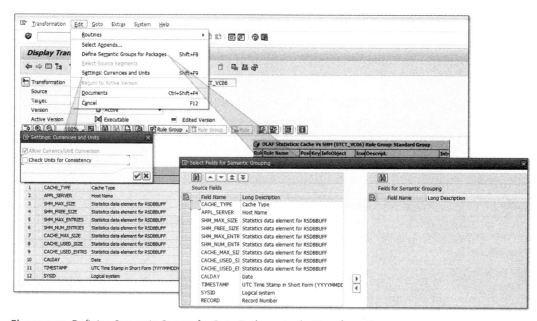

Figure 5.39 Defining Semantic Groups for Data Packages in the Transformation

Coding in the start routine or end routine is preferred over field-specific coding in individual transformation routines for several reasons. First, coding logic in the start or end routines can offer better performance than individual routines because more information is available and internal tables can be filled, reducing the number of database accesses. Second, the logic is easier to maintain if it is in a single routine and not distributed among different field mappings in the transformation.

However, if it is necessary to code logic in individual transformation routines, it is important to confirm that the coding does not impair performance. In our combined experience, poor coding practices and disjointed logic implementation in the transformation rules typically account for a significant chunk of any performance optimization opportunity.

Regardless of where the logic is coded, if it involves more than a few lines of simple coding (such as concatenating fields or filtering records), the logic should be written in a class method, function module, or program include. For more details and for recommended coding standards, refer to Section 5.2.4.

5.2.3 Load Processing

After data has been extracted and transformed, it is loaded into persistent data targets, such as InfoObjects, DSOs and InfoCubes. The sequence in which these different objects are loaded can make a difference in data loading performance.

First, master data should always be loaded before transaction data because this ensures that the SIDs are created before and not during the transaction data loads. Because the SID creation process is resource intensive, creating SIDs during loads with less volume and shorter record lengths reduces the burden on system resources and results in better performance overall.

Following this philosophy, master data loaded in the following sequence provides the best overall performance: texts, attributes, and hierarchies. Loading texts first creates the SIDs for all key characteristics, and subsequently loading attributes creates the SIDs for all attribute values. However, better performance does not always mean shorter duration. Recall from Chapter 2 that all non-essential loads should be removed from the critical path. Over time, the critical path evolves, so continuous monitoring of data load durations and performance is necessary to ensure that data loads do not exceed loading windows.

To facilitate the creation of SIDs for master data objects with a high volume of new values, such as document numbers, SID values can be buffered so that they do not need to be fetched from the database, as covered in Chapter 3, Section 3.1. When loading history or mass volumes to InfoCubes during cutover, increase the number-range buffer for the DIMIDs of high-cardinality dimensions, as well. If possible, reset these number-range buffers after loading to prevent unnecessary memory consumption.

Loading InfoCubes

To optimize performance when loading and deleting data from InfoCubes, consider adopting the following recommendations:

▸ **Compress InfoCube data regularly.**
During compression, all records with the same key values across the data package partitions in the F-fact table are aggregated into a single record in the E-fact table. In this way, the data volume of the InfoCube can be managed when a high number of delta records results in substantial growth. Compression provides benefits from a data loading perspective as well as a reporting perspective. When F-fact table requests are compressed, their respective data partition is dropped from the F-fact table.

Ideally, compression should be executed after each data load, although it is not necessarily a critical path item. The more frequently an InfoCube is compressed, however, the quicker it is to execute. The only reason not to compress data is that the request may need to be dropped from the InfoCube and reloaded from the source. However, since data should always be staged in a DSO before feeding a cube, this reasoning is without merit.

Recommendation

When compressing an InfoCube for the first time, select a single request only. After the first compression, select more than one request as needed.

▸ **Refresh database statistics routinely.**
The database statistics are used by the system to optimize both query and compression performance. Even when the InfoCube is indexed in BWA, it is important to keep the database statistics up to date. It is possible to schedule automatic recalculation of the database statistics after each data load in the process chains. At a minimum, it is recommended that you update the statistics after every one million new records have been loaded into an InfoCube.

The status of the database statistics can be checked from the InfoCube maintenance screen. The button CHECK STATISTICS confirms whether the statistics are up to date (green), out of date (yellow) or do not exist (red). Use RECALCULATE STATISTICS to create or update statistics in the background.

Recommendation

It is possible to configure the percentage of InfoCube data that is used to create the statistics; the default value is 10%. In general, the larger the InfoCube, the smaller the percentage should be to minimize the demands on the system. For smaller InfoCubes (up to 10 million records), set the percentage of data used for creating statistics to 100%.

- **Delete database indexes before loading.**
  The process chain variants and maintenance functions for deleting and rebuilding database indexes in batches affect only the secondary indexes on the F-fact table, not the E-fact table. Therefore, if InfoCubes are compressed regularly, the F-fact table and its database indexes should be small. In most cases, deleting the indexes before loading and rebuilding them after loading delivers better overall load performance than leaving them active during loading. There are two main reasons to delete InfoCube database indexes before loading InfoCubes:

  - First, when data is loaded into an InfoCube, or, more specifically, when records are inserted into the F-fact table, the database indexes on the F-fact table for each dimension table are updated. The performance of these updates can suffer if the data volume being loaded is large, which can result in data load errors if any updates exceed their allotted time. However, if the index has been deleted before the load, there is no active index to update, and all the records are inserted into the fact table.

  - Second, because the indexes can be updated only serially, their existence prevents parallel loading into standard InfoCubes. Therefore, deleting the indexes enables parallel loading into the InfoCube (multiple requests at the same time).

Recommendation

If the F-fact table contains more than 50 million records, as a rule, you should refrain from deleting and recreating indexes until data is compressed to the E-fact table.

The status of the database indexes can be checked from the InfoCube maintenance screen (see Figure 5.40). The button CHECK INDEXES confirms whether the indexes are the correct bitmap type (green), the wrong type (yellow), or do not exist (red). Use DELETE DB INDEXES (BATCH) to delete the F-fact table indexes or DELETE DB INDEXES (IMMEDIATELY) to delete both the E-fact and the F-fact indexes. With BUILD DB INDEXES (BATCH), the indexes of the F- and E-fact tables are rebuilt.

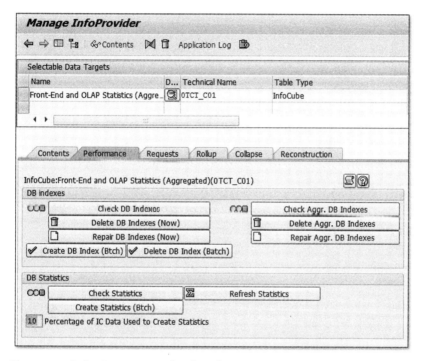

Figure 5.40 Index Functions in InfoCube Administration (Transaction RSA11)

Load Balancing

During data loading windows, especially in global systems where data loads execute all day, competition with end users for system resources can result in memory, CPU, or I/O bottlenecks. During these periods of intense resource demand, the performance and stability of the system can be seriously impaired.

To mitigate the risk that any server will reach its limit, a load-balancing strategy should be implemented in all systems with multiple application servers. The workload of loading processes and other data warehouse processes can be balanced in the way that best meets a variety of requirements. For example, it might be best to balance all processes across all available application servers or restrict some processes to specific application servers.

A successful strategy makes the best use of all physical hardware hosts and application server instances available in the BI system. Several different load-balancing scenarios can be employed to facilitate loading large volumes of data. If data load processes are split into packages for parallelization, they can be distributed among different applications server instances. In other words, parallel processing and load balancing are possible not only across multiple processes but also within a single process.

To configure load balancing in SAP BW for extractions from SAP source systems, choose one of the following scenarios and implement the approach as specified:

▶ **Scenario 1: A single host or instance for loading processes**
In this scenario, a single instance (normally the database instance) is dedicated for data loading processes, while the other instances are used for reporting and analysis. Limiting loading processes to the database host minimizes network traffic during data loads while freeing capacity for end-user reporting on the remaining instances. Use this scenario when data loading occurs at the same time as reporting and analysis, but ensure that the capacity of the dedicated host is sufficient to handle all loading processes.

To implement this approach, specify the target host and system number of the database instance of the BW system in the RFC destination of all source systems (Transaction SM59). Select No for the Load Balancing radio button.

▶ **Scenario 2: Multiple hosts or instances for loading processes**
In this scenario, data-loading processes are balanced across multiple hosts or instances in order to optimize the loading processes. This approach requires a logon group to balance the load equally over all instances in the logon group.

To implement this approach, create a logon group, as illustrated in Figure 5.41 (Transaction SMLG); assign instances to it; and activate dynamic load balancing by editing the logon group definition in table RZLLICLASS. Set field FAVTYPE (Logon group: Method for determining preferred server) to R for round robin. This setting means that the next instance in the list is used for the next logon.

In the source systems, set the LOAD BALANCING radio button to YES for the SAP BW RFC destination. Specify the target system, message server, and logon group.

When you load data, the global work process overview (Transaction SM66) shows how the tasks are balanced over the instances defined in the logon group for the loading processes.

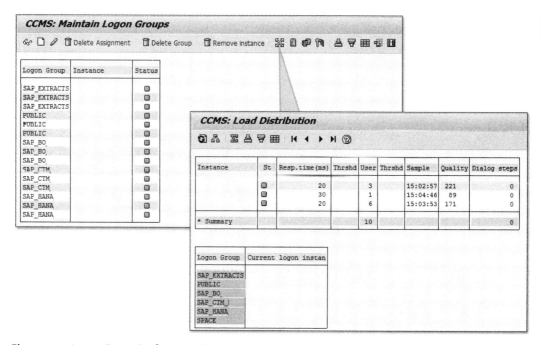

Figure 5.41 Logon Group Configuration (Transaction SMLG)

To achieve optimized balancing of system resources for background processing of BI processes (data staging processes within SAP BW), it is necessary that you use an RFC server group for background processing. Using Transaction SM61, create a server group and assign the relevant instances in the BI system (see Figure 5.42). To set up load balancing using instances of the RFC group, specify the RFC group in the default runtime parameters in BI background management with Transaction RSBATCH.

BI background management then executes work processes that have been split from the main process on the server(s) specified. If no settings for load balancing have been specified, the load is automatically balanced by BI background management. For each background job that is created, BI background management selects the server with the most free background work processes to process the job.

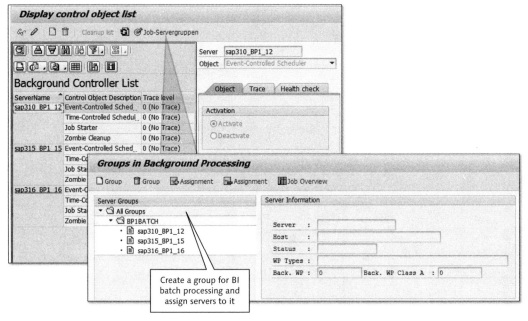

Figure 5.42 Server Group Administration (Transaction SM61)

When you execute manual loads, it is possible to overwrite the default RFC server group and specify which server(s) to execute the work processes on. You can make this alternate setting in the SERVER FOR SCHEDULING dialog box, which appears when manually executing BI processes and when configuring parallel processing settings in BI background management (Transaction RSBATCH).

5.2.4 ABAP Guidelines

In the BI system and SAP source systems, there are a number of places where customized ABAP code can be written in customer exits, BAdIs, and routines in transfer rules, update rules, and transformations. Wherever code is required to meet ETL or reporting and analytical requirements in SAP BW systems, ABAP development should endeavor to meet the following objectives:

1. **Efficiency**

   Improve processing time for all extractor user exits and transfer rule code, transformations, and update rules by adhering to best-practice coding standards. For more detailed programming guidelines, see other SAP Press books on this subject.

2. **Portability**

   Reduce the amount of redundant code in the system by putting common code such as lookups from master data tables or DSO tables in includes, function modules, or class methods.

   Replace hard-coding in ETL code with dynamic selections defined in range tables (like `TVARVC`) so that the same filters can be applied consistently in multiple transformations.

3. **Maintainability**

   For customer exits, minimize the impact of syntax errors in one variable or DataSource by implementing calls to independent executable programs.

   For transformations, transfer rules, and update rules, enable version history and version management by coding logic in includes, methods, and function modules instead of directly in the routines.

   For all development, adopt a consistent approach so that the support team can easily transition from one subject area to another and focus on the business logic without wasting time and effort to understand how the approach works.

To code efficient ABAP for optimal performance during BW ETL, developers should adhere to the lessons learned over the past fifteen years. There are many coding best practices for ensuring the best possible performance:

▶ **Avoid unnecessary loops—especially nested loops.**

   During transfer rules, update rules, and transformations, each data package is already being processed in a loop. Any loops coded in start and end routines are additional loops, while those coded in the field routines are nested loops. For example, to delete records from an internal table, do not loop through the data package; instead, use a single `delete` statement against the entire data package.

   Use field symbols instead of header records for faster table access and updates to data package fields (see in Figure 5.43).

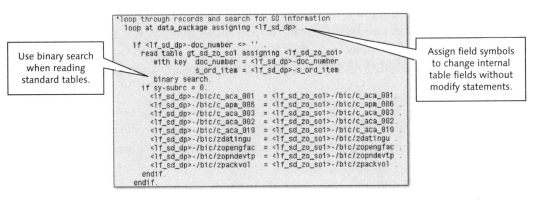

Figure 5.43 Loop Processing Best Practices in BW ABAP

▶ **Minimize database accesses while avoiding nested selects.**

Use array operations rather than SELECT SINGLE statements when reading the database. In other words, select data only once (i.e., during the start routine) and save it in global internal tables so that it can be accessed from memory during field routines instead of reading directly from the database. Limit the size of each internal table to prevent memory to disk swapping. For small-volume master data tables, read data into internal tables once per load—do not refresh these tables for every data package.

For large-volume master data and DSO tables, select only the records needed from the database using the FOR ALL ENTRIES statement instead of subqueries for each data package, as shown by ❶ in Figure 5.44. Always confirm that the data package is not empty before executing a FOR ALL ENTRIES statement; otherwise, all data is selected from the database. Where applicable, use aggregate functions and grouping functions (SUM, MAX, MIN or GROUP BY, ORDER BY, HAVING). Refresh these internal tables when processing each individual data package.

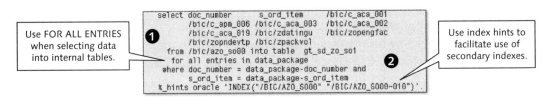

Figure 5.44 Select Statement Optimization Techniques

▶ **Avoid full table scans.**

When accessing database tables directly, specify the entire key in the WHERE condition (to use the primary index) or all the fields in an available secondary index. Where possible, avoid using NOT in the WHERE condition because table indexes are not supported for this type of access. If necessary, use index hints in the SELECT statement.

When reading internal tables, use the table key or binary search or otherwise define them as sorted or hash tables (see ❷ in Figure 5.44). Hash tables are useful for accessing individual records, especially if data in the table changes frequently. Sorted tables are useful for accessing ranges and normally require less memory space than hash tables.

When coding directly in start and end routines, the SAP ABAP system does not maintain versions. To have better management of code and keep track of code changes, create includes, class methods, or function modules for coding transformation routines in update rules, transfer rules, and transformations. If the change is only to the logic, the code can be modified, SAP maintains a new version, and only the program code needs to be transported—there is no need to transport SAP BW ETL objects.

Last but not least, to ensure that the coding can be supported, add comments to explain complex logic. To ensure that the code is legible, use PrettyPrinter to indent code and add line breaks where necessary.

This concludes our coverage on getting data in the data warehouse, as well as data modeling and data loading performance optimization techniques. In the next chapter, we will cover how to get data out of the data warehouse, focusing on how to design and implement queries and reports for optimal response time.

Reports are a key touch point with users. Let's turn our attention to identifying and resolving reporting performance problems in the SAP BW system.

6 Reporting Performance Tuning

An SAP BW system must provide great reporting performance. This is what the end users see every time they run reports, so a system that does not have good reporting performance will not be adopted by the users. They will instead start to find other solutions or just use the SAP BW system to extract data into other reporting solutions with better performance. This chapter will focus on identifying and resolving reporting performance problems in the SAP BW system.

The chapter is divided into two sections. In Section 6.1, we will cover the tools available to identify performance problems in the SAP BW system, and in Section 6.2, we will cover best practices and specific performance tuning guidelines.

Let's begin!

6.1 Identifying Performance Problems

To resolve performance problems related to reporting, you need to continuously identify and address these problems. SAP BW includes several tools that can be used to monitor performance and identify performance problems.

6.1.1 Using SAP BW-Specific Tools

Let's look at the SAP BW-specific tools, as well as some of the most used general SAP tools for performance analysis:

- SAP BW Statistics is a specific SAP BW tool to gather and monitor detailed SAP BW performance and usage statistics.
- SAP BW Technical Content is delivered in addition to the SAP BW statistics. You must activate the BW Technical Content in any SAP BW system because it is used in both SAP EarlyWatch and other services provided by SAP.

▸ The SAP BW Administration Cockpit is an optional tool that provides standard iViews to monitor and analyze performance and trends in the SAP BW system.

Let's explore each in more detail.

BW Statistics

Activate the collection of statistics data in the SAP BW system in Transaction RSDDSTAT. This is easily done for all objects: click the ACTIVATE STATISTICS button. Then, this button displays as DEACTIVATE STATISTICS (CURRENTLY ACTIVE), as shown in Figure 6.1.

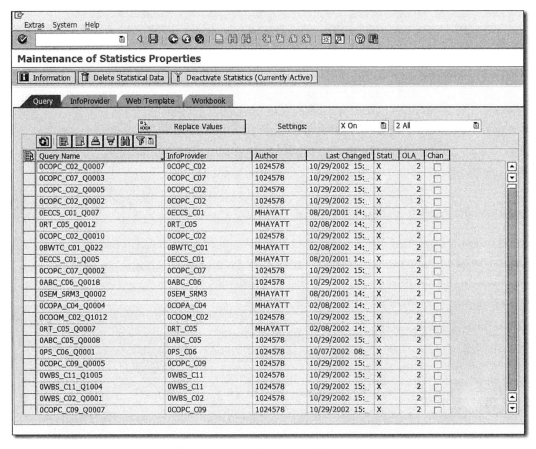

Figure 6.1 Activation of BW Statistics Collection (Table RSDDSTAT)

BW Statistics collects runtime information about the following:

1. BEx queries (actions on the frontend tools and in the OLAP engine, including planning)
2. Sub-processes in SAP HANA/BWA index maintenance and analytic indexes
3. Data transfer and data processing in the Data Warehouse, as well as their status
4. Planning functions

The statistics data is collected in tables RSDDSTAT* or UPC_STATISTIC*.

> **Recommendation**
>
> The system always records statistics on the runtimes and status of data transfer and data processing in the Data Warehouse. This is not the case for statistics for the data transfer process. These are deactivated in the default setting and can be activated in table RSDDSTATOBJLEVEL. See SAP Note 966964 for more information.

It is possible to control the specific statistics settings by the different object types and objects in the QUERY, INFOPROVIDER, WEB TEMPLATE, and WORKBOOK tabs.

To get the best statistics reporting capability, you should make sure all of these are active and set to default when the statistics collection is activated.

For queries, select the detail level for the statistics data from the following:

▶ **0: Aggregated data**
   The system aggregates all OLAP events (except events 3010 and 3100, which are needed to calculate the query counter) for the query in event 99999. This contains all times in the OLAP processing for this query. The system does not record data from the aggregation layer of the analytic engine.

▶ **1: Only frontend/calculation layer data**
   The system records all OLAP events, but not separate data from the aggregation layer of the analytic engine. The system writes only the general data manager event 9000 in the OLAP context, as well as the aggregation information. This is the recommended setting for most BW systems because it collects enough detail to analyze performance issues without generating too much information!

▶ **2: All**

The system records all data from the area for the frontend and calculation layer, as well as data from the area for the aggregation layer and aggregation information. We don't recommend this because too much data is recorded, which results in rapid growth of the RSDDSTAT* tables.

▶ **9: No data**

Data is recorded for the BEx web templates and workbooks, depending on the setting. The system does not record any data from the frontend and calculation layer or from the aggregated event 99999.

When new objects are created in SAP BW, they are assigned to the default setting. Therefore, it is important that the default setting is to collect statistics to ensure that new objects collect statistics from day one when they are implemented.

The DELETE STATISTICAL DATA button allows you to delete the collected data based on its age. This can also be scheduled with program RSDDSTAT_DATA_DELETE. This program should be scheduled to run regularly to clean up statistical data from the system because the statistics tables can grow rapidly in a system with heavy usage. We recommend that you keep a maximum of 30 days and a minimum of eight days of statistical data in the BW statistics tables.

SAP BW Technical Content Activation

SAP BW Technical Content is part of the standard SAP BW content. Although it can be installed like any other business content, SAP has also provided a quick installation program that can be called from Transaction RSTCO_ADMIN.

Use the START INSTALLATION button, shown in Figure 6.2, to trigger the installation. A background job is started that will perform the installation. The installation normally takes an hour or two, depending on the database platform. It is important to check the log after the installation is complete to ensure that all objects were installed without error. The log provides details about the installed objects, as well as the installation status for each object, as shown in Figure 6.3.

Recommendation
Warnings can occur due to impact when you activate the SAP BW Technical Content after upgrades. These warnings should be reviewed, but generally no action is required. You should always resolve errors because they do impact BW system operation.

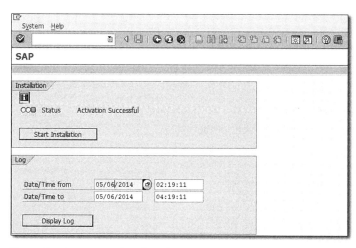

Figure 6.2 Activation of Technical Content (Transaction RSTCO_ADMIN)

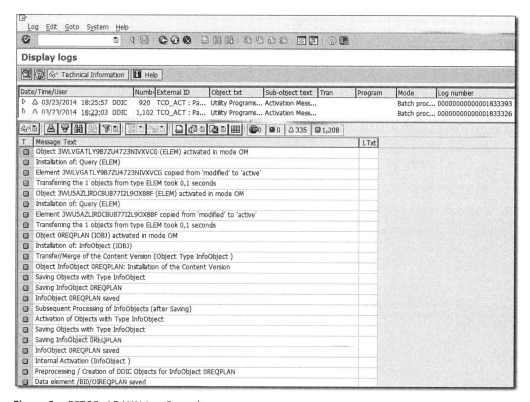

Figure 6.3 RSTCO_ADMIN Log Example

BW Administration Cockpit

The BW Administration Cockpit is built on the BW Statistics Technical Content. It includes several standard monitoring reports that provide insight into short- and long-term system performance.

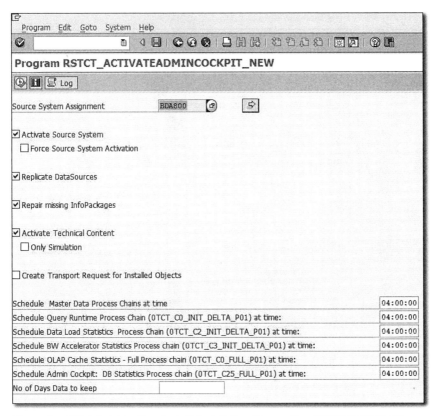

Figure 6.4 BW Administration Cockpit Installation (Transaction RSTCT_INST_BIAC)

Install the BW Administration Cockpit with Transaction RSTCT_INST_BIAC, as shown in Figure 6.4. This should be done in addition to the technical content installation.

When installing BW Administration Cockpit, you should check all the boxes in the activation tool so that it also schedules the process chains used to load the BW statistics data into the Technical Content. Again, you can specify how many days are to be kept in the BW statistics tables; we suggest between eight and 30 days.

You can also attach the objects to a transport request. This should be done in development so that the object can be transported to subsequent systems following a normal change management procedure.

The BW Administration Cockpit is included in the standard system administration portal role in the BI Java system. This role should be assigned to administrators to give them access to the standard iViews that are part of the BW Administration Cockpit. In addition, a separate BI administrator role provides access to these iViews. Figure 6.5 shows the iViews that are part of the BW Administration Cockpit.

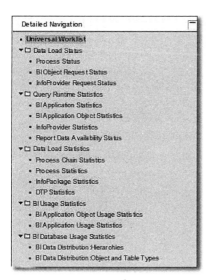

Figure 6.5 BI Administration Cockpit iViews

Installation of the Technical Content and the BW Administration Cockpit activates quite a few SAP BW objects in the system, as listed in Table 6.1.

Object Type	Count of Objects
iViews	15
Web Templates	33
Queries	196
MultiProviders	18
InfoCubes	15

Table 6.1 BW Technical Content Objects

You are not limited to using only the queries and objects installed by the standard content. They provide an excellent base for enhancements to add your specific organizations characteristics or groupings to the analysis.

The main objects you'll use are the MultiProviders, listed in Table 6.2 with the latest available content release.

InfoProvider Technical Name	Content Release	Long Description
0TCT_MC01	7.30/00	Frontend and OLAP Statistics (Aggregated)
0TCT_MC02	7.30/00	Frontend and OLAP Statistics (Details)
0TCT_MC03	7.30/00	Data Manager Statistics (Details)
0TCT_MC05	7.03/00	OLAP Statistics: Cache Type Memory Consumption
0TCT_MC06	7.30/00	OLAP Statistics: Cache vs. SHM
0TCT_MC07	7.30/00	OLAP Statistics: Query Memory Consumption
0TCT_MC11	7.30/00	BI Object Request Status
0TCT_MC12	7.30/00	Process Status
0TCT_MC14	7.30/00	Report Availability Status
0TCT_MC15	7.30/00	MPRO—Data Storages with Inconsistent and Incomplete Data
0TCT_MC21	7.30/00	Process Statistics
0TCT_MC22	7.30/00	DTP Statistics

Table 6.2 Technical Content Multiproviders

InfoProvider Technical Name	Content Release	Long Description
0TCT_MC23	7.30/00	InfoPackage Statistics
0TCT_MC25	7.30/00	Database Volume Statistics
0TCT_MC31	7.30/00	BWA Statistics: CPU Consumption
0TCT_MC32	7.30/00	BWA Statistics: InfoProvider Memory Consumption
0TCT_MCA1	7.30/00	Frontend and OLAP Statistics (Highly Aggregated)
0TCT_MCWS	7.40/00	Workspace MultiProvider

Table 6.2 Technical Content Multiproviders (Cont.)

InfoProviders 0TCT_MC01 through 0TCT_MC07 provide query, workbook, and web application performance statistics. The delivered queries include queries to monitor short- and long-term trends.

With the SAP BW-specific tools installed and activated, it is now possible to analyze the performance and find bottlenecks in reporting.

Table 6.3 lists the main queries provided for analyzing the reporting performance in SAP BW.

InfoProvider Technical Name	Query Technical Name	Query Description
0TCT_MC01	0TCT_MC01_Q0413	Short-Term Trends in Total Runtimes of a BI Application
0TCT_MC01	0TCT_MC01_Q0122	Deviations in Runtimes of BI Application Objects
0TCT_MC02	0TCT_MC02_Q0200	Detailed Query Runtime Statistics: Analysis
0TCT_MC01	0TCT_MC01_Q0423	Short-Term Trends in Total Runtimes of a BI Application Object
0TCT_MC01	0TCT_MC01_Q0131	Runtimes of InfoProviders
0TCT_MC01	0TCT_MC01_Q0200	Aggregated Query Runtime Statistics: Analysis
0TCT_MC01	0TCT_MC01_Q0112	Deviations in Runtimes of BI Applications

Table 6.3 Technical Content Performance Analysis Queries

InfoProvider Technical Name	Query Technical Name	Query Description
0TCT_MC05	0TCT_MC05_Q0101	Memory Consumption of Cache Types
0TCT_MC05	0TCT_MC05_Q0102	Memory Consumption of Cache Types (Graphical)
0TCT_MC06	0TCT_MC06_Q0101	Memory Consumption of Cache vs. SHM
0TCT_MC06	0TCT_MC06_Q0102	Entries of Cache vs. SHM
0TCT_MC07	0TCT_MC07_Q0101	Query Memory Consumption
0TCT_MC01	0TCT_MC01_Q0414	Long-Term Trends in Total Runtimes of a BI Application
0TCT_MC05	0TCT_MC05_Q0200	OLAP Cache Status Overview
0TCT_MC01	0TCT_MC01_Q0132	Deviations in Runtimes of InfoProviders
0TCT_MC01	0TCT_MC01_Q0424	Long-Term Trends in Total Runtimes of a BI Application Object
0TCT_MC01	0TCT_MC01_Q0133	Short-Term Trends in Total Runtimes of InfoProviders
0TCT_MC01	0TCT_MC01_Q0123	Short-Term Trends in Total Runtimes of BI Application Objects
0TCT_MC01	0TCT_MC01_Q0134	Long-Term Trends in Total Runtimes of Info-Providers
0TCT_MC01	0TCT_MC01_Q0501	Query Performance: Daily Overview
0TCT_MC01	0TCT_MC01_Q0502	Query Performance: Weekly Overview
0TCT_MC01	0TCT_MC01_Q0125	BI KPI Monitoring: Run Times of BI Application Objects
0TCT_MC01	0TCT_MC01_Q0115	BI KPI Monitoring: Run Times of BI Applications
0TCT_MC01	0TCT_MC01_Q0503	Query Performance: Monthly Overview
0TCT_MC01	0TCT_MC01_Q0303	Long-Term Trends in Total Runtimes of BI Application Objects
0TCT_MC01	0TCT_MC01_Q0113	Short-Term Trends in Total Runtimes of BI Applications

Table 6.3 Technical Content Performance Analysis Queries (Cont.)

InfoProvider Technical Name	Query Technical Name	Query Description
0TCT_MC01	0TCT_MC01_Q0121	Runtimes of BI Application Objects
0TCT_MC01	0TCT_MC01_Q0111	Runtimes of BI Applications
0TCT_MC03	0TCT_MC03_Q0202	Missing Aggregate Report for Queries
0TCT_MC03	0TCT_MC03_Q0200	Data Manager Statistics: Analysis
0TCT_MC01	0TCT_MC01_Q0434	Long-Term Trends in Total Runtimes of an InfoProvider
0TCT_MC01	0TCT_MC01_Q0202	BI Application Object Runtimes Overview
0TCT_MC01	0TCT_MC01_Q0124	Long-Term Trends in Total Runtimes of BI Application Objects
0TCT_MC01	0TCT_MC01_Q0433	Short-Term Trends in Total Runtimes of an InfoProvider
0TCT_MC01	0TCT_MC01_Q0114	Long-Term Trends in Total Runtimes of BI Applications
0TCT_MC01	0TCT_MC01_Q0201	BI Application Runtimes Overview
0TCT_MC03	0TCT_MC03_Q0201	Missing Aggregate Report for InfoProvider

Table 6.3 Technical Content Performance Analysis Queries (Cont.)

Some queries are used more frequently than others:

▶ The Long-Term Trends in Total Runtimes of a BI Application Object query provides a view of the long-term (30 days) trend for report runtimes. This is a good starting point to find reports that are trending upwards in runtime or having long runtimes.

▶ The Query Performance: Daily, Weekly and Monthly Overview queries provide details of total and average duration, as well as number of executions by query on a day, week, or month.

▶ The Detailed Query Runtime Statistics: Analysis query provides details on query runtime and count of executions and includes breakdown by various details, such as InfoProvider, query, query step, date, and so on. Conditions can be used to set up a bookmark that provides a list of queries with execution times higher than a certain threshold to immediately identify long-running queries.

6.1.2 Using Workload Monitors

Workload monitors provide detailed information about the current system workload and historical data about workload.

Here, we will cover the following standard SAP tools:

- ▶ SAP Workload Business Transaction Analysis (Transaction STAD)
- ▶ SAP Workload Monitor (Transaction ST03N)
- ▶ Snapshot Monitoring Tool (program /SDF/MON)
- ▶ SAP Solution Manager Wily Introscope

These tools provide details about server workload and memory utilization. Let's first look at general SAP workload analysis tools.

The SAP Workload Monitor is a great tool to monitor the workload in the SAP BW system. It provides the general SAP NetWeaver application workload monitor with the options displayed in Figure 6.6.

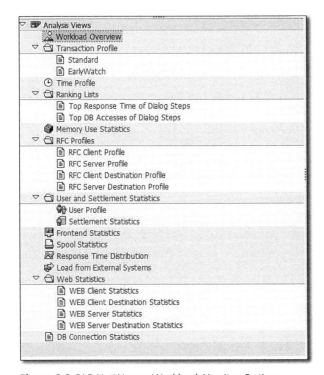

Figure 6.6 SAP NetWeaver Workload Monitor Options

Let's take a look at a few of these options. The WORKLOAD OVERVIEW option provides overall system details about response times, database times, and roll time, as displayed in Figure 6.7. These workload statistics are general for all SAP processes and do not focus on the BW-specific workload.

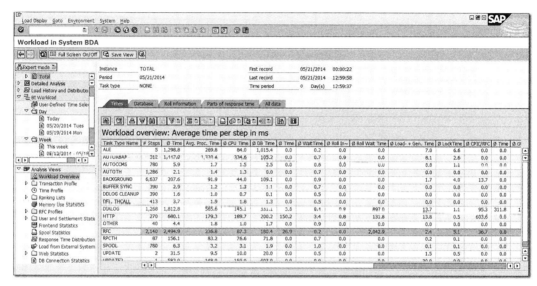

Figure 6.7 Workload Overview Analysis (Transaction ST03N)

SAP BW reporting makes use of the task type RFC to communicate with the SAP BW server from the frontend tools. However, a lot of other processes, such as data loading and internal processes in SAP, also make use of this task type, so it does not provide a good indication of the reporting performance in the SAP BW system.

It does, however, give a good overview of trends for RFC workload tasks in the system and can provide insight into potential issues in the RFC setup (for example, too few parallel processes defined for qRFC).

SAP Workload Business Transaction Analysis

SAP Workload Business Transaction Analysis, also accessible via Transaction STAD, provides details for each business transaction executed in the system. The SAP workload transaction analysis can also be used to monitor the workload of the data loading processes.

The transaction analysis can be executed with the following display options, as displayed in Figure 6.8:

▶ SHOW ALL STATS RECORDS, SORTED BY TIME

▶ SHOW ALL RECORDS, GROUPED BY BUSINESS TRANSACTION

▶ SHOW BUSINESS TRANSACTION TOTALS

You can also select only transactions with response times above certain thresholds.

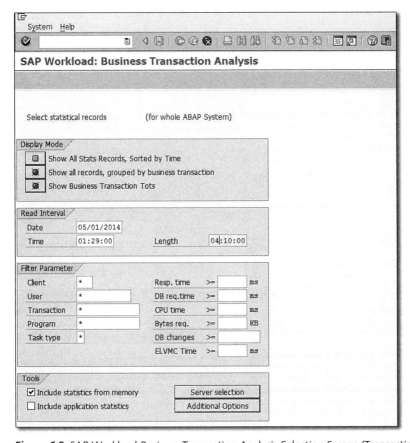

Figure 6.8 SAP Workload Business Transaction Analysis Selection Screen (Transaction STAD)

The report shown in Figure 6.9 provides details on each transaction execution and a breakdown of the response times. This can provide details about a specific user transaction that has had a performance problem, such as when a user has reported a performance problem to the help desk.

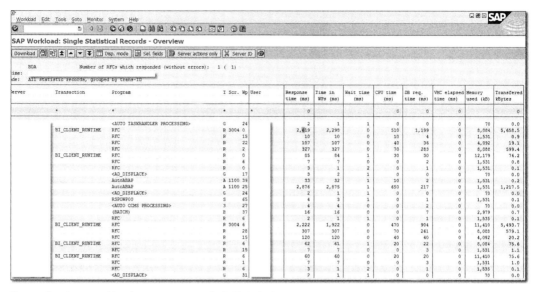

Figure 6.9 SAP Workload Transaction Analysis Details (Transaction STAD)

The time profile displayed in Figure 6.10 provides a breakdown of the workload in time buckets of the day.

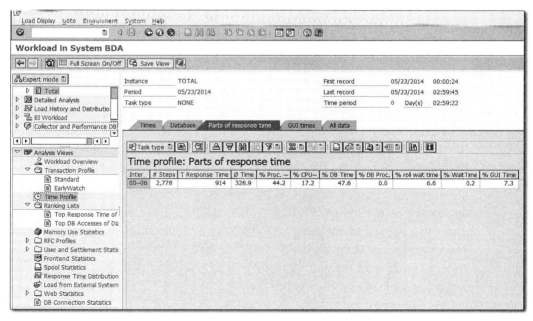

Figure 6.10 Time Profile (Transaction ST03N)

This view shows when the peak workload in the system occurs and can help provide focus on a time frame during the day that has worse performance, such as when data loading occurs at the same time as reporting.

The top response-time view provides details about the programs and transactions that have the longest runtimes in the system and a breakdown by type of response time. This view can help find programs that could impact reporting performance (for example, when a query is used in an APD or when RFCs are executed from within programs to read BW data). An example is displayed in Figure 6.11.

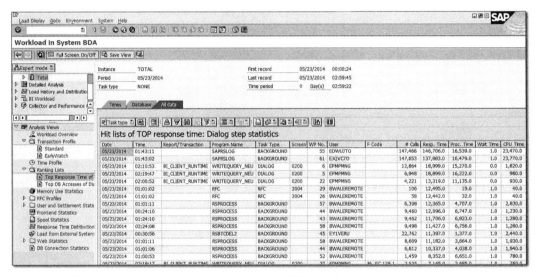

Figure 6.11 Top Response Times (Transaction ST03N)

Because SAP BW reporting makes use of the RFC task type, it can be useful to review the RFC client profile displayed in Figure 6.12 to get a breakdown of the RFC performance statistics. You should evaluate the report BI_CLIENT_RUNTIME in particular because it captures most of the reporting tools activity.

The frontend statistics analysis, as displayed in Figure 6.13, provides a workload analysis by each frontend server or workstation that accesses the SAP BW system. This can help you identify specific end users or application servers with performance problems. Many corporate workstations might have names that also indicate the location of the end user; this can help identify potential network problems to specific IP addresses or locations in the corporate network.

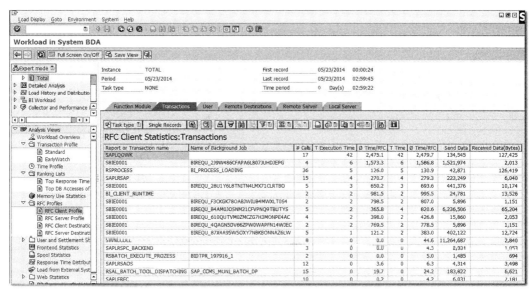

Figure 6.12 RFC Client Profile (Transaction ST03N)

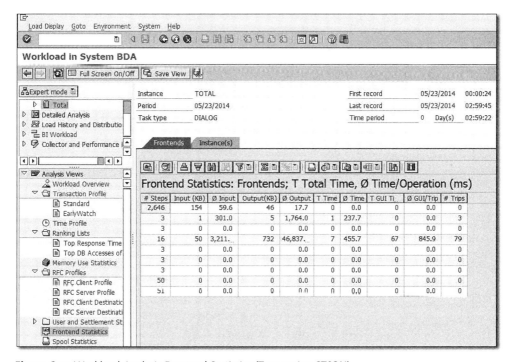

Figure 6.13 Workload Analysis Frontend Statistics (Transaction ST03N)

Having reviewed the general SAP workload analysis tools, we will now focus on the tools that are specific to the SAP BW workload analysis.

SAP Workload Monitor (Transaction ST03N)

The workload monitor (Transaction ST03N) includes some SAP BW-specific views that focus specifically on the SAP BW workload statistics. These make use of the technical content and require activation of SAP BW statistics and installation of the technical content in the system, as described earlier in this chapter.

Figure 6.14 provides an overview of the SAP BW-specific workload views in Transaction ST03N. These are arranged in the following groups:

▸ WORKLOAD OVERVIEW

▸ QUERY RUNTIMES

▸ LOAD DATA

▸ PROCESS CHAINS

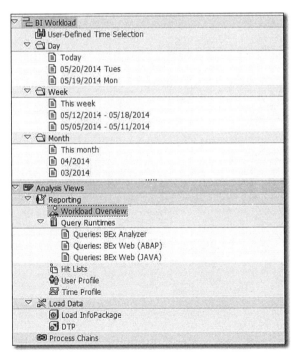

Figure 6.14 Analysis Views (Transaction ST03N)

The BI workload overview provides a runtime breakdown by frontend type to provide an overview of which tools are being used most in the system. The overview can help focus further analysis on which tools should be reviewed for performance problems.

Let's look at an example. In Figure 6.15, notice that the BEx analyzer accounts for 60% of the runtime, and BEx Java accounts for less than 8%. A KPI for the number of queries with runtimes longer than 20 seconds is included as the last column. In general, there should be very few queries with a runtime longer than 20 seconds, so this KPI provides a benchmark for general performance in each tool.

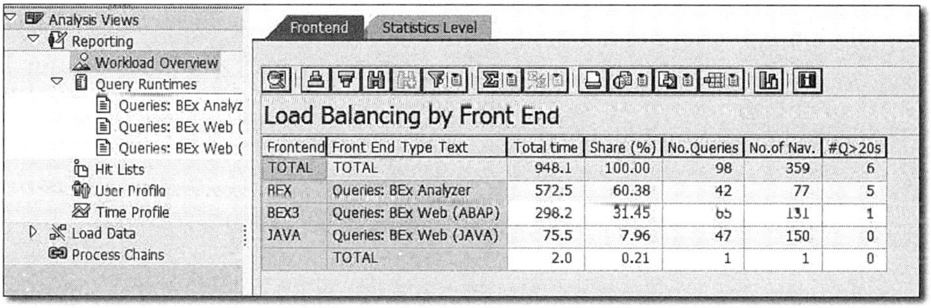

Frontend	Front End Type Text	Total time	Share (%)	No.Queries	No.of Nav.	#Q>20s
TOTAL	TOTAL	948.1	100.00	98	359	6
BEX	Queries: BEx Analyzer	572.5	60.38	42	77	5
BEX3	Queries: BEx Web (ABAP)	298.2	31.45	65	131	1
JAVA	Queries: BEx Web (JAVA)	75.5	7.96	47	150	0
	TOTAL	2.0	0.21	1	1	0

Figure 6.15 Workload Overview (Transaction ST03N)

The next step is to analyze the specific query tool runtime statistics. The Query Runtimes screen shows each of the tools by InfoProvider and query, with breakdowns by number of executions; total runtime; and percent used by frontend, DB, and OLAP engine. The Average Times (AVG) tab, displayed in Figure 6.16, is very useful for finding the queries and InfoProviders with a general performance problem, such as poor query or InfoProvider design.

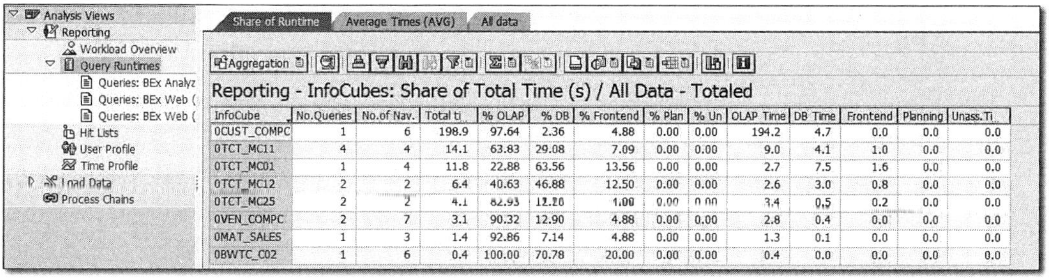

InfoCube	No.Queries	No.of Nav.	Total ti	% OLAP	% DB	% Frontend	% Plan	% Un	OLAP Time	DB Time	Frontend	Planning	Unass.Ti
0CUST_COMPC	1	6	198.9	97.64	2.36	4.88	0.00	0.00	194.2	4.7	0.0	0.0	0.0
0TCT_MC11	4	4	14.1	63.83	29.08	7.09	0.00	0.00	9.0	4.1	1.0	0.0	0.0
0TCT_MC01	1	4	11.8	22.88	63.56	13.56	0.00	0.00	2.7	7.5	1.6	0.0	0.0
0TCT_MC12	2	2	6.4	40.63	46.88	12.50	0.00	0.00	2.6	3.0	0.8	0.0	0.0
0TCT_MC25	2	2	4.1	82.93	12.20	1.00	0.00	0.00	3.4	0.5	0.2	0.0	0.0
0VEN_COMPC	2	7	3.1	90.32	12.90	4.88	0.00	0.00	2.8	0.4	0.0	0.0	0.0
0MAT_SALES	1	3	1.4	92.86	7.14	4.88	0.00	0.00	1.3	0.1	0.0	0.0	0.0
0BWTC_C02	1	6	0.4	100.00	70.78	20.00	0.00	0.00	0.4	0.0	0.0	0.0	0.0

Figure 6.16 Query Runtimes (Transaction ST03N)

You should focus on all queries that have an average runtime of more than 20 seconds because these should be the exception in a well-tuned SAP BW system.

The Hit Lists view, as displayed in Figure 6.17, further focuses attention on the top problematic queries. The default is to focus on the top 10 worst-performing queries in the system. The hit list should be reviewed weekly or monthly to ensure that performance problems are caught before the end users start reporting them. This view is one of the most helpful when you are performing day-to-day performance monitoring.

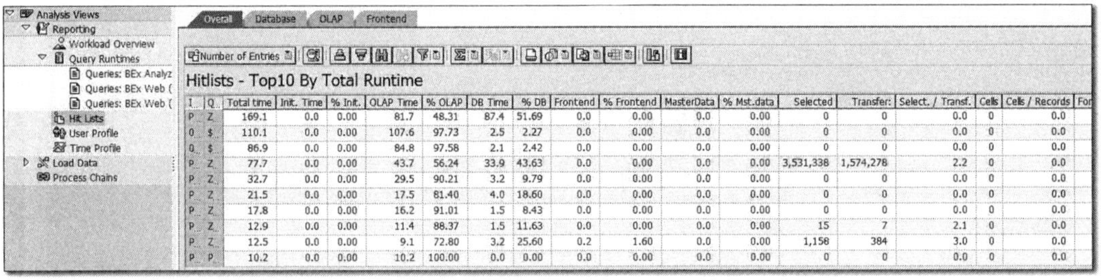

Figure 6.17 Hit Lists (Transaction ST03N)

Another great view for monitoring the users' change in behavior in an SAP BW system is the BI workload user profile, as displayed in Figure 6.18. This provides a breakdown of how many users are using the system heavily vs. how many use it more sporadically.

You should monitor this view frequently because more users with heavy workloads can impact the resource requirements in the system. For example, systems that have heavy finance use cases could have a varied user profile across the month, with heavy workload during the financial period-end closing and then declining use during the month, with a pick up during the end of the month again. Therefore, we recommend that you create a query view using the technical content queries to display daily usage trends across the days of the month.

Daily usage isn't the only thing that can differ; usage within the workday itself can, as well. The time profile view provides the breakdown of navigation steps, total time, and average time by hours of day and even within the hours. This view helps correlate reporting performance with the potential impact of data loads being executed at the same time. The example in Figure 6.19 shows more use in the morning but performance problems for some queries executed in the afternoon, around 14:00.

Category	Number of Users	No.of Nav.
10	4	16
20	1	16
30	1	26
40	1	38
50	1	45
90	1	84
300	1	236

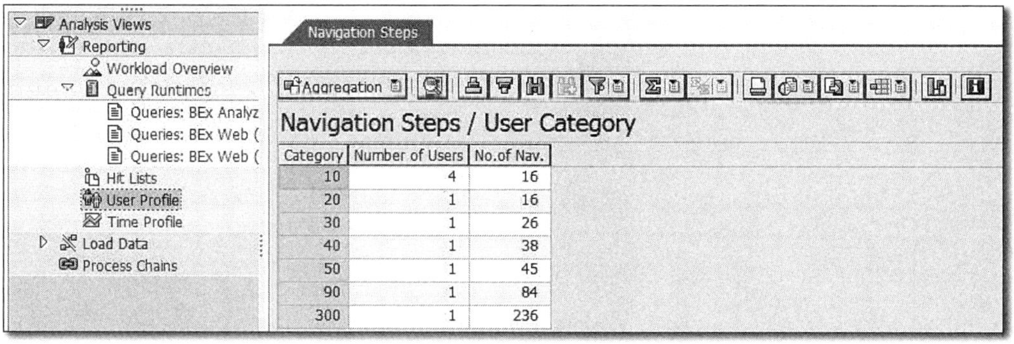

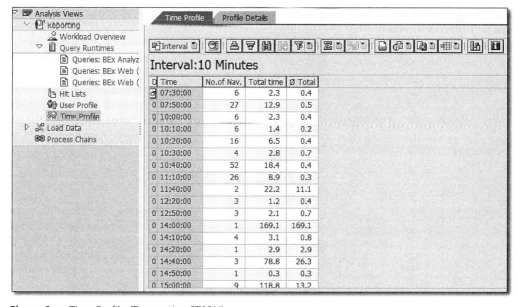

Figure 6.18 User Profile (Transaction ST03N)

D	Time	No.of Nav.	Total time	Ø Total
	07:30:00	6	2.3	0.4
0	07:50:00	27	12.9	0.5
0	10:00:00	6	2.3	0.4
0	10:10:00	6	1.4	0.2
0	10:20:00	16	6.5	0.4
0	10:30:00	4	2.8	0.7
0	10:40:00	52	18.4	0.4
0	11:10:00	26	8.9	0.3
0	11:40:00	2	22.2	11.1
0	12:20:00	3	1.2	0.4
0	12:50:00	3	2.1	0.7
0	14:00:00	1	169.1	169.1
0	14:10:00	4	3.1	0.8
0	14:20:00	1	2.9	2.9
0	14:40:00	3	78.8	26.3
0	14:50:00	1	0.3	0.3
0	15:00:00	9	118.8	13.2

Figure 6.19 Time Profile (Transaction ST03N)

Snapshot Monitoring Tool (Program /SDF/MON)

When a specific performance problem—say, a correlation between data loading and reporting performance—is being analyzed, it can be helpful to collect detailed statistics in the system every day during a specific time interval. The Snapshot

Monitoring Tool provides great system statistics and can be configured to capture snapshots down to every 10 seconds. It can also be used to capture performance snapshots during specific testing executions, such as performance testing.

To configure a daily monitoring job, go to Transaction SE38 and execute report /SDF/MON, as displayed in Figure 6.20.

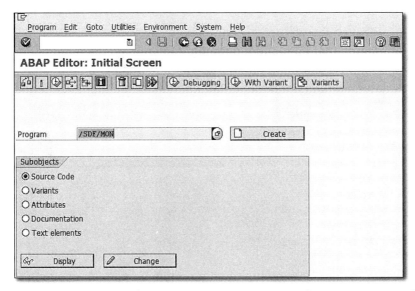

Figure 6.20 Executing Daily Monitoring (Transaction SE38 and Program /SDF/MON/)

The next screen in Figure 6.21 displays the option to schedule new monitoring or display the results from an existing monitoring job.

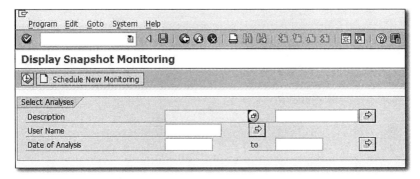

Figure 6.21 Display or Schedule a New Snapshot Monitoring (Program /SDF/MON/)

Click the SCHEDULE NEW MONITORING button if you have not yet scheduled a monitoring job. This takes you to the selection screen to choose the monitoring parameters, as displayed in Figure 6.22.

Selecting additional details for the work process, such as CPU per work process, SQL statements, and ABAP references, increases the workload from the tool, so choose these with caution. However, they do provide great details that can help pinpoint a specific problem in a program or query execution, such as a long-running select statement or a problem in the OLAP engine execution. You should set most of the statistics settings to the default when collecting every 10 seconds to avoid causing too much workload on the system.

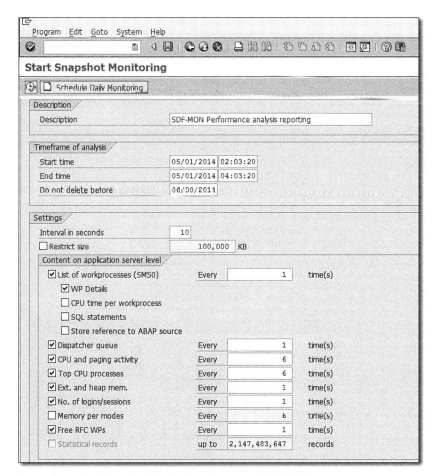

Figure 6.22 Start Snapshot Monitoring (Program /SDF/MON/)

You can also select specific servers for collecting the statistics and specific SAPOSCOL destinations, as displayed in Figure 6.23.

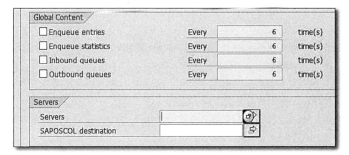

Figure 6.23 Start Snapshot Monitoring Server Selection (Program /SDF/MON/)

Once Snapshot Monitoring has collected statistics, you can analyze the collected statistics by executing the program and selecting the analysis from the overview, as displayed in Figure 6.24.

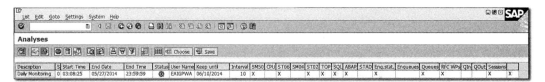

Figure 6.24 Display Analysis Selection (Program /SDF/MON/)

The selected analysis results are then displayed, as shown in Figure 6.25, with details for each snapshot on work processes, CPU workload, memory usage, paging, and sessions.

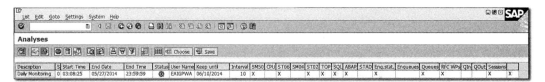

Figure 6.25 Display Analysis (Program /SDF/MON/)

The analysis result is context sensitive, so double-clicking on specific cells provides drilldown to the details captured in the snapshot, such as active work processes and CPU processes (shown in Figure 6.26 and Figure 6.27).

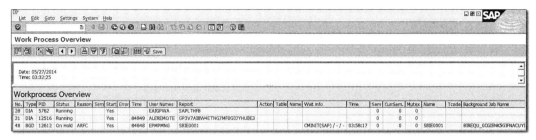

Figure 6.26 Work Processes (Program /SDF/MON/)

Top CPU Processes

Date: 05/27/2014
Time: 03:32:35

Top CPU Processes

Server Name	Type	Subtype	saposcol	PROC_ID	User	Process Name	CPU_UTIL	CPU Time	RES_SIZE	PRIORITY	PRIV_PAGES
sap-0064_BDA_81	105	1	0	12,516	bdaadm	dw.sapBDA_DVEBMGS81	9,987	1413:10	511,568	20	0
sap-0064_BDA_81	105	1	1	5,708	bdaadm	dw.sapBDA_DVEBMGS81	21	000:05	375,724	20	0
sap-0064_BDA_81	105	1	2	5,762	bdaadm	dw.sapBDA_DVEBMGS81	11	000:05	324,348	20	0
sap-0064_BDA_81	105	1	3	5,785	bdaadm	dw.sapBDA_DVEBMGS81	9	000:03	307,716	20	0
sap-0064_BDA_81	105	1	4	14,539	bdaadm	dw.sapBDA_DVEBMGS81	9	000:01	143,728	20	0
sap-0064_BDA_81	105	1	5	5,923	bdaadm	dw.sapBDA_DVEBMGS81	6	000:11	298,684	20	0
sap-0064_BDA_81	105	1	6	5,819	bdaadm	dw.sapBDA_DVEBMGS81	6	000:10	320,504	20	0
sap-0064_BDA_81	105	1	7	7,555	bdaadm	dw.sapBDA_DVEBMGS81	6	000:03	202,488	20	0
sap-0064_BDA_81	105	1	8	14,434	bdaadm	dw.sapBDA_DVEBMGS81	6	000:02	192,832	20	0
sap-0064_BDA_81	105	1	9	3,370	bdaadm	collectd	4	042:40	1,700	20	0
sap-0064_BDA_81	105	1	10	19,997	root	saposcol -l -w60 pf	4	037:37	4,224	20	0
sap-0064_BDA_81	105	1	11	5,782	bdaadm	dw.sapBDA_DVEBMGS81	4	000:04	326,072	20	0

Figure 6.27 CPU Processes (Program /SDF/MON/)

SAP Solution Manager with Wily Introscope Tool

Additional performance statistics can be collected via SAP Solution Manager. We will only cover a few examples here; these are related to statistics captured in the

SAP Solution Manager diagnostics agent and analyzed with the Wily Introscope Tool, which is part of SAP Solution Manager.

When you monitor SAP BW using SAP Solution Manager, you can access additional long-term trend analysis capabilities that are part of the standard statistics capture in SAP Solution Manager via the diagnostics agent. The diagnostics agent should be installed on each server that should be monitored because the statistics are collected at the OS level and sent to the SAP Solution Manager server.

The following kinds of statistics are captured and available for analysis in Wily Introscope:

▶ CPU usage

▶ Memory usage

▶ Disk IO times

▶ LAN network load

The trend analysis can cover several days, weeks, or even months to enable comparison over a longer period. Let's explore a few examples of the charts captured in Wily Introscope.

The CPU trend displayed in Figure 6.28 shows that CPU is completely used during certain times. This causes performance problems during SAP BW report execution because no CPU is available to handle the query request. A problem like this causes severe performance problems during the high workload and should be avoided in any production system. It requires an increase of CPUs or a rebalancing of the workload.

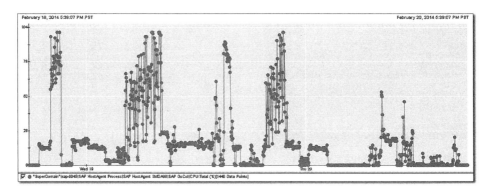

Figure 6.28 CPU Trend Analysis with Wily Introscope

The memory statistics displayed in Figure 6.29 indicate that all the memory is consumed. This could cause performance problems in the system because memory is not available to processes the queries in the OLAP engine.

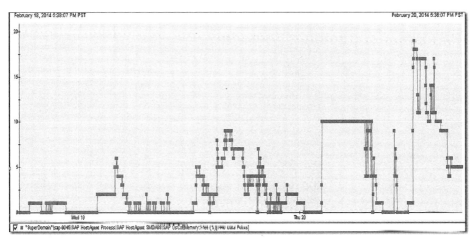

Figure 6.29 Memory Trend Analysis with Wily Introscope

The LAN statistics displayed in Figure 6.30 show that the network is heavily loaded at times, which could cause delays in reporting performance.

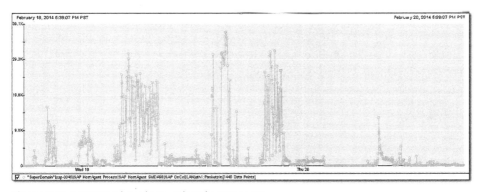

Figure 6.30 LAN Trend Analysis with Wily Introscope

The disk I/O displayed in Figure 6.31 shows that the I/O from a particular disk is causing a delayed in response time. This could be due to the layout of the data files, also known as a disk I/O hotspot.

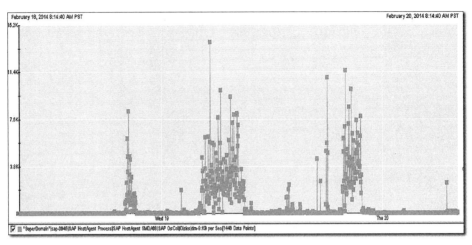

Figure 6.31 Disk I/O Trend Analysis with Wily Introscope

6.1.3 Performance Testing

We have now reviewed some of the most used tools to find performance problems in an SAP BW system. One additional way to find performance problems is by executing performance testing prior to go-live to preempt performance problems in the system.

Prior to normal system operation go-lives, it can be difficult to capture detailed performance statistics. Therefore, we recommend that you execute a stress and volume test prior to go-live to ensure that the system can accommodate the planned workload. The stress and volume testing should provide guidelines for how the BW system operates when certain workloads are put on the system, as follows:

- ▶ Reporting navigation steps
- ▶ Data loading processes
- ▶ A combination of these

The reporting navigation step execution can be done with a tool like Loadrunner, which can simulate report executions, including wait times. The BW RS Trace Tool (Transaction RSTT) is also an option through which query executions can be recorded as traces and replayed.

The tools available for monitoring the workload and performance when executing stress and volume testing are general SAP tools combined with the output of the BW statistics data collection. For specific SAP BW performance KPIs such as query runtime and data records processes in DTPs, you should use the SAP BW statistics data.

6.1.4 Analyzing Query-Specific Performance Issues

Once you identify a performance issue for a specific query or report, the next step is to analyze the problem in detail. This section will focus on the analysis of specific performance problems. We will look at how to perform more detailed analysis of the performance issue and then consider optimizations that can be implemented to improve performance.

Here, we will look at a few different ways to analyze the following specific performance issues:

▸ The Query Monitor (Transaction RSRT)

▸ Analysis & Service Tools Launchpad (Transaction ST13)

▸ HTTPWATCH for Web Page Rendering Times

Let's begin.

Query Monitor (Transaction RSRT)

The SAP BW query monitor is the main tool for troubleshooting query problems. The query monitor can be used for many types of problems, such as an incorrect query result, navigation errors, variable debugging, and performance problems.

You can access it via the following transactions:

▸ Transaction RSRT: Main Query Monitor

▸ Transaction RSRT1: Query Monitor for Query Views

▸ Transaction RSRT2: Main Query Monitor

These different transaction codes provide access to the same functionality but with different start points. Figure 6.32 and Figure 6.33 display the different screens you see when accessing the different transaction codes.

In Figure 6.32, you can see that there are several options for executing the query display. We'll describe this in more detail shortly.

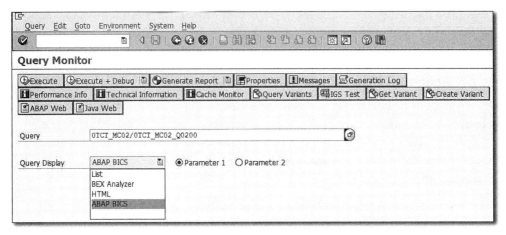

Figure 6.32 Query Monitor Main Screen (Transaction RSRT or RSRT2)

When executing the query monitor via Transaction RSRT1, as displayed in Figure 6.33, you can also enter a query view. This enables problem analysis if query views are used to provide quick access to a specific problem in the system. Note that the query view functionality makes use of SAP BW 3.x functionality, which is no longer fully supported in SAP BW 7.40.

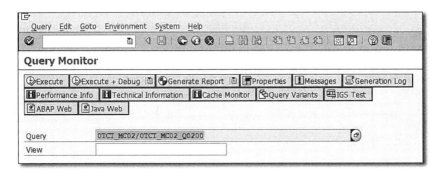

Figure 6.33 Query View (Transaction RSRT1)

The four query display options provide different outputs. Figure 6.34 displays the output from the LIST display option. This is the most basic option and was the first display option available in the query monitor when the tool was introduced in

early releases of SAP BW. Advanced navigation features can be accessed via the
MENU button, which provides a context-sensitive list of navigations possible for
the highlighted field in the LIST display.

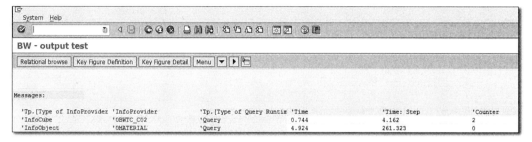

Figure 6.34 Execute List Display Option

The list display also has a button to display the key figure definition. This feature
gives a breakdown of the restrictions and calculations performed in the key figure
in the display. When you analyze performance problems, this can help you under
stand why certain restrictions are applied and what calculations are performed in
the query. Figure 6.35 shows an example of the key figure definition for a specific
result cell.

Key Figure Tree	Value	Techn.name	FE	Si	O	Lower Limi	U	Hi	Hi	Ke	LE	Ke	SE
▽ 🔏 Key figure		ROOT									0	0	
▽ ⬦ Selection of Drilldown Characteristics		SELECTION 0000									0	0	
▽ ⬚ BI Object Type		0TCTBWOTYPE									0	0	
⬛ I EQ			I	EQ							0	0	1
▽ ⬚ InfoProviders Used		0TCTIFPROV									0	0	
⬛ I EQ Product Analysis - Fiscal '		BDA800/CUBE/...	I		EQ	Product A...					0	0	1
▽ ⬚ InfoProvider Type		0TCTIFTYPE									0	0	
⬛ I EQ InfoCube		CUBE	I		EQ	InfoCube					0	0	1
▽ ⬚ Query Runtime Object, e.g Quer		0TCTSTATOBJ									0	0	
⬛ I EQ BDA800/Not assigned/A,		BDA800/#/A/R...	I		EQ	BDA800/N...					0	0	1
▽ ⬦ Fixed Filter		SELECTION 0000									0	0	
▽ ⬚ InfoProvider		0INFOPROV									0	0	
⬛ I EQ 0TCT_C02		0TCT_C02	I		EQ	0TCT_C02					0	0	1
▽ ⬚ Object Version		0TCTOBJVERS									0	0	
⬛ I EQ Active		A	I		EQ	Active					0	0	1
▽ ⬚ UTC Time Stamp		0TCTTIMSTMP									0	0	
[] I BT 06/02/2014 05:07:44 0		06/02/2014 0...	I		BT	06/02/201... 06...					0	0	3
▽ 🔏 Time		0TCTSTATTIM...	1								0	1	
🔏 0TCTSTATTIM		ITEM00000005	1								0	0	

Figure 6.35 Key Figure Definition Analysis

The HTML and BEx display options shown in Figure 6.36 provide the same output, which is based on the standard 3.x web template set in the system via Cus-

tomizing in Transaction RSCUSTV21. If you don't select a custom template, the default template 0ADHOC is used.

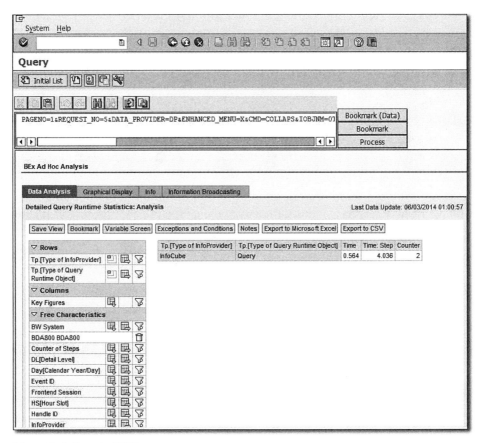

Figure 6.36 Execute HTML

The HTML and BEx Analyzer give access to the navigation features available in the template, so we recommend that you use either the standard 0ADHOC template or at least a template that provides access to all the same navigation features.

The ABAP BICS display option added in SAP BW 7.30 provides a new interface that makes use of the ABAP BI Consumer service. ABAP BICS is used in the BEx web application data access and when interfacing to other tools, like SAP BusinessObjects platform. This display option is still being developed and is recommended for analyzing performance problems in SAP BW release 7.40 and later.

The navigation is similar to that in the HTML and BEx Analyzer options, but there are differences in the code executed in the system that could render different performance results. Figure 6.37 gives an example of the ABAP BICS result display option.

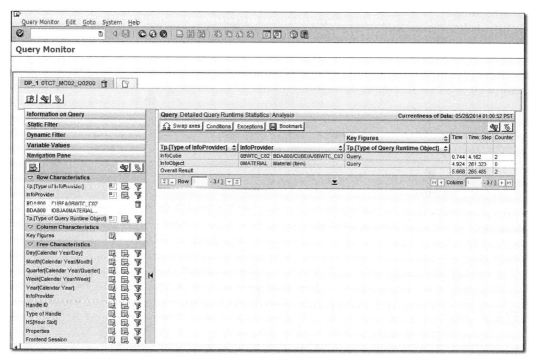

Figure 6.37 Execute ABAP BICS

The most used functionality in the query monitor for performance analysis is the EXECUTE AND DEBUG BUTTON. This lets you not only execute the query, but also set breakpoints and change the runtime settings in the system for that particular execution. A great, additional feature is the capability to immediately display the runtime statistics after the query is executed, which is the DISPLAY STATISTICS DATA option, found under the GENERAL EXECUTION OPTIONS list in Figure 6.38.

Figure 6.39 shows the result of the query runtime. Here, you can see the breakdown for each event in the query execution that is captured in SAP BW statistics, as well as the details for the data manager execution time and SAP HANA calculation time, because this example is executed on a system that runs on SAP HANA.

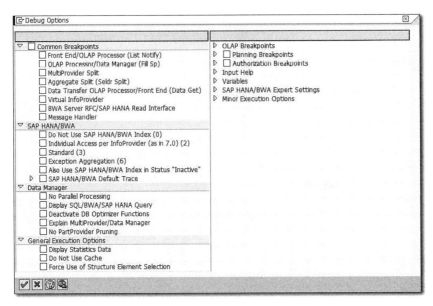

Figure 6.38 Execute and Debug

Session UID	Step UID	Ste	St	U	S	Ha.	Han	InfoProvider	Object Na.	D	Event ID	Event Text	Duration	Counter	Event Counter
0002TFZI.	0002TFZI5.	1	E	C			DFLT			2		Not Assigned	0.169744	0	1
0002TFZI.	0002TFZI5.	1	E	C	4	DP				2	13050	ABP Init.	0.022773	0	3
0002TFZI.	0002TFZI5.	1	E	C	4	DP				2	13052	Set ABAP Status Java	0.023893	0	31
0002TFZI.	0002TFZI5.	1	E	C	4	DP				2	13051	Load ABAP Status	0.001911	0	1
0002TFZI.	0002TFZI5.	1	E	C	4	DP				2	13056	Set ABP Hier.	0.008502	0	25
0002TFZI.	0002TFZI5.	1	E	C	4	DP				2	13054	ABP Result Set	0.030946	0	2
0002TFZI.	0002TFZI5.	1	E	C	4	OL.	0TCT_MC02	0TCT_MC0.	2	3010	OLAP: Query Gen.	0.026039	0	1
0002TFZI.	0002TFZI5.	1	E	C	4	OL.	0TCT_MC02	0TCT_MC0.	2	3999	OLAP Other Time	0.239050	0	30
0002TFZI.	0002TFZI5.	1	E	C	4	OL.	0TCT_MC02	0TCT_MC0.	2	4600	Authorization Buffer	0.020702	0	1
0002TFZI.	0002TFZI5.	1	E	C	4	OL.	0TCT_MC02	0TCT_MC0.	2	3510	OLAP: EXIT Variables	0.009584	0	3
0002TFZI.	0002TFZI5.	1	E	C	4	OL.	0TCT_MC02	0TCT_MC0.	2	3500	OLAP Initialization	0.022990	0	13
0002TFZI.	0002TFZI5.	1	E	C	4	OL.	0TCT_MC02	0TCT_MC0.	2	3000	OLAP: Settings	0.026784	0	29
0002TFZI.	0002TFZI5.	1	E	C	4	OL.	0TCT_MC02	0TCT_MC0.	2	3121	OLAP: cha-const Prun	0.005702	0	1
0002TFZI.	0002TFZI5.	1	E	C	4	OL.	0TCT_MC02	0TCT_MC0.	2	3122	OLAP: meta data Prun	0.003417	0	1
0002TFZI.	0002TFZI5.	1	E	C	4	OL.	0TCT_MC02	0TCT_MC0.	2	2515	Delete Cache	0.006191	0	1
0002TFZI.	0002TFZI5.	1	E	C	4	OL.	0TCT_MC02	0TCT_MC0.	2	2505	Read Cache	0.006104	0	2
0002TFZI.	0002TFZI5.	1	E	C	4	OL.	0TCT_MC02	0TCT_MC0.	2	2525	Cache Read Access	0.000000	0	1
0002TFZI.	0002TFZI5.	1	E	C	4	OL.	0TCT_MC02	0TCT_MC0.	2	2510	Write Cache	0.016974	0	8
0002TFZI.	0002TFZI5.	1	E	C	4	OL.	0TCT_MC02	0TCT_MC0.	2	2500	Cache Generation	0.010572	0	6
0002TFZI.	0002TFZI5.	1	E	C	4	OL.	0TCT_MC02	0TCT_MC0.	2	2502	Cache search	0.012088	0	11
0002TFZI.	0002TFZI5.	1	E	C	4	OL.	0TCT_MC02	0TCT_MC0.	2	9000	Data Manager	0.161364	0	2
0002TFZI.	0002TFZI5.	1	E	C	4	OL.	0TCT_MC02	0TCT_MC0.	2	9010	Total DBTRANS	0.000000	198	1
0002TFZI.	0002TFZI5.	1	E	C	4	OL.	0TCT_MC02	0TCT_MC0.	2	9011	Total DBSEL	0.000000	1,944	1

Figure 6.39 Display Statistics Data

Another great function of the EXECUTE AND DEBUG button is switching on and off in SAP HANA/BWA and in the Data Manager; this can help pinpoint whether a performance problem is caused by the optimized SQL access to the underlying database system.

Click the QUERY PROPERTIES button to review and change the properties of the query. The QUERY PROPERTIES screen is displayed in Figure 6.40.

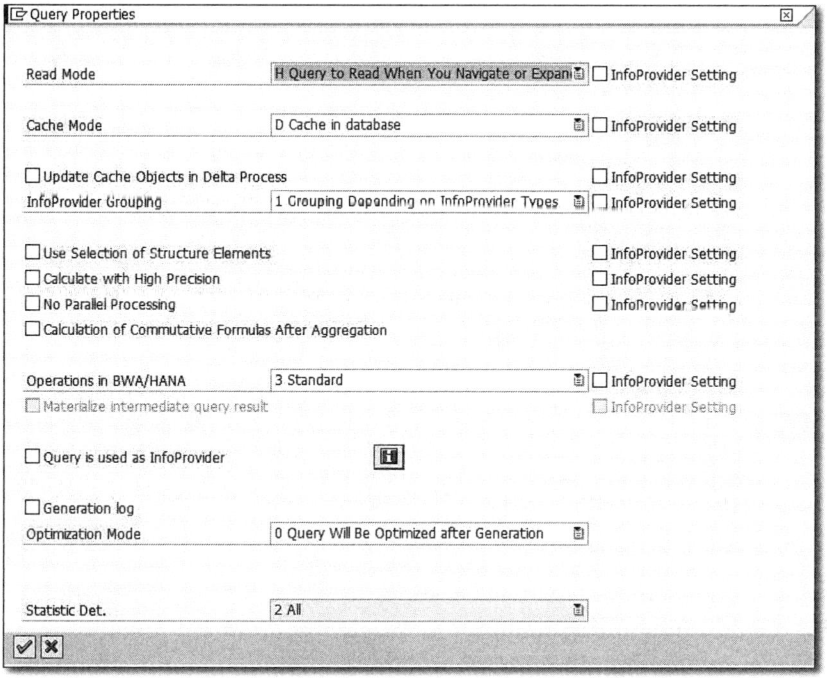

Figure 6.40 Query Monitor Properties

Table 6.4 lists the few key settings that impact query performance, along with our recommendations for you.

Setting	Recommended Value
Read mode	H—QUERY READ when you navigate or expand hierarchies. This setting provides the most optimal read of data for the initial display and reads only the needed data in subsequent navigation steps.

Table 6.4 Query Properties and Recommended Values

Setting	Recommended Value
Cache mode	D — CACHE IN DATABASE The database cache provides access to the cached data on all application servers, whereas local cache provides access only on the server where it is cached.
Use selection of structure elements	Checked Set this when selections in structures can provide additional restrictions for the query execution. This can provide a large performance increase when only a few key figures are displayed out of a long list of key figures in the query definition.
Calculate with high precision	Unchecked Not much impact on performance, but does impact memory usage. This should be set only when high-precision calculations are required.
No parallel processing	Unchecked Queries are always executed in parallel based on the query and Info-Provider design. Deactivating the parallel processing has significant impact on performance. The maximum degree of parallel processing determines the maximum number of work processes used for each query. In the default setting, this is set to 6. The maximum value can be changed to between 1 and 100 in the QUERY_MAX_WP_DIAG entry in table RSADMIN.
Operations in SAP HANA/BWA	3 — STANDARD Certain OLAP functions can be executed in SAP HANA or BWA. You can switch this off by changing this setting. SAP HANA/BWA normally provides significant performance benefit when these functions are executed there.
Optimization mode	0 — QUERY WILL BE OPTIMIZED AFTER GENERATION This allows for re-use of the generation settings for memory use over 31 days before the system optimizes the memory use again.

Table 6.4 Query Properties and Recommended Values (Cont.)

The PERFORMANCE INFO button in the query monitor can be used to display the query performance information compared to the standard settings and thresholds provided by SAP. As you can see in Figure 6.41, the virtual provider 0TCT_VC02 could be a performance problem because it can't use aggregates, and the delta cache should be activated to improve performance.

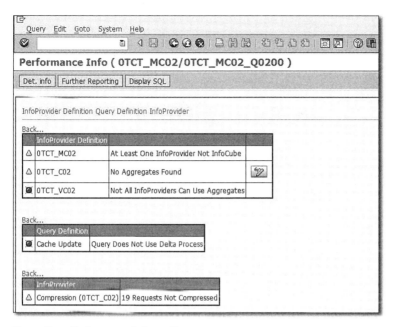

Figure 6.41 Performance Information

The query monitor also provides access to technical information about the query. Figure 6.42 displays general data and data from the query definition.

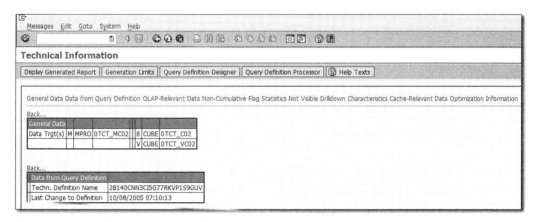

Figure 6.42 General Data and Query Definition

The number of part providers can impact the performance of the query. You should always have fewer than 10 part providers per MultiProvider.

The OLAP-relevant data includes information about query definition object that might impact performance. Yellow or red shapes like those shown in Figure 6.43 indicate that the definition can cause performance or other problems in the query.

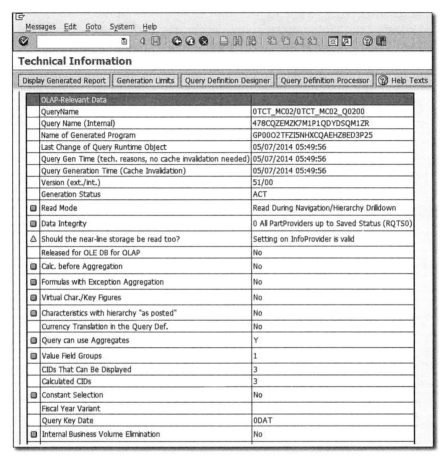

Figure 6.43 OLAP-Relevant Data

Non-cumulative cubes (see Figure 6.44) have longer runtimes because they require historical data to be read according to the validity slice. You should define the validity slice as simply as possible because it otherwise requires many sub-queries to be executed.

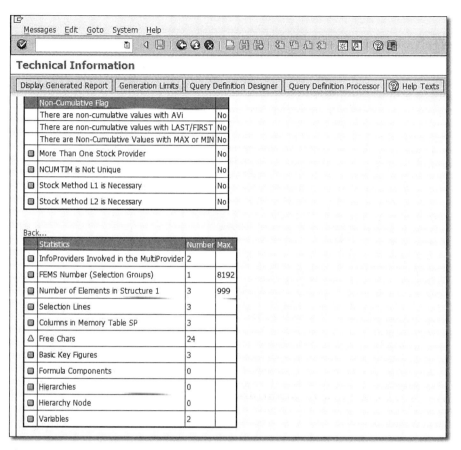

Figure 6.44 Non-Cumulative Data and Statistics

The statistics section of the technical information in Figure 6.44 provides details on objects and functionalities used in the query definition. Here, too, yellow and red indicate items that could impact performance. For example, many free characteristics impact query initialization performance and rendering performance.

The visible drilldown characteristics shown in Figure 6.45 also indicate potential performance issues; many drilldowns result in many result lines.

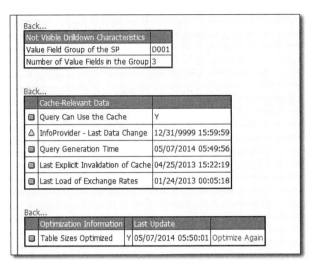

Figure 6.45 Hidden Characteristics, Cache, and Optimization

Cache-relevant data provides details on the cache settings and when the cache was last updated, and the optimization information provides details about when the memory optimization was last executed (see Figure 6.46).

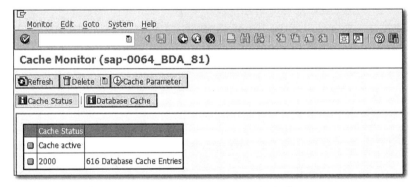

Figure 6.46 Cache Monitor Status (Transaction RSRCACHE)

You can access the cache monitor via Transaction RSRT or Transaction RSR-CACHE, as shown in Figure 6.47.

Set the cache parameters for the system by clicking the CACHE PARAMETERS button. You should set a DB cache limit number to avoid getting too many cache entries, which will impact performance of the system. There is no limit if the parameter is not set. The settings are displayed in Figure 6.48; check the RECORD STATISTICS checkbox if you want to capture statistics on how often the cache is used in the system.

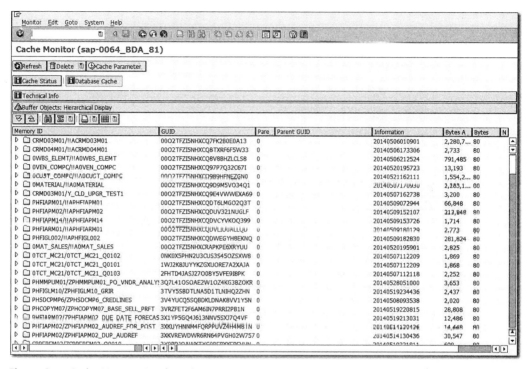

Figure 6.47 Cache Monitor Database (Transaction RSRCACHE)

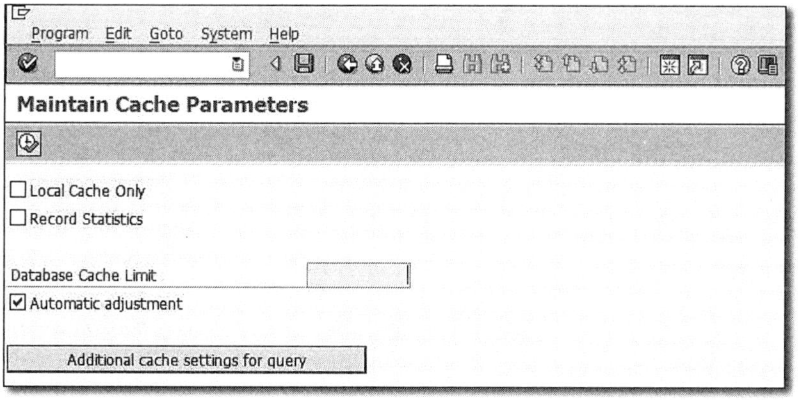

Figure 6.48 Cache Monitor Parameters (Transaction RSRCACHE)

Runtime Analysis (Transaction SE30)

The previous section provided an overview of how to use the query monitor to investigate performance issues. You can also use the query monitor in conjunction with the ABAP Runtime Analysis tool, Transaction SE30.

Select the query monitor transaction from the RUNTIME ANALYSIS screen, shown in Figure 6.49. Then, execute the query with the required display option and perform the navigation that caused the slow performance.

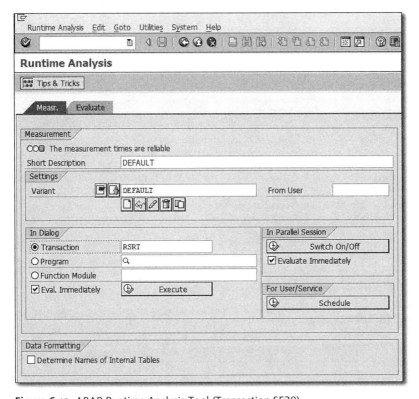

Figure 6.49 ABAP Runtime Analysis Tool (Transaction SE30)

Once the navigations are completed, you can see the runtime performance details for each ABAP call and DB call, as shown in Figure 6.50.

The runtime analysis tool result can be downloaded and provided to SAP if the performance problem is caused by a problem in the OLAP engine. This can help speed up the time SAP needs to resolve the problem.

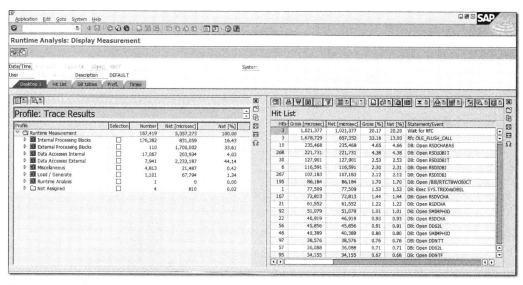

Figure 6.50 Evaluate Runtime Analysis (Transaction SE30)

Analysis and Service Tools Launchpad (Transaction ST13)

The Analysis and Service Tools Launchpad provides access to several SAP BW-specific tools. The following tools provide some functionality that can be used to analyze specific performance problems in the SAP BW system:

▸ BIIPTOOLS—BI-IP Performance Toolset

▸ BW-TOOLS—BW Tools

▸ BWATOOLS—BWA Support Tools

▸ BWQUAC_CUST—BW Query Alert Collector Customizing

▸ BW_QUERY_ACCESSES—BW: Aggregate/InfoCube accesses of queries

▸ BW_QUERY_USAGE—BW: Query usage statistics

We will cover some of the ways to use the BI-IP Performance Toolset in this section: this provides some useful functions to investigate performance issues. The BIIPTOOLS are accessed via Transaction ST13, as displayed in Figure 6.51.

When you start BIIPTOOLS, it displays a list of options, as shown in Figure 6.52 and Figure 6.53.

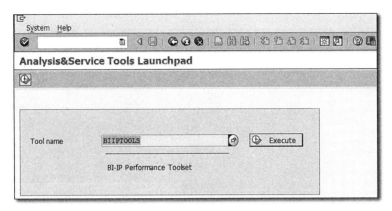

Figure 6.51 Analysis and Service Tools Launchpad (Transaction ST13)

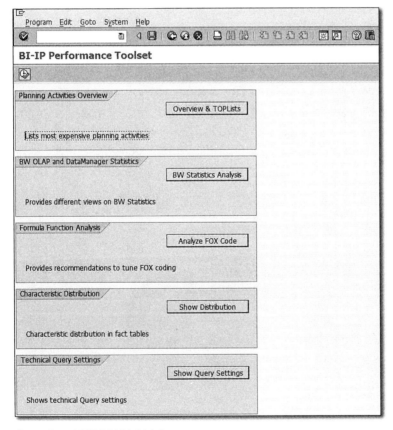

Figure 6.52 BIIPTOOLS Initial Screen

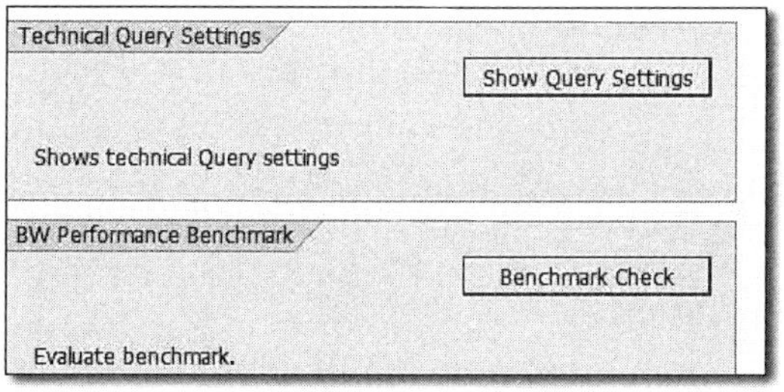

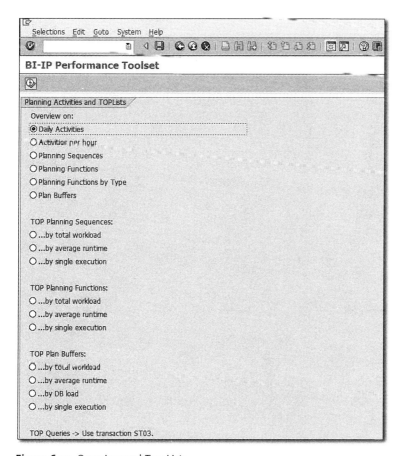

Figure 6.53 BIIPTOOLS Initial Screen

The planning activities and TOP lists, shown in Figure 6.54, can be used to list the top planning activities based on performance in the system.

Figure 6.54 Overview and Top Lists

You can use the BW Statistics Analysis (shown in Figure 6.55) to access the BW OLAP and data manager statistics data. Compared to accessing the tables directly, this option provides a better interface to the data than Transaction SE16.

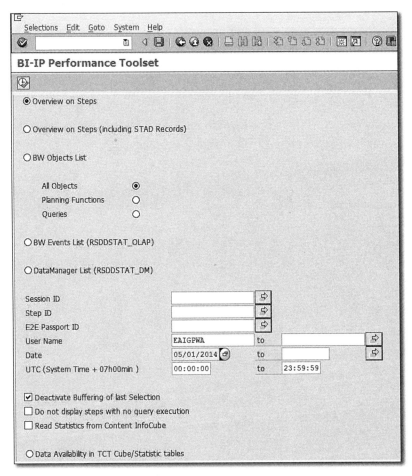

Figure 6.55 BW Statistics Analysis

The cube distribution, shown in Figure 6.56, can be very helpful when you are analyzing a performance problem. It provides the data distribution for a characteristic in the fact table and so can be used to improve aggregates and decide which aggregates might be needed in the system.

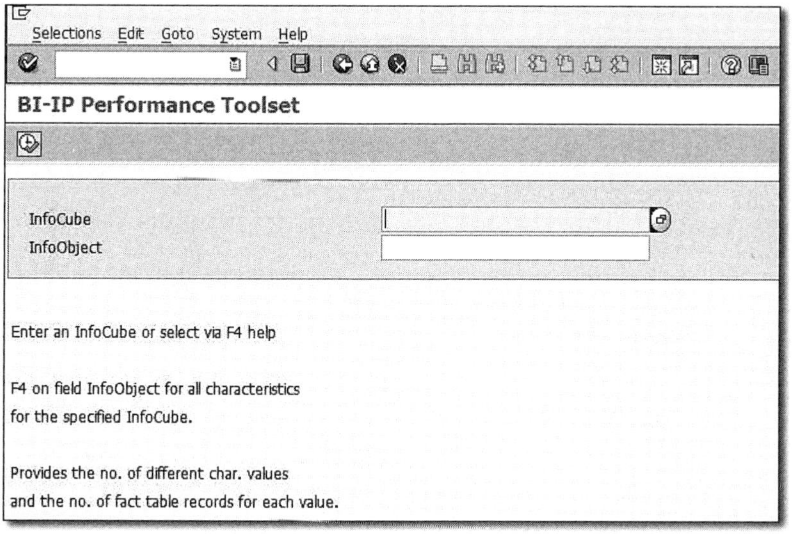

Figure 6.56 Cube Distribution

The query settings in Figure 6.57 provide a list of the settings for all the selected queries. It can be helpful to confirm that all queries are following the recommended settings. Alternatively, you can use Transaction SE16 and browse the RSRREPDIR table, which also provides access to these settings.

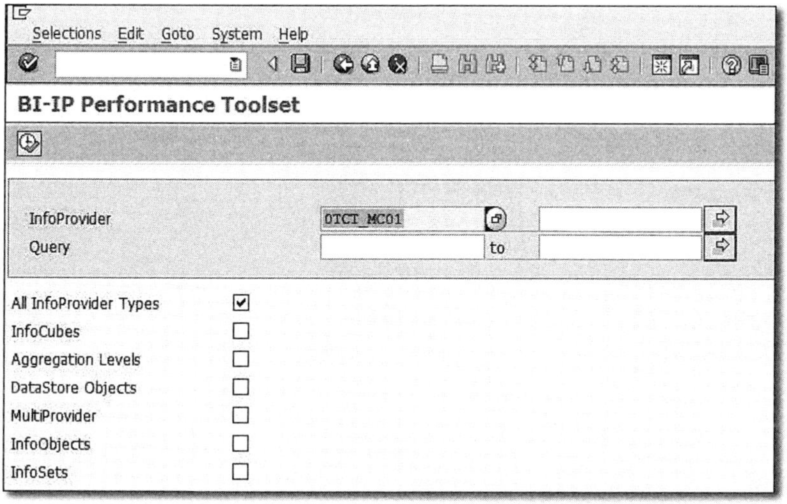

Figure 6.57 Query Settings

As you can see in Figure 6.58, it's easier to read the list output in the BIIPTOOLS than the Transaction SE16 display.

BI-IP Performance Toolset

Query Properties

InfoProvider	Query	Read Mode	Request Status	Cache Mode	Persistence Mode	Delta Cache	SP Grouping
0TCT_MC01	0TCT_MC01_Q0333	H		1	1		1
0TCT_MC01	0TCT_MC01_Q0413	H		1	1		1
0TCT_MC01	0TCT_MC01_Q0122	H		1	1		1
0TCT_MC01	0TCT_MC01_Q0313	H		1	1		1
0TCT_MC01	0TCT_MC01_Q0423	H		1	1		1
0TCT_MC01	0TCT_MC01_Q0131	H		1	1		1
0TCT_MC01	0TCT_MC01_Q0200	H		1	1		1
0TCT_MC01	0TCT_MC01_Q0112	H		1	1		1
0TCT_MC01	0TCT_MC01_Q0414	H		1	1		1
0TCT_MC01	0TCT_MC01_Q0132	H		1	1		1
0TCT_MC01	0TCT_MC01_Q0133	H		1	1		1
0TCT_MC01	0TCT_MC01_Q0123	H		1	1		1
0TCT_MC01	0TCT_MC01_Q0324	H		1	1		1

Figure 6.58 Query Settings Result

Note that you should use the Query Monitor (Transaction RSRT) if you need to change query settings.

Web Page Rendering with HTTPWATCH

The SAP BEx BI Java runtime environment can be difficult to analyze when there is a performance issue with standard SAP tools. HTTPWATCH is a good tool to use for analyzing web rendering performance issues.

The HTTPWATCH basic tool is a good starting point for analyzing performance issues in web rendering for the BEx BI Java runtime. It is installed as an add-in to the Internet Explorer browser (see Figure 6.59) and can be switched on and off from the Internet Explorer toolbar. It is also available for other browsers, such as Firefox, and as apps for iOS and Android.

The longest-running step is the POST method, which executes the query on the SAP BW system. This corresponds with the query runtime in SAP BW statistics. You can also see that several of the JavaScripts, style sheets, and images are cached locally on the workstation, which provides faster rendering time for the report page. If a lot of items are being loaded without being cached, you should review the cache settings in the Portal server to increase the cache validity.

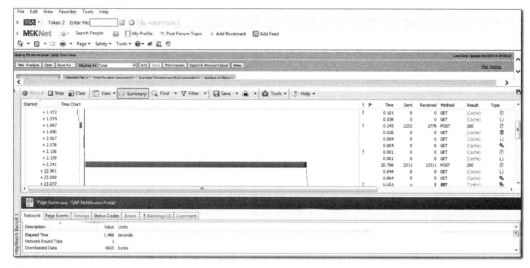

Figure 6.59 BI Java Report Example of HTTPWATCH Timechart

Although HTTPWATCH cannot be used as the only tool to analyze performance problems, it does provide additional insight into the web page rendering time, including network and other workstation-specific bottlenecks.

6.2 Reporting Performance Tuning

We have looked at the tools that can be used to identify and troubleshoot SAP BW reporting performance problems. This section will cover best practices and tips for improving reporting performance in the SAP BW system.

We will look at best practices for query definition, database read time, and frontend tool processing time.

6.2.1 Database Optimizations

The reporting performance in SAP BW is greatly impacted by the database read time to get the data needed to generate the report. This is mainly because reports normally access large volumes of data and, therefore, require reading the data into memory to then process the data.

Compression

InfoCube compression is a must-do maintenance activity in all SAP BW systems. The reporting performance impact of *not* compressing the InfoCubes can be query runtimes several times longer because the F-fact table partitions are read sequentially. You can easily find uncompressed InfoCubes using the standard SAP program SAP_INFOCUBE_DESIGNS.

Aggregates

When SAP BW 1.2a was released in 1998, it was possible to generate aggregates that would be accessed seamlessly by the application. This was quite revolutionary because aggregates provided great performance benefits when accessing relational databases.

Aggregates should generally provide at least a 10-time aggregation over the base InfoCube that the aggregate is built on. This is, however, not a hard requirement, and it can sometimes be good to generate aggregates with lower aggregation levels to speed up many queries.

You can generate as many aggregates as necessary for each InfoCube, but you must review and maintain the aggregates—an additional maintenance task to be executed in the system. Delete aggregates that are never used or used infrequently because the maintenance and devoting additional database space to store the aggregates negate the benefit of the aggregate.

It is possible to generate aggregate proposals based on queries with long runtimes. The technical content provides details about queries that are executed in the system and their runtimes. Figure 6.60 shows how the maintenance screen for aggregates can be accessed for a specific InfoCube.

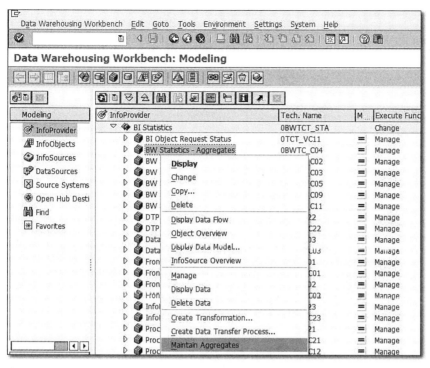

Figure 6.60 Creating Aggregates for InfoCubes (Transaction RSA1)

When accessing InfoCube maintenance, you have to decide how to create aggregates—either to GENERATE PROPOSALS or CREATE BY YOURSELF, as displayed in Figure 6.61. You should use the GENERATE PROPOSALS when queries for an InfoProvider have been in production for at least 30 days because, otherwise, there would be few statistics available upon which to generate a proposal. If you implement new queries and want to create an aggregate, choose the option to create it by yourself.

When you select a proposal generation method, you have to select the BW statistics parameters on which to generate the proposal. Use as long a time period as possible—at least 30 days; we also recommend that you initially optimize only queries that have a runtime longer than 100 seconds, as displayed in Figure 6.62.

The aggregate proposal is then generated and displayed. Some proposed aggregates might not provide the desired aggregation level, and we recommend that you review the aggregates and try to optimize them by combining some very like aggregates into larger aggregates.

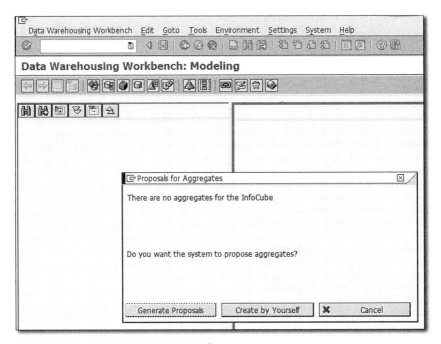

Figure 6.61 Generate Aggregate Proposal

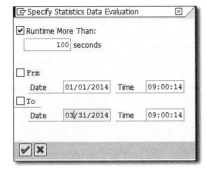

Figure 6.62 Select Parameters to Generate Aggregate Proposal

Aggregates are still available today and should be used if neither the BW Accelerator nor SAP HANA is used in the system.

Database Partitioning

Database partitioning improves reporting performance when the database can prune the SQL statement to access only the required partitions. This requires that the partitioning be done on characteristics that are part of almost all query selections, such as the following:

▸ Time (month, period, year)

▸ Region (Americas, Europe, Africa, Asia)

Partitioning also allows for parallel processing of the SQL statements on some database management systems in addition to partition pruning.

In SAP HANA, you may have to use database partitioning to overcome the two-billion row limitation for a single table or table partition. SAP BW, by default, partitions some objects during an SAP HANA migration, but executing SAP HANA redistribution is another way to get tables partitioned. Another benefit of partitioning in SAP HANA is that table partitions can be distributed across server nodes, allowing for parallel processing across multiple SAP HANA nodes in a scale-out SAP HANA system.

MultiProviders

You should always use MultiProviders because they provide flexibility on how the data model can evolve over time. Maybe you only defined one part provider initially, but new requirements could lead to additional part providers to be included.

Note that MultiProviders come with some overhead to process the part providers and the merge (union) that results from each part provider into a single result set. However, MultiProviders also provide improved capability for parallel processing when large datasets need to be processed. This is the main reason to use Multi-Providers for all reporting in SAP BW.

When using MultiProviders, you'll realize some performance improvement by using MultiProvider hints if the part providers are storing logical partitioned sets of data (for example, partitioned by region or customer group). A MultiProvider hint can be entered in table RRKMULTIPROVHINT via Transaction SM30, and it makes sense to avoid the MultiProvider split executing select statements on all part providers when the part providers are logically partitioned.

Logical Partitioning

As mentioned in the previous section, it can be beneficial to logically partition one InfoProvider into several that hold specific slices of data. This provides similar benefits because the database partitioning also provides the benefit that sub-queries are generated by the OLAP engine and executed in parallel. It also simplifies data management in the long term. Logical partitioning can be done with semantic partitioning objects as of SAP BW release 7.30.

Semantic Partitioning Objects

Semantic partitioning objects (SPOs) were introduced in SAP BW version 7.30. This provides the capability to define an object once, and it then generates a set of duplicate objects in the database that make use of the same transformations and object definition. This minimizes the effort to maintain the partitioning and still provides the benefits similar to the logical partitioning.

BW Accelerator

SAP released the BW Accelerator in 2006 as an add-on to SAP BW that provides in-memory processing for InfoCubes. BWA provides significant performance improvement over relational databases and was a predecessor to the SAP HANA database that was released in 2011.

The downside to using BWA is that the InfoCube data has to be replicated to the BWA server. In addition, you can anticipate additional license and hardware costs on top of the SAP BW system.

SAP HANA

The SAP HANA database can be used as the DBMS for SAP BW as of release 7.30 SP5. The SAP HANA in-memory platform provides fast data access to large volumes of data with sub-second runtime. Compared to SAP BW on Oracle, measurements from SAP BW on HANA show that query times are generally 20-100 times faster—and can be up to one thousand times faster.

SAP IQ

The SAP SIQ, formerly known as Sybase IQ, can also be used as the DBMS for SAP BW systems. The IQ database is a columnar database similar to SAP HANA, but it does not store the data in memory. It does, however, provide all the columnar database benefits that SAP HANA provides with regard to compression and aggregation of data. This can provide much faster database time for query executions compared to databases such as Oracle and Microsoft SQL.

6.2.2 Query Optimization

A big part of the SAP BW reporting performance is related to the query performance. We will now cover the following specific optimizations you can apply in the query design to improve the query performance:

- General query definition best practices
- Characteristics and navigational attributes
- Key figures
- Structures
- Exception aggregation
- Cell definition
- Hierarchies
- Unit of measure and currency translations

General Query Definition Best Practices

SAP BW queries can range from being very simple to very complex. The SAP BW OLAP engine provides a lot of different functionalities that, when used, can impact performance both negatively and positively. We offer the following basic recommendations:

- Keep the query simple, with only a few characteristics and key figures, to help improve performance.

▸ Use mandatory selections on time (for example, fiscal period or month) to limit the result set returned. Additional variables can also help limit the result set, but there is an overhead per variable. Therefore, it is not recommended to have too many variables in a query.

▸ Avoid too many drilldowns (rows and columns) because this returns too many result cells.

▸ Suppress zero rows to avoid rendering them.

Characteristics and Navigational Attributes

The number of characteristics in the query definition causes an overhead when you initialize the query and when you render the end result to the frontend. Consequently, we discourage you from having more than 20 characteristics in a single query.

Navigational attributes can cause performance problems because they are accessed via several joins instead of being stored directly in the DSO or fact/dimension tables. You can build aggregates or secondary indexes if navigational attributes are used heavily for selection in queries.

Key Figures

The number of key figures also impacts the initialization time and the time to render the query result. One best practice is to limit the number of key figures to those necessary for the report and avoid having key figures in the query definition that are not displayed.

Calculated key figures require the OLAP engine to execute the calculation and, hence, add runtime to the query execution. Very complex calculations on large result sets can increase runtime significantly and cause performance issues. Restricted key figures can help limit the result. It is, however, very important for restrictions that can be made global be made at the global level to avoid processing a lot of zero cells.

Structures

With BEx structures you can build predefined aggregation groupings or groupings of key figures directly in the query definition. This is a key component of the SAP

BEx query designer, but it can lead to poor performance if very complex structures are defined at the query level, since this leads to long OLAP processing time.

In addition, remember that you should always save structures as global structures to make them reusable and to improve performance since reusable structures can be optimized by the OLAP engine and selections are processed earlier in the OLAP engine processing.

Exception Aggregation

Exception aggregation has generally been a big performance problem in queries that make use of this feature. In SAP BW 7.40, it is possible to have exception aggregation executed in SAP HANA or BWA, which dramatically improves performance. You can also build specific aggregates to improve performance for exception aggregation key figures.

Cell Definition

Cell definition is one of the features that can cause performance issues if it is used incorrectly. When creating a cell definition, it is important to keep in mind that the cell calculation is done at the end of the OLAP processing.

Hierarchies

Using hierarchies in query definitions can be very useful—but can also provide some performance problems, especially when hierarchies are used in structures and restricted key figures.

You can use display hierarchies to provide the end user with a guided analysis with many characteristics in the drilldown but still have a small result set as the hierarchy is collapsed.

Unit of Measure and Currency Translations

Currency and unit of measure translations performed during query runtime can dramatically impact performance because additional data is required for the processing and additional processing steps are performed at runtime.

A currency translation that performs a translation based on a date in the dataset requires that those date characteristics are included in the result set processed by the OLAP engine. If a specific reporting currency like EUR or USD is generally used during reporting, you should perform the currency translation during data loading and store the original value as well as the converted value in the DSO or InfoCube.

The same recommendation is applicable for unit of measure conversions, where a standard measure can be stored in the database during data loading to avoid performing the translation during runtime.

6.2.3 Frontend Tool Optimization

The SAP BW frontend tools provide the end user interface to the data and require performance considerations

BEx Web Templates

The SAP BEx web templates can cause severe performance problems if they are not designed correctly. In general, we have measured that adding a query as a Data Provider into a web template causes a half- to one-second increase in runtime because the query needs to be initialized when the template is called.

Table 6.5 lists the general impact of adding some of the different web items to an SAP BW web template.

Web Item Type	Performance Impact
Query as data provider	0.5-1.0 second
Table	1.0 second
Chart	1.0-1.5 seconds
Filter	0.2-0.5 seconds
Dropdown	0.2-0.5 seconds
Button	0.2-0.3 seconds
Map	1.5-2.0 seconds
Other components	0.1-1.0 second
MIME objects (pictures)	0.1-0.3 seconds

Table 6.5 General Web Item Performance Impact

Note that the times in Table 6.5 are in addition to the query execution time and rendering time. Consequently, it is important to limit the number of web items used in a web template to get response time below 10 seconds for every report execution.

You can minimize the runtime impact of company logos and other MIME objects by caching the objects on the client. The caching is set in the MIME repository, as well as in the BI Java server.

We generally recommend that you cache objects for 30 days to avoid having to load the objects too frequently. One thing to note when JavaScripts are cached is that changes to the objects are only reflected in the client when the cache expires or is manually deleted on the client. Therefore, you must provide guidance on a manual procedure or script to execute when the SAP BW system is updated with patches or upgraded to avoid problems with the scripts. You can identify the caching time by using HTTPWATCH to display the details for the files loaded when a BEx web report is loaded in the browser.

BEx Analyzer Excel Workbooks

The SAP Business Explorer Analyzer (BEx Analyzer) is an add-in to Microsoft Excel, so it makes use of some Excel functionality on top of the add-in component functionality.

A general problem when using the BEx Analyzer is that Excel refresh time can be very long. This is normally caused by Excel formulas created to make use of the result area that the BEx add-in provides in the Excel worksheets, which causes a recalculation for every cell when it is updated. Analyzing this problem is normally quite easy because the query runtime is fast but the runtime in the particular workbook is slow.

The solution to this problem is also quite simple, requiring only that you deactivate the recalculation feature in the workbook when the SAP BW data is refreshed. To automate this, add a button to a standard Excel template that deactivates the recalculation before SAP BW data is refreshed and activates recalculation after the SAP BW data has been refreshed completely. Listing 6.1 shows the code for that button.

```
Public Sub Refresh_BW_Data()
'This routine refreshes all queries within this workbook
    ActiveCell.Activate
    'Keep calculation setting
    CalculationStatus = Application.Calculation
    'turn off automatic calculation
    Application.Calculation = xlCalculationManual
    ' Refresh BW data
    Run "BExAnalyzer.XLA!MenuRefreshVariables"
    ' Message to explain that the BW data has been refreshed and that
data will now be processed in Excel.
    '       MsgBox "The data has been refreshed from BW." & vbLf _
    '       & "Please wait while the data is processed in Excel." & vbLf _
    '       & "This may take a few minutes.", _
    '       vbInformation, "Excel is processing all worksheets with new data."
    ' Reset calculation to what it was before refreshing BW data
    Application.Calculation = CalculationStatus
    ' Make sure that we stay in the instructions sheet
    Range("F14").Select
End Sub
```

Listing 6.1 Recalculation Deactivation and Reactivation Refresh Button

The button can be inserted in the standard template provided by SAP, as shown in Figure 6.63.

Figure 6.63 BEx Analyzer Standard Workbook Template with Refresh Button

Another problem that can increase processing time to open BEx Analyzer workbooks is the size of the files. Even when you delete the result set from the file prior to saving them to the SAP BW server, they retain the result area as used; this can cause very large workbooks to be stored on the SAP BW server, taking up database space and causing long wait times when accessing the stored workbooks. Listing 6.2 shows how to clear the result set cells completely.

```
Sub Reset_LastCell()
    Dim LastCell As Range
    ' Save the lastcell and start there.
    '...next line would need to be changed based on worksheet name
    'included to put focus back to worksheet after button click
  Excel.ThisWorkbook.Sheets("Worksheet-1").Cells(1, 2).Select
  Set LastCell = Cells.SpecialCells(xlLastCell)
    ' Set the rowstep and column steps so that it can move toward
    ' cell A1.
    rowstep = -1
    colstep = -1
    ' Loop while it can still move.
    While (rowstep + colstep <> 0) And (LastCell.Address <> "$A$1")
        ' Test to see if the current column has any data in any
        ' cells.
        'no need to loop through all the rows since data has been cleared
        'added this If statement since there should be less than
        '200 rows after the data has been cleared
        If LastCell.Row > 200 Then
          Set LastCell = LastCell.Offset(200 - LastCell.Row)
        End If
        If Application _
            .CountA(Range(Cells(1, LastCell.Column), LastCell)) _
            > 0 Then colstep = 0 'If data then stop the stepping
          ' Test to see if the current row has any data in any cells.
          ' If data exists, stop row stepping.
        If Application _
            .CountA(Range(Cells(LastCell.Row, 1), LastCell)) _
            > 0 Then rowstep = 0
          ' Move the lastcell pointer to a new location.
          Set LastCell = LastCell.Offset(rowstep, colstep)
          ' Update the status bar with the new "actual" last cell
          ' location.
          Application.StatusBar = "Lastcell: " & LastCell.Address
    Wend
```

```
' Clear and delete the "unused" columns.
With Range(Cells(1, LastCell.Column + 1), "IV65536")
    Application.StatusBar = "Deleting column range: " & _
      .Address
    .Clear
    .Delete
End With
' Clear and delete the "unused" rows.
With Rows(LastCell.Row + 1 & ":65536")
    Application.StatusBar = "Deleting Row Range: " & _
      .Address
    .Clear
    .Delete
End With
' Select cell A1.
Range("a1").Select
' Reset the status bar to the Microsoft Excel default.
Application.StatusBar = False
End Sub
```

Listing 6.2 Clearing the Result Set Cells

As with the REFRESH button, you can insert this button in a standard workbook template for all users creating SAP BW BEx Analyzer workbook reports.

Network Optimization

When users are located in various parts of the world with different network capabilities, network speed can have tremendous impact on the reporting performance. Some network connections might still be based on legacy dial-up technology and, hence, cause a long delay in rendering or transferring the result set to the client.

Fortunately, most corporate networks make use of better network technology and global network providers that provide high-speed connections in almost all parts of the world. But even with high-speed connections to remote locations, you may need to prioritize SAP BW network traffic to ensure that it does not get delayed due to users downloading data from shared network drives or non-essential backups that are running during business hours.

Several tools are available for prioritizing network traffic on a corporate network. We will not go into specific tools in this book, but instead emphasize that you should prioritize the traffic from all the SAP BW servers—both ABAP and Java— because they all communicate out to the end users for different tools.

In our experience, network delay in some locations has such an impact on response times that, for global implementations, prioritizing network traffic can improve overall reporting response times in some locations by up to 50%.

SAP BW provides open interfaces to other reporting tools, including interfaces to the SAP BusinessObjects BI Platform tools. The following interfaces make use of different technologies in the SAP BW system:

▶ BI Consumer Services (BICS)

▶ OLE DB for OLAP

▶ Web services

We will now cover some basic optimization techniques for these specific interfaces.

BI Consumer Services

SAP BW provides an interface option called BI Consumer Services (BICS). It is a service-based interface method used for SAP BEx tools as of release 7.0 that can also be used by other tools, such as SAP BusinessObjects tools.

The BICS connection provides all the access to the SAP BW OLAP engine used in the BEx tools, so it can have some of the same performance bottlenecks as the BEx tools.

This causes some tools to generate value lists for all these characteristics, which dramatically slows down the performance for the initial load of the reports. Some tools like SAP BusinessObjects Web Intelligence have added features to avoid this behavior by stripping the query down to the needed characteristics. We definitely recommend that you make use of this setting in SAP BusinessObjects Web Intelligence.

OLE DB for OLAP

OLE DB for OLAP is a Microsoft standard for accessing multi-dimensional data. Implementation in SAP BW makes use of either an MDX parser, which is part of SAPgui, or direct access to the ABAP system via the OLAP BAPI.

The MDX parser in SAPgui has a tendency to add a large overhead on the query runtime because the transfer of data has to go via the MDX add-in in SAPgui. SAPgui is built as a frontend tool for a single user, and when it is installed on a server that executes many requests in parallel with large volumes of data, it introduces a performance bottleneck.

The OLAP BAPI circumvents the SAPgui add-in, so it does not have the same performance bottlenecks as the SAPgui limitations. However, the OLAP BAPI still has to translate the MDX statements to be parsed to the SAP BW OLAP engine, which causes an overhead in runtime.

Another general concern when using the OLAP BAPI and MDX parser is the impact of having many navigational characteristics in the query definition because some tools generate value lists for all the characteristics.

A good way to test the performance is by using the Transaction MDXTEST with the specific MDX statement to simulate the SAP BW processing time as displayed in Figure 6.64.

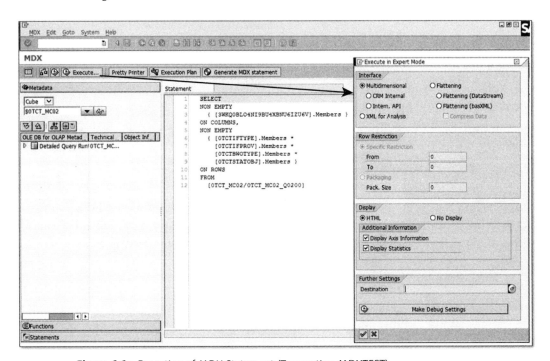

Figure 6.64 Execution of MDX Statement (Transaction MDXTEST)

The result of the MDX execution in Transaction MDXTEST provides two things: the result output of the query, and details about the runtime of the different MDX BAPI calls that are executed during processing as displayed in Figure 6.65. This can provide details on a possible performance problem in the OLAP BAPI or pinpoint the part of the MDX statement that is causing the performance problem.

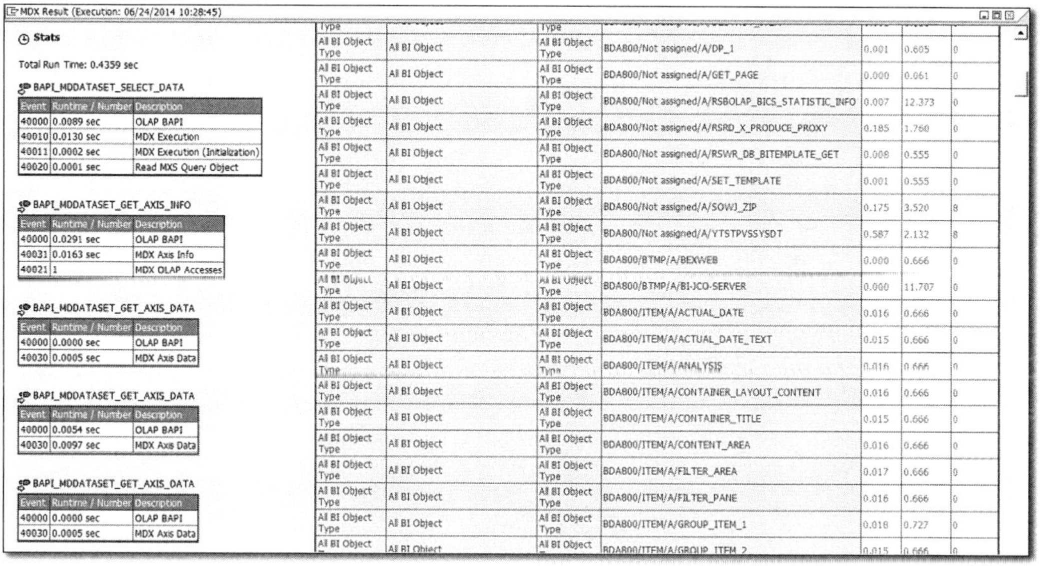

Figure 6.65 MDX Result including Runtime for BAPI Calls (Transaction MDXTEST)

Web Services

Web services make use of MDX statements like OLE DB for OLAP; all optimization techniques applied to OLE DB for OLAP are also valid for web services. In addition to the OLE DB for OLAP optimizations, we recommend that you review the web service requests to ensure that they are optimal. A common mistake in web service implementation is to request more data than needed and then filter the data in the web service.

You can normally use the frontend time in the technical content to monitor the time used by the web service. However, this is not always the case when the web service is executed to process the data after the request is completed to the SAP BW server.

We have covered a lot of information about finding and resolving performance problems in SAP BW reporting in this chapter. Remember that performance tuning is a never-ending effort. Whenever a problem has been resolved, it uncovers another bottleneck in the system—so you should continuously monitor performance and implement a procedure that takes care of the top performance problems.

The next part of this book will focus on administration tasks that should be performed in live SAP BW systems to keep them running smoothly with good performance.

Part III
Administration Tasks in Your SAP BW System

Proactive monitoring allows support organizations to identify and anticipate technical issues affecting end users before they are escalated. Daily monitoring and resolution of these issues can give support organizations credibility in the eyes of their stakeholders, which can be a very valuable asset.

7   Daily Tasks

In many companies, IT support for SAP BW is divided between the project delivery team(s) and a support organization. The support organization's main role is to ensure that the system operates within defined *service-level agreement* (SLA) parameters. The SLA parameters usually specify how long the support organization has to address incidents by severity. For example, they may have four hours for a "very high" severity incident, 24 hours for "high," one week for "medium," and four weeks for "low." Support organizations that proactively monitor and resolve issues are much more successful at meeting SLA parameters than those that don't.

This chapter will focus on daily administration (Section 7.1) and monitoring (Section 7.2) tasks, which should be performed by SAP Basis, SAP BW technical and/ or data load monitoring sub-teams within the support organization, which will be covered in more depth in Chapter 12 on the BI Competency Center. Some of these tasks need to be performed only once daily, but others may need constant supervision, such as data load monitoring. You should consider any opportunity to automate daily tasks, such as leveraging SAP Solution Manager to configure thresholds and send alerts by email.

7.1   Daily Administration Tasks

The first technical resource to arrive in the office every morning should conduct routine daily administration checks manually as a quick health check of the system.

If the system is monitored globally, 24/7, the technical team receiving handover should conduct the check at the beginning of every shift. Over time, thresholds for normal behavior will be apparent; technical resources should document these thresholds and note and follow up on any abnormal behavior or deviations above or below normal.

In addition, when performance or systematic issues are reported, these checks should be executed first so that the technical team is knowledgeable and aware of the system's operational health.

This section will highlight a few important administrative checks to execute on a daily basis:

▶ Check database storage

▶ Check workload

▶ Check BWA

▶ Perform system checks

▶ Automate daily tasks

7.1.1 Checking Database Storage

Every database grows consistently when in operational use. In SAP BW systems, there are usually four main reasons for growth:

▶ Organic growth

▶ New development/content-related growth

▶ System administration table growth

▶ Lack of management by projects and/or support

The final contributor to growth—lack of management by project or support teams—is completely preventable. This type of growth is usually the result of negligent housekeeping, such as failing to delete PSA or change-log tables after they are no longer valuable. Following the data management principles covered in Chapter 3, as well as the guidelines in this section, should help you not only eliminate this type of growth from your system, but also manage the other three types of growth.

When usage of the database grows more quickly than it has capacity for, you can expect significant performance or operational problems. It is therefore extremely important to monitor free space (or its absence) in the database. In many cases, free-space monitoring can be automated, and tablespaces can be extended automatically as soon as certain thresholds are met. However, if there is no more storage space to allocate, these automations will fail.

Free Space Analysis

The total size and free space of the database can be found on the overview screen of the Database Monitor (Transaction DB02). Figure 7.1 shows the database monitor for an SAP BW system on an Oracle database with a size of 58TB and free space of 18TB. Although this database is large, there is ample room to grow.

There are two important items to check in the overview screen. The first is the largest tablespace, and the second is the date of the last statistics update, which should be scheduled daily. If the statistics are out of date, the DB optimizer may not use the best SQL paths to retrieve data, resulting in performance issues in the system. The next item to check is the free space of each tablespace, which you can analyze by drilling down into the SPACE • TABLESPACES menu item on the left pane in Figure 7.1.

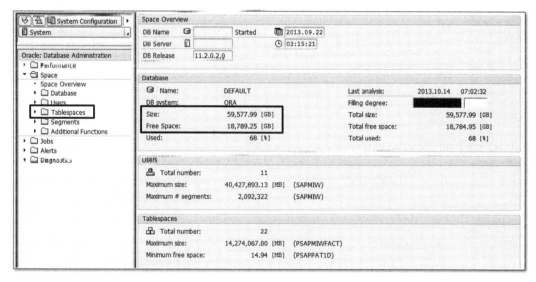

Figure 7.1 The Database Monitor in an Oracle System (Transaction ST03N)

BW Table Analysis

Under the ADDITIONAL FUNCTIONS folder in Figure 7.2, there is a BW ANALYSIS view that identifies the storage space consumed by BW object table types. This analysis is useful for monitoring the growth of DSO and InfoCube table sizes against the total database growth. If these tables are not growing at the same rate, it is likely there are PSA, change log, or system administration tables in the system that can be cleansed.

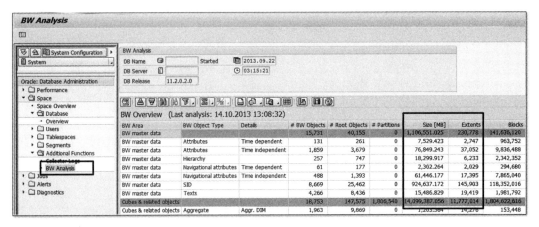

Figure 7.2 BW Analysis in the Database Monitor (Transaction DB02)

There are many other important and valuable functions in the database monitor, such as missing tables, indexes, and alerts. Each of these functions should be checked routinely.

SAP HANA Memory Consumption

Figure 7.3 shows that, in an SAP BW system on SAP HANA, the database monitor gives a completely different view. The information contained in the database monitor is the same information available in SAP HANA Studio.

There are a few key things to check in SAP HANA databases, which are labeled in Figure 7.3, although not necessarily in a specific priority. The first item to confirm is the operational state ❶. Second, check the overall memory consumption for all hosts ❷ — this is the same as the total database size in Oracle. Third, check the disk usage for all hosts ❸, and finally, check the alerts ❹.

Each of these items has a detailed view. In a scale-out or distributed system (the example has 28 hosts), it is more important to monitor memory consumption by host than overall. It is possible that memory on a single host could be overloaded while others are under-utilized. In this case, a reorganization or redistribution may be necessary.

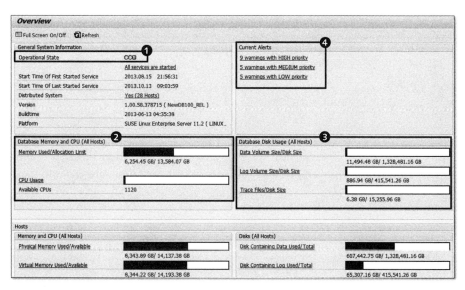

Figure 7.3 The Database Monitor in an SAP HANA System (Transaction DB02)

To see memory consumption by host, go to the menu item CONFIGURATION • SERVICES, shown in Figure 7.4. In this view, the memory consumption of each service on each host is specified. Pay particular attention to any index server consuming more than 75% on any single host.

Active	Host	Port Numbe	Service Name	Process ID	Detail	SQL Port N	Timestamp	Process CP	Total CP	Σ Process Me	Total Memo	Available	Physical M
	km3hf103	30,200	daemon	5,709		0	2013.08.15 21:56:32	1-	1	0.00	0.00	0.00	0.00
		30,201	nameserver	5,733	master	0	2013.08.15 21:56:33	0		18.79	98.41	506.90	504.90
		30,202	preprocessor	14,072		0	2013.08.15 21:57:20	0		15.38	98.41	506.90	504.90
		30,203	indexserver	40,226	master	30,215	2013.08.28 19:46:12	1		276.32	98.41	506.90	504.90
		30,205	statisticsserver	47,921	master	30,217	2013.10.13 09:03:59	0		33.92	98.41	506.90	504.90
		30,207	xsengine	14,277		0	2013.08.15 21:57:22	0		18.59	98.41	506.90	504.90
	km3hf104	30,200	daemon	1,425		0	2013.08.15 21:56:34	1-	1	0.00	0.00	0.00	0.00
		30,201	nameserver	1,448		0	2013.08.15 21:56:35	0		15.09	365.35	506.90	504.90
		30,202	preprocessor	9,846		0	2013.08.15 21:57:24	0		12.38	365.35	506.90	504.90
		30,203	indexserver	9,862		30,215	2013.08.15 21:57:26	0		368.39	365.35	506.90	504.90
	km3hf105	30,200	daemon	9,439		0	2013.08.28 12:37:54	1-	1	0.00	0.00	0.00	0.00
		30,201	nameserver	9,462		0	2013.08.28 12:38:00	0		15.09	295.94	506.90	504.90
		30,202	preprocessor	9,518		0	2013.08.28 12:38:09	0		8.99	295.94	506.90	504.90
		30,203	indexserver	9,534		30,215	2013.08.28 12:38:11	0		297.69	295.94	506.90	504.90
	km3hf106	30,200	daemon	1,648		0	2013.08.15 21:56:32	1-	1	0.00	0.00	0.00	0.00
		30,201	nameserver	1,671		0	2013.08.15 21:56:33	0		15.10	359.35	506.90	504.90
		30,202	preprocessor	9,851		0	2013.08.15 21:57:22	0		15.14	359.35	506.90	504.90
		30,203	indexserver	10,087		30,215	2013.08.15 21:57:24	0		360.88	359.35	506.90	504.90
	km3hf107	30,200	daemon	1,582		0	2013.08.15 21:56:33	1-	1	0.00	0.00	0.00	0.00
		30,201	nameserver	1,605		0	2013.08.15 21:56:35	0		15.08	267.77	506.90	504.90
		30,202	preprocessor	7,863		0	2013.08.15 21:57:23	0		14.77	267.77	506.90	504.90
		30,203	indexserver	9,768		30,215	2013.08.15 21:57:25	0		270.01	267.77	506.90	504.90
	km3hf108	30,200	daemon	1,396		0	2013.08.15 21:56:32	1-	1	0.00	0.00	0.00	0.00
		30,201	nameserver	1,419		0	2013.08.15 21:56:34	0		15.09	235.15	506.90	504.90

Figure 7.4 Memory Consumption by Host in a Distributed SAP HANA Database (Transaction DB02)

The memory consumption for each service includes memory used by the following components:

- Database administration
- Code and stacks
- Column store tables
- Row store tables

A more detailed memory consumption report can be executed to identify how much memory each component is using. This report is available under the menu item SYSTEM INFORMATION and is called *memory consumption by component*. Using this report can help identify memory leaks when components that are normally small grow suddenly large.

> **Recommendation**
>
> The row store tables may need to be compacted if they have been cleansed since migration to SAP HANA. Check SAP Note 1813245 for instructions on how to check whether row store compaction is recommended.

7.1.2 Checking Workload

After checking the database, the next step is to check the workload on the system's application servers. It is always good to understand what jobs or transactions are running in the system and who is running them.

Process Overview

The easiest place to find this information is in the process overview transactions. Transaction SM66 provides a list of all actively used processes in the system across all application servers. This complements Transactions SM50 and SM51 well; all processes (both used and available) for each individual application server can be monitored.

As seen in Figure 7.5, the process overview (Transaction SM50) provides an overview of all work processes for a specific application server (Transaction SM51 displays all available application servers; Transaction SM50 can be reached by selecting one application server from the list). In the process overview, pay particular attention to long-running activity. Any job that runs for more than 500 seconds appears in this screen with a red status.

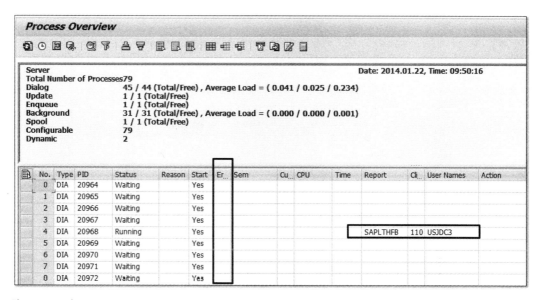

Figure 7.5 The Process Overview (Transactions SM51 and SM50)

In addition, check the ERROR column for any number greater than zero, which indicates the number of times the work process has been killed at the operating-system level since the last restart. If many work processes have been killed, there may be a systematic performance issue affecting the system.

Workload Statistics

Armed with the knowledge about what is running in the system, the next check should be to review the workload and performance statistics being captured by all workload components. The workload monitor in Transaction ST03N is available for this purpose, as you can see in Figure 7.6.

The workload overview ❶ provides valuable information about response times of all work processes ❷. Notice that the average time for background processes is 42,468.1 milliseconds, or 42.5 seconds: background processing should be the primary area of focus for improving response time. This transaction also provides load history and distribution, so you can also perform a statistical analysis of different servers by different time periods.

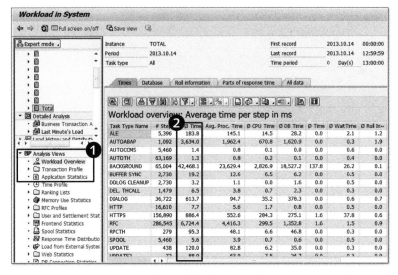

Figure 7.6 Response Time in the Workload Monitor (Transaction ST03N)

Performance Overview

More detailed database performance information, such as SQL execution history and wait event analysis, can be evaluated in the performance overview (Transaction ST04), as seen in Figure 7.7.

Figure 7.7 Performance Overview (Transaction ST04)

This transaction provides historical data and statistics, such as cache hit rates, buffer sizes, and the number of database reads and writes in the performance overview. If there are known database performance issues in the system, you can conduct a performance analysis using this transaction.

Memory Tuning Analysis

To evaluate whether the system profile parameters related to memory usage have adequate values for the system needs, check the tune summary (Transaction ST02) shown in Figure 7.8.

Tune Summary

Current parameters   Detail Analysis Menu

System:
Date + Time of Snapshot: 2014.01.22   09:23:25   Tune summary
Startup: 2014.01.16 02:44:40

Buffer	HitRatio %	Alloc. KB	Freesp. KB	% Free Sp.	Dir. Size	FreeDirEnt	% Free Dir	Swaps	DB Accs
Nametab (NTAB)								0	
Table definition	99.39	60,491	41,094	81.17	180,000	146,089	81.16	0	465,315
Field definition	99.94	264,062	191,535	76.61	180,000	155,051	86.14	0	30,476
Short NTAB	99.97	20,625	14,087	93.91	45,000	41,890	93.09	0	3,117
Initial records	74.20	35,625	23,061	76.87	45,000	30,394	67.54	0	17,005
								0	
program	99.68	1,300,000	5,574	0.47	325,000	293,585	90.33	24,461	181,536
CUA	99.47	30,000	16,013	67.34	15,000	13,846	92.31	0	2,310
Screen	99.79	58,594	27,155	47.16	10,000	9,016	90.16	0	2,115
Calendar	100.00	488	472	98.74	200	198	99.00	0	2
OTR	94.96	4,096	3,261	99.94	2,000	1,997	99.85	0	
								0	
Tables								0	
Generic Key	99.83	585,938	56,204	9.74	40,000	1,333	3.33	48	941,396
Single record	91.92	300,000	228,323	76.24	2,000	759	37.95	0	8,317,641
								0	
Export/import	99.18	400,000	332,693	83.87	8,000			126,678	
Exp./ Imp. SHM		204,800	192,373	100.00	30,000	30,000	100.00	0	

SAP Memory	Curr.Use %	CurUse[KB]	MaxUse[KB]	In Mem[KB]	OnDisk[KB]	SAPCurCach	HitRatio %
Roll area	2.26	23,724	79,360	262,144	786,432	IDs	98.60
Page area	0.59	6,188	45,568	262,144	786,432	Statement	95.00
Extended memory	37.37	7,835,648	14,802,944	20,967,424	0		0.00
Heap memory		0	7,812,495	0	0		0.00

Figure 7.8 Memory Swaps Tune Summary (Transaction ST02)

This transaction contains information on buffer size, swap usage, and extended heap memory. The most obvious item to check is whether swap space is being used, which would indicate that existing buffer sizes are too small and need to be increased. Figure 7.8 shows an example in which swap space is being used for the program buffer and the export/import buffer.

In these cases, you can identify the profile parameters that need to be tuned by double-clicking the buffer line item in the tune summary to go to the TUNE DETAIL ANALYSIS screen. In the detail screen, click the CURRENT PARAMETERS button, as indicated by ❶ and ❸ in Figure 7.9. The next screen displays the profile parameters that control the buffer size and current values, as indicated by ❷ and ❹. From this last screen, it is also possible to maintain the profile parameter directly.

Some parameters can be changed and are active immediately, while others require a system restart. Regardless, all parameter changes should be tested for efficacy before being enacted directly in a production environment.

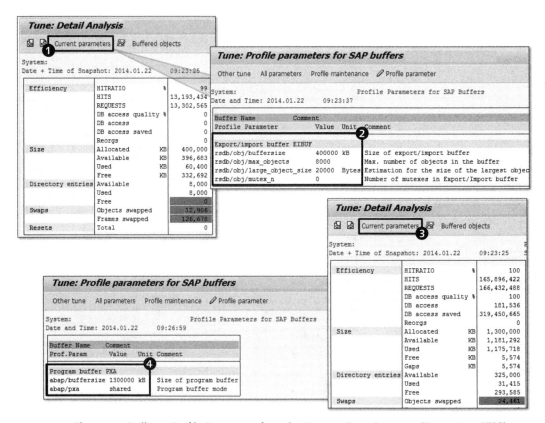

Figure 7.9 Drill into Profile Parameters from the Memory Tune Summary (Transaction ST02)

Figure 7.10 offers an example of a well-tuned system. This system has quite a lot of memory allocated to each buffer but only a few swaps. Ideally, there would be no swaps at all.

Tune Summary

Current parameters   Detail analysis menu

System: Tune summary
Date + Time of Snapshot: 2013.10.14   13:11:09   Startup: 2013.09.22 03:25:27

Buffer	HitRatio %	Alloc. KB	Freesp. KB	% Free Sp.	Dir. Size	FreeDirEnt	% Free Dir	Swaps	DB Accs
Nametab (NTAB)								0	
Table definition	99.22	58,825	28,196	57.29	175,000	100,255	57.29	0	4,236,884
Field definition	99.97	413,672	62,923	15.73	175,000	114,148	65.23	0	64,439
Short NTAB	99.99	15,469	8,570	85.70	43,750	38,156	87.21	0	5,846
Initial records	63.61	35,469	10,795	35.98	43,750	11,703	26.75	0	34,428
								0	
program	99.64	4,194,304	1,008,774	27.40	1,040,667	987,062	94.13	0	210,411
CUA	99.93	75,000	54,334	88.75	37,500	36,619	97.65	0	8,583
Screen	99.96	68,359	60,010	89.11	10,000	9,623	96.23	0	1,995
Calendar	99.87	684	201	29.96	250	83	33.20	0	418
OTR	49.02	4,096	3,352	100.00	2,000	2,000	100.00	0	
								0	
Tables								0	
Generic Key	99.97	2,539,063	1,388,389	55.72	200,000	6,186	3.09	4	1,242,786
Single record	87.80	1,000,000	676,359	67.81	10,000	6,594	65.94	0	172,714,952
								0	
Export/import	98.54	1,250,000	833,840	70.00	160,000	26,123	16.33	0	
Exp./ Imp. SHM	90.18	250,000	38,893	16.03	20,000	17,252	86.26	0	

SAP Memory	Curr.Use %	CurUse[KB]	MaxUse[KB]	In Mem[KB]	OnDisk[KB]	SAPCurCach	HitRatio %
Roll area	0.75	7,905	35,872	131,072	917,504	IDs	98.43
Page area	0.18	4,246	1,293,360	524,288	1,875,712	Statement	97.00
Extended memory	2.69	4,505,600	39,223,296	167,772,160	0		0.00
Heap memory	0		1,953,118	0	0		0.00
Ext. global memory		347,701	374,691	2,093,056	0		0.00
Shared objects		48,516	0	231,016	0		0.00

Figure 7.10 A Large but Well-Tuned System (Transaction ST02)

All the memory controlled by profile parameters is SAP application-level memory. To monitor the memory usage by all servers, you must to go to the operating system.

Operating Systems Monitor

The operating system can be checked in the operating systems monitor using Transaction ST06. In this OS monitor, check the current capacity and analyze average and peak CPU utilization. If it routinely exceeds 70-80%, additional capacity is likely needed before rolling out additional functionality or content. Figure 7.11 offers a snapshot of good system CPU utilization.

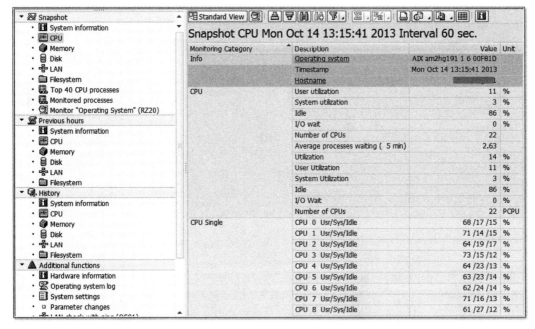

Figure 7.11 Snapshot of System CPU Utilization (Transaction ST06)

As a rule, 20% of the processes cause 80% of the load, so monitoring the top 40 processes (also in this transaction) identifies the areas needing the most focus. If an analysis in the OS monitor indicates a need for more CPU capacity, you can extend existing hardware in the following ways:

▶ Add application servers

▶ Add CPUs

▶ Replace existing CPUs with faster ones

All of these solutions can require long lead times, so you would be wise to monitor CPU proactively to identify bottlenecks before they crash the system.

From an operating system perspective, it is also necessary to monitor memory capacity and usage of the following:

▶ Physical memory

▶ Swap size

▶ Free memory

▶ Virtual memory

The operating systems monitor also provides information on the current memory capacity and enables analysis of average and peak memory utilization. Figure 7.12 offers a snapshot of current memory use in a sample system with 240 GB of physical memory allocated.

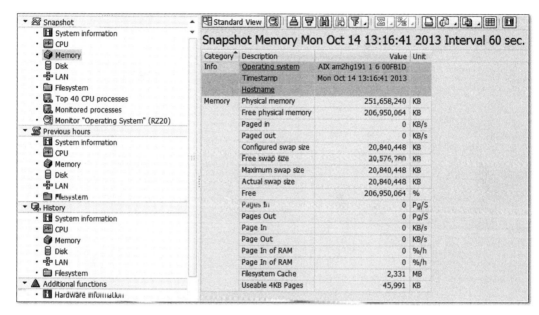

Figure 7.12 Snapshot of System Memory Utilization (Transaction ST06)

7.1.3 Checking BWA

The BWA Monitor provides a central point of access to the monitoring and administration functions for BWA (Transaction RSDDBIAMON2), as seen in Figure 7.13. This transaction provides an overview of the current status and a detailed technical overview of the hardware, the BWA services, all existing trace files, and the BWA indexes.

The BWA Monitor also displays the results of consistency checks. These checks are run on BWA periodically. If errors occur, the system automatically proposes corresponding measures, actions, or repair functions.

In the BWA Monitor, it is not possible to maintain the BWA indexes directly. Individual index maintenance at the InfoProvider level can be done from the InfoProvider maintenance screens or directly via the BW Accelerator index maintenance transaction (Transaction RSDDB).

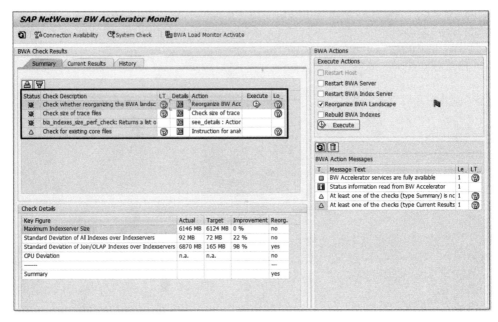

Figure 7.13 BWA Monitor (Transaction RSDDBIAMON2)

To see a status of all BWA indexes, go to Transaction RSDDB (see Figure 7.14). Here, each index can be checked for load status and number of records.

Information about BWA Indexes

BWA Index	Ind	V	St	Table Name	Table Size	In	Bo	Changed by	Time Stamp	Number
0BAL_FLAG	MDR			/BIO/SBAL_FLAG	2			INITH1	20,140,109,110,055	0
0CALMONTH	MDR			/BIO/SCALMONTH	617			ALEREMOTE	20,140,113,134,403	0
0CALMONTH2	MDR			/BIO/SCALMONTH2	13			ALEREMOTE	20,131,207,141,326	0
0CALQUART1	MDR			/BIO/SCALQUART1	5			ALEREMOTE	20,131,207,141,330	0
0CALQUARTER	MDR			/BIO/SCALQUARTER	116			ALEREMOTE	20,131,207,141,333	0
0CALWEEK	MDR			/BIO/SCALWEEK	1,179			ALEREMOTE	20,140,111,011,055	0
0CALYEAR	MDR			/BIO/SCALYEAR	61			ALEREMOTE	20,131,207,141,341	0
0CHRT_ACCTS	MDR			/BIO/SCHRT_ACCTS	31			INITH1	20,140,109,110,027	0
0CS_CHART	MDR			/BIO/SCS_CHART	5			S_EID_L3_03	20,131,209,022,222	0
0CURRENCY	MDR			/BIO/SCURRENCY	228			ALEREMOTE	20,131,207,141,345	0
0DATE	MDR			/BIO/SDATE	16,340			ALEREMOTE	20,140,117,053,224	0
0FISCPER	MDR			/BIO/SFISCPER	62,067			ALEREMOTE	20,140,102,131,236	0
0FISCPER3	MDR			/BIO/SFISCPER3	58			INITH1	20,131,208,055,745	0
0FISCVARNT	MDR			/BIO/SFISCVARNT	13			INITH1	20,131,208,055,748	0
0FISCYEAR	MDR			/BIO/SFISCYEAR	2,003			ALEREMOTE	20,140,117,114,739	0
0FUNC_AREA	MDR			/BIO/SFUNC_AREA	116			INITH1	20,140,109,110,047	0

Figure 7.14 BWA Index Overview Screen (Transaction RSDDB)

7.1.4   Performing System Checks

Not all daily administration tasks can be categorized under database storage or workload analysis. The system checks covered in this section represent all other categories of health checks, which are no less important. In fact, you may prefer to execute these checks first before checking database storage and system workload.

Short Dumps

The frequency of runtime issues encountered by users and batch processes in the system is indicative of the stability of the system. Check the number of runtime errors, or short dumps, using the ABAP RUNTIME ERROR analysis (Transaction ST22) to list the ABAP runtime errors that have occurred recently.

Figure 7.15 gives an example of short dumps in a BW system. You can easily access the current day's short dumps for all users by clicking the button TODAY ❶. There are two runtime errors represented ❷.

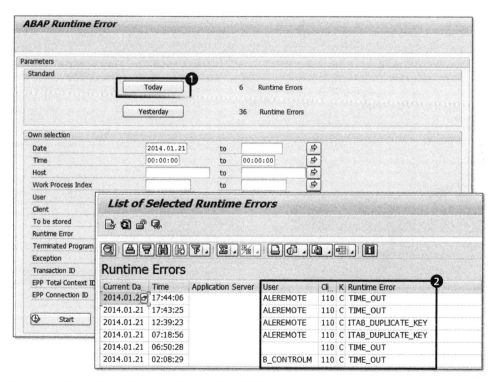

Figure 7.15 Short Dump Overview (Transaction ST22)

The time-out error indicates a performance issue that could be related to external RFC connections. The duplicate key issues indicate a data load error that could be resolved programmatically by checks in the ETL logic.

System Log

SAP systems log all system errors, warnings, user locks (due to failed logon attempts from known users), and process messages in the system log. There are to two different types of logs created by the system log:

▶ **Local logs**

Each application server has a local log for all the messages output by this server. The system log records these messages in a circular file. When this log file reaches the maximum permissible length, the system log overwrites it, starting over from the beginning.

▶ **Central logs**

Central logs are optional; when configured, the central log maintains a file on a selected application server. Each application server then sends local log messages to the central log server, which collects the messages and writes them to the central log. The central log consists of two files: the active file and the old file.

The active file contains the current log. When it reaches the maximum size, the system performs a *log file switch*. It deletes the old log file, makes the previously active file the "old" file, and creates a new active file. The switch occurs when the size of the active log file is half the value specified in the `rslg/max_diskspace/central` parameter.

> **Note**
>
> The location of the local log is specified in the `rslg/local/file` profile parameter. The location of the central log active file is specified in the `rslg/central/file`profile parameter; the location of the old file is specified in the `rslg/central/old_file` parameter.

Use Transaction SM21 to access the system log output screen. With this transaction, it is possible to read all the messages contained in any of the system logs by choosing SYSTEM LOG • CHOOSE • ALL REMOTE SYSTEM LOGS ❶, as shown in Figure 7.16. Enter the date and time ❷ to start reading the log and click the REREAD SYSTEM LOG button.

The resulting list can be restricted for PROBLEMS ONLY, PROBLEMS AND MESSAGES, or ALL MESSAGES ❸. The information in this list, such as transaction code and user, can be used to analyze the errors indicated with a red icon in the PRIORITY column. Double-clicking any line opens the detail text and provides more information.

Each error message in the log should be scrutinized for root cause analysis. Errors that are not resolved continue to consume system resources (CPU, memory, and storage space), which may lead to unrelated follow-up issues. Sometimes, log entries point to more information in a runtime error dump (Transaction ST22) or other location.

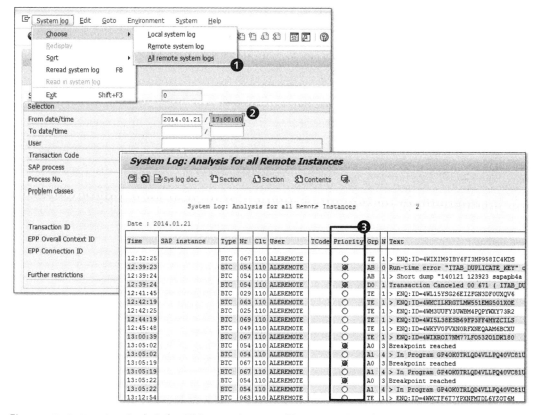

Figure 7.16 System Log Analysis for All Remote Instances (Transaction SM21)

Job Overview

The JOB OVERVIEW screen is a single, central area for completing a wide range of tasks related to monitoring and managing background jobs, including the following:

- ▸ Defining jobs
- ▸ Scheduling, rescheduling, and copying existing jobs
- ▸ Rescheduling and editing jobs and job steps
- ▸ Repeating jobs
- ▸ Debugging active jobs
- ▸ Reviewing information about jobs
- ▸ Canceling a job's release status
- ▸ Canceling and deleting jobs
- ▸ Comparing the specifications of several jobs
- ▸ Checking the status of jobs
- ▸ Reviewing job logs
- ▸ Releasing jobs to run

Jobs should be monitored for errors on a daily basis. In the case of errors, spool output files or job logs should be evaluated for the cause of the error.

To reach the JOB OVERVIEW screen, call Transaction SM37. Enter an asterisk (*) as a wildcard in the mandatory selection criteria fields JOB NAME and USER NAME, as indicated in ❶ of Figure 7.17. Deselect all job status checkboxes except ACTIVE and CANCELED ❷. Enter a date for analysis and then execute to get a list of all failed jobs plus those currently running. Analyze any error logs found.

Database Backup

The DBA Cockpit is a platform-independent tool used to monitor and administer activity in the database. The DBA Cockpit offers a subset of the functionality of DB management tools (such as SAP HANA Studio) and can be used to schedule database backups and database system checks. You can access the DBA Cockpit by calling Transaction DBACOCKPIT.

In the DBA Cockpit, the central calendar provides an overview of scheduled database administration actions on all the databases in the SAP system. The available actions differ depending on the database platform.

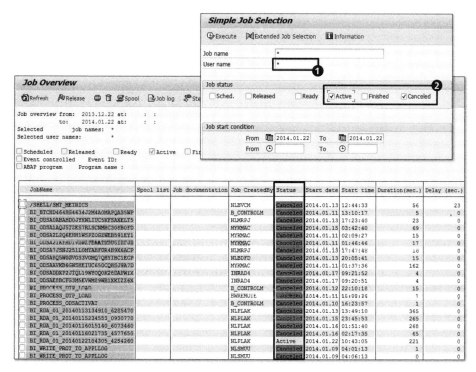

Figure 7.17 Active and Failed Jobs in the Job Overview (Transaction SM37)

The following tasks are available with the central calendar:

▶ Manage local system databases in real time

▶ Manage remote databases of different types and versions, including non-ABAP SAP systems

▶ Manage databases for different versions of an SAP system

▶ Quickly check whether actions were executed successfully

▶ Quickly check the number of actions and the actions with the highest status severity for each system

In the production system, check the status of database backups and system checks using the DBA Cockpit by viewing the central calendar (see Figure 7.18). All successful actions show as green, and failed actions show as red. Take an appropriate action for failed actions.

Figure 7.18 DBA Cockpit Central Calendar (Transaction DBACOCKPIT)

Expensive Statements

If you encounter specific performance issues, check the expensive statements in Transaction DB02 under the PERFORMANCE • EXPENSIVE STATEMENTS menu item in Figure 7.19.

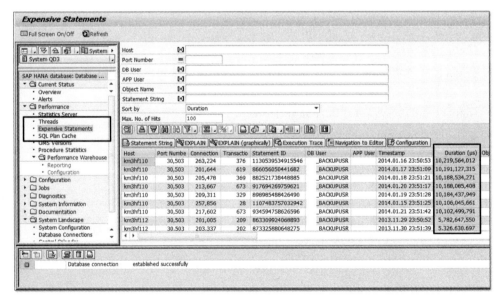

Figure 7.19 Expensive Statements in the Database Monitor (Transaction DB02)

This figure shows an example from an SAP HANA database indicating that specific statements executed by the DB backup user are running for more than 10 seconds.

Expensive statements should be traced to identify why they are taking so long. Transactions ST04 and ST05 can be used to complement the analysis performed in the Database Monitor.

7.1.5 Automating Daily Tasks

Many of these daily tasks can and should be automated using alerts available in SAP Solution Manager, in which effective measurement and reporting is the basis for a well-integrated system optimization process. There are four core elements of this process:

- Proactive real-time monitoring
- Reactive handling of critical events
- Lower mean time to problem resolution
- Optimized excellence of technical operations

Manual monitoring is a highly effort-intensive approach that usually requires expert involvement. Analysis and statistical tools are used to capture measurement points and evaluate them on an experience basis. Appropriate actions are then applied to counteract critical events. Automating monitoring processes involves defining and measuring KPIs and comparing and evaluating them with predefined threshold values.

The quality of the automated monitoring concept largely depends on the selected KPIs and definition of relevant threshold values. With fully automated monitoring, suitable countermeasures are initiated as soon as threshold values are exceeded. Incidents can also be reported to IT service desks.

The appropriate degree of automation depends on the effort and benefits involved. Manual expert monitoring is advisable to verify automated monitoring. If an adequate definition has not been made for certain KPIs and their threshold values, you should adjust the monitoring concept; otherwise, alerts will either be ignored or never be raised.

7.2   Daily Data Load Monitoring Tasks

The days of batch processing at night are a distant memory for most 21ˢᵗ-century SAP BW installations. In most systems, data loads are running around the clock because users are global, up-to-date information is critical, or volumes are so large that loads cannot be restricted to a nighttime operational window.

As a result, data load monitoring has become a critically important responsibility. In some systems, third-party tools are used to monitor process chains, but in many, no external tools are used, and monitoring is conducted within the Data Warehousing Workbench, where a host of monitors are available to help determine the current operational status, identify data load and BW object issues, and facilitate resolution.

In this section, we'll cover the following daily data load monitoring tasks:

▶ Monitor SAP BW Computing Center Management System (CCMS) alerts

▶ Monitor process chains

▶ Monitor InfoPackages and RDA daemons

▶ Monitor DSO activations

▶ Check aggregates

This list is not meant to be comprehensive; each system or implementation may have specific and unique data load monitoring requirements. However, these monitoring tasks represent the minimal list of tasks that should be performed to ensure that data is loading successfully into your system. Let's start by monitoring alerts raised in the Computing Center Management System.

7.2.1   Monitoring SAP BW CCMS Alerts

The Computing Center Management System (CCMS) has an alert monitor to help operate SAP BW systems. The CCMS BI MONITOR contains a selection of SAP BW-relevant monitoring trees for process chains and RSRV consistency checks. These alerts can be used to provide an overview of related issues in the system.

The monitoring trees in the BI Monitor come standard with the following alerts, as seen in Figure 7.20.

▶ **Process chains**
This alert contains all process chains executed in the system since it was last started or, if it was recently restarted, for up to seven days before the last restart.

After a system is restarted, the monitor contains the last seven days of PC logs before the restart. You can configure this setting by changing the transfer parameter for method execution DAYS_TO_KEEP_LOGS in method definition RSPC_CCMS_STARTUP. Go to the method definition, run Transaction RZ21, and then select menu item METHODS • DEFINITIONS. Once you set the parameter to OFF, process chains are not monitored in CCMS.

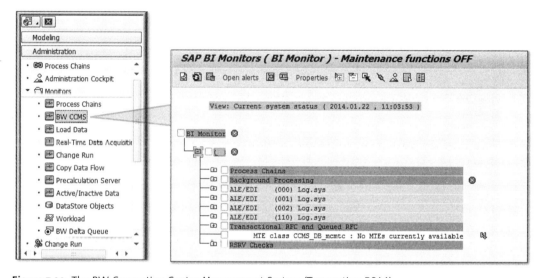

Figure 7.20 The BW Computing Center Management System (Transaction RSA1)

▶ **Background processing**
This alert agent runs every hour and monitors all the batch jobs in the system.

You can configure the frequency of this agent by changing the periodicity of batch job SAP_CCMS_MONI_BATCH_DP. By default, it is scheduled to run hourly, but it can be set in Transaction SM37 to run as frequently as every ten minutes.

▶ **RSRV checks**
This alert displays the messages for the consistency checks that have been executed in the analysis and repair environment (Transaction RSRV). The consistency checks have to be scheduled manually.

7.2.2 Monitoring Process Chains

While CCMS provides an overview of all process chain runs, from a daily data load monitoring perspective, it is most important to monitor only the last execution of each chain. There is a process chains monitor in the Data Warehousing Workbench, under ADMINISTRATION. This monitor provides only the current status ❷ for each process chain ❶ in the system, as seen in Figure 7.21.

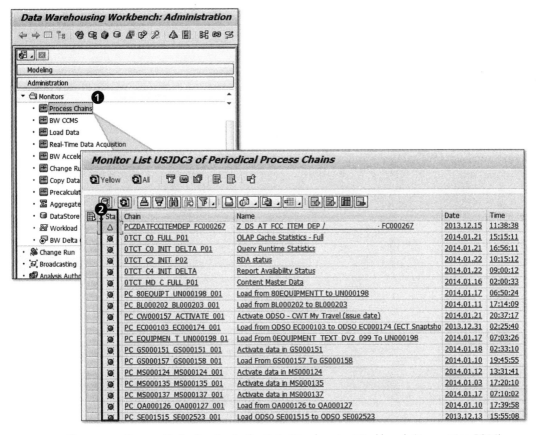

Figure 7.21 Process Chain Monitor in the Data Warehousing Workbench (Transaction RSA1)

The process chain monitor can also be accessed directly via Transaction RSPCM. Each active process chain in the system is listed here with a green, yellow, red, or gray status—gray means the chain has never been executed. If the status is yellow, the chain is currently running. The transaction does not distinguish between meta-chains and local chains, so all chains are displayed here.

Filtering the result list by chains in a specific status can be accomplished as shown in Figure 7.22. This can help narrow the focus to find only errors if there are too many chains in the list in another status.

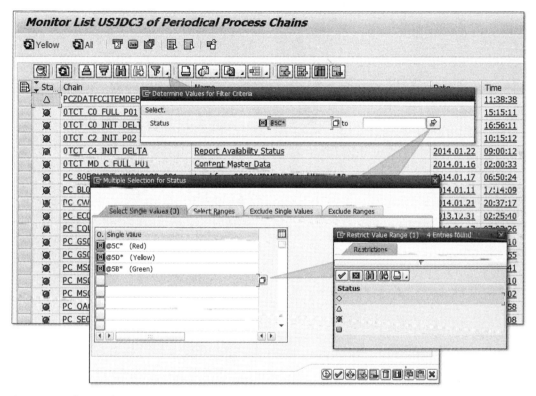

Figure 7.22 Filtering the Process Chain Monitor Based on Status (Transaction RSPCM)

7.2.3 Monitoring InfoPackages and RDA Daemons

On a more detailed level, monitoring InfoPackages and RDA daemons for errors can help facilitate resolution of source-data errors or configuration errors. Checking these monitors daily can provide valuable information on the status of data extractions into the SAP BW system.

You can check the InfoPackage status using the load data monitor in the Data Warehousing Workbench in the ADMINISTRATION section. In Figure 7.23, Info-Package errors on both the 20th and 21st of January indicate that an unresolved data extraction issue needs to be addressed.

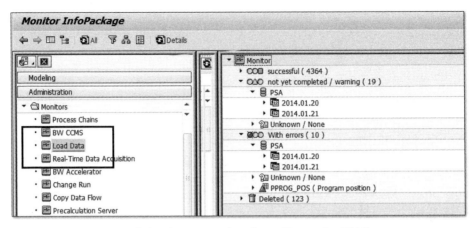

Figure 7.23 Monitoring Failed and Running InfoPackages (Transaction RSA1)

You can check the status of daemons using the Real-Time Data Acquisition (RDA) monitor. See Figure 7.24 for an issue-free example of RDA monitoring for all connected source systems. Notice that there are zeroes in the ERROR column down the middle.

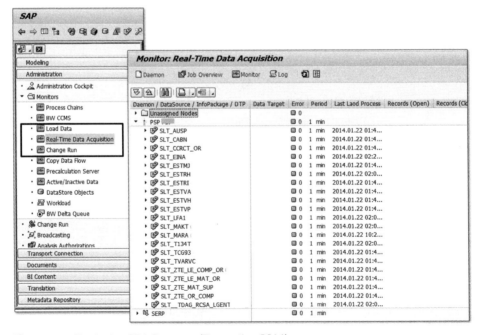

Figure 7.24 Monitoring RDA Daemons (Transaction RSA1)

7.2.4 Monitoring DSO Activations

Since DataStore objects continue to form the foundation of the EDW layer in the LSA and LSA++ architectures, they should be monitored independently for data load and activation issues. DSO issues prevent deltas from loading to subsequent data targets and may require reloads to resolve, so DSOs are critical to the successful processing of data throughout the data flow.

In the Data Warehousing Workbench, under the ADMINISTRATION section (see ❶ in Figure 7.25), the DSO monitor provides a status overview of all DSOs in the system. Here, it is quick and easy to identify any data load or activation errors throughout the data flow for one particular DSO ❷.

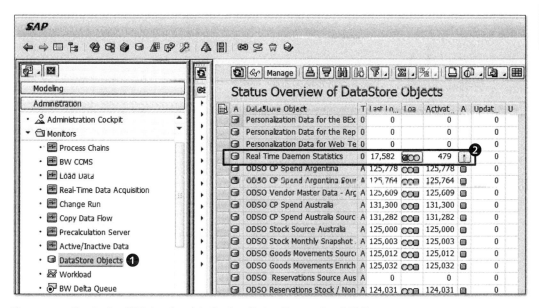

Figure 7.25 Monitoring DSO Load and Activation Status (Transaction RSA1)

7.2.5 Checking Aggregates

Before updated master data (attributes and hierarchies) can be available for use in reporting, it must be activated via a change run, as covered in Chapter 2. Therefore, to ensure that no InfoObjects are omitted and all data is activated in a timely manner, you should monitor change runs daily. Every time master data is loaded, the relevant change runs should be monitored to ensure completion.

The change run monitor is an efficient way to monitor the current status of outstanding change runs. You can access it directly by running report RSDDS_ CHANGERUN_MONITOR, as indicated in ❶ in Figure 7.26, and it can also be accessed in the Data Warehousing Workbench under ADMINISTRATION ❷.

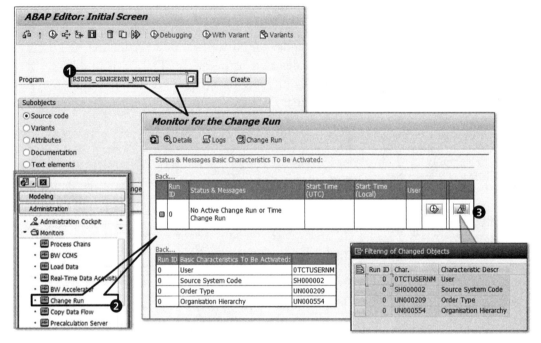

Figure 7.26 Accessing the Change Run Monitor to View the Current Status of CRs (Transactions SE38 and RSA1)

This monitor shows whether a change run is currently in process, as well as the list of InfoObjects that are waiting for a change run or being processed. In Figure 7.26, there is no CR running, but there are four characteristics waiting for a change run. By clicking the InfoObject button ❸, you can select any or all of the characteristics for processing and then execute a change run directly in this monitor.

Aggregates are dependent on CRs for correct and updated data, so all change runs should be processed before checking their status. When the CRs are confirmed as complete, the aggregates monitor can be checked in the Data Warehousing Workbench. You can also access the aggregates monitor directly via Transaction RSDDV.

This monitor quickly shows which aggregates are active and which are filled with data, as seen in Figure 7.27. Any aggregates with a red indicator are not available for reporting or have antiquated data and should be filled, rolled up, or rebuilt.

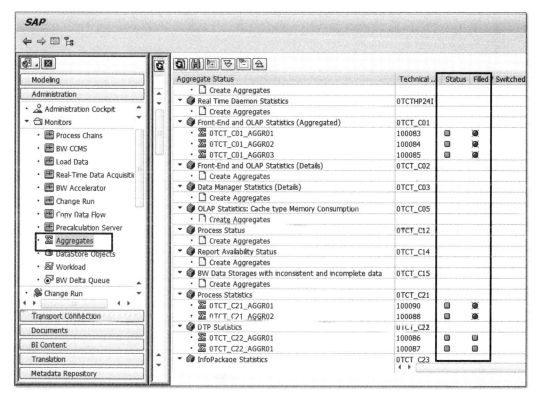

Figure 7.27 Aggregate Status Monitor in the Data Warehousing Workbench (Transaction RSA1)

This concludes our coverage of daily administration and data load monitoring tasks. In the next chapter, we will cover weekly administration and performance-tuning tasks to keep your SAP BW system running smoothly.

Weekly monitoring and administration can prevent small issues from growing into critical issues. Consistent housekeeping keeps the database small and the system operating within healthy limits.

8 Weekly Tasks

This chapter will split its focus between weekly administration tasks (Section 8.1) and weekly performance tuning tasks (Section 8.2).

All of these tasks should be performed by a combination of BW Basis, BW Technical, and/or data load monitoring sub-teams within the support organization. While some of these tasks only need to be performed once weekly, others, such as process chain monitoring, may need constant supervision. We recommend that you consider any opportunity to automate weekly tasks, such as by leveraging SAP Solution Manager to configure thresholds and send alerts by e-mail.

Reporting of performance or systematic issues for weekly checks should be handled the same way as for issues with daily checks. Any sensitive or critical checks should be executed first so that the technical team is knowledgeable and aware of the system's operational health.

Let's first look at weekly administration tasks.

8.1 Weekly Administration Tasks

The first technical resource in the office every Monday should conduct routine weekly administration checks manually as a quick health check of the system's weekend processing. If the system is monitored globally, 24/7, the weekly checks should be scheduled at a time when corrective action is most likely to be taken so that problems can be fixed immediately. Over time, thresholds for normal behavior will be apparent; these thresholds should be documented, and any abnormal behavior or deviations above or below normal should be noted and investigated.

In this section, we will review the following weekly administration tasks:

- Review EarlyWatch Alert
- Rebuild BWA indexes
- Clean up PSA and change logs
- Clean up application logs and trace files
- Execute housekeeping tasks
- Execute RSRV consistency checks

The majority of these administration tasks, such as rebuilding BWA indexes, cleaning up logs, and housekeeping tasks, ensure that your system is operationally healthy and stable enough to support future demand. The remaining administration tasks, such as reviewing the EarlyWatch Alert and executing Transaction RSRV consistency checks, arm you with information about the relative health of your system. Depending on the complexity of your system or the expected resolution, acting on the information provided may need to be handled in a more structured way, such as a project or simply planned in advance as part of the monthly, quarterly, or yearly administration tasks. The first weekly task should always be to check the EarlyWatch Alert for any information.

8.1.1 Reviewing SAP EarlyWatch Alert

The SAP EarlyWatch Alert (EWA) is a free preventive service included in the standard maintenance agreement with SAP. It is designed to help customers take rapid action before potential problems lead to unplanned downtime. The EWA provides customers with information about the stability and performance of their SAP systems, and it focuses on the following aspects:

- Server analysis
- Database analysis
- Configuration analysis
- Application analysis
- Workload analysis

The SAP EarlyWatch Alert is fully integrated with SAP Solution Manager, but it must be activated and scheduled. The EWA collects performance data by running background jobs in each SAP production system. The collected data is sent from each satellite system to the central SAP Solution Manager system for processing and evaluation. The resulting reports provide historical trends of each system's performance to aid in the analysis of performance related issues, as seen in Figure 8.1.

2 Performance Indicators

The following table shows the relevant performance indicators in various system areas.

Area	Indicators	Value	Trend
System Performance	Active Users	785	↘
	Avg. Response Time in Dialog Task	1253 ms	↘
	Max. Dialog Steps per Hour	5351	↘
	Avg. Response Time at Peak Dialog Hour	1054 ms	↗
	Avg. Availability per Week	83 %	→
	Average Response Time in RFC Task	6116 ms	↗
	Max. number of RFCs per hour	64436	↘
	Avg. RFC response time at peak work hour	6129 ms	↗
Hardware Capacity	Max. CPU Utilization on DB Server	41 %	↘
	Max. CPU Utilization on Appl. Server	60 %	→
Database Performance	Avg. DB Request Time in Dialog Task	783 ms	↗
	Avg. DB Request Time in Update Task	39 ms	↗
	Average DB time for RFC	760 ms	→
Database Space Management	DB Size	34626.60 GB	→
	DB Growth Last Month	1713.12- GB	→

Figure 8.1 Historical Trends Shown in Performance Indicators of the EWA

Recommendation

Further analysis services are based on the resulting EWA for each satellite system, such as EarlyWatch Alert for Solutions and Service Level Reporting. See SAP Note 1040343 for more information on EarlyWatch Alert for Solutions.

After the initial configuration and activation in SAP Solution Manager, the first EWA session is automatically created for each system marked for monitoring. By default, all subsequent EWA sessions are scheduled once a week, on Mondays. If the overall rating of the EWA is red, as can be seen by item ❶ in Figure 8.2, the service results are automatically sent to SAP Support. If the overall rating is yellow ❷ or green, results are sent to SAP Support only once every four weeks. It is also possible to have the reports e-mailed automatically to specific e-mail addresses.

If the EWA issues a red or yellow rating, the reasons for the rating are specified right below the rating in the alert overview (see Figure 8.3). More information is provided in the subsequent sections where the alerts were evaluated. Investigate the root cause of the issues and take corrective action.

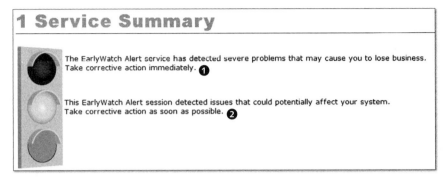

Figure 8.2 Red and Yellow Rating Messages in the EWA

Alerts Decisive For Red Report

▣	Based on the number of SIDs (> 1billion) in your InfoObject(s), system stability problems are expected.

Alert Overview

▣	Secure password policy is not sufficiently enforced.
▣	Security-related SAP HotNews have not been applied in the system.
①	Expensive SQL statements cause load on the database server.
①	Based on the number of aggregates recommended to build or delete, performance problems might exist or are expected.
①	Based on the number of requests (> 15.000) in your InfoProvider(s) severe performance problems might exist or are expected.
①	We found more than 30 ABAP dumps in your system.
①	Standard users have default password.
①	Security weaknesses identified in the Gateway or the Message Server configuration.
①	A high number of users have critical authorizations
①	Hardware resources may have been exhausted with the risk of performance degradation.
①	Based on response times in your ABAP system performance problems may occur.
①	Based on worsened response times in your ABAP system in atleast one time window a bottleneck was detected.

Figure 8.3 The Alert Overview's Justification for the EWA Report Rating

In our experience, many customers ignore EWA reports because the rating does not reflect a specific business need or use case. For example, if the report is always red because of a known and accepted issue, the monitoring team becomes falsely accustomed to the red rating and does not recognize when critical issues do indeed arise. This is a common behavior, but it is extremely reckless! In many cases, the thresholds for specific alerts and their ratings can be adjusted in SAP Solution Manager. If the issue cannot be resolved or is deemed an accepted risk, adjust the rating so that the monitoring team is not lulled into inaction.

In SAP BW systems, the EWA provides a section that analyzes the design, administration, and management of BW-specific areas (see Section 16 in Table 8.1, which lists all the EWA sections and subsections for an SAP BW 7.30 system). The BW Checks section has three subsections:

▸ **BW Administration and Design**

This subsection reports important KPIs specific for SAP BW; identifies the largest SAP BW objects; analyzes the number and types of each InfoProvider; analyzes configuration and design settings that could impact performance; analyzes partitioning, aggregates, and BWA; identifies important SAP Notes that should be applied; reviews number-range buffering; analyzes SAP BW statistics; and reviews SAP BW-specific workloads.

▸ **BW Reporting and Planning**

This subsection analyzes SAP BW runtime statistics and frontend distribution, checks query profiles, identifies the most popular queries and poorest-performing queries, analyzes query definitions, and analyzes OLAP cache usage.

▸ **BW Warehouse Management**

This subsection analyzes dataload statistics; identifies top DTPs, largest requests, and top InfoProviders by load requests and upload volume; and reviews process chain and change run performance.

Section	Title	Subsections
1	Service Summary	▸ Alert Overview ▸ Check Overview
2	Performance Indicators	▸ Performance KPIs
3	Landscape Overview	▸ Products and Components ▸ Servers ▸ Hardware Configuration
4	Service Preparation and Service Data Quality	▸ Service Data Control Center ▸ ST-PI and ST-A/PI Plug-ins ▸ Service Preparation Check ▸ Performance DB ▸ Landscape Service Information ▸ Hardware Capacity Data
5	Software Configuration	▸ Application Release Maintenance ▸ ABAP SP Maintenance ▸ Java SP Maintenance ▸ Database Maintenance ▸ Operating System Maintenance ▸ SAP Kernel Release

Table 8.1 EWA Sections for an SAP BW 7.30 System on Oracle

Section	Title	Subsections
6	Hardware Capacity	▶ Overview System
7	Workload Overview	▶ Workload by Users ▶ Workload by Task Types ▶ Top Applications
8	Performance Overview	▶ Performance Evaluation
9	Trend Analysis	▶ Response Time Trends ▶ Application Profile
10	SAP System Operating	▶ Update Errors ▶ Program Errors (ABAP Dumps)
11	Security	▶ SAP Security Notes ▶ Default Passwords—Standard Users ▶ Password Policy ▶ Gateway and Message Server Security ▶ Users with Critical Authorizations
12	Software Change Management	▶ SAP NetWeaver AS ABAP ▶ SAP NetWeaver AS JAVA
13	Database Performance	▶ Load per User ▶ I/O Performance ▶ Database Parameters
14	Database Administration	▶ Database Growth ▶ Database Release
15	Java System Data	▶ Java VM Heap Size ▶ Availability of Performance Data
16	BW Checks	▶ BW Administration and Design ▶ BW Reporting and Planning ▶ BW Warehouse Management
17	Expensive SQL Statements	▶ Analysis of DB SQL Cache

Table 8.1 EWA Sections for an SAP BW 7.30 System on Oracle (Cont.)

Section	Title	Subsections
18	Trend Analysis	▸ System Activity
		▸ System Operation and Hardware Capacity
19	Appendix	▸ Analysis of Aggregates

Table 8.1 EWA Sections for an SAP BW 7.30 System on Oracle (Cont.)

The EWA is an essential tool for any technical team supporting and monitoring an SAP BW system. It is always the first document that should be requested to assess the status of an existing system because it provides an overview supported by the exact details of every facet of the system, and it usually provides specific clues to solve performance issues and preserve operational health.

By routinely running, monitoring, and acting on the EWA, you can increase system stability and performance for your entire solution landscape. For this reason, we strongly recommend activating and monitoring the EWA for all productive systems.

8.1.2 Rebuilding BWA Indexes

You should routinely monitor BWA indexes to ensure that they are using the appropriate amount of BWA memory. Over time, BWA indexes can grow and become much larger than fact tables in the BI system. Any InfoCube that is fully reloaded after data is selectively deleted (not dropped) is a prime scenario in which the BWA index could double in size after every reload. Another slower growth scenario is an InfoCube, which is compressed with the elimination of zeroes. In both of these scenarios, the deleted or eliminated data still remains in the BWA index but is not used for reporting. As a result, the BWA index consumes more memory than necessary.

To identify these indexes, execute the BI and BWA table comparison check in Transaction RSRV on a periodic basis (see ❶ in Figure 8.4) and rebuild indexes for which there is a significant deviation. In addition to index growth, you should also adjust or rebuild indexes after changes are made to the relevant InfoProvider. If delta indexes are used, routinely merge them with the main index.

Regardless of an index size compared to the fact table, you would be prudent to rebuild the entire index routinely to ensure that memory is being released from the delta indexes. As seen in ❷ in Figure 8.4, Transaction RSRV has a BWA repair utility; it can be scheduled routinely to delete and rebuild all BWA indexes. Due to potentially long run times and the impact on query performance, you should schedule this utility during a period of low system usage by end users when possible.

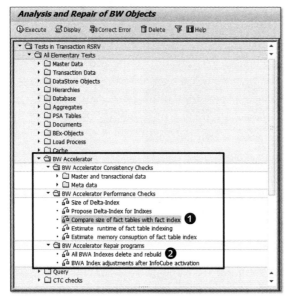

Figure 8.4 BWA Consistency Checks (Transaction RSRV)

However, if the rebuild time for all indexes exceeds any weekly available outage window, it is best to divide indexes into groups and schedule the rebuild of each group of indexes in an alternating manner. For example, in a scenario with two groups, A and B, the rebuilds of one group (A) can be scheduled during the first and second weeks of every month, and the rebuilds of the second group (B) can be scheduled during the third and fourth weeks. When necessary, individual index rebuilds can be deleted and re-created manually in Transaction RSDDB (see Figure 8.5).

Use Transaction RSDDBIAMON2 to access BWA and monitor the indexes on it. As indexes grow in size, you may find that you need to reorganize or redistribute indexes across the blades in the appliance. This capability can be launched from the BW Accelerator Monitor RSDDBIAMON2 as displayed in ❶ of Figure 8.6. The same messages from the monitor can also be seen in the system checks in Transaction RSRV ❷.

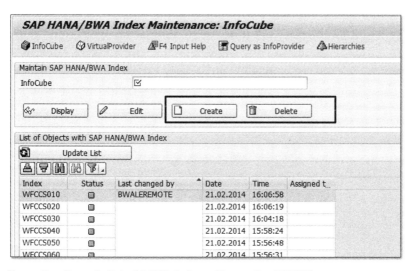

Figure 8.5 Manually Rebuild BWA Indexes (Transaction RSDDB)

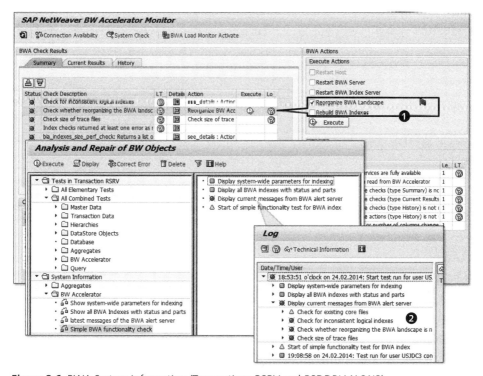

Figure 8.6 BWA System Information (Transactions RSRV and RSDDBIAMON2)

There are additional Transaction RSRV consistency checks available for BWA indexes, which should be used in conjunction with BWA alerts. BWA alerts can be configured via the TREX Admin tool on the BWA itself. These checks can also be executed directly from the index maintenance screen in Transaction RSDDB (see Figure 8.7). These consistency checks should be scheduled on a routine basis.

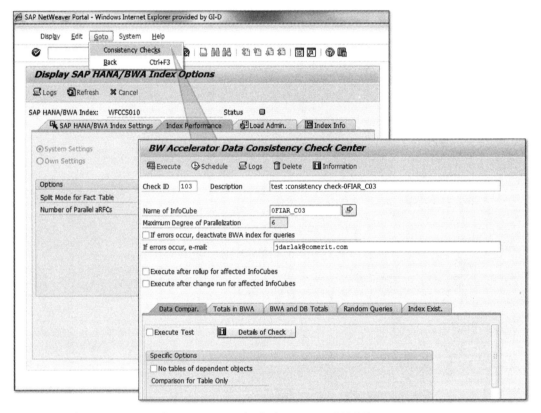

Figure 8.7 BWA Index Consistency Checks (Transaction RSDDB)

8.1.3 Cleaning PSA and Change Logs

During the load processing of large volumes of master and transaction data into SAP BW, there is usually a significant amount of storage consumed by temporary transaction data and system-related metadata. Routine housekeeping activities should remove unused, unwanted, and unneeded data. Regularly performing these activities ensures optimum utilization of system resources and increased system performance.

According to SAP Data Volume Management (DVM) Service, data deletion is one of the four recommended methodologies to check potential database growth. (The other methodologies are avoidance, summarization, and archiving.) Recall from Chapter 2 that one-third of the storage space in the average BW database is temporary data held in PSA and DSO change log tables.

Large PSA and DSO change log tables impact data load performance, increase the downtime for maintenance, and increase the cost of data storage. The size of the PSA and change logs can be explained by the fact that entries in these tables are never updated or overwritten. The only operations on these tables are inserts or deletions. For example, full loads on a periodic basis increase the size of the PSA table much faster than the actual data target, which is either overwritten in the case of a DSO or InfoObject, or dropped and reloaded in the case of an InfoCube. For delta loads, changes to previously extracted records are overwritten in DSOs and InfoObjects or compressed into a single record in InfoCubes (assuming that compression occurs routinely).

From a strategic perspective, the only reasons to retain entries in the PSA tables are to facilitate error resolution and to mitigate the need to re-extract data from sources that are either poor performing or delta capable. In the case of full loads, only the latest PSA entry should be retained, and all other entries can be deleted once the latest entry is successfully loaded into the PSA. For delta loads, a retention period for PSA data should be set based on the risk of data loss (i.e., data should not be deleted from the PSA before it is loaded to all subsequent data targets). In most cases, 15 days is more than sufficient to mitigate this risk. In many cases, a full repair load can be executed to recover any lost deltas without a significant performance impact, so this risk is usually applicable for delta DataSources that require the population of setup tables in the source system, such as LIS DataSources in the logistics cockpit, before full repairs can be carried out.

The deletion strategy for PSA tables should differentiate between master data and transaction data, full loads and delta loads, and DataSources and setup tables. Change logs should be treated like delta loads for transaction data. An additional consideration should be the periodicity of the data load from the source. For example, if a full InfoPackage is loaded monthly, the previous month's load should be retained in the PSA, so the retention period should be 31 days. Table 8.2 illustrates a sample deletion strategy for daily loads in a typical BW system.

Table Type	DataSource	Extraction Mode	Delete Entries Older Than...
PSA	Master data	Full	1 day
PSA	Master data	Delta	3 days
PSA	Transaction data	Full	1 day
PSA	Transaction data	Delta	8 days
PSA	Transaction data with setup table	Delta	15 days
Change log	Transaction data	Delta	8 days

Table 8.2 Sample Deletion Strategy for Daily Load PSA and Change Log Tables

The best way to delete data from the PSA and change log tables is by scheduling the relevant deletion process variants in the process chains after data has been loaded successfully (see Figure 8.8).

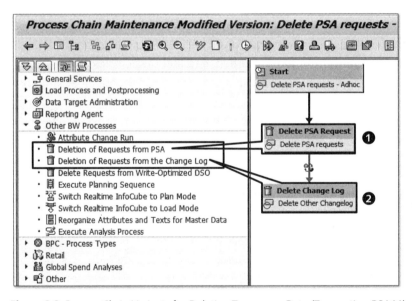

Figure 8.8 Process Chain Variants for Deleting Temporary Data (Transaction RSA11)

These process variants enable flexible deletion using selection criteria, and the parameter screens accept parameters with patterns on DataSource (for PSA tables) and DSOs (for change logs), as illustrated by ❶ in Figure 8.9. The number of days to retain each PSA can be specified in the column identified by ❷, and the deletion can be limited to only those requests that are successfully updated ❸.

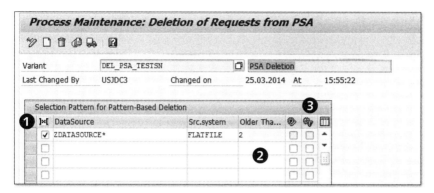

Figure 8.9 Process Variant for Deletion of Requests from the PSA

Even though the acceptance of patterns in the selection criteria simplifies maintenance of the deletion jobs, PSA and change log tables are still too easily omitted from cleansing. To combat this, custom programs published on SCN can help identify those tables with entries that are "unmanaged" or otherwise excluded from existing deletion variants.

For one-time use, PSA tables can be deleted using either program RSPSADEL1 or function module RSATREE_PSA_DELETE_BATCH. We do *not* recommend that you use these programs routinely because PSA deletions should not be scheduled while data is being loaded. Therefore, it is best to schedule the relevant process variants directly in the process chains after data has been loaded. This helps mitigate the risk of database contention by ensuring that these conflicting jobs do not overlap.

Schedule a weekly PSA and change log deletion process chain to "catch" any data loads for which deletions are not scheduled as part of the load process chains. This helps mitigate the risk that a PSA table or change log could grow exponentially, thereby keeping the database growth in check and optimizing system resources.

8.1.4 Cleaning Application Logs

In all SAP systems, there are many log and trace tables that, if left untended, grow over time. Keeping these tables cleansed on a weekly basis ensures optimal performance of the ABAP system overall. This section will cover routine housekeeping jobs that should be executed routinely to minimize the impact of log and trace growth over time.

All application logs are written to table BALDAT—this table is usually one of the largest system tables in most systems. Ironically, many routine housekeeping jobs generate more application logs, which can consume more storage capacity than the housekeeping jobs free up. For example, every request that is deleted from the PSA or change log generates an application log. Therefore, it is important to clean application logs as part of every housekeeping effort. Before cleansing, consider the utility that application logs serve during root cause analysis; some application logs should be retained long enough to be helpful when investigating system events.

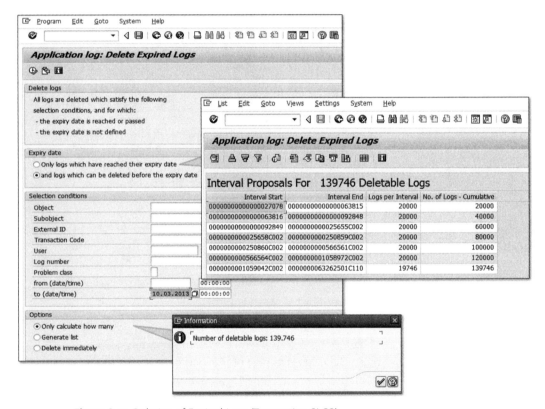

Figure 8.10 Deletion of Expired Logs (Transaction SLG2)

Regardless of their potential utility, at some point, application logs should be cleansed to reclaim that storage capacity and improve the overall performance of administering the system. Remember—the fewer logs in the table, the quicker it is to search for them.

To cleanup application logs, execute Transaction SLG2 or run report SBAL_ DELETE, enter an appropriate date from which to cleanse logs, and select the checkbox to delete logs that can be deleted before their expiry date, as shown in in Figure 8.10. Use the option ONLY CALCULATE HOW MANY to show how many logs can be deleted. Schedule report SBAL_DELETE to delete the application logs on a weekly basis.

8.1.5 Executing BW Housekeeping Task List

As covered in Chapter 1, the task list SAP_BW_HOUSEKEEPING is available for scheduling routine housekeeping tasks that should be executed weekly in all SAP BW systems. By default, the housekeeping task list contains tasks that do the following:

- Repair indexes on InfoCube fact table(s) at the Data Dictionary level
- Re-assign requests written into the incorrect PSA partition
- Ensure request consistencies throughout the PSA landscape
- Ensure that partitioned tables are correctly indexed for the PSA
- Verify DataSource segments' assignment to PSA
- Delete entries that are no longer required in table RSIXW
- Reorganize and delete bookmark IDs and view IDs
- Delete RSTT traces
- Delete BW statistical data
- Check BW metadata with regard to the DDIC
- Clear all OLAP Cache parameters

> **Note**
>
> The coding for the SAP_BW_HOUSEKEEPING task list can be implemented via SAP Note 1829728 for SAP BW 7.x systems.

You can execute and schedule the housekeeping task via Transaction STC01, as shown in ❶ in Figure 8.11. Some of the tasks in this task list require that parameters be entered; these tasks each contain a "text editing" icon in the parameter column, as illustrated by ❷.

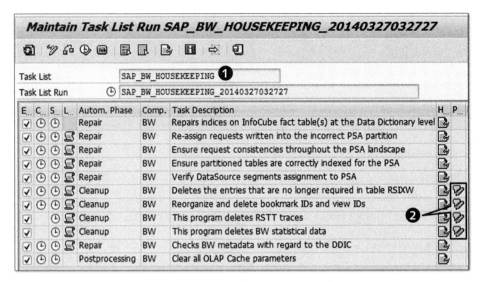

Figure 8.11 Task List SAP_BW_HOUSEKEEPING (Transaction STC01)

Enter the parameter values based on the data-retention strategy and save the entries as a variant so that the same values can be used when scheduling the task list. To check the status or logs of any current or previous task list execution, use Transaction STC02.

8.1.6 Executing Other Housekeeping Tasks

In addition to cleansing application logs and executing the SAP BW housekeeping task list, you should execute the jobs listed in Table 8.3 on a weekly basis. In most cases, the report can be scheduled, but the results should be monitored for exceptions or errors.

Report/Transaction	Administration Task
RSBATCH_DEL_MSG_PARM_DTPTEMP (use parameters DEL_MSG = 3, DEL_PAR = 3 and DEL_DTP = X)	Delete BW background management messages and parameters
RSSM_ERRORLOG_CLEANUP	Reorganize PSA error log
RSAR_PSA_CLEANUP_DEFINITION	Check and clean PSA tables

Table 8.3 Additional Housekeeping Jobs

Report/Transaction	Administration Task
RSB_ANALYZE_ERRORLOG	Analyze DTP error log
RSBM_ERRORLOG_DELETE	Delete inconsistent Error DTPs
RSPC_INSTANCE_CLEANUP	Delete old Process Chain logs
RSPC_LOG_DELETE	Delete old Process Chain logs
RS_FIND_JOBS_WITHOUT_VARIANT	Delete jobs without variant
RSBTCDEL2	Delete old job logs
RSSODFRE	Reorganize hidden folder Office Documents
RSBCS_REORG	Reorganize SAP Office/Business Workplace documents
RSTBPDEL	Check and clean up table change logs (DBTABLOG)
Transaction SM58	Check and delete old tRFC Queues
SAP_DROP_TMPTABLES	Delete temporary BW database tables
RSPO1041 (first run the consistency check from TemSe Data Storage in Transaction SP12)	Reorganize TemSe and Spool
RSTS0024	Delete orphaned job log
RSTT_TRACE_DELETE	Delete BW RSTT Traces
RSAN_UT_RESULT_DROP_RESULTS	Purge intermediary results from APD
RSBPSTDE	Delete statistic data from job runtime statistics
RSM13002	Delete update requests
RSARFCER	Delete old tRFC entries
SWNC_COLLECTOR_CLEAN_SWNCMONI	Delete old Transaction ST03N source system data
RSAR_PSA_NEWDS_MAPPING_CHECK	Check and repair inconsistent PSA request/tables
Transaction RSECADMIN	Delete authorization logs and disable log recording for all users

Table 8.3 Additional Housekeeping Jobs (Cont.)

As an alternative, create a custom task list in Transaction STC01 to include as many of these tasks as feasible, or enhance the default housekeeping task list.

8.1.7 Executing RSRV Consistency Checks

In Chapter 3, we covered elementary Transaction RSRV checks for master data and transaction data, which are perfect for investigating specific issues. Scheduling so many elementary tests for each InfoProvider would be a laborious burden and likely not worth the effort. Fortunately for you, SAP has provided combined tests (see Figure 8.12), which bundle many of the important elementary tests for ease of scheduling. These combined tests should be evaluated and scheduled for routine batch processing.

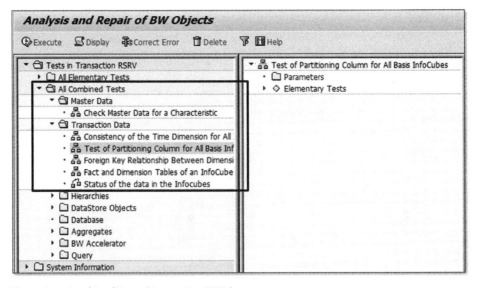

Figure 8.12 Combined Tests (Transaction RSRV)

Batch scheduling the combined tests proves valuable only if the logs are analyzed for errors or warnings. Therefore, you should analyze the logs using Transaction SLG1 for any combined tests that are deemed valuable to schedule on a weekly basis, as shown in Figure 8.13. The results of combined checks can also be monitored in the CCMS, as covered in Chapter 6.

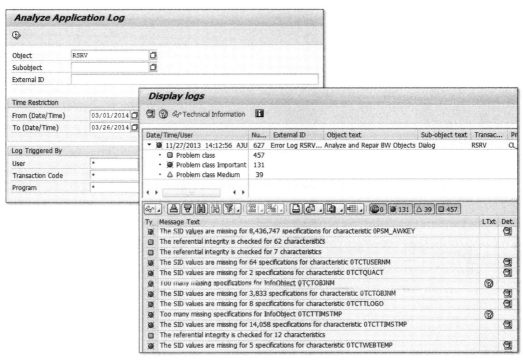

Figure 8.13 Viewing Application Logs (Transaction SLG1)

8.2 Weekly Performance Tuning

Let's take a look at tasks that are critical to maintaining optimal performance in the system for both end users who are running reports and support teams who are executing data loads and administering the data warehouse. We'll examine the following:

▶ Monitoring BI statistics

▶ Compressing InfoCubes

▶ Rebuilding DB indexes and statistics

▶ Monitoring cache usage

The first task is monitoring BI statistics.

8.2.1 Monitoring BI Statistics

SAP BW records runtime statistics for processes and events in SAP BEx, the Online Analytic Processor (OLAP), and warehouse management. The system records runtimes for statistical events by calculating the difference between the start and end times and subtracting the times for other events called from within each event. Technical BI Content delivers predefined SAP BW objects for analyzing statistics data.

The BW Administration Cockpit provides a central point of entry for monitoring the performance of SAP BW systems. Based on the technical BI Content, this enables runtime analysis and status of SAP BW objects and processes in the SAP Enterprise Portal or using SAP BusinessObjects Dashboards.

> **Note**
>
> For more information, see SAP Note 934848, "Collective note: (FAQ) BI Administration Cockpit)."

SAP BW statistics are recorded for the following areas:

- ▶ SAP BEx query runtimes (actions on the front end and in the Online Analytic Processor, including BW Integrated Planning)
- ▶ Runtimes of sub-processes in SAP HANA/BWA index maintenance
- ▶ Runtimes of sub-processes of analytic indexes
- ▶ Runtimes for performing planning functions
- ▶ Runtimes and status of data transfer and data processing in the Data Warehouse

> **Note**
>
> The system always records runtime and status statistics of data loading and data processing but does not, by default, record statistics for the DTPs. These are deactivated in the default setting and can be activated in table RSDDSTATOBJLEVEL. For more information, see SAP Note 966964.

Depending on the area, the system records statistics in tables RSDDSTAT* or UPC_STATISTIC*. For statistical analyses in warehouse management processes, technical BI Content uses tables RSMDATASTATE, RSMDATASTATE_EXT, RSDDSTATDTP, RSBKREQUEST, RSBSOURCEPROP, RSPCLOGCHAIN, and RSPCPROCESSLOG.

The data from these statistics tables is stored in technical BI Content InfoProviders, which are then assigned to one of the MultiProviders listed in Table 8.4. Technical BI Content queries and web templates provide ready-made views of the information for flexible analysis.

MultiProvider	Object Description
0TCT_MC01	Front-end and OLAP statistics (aggregated)
0TCT_MC02	Front-end and OLAP statistics (details)
0TCT_MC03	Data manager statistics (details)
0TCT_MC05	OLAP statistics: cache-type memory consumption
0TCT_MC06	OLAP statistics: cache vs. SHM
0TCT_MC07	OLAP statistics: query memory consumption
0TCT_MC11	BI object request status
0TCT_MC12	Process status
0TCT_MC14	Report availability status
0TCT_MC15	Data storages with inconsistent and incomplete data
0TCT_MC21	Process statistics
0TCT_MC22	DTP statistics
0TCT_MC23	InfoPackage statistics
0TCT_MC25	Database volume statistics
0TCT_MC31	BWA statistics: CPU consumption
0TCT_MC32	BWA statistics: InfoProvider memory consumption
0TCT_MCA1	Front-end and OLAP statistics (highly aggregated)
0TCT_MCWS	Workspace MultiProvider

Table 8.4 Technical BI Content MultiProviders

While analyzing the statistics data using the technical BI Content provided is mandatory, customers can and should define their own queries and web templates for specific analysis scenarios. See Figure 8.14 for an example of a simple query on aggregated OLAP statistics showing the percentage of runtime by component for a rolling 24 months. This data is reported from InfoCube `OTCT_C01` and shows that DB TIME has been steadily increasing over time. This indicates that database growth has been adversely impacting query performance, and steps should be taken to slow, stop, or reverse this trend. Potential solutions include compressing InfoCubes, rebuilding DB indexes, and tuning aggregates. If none of these solutions are satisfactory, consider installing BWA (which may be a regretful purchase) or migrating to SAP HANA.

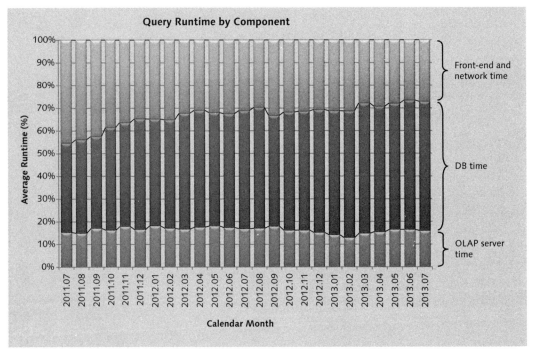

Figure 8.14 Front-End Query Statistics

Statistics queries and web reports should be executed and monitored for exceptions to average runtimes on a weekly basis. You should investigate and resolve any significant exceptions or deviations from normal.

8.2.2 Compressing InfoCubes

During compression, all records with the same key values across the data-package partitions in the F-fact table are aggregated into a single record in the E-fact table. When F-fact table requests are compressed, their respective data partitions are dropped from the F-fact table. In this way, the data volume of the InfoCube can be managed when a high number of delta records results in substantial growth. Compression provides performance benefits from a data loading perspective, as well as from a reporting perspective.

Ideally, you should execute compression after each data load, although it is not necessarily a critical path item. The more frequently an InfoCube is compressed, however, the quicker both queries against it and data loads to it execute. The only reason not to compress data is that the request needs to be dropped from the InfoCube and reloaded from the source. However, because data should always be staged in a DSO before feeding a cube, this reasoning is usually without merit.

Schedule a weekly compression process chain to compress all InfoCubes for which compression is not executed immediately after each data load. In most cases, compression with elimination of zeroes provides the most benefit by deleting all records from the E-fact table for which all key figures equal zero—as long as the zero-records are not required for business logic in reporting. Monitor this process chain exactly like any other process chain. If BWA indexes are also rebuilt weekly, ensure that you execute compression before rebuilding the index.

8.2.3 Rebuilding DB Indexes and Statistics

Like BWA indexes, database indexes can grow and become cumbersome over time. To combat this phenomenon, you should also rebuild DB indexes on a routine basis. While DB indexes can be rebuilt manually when managing InfoCubes ❶, as seen in Figure 8.15, the deletion and rebuilding of indexes should be scheduled via process chains on a weekly basis. You can delete and repair DB indexes in dialog mode or delete and re-create them in a batch.

The database statistics are used by the system to optimize both query and compression performance. Even when the InfoCube is indexed in BWA, it is important to keep the database statistics up to date. It is possible to schedule automatic recalculation of the database statistics after each data load in the process chains. At a minimum, we recommend that you update the statistics after every one million new records have been loaded into an InfoCube.

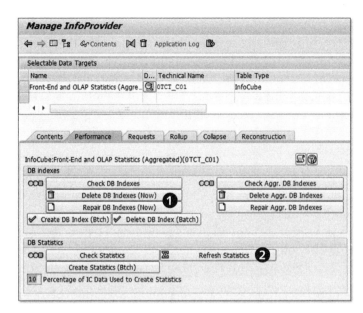

Figure 8.15 DB Index Rebuilding Using the InfoCube Manage Screen

The status of the database statistics can be checked from the InfoCube maintenance screen, as seen by ❷ in Figure 8.15. You can adjust the sample size as
needed. The button CHECK STATISTICS confirms whether the statistics are up to date
(green), are out of date (yellow), or do not exist (red). Use RECALCULATE STATISTICS
to create or update statistics in the background.

Calculating statistics for InfoProviders should also be scheduled weekly via process chains or directly via an OS-level command for the database installed, where
it may be possible to specify thresholds to limit the job to InfoProviders for which
only a specific percentage (usually 5-20%) of the base data has changed.

8.2.4 Monitoring Cache Usage

In SAP BW systems, the size of the global cache depends on the shared memory
buffer, which is defined by the profile parameter `rsdb/esm/buffersize_kb`. The
global cache setting can be maintained in Transaction RSRCACHE and should not
exceed 90% of the shared-memory buffer.

The cache monitor can be accessed via Transaction RSRT, as shown in Figure 8.16.
Check the size of the global and local cache buffers and the number of objects in
their consumption.

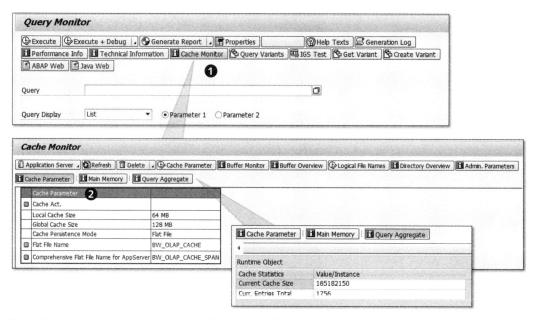

Figure 8.16 Access to the Cache Monitor (Transaction RSRT)

Alternatively, you can access the cache monitor directly via Transaction RSR-CACHE, as shown in Figure 8.17. From the hierarchical display of the MAIN MEMORY overview, the cache buffer size of every query object can be checked. Identify extraordinarily large query object buffer sizes and remediate, if necessary.

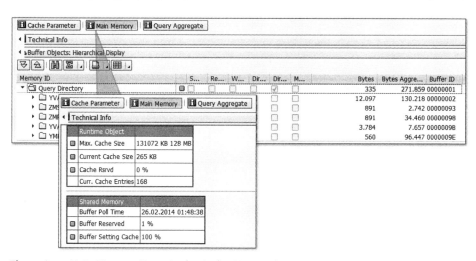

Figure 8.17 Main Memory Usage in the Cache Monitor (Transaction RSRCACHE)

Our next chapter covers monthly administration and performance-tuning tasks to keep your SAP BW system running smoothly.

Monthly monitoring and administration tasks take more effort and dedication than weekly or daily tasks. While these monthly tasks are not always easy to tackle, the results pay huge dividends.

9   Monthly Tasks

This chapter will split its focus between monthly administration monitoring tasks (Section 9.1) and monthly performance tasks (Section 9.2). As with previous chapters, all of these tasks should be performed by a combination of SAP Basis, SAP BW technical, and/or data load monitoring sub-teams within the support organization. While most of these tasks need to be performed only once monthly, others, such as archiving or near-lining storage, may need constant execution. Any opportunity to automate monthly tasks, such as leveraging SAP Solution Manager to configure thresholds and send alerts by e-mail, should be considered.

Monthly tasks generally require more planning and coordination to execute than a single technical resource can handle on a single day. Usually, these tasks are conducted once per month, but not all at once.

Reporting of performance or systematic issues for monthly checks should be handled the same as for issues with daily or weekly checks. Any sensitive or critical checks should be executed first so that the technical team is knowledgeable and aware of the system's operational health.

Wherever possible, assign responsibility for each task to a specific resource and set expectations by providing clear and attainable goals, such as "remove all red results from RSRV checks within six months" or "prepare a monthly forecast of storage capacity by the last day of each month." These types of instructions help ensure that these tasks are not swept under the rug when they become challenging to complete.

Like weekly tasks, monthly tasks can be divided into administration and performance tuning tasks, although the differentiation is not always crystal clear. Many administration tasks improve performance, while the performance tasks can also be quite administrative in nature. Let's begin by examining the monthly administration tasks.

9.1   Monthly Administration Tasks

In this section, we will review the following monthly administration tasks in no particular order of importance:

- Schedule a system restart
- Change portal settings
- Collect BWA usage
- Check SAP Notes
- Execute RSRV cleanup tasks
- Action EWA issues
- Forecast storage capacity

Completing these administration tasks on a monthly basis not only improves the overall health of your SAP BW system, but also provides a measure of stability and helps prepare the application for future growth.

9.1.1   Scheduling System Restart

The first administration task that should be carried out on a monthly basis is a full restart of the SAP BW system and its related applications. Over time, the accumulation of changes made to SAP applications and their databases can present the risk that the system will not restart properly in the event of an outage. On one hand, some profile parameters do not take effect until the system is restarted—if they are changed without an immediate restart, the change may be forgotten the next time the system is restarted. If the changed memory parameters are incorrect or invalid, the system may not start or may suffer other performance issues, and no one will know why. On the other hand, in UNIX systems, some changes can be made while the system is running that are not permanent unless coded in a text file. If these temporary changes are not made permanent and are also forgotten, the system may not perform well after the next restart, and no one will know why.

To mitigate the risk of these types of changes being forgotten, you should restart the system on a monthly basis. Schedule a monthly outage time, agreed upon by both the business and IT sides, when all the SAP systems in the landscape can be recycled—that is, stopped and restarted. This practice provides a scheduled opportunity to activate profile parameter changes, limit the impact of any temporary OS-level changes, and confirm that the system can be restarted.

> **Recommendation**
>
> A scheduled monthly restart is the best way to mitigate the risk that the system will not restart. The restart should be scheduled during a period of low usage, such as early Sunday mornings during the third weekend of each month.

Before restarting any SAP NetWeaver system, check the status of any running jobs (both batch jobs and data loads) and check for any users who may be logged on. Any running jobs will be terminated by the restart and will need to be rescheduled manually. Any data loads that are terminated will need to be cleansed from data targets before being restarted. Any jobs scheduled for the time the system is down will start automatically when the system is up and running. To check the activity on the SAP system, conduct the following checks:

▸ **Global process overview**

Check all system activity by calling the global process overview via Transaction SM66, as shown in Figure 9.1. This transaction shows all activity running in the system across all application servers. For more detail on activity using background processes, check for actively running jobs by calling the Job Overview via Transaction SM37, as shown previously in Figure 7.17. If the running jobs are data loads, check their status by calling Transaction RSMO.

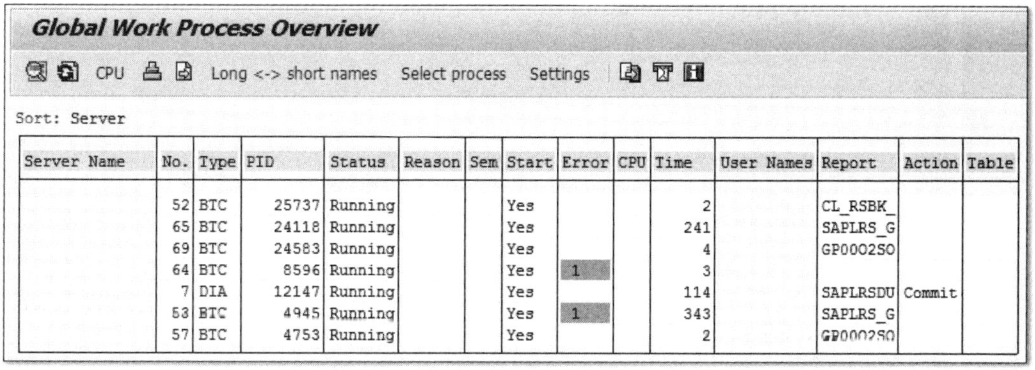

Global Work Process Overview

CPU   Long <-> short names   Select process   Settings

Sort: Server

Server Name	No.	Type	PID	Status	Reason	Sem	Start	Error	CPU	Time	User Names	Report	Action	Table
	52	BTC	25737	Running			Yes			2		CL_RSBK_		
	65	BTC	24118	Running			Yes			241		SAPLRS_G		
	69	BTC	24583	Running			Yes			4		GP0002SO		
	64	BTC	8596	Running			Yes	1		3				
	7	DIA	12147	Running			Yes			114		SAPLRSDU	Commit	
	53	BTC	4945	Running			Yes	1		343		SAPLRS_G		
	57	BTC	4753	Running			Yes			2		GP0002SO		

Figure 9.1 Global Work Process Overview (Transaction SM66)

In most cases, the restart should be deferred until the running jobs are finished and the system is idle. If an external job scheduler is used to trigger batch jobs and data loads, ensure that the external system has put all jobs on hold during the restart procedure.

▸ **Active users**

Check which users are logged on by calling the USER LIST via Transaction SM04 (by application server) and/or Transaction AL08 (system-wide). As shown in Figure 9.2, this transaction identifies the total number of users logged on, from which terminals, and to which client. It also shows the most recent transaction each user has called.

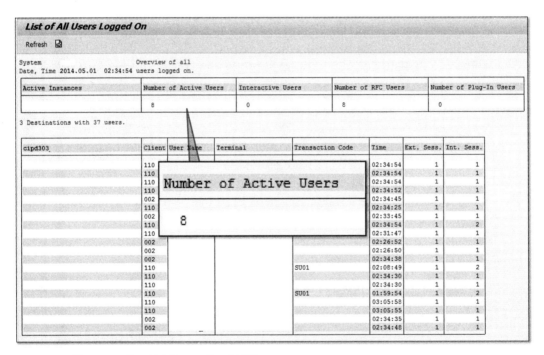

Figure 9.2 User List (Tranasction AL08)

Before stopping the system or performing any maintenance, it is always a good habit to inform users by posting a system message. You can post system messages by calling Transaction SM02, as shown in Figure 9.3.

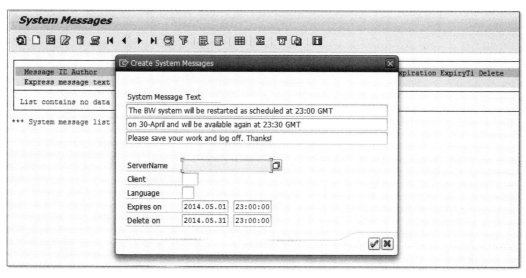

Figure 9.3 Posting a System Message (Transaction SM02)

To ensure that no requests or data are lost when restarting the system, use the soft shutdown utility—this is also known as a "graceful shutdown." A *soft shutdown* executes actions, known as states, in a specific order, as documented in Table 9.1. Some states have a timeout that can be configured using profile parameters. If the timeout is exceeded, the soft shutdown stops waiting and moves on to the next state.

State	Description	Wait Type
CHECK_SERVER	Check if server can be shut down	Waiting without timeout
CHANGE_STATE	Change server state from *active* to *shutdown*	No waiting
WAIT_FOR_LOAD_BALANCE_UPDATE	Wait for RFC/HTTP clients to stop calling server for load balancing	Waiting with timeout
J2EE_SHUTDOWN	Trigger AS Java shutdown (dual stack only)	No waiting
DISABLE_EXTERNAL_LOGIN	Disable external SAPgui logins	No waiting

Table 9.1 Soft Shutdown Actions in Sequence

State	Description	Wait Type
DISABLE_SCHEDULES	Deactivate scheduling (batch jobs, BG-RFC, QRFC)	No waiting
WAIT_FOR_END_OF_LONG_RUNNER	Wait for end of long-running tasks (BTC, UPD, etc.)	Waiting without timeout
WAIT_FOR_END_OF_EXCLUSIVE_ACTIONS	Wait for end of exclusive actions (kernel and ABAP)	Waiting with timeout
WAIT_FOR_END_OF_SESSIONS	Wait for end of active RFC/ITS sessions	Waiting without timeout
TERMINATE_PERIODIC_TASKS	Terminate kernel-internal periodic tasks	No waiting
WAIT_FOR_END_OF_J2EE	Wait for end of J2EE (dual stack only)	Waiting with timeout
J2EE_HARD_SHUTDOWN	Terminate AS Java with hard shutdown (dual stack only)	No waiting
CLOSE_LISTEN_PORTS	Close ports to GUI, RFC, and HTTP communication	No waiting
WAIT_FOR_IDLE_WPS	Wait until all work processes are idle and dispatcher queue is empty	Waiting with timeout
HALT	Shutdown servers	No waiting

Table 9.1 Soft Shutdown Actions in Sequence (Cont.)

Note

Because some states do not have a timeout, the soft shutdown cannot be guaranteed to complete by a specific time.

You can access the soft shutdown function by calling the Computing Center Management System (CCMS) Transaction RZ03, as illustrated in Figure 9.4. In SAP BW systems, process chains continue to run during the wait time for long-running jobs, but the background scheduler will not start new process chains during the soft shutdown.

During a soft shutdown, background jobs for real-time data acquisition (RDA) daemons are terminated early, but the daemons are not stopped, and open requests are not closed. Instead, open requests for daemons are scheduled using immediate start but do not run until the system is restarted. To stop the daemons and close requests during the shutdown, use the BW-specific report RS_SYSTEM_SHUTDOWN before the soft shutdown and after the restart. This report stops and restarts process chains and RDA daemons and closes open requests (see Figure 9.5).

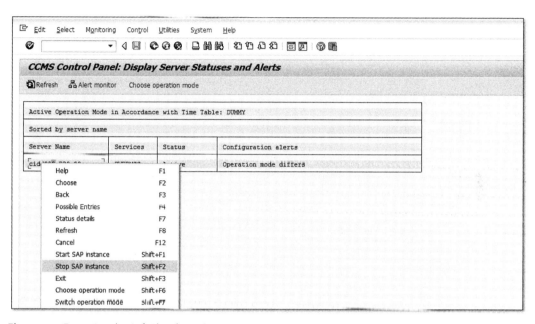

Figure 9.4 Executing the Soft Shutdown (Transaction RZ03)

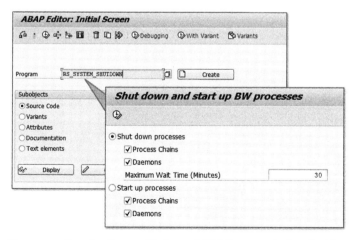

Figure 9.5 Stopping Process Chains and RDA Daemons before Shutdown (Transaction SE38)

487

If the soft shutdown cannot be used due to timing issues (i.e., if there is no time to wait for all the states to complete), the startsap and stopsap commands can be used from the OS-level command line. The command line syntax and options for the new style of these commands are as follows:

```
stopsap | startsap [-t | -task <task>] [-i | -instance <instance>] [-v |
-vhost "<virtual hostname>[ <virtual hostname>]*"][-c | -check] [-h |
-help] [-V | -VERSION] [-C | -checkVHost]
```

Table 9.2 gives a list of valid values for the instance parameters in the command line syntax.

Parameter Name	Description
DVEBMGS<nn>	ABAP central instance
D<nn>	ABAP dialog instance
ASCS<nn>	ABAP central services instance (ASCS instance)
SCS<nn>	Java central services instance (SCS instance)
J<nn>	Java central instance
TRX<nn>	TREX instance
ERS<nn>	Enqueue replication server instance (ERS instance)
SMDA<nn>	Diagnostics agent instance
W<nn>	Web services instance
G<nn>	Gateway instance

Table 9.2 Parameters for <instance>, Where <nn> Is the Instance Number

Recommendation

If the soft shutdown is not possible, execute reports BTCTRNS1 and RS_SYSTEM_SHUTDOWN before the shutdown to ensure that no new jobs are started during the shutdown. Execute reports RS_SYSTEM_SHUTDOWN and BTCTRNS2 after the restart to schedule the jobs again and start jobs that were scheduled to start during shutdown.

While the SAP BW system is recycled, all other related and dependent systems, such as pre-calculation servers, the Java stack, and the portal should also be recycled. Whenever these dependent systems are restarted, it is also a good opportunity to activate changes to them. However, some systems, such as the SAP Enterprise Portal, require additional considerations, which are covered in the next section.

9.1.2 Changing Portal Settings

Whether or not the portal is being recycled, you should implement changes to the portal settings at least once per month, or end-user performance may suffer — especially if client-side caching is enabled. Caching improves response time and overall system performance by reducing the load on the information source in the portal. Client-side caching further enhances the performance of the portal by storing web content on the client browser.

Client-side caching is a critical tool used to combat high response times and is extremely useful in global networks with high latency at remote sites. Of course, the users' browser settings must not be set to clear the cache every time they exit the browser, or the client-side caching will have no effect on performance, and all portal content will need to be downloaded every time the users restart their browsers.

For caching to be effective, the cache validity period must be set to an appropriate length of time. This is a difficult balance to achieve because the validity period must be set long enough that unchanged content is not downloaded frequently, but not so long that changes are never downloaded without manual intervention. If the content is changed but the validity period never expires, the changed content is never downloaded to users' browsers, which could result in reporting inconsistencies, incompatibilities between content objects, or even explicit errors when running reports. The only solution is to have users clear their browser caches, but this can communicate the wrong message.

Recommendation

If the client-side caching validity period is set to 7 days, new content is downloaded only after seven days: the validity period of seven days is then resident in every object downloaded on the user's PC, so changes to those objects are not downloaded until seven days have elapsed and the validity of those objects has expired. To make changes effective on a specific date, you must change the validity period seven days in advance by setting the validity period to 1 day. After seven days, the validity period expires in all users' browsers. Users then automatically download the objects again, with a one-day validity period. If the content is changed at this point, all portal users download the new content within the next 24 hours. After the content is changed, the validity period should be reset to 7 days.

This recommended process slightly impacts performance for end users during the seven days preceding the change, but only during the first access for each day. Less than optimal performance for seven days is more tolerable than instability and errors caused by inconsistencies in the users' cache for seven days after the change!

The remaining administration tasks have limited impacts on the end users and do not require system downtime. The remaining administration tasks all share one attribute in common: they all include monitoring aspects of the current system's health and behavior. The next task ensures that no known high-priority issues with the SAP application are unresolved in the system.

9.1.3 Checking SAP Notes

Applying SAP Notes to any SAP BW system should not be seen as a one-time endeavor to be performed as part of the upgrade to SAP BW 7.40 or the application of a new *support package stack* (SPS). Applying SAP Notes should be considered an important monthly activity to keep known issues from affecting the stability of the BI system.

The first step in this activity is to check the SAP Service Marketplace for relevant SAP Notes for each support pack in the system. Even after an SPS upgrade, especially if the BI upgrade strategy is to go to support pack $n - 1$, where n is the currently available support pack, there are already hundreds of SAP Notes released for that stack level.

Note

As of the writing of this chapter, Support Package 6 (SP6) was available for SAP BW 7.40, and SAP Notes were already published for SP7, SP8, and SP9.

The easiest way to check the SAP Service Marketplace for all relevant notes is to search on the technical name for the subsequent support packages that have not been applied in the system. For example, any SAP BW system at the latest support package (currently SP6) would search for notes delivered by SP7, SP8, and SP9. To do this, execute three separate searches on SAPKW74007, SAPKW74008, and SAPKW74009, as illustrated by ❶ in Figure 9.6. The results list specified the number of relevant notes ❷, which can be downloaded as a CSV file ❸.

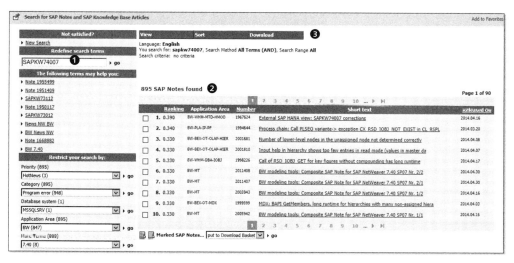

Figure 9.6 Check the SAP Service Marketplace for Relevant SAP Notes

After downloading the SAP Notes to a CSV file and formatting it in Excel, you can filter the list of notes for those that should be applied to the system, as illustrated in Figure 9.7. First, identify the relevant application areas ❶ and then filter on the category ❷ and priority ❸. At a minimum, choose category PROGRAM ERROR and priority CORRECTION WITH HIGH PRIORITY. The resulting list of notes can be checked against the SAP Note browser in Transaction SNOTE to confirm whether they have already been applied. As part of this monthly activity, you should download and apply any that are not already in the system.

Application Area	SAP Note Number	Version	Short Text	Changed on	Category	Priority
BW-BEX-OT-DBIF	1989112	2	Listcube functionality when downloading entries to adhoc DB	20140403	Program error	Correction with high priority
BW-BEX-ET-XC	1990572	3	Errors when publishing or transporting Xcelsius Dashboards	20140320	Program error	Correction with high priority
BW-BCT-TCT	1463442	7	Changes to RSTC webdynpro controller classes	20140327	Program error	Correction with high priority
BW-WHM-DBA-MD	1997021	3	InfoObject master data maintenance - collective corrections #3	20140402	Program error	Correction with high priority
BW-BEX-OT-OLAP	1997200	2	Query result does not show any data after upgrading	20140407	Program error	Correction with high priority
BW-BEX-OT	1999988	1	Infoprovider defaults for Request Status or Nearline Storage not used after BW7	20140417	Program error	Correction with high priority
BW-WHM-DST-TRF	2001332	3	Write-Optimized DSO: Missing table entries for partitioning	20140404	Program error	Correction with high priority
BW-WHM-MTD-HMOD	2006703	1	Access using a 'ZERO' object reference is not possible	20140417	Program error	Correction with high priority
BW-WHM-DST-TRF	2009927	1	SP33:Syntax errors during migration of transfer or update rules to transfromati	20140429	Program error	Correction with high priority
BW-WHM-DST-DTP	2012405	2	VirtualProvider: Runtime error OBJECTS_NOT_CHAR in program SAPLRSOA	20140502	Program error	Correction with high priority
BW-BEX-OT-BIA	2012482	1	Error during batch parallelization	20140502	Program error	Correction with high priority
BW-BEX-ET-WJR-BICS	1864140	3	BICS: Linked node instead of "real" node used for slicer	20140406	Program error	Correction with high priority
BW-BEX-OT-OLAP	1963880	2	Formula exception aggregation: _LRECH_BEFORE_XFEMS-03-	20140113	Program error	Correction with high priority
BW-WHM-DST-ARC	1966432	1	Event-based Backup Automation does not work anymore with IQ 16.0 SP 3	20140127	Program error	Correction with high priority

Figure 9.7 Identifying Relevant SAP Notes in Excel

491

While the example in Figure 9.6 and Figure 9.7 deals with only the component SAP_BW, the same process of identifying important SAP Notes and applying them to the system can and should be conducted for all components installed in the SAP NetWeaver system, including SAP_BASIS, SAP_ABA, and SAP_GWFND. Identify the support package level for all installed software components by going to menu item SYSTEM • STATUS and clicking the DETAIL button under the COMPONENT VERSION field (see Figure 1.1 for an example). Then, search on increments of the installed support package levels in the SAP Service Marketplace.

In addition to applying new notes, you may need to reapply existing notes. Over time, SAP releases updates to existing SAP Notes that may have already been applied to the system during the last support package stack application, as part of this monthly activity, or to resolve specific issues. To check for inconsistent notes, call Transaction SNOTE and click the button DOWNLOAD SAP NOTES AGAIN in Figure 9.8.

The system checks with the SAP Service Marketplace for new versions of previously applied notes and prepares a list of those that have been updated. After you download the list of updated SAP Notes, those with updated solutions (not simply updated note descriptions) are labeled as INCONSISTENT and should be re-applied immediately.

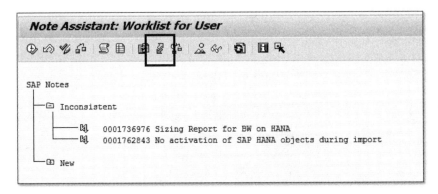

Figure 9.8 Checking for Inconsistent SAP Notes (Transaction SNOTE)

Considering that it is usually quite difficult to explicitly test the changes applied via SAP Notes, a standard set of test scripts for regression testing should be developed for the critical data loads, reports, and activities performed in the system. The regression test scripts can then be executed to determine whether the applied SAP Notes have introduced any issues before promoting them to production.

Alternatively, applying the notes; leaving them in the development and QA systems for an extended period of time, such as two to four weeks; and monitoring for issues may provide enough assurance that no bugs have been introduced. The efficacy of this approach depends on the level of activity on-going in the development and QA systems and, therefore, may be a risky approach to regression testing.

With the SAP application up to date with respect to SAP-provided bug fixes for known issues and the latest round of important SAP Notes, it is time to take action on the system-specific issues identified during the weekly checks.

9.1.4 Taking Action on the EarlyWatch Alert

Recall from the previous chapter that we recommend reviewing the EWA on a weekly basis; it should be e-mailed directly to a designee who is responsible for reviewing and escalating any warnings or alerts raised by SAP about the BW system or its usage.

However, like the consistency checks in the previous section, resolution of issues identified by the EWA may take considerable planning and effort to resolve. All EWA issues should be captured in a backlog issue list; categorized by responsible team (infrastructure, Basis, BW application, etc.); prioritized; and worked using a tactical approach, such as the agile scrum methodology, which is discussed in more detail in Chapter 12.

You should hold progress reviews as often as necessary to ensure that progress is being made, but no less frequently than monthly. As higher-priority items are resolved, medium- and lower-priority items can be addressed.

The next level of system-specific issues relates specifically to the data quality in the SAP BW application. These data quality and consistency issues are also identified as part of another weekly administration task.

9.1.5 Executing RSRV Cleanup Tasks

As covered in the previous chapter, Transaction RSRV consistency checks should be scheduled and executed on a weekly basis and monitored for errors. In many cases, errors can be resolved by running the failed Transaction RSRV check in repair mode. For tasks that can be repaired easily, there is no reason to delay once the error is known. If an error is found during the weekly check, it should also be resolved during the weekly check.

However, for some of the consistency checks, error resolution requires manual tasks and considerably more effort than simply executing the check in repair mode. For these errors, resolution must be planned in advance and may require some sort of downtime, such as a period of no data loading or a period when no end users are logged on to the system and executing queries.

These types of errors should be planned for and resolved on a monthly basis when downtime can be scheduled, if necessary. The first part of this activity is to plan which errors will be resolved in a given month. The easiest way to identify which consistency checks have resulted in errors is to use the BI monitor in the CCMS. The BI monitor should be active in all SAP BW systems since version 7.30, but if not, you can configure it by calling Transaction RZ20, as shown in Figure 9.9. The BI Monitor can be found under SAP BI Monitors ❶. There are additional standard CCMS monitor templates that may also be of interest ❷.

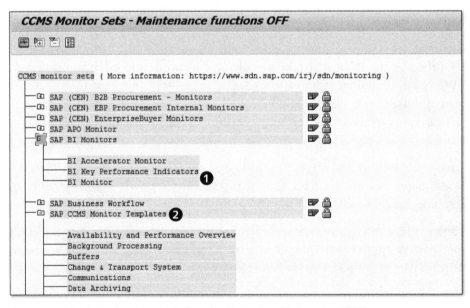

Figure 9.9 CCMS Monitor Sets, Including the BI Monitor (Transaction RZ20)

Assuming the BI monitor is indeed active, you can access it directly by calling Transaction BWCCMS or indirectly through the Data Warehousing Workbench. The results for the last execution of every consistency check can be found under the node labeled RSRV Checks (see Figure 9.10), making this transaction a convenient tool to identify the number and extent of existing issues identified by the consistency checks.

When all errors have been identified and verified, they should be prioritized for resolution. Assign each a high, medium, or low priority level and then plan to tackle the high-priority items first. Resolution of each error can involve many skills or tasks and depends on the specific error, so this activity does not provide specific resolution steps.

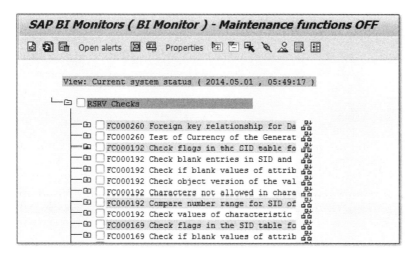

Figure 9.10 RSRV Checks in the BI Monitor (Transaction BWCCMS)

Once you resolve an error, be sure to re-run the consistency check to clear the error from the BI monitor and validate that the issues has been resolved. It is a good idea to add resolutions to each error to the team's knowledge database or how-to library, if one exists.

With system-specific issues resolved, the remaining monthly administration tasks are designed to make the most efficient use of system resources by monitoring database usage and growth, including BWA.

9.1.6 Collecting BWA Usage

In systems using SAP BW Accelerator (BWA), statistics are generated for each InfoProvider that capture whether the queries executed against it read data from BWA. In cases in which data is not read from BWA, the reasons are also captured. This statistical information is written to the database table RSDDSTATBIAUSE. The statistics table has the fields listed in Table 9.3.

Field	Description
INFOPROV	The name of the InfoCube from which the data is read
CALDAY	The calendar day; one entry is generated and counted for each Info-Cube, each day.
BIA_USED	A counter to indicate how many times during query execution the BWA index of the InfoCube is used
BIA_TECHINA	A counter to indicate how many times during query execution the BWA index is active and filled but has the status INACTIVE (CANNOT BE USED FOR QUERIES) BWA indexes cannot be used in the following cases: ▸ Data load processes are running ▸ Metadata change processes are running ▸ Request deletion processes are running ▸ Master data activation is running
BIA_INA	A counter to indicate how many times during query execution the BWA index is active and filled but is either manually set to INACTIVE or the user is prevented from using BWA by the system parameters during query execution
DB_FALLBACK	A counter to indicate how many times during query execution the BWA index is active and filled but the DB fallback is currently active and all queries are reading from the database
BIA_NOTPOSSIBLE	A counter to indicate how many times during query execution that queries cannot read from the BWA data: ▸ Queries contain aggregations not supported by BWA, such as calculation before aggregation or NOP key figures ▸ Queries using data mart or open hub read accesses ▸ Queries executed with debug options in Transaction RSRT, such as "Do Not Use BWA Index" or "Do Not Use Aggregates" ▸ Queries reading from an open request in the InfoCube ▸ Queries containing characteristics Request ID, Change ID, or Record TP in the drilldown or filter ▸ Queries using delta cache to read from a transactional InfoCube that does not have all its green requests rolled up
NO_BIA	A counter to indicate how many times during query execution there is (currently) no BWA index for this InfoCube

Table 9.3 Fields of Table RSDDSTATBIAUSE

The statistics data captured for BWA usage is not a detailed runtime analysis of the queries in the BI system—use the query runtime statistics for those details. Rather, these new statistics enable you to investigate the BWA usage by InfoProviders quickly and easily. Data from this table is available for reporting from the Virtual InfoCube 0TCT_V26 (BWA Usage Statistics).

BWA usage statistics should be analyzed on a monthly basis for InfoProviders that are indexed in BWA but not used during query execution. This insight can help determine which InfoProvider indexes are candidates for removal from BWA— the in-memory space in BWA is expensive real estate and should be used for Info-Providers only when it provides value in terms of better query performance. Alternatively, this information can also help identify InfoProviders with BEx queries that may need to be tuned or optimized for use with BWA.

As part of this monthly activity, take action based on the results of the statistical analysis. Develop a process that communicates to the project delivery and service delivery teams the outcome of the analysis and actions taken to ensure that Info-Providers that do not provide a performance improvement when indexed in BWA do not find their way back into the accelerator at a later date.

9.1.7   Forecasting Storage Capacity

Forecasting database growth is an important administration task that serves to maintain the desired server and database performance. Effective storage management requires administrators to calculate reasonably accurate future capacity needs in order to ensure a robust and reliable system.

You'll find that it's important to keep a check on database growth and forecast future requirements for a number of reasons, as follows:

▶ Forecasting database growth is important to maintain the stability of the system and smooth operation of the BI applications.

▶ DBAs need to communicate disk space requirements well in advance to secure funds in the IT budget and/or procure necessary infrastructure.

- When armed with a forecast, the database administrators can prepare for sufficient capacity before the disk runs out of space.

- Any delays, however slight, in arranging for sufficient backup infrastructure may introduce an unacceptable risk that a recovery may fail in the aftermath of a disaster.

There are two main components to database growth, and both must be considered if there is to be any hope of calculating a reasonably accurate estimate:

1. *Organic growth* is growth attributed to ongoing data loading and reporting usage of existing content in the data warehouse. This growth may be negative, especially if a data archiving has been recently implemented, but it is usually linear and quite predictable.

2. *Inorganic growth* is growth attributed to projects delivering reporting content on new sources of data or new business areas from existing sources. Inorganic growth is usually more difficult to predict than organic growth.

To calculate the organic growth rate, analyze the current database growth patterns and forecast the future database sizes for all SAP BW systems in the landscape. A good formula to use relies on averaging the growth rates over the last six months, excluding the months with the highest and lowest growth.

To calculate the inorganic growth rate, have project teams provide sizing estimates for new data extraction and staging throughout the landscape before the projects go live. Be sure to take into consideration projects that archive and/or compress existing data. These calculations can be added to the organic growth rate already calculated.

As an example, see the storage capacity growth trend illustrated in Figure 9.11 from a production SAP BW system. The solid line represents the actual database growth, and the dotted line represents the forecasted growth.

Over the three-year period the chart represents, the forecast aligns quite well with actual capacity growth. However, there is one notable exception identified by ❶. The explanation for this exception is simple enough: a new project was delivered in production, but deletion of PSAs and change logs for the new content was overlooked. The database grew unchecked for several months until the omission was discovered and addressed. At that point, the database returned to the forecasted size.

Another interesting data point is identified by ❷, when Oracle Advanced Compression was activated on the database. At that point in time, the storage capacity requirement was immediately reduced by 52%—a significant achievement by all standards!

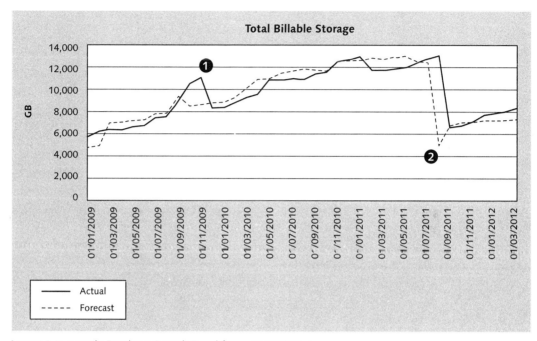

Figure 9.11 Sample Database Growth Trend for an SAP DW System

With all administration tasks completed and a stable system with no specific issues, we can shift our focus toward monthly performance-tuning activities.

9.2 Monthly Performance Tuning

The tasks covered in this section are critical to maintaining optimal performance in the system for both end users running reports and support teams executing data loads and administering the data warehouse. We'll take a look at the following:

- Conducting file system housekeeping
- Archiving or near-lining data
- Monitoring data load statistics

Let's begin with file system housekeeping.

9.2.1 Conducting File System Housekeeping

Not all storage capacity associated with an SAP BW system is allocated to the database. Additional storage capacity is required for the file system. Approximately 200 GB is used by the SAP kernel, but much more than that is required for backups, logs, archives, core dumps, transports, and data files (flat files), which are transferred to the application server for preparation and/or loading.

While all data warehouses should have a data retention strategy and process in place, most usually overlook the storage requirements reserved for the file system. However, the file system should not only be included in the data retention strategy, but also cleansed during routine monthly housekeeping.

For administrators without OS-level access, the file system can be monitored by calling Transaction AL11, as shown in Figure 9.12. Note that the file highlighted in the figure, which is a full-system info-dump file in the */tmp* directory, is 220 GB by itself. While this file was deliberately created to help in the root cause analysis of a specific issue, it should be purged from the file system as soon as it is outdated and no longer of value. In fact, in this example, there are a large number of files in the same temp directory that are candidates for cleansing.

Figure 9.12 Monitoring File Systems and Their Content (Transaction AL11)

Before cleansing any files the first time, you should review all the custom and temporary file directories in the file system(s) and identify those that can be deleted or archived. Define a file-retention strategy by file type that considers the intrinsic value, life cycle, and ease of replacement for each type of file. Over time, revisit that strategy and adjust as needed to mitigate both the risk of deleting files that may still be needed and the risk of retaining files that are no longer required.

The files related to transport change requests deserve special attention in the file-retention strategy. Each transport change request generates two files when it is released: a data file containing the object definitions and a co-file containing export and import logs. The data and co-files are stored in the */usr/sap/trans/data* and */usr/sap/trans/cofiles* directories, respectively. In many large systems, it is necessary to purge these directories to maintain transport management system performance.

> **Recommendation**
>
> Do not cleanse data or co-files unless there is no doubt they will ever be needed again.

Because co-files contain only export and import logs, they are generally quite small in size (bytes), but they are immensely useful during root cause analysis because they capture the systems into which each transport has been imported, along with the status of each import. For example, co-files can help explain why an object may not have the same definition in production as it does in develop ment, which, unfortunately, is not an uncommon scenario.

Data files, on the other hand, contain the actual definition (i.e., table entries and code) of every included object as of the release date and time and can be quite large in size. While data files do not assist in forensic analysis, they should never be purged from the file system unless they have been imported into every system in the landscape.

> **Note**
>
> If the data file has been deleted before the change request can be imported into pro-duction, it can never be imported, and there is a risk that the objects in the production system will never again align completely with development.

Identifying which change requests have been imported into all systems can be more difficult than it sounds. This information is stored at the co-file level, so there is no single source where the status of every transport in the landscape can be monitored. From within any single system, it is possible to see only which transports have been imported into that system—this can be checked in table E070, as shown in Figure 9.13.

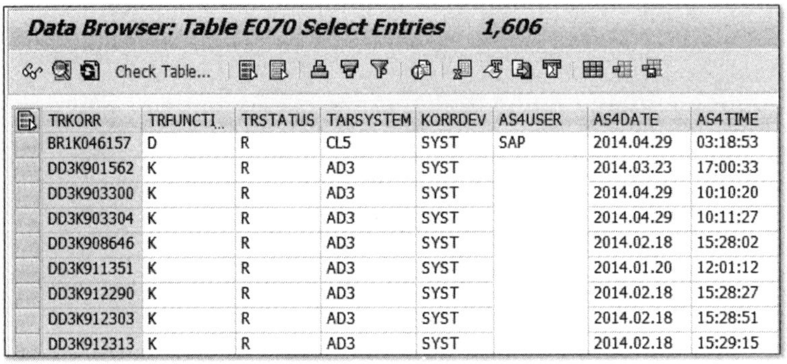

Data Browser: Table E070 Select Entries 1,606

TRKORR	TRFUNCTI...	TRSTATUS	TARSYSTEM	KORRDEV	AS4USER	AS4DATE	AS4TIME
BR1K046157	D	R	CL5	SYST	SAP	2014.04.29	03:18:53
DD3K901562	K	R	AD3	SYST		2014.03.23	17:00:33
DD3K903300	K	R	AD3	SYST		2014.04.29	10:10:20
DD3K903304	K	R	AD3	SYST		2014.04.29	10:11:27
DD3K908646	K	R	AD3	SYST		2014.02.18	15:28:02
DD3K911351	K	R	AD3	SYST		2014.01.20	12:01:12
DD3K912290	K	R	AD3	SYST		2014.02.18	15:28:27
DD3K912303	K	R	AD3	SYST		2014.02.18	15:28:51
DD3K912313	K	R	AD3	SYST		2014.02.18	15:29:15

Figure 9.13 Imported Change Requests Captured in Table E070 (Transaction SE16)

Transports that have not been imported but are waiting for approval can be found in the import buffer. The contents of the import can be viewed in Transaction STMS, as shown in Figure 9.14, or Transaction STMS_QA if it is being used to approve requests for import into production.

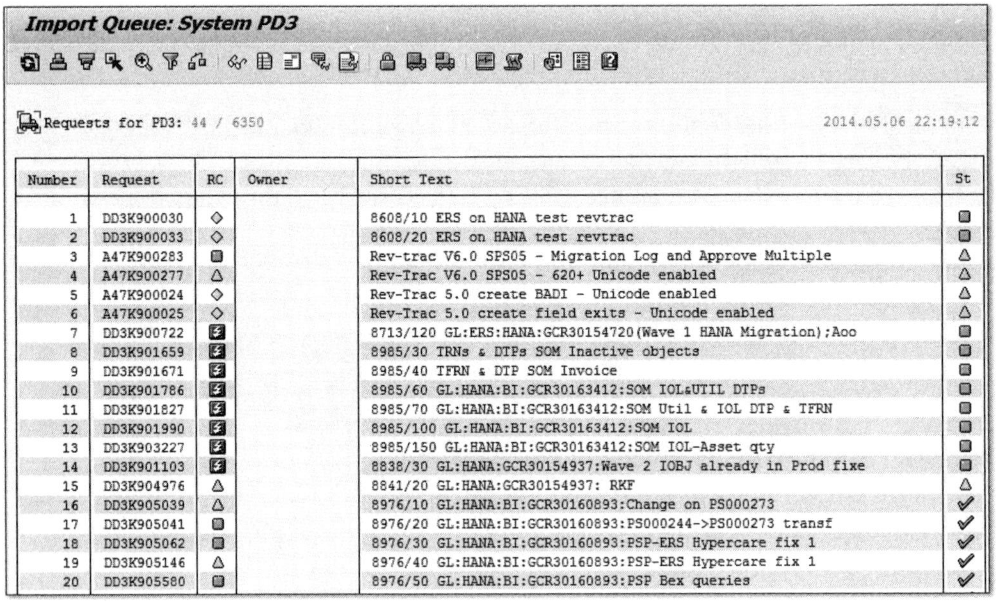

Import Queue: System PD3

Requests for PD3: 44 / 6350 2014.05.06 22:19:12

Number	Request	RC	Owner	Short Text	St
1	DD3K900030			8608/10 ERS on HANA test revtrac	
2	DD3K900033			8608/20 ERS on HANA test revtrac	
3	A47K900283			Rev-trac V6.0 SPS05 - Migration Log and Approve Multiple	
4	A47K900277			Rev-Trac V6.0 SPS05 - 620+ Unicode enabled	
5	A47K900024			Rev-Trac 5.0 create BADI - Unicode enabled	
6	A47K900025			Rev-Trac 5.0 create field exits - Unicode enabled	
7	DD3K900722			8713/120 GL:ERS:HANA:GCR30154720(Wave 1 HANA Migration);Aoo	
8	DD3K901659			8985/30 TRNs & DTPs SOM Inactive objects	
9	DD3K901671			8985/40 TFRN & DTP SOM Invoice	
10	DD3K901786			8985/60 GL:HANA:BI:GCR30163412:SOM IOL&UTIL DTPs	
11	DD3K901827			8985/70 GL:HANA:BI:GCR30163412:SOM Util & IOL DTP & TFRN	
12	DD3K901990			8985/100 GL:HANA:BI:GCR30163412:SOM IOL	
13	DD3K903227			8985/150 GL:HANA:BI:GCR30163412:SOM IOL-Asset qty	
14	DD3K901103			8838/30 GL:HANA:GCR30154937:Wave 2 IOBJ already in Prod fixe	
15	DD3K904976			8841/20 GL:HANA:GCR30154937: RKF	
16	DD3K905039			8976/10 GL:HANA:BI:GCR30160893:Change on PS000273	
17	DD3K905041			8976/20 GL:HANA:BI:GCR30160893:PS000244->PS000273 transf	
18	DD3K905062			8976/30 GL:HANA:BI:GCR30160893:PSP-ERS Hypercare fix 1	
19	DD3K905146			8976/40 GL:HANA:BI:GCR30160893:PSP-ERS Hypercare fix 1	
20	DD3K905580			8976/50 GL:HANA:BI:GCR30160893:PSP Bex queries	

Figure 9.14 Production System Import Buffer (Transaction STMS)

The important takeaway from this section is that the file system needs to be monitored and cleansed on a routine basis because it can grow quite rapidly and affect performance. By defining a file retention strategy for each type of file, you can mitigate the risks of poor performance. However, determining which files can be deleted may take specialized skills and more effort than anticipated because there is no readily available automated solution.

9.2.2 Archiving/Near-Lining Data

For data stored in the SAP BW database, solutions covered in previous chapters, such as archiving objects, near-line storage, and other data processing options like historical and summary InfoProviders (covered in Chapter 3 on Data Management) check data growth.

Leverage archiving objects to schedule the archiving of request administration data, IDocs, BI authorization logs, and authorization change logs. There is no need to wait until a database migration, system copy, or upgrade is imminent before archiving this system information. Much of this data is rarely used after several months—duration should be determined based on specific circumstances and environment—so it can be archived on a monthly basis.

Archiving is a two-step process, as follows:

1. The data to be archived is written to the archive file, as indicated by ❶ in Figure 9.15. The archive file is written to a specific directory in the file system, which must be configured prior to archiving. To create the archive file, specify the parameters for archiving (i.e., the age of the IDocs that should be archived) ❷, where the variant is configured so that all IDocs older than 180 days are archived.

2. The archived data needs to be deleted from the source tables ❸. Logically, this step can be executed only after the archive file has been written successfully— the file, or archive selection, must be explicitly identified in the parameters for you to execute a deletion.

> **Recommendation**
>
> Archived data is written to the file system. While archived data is recoverable if needed, odds are that it will never need to be recovered. At some point, archive files should be deleted from the file system. Before archiving, specify a firm end of life for the files of each archiving object; otherwise, they may live in the file system forever.

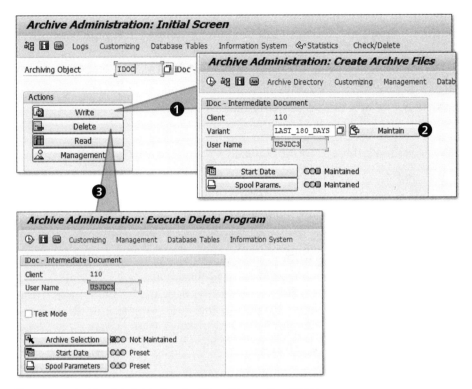

Figure 9.15 Archive Administration for IDocs (Transaction SARA)

Archiving system administration data is one thing, but business transaction data loaded into the data warehouse is another. Recall from Chapter 3 that there are better options available than archiving for business transaction data. Regardless of the source, as data ages, details lose relevance. Keeping irrelevant data on-line not only adversely impacts performance, but also increases administration and maintenance efforts and costs. For systems with a defined data-retention strategy, business transaction data should be summarized, near-lined, or deleted on a monthly basis, if not more frequently.

To automate data movements to adhere to a defined retention strategy, build process chains and schedule them on a monthly basis. Process chains can be used to move data from detailed InfoProviders to historical or summary InfoProviders and delete the data from the original InfoProviders. Process chains can also be used to archive data to NLS or simply delete it from any data target; Figure 9.16

shows the process variant available in Transaction RSPC for this activity. Because data deletion is involved in all of these approaches, it is vital that you monitor these chains closely and validate the results.

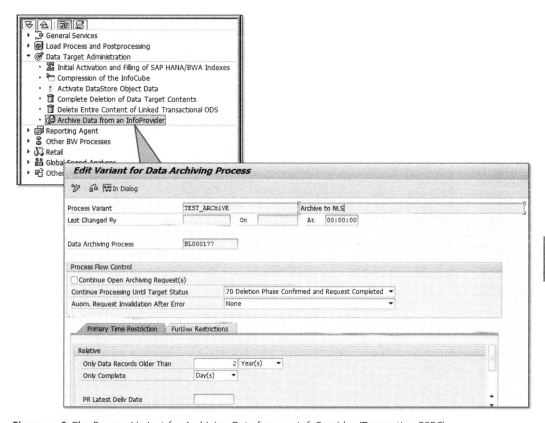

Figure 9.16 The Process Variant for Archiving Data from an InfoProvider (Transaction RSPC)

9.2.3 Monitoring Data Load Statistics

In addition to monitoring archiving and near-lining activities within the system, a monthly evaluation of data load statistics should be performed to ensure that the critical path has not evolved and that no new performance issues have surfaced. Several technical content InfoProviders dedicated to data load performance statistics are shown in Figure 9.17.

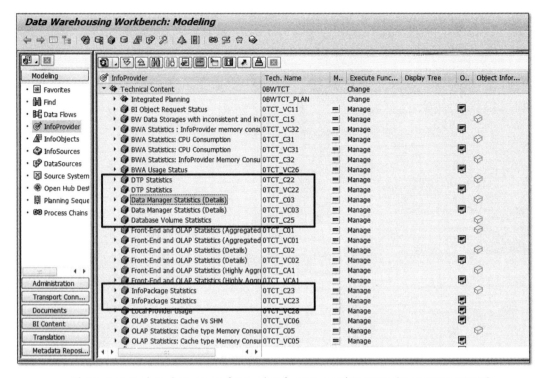

Figure 9.17 Technical Content InfoProviders for Data Load Statistics (Transaction RSA11)

As highlighted in the figure, there are technical content InfoCubes for the following areas:

- DTP statistics
- Data manager statistics
- Data volume statistics
- InfoPackage statistics

Use the technical content queries or build custom queries and reports to leverage the data available in the technical content InfoCubes. Design the queries to use conditions and exceptions so that they identify poor-performing data flows and/or overall systematic performance issues. For an example, see Figure 9.18, which shows a dashboard illustrating trends for process chain runtimes.

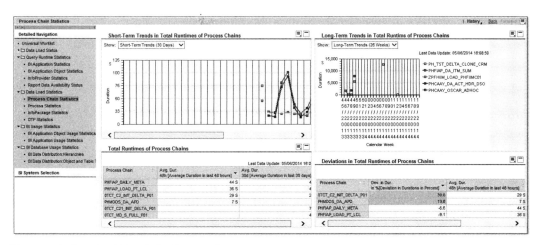

Figure 9.18 Data Load Trends for Process Chains

The specification of thresholds regarding poor performance is specific to each system and environment considering their CPU and memory capacity, network bandwidth, and data volumes. When data load performance issues occur, take necessary steps to identify the root cause and create an action plan to address the issue. Not all performance problems can be resolved overnight, but planning for a solution should not be delayed simply because the issue cannot be easily resolved.

This concludes our coverage of monthly administration and data load performance tuning tasks. In the next chapter, we will cover quarterly administration and performance-tuning tasks for your SAP BW system.

Quarterly tasks should be in place to lower long-term costs, such as license costs, or remove unused objects from the system.

10   Quarterly Tasks

Some tasks should be planned and executed quarterly to improve administration and performance of the SAP BW system.

Quarterly tasks are very important because they implement larger changes in the system and help improve performance in the long term by addressing configuration and parameter changes, as well as software updates. It is also the quarterly tasks that help reduce the total cost of ownership of the system by making sure that the system is in a supportable state and that licenses are managed correctly to avoid additional charges for unused user IDs or software licenses.

In this chapter, we'll walk you through them. We will first go through the quarterly administration tasks (Section 10.1) and then follow up with the quarterly performance tuning tasks (Section 10.2). To optimize the testing effort involved in the tasks, we highly recommend that you implement a quarterly release schedule that these tasks can be part of. That release schedule would include implementation of new content, administrative system updates, and performance improvements.

10.1   Quarterly Administration Tasks

These quarterly administration tasks help lower the cost and improve the reliability of the system. We will cover the following administration tasks:

- Managing users and licenses
- Refreshing test systems from production systems
- Maintaining hardware

- ▶ Updating SAP kernels
- ▶ Applying database updates
- ▶ Patching operating systems
- ▶ Validating system parameters
- ▶ Reviewing open transport requests

Let's look at a few detailed steps to execute the tasks.

10.1.1 Managing Users and Licenses

The SAP license cost is based on users in the system. You should review the users quarterly to ensure that the user licenses are in compliance with the number of licenses that your company has available, as well as avoid paying for licenses for users who are not using the SAP BW system and remove users who are no longer employed in the organization.

We will first look at how to review users against active users in the organization, and then look at how to review active users in the system. Once the users that require action have been identified, you have to lock them and then mark them for deletion. We will also go through the process of actually executing the deletion of the users in the system.

Identify Users Who Are No Longer with the Organization

Most companies maintain a central user database, like Microsoft Active Directory or another tool. To review the SAP BW users who are no longer in the central database, you must get an extract of the current active users from the central database and compare it with the current users in the SAP BW system. You can extract the SAP BW users using Transaction RSUSR200.

Select the USERS VALID TODAY checkbox, set the USER LOCKS (ADMINISTRATOR) field to NOT SET, and select the DIALOG USERS checkbox, as displayed in Figure 10.1.

The returned list includes all user IDs in the system that require licenses. Note that user IDs with expired validity dates or administrator locks set don't require a user license.

You can compare the report result list, as displayed in Figure 10.2, with the list extracted from the central user repository.

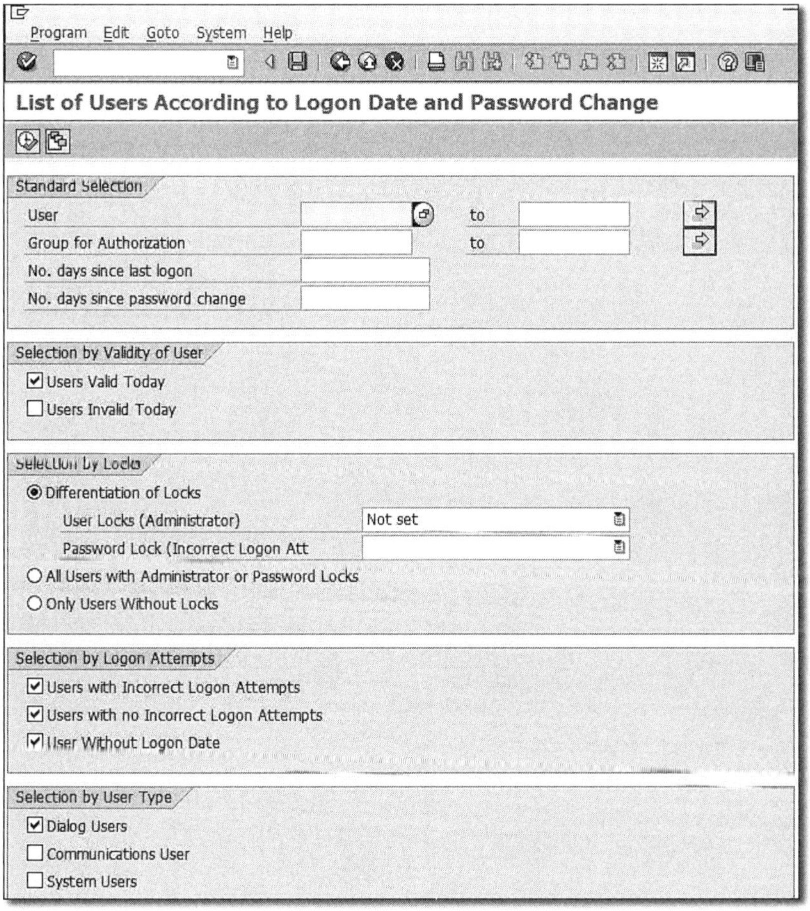

Figure 10.1 Selection Screen to Valid Users (Transaction RSUSR200)

User IDs of users who are no longer with the organization can be locked, and a validity date can be set accordingly to indicate that the user IDs are no longer required. This provides a two-pronged defense against unauthorized access, while also preventing those users from being counted against your licenses.

To set the validity date for a large number of users, use Transaction SUID10, as shown in Figure 10.3. Users cannot log on outside the validity date range, so setting validity period expiration dates is a simple way to ensure that user IDs are not used after a user has left the organization. You can validate that these users are no longer in the license selection by re-running the report.

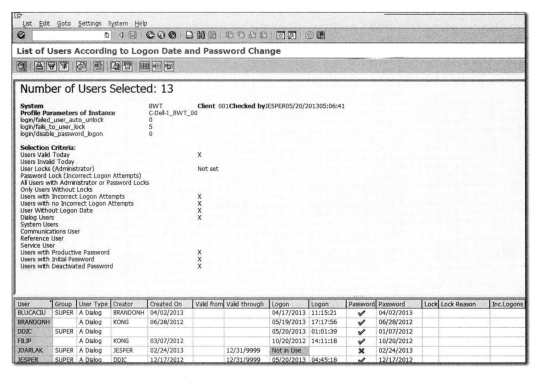

Figure 10.2 Report Result (Transaction RSUSR200)

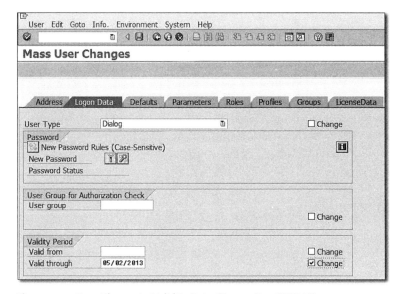

Figure 10.3 Mass Change to Validity Date (Transaction SUID10)

Review Active Users

You should review active users in the system after identifying users who are no longer in the organization. Transaction RSUSR200 is also used for this review, but with slightly different selections.

Most organizations try to minimize the license cost by deactivating the access for inactive users in the system. Inactive users are normally identified as users who have not logged on to the system for a predefined period, such as three months.

User Locks and Validity Dates

To mass lock user IDs, use Transaction SUID10 and go to menu item Users • Locks, as shown in Figure 10.4. You can also use Transaction SUID10 to update the validity date of the user IDs. Choose USER • CHANGE to apply changes to all the users selected. Update the validity date in the LOGON DATA tab and check the CHANGE box next to the validity date fields, as displayed in Figure 10.4.

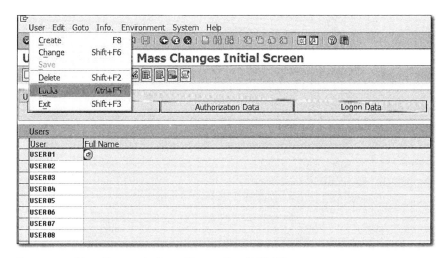

Figure 10.4 Mass Changes to Users (Transaction SUID10)

Click SAVE to save the changed validity dates for all the user IDs.

Delete Inactive Users

Deleting users in the SAP BW system also deletes all user-specific settings, parameters, and menus that the user has maintained. Since there are a number of valid reasons a user may not use the system for an extended period of time, we recommend that you only delete user IDs of users who have left the organization or been locked for the past three months to avoid losing user-specific information that might be valuable to the inactive users. It is not uncommon for users to request access again the day after their user IDs have been deleted!

Transaction SUID10 is also the recommended way to mass delete user IDs. Select the users IDs to delete and go to menu item USERS • DELETE to execute the deletion of the user IDs, as displayed in Figure 10.5.

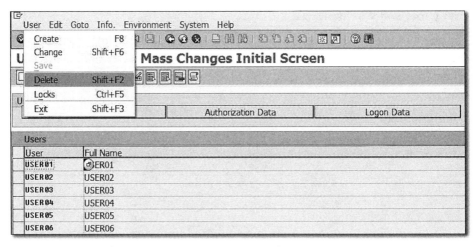

Figure 10.5 Mass Deleting User IDs (Transaction SUID10)

Once a user ID is deleted, it can be re-created in the system, if needed. The change log for the user is still available via Transaction SU01 • INFO. • CHANGE DOCUMENTS FOR USERS, as displayed in Figure 10.6.

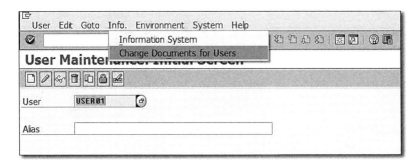

Figure 10.6 Displaying User Change Documents (Transaction SU01)

There is no limit to the number of user IDs that can be created in the system, so it is entirely possible to create more than you are licensed for. Once you have reviewed all users, verify that the number of registered users is within the number of user licenses you have purchased from SAP to avoid possible penalties in case of a license review.

You should also review licenses for other software components, such as databases and operating systems.

10.1.2 Testing System Refresh

SAP BW system landscapes normally include one or more pre-production test systems. These systems are used to test whether changes and fixes developed in the development system are working as expected prior to moving transports to the production system. We recommend that you refresh the pre-production test systems to ensure that the tests reflect the same impacts and results as in the production system. The refresh should occur at least twice each year, but quarterly refreshes improve testing capabilities and stability in the production system by avoiding possible errors introduced by changes.

There are two procedures for system copies:

▶ Homogeneous system copies, in which the operating system and database of both the source and target are the same

▶ Heterogeneous system copies, in which the operating systems and/or the databases of the source and target are different

Recommendation

We recommend the following SAP Notes for more information about system copying:
▶ Note 888210—NW 7.**: System Copy (supplementary note)
▶ Note 1768158—System Copy of Systems Based on SAP NW 7.0/7.0 EHP 1-3
▶ Note 1738258—System Copy of Systems Based on SAP NetWeaver 7.1 and Higher

BW Post Copy Automation

SAP BW Post Copy Automation (BW-PCA) lets you automate processing related to system copies. BW-PCA requires an SAP Landscape Virtualization Management enterprise edition license. It is an add-on installation on the system and is

515

installed using Transaction SAINT. The procedure is described in SAP Note 1621867—Installation of PCAI_ENT 100.

There are a lot of prerequisite notes to use BW-PCA without problems. These are described in SAP Note 1614266—System Copy: Post Copy Automation (PCA)/LVM.

The BW-PCA tools provide a set of task lists that are accessed via Transaction STC01. One of these is SAP_BASIS_COPY_REFRESH, which provides automation of export, cleanup, import, and configuration tasks, as displayed in Figure 10.7.

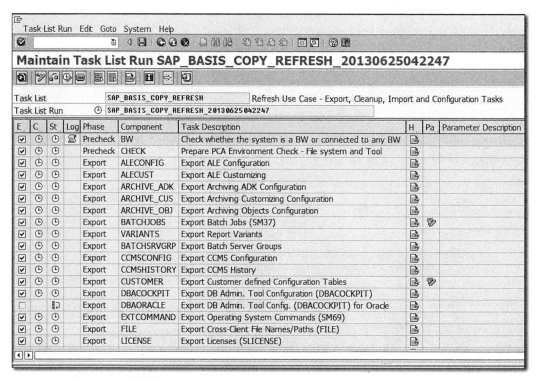

Figure 10.7 BW-PCA System Refresh Task List

To use the task list, set the `ctc/allow_systemcopy_postconfig = 1` parameter in the instance profile.

The task list contains the tasks in Table 10.1, which can be used as a checklist for executing system copies without the use of BW-PCA.

Phase	Component	Task Description
Pre-check	BW	Check whether the System is a BW or Connected to any BW
	CHECK	Prepare PCA Environment Check—File System and Tool
Export	ALECONFIG	Export ALE Configuration
	ALECUST	Export ALE Customizing
	ARCHIVE_ADK	Export Archiving ADK Configuration
	ARCHIVE_CUST	Export Archiving Customizing Configuration
	ARCHIVE_OBJ	Export Archiving Objects Configuration
	BATCHJOBS	Export Batch Jobs (SM37)
	VARIANTS	Export Report Variants
	BATCHSRVGRP	Export Batch Server Groups
	CCMSCONFIG	Export CCMS Configuration
	CCMSHISTORY	Export CCMS History
	CUSTOMER	Export Customer-Defined Configuration Tables
	DBACOCKPIT	Export DB Admin. Tool Configuration (DBA-COCKPIT)
	DBAORACLE	Export DB Admin. Tool Configuration (DBACOCKPIT) for Oracle
	EXTCOMMAND	Export Operating System Commands (SM69)
	FILE	Export Cross-Client File Names/Paths (FILE)
	LICENSE	Export Licenses (SLICENSE)
	LOGONGROUP	Export Logon Groups (SMLG)
	OPMODE	Export Operation Modes (RZ04)
	PRINTER	Export Spool Configuration (SPAD)
	PROFILE	Export System Profiles (RZ10)
	RFC	Export RFC Connections (SM59)

Table 10.1 SAP_BASIS_COPY_REFRESH Tasks

Phase	Component	Task Description
Export	RFC_IN	Export RFC Inbound Queue Configuration (qRFC)
	RFC_OUT	Export RFC Outbound Queue Configuration (tRFC and qRFC)
	BGRFC	Export Background RFC (bgRFC)
	SLD_RZ70	Export SLD Data Supplier Configuration (RZ70)
	SCOT	Export SAPconnect Configuration (SCOT)
	SICF	Export HTTP Service Configuration (SICF)
	SLD_APICUST	Export SLD Access Data Configuration (SLDAPICUST)
	SM14	Export Update Program Administration (SM14)
	SM19	Export Security Audit Profile Configuration (SM19)
	STRUST	Export Trust Manager Configuration (STRUST)
	TMS	Export Transport Management System Configuration (STMS)
	TMSQA	Export TMS Quality Assurance Configuration
	USER	Export Users (SU01)
	VERSDEV	Export Version Management
	VIRUSSCAN	Export Virus Scan Definitions (VSCAN)
	WEBSERVICE	Export Web Service Configurations (SOA-MANAGER)
	ECATT	Export Test Workbench Configuration (CATT, eCATT, STWB)
	IAC	Export Internet Transaction Server Configuration (IACOR, ITS)
	LOGINSCREEN	Export Login Screen Information

Table 10.1 SAP_BASIS_COPY_REFRESH Tasks (Cont.)

Phase	Component	Task Description
Export	PROJECTS	Export Project Configuration (SPRO)
	SCC4	Export Client Configuration (SCC4)
	SXMB_ADM	Export Integration Engine Configuration (SXMB_ADM)
	SOLMAN_MS	Export SolMan Configuration in Managed System
	TC_TASKRUN	Export Task List Runs
	TC_TASKVARI	Export Task List Variants
	CRM	Export CRM Configuration
	CRMINERP	Export CRM Configuration in ERP
	SCM	Export SCM Configuration
	SCMINERP	Export SCM Configuration in ERP
Cleanup	MANUAL_STEP	Confirmation: System Copy executed?
Pre-check	CHECK	Initial Consistency Check (SICK)
Prepare	USER	Lock Client Against Logon
	BATCHJOBS	Set Batch Jobs to Released/Suspended via BTCTRNS1
Cleanup	BW	Disconnect This Source System from Not Copied BW Systems
	BATCHJOBS	Cleanup of Batch Jobs (SM37)
	MONI	Cleanup of Operating System Monitoring Configuration (MONI)
	CCMSCONFIG	Cleanup of CCMS Configuration
	CCMSHISTORY	Cleanup of CCMS History
	CUSTOMER	Cleanup of Customer defined Configuration Tables
	OTHERS	Cleanup of ABAP Basis Tables
	DBACOCKPIT	Cleanup of DB Admin. Tool Configuration (DBACOCKPIT)

Table 10.1 SAP_BASIS_COPY_REFRESH Tasks (Cont.)

Phase	Component	Task Description
Cleanup	DBAORACLE	Cleanup of DB Admin. Tool Configuration (DBACOCKPIT) for Oracle
	RFC_IN	Cleanup of RFC Inbound Queue Configuration (qRFC)
	RFC_OUT	Cleanup of RFC Outbound Queue Configuration (tRFC and qRFC)
	BGRFC	Cleanup of Background RFC (bgRFC)
	SCOT	Cleanup of SAPconnect Configuration (SCOT)
	PRINTER	Cleanup of Spool Configuration (SPAD)
	STRUST	Cleanup of Trust Manager Configuration (STRUST)
Import	TMS	Cleanup of Transport Management System Configuration (STMS)
Cleanup	TC_TASKRUN	Cleanup of Task List Runs
	TC_TASKVARI	Cleanup of Task List Variants
	WEBSERVICE	Cleanup of Web Service Configurations (SOAMANAGER)
Import	LICENSE	Import Licenses (SLICENSE)
	RFC	Import RFC Connections (SM59)
	RFC_IN	Import RFC Inbound Queue Configuration (qRFC)
	RFC_OUT	Import RFC Outbound Queue Configuration (tRFC and qRFC)
	BGRFC	Import Background RFC (bgRFC)
Cleanup	SECURESTORE	Cleanup of Secstore (SAP Note 1532825)
Import	ALECONFIG	Import ALE Configuration
	ALECUST	Import ALE Customizing
	ARCHIVE_ADK	Import Archiving ADK Configuration
	ARCHIVE_CUST	Import Archiving Customizing Configuration

Table 10.1 SAP_BASIS_COPY_REFRESH Tasks (Cont.)

Phase	Component	Task Description
Import	ARCHIVE_OBJ	Import Archiving Objects Configuration
	BATCHJOBS	Import Batch Jobs (SM37)
	VARIANTS	Import Report Variants
	BATCHSRVGRP	Import Batch Server Groups
	CCMSCONFIG	Import CCMS Configuration
	CCMSHISTORY	Import CCMS History
	CUSTOMER	Import Customer-Defined Configuration Tables
	DBACOCKPIT	Import DB Admin. Tool Configuration (DBA-COCKPIT)
	DBAORACLE	Import DB Admin. Tool Configuration (DBA-COCKPIT) for Oracle
	EXTCOMMAND	Import Operating System Commands (SM69)
	FILE	Import Cross-Client File Names/Paths (FILE)
	LOGONGROUP	Import Logon Groups (SMLG)
	PROFILE	Import System Profiles (R710)
	OPMODE	Import Operation Modes (RZ04)
	PRINTER	Import Spool Configuration (SPAD)
	SLD_RZ70	Import SLD Data Supplier Configuration (RZ70)
	SCOT	Import SAPconnect Configuration (SCOT)
	SICF	Import HTTP Service Configuration (SICF)
	SLD_APICUST	Import SLD Access Data Configuration (SLDAPICUST)
	SM14	Import Update Program Administration (SM14)
	SM19	Import Security Audit Profile Configuration (SM19)

Table 10.1 SAP_BASIS_COPY_REFRESH Tasks (Cont.)

Phase	Component	Task Description
Import	STRUST	Import Trust Manager Configuration (STRUST)
	TC_TASKRUN	Import Task List Runs
	TC_TASKVARI	Import Task List Variants
	TMS	Import Transport Management System Configuration (STMS)
	TMSQA	Import TMS Quality Assurance Configuration
	USER	Import Users (SU01)
	VERSDEV	Import Version Management
	VIRUSSCAN	Import Virus Scan Definitions (VSCAN)
	WEBSERVICE	Import Web Service Configurations (SOA-MANAGER)
	ECATT	Import Test Workbench Configuration (CATT, eCATT, STWB)
	IAC	Import Internet Transaction Server Configuration (IACOR, ITS)
	LOGINSCREEN	Import Login Screen Information
	PROJECTS	Import Project Configuration (SPRO)
	SCC4	Import Client Configuration (SCC4)
	SXMB_ADM	Import Integration Engine Configuration (SXMB_ADM)
	SOLMAN_MS	Import SolMan Configuration in Managed System
	CRM	Import CRM Configuration
	CRMINERP	Import CRM Configuration in ERP
	SCM	Import SCM Configuration
	SCMINERP	Import SCM Configuration in ERP
	TABLE_BUFFER	Reset SAP Table Buffer

Table 10.1 SAP_BASIS_COPY_REFRESH Tasks (Cont.)

Phase	Component	Task Description
Configuration	SECURESTORE	Configuration of Secure Store (SECSTORE)
	TMS	Schedule Dispatcher Job for Transport Programs (RDDIMPDP)
	SGEN	Perform Load Generation (SGEN)
Post-processing	ICM	Trigger ICM Restart
	USER	Unlock Client for Logon
	BATCHJOBS	Set Batch Jobs to Released via BTCTRNS2
Verification	CHECK	Final Consistency Check (SICK)

Table 10.1 SAP_BASIS_COPY_REFRESH Tasks (Cont.)

You can copy the task lists included in BW-PCA and add or remove steps. This allows for a more standardized procedure for executing system refreshes, which we highly recommend.

10.1.3 Maintaining Hardware

Hardware maintenance is important for ensuring that the capacity and maintainability of the hardware solution are sustainable.

A quarterly hardware capacity review starts with reviewing the current system utilization in the following main areas:

▸ Database space or memory space for SAP HANA

▸ Peak, hourly, and daily CPU utilization

▸ Peak, hourly, and daily memory utilization

Once you've reviewed the current utilization, you should look at future projects that might add additional data and workload to the system. Each new project or content added to the system should be required to provide an estimate of capacity increase that the project will require in order not to impact the current utilizations in the system for each of these three categories.

Once you know the current capacity utilization and the expected future capacity increase, you can plan for any required capacity increases and start the process of adding the additional hardware when it is needed.

10.1.4 Updating SAP Kernels

Implementing SAP Kernel updates is important for a stable, well-performing SAP BW system. SAP Kernel updates consist of two main sets of operating system-specific Kernel files:

- Database-independent
- Database-specific

You should apply both sets of files at the same time by following the steps outlined in SAP Note 19466 for ABAP Kernel, as follows:

1. Download the Kernel patch files from the SAP Service Marketplace (*https://service.sap.com/swdc*).
2. Copy the patch into a temporary directory on your system.
3. Unpack the patch using *sapcar.exe*.
4. Stop the SAP system. Consider a graceful shutdown, as covered in the previous chapter. With Windows NT, you may also have to stop the SAP services using the Control Panel.
5. Save the Kernel directory by backing up or copying into a separate backup directory, as follows:
   - UNIX: */usr/sap/<SAPSID>/sys/exe/run*
   - NT: *<drive>:\usr\sap\<SAPSID>\sys\exe\run*

   If you use an SAP system 6.20 or higher (32-bit or 64-bit, Unicode or non-Unicode), there are also the following kernel directories:
   - NT: *<drive>:\usr\sap<SAPSID>sys\exe\nuc\<platform>* (non-Unicode)
   - NT: *<drive>:\usr\sap<SAPSID>sys\exe\uc\<platform>* (Unicode)

   This way, you always have the option of returning to the old kernel version if problems occur with the new patch.
6. Copy or move the unpacked programs into the SAP Kernel directory.
7. Restart SAP and execute routine system health checks.

Recommendation

To install Kernel updates for Java, we recommend that you use the SAP Software Update Manager (SUM). Using the SAP SUM is described in Chapter 11.

10.1.5 Applying Database Updates and Parameters

Database software updates and parameter information is updated frequently from the vendors. You should apply them to take advantage of fixed functionality and performance improvements in the database platforms. We'll give you a few more details about the most common vendors next.

Oracle

Oracle is currently the most-used database platform for SAP BW. Oracle releases fixes for the database regularly, and these should be applied quarterly to take advantage of the quarterly release testing process.

Table 10.2 contains some useful SAP Notes for planning and executing updates or upgrades to the Oracle Database.

SAP Note	Short Text
1171650	Automated Oracle DB Parameter Check
1013912	FAQ: Oracle BW Performance
682926	Composite SAP Note: Problems with "Create/Rebuild Index"
1175996	Oracle 10g/11g Patches Check
1696869	Patching of Oracle Homes with Minimal Downtime
1431797	Oracle 11.2.0: Troubleshooting the Database Upgrade

Table 10.2 SAP Notes for Oracle Databases

You should also review the Oracle parameters—specifically, the performance-related parameters. SAP Note 1013912 provides a good overview of performance for SAP BW and possible improvements.

Table 10.3 offers two notes for MSSQL databases.

SAP Note	Short Text
1654613	SQL Server Parallelism for SAP BW
1237682	Configuration Parameters for SQL Server 2008

Table 10.3 SAP Notes for MSSQL Databases

IBM DB2

The DB2 database platform from IBM has been around for many years. It is a stable database, but IBM is continuously developing new features and fixes for the platform. Table 10.4 offers some notes you should review regarding supported fix packs and procedures for updating the DB2 database.

SAP Note	Short Text
977845	DB6: Known Errors and Available Fixes in DB2 9.1 LUW
544274	FAQs: DB2/UDB 64-Bit Support
544312	FAQs: DB2/UDB Patches
1708037	DB6: Installing Fix Packs for DB2 10.1 (UNIX + Linux)
101809	DB6: Supported Fix Packs DB2 for Linux, UNIX and Windows
1836613	DB2-z/OS: Requirements for nZDM with SUM 1.0 SP7

Table 10.4 SAP Notes for DB2 Databases

We recommend that you start using SAP SUM for database updates. SAP Note 1836613 describes the requirements for using it for DB2-z/OS updates.

SAP MaxDB

The SAP MaxDB database provides a good platform for SAP BW; in fact, it was used as the base for some of the SAP HANA development. SAP still develops the SAP MaxDB database, and updates and fixes are released frequently. We recommend that you review the notes shown in Table 10.5.

SAP Note	Short Text
1020175	FAQ: SAP MaxDB Installation/Upgrade or Applying a Patch
832544	FAQ: MaxDB Hints
928037	FAQ: SAP MaxDB Indexes
927882	FAQ: SAP MaxDB Update Statistics
1004886	MaxDB Version 7.7 Parameter Recommendations
819324	FAQ: SAP MaxDB SQL Optimization

Table 10.5 SAP Notes for SAP MaxDB Databases

SAP Note	Short Text
912905	FAQ: Storage Systems Used with MaxDB
814704	MaxDB Version 7.6 Parameter Settings for OLTP/BW

Table 10.5 SAP Notes for SAP MaxDB Databases (Cont.)

Because they change over time, you should review specific parameter recommendations for SAP BW quarterly.

SAP HANA

In contrast, new revisions are released for SAP HANA frequently. Sometimes, more than one revision is released within one week. The SAP HANA revisions include fixes to bugs in SAP HANA but also offer new functionality that, together with application notes or support packages, delivers new, advanced functionality for systems powered by SAP HANA. You should update SAP HANA revisions quarterly to take advantage of the new functionality and bug fixes.

The revision update of SAP HANA used to be done with HDPUPD. This process is no longer supported, and SAP SUM should be used to perform the update of SAP HANA revisions. Using SAP SUM ensures that all the SAP HANA components are updated to compatible versions.

Consider the SAP Notes mentioned in Table 10.6 before using SAP SUM for SAP HANA revision updates.

SAP Note	Short Text
1793303	Install and Configure SUM for SAP HANA
1545815	SAP Release Note for SUM for SAP HANA 1.0

Table 10.6 SAP Notes for SAP HANA Update Process

SAP BWA

Revisions for SAP BW Accelerator (BWA) are generally released less frequently than the SAP HANA revisions for two reasons: because the product is more stable and because development from SAP has been switched toward SAP HANA since it provides long-term superior functionality compared to BWA.

You can download the latest BWA revision from SAP Service Marketplace and place it on the BWA appliance. The update procedure requires only a few steps:

1. Log on as super user (root) in the folder that you have created for downloading the file *BIA7xx_<revision>.SAR*.

2. Unpack this SAR file using SAPCAR. After the unpacking has finished, you can find the installation script `install.sh`.

3. Enter the command `sh install.sh update` for starting the update procedure.

4. In the event of several installed BWA instances, you are asked to choose one of them to be updated.

Review the two important SAP Notes shown in Table 10.7 about the latest BWA revisions every quarter.

SAP Note	Short Text
1856857	Latest Revision for BWA 7.00
1845809	Latest Revision for BWA 7.20

Table 10.7 SAP Notes for BWA Revisions

The implementation of a BWA revision update normally takes an hour or less to execute.

10.1.6 Patching Operating System

The operating system used by your SAP BW system requires patching, as well. We recommend that you keep up with patches on a regular basis and apply the patches at least monthly. Testing related to the patches should be done together with the quarterly release.

10.1.7 Validating System Parameters

Review the system parameters in the SAP BW system to ensure that they are still valid and optimal.

The general review should consist of the following validations:

1. Check RZ10 profiles.

2. Review memory parameters in Transaction ST02.

3. Check parameters changed since the last quarter.

4. Compare against SAP-recommended parameter settings.

You can find SAP-recommended parameters in the general SAP Note for SAP BW parameter (Note 192658, Setting Parameters for BW Systems).

Avoid any swapping activity with the parameter settings because it causes severe performance problems in the SAP BW system.

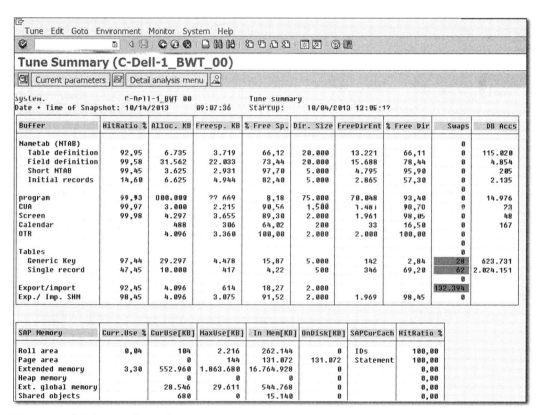

Buffer	HitRatio %	Alloc. KB	Freesp. KB	% Free Sp.	Dir. Size	FreeDirEnt	% Free Dir	Swaps	DB Accs
Nametab (NTAB)								0	
Table definition	92,95	6.735	3.719	66,12	20.000	13.221	66,11	0	115.020
Field definition	99,58	31.562	22.033	73,44	20.000	15.688	78,44	0	4.854
Short NTAB	99,45	3.625	2.931	97,70	5.000	4.795	95,90	0	205
Initial records	14,60	6.625	4.944	82,40	5.000	2.865	57,30	0	2.135
								0	
program	99,93	000.000	22.669	8,18	75.000	70.048	93,40	0	14.976
CUA	99,97	3.000	2.215	90,56	1.500	1.481	90,70	0	23
Screen	99,98	4.297	3.655	89,30	2.000	1.961	98,05	0	48
Calendar		488	306	64,02	200	33	16,50	0	167
OTR		4.096	3.360	100,00	2.000	2.000	100,00	0	
								0	
Tables								0	
Generic Key	97,44	29.297	4.478	15,87	5.000	142	2,84	28	623.731
Single record	47,45	10.000	417	4,22	500	346	69,20	62	2.024.151
								0	
Export/import	92,45	4.096	614	18,27	2.000			132.394	
Exp./ Imp. SHM	98,45	4.096	3.075	91,52	2.000	1.969	98,45	0	

SAP Memory	Curr.Use %	CurUse[KB]	MaxUse[KB]	In Mem[KB]	OnDisk[KB]	SAPCurCach	HitRatio %
Roll area	0,04	104	2.216	262.144	0	IDs	100,00
Page area		0	144	131.072	131.072	Statement	100,00
Extended memory	3,30	552.960	1.863.680	16.764.928	0		0,00
Heap memory		0	0	0	0		0,00
Ext. global memory		28.546	29.611	544.768	0		0,00
Shared objects		680	0	15.140	0		0,00

Figure 10.8 Database Buffers and Memory Parameters (Transaction ST02)

Transaction ST02 provides a good overview of database buffers and hit ratios, as well as whether there is swap activity for the specific buffer in the SWAPS column, shown in Figure 10.8.

10.1.8   Reviewing Open Transport Requests

Changes made in the development system are captured in the SAP Change and Transport Management System (CTS). The transport requests lock the objects until the request is released.

Perform a quarterly review of open transport requests to check whether old transport requests are lingering in the development system. These old requests could cause support issues because a change has been performed to an object but has not yet been tested and moved through to the production system.

We recommend that you review the following:

1. Transport creation dates older than two months
2. Number of objects included in the transport
3. Whether the objects are used in production
4. Documentation maintained for the change
5. Whether the change should be reversed, deleted, or promoted to production

These criteria have been evaluated; the transport should be either deleted or migrated to the production system. Transport requests older than six months should not occur in a production support landscape.

10.2   Quarterly Performance Tuning Tasks

System performance changes over time, so you should perform quarterly reviews of some configuration settings and the database layout to ensure good system performance. To free up capacity for the used content in the system and avoid spending time on performance problems related to the objects, clean obsolete objects out of the system. We'll examine the following quarterly tasks:

▶ Reorganizing the database
▶ Deleting obsolete queries and reports
▶ Deleting obsolete data flows
▶ Reviewing configuration settings

Let's begin!

10.2.1 Reorganizing the Database

Some database systems can require reorganization to remove degeneration of tables across too many data files. This doesn't happen frequently in the current DBMS versions on the market, but it might still be required for large tables that you identify as performance bottlenecks in the system.

Database reorganization offers the following benefits:

▶ Index full scans run faster after index reorganization whenever the density of the index entries becomes greater. In other words, for example, it takes less time to read 100,000 entries from a 100-block index than reading the entries from a 500-block index.

▶ Multi-block index range scans run far faster when the data blocks are arranged in index-key order.

▶ Large-table, full-table scans run faster after reorganization when the table has excessive chained or relocated rows, or low block density after massive updates and deletions.

▶ Table updates run faster after reorganizations.

▶ Database space can be reclaimed and re-purposed. A smaller database size has a positive ripple effect throughout the system, such as reducing both the backup size and performance.

A few key SAP Notes help shed light on the procedures for reorganizing some different databases. These are shown in Table 10.8.

DBMS	SAP Note
Oracle	Note 646681—Reorganizing tables with BRSPACE Note 541538—FAQ: Reorganization
SAP HANA	Note 1813245—SAP HANA DB: Row store reorganization
DB2	Note 169301—DB6: Online Reorganization with DB2 UDB Note 975352—DB6: Reorganizations in DB2/Using DB2 Auto REORG

Table 10.8 SAP Notes for Database Reorganization

Reorganization is also required for the SAP HANA row store tables. The objective here is mainly to reclaim space, but also to improve performance; these are similar to relational database tables.

10.2.2 Deleting Obsolete Queries and Reports

Reports are being developed over time; sometimes, a report becomes obsolete. This happens more frequently for power user–developed ad hoc reports, and it is important that these are cleaned up regularly to ensure that runtimes for other reports are optimal.

Normally, a process is defined that identifies the obsolete queries and reports as objects that have not been used for six to 12 months. This time interval is then used to select the objects to be deleted in the SAP BW system in Transaction RSZDELETE. The selection screen for the transaction is displayed in Figure 10.9.

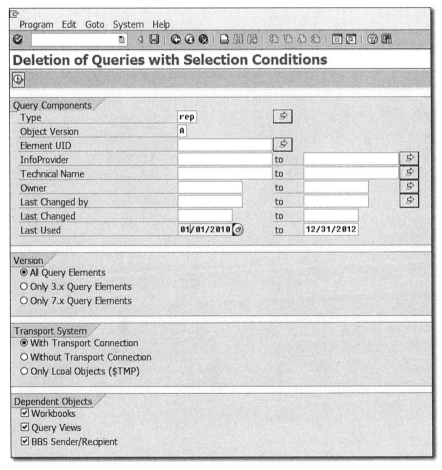

Figure 10.9 Deletion Selection for Queries and Reports

To get a list of objects, make the following selections:

▶ Object type: REP

▶ Last used: Date interval from system start to 6–12 months ago, depending on the procedure defined.

▶ Version: All query elements

▶ Transport system: With Transport Connection so that the deletions can be moved through to production

▶ Dependent objects: Check all options

When the report is executed, a list of queries that meet the criteria and their dependent objects is displayed, as shown in Figure 10.9.

Technical Name	Deletable	Delete	Type	InfoProvider	Technical ID	Person Responsible	Last Changed By	Last Used On	Last Changed On
OIC_C03_Q001;	▣	☑	ELEM...	OIC_C03	DUBSLTJKN...	SAP	NICKL	10/22/2012	10/22/2012
OIC_C03_Q003(	▣	☑	ELEM...	OIC_C03	7UYCRJ91X...	SAP	SAP	10/22/2012	10/20/2012
0TCTHP24_Q0!	▣	☑	ELEM...	0TCTHP24	7KU36MOU...	SAP	SAP	03/31/2010	01/08/2012
0TCTHP24_Q0!	▣	☑	ELEM...	0TCTHP24	7KU36MOU...	SAP	SAP	03/31/2010	01/08/2012
0TCTHP24_Q0!	▣	☑	ELEM...	0TCTHP24	7KU36MOU...	SAP	SAP	02/16/2012	01/08/2012
0TCT_MC01_Q(	▣	☐	ELEM	0TCT_MC01	5DRTXQQT...	SAP	SAP	08/31/2010	01/08/2012
0TCT_MC01_Q(	▣	☑	ELEM...	0TCT_MC01	7MODTUOA.	SAP	SAP	08/31/2010	01/08/2012
0TCT_MC01_Q(	▣	☑	ELEM...	0TCT_MC01	7KU36MOU...	SAP	SAP	03/31/2010	01/08/2012
0TCT_MC01_Q(	▣	☑	ELEM...	0TCT_MC01	7KU36MOU...	SAP	SAP	03/31/2010	01/08/2012
0TCT_MC03_Q(	▣	☑	ELEM...	0TCT_MC03	90CVDM03K...	SAP	SAP	04/07/2010	01/08/2012
0TCT_MC03_Q(	▣	☑	ELEM...	0TCT_MC03	F0LBV3VDQ...	SAP	SAP	02/01/2010	01/08/2012
0TCT_MC03_Q(	▣	☑	ELEM...	0TCT_MC03	8SL9ZPENG7...	SAP	SAP	04/07/2010	01/08/2012
0TCT_MC15_Q(	▣	☑	ELEM...	0TCT_MC15	7MODTUOA...	SAP	SAP	04/30/2010	01/08/2012
0TCT_MC15_Q(	▣	☑	ELEM...	0TCT_MC15	7MODTUOA...	SAP	SAP	04/21/2010	01/08/2012
0TCT_MC21_Q(	▣	☐	ELEM...	0TCT_MC21	7MODTUOA...	SAP	SAP	06/24/2010	01/08/2012
0TCT_MC21_Q(	▣	☑	ELEM...	0TCT_MC21	22PGH4RQK...	SAP	SAP	04/05/2010	01/08/2012
0TCT_MC21_Q(	▣	☑	ELEM...	0TCT_MC21	7MODTUOA...	SAP	SAP	06/25/2010	01/08/2012
0TCT_MC21_Q(	▣	☑	ELEM...	0TCT_MC21	7KU36MOU...	SAP	SAP	03/31/2010	01/08/2012
0TCT_MC21_Q(	▣	☑	ELEM...	0TCT_MC21	7KU36MOU...	SAP	SAP	03/31/2010	01/08/2012
0TCT_MC25_Q(	▣	☑	ELEM...	0TCT_MC25	7MODTUOA...	SAP	SAP	06/21/2010	01/08/2012
0TCT_MCA1_Q	▣	☑	ELEM...	0TCT_MCA1	7MODTUOA...	SAP	SAP	06/23/2010	01/08/2012
0TCT_MCA1_Q	▣	☑	ELEM...	0TCT_MCA1	473PM73D8...	SAP	SAP	06/21/2010	01/08/2012
0TCT_MCA1_Q	▣	☑	ELEM...	0TCT_MCA1	473POF3UQ...	SAP	SAP	06/21/2010	01/08/2012
0TCT_MCA1_Q	▣	☑	ELEM...	0TCT_MCA1	7MODTUOA...	SAP	SAP	11/02/2010	01/08/2012
REP_201201080	▣	☑	ELEM...	@10D NW ...	B531MC02H...	KONG	KONG	01/08/2012	01/08/2012

Figure 10.10 Queries and Dependent Objects to Delete

It is possible to deselect queries that should not be deleted within the list. In fact, we recommend that you send the list of queries out to the user who created the object so that they are aware that the object is about to be deleted. This allows them to access the object and, if they still want to keep it in the system, remove it from the list.

You can start the deletion by executing the selection list once the selection is confirmed. This performs the deletion of the objects; you can't undo this step except via a database restore.

Query objects can also become inconsistent. This normally happens when objects are created in older versions of SAP BEx tools or queries are deleted. SAP has released program ANALYZE_RSZ_TABLES for cleaning up these inconsistencies, and we recommend that you execute this program quarterly to ensure that access to query definitions is optimal. The program is executed from Transaction SA38 and provides a list of selections, as displayed in Figure 10.11.

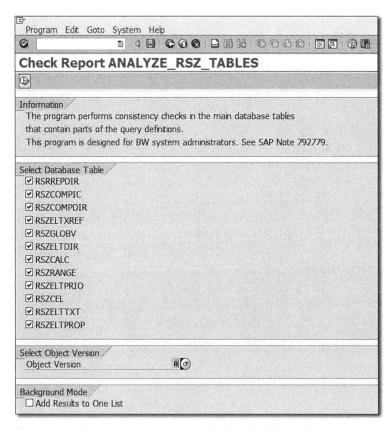

Figure 10.11 Selection Screen in Program ANALYZE_RSZ_TABLES

We recommend that you execute the report for all the database tables to correct all errors. SAP Note 1506560 (ANALYZE_RSZ_TABLES: Improvements and Enhancements) displays the report and describes how to correct the errors.

You would generally expect to get a report without errors once all the issues have been resolved, as displayed in Figure 10.12. Note the repeated message No ERRORS FOUND at the bottom.

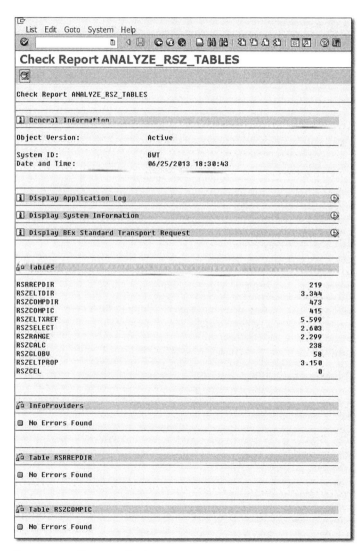

Figure 10.12 Clean Result of ANALYZE_RSZ_TABLES

The first execution normally has quite lot of errors requiring resolution, but future executions have fewer errors—sometimes even no errors at all.

10.2.3 Deleting Obsolete Data Flows

As the SAP BW system becomes more mature, some content might become obsolete. This includes the data flows containing InfoObjects, DSOs, and InfoCubes. You should review the usage statistics against the data load schedule and evaluate whether any data flows are obsolete.

Follow this procedure:

1. Execute SAP BW statistics report by InfoProvider to get a list of InfoProviders used for reporting.
2. Execute SAP BW statistics report for data loading by InfoProvider to get a list of objects that are being loaded with data.
3. Compare the two lists to get a list of object being loaded with data that are not used for reporting.
4. Work with the SAP BW application support team and end users to determine whether these objects and associated reports can be deleted.
5. Stop the data loading to the objects.
6. Verify that the reports are still not accessed after three months.
7. Delete the data content of the objects in the production system.
8. Delete the object three months after the data loading has been stopped in the development, and transport the deletion through the system landscape.

Ensure that the deletion of objects is executed in the development system and tested in the test system prior to being implemented in the production system.

10.2.4 Reviewing Configuration Settings

SAP BW configuration is normally done once during the system setup. You should review some of the configuration settings quarterly to ensure that they are still valid and confirm that they are aligned with the best practices for these configuration settings.

Here, we will cover some of the main settings in an SAP BW system. The configuration settings can be access via Transaction SPRO and are grouped under the PERFORMANCE SETTINGS folder, shown in Figure 10.13.

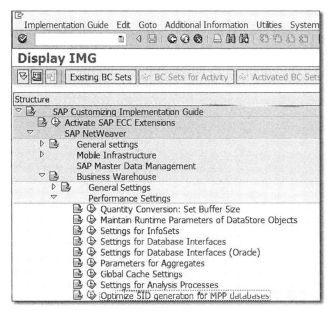

Figure 10.13 Performance Configuration for SAP BW

In addition to these configuration settings, we will also look at the RSADMIN table configuration and configuration settings for data transfer.

Quantity Conversion Buffer Size

This parameter controls the buffer size of the internal table used for quantity conversion. You should set the value between 400 and 1000. Higher values could negatively impact performance of the quantity conversion. Figure 10.14 displays the setting with a value of 500, which is a good starting point for this setting.

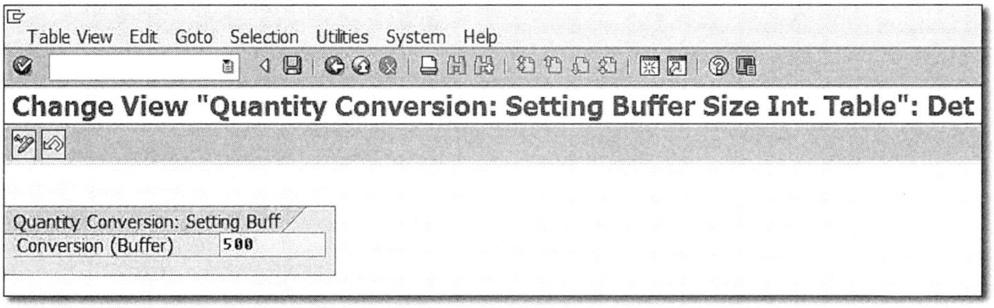

Figure 10.14 Quantity Conversion Buffer Setting

537

DSO Runtime Parameters

Transaction RSODSO_SETTINGS is used to control settings for DSOs. It is possible to set default system settings but also maintain specific settings for each DSO to improve the performance for that specific object.

To maintain the system-wide settings, click the EDIT SYSTEM SETTING button shown in Figure 10.15.

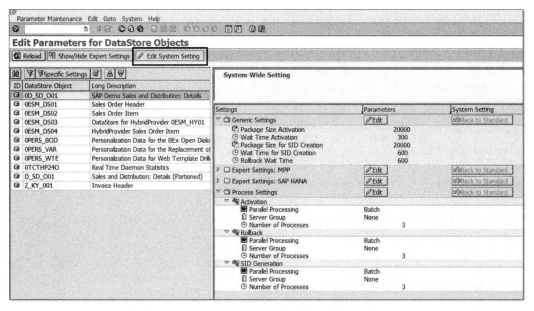

Figure 10.15 Editing Parameters (Transaction RSODSO_SETTINGS)

Double-click a DSO to maintain specific settings for that object. Let's walk through a few parameters:

▶ GENERIC SETTINGS cover package sizes and wait times, as follows:

 ▶ PACKAGE SIZE ACTIVATION: Specify the minimum number of data records per data package when activating data in the DSO. The default value of 10000 is used when no package size is set or the package size that is set is smaller than 10000.

 ▶ WAIT TIME ACTIVATION: Specify the maximum wait time, in seconds, when activating data in the DSO. This is the time that the main process (batch process) waits for the parallel dialog process before it classifies it as having errors.

- ▶ PACKAGE SIZE FOR SID GENERATION: Select the minimum number of data records per data package when generating the SID in the DSO.

- ▶ WAIT TIME FOR SID GENERATION: Select the maximum wait time, in seconds, when generating the SID in the DSO.

- ▶ ROLLBACK WAIT TIME: This is the time, in seconds, the batch process waits before it considers the parallel process lost and performs a rollback.

▶ PROCESS SETTINGS are for activation, rollback, and SID generation.

- ▶ PARALLEL PROCESSING: Specify parallel (batch) or parallel (dialog). *Batch* and *dialog* indicate which type of process is used for the processing. Batch is recommended when users access the system during data loading to avoid using all the dialog processes for data load processing.

- ▶ SERVER GROUP: Specify the group of servers to be used for the parallel processing of data in DSOs. This makes several dialog processes available to you. You need to have already created the server group in Transaction SM59. Choose RFC • RFC GROUPS from the main menu.

  If you specify nothing here, processing runs on the one on which the batch process was started. Processing is terminated if a server belonging to the server group is not active.

- ▶ NUMBER OF PROCESSES: Specify the maximum number of parallel processes allowed when activating data in the DSO. The upper limit is the number of dialog processes that exist in the system. If all dialog processes are involved in activation, the system is fully occupied.

There are some additional settings available for DSO massive parallel processing (MPP) and SAP HANA.

You can define the following expert settings for MPP:

- ▶ CLASSIC ACTIVATION: This deactivates MPP activation and switches back to standard activation.

- ▶ LOG SQL: By logging the generated native database statements, you can display them in Transaction RSODSO_SQLTRACE.

- ▶ ACCESS FOR SID HANDLING: This is used to specify which database access is used from the options STANDARD, FULL TABLE SCAN, DISTINCT VALUES, or ANTIJOIN.

Define the following expert settings for SAP HANA:

- ▶ PACKAGE SIZE FOR DATA RESTRICTION: This is the package size used for the SAP HANA-optimized and memory-optimized (memory consumption reduced, or

MCR) activation of requests. This is important when users run queries at the same time as data loads take place.

▶ NUMBER OF PACKAGES: This is the number of packages that are processed in parallel during SAP HANA request activation. It is another important parameter when users run queries during data load processing.

▶ ACCESS FOR SID HANDLING: In the context of SAP HANA DSO activation, SID generation supports various access methods for reading characteristic values for further processing from the active data/activation queue. The options are STANDARD, FULL TABLE SCAN, DISTINCT VALUES, or ANTIJOIN.

▶ COMPRESS CHANGE LOG: This option should be set only if you want to write change log entries for activated records and the activation of these records has actually changed the status of the active data.

These DSO settings should be reviewed, especially if DSO-specific settings are maintained, to ensure that they are following best practices. You should review SAP Note 1118205, RSODSO_SETTINGS Maintain Runtime Parameter of Data Store Obj., which contains some specific settings recommendations.

InfoSet Settings

This parameter is obsolete as of SAP BW version 7.0.

When InfoSets are used for reporting, performance issues may arise when a large number of single values are included in the selection. This configuration setting can be used to specify a numerical value to represent the upper limit for single-value selections (e.g., 100). If a characteristic has 100 or fewer single-value selections, it is included in the where condition; if it has more than the specified number, a virtual provider is generated dynamically and added to the join. This can improve performance dramatically. Check out SAP Note 673575 for more information.

Database Interface Settings

You use this configuration to make settings regarding the performance of the database interface, as displayed in Figure 10.16 and as follows:

▶ DB STATISTICS: This setting is obsolete and should not be used.

▶ QUERY-SQL SPLIT: You use this parameter to split complex queries into several SQL statements. The default value is 50, and it is not recommended to go beyond this value.

▶ DATA MART-QUERY SPLIT: You use this parameter to split complex data mart statements into several SQL statements. The default value is 20, and it is not recommended to set it higher than this.

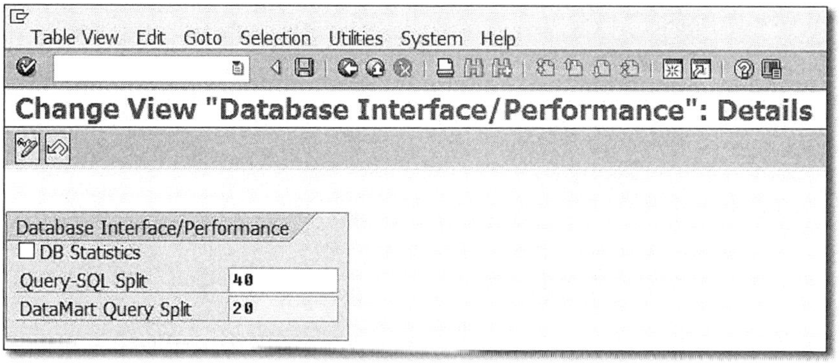

Figure 10.16 Settings for Database Interfaces

Additional information is available in SAP Note 514907.

If the SAP BW system is running on an Oracle database platform, there are some specific settings available to improve performance, as displayed in Figure 10.17 and as follows:

▶ LOGGING WITH INDEX: This indicator is used to control whether an index build is written to the database backup. If the indexes are written to backup, performance could improve when you rebuild indexes. However, it takes longer to build the indexes. Generally, you shouldn't set this indicator unless requests are not compressed frequently. As the default setting, Oracle database logging for the index build is switched off. This means that indexes cannot be rebuilt from the database backup. You must rebuild them afterward, using Transaction RSRV.

▶ DEGREE: This parameter determines the number of parallel processes that can be used when building Oracle aggregates and indexes. It is recommended to set this parameter if you want it to be different from the default parameter maintained in Oracle configuration PARALLEL DEFAULT.

These settings have no impact if the database platform is not Oracle.

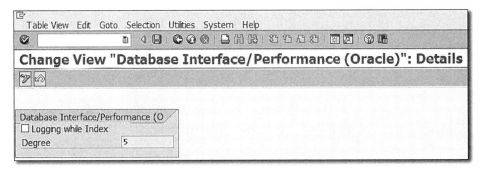

Figure 10.17 Database Interfaces and Performance Settings for Oracle

Aggregate Parameters

The parameters for aggregates can help improve performance for the aggregate rollup and attribute change run. In this activity, you change the parameters that control how aggregates are structured and changed. The settings are maintained via Transaction RSCUSTV8, as displayed in Figure 10.18 and as follows:

▶ PERCENTAGE CHANGE IN THE DELTA PROCESS: This setting controls when aggregates are adjusted via a delta update or full reconstruction of the aggregates. When a delta update is used, the old records are negated, and the new records inserted. The process that is used depends on, among other things, how much data has been changed. This parameter specifies as of which change percentage the system switches from a delta process to a reconstruction, and it is a number between 0 and 99. This allows you to optimize the performance of the change run. The recommended start value is 20, but this should be optimized when testing various values.

▶ BLOCK SIZE: The block size setting controls the size of each block of data used to build aggregates when the source the aggregate is built from (InfoCube or aggregate) is very large. The system then reads that data a block at a time based on this parameter value. There is no general recommendation for the block size: it depends on the database platform used in the SAP BW system. If no value is maintained for the BLOCKSIZE parameter, the default value of 100,000,000 is used (exception: DB6 = 10,000,000).

▶ WAIT TIME: This is the length of time a process waits before it terminates when another process is already locking an aggregate.

▶ REPORTING LOCKS: This is a parameter that is relevant only for installations with an Oracle database to avoid the problem of overflow database rollback segments when a large amount of master data changes are activated. This parameter, set to X, triggers that database commits are executed when the master data is activated. This prevents an overflow of rollback segments. Reporting is locked during this time because data is temporarily inconsistent. It is recommended to set this check only if problems with large rollback segments are encountered.

Recommendation

Aggregates are obsolete when SAP BW powered by SAP HANA is used because the performance of SAP HANA supersedes the performance of aggregates.

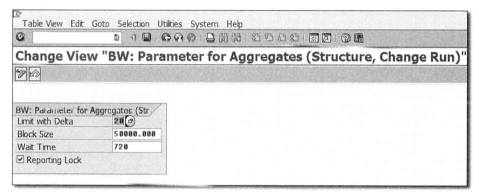

Figure 10.18 Parameter Settings for Aggregates (Transaction RSCUSTV8)

Global Cache Settings

Recall from Chapter 1 that the cache settings depend on the shared memory buffer. If the memory buffer has changed, the cache parameters should also be updated. You can maintain the global cache parameters by calling Transaction RSRCACHE. The following parameters should be reviewed for consistency with the current memory buffer size and cache usage:

▶ CACHE INACTIVE: If you set this parameter, the cross-transactional cache is deactivated centrally.

▶ LOCAL SIZE IN MB: This parameter determines the memory size, in megabytes, of the local OLAP processor cache. The local cache is used if you cannot save in the cross-transactional cache because it is not active or if the InfoProvider cache or query cache has been deactivated.

▶ GLOBAL SIZE IN MB: This parameter determines the maximum memory size, in megabytes, that is available for all objects to use in the cross-transactional cache. The memory size relates to the memory that is used for runtime objects. Therefore, the actual memory usage is generally smaller because the runtime objects are compressed when written to the cross-transactional application buffer.

The actual size of the cross-transactional cache depends on the size settings of the cross-transactional application buffer: the maximum cache size is the minimum from the GLOBAL SIZE IN MB parameter and the memory size that is actually available in the cross-transactional application buffer.

▶ PERSISTENCE MODE: You use the persistence mode to determine whether and in what form cache data is to be stored, as follows:

  ▸ FLAT FILE: The cached data is stored as a file in a directory on the application server or cross-application server in the network.

  ▸ CLUSTER TABLE/TRANSPARENT TABLE (BLOB): The cached data is stored in the database as a non-transparent cluster table or transparent table with binary logical object (BLOB).

Analysis Processes Settings

In this activity, you can specify a server, server group, or host executing analysis processes in the background. In this way, you can control the distribution of load for the background processes of analysis processes (including calculation of intermediate results in the background) by determining an application server or server group.

MPP Database SID Generation

You can optimize the performance of SID generations for MPP databases by defining a threshold value for the number of records that triggers mass access.

If more values are simultaneously selected than the threshold value allows, mass access is executed. If the threshold value is not exceeded, the records are selected individually. You should follow SAP's recommendations.

SID tables are usually buffered on a record-by-record basis. If a large number of values need to be read in the SID table, single-record access (select SINGLE) is considerably faster than mass access (select FOR ALL ENTRIES), provided that all the values to be read are contained in the single-record buffer. If the values are not contained in the buffer, mass access is considerably faster than single-record access. The relative access times depend very much on the database used.

RSADMIN Parameters

The RSADMIN table is used to control specific functionality in SAP BW. It is also used implement exceptions in functionality via SAP Notes, which can become obsolete with the implementation of support packages.

We recommend reviewing the parameters specified in table RSADMIN to ensure that the corresponding SAP Notes are still valid. A good starting point is SAP Note 912367 (Composite Note: RSADMIN Parameter), which contains the majority of the RSADMIN parameters and links to the corresponding SAP Notes.

There are also some parameters that are specific for DB2. These can be found in SAP Note 594263 (DB2/zOS: BW: RSADMIN parameter documentation).

Data Transfer Control Parameters

You can improve performance during data loading using the control parameters for data transfer.

For SAP source systems, you change the control parameter settings in the source system in Transaction SBIW (Customizing for Extractors), under Business Information Warehouse • General Settings • Maintain Control Parameters for Data Transfer:

▶ Maximum Size of Data Packages: For data transfer into SAP BW, the individual data records are sent in packages of variable sizes. You use these parameters to control how large such a data package typically is. If no entry is maintained, the data is transferred with a standard setting of 10,000 kilobytes per data package. The memory requirement depends on not only the setting for data package size, but also the width of the transfer structure and memory requirement of the relevant extractor.

▶ Frequency: With the specified frequency, you determine after how many data IDocs an info IDoc is sent to the SAP BW monitor. The frequency is set to 1 by default, but it is recommended to increase this to between 5 and 10, but not greater than 20. The larger the package size of a data IDoc, the lower you must set the frequency. In this way, you ensure that, when loading data, you receive information on the current data load status at relatively short intervals.

▶ MAXIMUM NUMBER OF PARALLEL PROCESSES FOR DATA TRANSFER: Select a number between 1 and 5. Generally, three parallel processes are recommended. More parallel processes increase the throughput of the data loading but also take up dialog processes.

The maintenance is displayed in Figure 10.19.

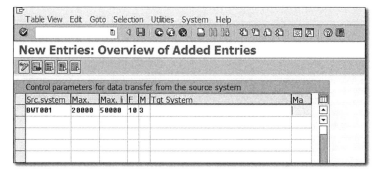

Figure 10.19 Maintaining Control Parameters for the Data Transfer

The setting in Transaction RSCUSTV6 in the SAP BW system controls the interfaces for external data, such as flat files, as displayed in Figure 10.20. One additional setting is available to control the size of a PSA partition. Here, you can set the number of records at which a new partition is generated. This value is set to 1,000,000 records by default and should generally be changed only if extremely large data loads are executed.

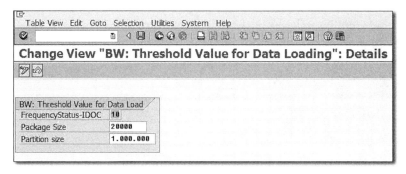

Figure 10.20 Maintain Control Parameters for External Systems

Now that we've looked at the quarterly tasks, we will take a look at the yearly tasks that also introduce large changes into the system.

Yearly administration and performance tuning tasks take the most effort of all the tasks covered in this book. It is advisable to execute these tasks as small projects to provide funding and accountability in order to guarantee success.

11   Yearly Tasks

Do not underestimate the importance or effort of the yearly tasks! Some of these tasks must be executed as projects and managed according to project management methodology.

Implementing support packages and performing version upgrades pave the way for future administration and performance tuning excellence and are required tasks in any SAP system. Performing a yearly system and performance review of the SAP BW system with an external consultant can provide great insight into performance problems and new ways of improving system performance.

As with the previous chapters, this chapter will also split its focus between yearly administration monitoring tasks (Section 11.1) and yearly performance tasks (Section 11.2). Yearly tasks generally require more planning and coordination to execute than any of the previous tasks covered, and most should be managed as small projects. In the next chapter on a BI Competency Center, we will cover the skills and team structure needed to deliver successful BI projects.

The administration tasks covered in this chapter are generally intended to keep the system up to date with SAP support and validate your organization's plans to keep the BI systems accessible in case of disruption. The performance tuning tasks covered in this chapter are required to prevent new content development, incremental changes over the past year, and organic growth from impacting acceptable performance standards. Let's start by reviewing the administrative performance tasks.

11.1   Yearly Administration Tasks

Some yearly administration tasks are major system changes and should be run as small projects. We will cover the following administration tasks:

▶ Upgrading SAP BW applications

▶ Using SAP BW support packs

▶ Using the Software Update Manager

▶ Running SAPgui maintenance

▶ High-availability and disaster recovery testing

▶ Assessing system risk

Let's look at a few detailed steps to execute the tasks.

11.1.1   Upgrading SAP BW

You can expect SAP BW application releases every two to three years. In general, we recommend that you update to the latest release within one to two years after a release is generally available. This ensures that your release of the SAP software is updated with the latest fixes and features required for maintaining a system without major issues.

SAP software upgrades should generally be done using the Software Update Manager (SUM). In the past, they were done using SAPup and SAPjup, which are now part of SUM.

Upgrading Project Planning

Planning a system upgrade can be a difficult task. It requires scheduling a time when the system can be shut down for a weekend, sometimes even an extended weekend. It also requires a team of resources from different functions to work together to get the project executed. When you intend to perform the SAP BW upgrade, you should plan the high-level tasks listed in Table 11.1.

Preparation	Review hardware sizing			3 days
	Prepare upgrade software	Review upgrade guide	2 days	5 days
		Create maintenance in solution manager MOPZ	1 day	
		Get SAP BW upgrade software (DVD or download)	2 days	
	Hardware installation, if required			3 days
	Other preparations	Impose freeze on new development	1 day	3 days
		Release all transports from Development and move to Production	1 day	
		Detailed system outage planning	1 day	
	Total			**14 days**
Upgrade activities	Upgrade sandbox system	Perform baseline testing	3 days	45 days
		Upgrade system	2 days	
		Perform regression testing and resolve issues	40 days	
	Development	Perform baseline testing	2 days	14 days
		Upgrade system	2 days	
		Perform regression testing	10 days	
	Test system	Perform baseline testing	2 days	7 days
		Upgrade system	1 day	
		Perform regression testing	4 days	
	Production system	Perform baseline verification	½ day	2 days
		Upgrade system	1 day	
		Perform system verification	½ day	
		Release system for general use	Immediate	
	Total			**68 days**

Table 11.1 SAP BW Upgrade High-Level Project Plan

Preparation Tasks

During the preparation phase, make sure to read through the SAP upgrade guide and the main SAP Upgrade notes. The upgrade guides can be found on the SAP Service Marketplace, along with specific SAP Notes mentioned in the guides, which should be read for the most up-to-date information.

You also need to acquire the software for the upgrade. Download it from the SAP Service Marketplace if you have a high-speed internet connection, or order it from your local SAP affiliate or partner.

Another very important task in the preparation of an upgrade is to review SAP Notes for future support packages and evaluate whether any of the SAP Notes should be implemented as part of the upgrade. You should always implement the SAP Notes with priority "Correction with high priority" and at least review the SAP Notes with priority "Correction with medium priority."

> **Recommendation**
>
> You can access SAP support package notes via *https://service.sap.com/sap/bc/bsp/spn/spat/index.htm?sp1=<SP technical name>*. For example, the support pack for SAP BW 7.30 SP10 is located at *https://service.sap.com/sap/bc/bsp/spn/spat/index.htm?sp1=SAPKW73010*.

Using the Software Update Manager

You can use the Software Update Manager (SUM) for the following system maintenance tasks:

▶ Upgrading to a new software release

▶ Installing enhancement packages

▶ Updating Support Packages (SPs) and Support Package Stacks

▶ Updating Java patches

> **Recommendation**
>
> The term *update* is the generic term used in the SUM documentation for all of these activities, but we will distinguish between upgrades to new versions and the application of enhancement packages (this section) and the application of support package stacks (the next section).

SUM can be used to update all SAP NetWeaver-based systems, including systems based on AS ABAP, AS Java, or both (in the case of a dual-stack system). During the maintenance—or update—procedure, you can prepare SUM and use it to execute the system update by following these seven simple steps:

1. Before you begin, plan the maintenance activity using the Maintenance Optimizer in SAP Solution Manager (Transaction MOPZ).
2. Download the SUM and documentation from *http://service.sap.com/sltoolset*.
3. Extract the archive to a folder on the primary application server/central instance of your SAP system.
4. Start the tool on the primary application server/central instance.
5. Connect to *http://<hostname>:4239* from your local computer using any browser.
6. Configure the SUM tool and point to the *stack.xml* file produced by the Maintenance Optimizer Transaction or to a directory with the set of support packages to be imported.
7. Execute the update of your system.

> **Recommendation**
>
> SAP Note 1732061 (Software Update Manager 1.0 SP07) contains important information on the SUM tool. We recommend that you update to the latest SUM SP level and read the corresponding SAP Note before using the tool for an update because not all update scenarios are supported.

Regression Testing Tasks

System regression testing is one of the most important tasks when it comes to performing an upgrade to a new SAP BW release. Table 11.2 lists the most important regression tests to execute in the upgrade project. The regression testing should be executed by the project team (and specifically by the test team) within the project.

Test	Description
Test data loads	Execute all or at least a 20% subset of all data loads that run in the system. This includes loads that are executed only monthly or yearly.

Table 11.2 Regression Testing Tasks

551

Test	Description
Generate all queries	A quick way to test queries in the system is to generate them all. This is done from Transaction RSRT • ENVIRONMENT • GENERATE QUERIES DIRECTLY. This executes program RSR_GEN_DIRECT_ALL_QUERIES. You should generate all queries both before and after the system upgrade so that query results can be compared to verify that there are no differences.
Test query results	A subset of all queries in the system should be tested before and after the upgrade to ensure that they give the exact same result. The best approach is to set up workbooks in SAP BEx Analyzer, refresh queries, and compare the results between the snapshots done before the upgrade to the result after the upgrade. You can accomplish a similar approach with bookmarks that are downloaded to Excel.
Test reporting tools	All reporting tools used to access the SAP BW system should be tested. This testing requires a set of standard test scripts, as well as users executing ad hoc analysis to ensure that as much functionality as possible is tested.
Test data load performance	To test data load performance, it is important that a few tests are set up prior to the upgrade, and that these can be replicated after the system change. You can do this by using a full load for a historical period as an example and then re-running the exact same parameters for the load after the change is implemented. Remember to test different types of data loads, such as master data, text, hierarchies, transaction data to DSO, and transaction data to InfoCube. You can compare the results from the data loading using the BW statistics data collected during the processing.
Test reporting performance	Testing the report performance requires that the same reports with the same selections be executed before and after the change. Select a subset of the reports and create specific performance testing bookmarks or workbooks using the SAP BEx tools. You can compare the results from the data loading using the BW statistics data collected during query execution.
Test interfaces	All interfaces should be tested. This means that interfaces related to different source systems should be tested for data loads. You should also test outbound interfaces that are receiving data from SAP BW.

Table 11.2 Regression Testing Tasks (Cont.)

Test	Description
Test security and authorization	Make sure that the security implemented in the system is still functioning. The best approach is to test reporting with user IDs that have limited access restrictions, rather than testing with support user IDs. This ensures that errors are identified early and not by end users during user acceptance testing or in production. You may need to review all roles because upgrades can introduce new authorization objects that are required to execute actions that did not require authorization in the previous release.
Test new functionality	An additional set of test scenarios should be defined for functionality that has either changed or been introduced in the new version. These tests might be less important if the functionality is not going to be used immediately after the system upgrade. It is, however, important to find issues with the functionality early to avoid starting implementation of the new functionality only to find out that it is not yet fully functional.

Table 11.2 Regression Testing Tasks (Cont.)

11.1.2 Applying SAP BW Support Packs

SAP BW support packages should be applied yearly, at the minimum. If you upgrade to a release within the first year of general availability, you should expect to update support packages every six months for the first year, and subsequently once every year.

You can apply support packages using the Support Packages Manager (Transaction SPAM), Transaction SAINT, or the SUM tool. To choose a method, you should review SAP Note 1803986 (Rules to Use SUM or SPAM/SAINT to Apply SPs for ABAP Stacks).

Planning Support Package Update

Planning a support package update is similar to planning a version upgrade, but it is normally executed much faster and with less impact on the system. A high-level project plan should include the tasks and proposed timeline shown in Table 11.3.

	Review hardware sizing			5 days
	Prepare upgrade software	Review SP notes	2 days	5 days
		Create maintenance in solution manager MOPZ	1 day	
		Download required Support packages	2 days	
	Other preparations	Impose freeze on new development	1 day	3 days
		Release all transports from Development and move to Production	1 day	
		Detailed system outage planning	1 day	
Total				**13 days**
	Upgrade sandbox system	Perform baseline testing	2 days	14 days
		Upgrade system	2 days	
		Perform regression testing and resolve issues	10 days	
	Development	Perform baseline testing	1 day	10 days
		Upgrade system	1 day	
		Perform regression testing	8 days	
	Test system	Perform baseline testing	1 day	5 days
		Upgrade system	1 day	
		Perform regression testing	3 days	
	Production system	Perform baseline verification	Half day	2 days
		Upgrade system	1 day	
		Perform system verification	Half day	
		Release system for general use	Immediate	
Total				**31 days**

Table 11.3 SAP BW Support Package Update High-Level Project Plan

The very accelerated timeline from the development system to the production system can be executed as long as good testing as been performed in the sandbox system. It is possible to start with updating the test system in cases when there is no sandbox system in place.

Applying Support Packages

The SUM is the main tool for applying updates to the SAP BW system. However, it does not support all scenarios, such as applying single ABAP support packages. For these updates, you still use the Support Packages Manager (Transaction SPAM).

To start a support package update, call Transaction SPAM in client 000 of the SAP BW system. This brings you to the screen shown in Figure 11.1. You should always update to the latest version of the SPAM before starting any updates. The latest version should be downloaded from the SAP Service Marketplace.

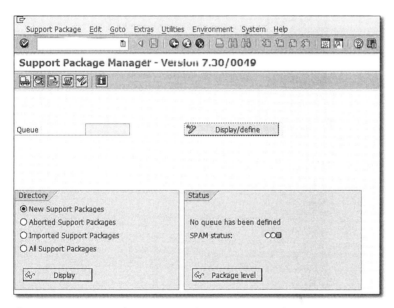

Figure 11.1 Support Package Manager (Transaction SPAM)

To apply the support packages, upload them to the system by choosing SUPPORT PACKAGE • LOAD PACKAGES • FROM FRONT END or FROM APPLICATION SERVER. This transfers the support packages to the correct folder on the server and decompresses the files.

Once the files are on the server, you can create an import queue. Choose DISPLAY/DEFINE to see a list of the installed components, as seen in Figure 11.1.

Double-click the components you want to update, as shown in Figure 11.2. The system checks whether the required support packages are on the server and calculates the queue to be imported. You can select a subset of the calculated import queue.

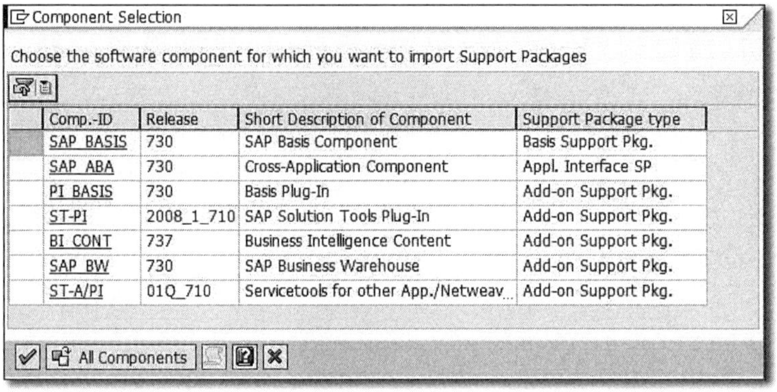

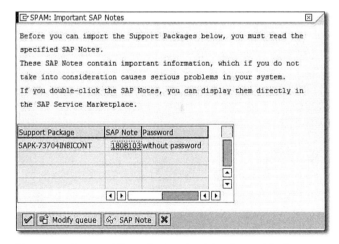

Figure 11.2 Selection of Component to Update

Some support packages require you to enter a password, which can be obtained from an SAP Note. This is normally the case if there are specific requirements or precautions to be taken when applying the support package to prevent problems that the support package could cause. Additional information is then contained in the same SAP Note as the password. A password is not required in the example shown in Figure 11.3, but you should still read the SAP Note.

Figure 11.3 Password Prompt when Applying Support Packages

Click OK; a prompt is displayed to allow for a modification adjustment transport to be imported as part of the support package process. A modification adjustment transport contains reversals of obsolete SAP Notes that have previously been implemented. Therefore, these modification adjustment transports should be imported in the test and production systems because the modification adjustments from previous, obsolete SAP Notes have already been implemented in the development system.

Modification adjustments must be transported to clear the enhancement info system and avoid errors when the support package is implemented. The modifications are reset or adjusted in Transaction SPAU for program modifications and Transaction SPDD for dictionary modifications.

The queue is now ready to be imported. Select SUPPORT PACKAGE • IMPORT QUEUE to start the import. A prompt displays to allow users to select whether the import should run in dialog or in the background. You should run the import in the background to avoid timeouts. Choose START OPTIONS • START IN BACKGROUND to schedule the import as a background job.

You can monitor the import status from the SPAM, as shown in Figure 11.4.

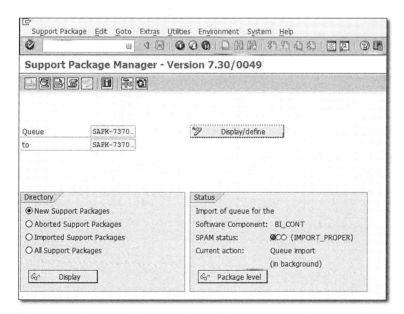

Figure 11.4 Monitoring the Import Status (Transaction SPAM)

If for any reason the import stops, try to restart it. This could be caused by objects being activated while also being in use by the SPAM. If that does not resolve the problem, you can perform further analysis by looking in the import logs. You can access the import logs from GOTO • IMPORT LOGS • QUEUE.

11.1.3 Performing SAPgui Maintenance

SAPgui is the main frontend interface for accessing the administration functions in SAP BW. This software should be updated regularly every six months, or at least yearly.

At the time of writing (Summer 2014), the latest version of SAPgui for Windows is 7.30. Version 7.20 went out of support in April 2013.

The SAP BW frontend tools are part of the SAPgui for Windows installation. These can be installed at the same time SAPgui is installed or installed later. We will go through the SAPgui installation process next.

Getting the SAPgui Software

Order an installation DVD from SAP or download the installation software from the SAP Service Marketplace following the path *http://service.sap.com/swdc* • INSTALLATIONS AND UPGRADES • MY COMPANY'S APPLICATION COMPONENTS • COMPLIMENTARY SOFTWARE • SAP GUI FOR WINDOWS • SAP GUI FOR WINDOWS 7.30 CORE • INSTALLATION.

Figure 11.5 shows the two zip files available for download. Download these files using SAP download manager and unzip them to generate a complete installation directory.

There are two options for installing SAPgui on a computer:

▶ Local installation using a DVD or similar media
▶ Installation from an installation server

The system requirements for SAPgui software installation are described in SAP Note 26417, and the installation procedures are described in the SAP Frontend Installation Guide, which is included in the *PRES1\GUI\WINDOWS\WIN32\ ReadMe* directory on the installation DVD.

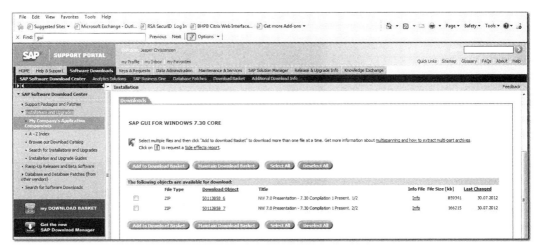

Figure 11.5 SAPgui Download Files in the SAP Service Marketplace

Local Installation of SAPgui

The simple installation option is to install SAPgui locally using the installation DVD or the downloaded installation files.

To start the installation, go to the *PRES1\GUI\WINDOWS\WIN32* directory on the DVD or in the unzipped download directory. Here, you will find the SAPSetup files to allow for different preconfigured installation procedures. To select your installation components, choose *SetupAll.exe*. This brings up the SAP frontend installer shown in Figure 11.6. Select the following components for SAP BW:

- SAPgui for Windows
- Business Explorer

Of course, if you have these tools in your organization, you can select them, as well. Once the selection is done, start the installation by clicking NEXT.

Distributing SAPgui Updates to Clients Using an Installation Server

SAP recommends that you set up an installation server for SAPgui software distribution to centrally administer the distribution of SAPgui onto client computers. The minimum operating system requirements for the installation server should be Windows version 2003 or higher. To install an installation server, use *NWCreateInstServer.exe* in the setup folder on the installation DVD.

Figure 11.6 SAPgui Installer (Selection of Components)

Upgrading SAPgui

Upgrading to a new SAPgui version requires uninstallation of the previous version and installation of the new version. The installation normally handles the uninstallation of the obsolete SAPgui. However, if there are problems after the installation, you should try to uninstall SAPgui completely yourself and then install it again.

Updating Patches for SAPgui Components

SAPgui patches are released regularly by SAP. These should be applied if you have specific problems with any of the SAPgui components.

You can download the SAPgui patches from SAP Service Marketplace by going to *http://service.sap.com/swdc* • SUPPORT PACKAGES AND PATCHES • MY COMPANY'S APPLICATION COMPONENTS • COMPLIMENTARY SOFTWARE • SAP GUI FOR WINDOWS • SAP GUI FOR WINDOWS 7.30 CORE • WIN32.

In addition to the SAPgui patches, you need to update the SAP BEx add-on component that contains SAP BEx from the SAP Service Marketplace, located at *http:/*

/service.sap.com/swdc • SUPPORT PACKAGES AND PATCHES • MY COMPANY'S APPLICA-
TION COMPONENTS • COMPLIMENTARY SOFTWARE • BI ADD-ON FOR SAP GUI • BI 7.0
ADD-ON FOR SAP GUI 7.30 • WIN32.

The patches are executable fields that can be executed on the client to update the
software.

On an installation server, you use *NWSAPSetupAdmin.exe* with the option PATCH
SERVER, as displayed in Figure 11.7, to update the patch onto the installation
server.

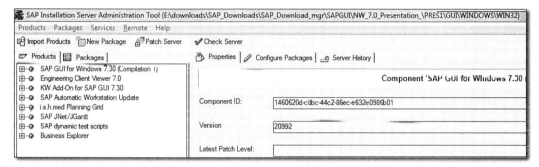

Figure 11.7 Patching the Installation Server from NWSAPSetupAdmin.exe

You can set up automatic updates from the installation server onto the clients
once the patch is updated. We recommend that you do, in fact, do this to ensure
that all clients get updated with the same patch version.

There are two options for the automatic update:

▶ Update notification when a user is logged on. The user has to OK the update.

▶ Update without a user logged on. The option also initiates a reboot, if required.

Both of these options require an installation server that can work as a file server.
The setup is done using *NWSAPSetupAdmin.exe*.

Troubleshooting SAPgui Issues

You can check the installed SAPgui using the SAPgui configuration in the control
panel of the client computer by going to CONTROL PANEL • SAP GUI CONFIGURATION •
SYSTEM INFORMATION • CHECK SAP GUI INSTALLATION, as displayed in Figure 11.8. A
file can be generated at the end of the check with information about the installation that can help your or SAP resolve installation issues.

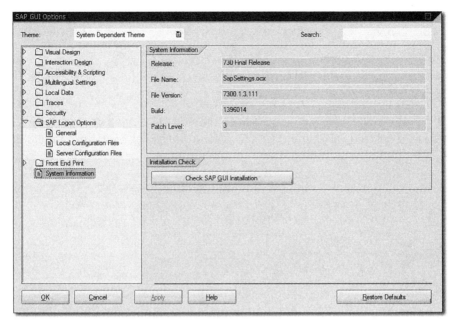

Figure 11.8 SAPgui Installation Check

A good source of installation information is the SAPgui application itself, as shown in Figure 11.9. When you start an SAPgui session, you can type ⎇Alt⎇+⎇F12⎇ and then select ABOUT.

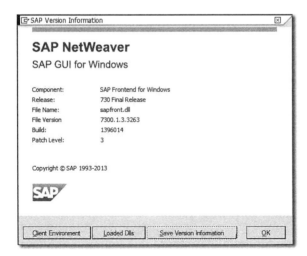

Figure 11.9 Getting SAPgui Version Information

It is possible for users to save the information into a file that can be used for further problem analysis.

11.1.4 Testing High Availability and Disaster Recovery

High availability (HA) describes systems that are configured with redundant hardware in case one piece of hardware or infrastructure fails. Then, the failover to the standby server is triggered upon detection of the failure without disruption to the end users.

Disaster recovery (DR) is the process, policies, and procedures related to preparing for recovery of your SAP BW system and data after a natural disaster at the data center where the infrastructure is hosted. Disaster recovery can involve the offsite storage of backups, the replication of data and logs to a dormant database in another location, and the separation of quality and production systems in different data centers.

If the SAP BW system has been set up with HA and/or DR (commonly called HADR), you should test it every year to ensure that the plans are executable in case a disaster occurs.

High-availability testing is normally simulated when no users are logged on to the system as if a server fails in the system. The HA setup should fail over to the HA server, and the system should be running normally after the fail over.

Disaster recovery testing is normally more comprehensive: it simulates that the data center is completely down and should include the following aspects when executed:

1. Full system recovery
2. All interfaces reconnected and working
3. Data loading schedule executed in restored system
4. Critical reports executed and validated

It is important that the HA and DR tests are executed from both a technical perspective and the application perspective because the plans should include clear guidelines on how the application is restored and operated after an HA or DR event.

11.1.5   Assessing System Risks

Most companies perform a system-risk assessment when a new system is implemented, but you should also update this risk assessment yearly to ensure that the system is maintained and monitored in accordance with how it is being used by the business. It is common for an SAP BW system to be classified as a non-critical system when it is initially implemented but subsequently become a critical system as more and more users rely on the business information in their daily work and for critical decision making.

Business continuity involves planning to keep all aspects of a business functioning in the midst of disruptive events. Your business continuity plan (BCP) should be updated as your SAP BW system evolves into a critical support system for business functions; the plan should take into account the results of your annual risk assessment.

11.2   Yearly Performance Tuning Tasks

Let's turn our attention to some recommended yearly performance tuning tasks. We'll examine the following yearly performance tuning tasks:

- ▶ Reviewing data flow
- ▶ Reviewing external performance and optimization
- ▶ Re-partitioning InfoProvider

These are more substantial efforts than the other performance tuning tasks and could be planned as small projects. They are normally organized as technical reviews performed by external expert resources or a team of internal resources. The outcome of the reviews is typically a list of short- and long-term actions that should be planned and implemented in the system.

11.2.1   Reviewing Data Flow

Performing a data flow review can be extremely beneficial for both data loading efficiency and process chain stability for the following reasons:

- ▶ Shortens data load duration and removes non-dependent tasks from the critical path
- ▶ Eliminates unnecessary and disruptive attribute change runs and reviews all chains that run in parallel without potential conflicts

The approach for the review centers on the following:

1. Reviewing data flows and compliance to best practices, such as LSA and LSA++

2. Reviewing the critical path for data loading and finding optimization candidates

3. Reviewing complex data flows

4. Reviewing InfoProvider usage and determining InfoProviders that are no longer used

5. Reviewing chains not used in the last six months and identifying candidates for deletion

6. Aligning production versions of chains with development and migrating through to production to ensure consistency

The data flow review normally leads to some quick actions that can improve the system performance, but it could require some more radical redesign to achieve the full benefits in the long run.

11.2.2 Reviewing External Performance and Optimization

An external performance and optimization review is normally organized as a two-week workshop when two to three external consultants are given access to two things: the system itself and support from key specialists such as the Basis administrator, SAP BW support and administration team, and SAP BW development team.

The following topics are normally covered during the review:

- DSOs layer analysis
- Database statistics
- DB indexes
- Partitioning
- Compression
- Cardinality
- PSA
- SID buffering
- MultiProviders with hints

- BWA management and reorganizations
- Query design
- Query read modes
- Caching
- Process chain scheduling and dependencies
- Network loads
- Database performance
- DSO and InfoCube design and configuration
- System statistics
- Integrated planning performance
- Data load performance
- Database locks
- I/O analysis
- Hardware capacity analysis
- Aggregate analysis
- Log files
- Data activation performance
- ABAP programming analysis

The outcome of the review is a detailed report of the system and a list of actions that should be planned for implementation. It should also include recommendations for future development and standards improvement.

One major benefit is that it is normally possible to implement some of the quick-win recommendations within the two weeks to achieve some immediate improvement in the system.

11.2.3 Re-Partitioning InfoProviders

SAP BW supports partitioning of InfoCubes and DataStore objects to improve the runtime during read and delete operations on the database. Partitioning is not required when using the SAP HANA database.

The following database platforms support partitioning:

- Oracle
- MSSQL
- Informix, where it is called fragmentation
- IBM DB2 for UNIX, Linux, and Windows, where it is called multi-dimensional clustering (MDC)

On Oracle and MSSQL, the F-fact table of InfoCubes is always partitioned dynamically using the package dimension. The partitioning of the E-fact table of Info-Cubes and DSOs is static, and you can do it using the maintenance interface before you activate the InfoProvider using the path EXTRAS • DB PERFORMANCE • DB PARTITIONING.

Two characteristics are supported for partitioning of the E-fact table or DSOs:

- 0CALMONTH (calendar month)
- 0FISCPER (fiscal period)

The master data IDs (SIDs) of these two partitioning characteristics are added to the two fact tables of InfoCubes as additional columns and filled according to the entries in the time dimension when you load new data requests. Since the fiscal variant influences the fiscal period, you should partition the E-fact tables only if the fiscal variant for the InfoCube is set to a constant value. The DSO requires one of the characteristics as part of the primary key to enable partitioning.

If data has already been loaded, you can no longer change the partitioning properties of an InfoProvider using the maintenance interface. However, there are a few reasons you may need to consider making changes:

1. Partitioning has become available for the database platform used. Therefore, you want to partition existing InfoProviders subsequently so that you can benefit from the advantages of partitioning for the existing InfoProviders (complete repartitioning).

2. Partitioning is already used, but you want to adjust it because the original partitioning schema no longer meets your requirements. For example, there may now be too much data in a partition because data growth has increased over time (complete repartitioning).

3. The time period for partitioning is too small, and you want to extend the partitioning schema for future years (adding partitions).

4. Several partitions contain no data records—or very few data records—and you want to merge them into fewer partitions (merging partitions).

5. A general yearly re-partitioning task is to add partitions to existing InfoProviders.

6. Re-partitioning can be done from Transaction RSA1 (Data Warehousing Workbench). Right-click the targeted InfoCube and then select ADDITIONAL FUNCTIONS • REPARTITIONING, as displayed in Figure 11.10. Another option is to execute program RSDU_REPART_UI directly from Transaction SE38.

Figure 11.10 Accessing Re-partitioning from the Admin Workbench

7. You can add partitions to an already-partitioned InfoProvider by using the ATTACHING PARTITIONS option, shown in Figure 11.11. Click INITIALIZE to start the processing. You are asked if you have backed up the database prior to starting the processing.

Recommendation

Always perform a database backup before executing any re-partitioning actions. Data loads and query execution should be stopped where an InfoProvider is being re-partitioned.

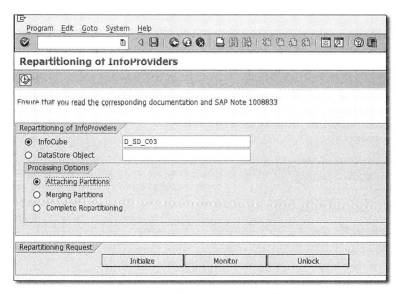

Figure 11.11 Adding Partitions to Already Partitioned InfoProvider

Specify up to which fiscal period or calendar month you want to extend partitions, as shown in Figure 11.12.

Once this is done, a job is scheduled in the background to process the re-partitioning. You can access the monitor to view the steps in the processing and the status of the processing request. The monitor displays the database operations that are performed to execute the re-partitioning, and it is very helpful in resolving errors. A failed re-partitioning request can also be restarted from the monitor, if needed, as shown in Figure 11.13. Requests can also be deleted or reset from within the monitor.

569

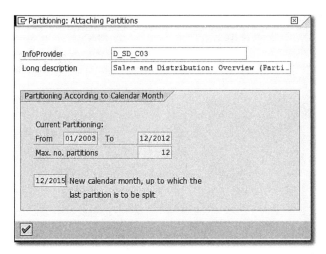

Figure 11.12 Extending Partitions up to a Future Calendar Month

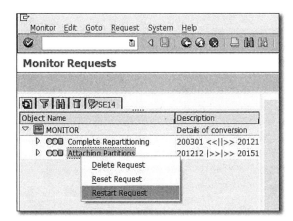

Figure 11.13 Restarting a Re-Partitioning Request if It Has Failed

To see the result of the re-partitioning, access Transaction SE14 directly from the monitor. Click EDIT • STORAGE PARAMETERS to see the partitions generated for the table, as displayed in Figure 11.14.

You can continue data loading and other activities on the InfoProvider once the partitions have been verified.

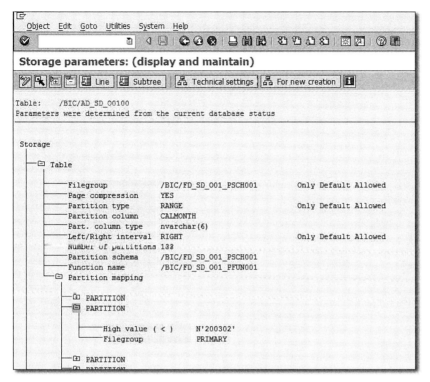

Figure 11.14 Displaying Partitions for a Table in Transaction SE14

This concludes our coverage of administration and performance tuning tasks that can help your system deliver value to the organization at a lower cost. We now turn our attention to supporting your SAP BW system.

Part IV
Support for Your BI Initiatives

A successful BI initiative delivers real business value by maximizing payback and mitigating risk. It all begins with defining and implementing a sound BI strategy to unite business objectives with technical capabilities.

12   BI Competency Center

The first step in launching a successful business intelligence (BI) initiative is to define a BI strategy that supports the strategic goals and objectives of the business. Linking the business strategy and the BI strategy drives alignment across processes toward these goals and objectives. The greater this alignment, the more successful the BI effort will be at generating positive business impact and acceptance throughout the business community.

Positive business impact can be generated only by companies with the skills, organization, and ability to drive changes based on BI insight. How resources are organized and which methods they use are critical for any company looking to leverage internal competencies and ensure the effectiveness of their BI investments. Resources from IT and the business must have in-depth skills in the business processes, BI strategy, and change management, and they must coordinate their actions so that the business can evolve.

The *BI Competency Center* (BICC) is an organizational structure that integrates business and IT to implement the BI strategy across an organization and deliver business value. The BICC is responsible for developing a plan to drive adoption of BI while helping as many user groups and business departments as possible. The goal of the BICC is to shift the corporate culture toward fact-based decision making.

The BICC is a tightly centralized, staffed, and organized group managing all BI initiatives. The benefits of implementing such tight central control are evident in the results of the Conference Board Survey, which determined that when more than one BI project was implemented, those managed centrally were 100% successful. However, only 24% of all organizations leveraged tight central control (as seen in Figure 12.1). Organizations that executed their projects independently reported that only 30% of their BI initiatives were successful.

The main risk with independently managed BI initiatives is that they create silos of skills, methodologies, and data, resulting in data inconsistencies and inaccuracies, as well as competition for funding and influence throughout the enterprise. The cost of silos to business strategy and management can be significant. To correct previously implemented silos, develop consolidation plans, and launch initiatives to address pre-existing BI problems, ensure that subsequent BI investments and skills stay aligned to the overall vision and BI strategy by defining a feedback and review process for business stakeholders to report to the BICC.

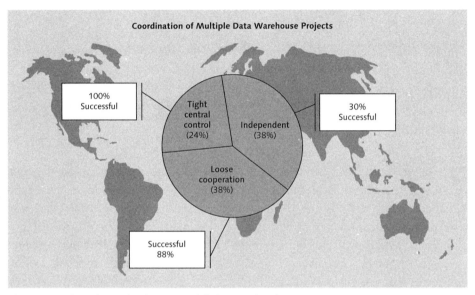

Figure 12.1 The Relationship between Global Control and Success

In addition to improving alignment between the business and IT, an integrated view of key processes and metrics can reduce liability exposure by increasing visibility. To achieve this, the right person needs to see the right data at the right time; they need to see a single version of the truth. BI can provide business value by helping companies identify risks early, as well as changes in business conditions that require attention.

Many companies struggle with BI and performance management initiatives. Defining a balanced, empowered BI organizational structure is critical to the success of delivering BI. This chapter covers how to organize a BICC to efficiently implement and support successful BI projects. It begins by examining the organizational structure of a BICC (Section 12.1), and then moves into the roles and skill sets (Section 12.2) and team structures (Section 12.3) that produce the best results. It closes with BICC best practices that organizations of all sizes can leverage (Section 12.4).

12.1   Centralized Support Organization

The formation of a BICC within most organizations facilitates success with BI by improving the skills, competency, and focus of its resources. These centers are chartered to advance BI from an IT-driven initiative into a business-driven, cross-organization initiative that encompasses a wide range of users, customers, and partners.

But a BICC requires investments in people and the time to develop standards, methodologies, skills, and competencies. There is also the cost (time, people, political capital) of bringing together diverse groups and getting them to agree to priorities and compromises across multiple business needs. In addition, there are compelling "hidden costs" to consider when deciding if a BICC investment is worthwhile.

But a BICC can offer clear cost advantages, like the following:

► A centralized resource pool could reduce duplicated BI resource effort and costs, if those resources are scattered across the organization and are not learning from each other.

► A centralized services model for BI tools could reduce TCO by consolidating infrastructure, maintaining a standard BI architecture and unifying application licensing.

► Developing and maintaining skills for a standard suite of tools costs less than for multiple overlapping tools.

► Building on a standard set of methodologies, definitions, processes, tools, and technologies leads to more consistent data quality, results, and insights, which, in turn, results in better decisions and delivers a higher return on BI investments.

The center develops the overall strategic plan and priorities for BI, sets the standards relating to process and technology, governs their use, and helps the organization interpret and apply the resulting insight to business decisions. Regardless of the organization's structure, the BICC should report directly to the CIO, CFO, or other C-level business executive. This executive sponsor should provide the BICC with a clear mandate to which both the business and IT will adhere.

Although BICC resources normally spend a considerable effort on program management tasks, such as defining requirements, securing funding, ensuring data quality, and architecting technological solutions, these tasks represent only a subset of the center's role. The majority of the effort expended by the center should focus on improving user adoption and acceptance in order to continue to receive funding. This effort includes non-technical tasks, such as training users; promoting the adoption of best practices, methodologies, tools, and applications; and marketing BI capabilities via management updates, user groups, and newsletters.

Achieving the full role of a BICC requires true integration between business and IT. A centralized support organization needs to deliver new BI capabilities, support existing BI capabilities, and govern and promote adoption of all BI initiatives. The governance tasks should be undertaken by the business with support from IT, whereas the project and service delivery should be undertaken by IT, with direction from the business, as indicated in Figure 12.2.

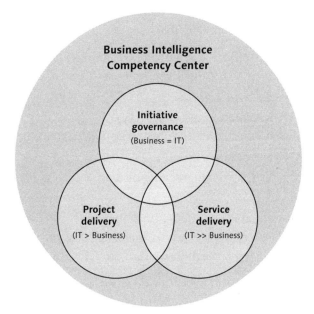

Figure 12.2 Business-IT Integration

12.1.1   BICC Governance

End users need BI tools and applications that are fit for purpose; that is, they need BI solutions that are tailored to their roles and the types of information they must analyze. The governance team must understand both the user population and the different BI technologies available. It is important to recognize that a single toolset will not meet the needs of all users, so organizations should strive to address the majority of needs with the minimal number of tools.

To ensure that the BICC is tackling strategic priorities and not simply reacting only to tactical issues, the governance team should prioritize projects, metrics, and business areas based on their impact on business objectives. The business areas and stakeholders that support BI and are aligned with the BI vision and strategy should be ranked high on the priority list, whereas those requiring cultural change should be ranked lower, as shown in Figure 12.3.

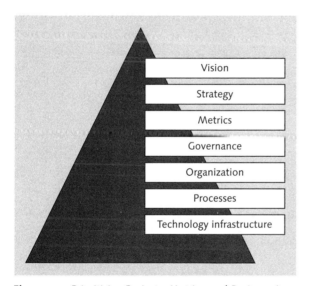

Figure 12.3 Prioritizing Projects, Metrics, and Business Areas

With a defined list of priorities, the BICC can respond more quickly to both tactical and strategic requests from different business areas. Any conflicts regarding priorities should first be negotiated within the BICC and then, if needed, escalated to the executive sponsor. The priority list should be evergreen, meaning it should be updated to reflect the current business strategy and objectives at any point in time.

> **Recommendation**
>
> We recommend the following best practices for this prioritization exercise:
>
> ► Map all BI-relevant business processes and identify which applications could be optimized to improve business value.
>
> ► Define well-articulated business objectives and KPIs to measure business process performance.
>
> ► Establish and enforce BI standards in both strategic and operational business processes.
>
> ► Identify an executive sponsor or steering committee to set priorities, govern and fund initiatives, commit resources, and audit the results.

For each initiative on the priority list that is chosen for implementation, the governance team is responsible for preparing that project for launch. The planning phase of the project should include the following tasks:

► Writing the business case

► Identifying key stakeholders

► Defining scope

► Choosing project methodology

► Writing a milestone plan

► Developing a staffing plan

► Determining target architecture

► Estimating costs and agreeing to the budget

► Identifying risks and critical success factors

► Preparing for on-boarding, training, and staffing issues

► Instituting an approval process

The governance team is also responsible for the post-implementation review of each project, which consists of the following tasks:

► Documenting lessons learned

► Updating BI-specific processes and procedures

In addition to supporting planning and post-implementation for projects launched by the BICC, the governance team is responsible for analyzing and understanding users' behaviors and needs, which may take significant investment. This team is also responsible for training and developing user skills and advocating for the existing and future BI capabilities delivered by BI initiatives and projects launched by the BICC. Ultimately, the governance team is responsible for driving adoption of BI and supporting the use and analysis of BI information as a way to achieve business objectives and transformation.

12.1.2 Project Delivery

BI initiatives come in all shapes and sizes. From *continuous improvement* projects, which serve to enhance existing initiatives, to new initiative implementations, whether it's a small local project or a large-scale global implementation, different types of BI initiatives may follow different methodologies. The methodology for each BI initiative should be chosen based on two basic dimensions, as illustrated in Figure 12.4. These are time to delivery and impact of failure.

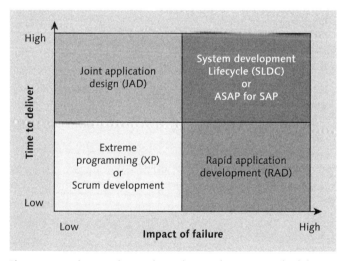

Figure 12.4 When to Choose the Right Development Methodology

Shown in the upper right quadrant, a *system development life cycle* (SDLC) methodology, such as ASAP for SAP, is the right approach when the impact of failure is high and the time to "get it right" is available. The ASAP methodology is a rigid structure that follows clearly defined deliverables and formal checkpoints in the form of "structured walkthroughs" and a formal approval process. This methodology is best suited for mission-critical application development.

Below it, the preferred development approach is the *rapid application development* (RAD) methodology if the time to delivery is compressed while the impact of failure remains high. RAD uses minimal planning in favor of rapid prototyping, which allows the application to be developed much faster—so users can see results earlier in the process—and makes it easier to change requirements. For projects with substantial complexity and/or a high level of dependency between SAP BI and other SAP products, the alternative ASAP methodology may be used.

Extreme programming (XP), shown in the bottom left, is a highly preferred agile development methodology when developing web pages and stand-alone applications because of the rapid development cycle and because most web and stand-alone applications can be rapidly rewritten with minimal disruption to the organization (the impact of failure is typically low). *Scrum* development is an iterative and incremental agile development methodology often preferred when delivering independent reports or bug fixes to existing applications.

The final methodology, *joint application design* (JAD), leverages group sessions to define requirements and transfers much of the design responsibility to the end users. It is an appropriate methodology when there is more time to deliver and the impact of failure is low. This technique usually leads to a community consensus rather than optimal requirements for applications, which is suitable for user-based applications. When the impact of failure is high, a better approach might be to prototype or have structured interviews, as proposed by the RAD and SDLC methodologies, respectively.

Most methodologies have some variation of these three basic phases of work, although multiple iterations can be included in a single project, as illustrated in Figure 12.5.

Let's walk through these three phases.

1. **Blueprint**
   The detailed requirements are captured and converted into the technical design. Project blueprint usually includes the following tasks:
   - Writing the detailed project plan
   - Gathering business requirements
   - Documenting functional designs
   - Conducting gap analysis
   - Documenting detailed designs
   - Monitoring quality/conducting design reviews

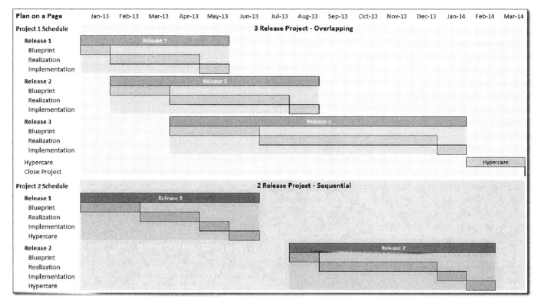

Figure 12.5 Multiple Release Projects by Phase

2. **Realization**

   A functional solution based on the blueprint design is developed and tested. Project realization usually includes the following tasks:

   ► Developing a solution

   ► Monitoring progress and risks

   ► Conducting unit, system, integration, and stress tests

   ► Conducting user-acceptance testing

3. **Implementation**

   The functional solution developed and tested in realization is prepared and deployed to the end-user audience. Project implementation usually includes the following tasks:

   ► Executing cutover and providing hypercare support

   ► Conducting end-user and power-user training

   ► Transitioning from project to service

   ► Post-implementation review and next steps

For the best chance of success, IT projects should be embedded in business projects. Therefore, the project teams must consist of business and IT representatives with the right mix of skills who can work together to implement the chosen BI methodology. These teams define and execute a detailed plan to improve business processes as specified by the scope of the project. The structure of project teams will be covered later, in Section 12.3.

12.1.3 Service Delivery

Unlike the governance and project delivery components of the BICC, the service delivery team is mostly IT representatives, with some influence from the business when initiatives require service optimization. The service delivery team provides end-to-end support for existing BI applications, ensuring that they function at an optimal level and meet the performance expectation of the organization. The BI service delivery team is often responsible for the following items:

- BI application support
  - Analyzing end-user activity
  - Scheduling and monitoring data loads
  - Resolving bugs and end-user issues
  - Managing BI project releases
  - Supporting critical business periods (financial close, etc.)
- User access
  - Maintaining roles, profiles, and authorizations
  - Assigning end users to roles
- Operations support
  - Managing BI system capacity
  - Managing BI system infrastructure
  - Maintaining BI application performance
  - Scheduling downtime for routine maintenance
- Process implementation
  - Defining BI-specific processes and procedures
  - Adopting best practices

- Licensing

  - Managing BI software licenses

  - Choosing service delivery team members for the project

Depending on the size of the BICC, it can be efficient to transfer resources from project to service after their project goes live during the transition to support. When a new project starts, service delivery team members can be chosen for the project based on the mix of required skills.

12.2 Roles and Skill Sets

The members of a BICC come from both IT and the business. While most members are dedicated full-time to the BICC, others may only be needed part time. Regardless, they should all possess a solid understanding of the value of BI and the critical role it plays in helping the company achieve its business objectives. In addition, business and IT leaders in the BICC need a unique mix of basic and advanced business skills, technical knowledge, and communication skills.

To ensure that the benefits of BI initiatives will continue, all BICC members will need to do the following:

- Communicate the value and importance of BI to executives and IT

- Promote the critical role BI plays in improving business management

- Facilitate communication across lines of business

- Ensure the integration of new BI applications with the BI architecture

- Enlighten business stakeholders that a robust BI architecture is needed to successfully deliver BI initiatives

- Solicit business support for an IT platform that can handle changing business requirements

- Convince IT that multiple BI tools are required to meet all analytical needs

- Encourage IT to work more closely with business users

Considering the evangelical role the BICC plays in communicating the value and importance of BI to both the business and IT, failure to include engaged business users in the center will result in a significant increase in the long-term cost of implementing and supporting BI. Enterprises that do not successfully integrate business members in the BICC will likely need to redefine their BI strategy and redesign their BI initiatives to reflect the true needs of the business users.

The following skills and competencies are required for all members of the BICC, regardless of whether they are from the business or IT:

▶ Strong communication and interpersonal skills

▶ A team player mentality

▶ An awareness and appreciation of social and cultural differences

▶ The ability to learn quickly in a hands-on environment

▶ A results-oriented work ethic to deliver on time, on scope, and on budget

▶ The ability to work under pressure

▶ The confidence to manage stressful situations effectively

▶ The ability to work independently on problems and issues

▶ The flexibility to work on a global team

The following sections will define various roles for business users, analysts, technical leaders, and support staff and specify responsibilities for each role.

12.2.1 Business Roles

While it is important to have business users included in the BICC, not just any business people will do. The business members in the BICC must have credibility, clout, and the ability to communicate to and persuade the executive level. The business members of the BICC should possess a mix of basic and advanced business skills and come from diverse backgrounds across the enterprise to better appreciate cross-functional issues as well as those across lines of business. It is particularly beneficial to have business users involved who are engaged in the management of business processes.

Ongoing stewardship of the BICC is the number-one priority of its business members. They need to preach the core message of the BI strategy to their colleagues; their evangelism drives standardization, adoption, and acceptance. In addition to their main focus, business members of the BICC are also expected to do the following:

▶ Recognize and understand which business processes can be supported and possibly improved by better data and analysis

- ▶ Facilitate the identification and definition of performance metrics for each functional area and line of business

- ▶ Prioritize BI initiatives and projects based on expected business impact

- ▶ Help develop business cases with positive returns on investment (ROI) for each eligible initiative

- ▶ Define business decisions in the scope of the overall business objectives

While some of these expectations might appear quite challenging at first, the business members should evolve to meet these more advanced business needs as the BICC gains momentum and establishes itself in the company.

Executive Sponsor

Ideally, BI initiatives are quite strongly aligned with both business objectives and corporate goals and metrics. It is equally important for them to be supported at the executive level by a sponsor who is actively involved in the BICC by providing guidance, direction, and leadership. The most effective executive sponsors are committed to their responsibilities and also promote the BI strategy with other executives. This level of engagement serves to further develop the BICC and its BI capabilities.

Since the makeup of the BICC should reflect the business objectives that drive the BI strategy and its initiatives, it is only logical that the BICC should report to the executive sponsor leading the primary focus of the business. While the CIO may be the first within a company to create the BICC, the CIO is usually not the best choice for an executive sponsor. For example, in companies where financial performance is paramount, the BICC should report to the CFO. Or, in companies where operational efficiency is vital, the BICC should report to the COO.

Business Process Owner

When implementing BI, most companies are looking to answer a long list of significant business questions or address an inventory of BI-relevant topics. In many cases, each *line of business* (LOB) or business process has its own priorities and may fund its own BI initiatives. Additional enterprise-wide initiatives, such as a need to reduce infrastructure cost, improve data quality, and achieve a "single version of the truth" may exist. Many times, all of these exclusive initiatives are competing for the same funding. As a result, the initiatives need to be evaluated and prioritized. Normally, the decision-making process varies from organization to organization because it tends to be rooted deeply in each organization's culture, leadership, skills, and management methodologies.

In order to centralize and consolidate the evaluation and prioritization of initiatives, it is important that you have LOB or business-process representation within the BICC. While their participation will not be full-time, their input should be solicited or required so that they can take some level of ownership and support the outcome of the prioritization effort.

Business Project Manager

The greatest challenge to implementing successful BI initiatives is having the right mix of management skills to deliver results. Skilled project managers can achieve the greatest benefit from complex BI technologies while overcoming the complex organizational dynamics associated with competing BI priorities. More simply put, implementing BI requires highly developed program management skills.

To provide the right mix of management skills, every project launched from within the BICC should have both a *business project manager* (BPM) and a *technical project manager* (TPM). The complexity of BI projects and required integration between business and IT demands that both roles be staffed on every BI initiative. The BPM decides with the TPM how work is split between them according to their respective strengths and weaknesses and the specific needs of the project.

The BPM is accountable for managing scope and avoiding cost and time overruns. The BPM is responsible for coordinating business inputs, outputs, and resources when necessary to ensure that they are delivered and/or available at the appropriate time to avoid risking a schedule delay. In addition, the BPM is charged with planning and executing all change management tasks, including training and go-live communication with the business. Lastly, the BPM is also expected to measure the benefits realized from the implementation and report these results to the BICC.

Business Analyst

In the BICC, the business analyst supports the reporting requirements related to a specific business processes. The business analyst is fluent in one or more processes and has insights into business needs, so he or she can work with users to gather and define BI reporting requirements. This role also focuses on the reporting and analysis of critical business information, so the analyst must leverage a combination of creative and interpretive skills when analyzing the wealth of available information.

In addition to business skills, the business analyst must demonstrate analytical and technological skills using different BI tools and technologies. He or she must understand how to use all SAP BusinessObjects reporting tools, BEx queries, and SAP BW data models to effectively communicate, or translate, the results of their analysis to the business audience.

The business analysts are responsible for the following tasks:

- Managing stakeholders in one or more business processes
- Understanding the data provider structures (InfoCubes, DSOs, etc.)
- Demonstrating competence in analytical techniques (from simple aggregation and filtering to statistical analysis and complex data mining)
- Understanding and articulating the relationship between analytics and KPIs
- Validating data and reports developed by both business power users and IT
- Navigating, exploring, and analyzing data in one or more business processes
- Producing sound business recommendations

In many cases, analysts do not need to be dedicated full time to the BICC. Instead, their involvement can be as dynamic and engaged as needed, according to the strategic and business focus of the BICC. All stakeholders should expect membership and projects in the BICC to be based on current needs to align with organizational and business objectives.

12.2.2 IT Roles

IT membership in the BICC needs to possess a depth and breadth of design, architectural, and technical skills to meet the expectation of today's business users, who can instantly satisfy queries on the Internet with sub-second response times or leverage apps on their phones or other mobile devices to provide instant results for whatever information they seek. The IT members of the BICC are responsible for BI application development and administration, including infrastructure and security. They are responsible for data modeling, data staging, ETL, data integration, data quality, master data management, warehouse management, and report writing. In summary, they are responsible for the performance and efficacy of the analytical solutions delivered by the BICC.

However, the IT members in the BICC cannot be only technical. They must also be business savvy and able to work and communicate with a number of different constituents. They facilitate requirements gathering and work closely with the business analysts to define analytical solutions. They need to have solid program management skills to deliver on time and on budget. And they can play a key role in cultural change management, particularly in terms of promoting BI within and across the IT organization. This role may include the following tasks:

- ▸ Communicating to the rest of the IT organization the role and opportunities of supporting BI applications as part of a BI strategy, as well as helping to build communication across lines of business and IT
- ▸ Helping people (users and IT) understand that BI initiatives need a robust BI architecture to be successful
- ▸ Getting the IT organization to realize that business users need multiple BI technologies to meet their varied analytical needs
- ▸ Ensuring that business users support the IT organization's need to provide a platform that can handle changing business requirements
- ▸ Working with the business to measure the use, effectiveness and value of the BICC

The following roles are commonly found in the BICC, either dedicated or part time. Some roles focus solely on project delivery, others focus solely on service delivery, and some are used in both.

Delivery Director

There is always a risk of BI strategy misalignment across LOBs, business processes, and teams. This can be the result of poor execution by the BICC with regard to specific initiatives, or it can simply be poor penetration into specific business groups that make independent purchasing decisions. Regardless of the cause, the enterprise may end up owning multiple BI tools that provide the same or similar functionality. Procuring, implementing, and supporting redundant tools introduces additional tangible costs, such as licensing and the service costs to support a wider range of skills, but also introduces intangible costs, such as those inhibiting collaboration.

The delivery director's role is to communicate BI technology and tool standards to ensure maximum consistency throughout the organization. The delivery director is responsible for controlling proliferation of non-standard tools and consolidating tools with functionality overlaps. The delivery director is the most senior IT person in the BICC, and all program, project, and SDMs report directly to him or her.

Technical Project Manager

Recall that the TPM is responsible for integrating complex technologies and using those technologies skillfully to gain the insight needed to make better decisions. The TPM is accountable for project results (on time, on scope, and on budget), detailed project planning, and technical delivery. The TPM provides project management skills, experience, and execution and also ensures that technical resources are available and productive.

The typical responsibilities of the TPM include the following:

▶ Creating and updating the detailed project plan
▶ Securing resources and infrastructure
▶ Mobilizing the project resources
▶ Continually assessing progress, risks, and costs
▶ Reporting progress to stakeholders and the steering committee
▶ Ensuring the quality of technical delivery
▶ Closing out the project

The TPM works closely with the BPM and splits project management responsibilities according to specific project needs and the respective strengths and weaknesses of each.

Service Delivery Manager

The service delivery manager (SDM) is responsible for managing the productive systems and support staff. The service delivery team handles incident management, root cause analysis, continuous improvement, and performance optimization for projects that have gone live and been transitioned to support.

The service team members do the following:

- Troubleshoot user-reported issues and develop bug fixes
- Conduct performance tuning, problem solving, debugging, and validation
- Escalate significant issues to the Data Architect and SDM
- Follow up with the BI governance and project delivery team
- Perform routine activities within one or more business processes
- Configure the SAP BW environment to facilitate reporting and data analytics
- Develop and drive the implementation of SAP BW best practices and standards
- Monitor data loads and resolve load issues
- Develop team competence and process compliance
- Receive knowledge transfer (KT) from project teams
- Provide relevant KT to other BICC members

In preparation for the team's responsibilities, the SDM is responsible for defining service-level agreements, which specify how quickly incidents of all priorities are resolved. In addition, the SDM is generally responsible for managing BI software licenses, supporting infrastructure and/or outsourcing contracts, scheduling outages with the business, and managing support staff costs.

BI Systems Architect

In the world of data warehousing, there are two different types of architects, and it is important to recognize the differences between them. The first is the systems architect, who is primarily responsible for technology selection, implementation, and integration. The systems architect is accountable for delivering a robust yet flexible infrastructure that can withstand change and facilitate rapid deployment of new BI projects and initiatives.

Because a significant effort in most BI implementations is spent dealing with infrastructure concerns and issues, the systems architect should design infrastructure to ensure efficiency and agility so that the BICC can react to changing business requirements. In a given SAP BW on SAP HANA environment, the systems architect may integrate the SAP BW system to its source systems using a combination of SAPI, SAP SLT, and SAP Data Services. The architect may also integrate it to SAP NLS, SAP BusinessObjects BI 4.1, SAP Enterprise Portal, Java, and a pre-calculation server to maintain efficiency and flexibility for BICC projects.

The BICC should empower the systems architect by placing an emphasis on controlling the infrastructure and driving toward a common BI architecture. This support helps avoid fragmented environments, consisting of independent data marts on different platforms. Such environments add significant cost and complexity to the BI environment and hamper abilities to adapt to changing business requirements. The systems architect, with the support of the BICC, can limit expensive data mart proliferation by tightly controlling infrastructure and minimizing BI platform fragmentation.

Data Architect

The second type of architect is the data architect. While the systems architect is responsible for the selection and integration of BI technologies, the data architect is responsible for championing best practices, guidelines, and processes within the chosen technologies. This position is absolutely critical within even the smallest teams and should be the most experienced IT member of the BICC. The data architect is not involved in day-to-day, hands-on project work or support work but provides guidance on decisions that could affect future direction, such as where or how to implement specific BI solutions, and gives recommendations on the use of BI tools.

In SAP BW, the data architect(s) defines the developmental guidelines for which all projects and enhancement must adhere. The guidelines should include the layered scalable architecture approach, directions for the use of semantically partitioned objects, and the naming conventions of object types, among other things.

The data architect has a broad, enterprise-wide perspective—or "big picture"—and should review and approve solutions designed by the project teams. To prevent design review bottlenecks, the architect can deputize other senior data modelers to perform these tasks but should still serve to encourage all projects to focus on proper planning and design.

Data Modeler

The data modeler has a knack for visualizing requirements and designing creative, long-term solutions to meet them. She gathers and clarifies business reporting requirements (with the aid of the business analyst) and translates those requirements into optimal data models and data flows.

The data modeler adheres to best practices to design and build high-quality data models that can be efficiently loaded and queried. She designs and builds data flows according to the LSA or LSA++ standards and strives to reduce data redundancy.

This role is responsible for converting the reporting solution into detailed technical design documents. The data modeler also implements the solution and conducts unit testing and integration testing.

ETL Developer

The ETL developer understands the source system tables and data structures and is highly skilled in efficient programming techniques. This role requires proficiency in ABAP because it is responsible for the extraction logic in the source and the transformation logic needed in SAP BW.

The ETL developer collaborates with architects, modelers, and business analysts to design optimal solutions according to best practices. This developer also conducts unit testing and integration testing in coordination with the architect and/ or modeler.

The ETL developer is also responsible for building process chains and related objects to load data, so he should be familiar with decision trees and critical paths. In smaller teams, the data modeler and the ETL developer may be a single person. In more complex scenarios, a good ETL developer is worth his weight in gold!

Presentation Developer

The presentation developer is skilled in the selection of available BI tools and applications. In general, the choice of tool for each solution should be based on the intended audience. Different user segments require different reporting tools; accountants prefer Excel-based tools such, as BEx Analyzer and Analysis for Office, marketing users prefer sophisticated analytic applications, and sales and logistics users prefer static reports. Identifying and deploying the proper mix of tools and applications is critical to successfully penetrating the user base to achieve high levels of BI adoption.

The presentation developer is responsible for designing, developing, and testing reports in the preferred tool for each user segment. This role requires advanced knowledge of visualization techniques to ensure that reports are designed and developed to clearly communicate the report's message or exceptions.

Security Administrator

Depending on the maturity of risk management in an organization, security in BI systems can be quite complex. The security administrator is responsible for defining the security policy within each BI tool and ensuring security integration between tools.

In SAP BW, the security administrator defines roles for IT developers and support staff, as well as business end users, by process and position. In SAP Business-Objects, she defines the method of authentication (i.e., whether Windows active directory authentication is used or whether roles are replicated from SAP BW).

The security administrator is responsible for striking the right balance between risk management and efficient policy. In many large organizations, she simply implements policy based on enterprise-wide standards.

Basis Engineer

Not all roles in the BICC have direct end-user contact. The Basis engineer is responsible for the optimal performance of each BI system in the landscape and possesses a wide range of skills. From the deep-Basis skills at the operating system-monitoring and database-administration levels to the SAP-application level, this role may require multiple engineers to cover all required skills.

The Basis engineer is responsible for executing all system-related performance tasks, such as monitoring capacity sizing, database growth, and network bandwidth. The Basis engineer is responsible for monitoring the SAP application for systematic errors using either SAP Solution Manager or other tools available directly in each system. The Basis engineer is responsible for maintaining database, operating system, and SAP kernel patch levels; applying support package stacks; and executing upgrades to the SAP applications.

The mark of a good Basis team is proactive monitoring and resolution of issues before they become catastrophic. The Basis engineers may not reside fully within the BICC; instead, they may be a team that is shared across all SAP applications within the enterprise.

12.3   Team Structure

The maturity and complexity of BI in an organization drives the size and membership in the BICC. Let's look at how a BICC team should be structured to take governance, project delivery, and service delivery into consideration.

12.3.1   BICC Governance

Recall from Section 12.1.1 that the governance team is responsible for prioritizing BI initiatives, preparing projects for launch, conducting post-implementation reviews, training and developing user skills, and ultimately driving adoption of BI to facilitate business transformation.

Given these responsibilities, the members of the governance team must be very close to the business and also possess an enterprise-wide perspective of the existing and future information technology landscape.

As illustrated in Figure 12.6, the governance team may not necessarily be organized in a particular structure and should act more like a steering committee for an indefinite project.

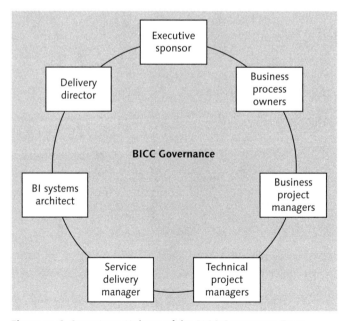

Figure 12.6 Committee Makeup of the BICC Governance Team

12.3.2 Project Delivery

When prioritized initiatives are prepared for launch, they are handed over from the BICC governance team to the project delivery team. This transition should be seamless because the business and technical project managers are typically members of the governance team and may have participated in the pre-project planning activities.

The project delivery team reports to the project steering committee, which might include BICC governance team members. As illustrated in Figure 12.7, the BPM and TPM generally manage business and IT resources, respectively, with the exception of the presentation developers, who may be more engaged with the business analysts and report to them for the sake of convenience.

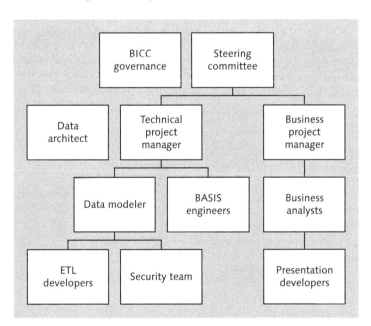

Figure 12.7 Organization Chart for a BI Project

In larger projects, there may be multiple data modelers, and each may be responsible for a specific business process or area. For example, there may be a finance team, a sales team, and an inventory team. In this case, the business analysts and data modelers would be assigned to process-specific teams.

12.3.3 Service Delivery

Because the service delivery team handles support for the productive systems and transition from projects, it requires a broad and deep set of skills. Essentially, every skill set required to deliver a project is required to support it productively for the long term. In fact, many project resources may be selected from the support team if the extra capacity exists.

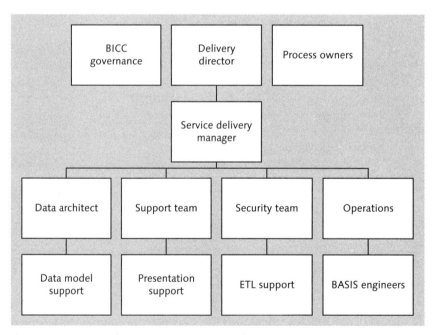

Figure 12.8 Service Delivery Team Organization Chart

As illustrated in Figure 12.8, the SDM reports to the delivery director but answers to key stakeholders in the business (process owners) and the BICC governance team, of which the SDM is a member. The data architect(s) reports to the SDM, as do data modelers, ETL developers, and presentation specialist, all of which are roles, not positions—one employee may assume multiple roles.

12.4　Best Practices

For the BICC to function efficiently as a driving force behind the adoption of BI throughout the business, it must create repeatable processes for delivering solutions that positively impact the business. Promoting the vision and strategy is only a small part of the effort; in fact, ensuring that BI projects and initiatives align with the strategies time and again in a stable and consistent manner enables the widest range of use cases for BI and the greatest possible penetration of BI into the business.

The most important best practice is to prepare for the BICC to be dynamic. Delivering BI and performance management needs to be driven by business objectives and goals. Business intelligence is defined for an organization by its strategy, business, people, process, services, and technologies, all of which change and evolve over time. The BICC needs to be able to evolve with the business and the needs of its audiences. While not all internal changes directly affect the BICC, it should constantly monitor its corporate environment for impact and adjust its membership and their roles and responsibilities accordingly.

As new technologies emerge and others wane, the BICC itself should adapt as needed to better serve its objectives. Establishing an enterprise-wide data warehouse, such as SAP BW, as the core data architecture for BI is the first step to achieving flexibility in BI capabilities. With such a stable and scalable platform in place, the BICC can focus on quality by defining best practices to govern the implementation of BI initiatives and projects, as well as the delivery of service. Quality can be achieved by adopting a project-delivery framework and standard methodology, standardizing the set of BI reporting tools used and adhering to best-practice guidelines and procedures for developing solutions in the BI environment—many of which are documented in this book.

12.4.1　Vision and Strategy

Many of the best practices discussed in this book come directly from our experience with different BI strategies used successfully by top companies. In many of these companies, the most challenging part of implementing BI was getting management to define their BI strategy. The BICC can facilitate this effort by leading discussions with senior managers and executives and demonstrating the benefits and business impact of BI initiatives.

The first step in defining a strategy is to define the company's BI vision statement (as illustrated in Figure 12.3). The vision statement should answer the question "what do we want to become?" It should clearly state the goals and objectives for business intelligence in the company. A good vision statement is aligned with business objectives, long-term and broad in perspective, not so specific that it limits its scope, and written in a brief and succinct manner without sounding generic.

Consider this example of a vision statement, which clearly states that the goal for BI is to improve the bottom line based on better information and analytics:

> *Provide business insights leading to better, faster, and proactive decisions in order to optimize corporate performance*

And here is another example, which clearly articulates that the goals for BI are to add value in an economic manner:

> *Build, implement, and support reliable, cost-efficient, and secure global information management systems that bring value to the company and its customers*

Once the vision is defined, the BI strategy simply describes how the goals will be achieved and by what resources. The BI strategy should answer the following questions:

▶ What are the BI objectives, challenges, and goals?
  ▷ What types of strategic and tactical decisions need to be made?
  ▷ Which user groups and user types will make these decisions?
  ▷ What sources of information will feed these decisions?
  ▷ What functionality will be needed to support these decisions?
  ▷ What technology will be needed to support these decisions?
▶ How will progress towards the goals be measured?
▶ Who will execute the strategy?

Because the answers to these questions may change over time, the BI strategy needs to be dynamic. The BICC should prompt the organization's management to revisit its BI strategy every couple of years to ensure that it remains relevant.

As the business strategy evolves, so too do the BICC and its initiatives. The BICC matures as it grows through the different phases of its lifecycle, and each phase requires a different focus (see Figure 12.9). During the "vision" phase, the BICC focuses on strategy, people, and metrics. The last phase is where the strategic goals are actually achieved. The middle three phases focus more on technology and process than strategy. During these phases, the BICC develops guidelines and its governance process.

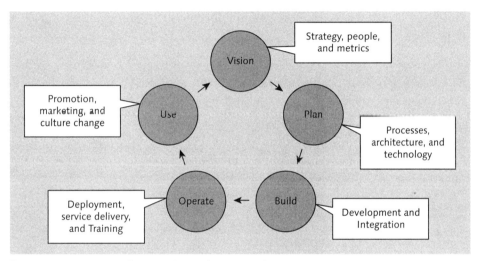

Figure 12.9 Focus Areas for Each Phase of a BICC's Lifecycle

12.4.2 Governance

The BICC should assume governmental control over all existing corporate BI applications that are included in the BI strategy. Each new initiative should be evaluated to ascertain its value and then ranked against other initiatives accordingly. The governance team should not allow BI initiatives to proceed unless they have clear links to one or more critical business objective and are aligned with the BI strategy.

In order to be effective in executing the BI strategy, the BICC must have strong governance over its BI technology, but there may be special applications over which the BICC has no governance. Most importantly, the BICC must try to limit the proliferation of data marts deployed outside its control. If a data mart deployment is justified, the BICC should, at a minimum, ensure that the tools, architecture, and data standards are consistent—published guidelines can help facilitate such consistency.

12.4.3 Guidelines

During the planning phase, the architects and IT staff of the BICC governance team should establish well-defined guidelines, templates, and procedures to facilitate quality during development, integration, and deployment of BI technology. Table 12.1 provides a list of these types of documents recommended for projects and service.

Used By	Guideline
BICC governance	Technology roadmap
	BI capabilities matrix
	BI roles & responsibilities
Project delivery	Project delivery framework
	Change management guidelines
	Functional specification template
	Technical specification template
	Development cost model
	Service delivery cost model
	Test script template
Project delivery and service delivery	Enterprise data architecture definition
	Layered scalable architecture guideline
	Modeling guidelines
	ABAP guidelines
	Naming conventions
	Performance tuning guidelines
	Development checklist

Table 12.1 Recommended Guidelines for BI Technology

Used By	Guideline
Service delivery	Monitoring tools manual
	Roles and authorization guidelines
	Service definition
	Housekeeping checklist
	Data load/reload procedure

Table 12.1 Recommended Guidelines for BI Technology (Cont.)

The larger a BI initiative is, the more important it is to have formally published and communicated guidelines to mitigate the risk of poor quality or unsuccessful solutions. Uniform definitions, adoption, and compliance are crucial. This book can serve as a resource for many of the recommended guidelines. The guidelines should not be so onerous or burdensome that their purpose is questionable. Instead, they should provide reasonable and prudent standards that are easily understood and valuable to follow. The goal of any guideline is to make it so valuable that it is considered an asset by those who are required to use it.

12.4.4 Compliance

As much as practical, adherence to the published guidelines should be rigidly enforced. The most efficient way to ensure world-class quality, optimal performance, and lower TCO is to follow proven development guidelines and repeatable procedures. On the other hand, failure to adhere to the best practices defined in the published guidelines could lead to lower quality, poor performance, and higher delivery and/or support costs.

A good practice to ensure alignment with strategy is to review the solution architecture with the systems architect prior to launching the project. This prevents an unsupported technology from being chosen and provides an opportunity for subsequent reviews by informing the system architect of impending changes to the BI toolset.

Another good practice for ensuring compliance is to require design reviews by a data architect (or a member of the architect's team) before development can be started in the system. This alone prevents many quality issues from ever being created.

> **Recommendation**
>
> Be very cautious about implementing a procedure that prevents developers from creating or releasing change requests in the SAP BW development system. Such authorization restrictions result in a loss of productivity and schedule delays without having any significant improvement in quality.

Appendices

A   **Checklists** 607

B   **Transaction Codes** 619

C   **Reports and Utilities** 629

D   **The Authors** 639

A   Checklists

In this section we will cover samples of the checklists referenced in Chapter 12, BI Competency Center. First we will review sample development checklists for front-end and back end designs and then sample housekeeping checklists summarizing the administration and performance tuning tasks covered in Parts II and III.

A.1   Development Checklists

Developers should use a development checklist when unit testing their work against the documented design. The results of the checklist should be documented for review by the data modeler or lead designer. Transport requests containing objects that have not been unit tested should be held until the unit test is completed.

The lead designer should start by reviewing the project documentation:

- Business requirements
- Functional design
- Detailed design

After reviewing the documentation, he should interview the project developer and ask the questions listed in Table A.1 for each report delivered. These questions should have been answered before the design phase, so if the developer has trouble answering any of them, it is a cause for concern.

Topic	Question(s)
Report description	What is the name of the report?
Purpose	What problem does the report solve?
	How is it used?
Audience	Who uses the report?
Security	Who should (or should not) have access to the report?
	On what basis should access be controlled?
	Are there any special authorizations?
Content	What data is presented?
	What calculations are performed?

Table A.1 Interview Questions for Each Report

Topic	Question(s)
Time periods	How is the data displayed? (Yearly, quarterly, monthly, weekly, daily, etc.)
Units/currencies	In what standard unit or currency should the facts be displayed?
Frequency	How often and when is the report needed?
Timeliness	How often and when should data be updated?
Sources	Where does the data come from (SAP ERP, SLT, BODS, other)? There should always be a system of record.
Functionality	What is the granularity of the report? What drill-down paths are needed to properly analyze the data?

Table A.1 Interview Questions for Each Report (Cont.)

After interviewing the project developer, he should review the technical implementation directly in the system. Check all BEx queries and reports. Look for obvious departures from defined standards. Confirm all queries are built on Multi-Providers to insulate them from changes to the physical InfoProviders.

The front-end development checklist in Table A.2 gives a complete list of items that should be checked during unit testing and peer reviews.

Item Area	Item Description
Report header	Confirm the logo, title, and last refresh date are correctly displayed.
	Confirm that the header buttons (i.e., GO BACK, GO BACK TO START, CHANGE SELECTION, SAVE BOOKMARK, SEND BOOKMARK, and HELP) work correctly.
Filter panel	Check that COLLAPSE and EXPAND work.
	Verify the order of characteristics in the filter panel (should be sequenced from coarse to fine granularity).
	Confirm that the filter panel functionality works as expected. When you APPLY FILTER, it should be reflected in both the table and the graph.
	Check GO TO button functionality: ▸ The receiver report should open up in a separate window. ▸ All filters applied in the sender report should be automatically passed to the receiver report.
	Check that key figure selection area is working as expected. Key figure changes should be reflected in both the chart and the table.
	Check that the CLEAR ALL button clears the dynamic filter selections.

Table A.2 Report Development Checklist

Item Area	Item Description
Global filter	Verify that global filters are implemented per report specification.
Report body	Check that ANALYZE BY works as expected: ▸ Characteristics should be in the correct sequence. ▸ Each one should affect the table and chart when chosen.
	Verify that BREAKDOWN BY works as expected.
	Check that the CHART TYPE work as expected.
	Validate that the EXPORT TO EXCEL button is working correctly.
	Check that the EXPORT TO PDF button is working correctly.
Analysis table	Check characteristic descriptions are consistent with other reports.
	Check characteristic display formats are consistent (key, key-text, text-key, or text).
	Check characteristic sort sequences are consistent.
	Check characteristic result properties are set correctly to display or suppress the result row.
	Check that decimal points are set correctly for all key figures: ▸ Numbers (e.g., no decimals) ▸ Percentage (e.g., 1 decimal) ▸ Amount/quantity (e.g., 2 decimals)
	Check that the scaling factor of all key figures is implemented per report requirements.
	Validate the RESULT ROW total is calculated correctly.
	Check that context menu items are working as expected.
Chart	Ensure 'Title' should not be displayed for the graph.
	Check that the ANALYZE BY dropdown has all the characteristics as per requirement.
	Ensure that labels for both the X-axis and Y-axis are displayed correctly.
	Check the legend is displayed correctly in the expected location.
	Check the color of the chart is correct.
Query	Validate the query output against the InfoProvider (use Transaction LISTCUBE to reconcile the results).
	Check that the authorization objects are assigned correct variables.

Table A.2 Report Development Checklist (Cont.)

Item Area	Item Description
Query	Validate that the calculations are working as expected.
	Check each column descriptions against the requirements.
	Check the list of free characteristics against the requirements.
	Check the list of key figures against the requirements.
	Verify the list characteristics for the following: ▸ Data ▸ Filter
Performance	Check that the report runtime is less than X seconds.
	Check whether the cache setting of the query uses the default value (or justify non-adherence to the standard).
Bookmark	Confirm that bookmarks do not open the variable screen window.
	Confirm report changes do not impact existing bookmarks.
Workflow	Go to the receiver report: ▸ Check that the correct report is called. ▸ Check that the filters are passed correctly. ▸ Check that the time dimension in the receiver is correct.
General	Check that the user authorization for the report works as expected.
	Check that zero suppression in enabled.
	Check the spelling for all items in the report.
Data quality	Validate all measures against the business requirement.
	Execute positive test scenarios unique to the report and record the results.
	Execute negative test scenarios unique to the report and record the results.

Table A.2 Report Development Checklist (Cont.)

After reviewing all reports, check the back-end development using the checklist in Table A.3 as a guide. Check all InfoCube data models. Are there any dimension high cardinality flags set? Is the InfoCube assigned to an appropriate data class? Is partitioning defined? How many InfoObjects are included? Are the dimensions evenly distributed? Is there an appropriate level of summarization (check granularity requirement)? Are all potential time characteristics included? What is the expected data volume (monthly, yearly, etc.)? If data volume is high, should the cube be semantically partitioned? If semantically partitioned, are SPOs used or are the appropriate characteristics set to a fixed value?

Check all DSOs. Do the key fields match the data being loaded? Are the key fields in the best order from a performance perspective? How many fields are included in the DSO? Should the DSOs be semantically partitioned? If manually semantically partitioned, are the appropriate characteristics set to a fixed value? If you are using an SPO, are the appropriate characteristics defined as key fields?

Item Area	Item Description
Extraction	Confirm the relevant unit for each key figure is included in the Data-Source.
	Validate extractor returns results in Transaction RSA3 as expected when compared to source table or view.
	Check user exit logic against the following: ▸ All appended fields as expected ▸ Performance benchmarks before/after code change
	Check delta extraction: ▸ Change all the custom fields of a source document (e.g., sales order) and confirm a delta is triggered. ▸ Confirm that all appended fields are populated correctly in the user exit (if applicable).
	Reconcile the number of records extracted compared to source table or view.
	Reconcile the data in PSA against source tables.
Transformation	Confirm all complex logic is designed between DSO layers: ▸ No logic should exist between PSA and DSOs. ▸ No logic should exist between DSOs and InfoCubes.
	Check performance of transformations against benchmark before change (or with no logic).
	Check InfoObject 0RECORDMODE is mapped correctly in the transformations.
	Reconcile the data in the data target against the PSA.

Table A.3 Back-End Development Checklist

Item Area	Item Description
Loading	Test full and delta process chains.
	Identify any load dependencies.
	Confirm process chain changes following best practices.
	Test compression of data with zero elimination (if applicable).
	Confirm that InfoCube database indexes are dropped before loading and rebuilt after loading.
	Confirm that all new PSA tables and change logs are added to deletion process variants.
	Confirm that all DTPs from PSA have extraction mode DELTA.
	Check that error handling adheres to the default NO UPDATE, NO REPORTING UNLESS OTHERWISE JUSTIFIED.
	Check that if loading master data from a DSO, the DTP is set to HANDLE DUPLICATE RECORDS.
Modeling	Check that all InfoObjects conform to source field definitions (such as data type, length, conversion routine, allowed characters, etc.).
	Confirm that all flags and dates are modeled appropriately as reference InfoObjects.
	Confirm that all free text fields in the source are modeled as ATTRIBUTE ONLY InfoObjects.
	Check that SID generation is only turned on for DSOs used for reporting: ▸ Valid options are DURING ACTIVATION or NEVER CREATE SIDs. ▸ The option DURING REPORTING should not be used.
	Confirm the UNIQUE RECORDS setting is not flagged in standard DSOs (use write-optimized DSOs instead).
	Confirm that secondary indexes are created to support lookups or DTP filters on multiple fields.
	Confirm that SPO DSOs are semantically partitioned based on key fields only.
	In SAP HANA, confirm InfoCubes are only used for non-cumulative key figures, Integrated Planning, BPC, or when the external write-interface (RSDRI) is required.
	Check that InfoCube dimensions are evenly distributed for best performance.

Table A.3 Back-End Development Checklist (Cont.)

Item Area	Item Description
Modeling	Check that no dimensions are flagged as HIGH CARDINALITY.
	Check that all potential time characteristics are included in the Info-Cubes and MultiProviders.
	Check that MultiProvider dimensions are modeled to benefit the report developer.
	Check the MultiProvider mapping for consistency and completeness.
	Check that the custom object naming convention has been correctly followed.
	Confirm that all physical InfoProviders are assigned to the correct data class.
	Confirm that all physical InfoProviders are configured for partitioning or multi-dimensional clustering.
ABAP	Check that no complex logic is directly coded in the transformation. Complex logic should only be coded in include programs or classes.
	Check that in-line documentation has been added to program changes.
	Check that select statements are used with right index.
	Confirm that best practices have been followed for custom ABAP development.
	Execute the EXTENDED SYNTAX CHECK for all include programs (Transaction SLIN).
General	Check whether the change will impact unintended reports.
	Check the WHERE-USED list to identify breadth of impact.
Transport	Check if all MultiProviders are collected.
	Check if all transformations and DTPs are collected.
	Check transport log for errors and warnings.

Table A.3 Back-End Development Checklist (Cont.)

Check all transformations to ensure development standards are followed. Is the data load process understandable? Are there lookups in the transformations that load to any InfoCube? All lookups should be insulated between DSOs and supported by secondary indexes where necessary. Are there lookups in the load to the first layer DSO? All lookups should be insulated between DSOs. How will changes to the field values being looked up trigger changes to the data in target InfoProvider?

Check all DataSources. If a DataSource is not delta-enabled, determine whether this is a technical limitation. Is it a custom-developed or business content Data-Source? If it is business content, has it been enhanced? If fields have been added, will changes to the field values trigger deltas? Could the fields be navigational attributes instead? Review any user exit code for compliance with best practices.

A.2   Housekeeping Checklists

To keep the system clean and healthy, follow these housekeeping checklists. The first checklist in Table A.4 lists all daily housekeeping tasks as covered in Chapter 7.

Daily Housekeeping Task	Report/Transaction
Check database growth, free space analysis, and SAP HANA memory consumption	Transaction DB02
Check process overview	Transaction SM66
Check workload statistics	Transaction ST03N
Check performance overview	Transaction ST04
Check performance tuning	Transaction ST02
Check operating systems monitor	Transaction ST06
Check BWA	Transaction RSDDBIAMON2
Check system short dumps	Transaction ST22
Check system log	Transaction SM21
Check job overview	Transaction SM37
Check database backup	Transaction DBACOCKPIT
Check expensive statements	Transaction DB02
Monitor BW CCMS alerts	Transaction BWCCMS
Monitor data loads	Transaction RSPCM
Monitor InfoPackages and RDA daemons	Transaction RSA1
Monitor DSO activations	Transaction RSA1
Monitor change run activity	RSDDS_CHANGERUN_MONITOR
Monitor aggregates	Transaction RSA1

Table A.4 Daily Housekeeping Tasks

Table A.5 contains all weekly housekeeping tasks covered in Chapter 8.

Weekly Housekeeping Task	Report/Transaction
Review SAP EarlyWatch Alert	N/A
Rebuild BWA indexes	Transaction RSDDB
Cleanup PSA tables and change logs	RSPSADEL1 for one-time use only (instead, schedule via Process Chain)
Cleanup application logs	Transaction SLG2
Execute SAP BW housekeeping task list	Transaction STC01
Delete SAP BW background management messages and parameters	RSBATCH_DEL_MSG_PARM_DTPTEMP (use parameters DEL_MSG = 3, DEL_PAR = 3 and DEL_DTP = X)
Reorganize PSA error log	RSSM_ERRORLOG_CLEANUP
Check and clean PSA tables	RSAR_PSA_CLEANUP_DEFINITION
Analyze DTP error log	RSB_ANALYZE_ERRORLOG
Delete inconsistent error DTPs	RSBM_ERRORLOG_DELETE
Delete old process chain logs	RSPC_INSTANCE_CLEANUP
	RSPC_LOG_DELETE
Delete jobs without variant	RS_FIND_JOBS_WITHOUT_VARIANT
Delete old job logs	RSBTCDEL2
Reorganize hidden folder *Office Documents*	RSSODFRE
Reorganize SAP Office/BW documents	RSBCS_REORG
Check and clean up table change logs (DBTABLOG)	RSTBPDEL
Check and delete old tRFC queues	Transaction SM58
Delete temporary SAP BW database tables	SAP_DROP_TMPTABLES
Reorganize TemSe and spool	RSPO1041 (first run the consistency check from TemSe Data Storage in Transaction SP12)
Delete orphaned job logs	RSTS0024
Delete RSTT traces	RSTT_TRACE_DELETE
Purge intermediary results from APD	RSAN_UT_RESULT_DROP_RESULTS

Table A.5 Weekly Housekeeping Tasks

Weekly Housekeeping Task	Report/Transaction
Delete statistic data from job runtime statistics	RSBPSTDE
Delete update requests	RSM13002
Delete old tRFC entries	RSARFCER
Delete old Transaction ST03N source system data	SWNC_COLLECTOR_CLEAN_SWNCMONI
Check and repair inconsistent PSA request/ tables	RSAR_PSA_NEWDS_MAPPING_CHECK
Delete authorization logs and disable log recording for all users	Transaction RSECADMIN
Check master data for characteristics	Transaction RSRV
Check consistency of the time dimension for all InfoCubes	Transaction RSRV
Check the status of the data in all InfoCubes	Transaction RSRV
Test partitioning columns for all Basis InfoCubes	Transaction RSRV
Monitor BI reporting statistics	N/A
Compress InfoCubes	N/A (schedule via process chains)
Rebuild DB indexes and statistics	N/A (schedule via process chains)
Monitor cache usage	Transaction RSRCACHE

Table A.5 Weekly Housekeeping Tasks (Cont.)

Table A.6 contains all monthly housekeeping tasks covered in Chapter 9.

Monthly Housekeeping Task	Report/Transaction
Restart SAP system	N/A
Change portal settings (as needed)	N/A
Reapply inconsistent SAP notes	Transaction SNOTE
Take action on SAP EarlyWatch Alert	N/A
Execute RSRV cleanup tasks	Transaction BWCCMS Transaction RSRV

Table A.6 Monthly Housekeeping Tasks

Monthly Housekeeping Task	Report/Transaction
Collect and review BWA usage	N/A
Forecast storage capacity	N/A
Conduct file system housekeeping	Transaction AL11
Archive system data and near-line transaction data	Transaction SARA
Monitor data load statistics	N/A (use BEx reporting)

Table A.6 Monthly Housekeeping Tasks (Cont.)

Table A.7 contains all quarterly housekeeping tasks covered in Chapter 10.

Quarterly Housekeeping Task	Report/Transaction
Manage users and licenses	Transaction RSUSR200 Transaction SUID10
Refresh QA system	N/A
Update SAP kernel	N/A
Apply database patches and parameters	N/A
Patch operating system	N/A
Validate system profile parameters	Transaction RZ10
Review open change requests	Transaction ST01
Reorganize database	N/A
Delete obsolete queries and reports	Transaction RSZDELETE
Delete obsolete data flows	Transaction RSA1
Review configuration settings	Transaction SPRO
Review DSO settings	Transaction RSODSO_SETTINGS
Review RSADMIN parameters	Transaction RSADMIN
Review data transfer control parameters	Transaction SBIW
Review query cache settings	Transaction RSRT

Table A.7 Quarterly Housekeeping Tasks

Last, Table A.8 contains the annual tasks covered in Chapter 11.

Yearly Housekeeping Task	Report/Transaction
Upgrade SAP BW	N/A
Apply support packs	N/A
Upgrade SAPGUI	N/A
Test high availability and disaster recovery	N/A
Assess system risks	N/A
Review and optimize data flow	N/A
Review and optimize external performance	N/A
Re-partition InfoProviders	RSDU_REPART_UI

Table A.8 Yearly Housekeeping Tasks

Leverage the tasks in these checklists to maintain the operational health of your system and keep your cost of ownership low.

B   Transaction Codes

This book has referenced many transaction codes that are useful from Basis administration, BW development, ABAP customizing, and performance monitoring perspectives.

Remember that the more often you use these transactions, the more easily you will remember them. However, it is always helpful to keep a short-list of transactions needed for your daily work. Please note all transaction codes in your system are contained in table TSTC.

We've listed them in Table B.1 alphabetically for ease of access.

Transaction Code	Description
/ASU/START	Start ASU Toolbox
/ASU/UPGRADE	Start ASU Toolbox in Upgrade Mode
AL08	Users Logged On
AL11	Display SAP Directories
AOBJ	Archiving Object Definition
BAPI	BAPI Explorer
BD53	Reduction of Message Types
BD54	Maintaining Logical Systems
BDLS	Convert Logical System Names
BW_DATASOURCE_CHECK	DataSource/InfoSource Check
BW_QUERY_ELEM_CHECK	Dev. Classes for Query Elements
BW_WORKBOOK_CHECK	Queries/Workbooks Check
BWCCMS	CCMS Monitor for BW
CMOD	Enhancements
CUNI	Units of Measure
DB01	Analyze Exclusive Lockwaits
DB02	Tables and Indexes Monitor
DB12	DBA Backup Logs
DB13	DBA Planning Calendar

Table B.1 Transaction Codes

Transaction Code	Description
DB15	Data Archiving: Database Tables
DB17	Configure DB Check
DB20	Update DB Statistics
DB21	Configure DB Statistics
DBACOCKPIT	Start DBA Cockpit
FILE	Cross-Client File Names/Paths
OMSL	C MM-BD Maintain TMCNV
PFCG	Role Maintenance
RRMX	Start the Business Explorer Analyzer
RS_CONV_ACTIVATE	Activate InfoObject Conversion
RS_PERS_ACTIVATE	Activation of BEx Personalization
RS09	Transport Browser for BI Objects
RS12	Overview of Master Data Locks
RS2HANA_VIEW	Settings for SAP HANA Views
RSA1	Modeling—DW Workbench
RSA10	Real-time Test Interface Source System
RSA11	DW Workbench: InfoProvider Tree
RSA12	DW Workbench: InfoSource Tree
RSA13	DW Workbench: Source System Tree
RSA14	BW Workbench: InfoObject Tree
RSA15	DW Workbench: DataSource Tree
RSA16	DW Workbench: Favorites Tree
RSA17	DW Workbench: General Search
RSA18	DW Workbench: Open Hub Destination
RSA19	DW Workbench: Data Flows
RSA2	SAPI DataSource Repository
RSA20	DW Workbench: Planning Sequences
RSA3	Extractor Checker
RSA5	Install Business Content
RSA6	Maintain DataSources

Table B.1 Transaction Codes (Cont.)

Transaction Code	Description
RSA7	BW Delta Queue Monitor
RSA8	DataSource Repository
RSA9	Transfer Application Components
RSABAPSC	Statistical Program Analysis for Search
RSABAUTH	Transfer of Authorization Groups
RSABTPGP	Authorization Groups
RSADMIN	RSADMIN Maintenance
RSANWB	Analysis Process Designer
RSARCH_ADMIN	BW Archive Administration
RSATTR	Attribute/Hierarchy Realignment Run
RSBATCH	Management of RSBATCH/SEARCHLOGS
RSBBS	Maintaining BW Sender-Receiver
RSBMO2	Open Hub Monitor
RSBO	Open Hub Maintenance
RSBPCADMIN	BPC Parameters
RSBWREMOTE	Create Warehouse User
RSCOPY	Data Flow Copy Processes
RSCUR	Start: Currency Translation Type
RSCUSTA	Maintain BW Settings
RSCUSTA2	ODS Settings
RSCUSTV1	BW Customizing—View 1
RSCUSTV21	BW Customizing—View 21
RSCUSTV27	Set Standard Web Templates
RSCUSTV28	Determine Settings for Web Templates
RSCUSTV6	BW Customizing—View 6
RSCUSTV8	BW Customizing—View 8
RSCUSTV9	BW Customizing—View 9
RSD1	Characteristic Maintenance
RSD2	Maintenance of Key Figures
RSD3	Maintenance of Units

Table B.1 Transaction Codes (Cont.)

Transaction Code	Description
RSD4	Maintenance of Time Characteristics
RSDANLCON	Set Up Near-Line Connections
RSDAP	Edit Data Archiving Process
RSDBC	DB Connect
RSDCUBE	Start: InfoCube Editing
RSDD_HM_PUBLISH	Publish SAP HANA Model
RSDD_LTIP	Administration of Analytic Indexes
RSDD_LTIP_PUBLISH	Publish a TREX Cube Index
RSDDAGGRCHECK	Maintenance of Aggregate Check
RSDDB	SAP HANA/BWA Index Maintenance
RSDDBIAMON	BW Accelerator Maintenance Monitor
RSDDBIAMON2	BW Accelerator Maintenance Monitor
RSDDBIAMON3	BW Accelerator Maintenance Monitor
RSDDG	Demo Data Generation
RSDDSTAT	Maintain the BW Statistics Settings
RSDDV	Maintaining Aggregates/BIA Index
RSDF	Edit Data Flows
RSDFWIZ	Data Flow Generation Wizard
RSDHAAP	SAP HANA Analysis Process Designer
RSDHAAP_MONITOR	SAP HANA Analysis Process Monitor
RSDHATR	SAP HANA Transformation
RSDHYBR	Initial Screen: Edit HybridProvider
RSDIOBC	Start: InfoObject Catalog Editing
RSDIOBJ	Initial Screen: InfoObject Editing
RSDIPROP	Maintain InfoProvider Properties
RSDMCUS	Data Mining Customizing
RSDMD	Master Data Maintenance
RSDMPRO	Initial Screen: MultiProvider Proc.
RSDODS	Initial Screen: ODS Object Processing
RSDS	DataSource

Table B.1 Transaction Codes (Cont.)

Transaction Code	Description
RSDV	Validity Slice Maintenance
RSECADMIN	Manage Analysis Authorizations
RSECAUTH	Maintenance of Analysis Auth.
RSECAUTH02	Mass Maintenance—Analysis Authorizations
RSECPROT	Maintenance of Analysis Auth.
RSECSY	Mass Maintenance—Analysis Authorizations
RSEIDOC2	IDoc List
RSEIDOCA	Active IDoc Monitoring with Workflow
RSEIDOCM	Variant for RSEIDOCA
RSENQ	Display of Lock Log
RSFC	Analytic Engine—Demo Content
RSH1	Edit Hierarchy Initial Screen
RSH3	Simulate Hierarchies
RSHDBMON	HDB Monitoring
RSHIER	Hierarchy Maintenance w/o Admin WB
RSIMG	BW IMG
RSISET	Maintain InfoSets
RSKC	Maintaining the Permitted Extra Characters
RSLGMP	Maintain RSLOGSYSMAP
RSLIMO	BW Lean Modeler Test UI
RSLIMOBW	BW Lean Modeler Test UI
RSM37	Job List with Program Variant
RSMD	Extractor Checker
RSMIGRHANADB	Conversion to In-Memory Optimized
RSMO	Data Load Monitor Start
RSMON	Administration—DW Workbench
RSO2	OLTP Metadata Repository
RSO3	Set Up Deltas for Master Data
RSODSO_SETTINGS	Maintenance of DSO Runtime Parameters
RSODSVIEW	Open ODS View

Table B.1 Transaction Codes (Cont.)

Transaction Code	Description
RSOR	BW Metadata Repository
RSPC	Process Chain Maintenance
RSPC1	Process Chain Display
RSPCM	Monitor Daily Process Chains
RSPCP	Process Log
RSPFPAR	Display Profile Parameter
RSPLAN	Modeling BI Integrated Planning
RSPLF1	Start: Function Type Editing
RSPLSA	BI Planning: Starter Settings
RSPLSE	BI Planning: Lock Management
RSPRECADMIN	BW Excel Workbook Pre-calculation Admin
RSPRECALCADMIN	Pre-calculation Server Administration
RSRCACHE	OLAP: Cache Monitor
RSRD_ADMIN	Broadcasting Administration
RSRD_LOG	Broadcaster Application Log
RSRD_REPLAY	Restart Broadcasting for Log Number
RSRDA	Real-Time Data Acquisition Monitor
RSREQARCH	Req. Archive Administration Dialog
RSRQ	Data Load Monitor for a Request
RSRT	Start of the Report Monitor
RSRT1	Start of the Report Monitor
RSRT2	Start of the Report Monitor
RSRV	Analysis and Repair of BW Objects
RSSDK	DB Connect
RSSM	Authorizations for Reporting
RSTCO_ADMIN	Technical BW Content
RSTCT_INST_BIAC	Installation of BI AC Content
RSTPRFC	Create Destination for After-Import
RSTT	RS Trace Tool Monitor
RSU7	Data Extraction: Maintain Parameters

Table B.1 Transaction Codes (Cont.)

Transaction Code	Description
RSUDO	Execution as Other User
RSUSR000	Currently Active Users
RSUSR007	List Users
RSUSR200	List of Users per Login Date
RSWBO004	Set System Change Option
RSWSP	Workspace Individual Processing
RSWSPW	Workspace Mass Processing
RSZC	Copying Queries between InfoCubes
RSZDELETE	Deletion of Query Objects
RSZTABLES	Call ANALYZE_RSZ_TABLES
RSZTREE	Hierarchical Display of CKF/RKF
RSZV	Call Up of View V_RSZGLOBV
RSZVERSION	Set Frontend Version
RZ10	Maintain Profile Parameters
RZ11	Profile Parameter Maintenance
RZ20	CCMS Monitoring
RZ21	CCMS Monitoring Arch. Customizing
SA38	ABAP Reporting
SAINT	Add-On Installation Tool
SALE	Display ALE Customizing
SARA	Archive Administration
SBIW	BIW in IMG for OLTP
SCC4	Client Administration
SCDO	Display Change Document Objects
SCOT	SAPconnect—Administration
SCUA	Central User Administration
SE01	Transport Organizer (Extended)
SE03	Transport Organizer Tools
SE06	Set Up Transport Organizer
SE09	Transport Organizer

Table B.1 Transaction Codes (Cont.)

Transaction Code	Description
SE11	ABAP Dictionary Maintenance
SE14	Utilities for Dictionary Tables
SE16	Data Browser
SE24	Class Builder
SE30	ABAP Objects Runtime Analysis
SE37	ABAP Function Modules
SE38	ABAP Editor
SE39	Split Screen Editor: (New)
SE51	Screen Painter
SE80	Object Navigator
SE91	Message Maintenance
SE92	Maintain System Log Messages
SE93	Maintain Transaction Codes
SGEN	SAP Load Generator
SICF	HTTP Service Hierarchy Maintenance
SICK	Installation Check
SLG1	Application Log: Display Logs
SLG2	Application Log: Delete Logs
SLICENSE	Administer SAP Licenses
SM02	System Messages
SM04	User List
SM12	Display and Delete Locks
SM13	Administrate Update Records
SM21	System Log
SM30	Call View Maintenance
SM31	Call View Maintenance Like SM30
SM36	Schedule Background Job
SM37	Overview of Job Selection
SM50	Work Process Overview
SM51	Server List

Table B.1 Transaction Codes (Cont.)

Transaction Code	Description
SM58	Asynchronous RFC Error Log
SM59	RFC Destinations (Display/Maintain)
SM61	Background Control Objects Monitor
SM66	System-wide Work Process Overview
SMLG	Maintain Logon Group Assignments
SMQ1	qRFC Monitor (Outbound Queue)
SMQ2	qRFC Monitor (Inbound Queue)
SMQ3	qRFC Monitor (Saved E-Queue)
SMQR	Registration of Inbound Queues
SMQS	Registration of Destinations
SNOTE	Note Assistant
SNRO	Number Range Objects
SP01	Output Controller
SPAD	Spool Administration
SPAM	Support Package Manager
SPAU	Display Modified DE Objects
SPDD	Display Modified DDIC Objects
SPRO	Customizing—Edit Project
SPUMG	Unicode Preconversion
SQ01	SAP Query: Maintain Queries
SQ02	SAP Query: Maintain InfoSet
ST01	System Trace
ST02	Setups/Tune Buffers
ST03G	Global Workload Statistics
ST03N	Workload and Performance Statistics
ST04	DB Performance Monitor
ST05	Performance Trace
ST06	Operating System Monitor
ST07	Application Monitor
ST13	Analysis and Monitoring Tool Collection

Table B.1 Transaction Codes (Cont.)

Transaction Code	Description
ST22	ABAP Dump Analysis
STAD	Statistics Display for All Systems
STC01	Task Manager for Tech. Configuration
STC02	Task List Run Monitor
STMS	Transport Management System
STMS_QA	TMS Quality Assurance
SU01	User Maintenance
SU01D	User Display
SU10	User Mass Maintenance
SU12	Mass Changes to User Master Records
SU21	Maintain Authorization Objects
SU25	Upgrade Tool for Profile Generator
SU3	Maintain Users Own Data
SU53	Evaluate Authorization Check
SUID10	Test Framework for Ident. API (MASS)
SUIM	User Information System
TCURMNT	Maintain Exchange Rates
TREXADMIN	TREX Administration Tool
UCCHECK	Unicode Syntax Check
UPSPL	Execute Generic Planning Folder
UPSPM	Edit Generic Planning Folder
UPSPMD	Display Generic Planning Folders
WE02	Display IDoc
WE06	Active IDoc Monitoring
WE07	IDoc Statistics
WE20	Partner Profiles
WE30	IDoc Type Development
WE40	IDoc Administration

Table B.1 Transaction Codes (Cont.)

C   Reports and Utilities

The reports and utility programs identified in Table C.1 are useful to help build and maintain your data warehouse. Many of these programs have been referenced in this book, although there are still many others that are noteworthy but have not been explicitly called out.

Program	Description
/ASU/ASUSTART	Application Specific Utilities and Tools
/ASU/MAINTAIN	XML Maintenance
/ASU/UPGRADE	Application Specific Upgrade—SAPUp
/IMO/CFS_START_BOM_PROC	Program /IMO/CFS_START_BOM_PROC
/SDF/HANA_BW_PC_CHECK	Test Report: Check Potential of BW Process Chains with HANA
/SDF/HANA_BW_SIZING	Determine DB Size Relevant for BW on HANA Sizing
/SDF/HDB_HOUSEKEEPING	Housekeeping for HDB Monitoring
/SDF/HDB_MON	Monitoring of Various HDB Metrics
AGR_REGENERATE_SAP_ALL	Regenerate SAP_ALL Profile in All Clients
AGR_XPRA_REGENERATE_SAP_ALL	Regenerate SAP_ALL Profile in All Clients
AGR_XPRA_REGENERATE_SAP_NEW	Generate SAP_NEW Profile in All Clients
ANALYZE_RSZ_TABLES	Check Report ANALYZE_RSZ_TABLES
BADI_RSANALYZE	Analysis Report for New BAdIs
BTC_EVENT_RAISE	Program BTC_EVENT_RAISE
BTCTRNS1	Transport: Move Jobs with Status "Rescheduled Due to Upgrade"
BTCTRNS2	Transport: Release Jobs with Status "Rescheduled Due to Upgrade"
CCUEVAL	Measurement of Concurrent Users: Analysis
CCUINIT	Measurement of Concurrent Users: Initialization

Table C.1 Useful Reports and Utility Programs

Program	Description
FUGR_ANALYZE	Function Group Analysis: Select Function Groups
HANA_ABAP_CUSTOMIZING	HANA: Parameters For HANA-ABAP Client
HANA_ABAP_PYTHON	HANA: Switch for ABAP-Python Flag
ODQ_CLEANUP	Reorganize Delta Queues
ODQ_DAEMON	ODS Daemon for Real Time Processing
ODQ_TASK	Program for Executing a Task
PFCG_MASS_DOWNLOAD	Bulk Role Download
PFCG_MASS_IMPORT	Bulk Role Import
PFCG_MASS_TRANSPORT	Role Transport
RBDLSMAP2	Tool: Conversion of Logical System Names
REPAIR_AFTER_IMPORT	Program REPAIR_AFTER_IMPORT
RODPS_LOAD_ACTIVATE_ALL	Activate All ODPs
RODPS_LOAD_ACTIVATE_SINGLE	Activate ODP Including Associated ODPs
RODPS_LOAD_ACTIVATION	ODP Activation
RODPS_LOAD_ACTIVATION_REPAIR	Reactivate ODPs to All Active Connectors
RODPS_LOAD_USER	User Settings for ODP Activation
RODPS_ODP_CHECK	Program RODPS_ODP_CHECK
RODPS_REBUILD_ALL_CONNECTORS	Rebuild All Connectors
RODPS_SHOW_INDEX_DATA	SAP HANA/BWA Data Display for ODPs
RODPS_SQL_STUDIO	Simple Browser for an Operational Data Provider
RRHI_HIERARCHY_ACTIVATE	Activation of a Hierarchy
RRMX_START_EXCEL	Starting Excel with BI Add-On and Empty Workbook
RRMX_WORKBOOKS_GARBAGE_COLLECT	BW InfoCatalog: Find/Delete Unreferenced Workbooks
RRMX_WORKBOOKS_UNTOUCHED_PURGE	BW InfoCatalog: Find/Delete Unreferenced Workbooks
RS_BW_POST_MIGRATION	Heterogeneous BW Migration, Invalidation of Generated Routines

Table C.1 Useful Reports and Utility Programs (Cont.)

Program	Description
RS_BW_PRE_MIGRATION	Analysis Before Migration of a BW System
RS_CREATE_BWREMOTE	Creates the BWREMOTE User and Enters it in the "RSADMIN"
RS_CREATE_INDEX	Program RS_CREATE_INDEX
RS_EARLYWATCH_STATISTICS	Test: EarlyWatch Statistics
RS_FIND_JOBS_WITHOUT_VARIANT	Find Jobs without Program Variants
RS_PERS_ACTIVATE	Activating/Deactivating Personalization in BEx
RS_PRECALC_ADMIN	Report RS_PRECALC_ADMIN
RS_SYSTEM_SHUTDOWN	Shut Down and Start Up BW Processes
RS_TEMPLATE_MAINTAIN_70	BW 7.0 Template Maintenance
RS_TEMPLATE_MASS_CHECK_70	BEx Web Template Check
RS2HANA_AUTH_CHECK_AUTHORIZED	Checks if Users are Authorized for Info-Providers
RS2HANA_AUTH_CHECK_CONSISTENCY	Checks Consistency of Filter Values and Generated Objects in HANA DB
RS2HANA_AUTH_RESET	Reset All Changes
RS2HANA_AUTH_RUN	Run BW2HANA Authorization Generation
RS2HANA_AUTH_SCHEDULE	Schedule Batch Job
RS2HANA_VIEW_SETTINGS	Settings for SAP HANA View for BW Info-Provider
RSAN_UT_RESULT_DROP_RESULTS	Purge Intermediary Results from APD
RSANAORA	Analysis of Oracle Tables for Creating Statistics
RSAR_AFTER_SYSTEMCOPY	Prepare BW System Copy for Data Extraction Again
RSAR_AFTER_SYSTEMCOPY_PART_2	Prepare Second Part of the System Copy for Data Extraction Again
RSAR_EXECUTE_BDLS_PSA_EXIT	Execute Logical System Conversion of PSA Manually
RSAR_LOGICAL_SYSTEMS_ACTIVATE	Activate All SAP Source Systems (After BW Upgrade)

Table C.1 Useful Reports and Utility Programs (Cont.)

Program	Description
RSAR_LOGSYS_CHANGE	BW Renamed Logical System Name
RSAR_ODS_TABLETYPE_REPAIR	Check and Repair TADIR Entry for PSA Table Types
RSAR_PSA_CLEANUP_DEFINITION	Report RSAR_PSA_CLEANUP_DEFINITION
RSAR_PSA_CLEANUP_DIRECTORY	PSA Directory Clean Up Program
RSAR_PSA_NEWDS_MAPPING_CHECK	Check and Repair Inconsistent PSA Request/Tables
RSAR_PSA_PARTITION_CHECK	Report RSAR_PSA_PARTITION_CHECK
RSAR_PSA_REQUEST_CHECK	Analysis of PSA Request (Transfer Method: PSA Only)
RSAR_REPAIR_BWINST	Repair the BWINST Logical System after Installation of 2.1C Systems
RSAR_RSTSRULES_CORRECTION	Report to Correct Orphaned RSTSRULES Entries
RSAR_TRANSTRUCTURE_CHECK	Find and Remove Inconsistent Transfer Structures
RSARFCER	Delete Old tRFC Entries
RSAU_UPDR_REACTIVATE_ALL	Report RSAU_UPDR_REACTIVATE_ALL
RSB_ANALYZE_ERRORLOG	Analyze Contents of Error Tables
RSBATCH_DEL_MSG_PARM_DTPTEMP	Delete Old Messages, Parameters and Temp. DTP Data
RSBATCH_EXECUTE_PROZESS	Execute Batch Process
RSBCS_REORG BCS	Reorganization of Documents and Send Requests
RSBK_CHECK_DELTAINIT_AFTERU730	Delta-Initialization Set Incorrectly
RSBK_REPAIR_BDLS	Report RSBK_REPAIR_BDLS
RSBKCHECKBUFFER	Clean up the DTP Runtime Buffer
RSBKDTPDELETELSYS	Delete All Orphaned DTPs from a Source System
RSBKDTPREPAIR	DTP Repair
RSBM_CHECK_REPAIR_RSBMNODES	Repair Missing Entries in Table RSBMNODES

Table C.1 Useful Reports and Utility Programs (Cont.)

Program	Description
RSBM_ERRORLOG_DELETE	Report RSBM_ERRORLOG_DELETE
RSBMON	Open Hub—Monitor
RSBPSTDE	Delete Statistics Data from the Job Runtime Statistics
RSBTCDEL2	Deletion of Jobs
RSCDS_NULLELIM	Report for Zero Elimination After Compression
RSCRMREPORT_BAPI	Batch Program for Carrying Out MDX Reports
RSCSAUTH	Maintain/Restore Authorization Groups
RSDD_EXEC_SQL	Example Native SQL Statements (without Host Variables, No Output)
RSDD_HANA_DELTA_INIT_TC	Fills/Changes HANA-Delta Indexes of Specified InfoProvider/Table
RSDD_IIM_PUBLISH	Publish SAP HANA Model
RSDD_LTIP_AIND_DELETE	Mass Deletion for Analytic Indexes
RSDDB_MASS_INDEX_CREATE	Fill BWA Index (All Types) Initially
RSDDCHECK	Recursive Consistency Check for DDIC Runtime Objects
RSDDK_AGGREGATE_STATUS_CHECK	Aggregate Status of all InfoCubes
RSDDS_AGGREGATES_MAINTAIN	Program RSDDS_AGGREGATES_MAINTAIN
RSDDS_CHANGERUN_MONITOR	Monitor for Change Run
RSDDSTAT_DATA_DELETE	Deletion of Data from the BW Statistics Tables
RSDDTREX_MEMORY_ESTIMATE	Estimate Memory Usage of BWA Index to InfoCubes
RSDELPART1	Execute InfoCube Aggregation
RSDG_AFTER_IMPORT_FOR_CORR	Starts the BW after Import Routine for a Request
RSDG_CUBE_ACTIVATE	Activation of InfoCubes
RSDG_DATCLS_ASSIGN	Assign Data Classes to InfoProviders

Table C.1 Useful Reports and Utility Programs (Cont.)

633

Program	Description
RSDG_HYBR_ACTIVATE	Activation of HybridProviders
RSDG_IOBJ_ACTIVATE	Activation of InfoObjects (w/o Automatic Transport Connection!)
RSDG_IOBJ_FILL_XY_TABLE	Filling Characteristic Attribute SID Table
RSDG_IOBJ_REORG	Repair InfoObjects
RSDG_MPRO_ACTIVATE	Activating MultiProviders
RSDG_ODSO_ACTIVATE	Activating/Repairing DataStore Objects (without Automatic Transport)
RSDG_TRFN_ACTIVATE	Activate Transformations
RSDHAR_ANALYSIS_EXECUTE	Load Data Target
RSDMDD_DELETE_FROM_MD_TABLE	Packetized Deleting of Master Data from Table
RSDRI_INFOPROV_READ_SERVICE	Program RSDRI_INFOPROV_READ_SERVICE
RSDS_DATASOURCE_ACTIVATE_ALL	Activate DataSources
RSDU_EXEC_SQL	SQL
RSDU_REPART_UI	Repartitioning of InfoProviders
RSDU_SET_FACT_ATTR_ADA	Set Fact Attribute for Fact Tables
RSDU_SET_FV_TO_FIX_VALUE	Subsequent Changing of Fiscal Variant in InfoCube to Fixed Value
RSDU_TABLE_CONSISTENCY	Program RSDU_TABLE_CONSISTENCY
RSDV_VALTAB_MAINTENANCE	Report on Validity Slice Maintenance
RSIMPCURR	Transfer Global Settings: Selection
RSIMPCUST	Transfer Global Settings: Selection
RSKC_ALLOWED_CHAR_MAINTAIN	Maintenance of the Permitted Extra Characters in BW
RSM13002	Tool for Analyzing and Processing VB Request
RSMDEXITON	Update InfoObject Conversion Routine
RSODSO_SETTINGS	Maintenance for DataStore Settings
RSPARAGEN	Report for Parallel Generation of ABAP Loads

Table C.1 Useful Reports and Utility Programs (Cont.)

Program	Description
RSPC_INSTANCE_CLEANUP	Report RSPC_INSTANCE_CLEANUP
RSPC_LOG_DELETE	Deletion of Process Chain Logs and Assigned Process Logs
RSPO0041	Delete Old Spool Requests
RSPO1041	Delete Old Spool Requests
RSPP_PART_MAINTAIN	Report RSPP_PART_MAINTAIN
RSPSADEL1	Delete PSA
RSR_CACHE_ADMIN_MAINTAIN	Maintain Cache Parameters
RSR_CACHE_QUERY_SETTINGS	Additional Cache Settings for Query
RSR_GEN_DIRECT_ALL_QUERIES	Regenerates All Queries Directly
RSR_MULTIPROV_CHECK	Delete or Rebuild Metadata Runtime (CL_RSD_MULTIPROV)
RSRD_BOOKMARK_REORGANISATION	Reorganization of Bookmarks/View IDs (Generated in Broadcasting)
RSRLDREL	Delete Links between ALE and IDocs
RSRV_JOB_RUNNER	Run RSRV Consistency Checks
RSSB_GENERATE_AUTHORIZATIONS	Generating Authorizations in BW from Data in the InfoProviders
RSSM_ERRORLOG_CLEANUP	Delete Error Log for All Requests that Are Not in the PSA
RSSM_OLTP_INIT_DELTA_UPDATE	Init-Delta Settings Written from RSSD-LINIT/Selection to OLTP
RSSM_REPAIR_PSADELETE	Repair Incorrect PSA References in PSADELETE
RSSM_SET_REPAIR_FULL_FLAG	Set Repair Indicator for Full Requests
RSSM_UPDATE_RSMDATASTATE	Report RSSM_UPDATE_RSMDATASTATE
RSSNAPDL	Reorganization Program for Table SNAP of Short Dumps
RSSODFRE	Delete Documents from Hidden Folder
RSTBPDEL	Table Log Database Management: Delete Logs

Table C.1 Useful Reports and Utility Programs (Cont.)

Program	Description
RSTCO_ACTIVATION_ADMIN	Technical BW Content Log Output/ Activation
RSTRAN_MIGRATION_REPAIR	Auto-Corrections for Transformation Created by Migration
RSTS0024	Finds and Deletes "Orphaned" Job Logs
RSTT_TDATA_TRANSFER	Transfer Test Data in BI Environment
RSTT_TRACE_DELETE	Report RSTT_TRACE_DELETE
RSTT_TRACE_EXEC	Execute Trace
RSUSR_CLEANUP_USER_TABLES	Display and Delete Unneeded Entries in User Tables
RSUSR_LOCK_USERS	Lock/Unlock Users
RSUSR_MAINT_SU10	User Mass Maintenance
RSUSR000	List of All Users Logged On
RSUSR002	Users by Complex Selection Criteria
RSUSR200	List of Users According to Logon Date and Password Change
RSUSR300	Set External Security Name for All Users
RSWB_ROLES_REORG	Reorganization of Workbook and Role Storage
RSWR_BOOKMARK_REORG	Reorganization of Bookmarks
RSZ_TEST_FUNCTION	Short Call FB Test Environment
RSZW_ITEM_MIGRATION_3X_TO_70	BW: Migrate Library Items (3.x) to Reusable Web Items
SAP_AGGREGATES_ACTIVATE_FILL	Activating and Filling the Aggregates of an InfoCube
SAP_AGGREGATES_DEACTIVATE	Deactivating the Aggregates of an Info-Cube
SAP_ANALYZE_ALL_INFOCUBES	Create DB Statistics for all InfoCubes
SAP_BW_MIGRATION	Report with Help Routines for Migrating a BW
SAP_CONVERT_NORMAL_TRANS	Conversion: Normal Transactional Info-Cube

Table C.1 Useful Reports and Utility Programs (Cont.)

Program	Description
SAP_CREATE_E_FACTTABLES	Creates Missing E-Fact Tables for Info-Cubes and Aggregates
SAP_DBSTATC_CLEANUP	Cleanup of DBSTATC Table (for Use with BRCONNECT)
SAP_DROP_EMPTY_FPARTITIONS	Locate/Remove Unused or Empty Partitions of an F-fact Table
SAP_DROP_TMPTABLES	Removes Temporary Database Objects
SAP_GENERATE_TMPTABLES	Generation of Temporary Tables for Read Without Commit
SAP_GLOBV_CHECK	Report SAP_GLOBV_CHECK
SAP_INFOCUBE_DESIGNS	Print a List of the Cubes in the System and their Layout
SAP_INFOCUBE_INDEXES_REPAIR	Repairs Identification of Existing Info-Cubes
SAP_PSA_PARTNO_CORRECT	Report SAP_PSA_PARTNO_CORRECT
SAP_QUERY_CHECKER_740	SAP Report Checker for Upgrade to 7.40
SAP_REFPOINT_COMPLETE	Repair Program for Missing Markers
SAP_RSADMIN_MAINTAIN	RSADMIN Administration
SAP_UPDATE_DBDIFF	SAP BW: Refreshing Table DBDIFF (Inconsistencies DDIC DB)
SBAL_DELETE	Application Log: Delete Expired Logs
SHDB_DISTRIBUTE_TABLES	Report SHDB_DISTRIBUTE_TABLES
SHDB_INDEX_ANALYZE	Analyzing Indexing in SAP HANA Systems to Derive Single Column Indexes
SHDB_INDEX_CHECK	Checking and Activating Single Column SAP HANA DB Indexes
SHDB_INDEX_CREATE	Creation of SAP HANA-Specific Single Column Indexes
SHDB_MIGRATION_CHECK	DB/DDIC Checks after Migration to HANA DB
SMIGR_CREATE_DDL	Report SMIGR_CREATE_DDL: Generate DDL Statements for Migration
TREX_ADMIN_TOOL	TREX Administration

Table C.1 Useful Reports and Utility Programs (Cont.)

Program	Description
ZBW_ABAP_ANALYZER	BW ABAP Analyzer (SAP Note 1847431)
ZBW_HANA_CHECKLIST	HANA Migration Checklist (SAP Note 1729988)
ZBW_HANA_MIGRATION_COCKPIT	HANA Migration Cockpit (SAP Note 1909597)
ZBW_TRANSFORM_FINDER	SAP NetWeaver BW Transform Finder (SAP Note 1908367)
ZRSDMD_CHECK_CHA_VIEWS	Check for Missing Views of Characteristics
ZRSTRAN_CHECK_TRANSPORT	Check/Repair Inconsistencies in Table RSTRAN (SAP Note 1923226)

Table C.1 Useful Reports and Utility Programs (Cont.)

D   The Authors

Joe Darlak, director at COMERIT, Inc., has been successfully implementing SAP BW at clients since 1998, including several large-scale, full-lifecycle global rollouts. He has significant experience increasing the capacity, reliability, and performance of BI systems, defining and implementing processes and controls to stabilize service and mitigate risk, and improving the competency and skill sets of implementation and client service teams. Recently, he has architected one of the largest SAP BW migrations to SAP HANA on record, and has been instrumental in defining best practices for SAP HANA at Fortune 100 clients. Over the past decade, he has presented at multiple conferences on various SAP BW performance tuning topics. He is a former principal consultant in the iAnalytics practice at PricewaterhouseCoopers and holds a masters of business administration from the McCombs School of Business at the University of Texas at Austin.

Jesper Christensen, director of Business Intelligence International at COMERIT, Inc., was part of the SAP BW Regional Implementation group at SAP that initially rolled out SAP Business Warehouse. He is an internationally recognized subject matter expert in business intelligence, a contributing author of international BI journals, and a frequent speaker at SAP and BI-related conferences. His leadership at COMERIT helped Tetra Pak win the Gartner Award of BI Excellence in 2009. Jesper has supported multi-year global projects as the lead architect with companies such as ExxonMobil, Chevron, Statoil, Ericsson, Tetra Pak, Shell, BHP Billiton, and McKesson, among others.

Index

A

ABAP, 613
ABAP BICS display, 388
ABAP development objectives, 352
ABAP Development Tools, 258
ABAP Dictionary, 52
ABAP Editor, 52
ABAP guidelines, 352
ABAP in Eclipse, 40
ABAP programs, 150
ABAP references, 379
ABAP Runtime Analysis, 398
ABAP Workbench, 52, 58
Access Control Lists (ACLs), 218
Activation queue, 281
Active data table, 281
Activity fields, 220
Administration tasks
  Daily, 425
  Monthly, 482
  Quarterly, 509
  Weekly, 455
  Yearly, 548
Administrator roles, 232
Administrator workbench, 222
Aggregate parameters, 542
Aggregates, 157, 194, 406, 451
Aggregation level, 291
Aggregation types, 342
  Overwrite, 343
  Summation, 342
ALE delta configuration, 322
ALPHA routine, 161, 162
Analysis authorizations, 225, 242
  Activity, 228
  Automatically generating, 229
  InfoObjects, 225
  InfoProvider, 228
  Roles, 238
  Users, 238
  Validity, 228
Analysis log, 246

Analysis Process Designer (APD), 290, 292, 293, 372
Analysis processes settings, 544
Analysis table, 609
Analytical index, 292, 314
Antijoins, 296
Application component, 205
Application data, 53
Application logs, 467
Application process category
  Data target administration, 145
  General services, 144
  Global spend analysis, 146
  Load process and post-processing, 144
  Other, 146
  Other SAP BW processes, 145
  Reporting agent, 145
  Retail, 145
Application processes, 143
Application programming interface (API), 290
Application server, 42, 436
  Instance, 81
Application-to-application (A2A), 40
Architected data mart layer, 119
  Business transformation, 119
  Reporting, 119
  Virtualization, 119
Archival, 157
  Archived data, 503
  Archiving objects, 201
Archiving request administration data, 202
AS ABAP, 42, 236, 551
AS ABAP authorizations, 218
AS Java, 42, 238, 551
ASAP methodology, 581
ASCII files, 330
Attribute change runs (ACRs), 138, 564
Attribute tables, 159
Authorization object, 217
Authorizations, 219
  Authorization check log, 246
  Authorization checks, 246
  Authorization concept, 217
  Authorization data, 230

Authorizations (Cont.)
  Authorization errors, 242, 246
  Authorization fields, 220
  Authorization flag, 228
  Authorization object, 217, 219, 220, 222,
    224, 242
  Authorization problems, 242
  Authorization-relevant, 165
Automation, 22

B

B*tree indexes, 274
Background processing, 431, 447
Backup domain controller, 64
BAPI, 312
Basis engineer, 595
Batch jobs, 483
BEx
  Analyzer, 415
  Objects, 72
  Web Templates, 414
BEx queries, 608
BI Basis Customizing, 103
BI Competency Center (BICC), 425, 547, 575
  Best practices, 599
  Compliance, 603
  Cost advantages, 577
  Governance, 579, 596
  Guidelines, 602
  Prioritization, 580
  Tactical issues, 579
  Team structure, 596
  Vision and strategy, 599
BI Consumer Services (BICS), 419
BI Content models, 35
BI governance, 601
BI Statistics, 474
BI strategy, 575
BI systems architect, 592
BICC members
  Expectations, 586
  Roles, 585
  Skills and competencies, 586
BI-IP Performance Toolset, 399
Binary logical object (BLOB), 544
Blueprint, 582

Bookmark, 610
Buffer size, 537
Business analyst, 588, 589
Business continuity plan (BCP), 564
Business Information Warehouse (BIW), 21
Business process owner, 587
Business project manager (BPM), 40, 588, 597
Business requirements, 254, 607
Business roles, 586
Business transformation logic, 118
Business-to-business (B2B), 40
BW Accelerator, 195, 410
  Alerts, 464
  Index maintenance, 437
  Indexes, 196, 461
  Monitor, 437, 462
  Sizing, 95
  Usage, 495, 497
BW Administration Cockpit, 363, 474
BW Basis, 455
BW checks, 458
  BW Administration and Design, 459
  BW Reporting and Planning, 459
  BW Warehouse Management, 459
BW housekeeping tasks, 469
BW Integrated Planning, 290
BW object metadata, 205
BW object types, 205
BW table analysis, 427
BW_QUERY_ACCESSES, 399
BW_QUERY_USAGE, 399
BWA, 614
BWATOOLS, 399
BW-EML, 84
BW-EML Benchmark, 90
BWQUAC_CUST, 399
BW-TOOLS, 399

C

Caching, 392, 489
  Client-side, 489
  Monitoring, 478
Calendar month, 567, 569
Candidate characteristics, 302
Cardinality InfoObjects, 163
Cell definition, 413

Centralized support organization, 577
Change and Transport System (CTS), 52, 58, 530
Change logs, 281, 464
   Tables, 465
Chart, 609
Classic InfoSet, 309
Client 000, 555
Client roles, 55, 58
Code and stacks, 430
Cold data, 214
Collection process, 135, 154
Column store tables, 430
Composite roles, 231
CompositeProvider, 257, 293, 294, 314
Compression, 273, 406, 477
Computing Center Management System (CCMS), 446, 486
Configuration settings, 536
Consistency checks, 472
Consolidation routes, 65
Continuous improvement, 581
Controlling area, 268
Cost center, 268
CPU, 379, 436
   Trend, 382
   Utilization, 523
Critical path, 137
Customizing client, 55
Customizing object, 59, 61
Customizing tools, 51, 58

D

Daisy chain, 297
Data architecture, 22, 110, 593
Data cleansing, 340
Data consistency, 23
Data consolidation, 340
Data deletion, 157
Data Dictionary objects, 76
Data flow, 110
   Components, 111
   Deletion, 536
   Design options, 111
   Diagram, 110
   Template, 127, 128

Data integrity, 22
Data load, 253, 317, 446, 483, 551, 612
   Automation, 134
   Duration, 564
   Performance, 157, 552
   Statistics, 505
Data management, 157
Data manager statistics, 506
Data Mart Benchmark (BI-D), 82
Data modeling, 253, 593, 612
   Enhanced, 257
Data propagation layer, 119
   Corporate memory, 119
Data quality, 610
Data replication, 157
Data retention strategy, 157, 205, 207, 208
   Data deletion, 198, 207
   Detail InfoProviders, 207
   History InfoProviders, 207
   Near-line storage, 207
   Summary InfoProviders, 207
   Traditional archiving, 207
Data sizing, 90
Data transfer control parameters, 545
Data transfer process (DTP), 114, 146, 332
   Original state, 336
   Statistics, 504
Data volume statistics, 506
Data Warehouse, 359
Data Warehousing Workbench, 28, 52, 58, 69, 125, 183, 204, 293
Database
   Administration, 430
   Backup, 442
   Indexing statistics, 477
   Interface settings, 540
   Parameter information, 525
   Reorganization, 531
   Software updates, 525
Database growth
   Forecasting, 497
   Inorganic growth, 498
   Organic growth, 498
   Storage capacity growth, 498
Database instance, 81
Database optimizations, 405
Database partitioning, 409
Database space, 531
Database storage, 426

Database table size, 205
DataSource, 75, 76, 112, 175, 198, 318
    Custom, 318
DataStore object (DSO), 194, 198, 230, 257, 611
    Activations, 451
    Modeling, 279
    Parameters, 538
    Templates, 230
DBA Cockpit, 442
Delivery director, 590
Delivery routes, 65
Delta type, 327
Denormalization, 157, 255
    Aggregates, 255
    BWA indexes, 255
    Materialized views, 255
    Star schemas, 255
Detailed design, 255, 607
development checklist, 608
Development methodology, 581
Development packages, 67, 75
Development system, 43
Development transfer rules, 45
Dimension IDs (DIMIDs), 32, 173, 185, 267
Dimensional characteristic, 270
Direct update, 116
Disaster recovery (DR), 563
Disk I/O, 383
Distributed process, 150
Domain, 120
DSO tables, 32
    Activation queue, 32
    Active data, 32
    Change log, 32
DSO type, 280
    Direct update, 289
    In-memory, 285
    Standard, 281
    Write-optimized, 287
Dynamic authorizations, 229
Dynamically switchable, 100

E

Eclipse-based modeling tools, 257
E-fact table, 185, 186, 188, 273, 348, 567
End routine, 344

End-user roles, 232
Enhanced Mixed Load Benchmark (BW-EML), 82, 85
Enterprise data warehouse, 109, 134, 254
Enterprise data warehouse layer, 118, 124
    Data acquisition, 118
    Data propagation, 119
    Quality and harmonization, 118
Enterprise reports, 72
Equal join, 298
Error resolution, 197
ETL developer, 594
Exception aggregation, 413
Executive sponsor, 587
Expensive statements, 444
Expert routine, 345
External performance and optimization, 565
Extract, transform, and load (ETL), 34, 317
Extraction, 611
Extraction processing, 317
Extreme programming, 582

F

Failed re-partitioning request, 569
F-fact table, 185, 186, 188, 273, 275, 347, 567
File system housekeeping, 500
File-retention strategy, 501
Filter panel, 608
Fiscal period, 567, 569
Flat file, 175
Free space analysis, 427
Frontend statistics analysis, 372
Frontend tool, 369
    Optimization, 414
Full-table scans, 531
Functional design, 254, 607

G

General, 610
Global cache, 543
Global control and success, 576
Global filter, 609
Global process, 483
Global settings and exchange rates, 106
Graphical modeling, 125

H

Hardware installation, 549
Hardware maintenance, 523
Hardware sizing, 549, 554
Header, 246
Hidden costs, 577
Hierarchies, 182, 413
   Hierarchy/attribute change run, 171
   Levels, 171
   Nodes, 229
   Tables, 159
High availability (HA), 563
High cardinality, 274
High-cardinality InfoObjects, 164
Hit lists, 376
Hot data, 214
Housekeeping task, 170
   Daily, 614
   Monthly, 616
   Quarterly, 617
   Weekly, 615
   Yearly, 618
HTTPWATCH Tool, 404
Hub-and-spoke, 297
HybridProvider, 257, 314
Hypercare, 583

I

IBM DB2, 185, 526
Implementation, 583
Implementation Guide (IMG), 51
Inactive users, 513
Index full scans, 531
InfoArea, 205, 220
InfoCube, 191, 406
   BWA-only, 275, 276
   Compressing, 477
   Data models, 610
   Index functions, 349
   Loading, 347
   Modeling, 256, 267
   Real-time, 278
   Standard, 272
   Type, 271

InfoObjects, 30, 113, 159
   Catalogs, 76
   Characteristics, 30
   Key figures, 30
   Technical characteristics, 31
   Time characteristics, 31
InfoPackage, 112, 325
   Data transfer, 329
   Monitoring, 449
   Statistics, 506
InfoProvider, 30, 113, 122, 220, 301
   Aggregation level, 33
   BEx Query, 33
   Check, 246
   CompositeProvider, 33
   DataStore objects, 32, 113
   HybridProvider, 33
   InfoCubes, 31, 113
   InfoSet, 34, 295
   Maintenance, 191
   MultiProvider, 34
   OpenODSViews, 114
   Partitioning, 184
   Query, 314
   Technical name, 365
   TransientProvider, 34
   Virtual, 291
   VirtualProvider, 34
Infoset, 35, 295
   Settings, 540
InfoSource, 122, 338
   Intermediate, 339
Infrastructure architecture, 22
Infrastructure costs, 206
Inner join, 293, 296
Instances, 24
   ABAP server, 25
   Central services, 25
   Dual-stack, 25
   Enqueue replication server, 25
   Java server, 25
   SAP NetWeaver Search and Classification (TREX), 25
   Web Dispatcher server, 25
Interfaces, 552
Interrupt process, 141
Invalid or incorrect master data values, 182

IT roles, 589
  Tasks, 590
iViews, 363

J

Java portal authorizations, 242
Job overview, 441
Join, 255
  Join types, 296
Joint application design, 582

K

Key figures, 302, 387, 412

L

LAN statistics, 383
Large-table scans, 531
Layer architecture, 111
Layered scalable architecture (LSA), 117, 123
  LSA++, 123
Left outer joins, 293, 296
Line of business (LOB), 587
Line-item dimension, 273
Load balancing, 349
Load processing, 346
Loading processes, 146
Loadrunner, 384
Log file switch, 440
Logical database size, 205
Logical partitioning, 410
Lower limit, 319
LSA, 254
  Architecture, 157
LSA++, 254
  Architecture, 276

M

Maintenance, 22, 206
Massive parallel processing, 539

Master data, 137, 157, 158, 159, 171
  Critical and dependent (C&D), 137
  Critical and non-dependent (C&ND), 137
  Dalues, 182
  Design, 159
  IDs (SIDs), 567
  Initial record, 178
  Loading, 170
  Maintenance, 176
  Non-critical (NC), 137
  Portability, 159
  Startup phase, 171
  Values, 182
  Work phase, 171
Memory capacity monitor, 436
Memory sizing, 93
Memory statistics, 383
Memory tuning analysis, 433
Memory utilization, 523
Metachain, 141, 150
Metadata, 159
Microsoft Active Directory, 510
MIME objects, 415
Mixed Load Benchmark (BI-MXL), 82, 85
Modeling
  CompositeProvider, 258
  Open ODS Views, 258
Monitoring tasks, 446
Monitoring trees, 446
Multi-block index range scans, 531
Multidimensional clustering (MDC), 284
Multidimensional modeling, 256
Multiple components in one database
  (MCOD), 307
MultiProvider, 210, 301, 364, 409
  Advantages, 302
  Technical BI Content, 475
MultiProviders, 608

N

Navigational attribute, 169, 171, 227, 302
Near-critical paths, 139
Near-line storage, 157, 212, 286
  Data, 503
  Database, 210
  Interface, 212

Network optimization, 418
Non-cumulative cubes, 394
Non-dependent data, 173
Non-persistent objects, 127
Normalization, 255

O

ODS View, 307
OLAP BAPI, 419
OLAP engine, 359
OLE DB for OLAP, 419
Online analytical processing (OLAP), 23
Open transport requests, 530
Operating systems monitor, 435
Operational Data Provisioning, 115, 184, 257,
   260
   Benefits, 261
Operational Delta Queue (ODQ), 115, 261
Optimization mode, 392
Oracle, 525
Oracle advanced compression, 498
Organic database growth, 205, 213

P

Package, 60
Parallel processing, 392
Partitioning, 185, 567
Partitions, 186
PartProvider, 301, 306
Password prompt, 556
Patching, 528
Performance, 610
Performance limits, 170
Performance testing, 384
Performance tuning tasks, 357, 473
   Monthly, 499
   Quarterly, 530
   Yearly, 547, 564
Persistent objects, 126
Persistent staging area (PSA), 112, 197, 330,
   331, 465
   Cleanup, 464
   Entry, 197
   Tables, 465

Planning Application Kit, 116
Portal settings, 489
Post-copy automation, 46, 515
Presentation developer, 594
Primary application server (PAS) instance, 81
Process chain, 114, 135, 446, 448, 487, 504
   Local, 150
   Remote, 150
   Structure, 135
Process instance, 140
Process type, 140
Process variant, 140, 198, 466
Processing sizing, 91
Production client, 55
Production system, 43
Productive sizing, 79, 90
Profile parameters, 98, 99
Project delivery, 581, 597
Project IMG, 101
Project preparation, 549
Promote to production strategy, 13, 14
Prototype or sandbox client, 58

Q

QA approval procedure, 67
qRFC, 369
Quality assurance, 63
   Client, 55
   System, 43
Queries, 195, 552, 609, 610
   Characteristics and navigational attributes,
      412
   Deletion, 532
   Elements, 72
   Frequently used, 367
   Monitor, 385
   Objects, 534
   Optimization, 411
   Pruning, 304
   Results, 552
   Runtimes, 375
   Views, 72
Quick Sizer, 79, 86

R

Rapid application development, 582
RDA daemons, 449
Read mode, 391
Realigning aggregates, 171
Realization, 583
Real-time data acquisition, 486
  Monitor, 450
Reference InfoObject, 160
Regression testing, 551
Relational database (RDBMS), 116
Repartitioning, 187
  InfoProviders, 566
  Processing steps, 188
  Types, 187
Report body, 609
Report description, 607
Report header, 608
Report RS_FIND_JOBS_WITHOUT_VARIANT, 615
Report RSAN_UT_RESULT_DROP_RESULTS, 615
Report RSAR_PSA_CLEANUP_DEFINITION, 615
Report RSAR_PSA_NEWDS_MAPPING_CHECK, 616
Report RSARFCER, 616
Report RSB_ANALYZE_ERRORLOG, 615
Report RSBATCH_DEL_MSG_PARM_DTPTEMP, 615
Report RSBCS_REORG, 615
Report RSBM_ERRORLOG_DELETE, 615
Report RSBPSTDE, 616
Report RSBTCDEL2, 615
Report RSDDS_CHANGERUN_MONITOR, 614
Report RSDU_REPART_UI, 618
Report RSM13002, 616
Report RSPC_INSTANCE_CLEANUP, 615
Report RSPC_LOG_DELETE, 615
Report RSPO1041, 615
Report RSSM_ERRORLOG_CLEANUP, 615
Report RSSODFRE, 615
Report RSTBPDEL, 615
Report RSTS0024, 615
Report RSTT_TRACE_DELETE, 615
Report SAP HANA, 614

Report SAP_DROP_TMPTABLES, 615
Report SWNC_COLLECTOR_CLEAN_SWNC-MONI, 616
Reporting authorizations, 224
Reporting performance tuning, 357
Reporting tools, 552
Reports
  Deletion, 532
Repository object, 59, 61
Request processing, 335
Reviewing data flow, 564
Risk mitigation, 22
Role templates, 233
  BW Administrator (development system), 234
  BW Administrator (productive system), 234
  Modeler (development system), 234
  Operator (productive system), 234
  Planner, 235
  Planning Administrator, 235
  Planning Modeler (development system), 235
  Reporting Developer (development system), 234
  Reporting User, 235
  Workspace Administrator, 235
  Workspace Designer, 235
  Workspace Query User, 235
Role-based authorizations, 231
Row store tables, 430
RSADMIN parameters, 545
RSRV cleanup tasks, 493

S

Safety intervals, 320
Sandbox system, 549, 554
SAP Application Performance Standard (SAPS), 84
SAP Basis, 79, 481
SAP Benchmarks, 82
SAP BEx tools, 28, 29
  SAP BEx Analyzer, 29
  SAP BEx Broadcaster, 29
  SAP BEx Query Designer, 29
  SAP BEx Report Designer, 29
  SAP BEx Web Application Designer, 29
SAP Business Planning and Consolidation (BPC), 137

SAP Business Suite, 79
SAP Business Warehouse Accelerator (BWA), 28
SAP BusinessObjects, 29, 79
  Analysis, 30
  Business Intelligence, 29
  Crystal Reports, 30
  Dashboards, 30
  Web Intelligence (WebI), 30
SAP BW, 21, 28
  Application releases, 548
  Support packs, 553
  Technical, 481
  Users, 510
SAP BW 7.30, 205, 262
SAP BW 7.40, 22, 37, 116
  Features, 38
SAP BW Accelerator (BWA), 95, 495, 527
SAP BW-specific table classifications, 205
SAP BW-specific tools, 357
  BW Administration Cockpit, 358, 362
  BW Statistics, 357, 358, 402, 474
  BW Technical Content, 357, 360, 455
SAP Data Services, 317
SAP Data Volume Management (DVM), 196, 465
SAP EarlyWatch Alert (EWA), 173, 456, 457, 493
SAP ERP, 22
SAP Gateway, 41
SAP GRC Access Control, 241
SAP HANA, 21, 36, 37, 48, 94, 115, 154, 164, 166, 256, 310, 410, 523, 527, 539, 543
  Analytical process, 116
  Calculation time, 389
  Cloud, 21, 40, 42
  Databases, 428
  DSOs, 286
  InfoCubes, 124
  Memory consumption, 428
  SAP HANA Studio, 40, 258
  SAP HANA XS, 42
  Smart Data Access, 115, 184, 257, 259
SAP Implementation Guide (IMG), 98
SAP Industry Solutions, 79
SAP Kernels, 524
SAP Landscape Transformation, 116
SAP Landscape Virtualization Management, 46, 515

SAP MaxDB, 526
SAP Mobile, 21
SAP NetWeaver, 79, 217
  SAP NetWeaver 7.0, 112
  SAP NetWeaver 7.30, 134
  SAP NetWeaver 7.31, 40
  SAP NetWeaver 7.40, 41
SAP NetWeaver Application Server, 24
SAP NetWeaver function area, 23
  SAP Auto-ID Infrastructure, 23
  SAP Gateway, 23, 41
  SAP Identity Management, 23
  SAP Information Lifecycle Management, 23
  SAP Master Data Management (MDM), 23
  SAP Portal, 23
  SAP Process Orchestration, 23
SAP Notes, 490, 525
SAP Process Integration (PI), 40
SAP Reference IMG, 101
SAP Service Marketplace, 79, 490, 524, 550, 555, 558
SAP SLT, 317
SAP Solution Manager, 23, 381, 445, 455, 457, 551
SAP Upgrade, 550
SAP Workload Business Transaction Analysis, 369
SAP Workload Monitor, 368, 374
SAPgui, 419, 558
  Maintenance, 558
SAPUI5, 40, 41, 42
Security administrator, 595
Security and authorization, 553
Security functions, 217
Semantic partitioning, 120, 209, 256, 262
Semantic partitioning object (SPO), 120, 184, 264, 266, 410
Server group, 544
Service delivery, 584
  BI application support, 584
  Licensing, 585
  Operations support, 584
  Process implementation, 584
  User access, 584
Service delivery manager (SDM), 591, 598
  Roles, 592
Service tools, 399
Service-level agreement (SLA), 205, 425

Short dumps, 439
SIDs, 346
   SID table, 159, 180
   SID values, 173
Single sign-on, 23
SIQ, 411
Sizing, 79
Snapshot Monitoring Tool, 377
Soft shutdown, 485
   Actions in sequence, 485
Software Update Manager (SUM), 524, 548, 550
SQL statements, 379
Standard authorization objects, 221
Star schema, 267
Start routine, 343
Statement optimization, 354
Storage capacity, 497
Storage requirement, 157
Structure elements, 392
Support package, 27, 554
   Stack, 28, 490
   Update, 553
Synchronous, 152
System, 24
   ABAP system, 24
   Dual-stack system, 24
   Java system, 24
System checks, 439
System copies, 515
   Heterogeneous system, 515
   Homogeneous system, 515
System development life cycle (SLDC), 581
System environment, 21
System landscapes, 42
System logs, 440
System parameters, 528
System refresh, 515
System restart, 482
System risks, 564
System settings, 98
System sizing, 78

T

Table updates, 531
TCO, 603

Technical project manager (TPM), 588, 591, 597
   Responsibilities, 591
Temporal joins, 297
Temporary data, 157, 196
Text table, 159
Third normal form, 255
Time profile, 371
Top response-time view, 372
Training client, 58
Transaction, 619
Transaction AL08, 484
Transaction AL11, 500, 617
Transaction AOBJ, 201
Transaction BD54, 104
Transaction BDLS, 49
Transaction BWCCMS, 494, 614, 616
Transaction CMOD, 104
Transaction data, 157, 184
Transaction DB02, 91, 349, 427, 444, 614
Transaction DBACOCKPIT, 442
Transaction FILE, 175
Transaction MOPZ, 551
Transaction OMSL, 103
Transaction PFCG, 231, 235
Transaction RS_CONV_ACTIVATE, 104
Transaction RS_PERS_ACTIVATE, 104
Transaction RSA1, 104, 304, 407, 568, 614, 617
Transaction RSA11, 506
Transaction RSA13, 106
Transaction RSA6, 324
Transaction RSADMIN, 617
Transaction RSBATCH, 149, 336, 351
Transaction RSCUSTV1, 104
Transaction RSCUSTV21, 388
Transaction RSCUSTV27, 104
Transaction RSCUSTV28, 104
Transaction RSCUSTV6, 104, 546
Transaction RSCUSTV8, 542
Transaction RSCUSTV9, 103
Transaction RSD1, 161, 307
Transaction RSDD_LTIP, 292
Transaction RSDDB, 462, 464, 615
Transaction RSDDBIAMON2, 437, 462, 463, 614
Transaction RSDDSTAT, 204, 358
Transaction RSDDSTAT*, 204

Transaction RSDIOBJ, 258
Transaction RSDMD, 175
Transaction RSDODS, 283
Transaction RSDS, 112, 331
Transaction RSECADMIN, 227, 228, 233, 238, 239, 241, 246, 249, 616
Transaction RSISET, 296
Transaction RSKC, 103
Transaction RSLGMP, 104
Transaction RSLIMOBW, 293
Transaction RSMDCNVEXIT, 181
Transaction RSMO, 483
Transaction RSO2, 322
Transaction RSODSO_SETTINGS, 104, 538, 617
Transaction RSODSVIEW, 308
Transaction RSPC, 505
Transaction RSPCM, 614
Transaction RSRCACHE, 104, 396, 543, 616
Transaction RSRT, 248, 385, 396, 404, 617
Transaction RSRT1, 385
Transaction RSRT2, 385
Transaction RSRV, 191, 196, 447, 456, 461, 472, 493, 616
Transaction RSTCO_ADMIN, 360
Transaction RSTCT_INST_BIAC, 103, 363
Transaction RSTPRFC, 104
Transaction RSTT, 304
Transaction RSUSR200, 510, 513, 617
Transaction RSZDELETE, 532, 617
Transaction RZ10, 99, 617
Transaction RZ11, 99
Transaction RZ20, 494
Transaction SA38, 534
Transaction SARA, 202, 617
Transaction SBACOCKPIT, 614
Transaction SBIW, 330, 617
Transaction SCC4, 55, 104
Transaction SCDO, 323
Transaction SE01, 61
Transaction SE03, 56
Transaction SE09, 59
Transaction SE11, 175
Transaction SE14, 570
Transaction SE16, 173, 402, 403
Transaction SE30, 398, 399
Transaction SE38, 378, 568

Transaction SLG2, 615
Transaction SM02, 484
Transaction SM04, 93, 484
Transaction SM21, 614
Transaction SM37, 483, 614
Transaction SM50, 430
Transaction SM51, 430
Transaction SM58, 615
Transaction SM61, 351
Transaction SM66, 483, 614
Transaction SMLG, 351
Transaction SMQS, 329
Transaction SNOTE, 491, 616
Transaction SNRO, 103, 174
Transaction SPAD, 103
Transaction SPAM, 553, 555
Transaction SPAU, 557
Transaction SPDD, 557
Transaction SPRO, 51, 281, 536, 617
Transaction ST01, 243, 244, 617
Transaction ST02, 93, 433, 529, 614
Transaction ST03G, 92
Transaction ST03N, 92, 374, 427, 431, 614
Transaction ST04, 432, 445, 614
Transaction ST05, 445
Transaction ST06, 92, 94, 435, 614
Transaction ST07, 94
Transaction ST13, 385, 399
Transaction ST22, 439, 441, 614
Transaction STAD, 92, 369
Transaction STC01, 49, 472, 516, 615
Transaction STC02, 49
Transaction STMS, 502
Transaction STMS_QA, 502
Transaction SU01, 236
Transaction SU21, 219
Transaction SU53, 242, 244
Transaction SUID10, 511, 513, 617
Transfer processing, 332
Transformation, 340, 611, 613
Transformation routines, 344
Transformation rules, 113, 209, 341
TransientProvider, 292, 308, 314
Transport, 613
Transport domain, 63
    Controller, 64
Transport group, 63

Transport layer, 64
Transport management system (TMS), 61, 63
Transport organizer, 58
Transport routes, 65
Transport schedule and strategy, 66
Transport workflow, 67
TREX Admin tool, 196, 464

U

Unified Modeling Tool, 258
Union, 293
Upgrade activities, 549
   SAP BW, 548
   SAPgui, 560
   software, 549, 554
Upper limit, 319
User administration, 236
   Tools, 241
User Information System, 241
User locks, 513
User management engine (UME), 242
User profile, 377
Users and licenses, 510

V

Validity dates, 513
Virtual data mart layer, 125
VirtualProvider, 257, 312

W

Warm data, 214
Web items, 72
Web services, 421
Web templates, 72
Wily Introscope Tool, 382
Workbooks, 72
Workflow, 610
Workload monitors, 368
Workload statistics, 431
Workspace Designer, 292, 293
Write-optimized DSO, 288

- 100 little-known time-saving tips and tricks

- Step-by-step instructions and guiding screenshots

- Practical, expert advice for anyone working in SAP NetWeaver BW

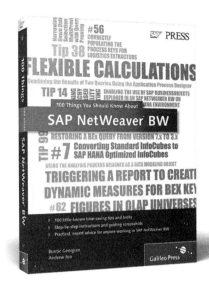

Buntic Georgian, Andrew Joo

SAP NetWeaver BW

100 Things You Should Know About...

If you're looking to take your knowledge of SAP NetWeaver BW to the next level, then this is the book for you! You'll benefit from expert information that reveals the secrets of SAP NetWeaver BW gurus as they provide the most useful tricks of working with the major task areas in SAP NetWeaver BW. These "100 Things" provide detailed screenshots, easy instructions, and a hands-on approach to quickly working with SAP NetWeaver BW.

367 pp., 2013, 49,95 Euro / US$ 49.95
ISBN 978-1-59229-447-3
www.sap-press.com

Galileo Press

- Learn about the three types of a BW on HANA implementation

- Get full step-by-step instructions for system preparation, installation, and post installation

- Find out how data modeling and reporting work in a BW on HANA system

Alexandra Carvalho

Implementing SAP BW on SAP HANA

There are a lot of different ways to go live with a BW on HANA system, and whether you're performing a new installation, a sidecar installation, or a full migration, this book will guide you on your way. With the help of practical instructions and screenshots, you'll learn how to choose the right scenario and perform all the necessary steps to accomplish it. Full speed ahead!

approx. 650 pp., 69,95 Euro / US$ 69.95
ISBN 978-1-4932-1003-9, March 2015
www.sap-press.com

■ Learn the basic principles and concepts of BW

■ Get step-by-step instructions for performing BW tasks

■ Download sample data and recreate a real-life business scenario to get hands-on experience

■ 2nd edition updated and

Amol Palekar, Bharat Patel, Shreekant Shiralkar

SAP NetWeaver BW 7.3—Practical Guide

Business analytics remains one of the hottest and most dynamic topics in enterprise software—so don't be left behind. With this comprehensive reference, you can get up to speed and stay up to date on the principles of SAP NetWeaver BW 7.3, from the basics to the advanced concepts. Thanks to a practical example that is carried throughout the course of the book, you'll do more than learn what DSOs, InfoCubes, or InfoProviders are: You'll learn what you can do with them, and how. If you want to master BW, this book is what you need.

789 pp., 2. edition 2013, 69,95 Euro / US$ 69.95
ISBN 978-1-59229-444-2
www.sap-press.com

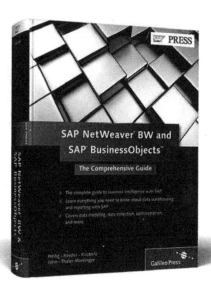

- The complete guide to business intelligence with SAP

- Learn everything you need to know about data warehousing and reporting with SAP

- Covers data modeling, data collection, administration, and more

Loren Heilig, Torsten Kessler, Thilo Knötzele, Peter John, Karin Thaler-Mieslinger

SAP NetWeaver BW and SAP BusinessObjects
The Comprehensive Guide

Finally—the entire SAP business intelligence world in one volume! Get the big picture, and get it from all angles: backend, frontend, and everything in between. Tools covered include BEx Query Designer, BEx Analyzer, BEx Web Analyzer, BEx Web Application Designer (WAD), Analysis, Web Intelligence, Crystal Reports, Dashboards (Xcelsius), and more. Based on SAP BusinessObjects 4.0 and SAP NetWeaver 7.3, this book will get you up to speed.

795 pp., 2012, 79,95 Euro / US$ 79.95
ISBN 978-1-59229-384-1
www.sap-press.com

Interested in reading more?

Please visit our website for all new
book and e-book releases from SAP PRESS.

www.sap-press.com